Dale and Appelbe's
Pharmacy Law and Ethics

Dale and Appelbe's Pharmacy Law and Ethics

NINTH EDITION

Gordon E Appelbe LL B, PhD, MSc, BSc(Pharm), BA, FRPharmS, Hon MPS(Aus), FCPP, FCPP (Hons)
Independent Pharmaceutical and Legal Consultant, London, UK
Joy Wingfield LL M, MPhil, BPharm, FRPharmS, Dip Ag Vet Pharm, FCPP
Special Professor of Pharmacy Law and Ethics, University of Nottingham, UK

London • Chicago **Pharmaceutical Press**

Published by the Pharmaceutical Press
An imprint of RPS Publishing

1 Lambeth High Street, London SE1 7JN, UK
100 South Atkinson Road, Suite 200, Grayslake, IL 60030-7820, USA

© 2009 jointly by Gordon E Appelbe, Joy Wingfield and the Pharmaceutical Press

(**PP**) is a trade mark of RPS Publishing

RPS Publishing is the publishing organisation of the Royal Pharmaceutical Society of
Great Britain

First published 1976
Second edition 1979
Third edition 1983
Fourth edition 1989
Fifth edition 1993
Sixth edition 1997
Seventh edition 2001
Eighth edition 2005
Ninth edition 2009

Typeset by Thomson Digital, Noida, India
Printed in Great Britain by TJ International, Padstow, Cornwall

ISBN 978 0 85369 827 2

A catalogue record for this book is available from the British Library.

Front cover image: © iStockphoto.com/DNY59.

Contents

Preface to the Ninth Edition

This book again seeks to provide in one volume an outline of the law that affects the practice of pharmacy in Great Britain, together with an account of the way in which British pharmacy has developed and maintained its standards of professional conduct. The authors hope that the book will prove useful not only to pharmacy undergraduates, preregistration students and pharmacists in all branches of the profession, but also to others in Britain and overseas who may need some knowledge of contemporary British law relating to medicines and poisons, and of the development of professional ethics in British pharmacy.

The period between the 8th and 9th editions, spanning the end of 2004 to the end of 2008, has reflected radical changes in policy towards health professionals as a whole, much arising from healthcare 'scandals' such as the Shipman Inquiry and similar inquiries into the quality of healthcare and staff at hospitals in Bristol and Liverpool (Alder Hey). Closer to home, legislative changes to enable the skills and training of community pharmacists to be valued and these professionals to make a proper contribution to healthcare and promotion are unpicking long established precedents in the Medicines Act that have been in place for more than 40 years. We pick out four major changes:

- revision and tightening up the Misuse of Drugs Regulations following the Shipman Inquiry;
- revision and replacement of the Royal Pharmaceutical Society's disciplinary powers and processes with fitness to practise procedures that parallel those of other health professions;
- proposals to separate the functions of the Society and create a regulator, the General Pharmaceutical Council (GPhC), and a new professional leadership body for pharmacy; and
- proposals to replace the concept of 'personal control' in the Medicines Act with that of the *responsible pharmacist* and subsequently to reinterpret the concept of 'supervision' to permit appropriately trained and registered supporting health professionals to carry out tasks in the community pharmacy, in the absence of a responsible pharmacist.

The first of these changes is, we believe, more or less complete and is covered in Chapter 17. Chapters 22, 23 and 24 capture the changes to the Society's powers in preparation for the creation of the GPhC, but they themselves are likely to undergo further change as the draft Pharmacy Order 2009 is implemented; we also provide an overview in these chapters of where these changes may occur. Proposals to change personal control are covered mostly in Chapter 5 but, as we went to press, it is likely that the Medicines Act itself will be reviewed in the next few years, meaning that the content and structure of all the chapters considering the Medicines Act may need an overhaul for any subsequent editions.

Not withstanding the above, new material has been added to most chapters. These include changes to the range of qualifications and reciprocal arrangements now recognised within the European Union (Chapter 1); new classes of prescriber and the use of electronic signatures to authorise prescribing (Chapter 8); a new regime for traditional herbal medicines (Chapter 12) and a new presentation of the law relating to veterinary medicines all in one Chapter (13). The advent of an *accountable officer* for all transactions in Controlled Drugs and many other changes to this legislation appears in Chapter 17; strychnine is now removed from Chapter 18, which now includes the law controlling pesticides (formerly under miscellaneous legislation). Changes in the description of alcoholic material are included in Chapter 19. Chapter 21 on miscellaneous legislation has been slightly reordered and now includes references to the vetting of health professionals in relation to working with children and vulnerable adults and a brief update on the disposal of waste from pharmacies.

Chapter 22, now called Pharmacy regulation and leadership, has been totally rewritten to reflect the ongoing process of splitting these functions by 2010. Chapter 23 on professional conduct reflects the now statutory 2007 Code of Ethics, and Chapter 24 covers the fitness to practise processes in place at the end of 2008. These are, however, subject to further change when the GPhC is established in 2010. In addition, discussion of 'old' disciplinary cases has been reduced and summarised and 'new' cases have been added where possible. In Chapter 25, discussing the regulation of other health professions, we have provided some background to the role of healthcare scandals in precipitating a wholesale review of this area of law, including the overarching scrutiny role of the Council for Healthcare Regulatory Excellence (CHRE), the development of revalidation and the role of the Office of the Health Professions Adjudicator (OHPA), both of which will be applied to the pharmacy profession sometime after 2010.

Chapter 26 on the NHS continues to be a challenge, recognising that some changes actually came and went in the period between the two editions and the fast diverging nature of practice, and hence underpinning legislation, now evident in community pharmacy contracts in England, Wales and Scotland.

Chapter 27 on important cases is also reduced in size to reflect the demise of the Pharmacy Act 1954 and outdated case law under the Medicines Act. We have also reduced the number of appendices, reflecting the now universal availability of detailed information on relevant websites.

The law is that of Great Britain except where otherwise stated in the text. The aim has been to state the law as concisely as accuracy permits, but it should be borne in mind that only the courts can give a legally binding decision on any question of interpretation. The responsibility for the text and any views expressed therein lies with the authors.

We gratefully acknowledge the help and advice we have received from numerous sources. In particular we thank Edward Mallinson concerning the NHS in Scotland, Sarah Cockbill concerning the NHS in Wales and Steve Lutener of the PSNC for his help on changes to the NHS contract and Terms of Service for community pharmacy. Thanks also go, once again, to our publishers, in particular to Christina De Bono and Louise McIndoe in coping with an uncertain legislative programme that takes no account of publication dates!

Gordon E Appelbe
Joy Wingfield
April 2009

Foreword

I first became truly aware of the complexity of pharmacy practice when I was asked to chair the working group overseeing the revision of the pharmacy profession's Code of Ethics. During our deliberations, it became increasingly clear that the ethical and legal responsibilities of pharmacy practitioners are both demanding and multifaceted. In addition to the need to conduct oneself at all times with the dignity and responsibility expected of a pharmacy practitioner, s/he must also navigate a complex and expanding body of statutory law against the backdrop of increasing common law liability imposed by the adoption of ever more significant professional roles.

Negotiating a path through the rights and responsibilities that result from professional status can be a daunting challenge. Support and information are both necessary to advise the pharmacy professional on how best to practise both ethically and legally, with due attention both to the interests of those they serve and their professional colleagues. In earlier editions of this book, the authors offered an extraordinary resource for pharmacy professionals by meticulously exploring these questions. In this revised and expanded 9th edition, the authors bring pharmacy professionals up to date with the plethora of legal changes that have been promulgated in recent years and explore the ethical obligations imposed on them.

This is a truly monumental task, which has been completed to great effect by the authors. The precise detail they offer in their analysis of relevant statutes and other legal regulation offers a comprehensive and accessible account of the legal requirements surrounding pharmacy practice, with many chapters helpfully including suggested further reading material. Moreover, they offer a comparative analysis of selected other professional groups engaged in healthcare with particular attention to the impact that inquiries into practice – particularly of medical practitioners – has had on the roles and responsibilities of all professionals involved in the delivery of healthcare. This is a comprehensive, informative and meticulously researched volume which will meet the intentions of the authors to offer a full account of the law regulating pharmacy practice and practitioners and the way(s) in which their roles and responsibilities have changed over the years.

Sheila A M McLean

International Bar Association Professor of Law and Ethics in Medicine

University of Glasgow

April 2009

About the authors

Gordon E Appelbe, LL B, PhD, MSc, BSc(Pharm), BA, FRPharmS, HonMPS (Aus), FCPP, FPP(Hons), is an independent pharmaceutical/legal consultant. He qualified as a pharmacist in 1956 and then worked for nine years in community pharmacy. He joined the staff of the Pharmaceutical Society in 1965, first as an inspector under the Pharmacy Acts and then, in 1971, as secretary to the Statutory Committee. He was appointed deputy head of the Law Department in 1974 and was head of the Law Department and Chief Inspector from 1978 to 1991.

Joy Wingfield, LL M, MPhil, BPharm, FRPharmS, Dip Ag Vet Pharm, FCPP, is Special Professor of Pharmacy Law and Ethics at the University of Nottingham and a independent pharmacy practice consultant She qualified as a pharmacist in 1971 and then worked for five years in community pharmacy. She joined the staff of the Pharmaceutical Society in 1976 as an inspector under the Pharmacy Acts. From 1986 to 1991, she was the senior administrator, and later head of Ethics Division in the Law Department, responsible for professional and registration matters. This was followed by nine years as the assistant pharmacy superintendent for Boots.

Introduction

Development of the law in relation to pharmacy, medicines and poisons

Between 1968 and 1978, the statutes relating to medicines, poisons and drugs were almost entirely repealed and replaced by new legislation. The Medicines Act 1968 now controlled the manufacture and distribution of medicines; the Poisons Act 1972 regulated the sale of non-medicinal poisons, while the Misuse of Drugs Act 1971 dealt with the abuse of drugs. In 1973, the National Health Service Reorganisation Act brought about a major revision in the pharmaceutical services of the National Health Service (NHS). A new National Health Service Act in 1977 together with many amending Health Service Acts now regulate the pharmaceutical services. All these Acts are described in detail in later chapters together with the orders and regulations which have been made under them. This introduction gives a brief account of how the law developed to this point, including references to most of the early statutes, all of which have now been repealed either wholly or in part.

Before the middle of the 19th century, there were no legal restrictions in England on the sale of poisons or drugs, and anyone could describe themselves as a pharmaceutical chemist. Statutory control over sales was first applied to arsenic because, as the preamble to the Arsenic Act 1851 stated, the unrestricted sale of arsenic facilitates the commission of crime. The first statute relating to pharmacy followed the next year. The Pharmacy Act 1852 confirmed the charter of incorporation of the Pharmaceutical Society of Great Britain, hereinafter called the Society, which had been granted in 1843 (see p. 319). The 1852 Act established the framework of the Society and gave it power to hold examinations and to issue certificates. It also restricted the use of the title pharmaceutical chemist to members of the Society, although it did not restrict the use of the titles chemist or druggist. The Society received its Royal prefix in 1988.

The Pharmacy Act 1868 brought new developments. It introduced a Poisons List (with 15 entries) and empowered the Society to add other substances to it, subject to the approval of the Privy Council. A poison was defined as any substance included in the Poisons List. Articles and preparations containing poisons could be sold by retail only by pharmaceutical chemists or by a new legal class of chemists and druggists. Both titles were protected by the Act. The class of chemists and druggists comprised (i) all those who before the passing of the Act had been engaged in the keeping of open shop for the compounding of the prescriptions of duly qualified medical practitioners, and (ii) all those persons who had been registered as assistants under the provisions of the Pharmacy Act 1852.

The Registrar of the Society was thereafter required to keep registers of pharmaceutical chemists, of chemists and druggists, and of apprentices or students. The qualification of chemist and druggist (the Minor examination) became the statutory minimum for persons carrying on a business comprising the sale of poisons. Chemists and druggists were eligible to be elected members or associates of the Pharmaceutical Society but did not have all the privileges of a member who had qualified as a pharmaceutical chemist (by passing the Major examination). That state of affairs continued – slightly modified by a statute of 1898 – until the Pharmacy Act 1953 combined the two qualifications in one Register of Pharmaceutical Chemists. The profession of pharmacy was now regulated by the Pharmacy Act 1954, which absorbed the 1953 Act. The 1954 Act was subsequently repealed by a section 60 Order under the Health Act 1999 (see Chapter 22).

The 1868 Act not only introduced the first list of poisons but also regulated the manner in which they could be sold, specifying more stringent restrictions on sale for the more dangerous poisons. Fixed penalties, recoverable in the civil courts, were prescribed for breaches of the Act. The list of poisons was extended by the Poisons and Pharmacy Act 1908, which also provided that poisons for agricultural and horticultural purposes could be sold by licensed dealers as well as by pharmacists. This Act also prescribed conditions under which corporate bodies could carry on the business of a chemist and druggist. This had become necessary because it had been held in the High Court in 1880 that an incorporated company was not covered by the word person as used in the 1868 Act and was, therefore, not liable for penalties under the Act (*Pharmaceutical Society* v. *London and Provincial Supply Association Ltd*, see p. 440).

Under the Pharmacy and Poisons Act 1933, a Poisons Board was established to advise the Secretary of State on what should be included in the Poisons List. Poisons in Part I of the list could be sold by retail only at pharmacies; poisons in Part II could be sold also by traders on a local authority list. Poisons were further classified by means of the Schedules to the Poisons Rules made under the Act. Schedule 4, for example, comprised a class of poisons which could be supplied to the public only on the authority of a prescription written by a practitioner. A Register of Premises was set up under the Act, and all registered pharmacists were required to be members of the Pharmaceutical Society.

One of the main features of the 1933 Act was the establishment of a disciplinary body (the Statutory Committee), which had authority not only over pharmacists who committed misconduct but also over pharmacists and corporate bodies convicted of offences under the Pharmacy Act. The Society was placed under a duty to enforce the Act, and was authorised to appoint inspectors for the purpose. Proceedings under the Act were to be taken in courts of summary jurisdiction and not, as previously, in the civil courts. The Pharmacy and Poisons Act 1933 was repealed by the Medicines Act 1968. The Poisons Act 1972 deals only with non-medicinal poisons (Chapter 18). The Statutory Committee and its cases has now been replaced by a Disciplinary Committee under a section 60 Order under the Health Act 1999 (see p. 350).

Pharmacy and poisons were firmly linked together by statute, but the sale and manufacture of medicines was not regulated in any way except for medicines containing poisons. Some control over quality was provided by a series of Food and Drugs Acts, culminating in the Food and Drugs Act 1955. Under those Acts, it was an offence to sell adulterated drugs, or to sell, to the prejudice of the purchaser, any drug not of the nature, substance or quality demanded. The effectiveness of those provisions was limited by the fact that most drugs were of vegetable origin and there were no precise standards for many of them. Furthermore, a manufacturer of a proprietary medicine did not have to disclose its composition, provided that s/he paid the appropriate duty by way of fixing the appropriate excise stamps to each bottle or packet as required by the Medicine Stamp Acts. That state of affairs was changed by the Pharmacy and Medicines Act 1941, which abolished medicines stamp duty and required, instead, a disclosure of composition of each container. It also restricted the sale of medicines to shops (as distinct from market stalls etc.) and made it unlawful to advertise any article for the treatment of eight named diseases, including diabetes, epilepsy and tuberculosis. This was the first statute in which pharmacy and medicines were directly linked. The 1941 Act, however, did not apply to animal medicines.

The Therapeutic Substances Act 1925 controlled by licence the manufacture (but not the sale or supply) of a limited number of products the purity or potency of which could not be tested by chemical means, for example vaccines, sera, toxins, antitoxins and certain other substances. The list was greatly extended when antibiotics came into use. It had not been held necessary to restrict the retail sale or supply of vaccines, sera and antitoxins, but penicillin and most other antibiotics were found to be substances which were capable of causing danger to the health of the community if used without proper safeguards. Consequently, the Penicillin Act 1947 and the Therapeutic Substances (Prevention of Misuse) Act 1953 permitted the supply of antibiotics to the public only by practitioners, or from pharmacies on the authority of practitioners' prescriptions. The Therapeutic Substances Act 1956 replaced the earlier Acts, so bringing under the control of one statute both the manufacture and the supply of therapeutic substances. It could be regarded as the precursor to the Medicines Act 1968, which replaced it.

Legislation relating to medicines developed in a piecemeal manner, each problem being dealt with as it arose, and the law was scattered throughout a number of statutes. However, rapid developments in pharmaceutical research after the Second World War made available an increasing number of potent substances for use in medicine, and a working party was set up by the government in 1959 to examine the need for new controls. The thalidomide tragedy in 1961 almost certainly precipitated proposals for new legislation, which was published in 1967 in a White Paper entitled *Forthcoming Legislation on the Safety, Quality and Description of Drugs and Medicines* (Cmnd.3395). The Medicines Act 1968, which was designed to replace all earlier legislation relating to medicines, was based on the proposals in the White Paper. It is considered in detail in Chapters 1 to 15.

European Community legislation has had, and still has, a large impact on UK law. The Treaty of Rome and the issue of regulations, directives, decisions and recommendations by the Council of Ministers in Brussels has led to amendments of pharmacy law in Great Britain, particularly with regard to the mutual recognition of pharmaceutical qualifications and the manufacture and distribution of medicines. This is discussed in Chapter 1, which also includes the principles and sources of law and the administration of justice

International agreement about the control of narcotics began with the International Opium Convention signed at The Hague in 1912, although the Convention was not implemented until after the First World War. A series of Dangerous Drugs Acts, beginning with the Dangerous Drugs Act 1920, brought the various international agreements into force in Great Britain. The Single Convention on Narcotic Drugs 1961 replaced all the earlier international agreements and was reflected in the Dangerous Drugs Act 1965.

The misuse of amphetamines and other psychotropic drugs widened the problems of abuse, and an International Convention on Psychotropic Substances was signed in 1971. In Great Britain, however, the Drugs (Prevention of Misuse) Act 1964 had provided a measure of control by making the unlawful possession of amphetamines, and certain other drugs, an offence. As problems of drug abuse continued to increase, the law was extended and recast in the Misuse of Drugs Act 1971, which repealed the various Dangerous Drugs Acts and the 1964 Act. The provision of the 1971 Act and the new regulations have been extensively amended since the 8th edition of this book, following the Shipman inquiry, and are described in detail in Chapter 17.

The National Health Service Act 1946 and the National Health Service (Scotland) Act 1947 provided for a comprehensive health service, including the provision of pharmaceutical services. There have since been numerous amending Acts particularly since the 8th edition of this book was published in 2005. In this present edition, because the primary and secondary healthcare systems are moving closer together, the opportunity has been taken to amalgamate the service requirements with those of the hospital service (Chapter 26). Miscellaneous legislation impinging on pharmacy is dealt with in Chapter 21, professional matters in Chapters 22 and 23 and fitness to practise/disciplinary matters in Chapter 24. A discussion on allied health professions is provided in Chapter 25. When this book went to press, the government was proposing new legislation, coming into force in 2010, which will split the Society's regulatory and professional functions into a new General Pharmaceutical Council and a new professional body (Chapter 22).

List of Statutes and Statutory Instruments

Statutes marked with an asterisk have been repealed.

Access to Health Records Act 1990	
Agriculture Act 1947	
Agriculture Act 1970	
Alcoholic Liquor Duties Act 1979	
Animal (Cruel Poisons) Act 1962	
SI 1963 No.1278	Animal (Cruel Poisons) Regulations 1963
Animal Health and Welfare Act 1984	
Animals (Scientific Procedures) Act 1986	
Apothecaries Act 1815	
Arsenic Act 1851	
Business Names Act 1985	
Competition Act 1998	
Companies Act 1985	
Consumer Protection Act 1987	
SI 1988 No.2078	Consumer Protection (Code of Practice for Traders on Price Indications) (Approved) Order 1988
SI 1994 No.3017	Medical Devices Regulations 1994
SI 1994 No.3119	Medical Devices (Consequential Amendments – Medicines) Regulations 1994
SI 1995 No.449	Medical Devices (Consultation Requirements) (Fees) Regulations 1995
	amended 1996/622; 1998/574; 1999/566

SI 1999 No.3042	Price Marking Order 1999
SI 2002 No.618	Medicines for Human Use and Medical Devices (Fees) Amendments) Regulations
	amended 2003/1687, 2007/400
Control of Pollution Act 1974	
SI 1992 No.588	Controlled Waste Regulations 1992
SI 1988 No.819	Collection and Disposal of Waste Regulations 1988 amended 1994/1056
SI 1996 No.972	Special Waste Regulations 1996 amended 1996/2019
Copyright Act 1956	
Criminal Justice Act 2003	
Criminal Justice (International Co-operation) Act 1990	
SI 1991 No.1285	Controlled Drugs (Substances Useful for Manufacture) Regulations 1991
	amended 1992/2914
SI 1993 No.2166	Controlled Drugs (Substances Useful for Manufacture) (Intra-Community Trade) Regulations 1993
	amended 2001/3683; 2004/850
Criminal Law Act 1977	
Customs and Excise Act 1952	
Customs and Excise Management Act 1979	
SI 1952 No.2229	Spirits Regulations 1952 amended 1991/2564
SI 1987 No.2009	Methylated Spirits Regulations 1987
Dangerous Drugs Act 1965*	
Data Protection Act 1984	
Data Protection Act 1998	
SI 2000 No.191	Data Protection (Subject Access) (Fees and Miscellaneous) Regulations 2000
SI 2000 No.413	Data Protection (Subject Access Modification) (Health) Order 2000
SI 2000 No.417	Data Protection (Processing of Sensitive Personal Data) Order 2000

European Decisions	
75/320/EEC	
85/434/EEC	
European Regulations	
90/2377/EEC	
90/3677/EEC	
93/2309/EEC	
726/2004/EC	
Finance Act 1920	
Fire Precaution Act 1971	
Food Act 1984	
Food and Drugs Act 1955	
Food and Drugs Act (Northern Ireland) Act 1958	
Food and Drugs (Scotland) Act 1956	
Food and Environment Protection Act 1985	
SI 1986 No.1510	Control of Pesticide Regulations 1986
	amended 1994/1142; 1995/887
Food (Northern Ireland) Order 1989	
Food Safety Act 1990	
Freedom of Information Act 2000	
Health Act 1995	
Health Act 1999	
Health Act 2006	
Health Act (Commencement Order No.2) 2006	
Health Authorities Act 1995	
Health and Personal Social Services (Northern Ireland) Order 1972	
Health and Safety at Work, etc. Act 1974	

SI 1974 No.1439	Health and Safety at Work etc. Act 1974 (Commencement No.1) Order 1974
SI 1975 No.1584	Employers Health and Safety Policy Statement (Exemptions) Regulations 1975
SI 1981 No.917	Health and Safety (First Aid) Regulations 1981
SI 1992 No.3004	Workplace (Health, Safety and Welfare) Regulations 1992
SI 1994 No.3247	Chemicals (Hazard Information and Packaging for Supply) Regulations 1994 amended 1996/1092; 1997/1460; 1998/3106; 1999/197; 2000/2381
SI 1998 No.1833	Working Time Regulations 1998
SI 1999 No.437	Control of Substances Hazardous to Health Regulations 1999
SI 2000 No.2381	Carriage of Dangerous Goods (Classification, Packaging & Labelling) Regulations 2000
Health and Social Care Act 2001	
Health and Social Care Act 2008	
Health and Social Care (Community Health and Standards) Act 2003	
Health Professions Order 2001 No.254	
SI 2003 No.1209	The Health Professions Council (Practice Committees) (Constitution) Rules Order of Council 2003
SI 2003 No.1572	The Health Professions (Registration and Fees) Rules Order of Council 2003
SI 2003 No.1573	The Health Professions (Screeners) Rules Order of Council 2003
SI 2003 No.1574	The Health Professions (Investigating Committee)Screeners) Rules Order of Council 2003
SI 2003 No.1575	The Health Professions (Conduct and Competence Committee) (Procedure) Rules Order of Council 2003
SI 2003 No.1576	The Health Professions (Health Committee)(Procedure) Rules Order of Council 2003
SI 2003 No.1577	The Health Professions(Functions of Assessors) Rules Order of Council 2003
SI 2003 No.1578	The Health Professions (Legal Assessors) Rules Order of Council 2003
SI 2003 No.1579	The Health Professions (Registration Appeals) Rules Order of Council 2003
SI 2003 No.1590	The Health Professions (Consequential Amendments) Rules Order of Council 2003

Health Professions Order (contd)	
SI 2004 No.2033	The Health Professions (Operating Department Practitioners and Miscellaneous Amendments) Order 2004
SI 2007 No.289	The Health Care Professions (The Pharmacists and Pharmacy Technicians) Order 2007
SI 2007 No.441	The Health Care Professions Royal Pharmaceutical Society of Great Britain (Registration Rules) Order of Council 2007
SI 2007 No.442	The Health Care Professions Royal Pharmaceutical Society of Great Britain (Fitness to Practise and Disqualification, etc Rules) Order of Council 2007
SI 2007 No.561	The Health Care Professions Royal Pharmaceutical Society of Great Britain (Fitness to Practise and Appeals Committees and their Advisers Rules) Order of Council 2007
SI 2007 No.1320	Health Service Medicines (Information Relating to Sales of Branded Medicines, etc) 2007
SI 2008 No.1938	Health Service Branded Medicines (Control of Prices and Supply of Information) 2008 Hearing Aid Council Act 1968
Hearing Aid Council (Amendment) Act 1989	
Hearing Aid Council Extension Act 1975	
Human Rights Act 1998	
Industrial and Provident Societies Act 1965	
Interpretations Act 1889	
Juries Act 1974	
SI 1987 No.1579	Jurors' Allowances Regulations 1987
Law Reform (Miscellaneous Provisions) (Scotland) Act 1980	
Limited Partnerships Act 1907	
Local Government Act 1972	
Lunacy Regulation Act (Northern Ireland) 1958	
Local Government and Public Involvement in Health Act 2007	
Medical Act 1858	
Medical Act 1983	

SI 2000 No.1803	Medical Act (Amendment) Order 2002 (Transitory Provisions) Order of Council 2003
SI 2003 No.1340	Medical Act (Amendment) Order 2000
SI 2003 No.1341	General Medical Council (Voluntary Erasure and Restoration) Regulations Order of Council 2003
SI 2003 No.1342	General Medical Council (Restoration and Registration Fees Amendment) Regulations Order of Council 2003
SI 2003 No.1343	General Medical Council Fitness to Practise Committees and Review Board for Overseas Qualified Practitioners (Amendment) Rules Order Order of Council 2003
SI 2003 No.1344	General Medical Council (Constitution of Fitness to Practise Committees)(Transitional Arrangements) Rules Order of Council 2003
Medical (Professional Performance) Act 1995	
Medicinal Products: Prescription by Nurses, etc. Act 1992	
Medicines Act 1960	
Medicines Act 1968	Medicines
SI 1970 No.746	Commission and Committees Regulations 1970
SI 1970 No.1256	(British Pharmacopoeia Commission) Order 1970
	amended 1982/1335
SI 1970 No.1257	(Committee on Safety of Medicines) Order 1970
SI 1971 No.974	(Application for Manufacturer's Wholesale Dealer's Licences) Regulations 1971
	amended 1977/1052; 1978/1140; 1983/1725; 1993/832
SI 1971 No.115	(First Appointed Day) Order 1971
SI 1971 No.1200	(Control of Substances for Manufacture) Order 1971 amended 1994/787
SI 1971 No.1267	(Surgical Materials) Order 1971 amended 1994/3119
SI 1971 No.1309	(Exportation of Specified Veterinary Products) Order 1971
SI 1971 No.1326	(Importation of Medicinal Products for Re-exportation) Order 1971
	amended 1977/640
SI 1971 No.1410	(Exemption from Licences) (Foods and Cosmetics) Order 1971
	amended 1973/2079

Medicines Act (*contd*)	
SI 1971 No.1445	(Retail Pharmacists – Exemption from Licensing Requirements) Order 1971
SI 1971 No.1450	(Exemption from Licences) (Special and Transitional Cases) Order 1971
	amended 1972/1200; 1978/1139; 1979/1585; 1989/1184; 1989/2323
SI 1971 No.1198	(Exportation of Specified Products for Human Use) Order 1971
SI 1972 No.640	(Exemption from Licences) (Wholesale Dealing) Regulations 1972
SI 1972 No.717	(Closing Date for Applications for Licences of Right) Order 1972
SI 1972 No.1200	(Exemptions from Licences) (Special Cases and Miscellaneous Provisions) Order 1972
	amended 1974/498; 1977/1161; 1978/1139; 1979/1585; 1989/2323
SI 1972 No.2076	(Data Sheet) Regulations 1972
	amended 1979/1760; 1981/1633; 1989/1183; 1994/3142; 1996/2420
SI 1973 No.367	(Extension to Antimicrobial Substances) Order 1973
	amended 2005/2754
SI 1973 No.1822	(Pharmacies) (Applications for Registration and Fees) Regulations 1973
	amended 2004/3197; 2005/3259; 2006/3264; 2007/3282
SI 1973 No.1849	(Pharmacies) (Appointed Day) Order 1973
SI 1974 No.1150	(Exemption from Licences) (Ingredients) Order 1974
SI 1975 No.298	(Advertising of Medicinal Products) Regulations 1975
SI 1975 No.533	(Dental Filling Substances) Order 1975
SI 1975 No.761	(Termination of Transitional Exemptions) (No.3) Order 1975
SI 1975 No.762	(Exemptions from Licences) (Wholesale Dealing in Confectionery) Order 1975
SI 1975 No.1169	(Medicines Act 1968 Amendment) Regulations 1975
SI 1975 No.1349	(Feeding Stuffs Additives) Order 1975
SI 1975 No.2000	(Child Safety) Regulations 1975
	amended 1976/1643; 1987/877; 1994/1402
SI 1976 No.31	(Feeding Stuff Limits of Variation) Order 1976

SI 1976 No.968	(Specified Articles and Substances) Order 1976
	amended 1994/3119
SI 1976 No.1726	(Labelling) Regulations 1976
	amended 1977/996; 1977/2168; 1978/41; 1978/1140; 1981/1791; 1983/1729; 1985/1558; 1985/2008; 1989/1183; 1992/3273; 1994/104; 1994/3114, 2005/2754
SI 1977 No.670	(Bal Jivan Chamcho Prohibition) (No.2) Order 1977
	amended 1997/856
SI 1977 No.1038	(Manufacturer's Undertakings for Imported Products) Regulations 1977
	amended 1992/2845; 1994/3144
SI 1977 No.1050	(Medicines Act 1968) Amendment Regulations 1977
SI 1977 No.1055	(Leaflets) Regulations 1977
	amended 1992/3274; 1994/104
SI 1977 No.1399	(Certificate of Analysis) Regulations 1977
SI 1977 No.1488	(Breathing Gases) Order 1977
SI 1977 No.2126	(Pharmacy and General Sale) (Appointed Day) Order 1977
SI 1977 No.2130	(Retail Sale or Supply of Herbal Remedies) Order 1977
SI 1977 No.2131	(Prohibition of Non-Medicinal Antimicrobial Substances) Order 1977
	amended 1992/2684
SI 1978 No.40	(Fluted Bottles) Regulations 1978
SI 1978 No.41	(Labelling and Advertising to the Public) Regulations 1978
SI 1978 No.1004	(Radioactive Substances) Order 1978
SI 1978 No.1006	(Administration of Radioactive Substances) Regulations 1978
	amended 1995/2147; 2005/2754; 2006/2407; 2006/2806
SI 1978 No.1138	(Intra-Uterine Contraceptive Devices) (Appointed Day) Order 1978
SI 1978 No.1139	(Intra-Uterine Contraceptive Devices) (Amendment to Exemption from Licence) Order 1978
SI 1978 No.1140	(Licensing of Intra-Uterine Contraceptive Devices) (Miscellaneous Amendments) Regulations 1978
SI 1978 No.1421	(Collection and Delivery Arrangements – Exemption) Order 1978

Medicines Act (contd)	
SI 1979 No.382	(Chloroform Prohibition) Order 1979
	amended 1980/263; 1989/1184
SI 1979 No.1114	(Exemption from Licences) (Assembly) Order 1979
SI 1979 No.1539	(Contact Lens Fluids and Other Substances) (Appointed Day) Order 1979
SI 1979 No.1585	(Contact Lens Fluids and Other Substances) (Exemption from Licences) Order 1979
	amended 1979/1745
SI 1979 No.1759	(Contact Lens Fluids and Other Substances) (Labelling) Regulations 1979
SI 1979 No.1760	(Contact Lens Fluids and Other Substances) (Advertising and Miscellaneous Amendments) Regulations 1979
SI 1980 No.1923	(Sale or Supply) (Miscellaneous Provisions) Regulations 1980
	amended 1982/28; 1990/1124; 1992/2938; 1994/2411; 1994/3144; 1995/3215; 1997/1831; 1997/2045; 1998/1045; 1999/644; 1999/2510; 2000/1070; 2000/1918; 2000/2494; 2001/3849; 2003/698; 2004/971; 2005/764; 2005/1520; 2005/2745; 2006/914; 2008/1162
SI 1980 No.1924	(Pharmacy and General Sale – Exemption) Order 1980
	amended 1982/27; 1989/1852; 1994/2409; 1994/3144; 1997/1350; 1998/107; 1998/2368; 2000/1919; 2003/697; 2004/1; 2004/1190; 2005/766; 2007/2179
SI 1981 No.1690	(Contact Lens Fluids and Other Substances) (Termination of Transitional Exemptions) Order 1981
SI 1982 No.626	(Stilbenes and Thyrostatic Substances) Regulations 1982 amended 1986/1980
SI 1983 No.1724	(Medicines Act 1968 Amendment) Regulations 1983
SI 1983 No.1727	(Leaflets for Veterinary Drugs) Regulations 1983
SI 1984 No.187	(Cyanogenetic Substances) Order 1984
SI 1984 No.673	(Exemption from Licences) (Importation) Order 1984
	amended 2005/2754
SI 1984 No.768	(Veterinary Drugs) (General Sale List) Order 1984
SI 1984 No.769	(Products other than Veterinary Drugs) (General Sale List) Order 1984
	amended 1985/1540; 1987/910; 1989/969; 1990/1129; 1992/1535; 1994/2410; 1995/3216; 1997/2043; 1998/2170; 1999/852;

	1999/2535; 2000/1092; 2000/2526; 2001/2068; 2001/4111; 2002/933
SI 1985 No.1403	(Control of Substances for Manufacture) Order 1985
SI 1985 No.1539	(Control of Substances for Manufacture) (Appointed Day) Order 1985
SI 1986 No.1180	(Exemption from Licences and Animal Test Certificates) Order 1986
SI 1988 No.705	(Hormone Growth Promoters) (Prohibition of Use) Regulations 1986
SI 1989 No.192 (C.6)	(Commencement) Order 1989
SI 1990 No.566	(Exemption from Licences) (Wholesale Dealing) Regulations 1990
SI 1991 No.1392	(Veterinary Drugs) (Prescription Only) Order 1991 amended 1991/2568
SI 1992 No.604	(Medicines Act 1968) (Amendment) Regulations 1992
SI 1992 No.605	(Application to Radiopharmaceutical-associated Products) Regulations 1992
SI 1992 No.606	(Committee on the Review of Medicines) (Revocation) Order 1992
SI 1992 No.755	(Applications for Grant and Renewal of Licences) (Miscellaneous Amendments) Regulations 1992
SI 1992 No.2844	(Exemptions from Licensing) (Radiopharmaceuticals) Order 1992
SI 1992 No.3271	(Medicines Act 1968) (Amendment) (No.2) Regulations 1992
SI 1993 No.834	(Medicines Act 1968) (Amendment) Regulations 1993
SI 1993 No.1227	(Veterinary Drugs) (Renewal Applications for Licences and Animal Test Certificates) Regulations 1993
SI 1993 No.2538	(Applications for Grant of Product Licences – Products for Human Use) Regulations 1993
SI 1994 No.102	(Advisory Board on the Registration of Homoeopathic Products) Order 1994
SI 1994 No.105	(Homoeopathic Medicinal Products for Human Use) Regulations 1994
	amended 1994/899; 1995/541; 1996/482; 1998/574; 1999/566; 2005/2753
SI 1994 No.276	(Medicines Act 1968) (Amendment) (No.2) Regulations 1994
SI 1994 No.1932	(Advertising) Regulations 1994
	amended 1996/1552; 1999/267; 2004/1480; 2005/2787

Medicines Act (*contd*)	
SI 1994 No.1933	(Monitoring of Advertising) Regulations 1994
	amended 1999/566; 1999/784
SI 1994 No.3119	(Consequential Amendments – Medicines) Regulations 1994
SI 1994 No.3142	(Marketing Authorisations for Veterinary Medicinal Products) Regulations 1994
	amended 2002/269; 2004/3193; 2004/3224; 2005/1520
SI 1994 No.3144	(For Human Use) (Marketing Authorisations, etc.) Regulations 1994
	amended 1998/3105; 2000/292; 2003/1618; 2004/3224; 2005/768; 2005/1520; 2005/2759
SI 1995 No.309	(Advisory Board on the Registration of Homoeopathic Products) Order 1995
	amended 2002/236; 2005/2753; 2006/2386
SI 1995 No.1116	(Products for Human Use – Fees) Regulations 1995
	amended 1996/683; 1998/574; 1999/566; 2000/592; 2000/3031; 2001/795; 2002/236; 2002/542; 2003/625; 2003/2321; 2004/666; 2004/1157; 2005/1124; 2006/2125
SI 1995 No.2321	(Amendment) Regulations 1995
SI 1997 No.321	(Registration of Homoeopathic Veterinary Medicinal Products) (Fees) Regulations 1997
SI 1997 No.1830	(Prescription Only Medicines) (Human Use) Order 1997
	amended 1997/2044; 1998/108; 1998/1178; 1998/2081; 1999/1044; 1999/3463; 2000/1917; 2000/2899; 2000/3231; 2001/2777; 2001/2889; 2001/3942; 2002/549; 2003/696; 2003/1590; 2003/2915; 2004/2; 2004/1189; 2005/765; 2006/915 2008/464; 2008/1161 and other Medicine for Human Use Prescribing Orders
SI 2000 No.1368	(Aristolochia and Mu Tong, etc.) (Temporary Prohibition) Order 2000
SI 2001 No.2889	The Prescription Only Medicines (Human Use) (Electronic Communications) Order 2001
SI 2002 No.236	(Codification Amendments etc.) Regulations 2002
	amended 2002/542
SI 2002 No.618	Medicines for Human Use and Medical Devices (Fees) Amendments) Regulations
	amended 2003/1687; 2007/400

SI 2002 No.3170	The Medicines for Human Use (Kava-kava) (Prohibition) Order 2002
SI 2003 No.2317	(Child Safety)Regulations 2003
	amended 2005/1520
SI 2003 No.3141	The Medicines (Pharmacies) (Application for Registration and Fees) Amendment Regulations 2003
SI 2004 No.1031	The Medicines for Human Use (Clinical Trials) Regulations 2004
	amended 2005/2754; 2006/2759; 2006/1928; 2006/2984
SI 2005 No.765	The Medicines for Human Use (Prescribing) Order 2005
	amended 2005/1507; 2005/3324; 2006/915
SI 2005 No.1094	The Medicines (Appointed Bodies) Regulations 2005
	amended 2005/2754; 2005/2788
SI 2005 No.1520	The Medicines (Sale or Supply) (Miscellaneous Amendments) Regulations 2005
SI 2005 No.1710	The Medicines (Provision of False and Misleading Information and Miscellaneous Amendments) Regulations 2005
SI 2005 No.2750	The Medicines (Traditional Herbal Medicinal products for Human Use Regulations 2005
	amended 2006/395
SI 2005 No.2789	The Medicines (Human Use) (Manufacturing, Wholesale Dealing and Miscellaneous Amendments) Regulations 2005
SI 2005 No.2791	The Herbal Medicines Advisory Committee Order 2005
SI 2006 No.1952	The Medicines for Human Use (National Rules for Homoeopathic Products) Regulations 2006
SI 2006 No.2407	The Veterinary Medicines Regulations 2006
SI 2006 No.2807	The Medicines for Human Use) Administration and Sale and Supply) Miscellaneous Amendments) Order 2006
	amended 2007/2178
SI 2007 No.2539	The Veterinary Medicines Regulations 2007
SI 2008 No.548	Medicines for Human Use (Prohibition) (Scencio and Miscellaneous Amendments) Order 2008
SI 2008 No.1692	The Medicines for Human Use (Prescribing by EEA Practitioners) Regulations 2008
SI 2008 No.2789	The Medicines (Pharmacies) (Responsible Pharmacist) Regulations 2008
Medicines Act 1971	

Medicines Act (*contd*)	
SI 1995 No.1116	(Products for Human Use – Fees) Regulations 1995
	amended 1996/683; 1998/574; 1999/566
SI 1998 No.2428	(Products for Animal Use – Fees) Regulations 1998
	amended 1999/2512; 2000/2250; 2004/2750; 2004/3081
SI 2006 No.494	(Products for Human Use and Medical Devices (Fees and Amendment) Regulations 2006
Mental Health Act 1959	
Mental Health Act 1983	
Mental Health (Scotland) Act 1960	
Merchant Shipping Act 1894	
Merchant Shipping Act 1970	
Merchant Shipping Act 1979	
SI 1995 No.1802	Merchant Shipping and Fishing Vessels (Medical Stores) Regulations 1995
	amended 1996/2821
Methylated Spirit (Sale by Retail) (Scotland) Act 1937	
SI 1998 No.1602 (S.87)	Deregulation (Methylated Spirits Sale by Retail) (Scotland) Regulations 1998
Mineral Workings (Off-Shore Installations) Act 1971	
Ministers of the Crown (Transfer of Functions) Act 1946	
SI 1968 No.1699	(Secretary of State for Social Services) Order 1969
Misuse of Drugs Act 1971	
SI 1971 No.2120 (C.57)	(Commencement No.1) Order 1971
SI 1973 No.771	(Modification) Order 1973
SI 1973 No.795 (C.20)	(Commencement No.2) Order 1973
SI 1973 No.796	Designation Order 1973
SI 1973 No.798	(Safe Custody) Regulations 1973
	amended 1974/1449; 1975/294; 1984/1146; 1985/2067; 1986/2332; 1999/1403

SI 1974 No.85 (L.1)	Tribunal (England and Wales) Rules 1974
SI 1975 No.421	(Modification) Order 1975
SI 1975 No.459 (Sch.59)	Tribunal (Scotland) Rules 1975
SI 1975 No.498	(Designation) (Amendment) Order 1975
SI 1977 No.1243	(Modification) Order 1977
SI 1977 No.1379	(Designation) Order 1977
SI 1979 No.209	(Modification) Order 1979
SI 1983 No.765	(Modification) Order 1983
SI 1984 No.859	(Modification) Order 1984
SI 1984 No.1144	(Designation) (Variation) Order 1984
SI 1985 No.1995	(Modification) Order 1985
SI 1986 No.416	(Licence Fees) Regulations 1986 amended 2003/611
SI 1986 No.2230	(Modification) Order 1986
SI 1990 No.2589	(Modification) Order 1990
SI 1993 No.2166	Controlled Drugs (Substances useful for Manufacture)(Intra Community Trade) Regulations 1993
	amended 2004/850
SI 1995 No.1966	(Modification) Order 1995
SI 1996 No.1300	(Modification) Order 1996
SI 1997 No.1001	(Notification of and Supply to Addicts) Regulations 1997
SI 1998 No.750	(Modification) Order 1998
SI 2001 No.3932	(Modification) Order 2001 (36 additions, phenylamine derivatives)
SI 2001 No.3997	(Designation) Order 2001
	amended 2005/1652
SI 2001 No.3998	Regulations 2001
	amended 2003/1432; 2003/1653; 2003/2429; 2005/271; 2005/1653; 2005/3178; 2005/3372; 2006/986; 2006/1450; 2006/2178; 2006/3331
SI 2003 No.1243	(Modification) Order 2003
SI 2003 No.3201	(Modification)(No.2) Order 2003
SI 2005 No.2864	Misuse of Drugs (Supply to Addicts) (Amendment) Regulations 2005

Misuse of Drugs Act (*contd*)	
SI 2006 No.3148	Controlled Drugs (Supervision of Management and Use) Regulations 2006
SI 2007 No.2154	Misuse of Drugs and Misuse of Drugs (Sale Custody) (Amendment) Regulations 2007
SI 2008 No.296	Controlled Drugs (Drug Precursors) (Community External Trade) Regulations 2008
Misuse of Drugs (Northern Ireland) Regulations 1974	
National Health Service Act 1946	
National Health Service Act 1977	
National Health Service Act 2006 (for England)	
National Health Service (Wales) Act 2006	
National Health Service (Consequential Provisions) Act 2006	
National Health Service Reform and Health Care Professions Act 2002	
National Health Service and Community Care Act 1990	
National Health Service	
SI 1981 No.597	(Standing Advisory Committees) Order 1981
SI 1985 No.304	Community Health Councils Regulations 1985
	amended 1990/1375
SI 1988 No.551	(Travelling Expenses and Remission of Charges) Regulations 1988
	amended 1999/767
SI 1989 No.419	(Charges for Drugs and Appliances) Regulations 1989
	amended 1990/537; 1993/420; 1994/690; 1994/2402; 1995/643; 1996/583; 1998/491; 1999/767; 2000/122
SI 1990 No.1718	Prescription Pricing Authority Constitution Order 1990
SI 1990 No.1719	Prescription Pricing Authority Regulations 1990
SI 1992 No.635	(General Medical Services) Regulations 1992
	amended 1992/2412; 1993/2421; 1994/2620; 1995/3093; 1997/981

SI 1992 No.662	(Pharmaceutical Services) Regulations 1992
	amended 1993/2451; 1994/2402; 1995/644; 1996/698; 1998/681; 1999/696; 1999/2563; 2000/121
SI 1992 No.664	(Service Committees and Tribunal) Regulations 1992
	amended 1993/2972; 1995/3091; 1996/703
SI 1996 No.70	Health Authorities (Membership and Procedure) Regulations 1996
SI 1996 No.708	(Functions of Health Authorities and Administration Arrangements) Regulations 1996
SI 1996 No.640	Community Health Council Regulations 1996
SI 1999 No.2794	(Penalty Charge) Regulations 1999
SI 2000 No.89	Primary Care Trusts (Membership, Procedure and Administration) Regulations 2000
SI 2001 No.2887	(Charges for Drugs and Appliances)(Electronic Communications) Order 2001
SI 2001 No.2888	(Pharmaceutical Services) and (Misuse of Drugs)(Electronic Communications) Order
SI 2001 No.2889	The Prescription Only(Human Use (Electronic Communications) Order 2001
SI 2001 No.2890	(General Medical Services)(Electronic Communications) Order 2001
SI 2001 No.3744	(Abolition of the NHS Tribunal(Consequential Provisions) Regulations 2001
SI 2001 No.3750	(The Family Health Appeal Authority (Procedures) Rules 2001
SI 2002 No.551	(Pharmaceutical Services) and (General Medical Sevices) (No.2) Amendment Regulations 2002
SI 2002 No.888	(Local Pharmaceutical Services) and Pharmaceutical Services) Regulations
	amended 2002/2016
SI 2002 No.1016	The NHS (Primary Care) Act (Commencement No.8) Order 2002
SI 2002 No.2375	(England: Functions of Strategic Health Authorities and Primary Care Trusts) Regulations 2002
SI 2002 No.2861	(Local Pharmaceutical Services etc) Regulations 2002
	amended 2005/641; 2006/552
SI 2003 No.1084	(Pharmaceutical Services) (General Medical Services) and (Charges for Drugs and Appliances) Amendment Regulations 2003

National Health Service (*contd*)	
SI 2003 No.2863	(General Medical Services, etc.) (Patients Forums) Amendment Regulations 2003
SI 2004 No.38	(Tribunal) (Scotland) Regulations 2004
SI 2004 No.39	(Pharmaceutical Services) (Scotland) Amendment Regulations 2004
SI 2004 No.569	Direct (Establishment and Constitution) Order 2004
SI 2004 No.629	NHS (GMS Contracts) (Prescription of Drugs) Regulations 2004
SI 2004 No.1768	(Complaints) Regulations 2004
National Health Service (Primary Care) Act 1997	
SI 1616	National Health Service (Primary Care) Act Commencement No.8) Order 2002
National Health Service Reorganisation Act 1973	
National Health Service (Scotland) Act 1947	
National Health Service (Scotland) Act 1972	
National Health Service (Scotland) Act 1978	
National Health Service Reform (Scotland) Act 2004	
SI 1973 No.691 (S.56)	(Determination of Areas of Health Boards) (Scotland) Order 1973
	amended 1974/266 (S.15)
SI 1989 No.326	(Charges for Drugs and Appliances) (Scotland) Regulations 1989
	amended 1998/609 (S.20); 1999/612 (S.36)
SI 1992 No.434	(Service Committees and Tribunal) (Scotland) Regulations 1992
	amended 1994/3038; 1995/3201; 1996/938 (S.103); 1999/53
SI 1995 No.414 (S.28)	(Pharmaceutical Services (Scotland) Regulations 1995
	amended 1996/840 (S.95); 1996/1504 (S.132); 1997/696 (S.55); 1998/3031 (S.174); 1999/57
SI 1995 No.416	(General Medical Services) (Scotland) Regulations 1995
Nurses and Midwives Order 2001 No.253	

SI 2003 No.1738	The Nursing and Midwifery Council (Practice Committees) (Interim Constitution) Rules Order of Council 2003
Nursing Homes Registration (Scotland) Act 1960	
Offices, Shops and Railway Premises Act 1963	
Opticians Act 1989	
SI 1984 No.1778	Sale of Optical Appliances Order of Council 1984
SI 2005 No.848	(Amendment) Order 2005
Partnership Act 1890	
Penicillin Act 1947*	
Pharmacists (Fitness to Practise) Act 1997	
Pharmacy Act 1852*	
Pharmacy Act 1868*	
Pharmacy Acts Amendment Act 1898*	
Pharmacy Act 1953	
Pharmacy Act 1954	
SI 1978 No.20	Pharmaceutical Society (Statutory Committee) Order of Council 1978
Pharmacy and Poisons Act 1933*	
Pharmacy and Poisons (Northern Ireland) Act 1925	
Pharmacy and Medicines Act 1941*	
Poisons Act 1972	
SI 1982 No.217	Poisons List Order 1982
	amended 1986/9; 1992/2292
SI 1982 No.218	Poison Rules 1982
	amended 1985/1077; 1986/10; 1986/1704; 1989/112; 1992/2293
Poisons and Pharmacy Act 1908*	
Protection from Eviction Act 1977	

Protection of Animals Acts 1911–1962	
Protection of Animals (Amendment) Act 1927	
Prevention of Damage by Rabbits Act 1939	
Public Health Act 1936	
Public Health (Scotland) Act 1897	
Rabies Act 1974* (Replaced by the Animal Health Act 1981)	
SI 1974 No.2212	Rabies (Control) Order 1974
Race Relations Act 1976	
Revenue Act 1889	
SI 470	Regulatory Reform (Sunday Trading) Order 2004
Sex Discrimination Act 1975	
Sex Discrimination Act 1986	
Ships (Airports) Act 1962	
SI 1977 No.1397	Airports Shops Order 1977
SI 1980 No.774	Cardiff–Wales Airport Shop Order 1980
Shops Acts 1950–1962	
Shops (Early Closing Days) Act 1965	
Single European Act 1987	
Smoking, Health and Social Care (Scotland) Act 2005 (asp 13)	
Social Work (Scotland) Act 1968	
Social Security Act 1986	
Statutory Declarations Act 1935	
Therapeutic Substances Act 1956*	
Sunday Trading Act 1994	
Trade Descriptions Act 1968	
Trade Descriptions Act 1972	

SI 1973 No.2031	Trade Descriptions (Indication of Origin) (Exemption No.5) Directions 1973
Trade Union Act 1876	
Trade Union and Labour Relations Act 1974	
Trade Union Reform and Employment Rights Act 1993	
Tribunal and Inquiries Act 1971	
SI 1973 No.1600	Tribunals and Inquiries (Misuse of Drugs Tribunals) Order 1973
SI 1974 No.1964	Tribunals and Inquiries (Misuse of Drugs Tribunals) Order 1974
SI 1986 No.176	Medicines Act 1968 (Hearings by Persons Appointed) Rules 1986
Trustee Investments Act 1961	
SI 2005 No.2745	The Veterinary Medicines Regulations 2005
SI 2005 No.2751	The Supply of Relevant Veterinary Medicinal Products Order 2005
Veterinary Surgeons Act 1948	
Veterinary Surgeons Act 1966	
SI 1973 No.308	Veterinary Surgery (Exemption) Order 1973
SI 1980 No.1951	Veterinary Surgery (Amendment) Order 1980
SI 1982 No.1267	Veterinary Surgery (Exemption) Order 1982
SI 1983 No.6	Veterinary Surgery (Blood Sampling) Order 1983
SI 1988 No.526	Veterinary Surgeons (Schedule 3 Amendment) Order 1988
SI 1990 No.2217	Veterinary Surgeons (Schedule 3 Amendment) Order 1990
SI 1991 No.1412	Veterinary Surgeons (Schedule 3 Amendment) Order 1991
SI 1992 No.696	Veterinary Surgeons (Epidural Anaesthesia) Order 1992
SI 2002 No.1479	Veterinary Surgeons Act 1966 (Schedule 3 Amendment) Order 2002
Water Resources Act 1991	
Weights and Measures Act 1985	
SI 1970 No.1897	Weights and Measures (Equivalents for Dealing in Drugs) Regulations 1970
	amended 1976/1664

Abbreviations and acronyms

AC	Appeal Court
All ER	All England Law Reports
AMS	Acute Medication Service
AMTRA	Animal Medicines Training Regulatory Authority
AVM	Authorised Veterinary Medicines
BERR	Department for Business, Enterprise and Regulatory Reform
BNF	*British National Formulary*
CEHR	Commission for Equality and Human Rights
Ch	Law Reports Chancery Division
CHAI	Commission for Health Care Audit and Inspection (Healthcare Commission)
CHI	Commission for Health Improvement (obsolete)
CHRE	Council for Healthcare Regulatory Excellence
cm	centimetre
Cmnd.	Command paper
CMS	Chronic Medication Service
COSHH	Controls on Substances Hazardous to Health
CPD	continuing professional development
CQC	Care Quality Commission
CSCI	Commission for Social Care Inspection
DEFRA	Department for Environment, Food and Rural Affairs
EEA	European Economic Area
EEC	European Economic Community
EU	European Union
FHSAA	Family Health Services Appeal Authority
fl.oz	fluid ounce
FTP	fitness to practise
g	gram
GMC	General Medical Council
GMP	Good Manufacturing Practice
GP	general practitioner
GPhC	General Pharmaceutical Council
INN	international non-proprietary name
iu	international unit
KB	Law Reports King's Bench Division
kg	kilogram

LHB	local health board
LINks	local involvement networks
LLP	limited liability partnerships
LPC	local pharmaceutical committee
LT	*Law Times Reports*
MAS	Minor Ailment Service
md	maximum dose
mdd	maximum daily dose
mg	milligram
MHRA	Medicines Healthcare Regulatory Authority
mL	millilitre
MRL	maximum residue limit
ms	maximum strength
MUR	Medicines Use Review
NHS	National Health Service
NICE	National Institute for Health and Clinical Excellence
P	Pharmacy Medicine
P&PT Order 2007	Pharmacists and Pharmacy Technicians Order 2007
PALS	Patient Advocacy and Liaison Service
PCT	primary care trust
PGD	Patient Group Direction
Pharm J	*Pharmaceutical Journal*
PHS	Public Health Service
POM	Prescription Only Medicine
PPRS	Pharmaceutical Price Regulation Scheme
PSNC	Pharmaceutical Services Negotiating Committee
QB	Law Reports, Queen's Bench Division
QIS	Quality Improvement Scotland
RAC	Registration Appeals Committee
reg.	Regulation
RPSGB	Royal Pharmaceutical Society of Great Britain
s.	section
S4BH	Standards for Better Health
Sch.	Schedule
SI	Statutory Instrument
SPC	Summary of Product Characteristics
SQP	suitably qualified person
v/v	volume in volume
v/w	volume in weight
w/v	weight in volume
w/w	weight in weight

1

Sources of law

Introduction

Since the accession of the United Kingdom (UK) (i.e. England, Scotland, Wales and Northern Ireland) to the European Treaty of Rome in 1973, almost all legislation relevant to pharmacy and medicines derives from the European Union (EU) (formerly the European Economic Community – EEC). Thus Europe is the highest legal authority for such law in the UK. Law emanating from the EU has then to be enacted into 'domestic' legislation to take effect in the UK. Domestic legislation in the UK operates at two levels: 'primary' law, that is, Acts of Parliament, and 'secondary' law, that is, detailed provisions implementing the broad provisions of an Act. Public bodies are also subject to further 'Directions' made under the authority of primary and secondary law. This hierarchy is reflected in the processes by which law is made, how it is enforced and interpreted and how it may be challenged. This chapter provides an overview of aspects of UK law as they relate to pharmacy.

European law

Following the Second World War, there was felt to be a need for trading agreements between the countries of Europe. In 1957, six member states signed the Treaty of Rome, which established the EEC – now the EU. The UK acceded to the Treaty in 1973, along with Denmark and Ireland; Greece acceded in 1981 and Portugal and Spain followed in 1986. Sweden, Finland and Austria signed up to the Treaty in 1996, and Latvia, Lithuania, Estonia, Cyprus, the Czech Republic, Slovakia, Poland, Hungary, Malta and Slovenia joined in May 2004, followed by Romania and Bulgaria in 2007, bringing the total number of member states to 27.

The Single European Act 1987 was designed to expedite a single internal market and to remove all the remaining barriers which exist to the free movement of people, goods, services and capital. It is the object of the Community to ensure that there is no impediment to these 'four freedoms' and, if there is, to remove it. Harmonisation is one method by which such obstacles can be overcome and this is shown in many of the Directives which have affected the production and distribution of pharmaceuticals.

The legislation implementing the Treaty is formulated by the Council of Ministers in four basic forms:

Regulations. These have a direct effect and are binding on all member states and on individuals in every respect.

Directives. These are binding as to their objectives but leave to member states the method of implementation. Such implementation may be legislative or administrative. Most directives include 'derogations' – a form of exception which member states may claim if they feel that their particular circumstances require it.

Decisions. These are binding on those to whom they are addressed and are often of an administrative nature.

Recommendations. These are self-evident and are persuasive.

The European institutions

There are five main institutions of the European Union.

The *Council of Ministers* is composed of politicians of each member state and in practice the minister attending changes according to the item under discussion. The Council makes the ultimate decisions on European law. The Council is supported by working parties which include civil servants from each state and which study proposals put forward by the Council or the Commission. The working party reports are sent to the Committee of Permanent Representatives, which makes the decision whether or not to put the proposal forward to a Council meeting.

The *Commission* comprises commissioners (civil servants), each with responsibilities for a particular area of interest, for example agriculture, internal affairs, environment. It has been called the Civil Service of the Community and proposes, executes and polices the policies of the Community as promulgated by the Council. Discussions between a commissioner's department and interested parties can lead to the formation of draft proposals. These are discussed by the Commission as a whole, which then decides on the form of any final proposal to be laid before the Council.

The *Parliament (Assembly)* is a directly elected chamber of members from the 27 states; member state representation is related directly to population size. It has three main functions: control over the Community's budget, power of censure over the Commission and scrutiny of the legislative process. The last function has been of importance in the promulgation of directives affecting pharmacy upon which the Parliament must be consulted. The detailed work is done by standing committees who have a *rapporteur*, responsible for preparing the draft response of the Committee and presenting it to the plenary session of the Parliament.

The *Economic and Social Committee* comprises representatives of economic and social groups in the member states. It is divided into three groups: employers, workers (trade unions) and a variety of interest groups, which includes the professions. The Economic and Social Committee has to be consulted before any final decision can be taken on proposed legislation. The work is mainly done in various specialist expertise sections (e.g. agriculture, transport). Within each section, there are study groups which deal with specific proposals. The section produces an 'Opinion' which is presented to a plenary session of the Committee before being forwarded to the Council.

The *European Court of Justice* is covered below, under Courts.

European law usually results from a request for action from an EU member state. The Commission then drafts proposed legislation that passes through a lengthy debate, amendment and consultation process until the Council agrees the final form of the legislation.

British law

The scope of this book does not extend to Northern Ireland. Therefore, the law covered relates to England Scotland and Wales only, although the law in Northern Ireland often replicates the British law. Law covering medicines and pharmacy practice generally applies across all of Britain but there is scope for differences. Law covering the administration of the National Helath Service (NHS) differs significantly in the three component countries of Britain and is likely to diverge further over time. There are two primary divisions in British law: statute law and civil law (Table 1.1). These may commonly be referred to as criminal and civil law, but there is a substantial body of statutory law that is not accompanied by criminal sanctions, but by administrative or professional sanctions.

The arrangements for the NHS and for professional discipline fall into these two categories. Legislation in Britain is made in the name of the Crown – the Queen. Properties owned by, and activities carried out by the state on her behalf, have in the past been subject to Crown immunity.

Crown immunity means complete immunity from prosecution under statutory legislation. This concept prevailed in the NHS hospitals for many years and many hospital pharmacists still have the false idea that it still applies and that they cannot be prosecuted for offences committed within NHS hospitals. This is not true as Crown immunity was formally removed from NHS hospital services in April 1991 and all the major pharmaceutical legislation now applies including the Medicines Act and the Misuse of Drugs Acts together with the subordinate legislation made under them. The prison health services and military health services are also expected to comply with UK legislation, other than in exceptional cases (see Chapter 26).

Table 1.1 Summary of UK law with relevance to pharmacy

	Statutory law			Civil law
	Criminal legislation	Administrative legislation	Professional legislation	Common law rights and duties, augmented by human rights
Enforcement agencies	Police officers RPSGB inspectors	Representatives of administrative body	Professional body RPSGB inspectors	Direct action by plaintiff
Action for breach	Prosecution in the criminal courts	Appearance before relevant tribunal	Appearance before professional tribunal	Being sued in the civil courts
Sanctions available	Fines Imprisonment	Loss of remuneration Loss of contract Loss of position	Removal from professional register	Having to pay compensation
Redress available	Appeal	Judicial review	Appeal	Appeal

Statute law

A statute, strictly speaking, is an Act of Parliament. There are two kinds, public and private, but this book is only concerned with public acts such as the Medicines Act, the Misuse of Drugs Act, the Poisons Act (appearing principally in Chapters 2 to 21). Acts are usually referred to as *primary* legislation since they are the primary authority for legislation in the UK. Statute law is also used to describe legislation which is subsidiary to an Act, normally in the form of Regulations or Orders. These are collectively known as Statutory Instruments (or SIs) or *secondary* legislation. Proposals to introduce new legislation come forward in the form of bills. Most are government bills but sometimes they are put forward by individual members of parliament (private member's bill). Before a bill is proposed, the government will normally signal its intentions in a 'white paper'. Sometimes this is preceded by a discussion document, called a 'green paper'. The programme of primary legislation is usually outlined in the Queen's speech when Parliament enters a new session in the autumn.

Each bill is normally introduced into the House of Commons at a formal first reading and then passes through a series of 'readings'. After the second reading, the content and object of the bill is open to debate, following which the bill goes to a committee stage which examines the detail clause by clause and any amendments suggested in debate. The Commons then consider the bill again at the report stage, followed by the third reading.

These stages are then repeated in the House of Lords. Once a bill passes both Houses it is ready for Royal assent. Acts are most often 'enabling'; that is, they give powers to the government, usually individual Secretaries of State, to do things. Major changes to an Act can normally only be made by another Act. An SI implements the detail of broad powers given by an Act. An SI does not go through parliamentary debate but is 'tabled' in the Parliament in the name of the Minister and will be passed if no objections are raised.

Administrative law

Administrative law (appearing principally in Chapters 24 and 26) is that body of law that regulates the activity of public bodies. Such bodies include NHS authorities such as primary care trusts (PCTs) in England and local authorities and education authorities. Every NHS body and PCT is set up by individual Regulation, thus conferring statutory powers such as power to manage budgets, hire and fire staff and enter into contracts. Strategic health authorities, ambulance and mental health care trusts are also individually created by statute. NHS Direct is a legally constituted special health authority to give it power to enter into formal contracts with PCTs (England). Administrative law comprises statutes (Acts, Regulations, Orders) supplemented by a substantial body of 'Directions' made by senior civil servants acting under the authority of the relevant minister. Policy statements and guidelines, all of which describe the standards to which the public sector is expected to work, supplement the legal framework further. Initially, the public authority itself usually enforces administrative law – a good example would be the enforcement of the NHS dispensing contract by the PCTs in England. Enforcement is often also pursued through tribunals, appeal authorities and the courts. Sanctions are administrative such as a fine (withholding of reimbursement for dispensing NHS scripts), which reverts to the public body, or loss of contract.

Action by public bodies is susceptible to *judicial review*; a process whereby a court determines whether the public body acted fairly and within its statutory powers, rather than reviewing the actual decision reached. Three types of criteria are considered namely:

- was a decision made by a public body lawful or not?
- was it a reasonable and rational one: had the body considered all the relevant facts and ignored those that were irrational?
- was it based on the correct procedures laid down in a particular case?

Decisions in Statutory Committee and disciplinary cases can be made subject to *judicial review* particularly if there has been a breach of proper procedures or where the penalty imposed has been irrational or unreasonable (see Chapter 24).

Professional law

Professional law (appearing principally in Chapters 22 to 25) comprises the law underpinning the powers to discipline health professionals such as pharmacists. The authority to discipline pharmacists lies in the Pharmacist and Pharmacy Technicians Order 2007 and associated rules. The notion of an expected standard of care, which also used in civil law cases (see below), is used by professional tribunals to judge whether a professional is guilty of professional misconduct. For pharmacists, these standards may principally be found in the profession's Code of Ethics and in the standards, guidelines and protocols laid down for NHS care.

Civil law

Civil law (referred to in Chapters 22 and 23) derives from the notion of duties and responsibilities owed between citizens (Latin *civitas*, citizen). In its turn, civil law has developed through court judgments based on the 'common law'. The common law developed during the Middle Ages as the King's courts gradually took the rule of law out into the shires to make judgments over the affairs of 'common' people. Action under civil law allows an aggrieved party to sue for compensation from another citizen who was alleged to have 'wronged' him. This concept of 'a civil wrong' is known in law as 'tort' (another archaic term from Old French). Some types of tort are now rarely seen in courts; breach of promise, for example. Libel, slander and trespass actions are all civil wrongs. In healthcare practice, the most likely actions are for clinical negligence and possibly breach of confidentiality and defamation. In a case of clinical negligence, the complainant (plaintiff) makes an allegation that the actions of another person (the respondent) has caused them damage or injury. To succeed, the plaintiff would have to prove that the health professional firstly owed him a duty of care, and then that the duty had been breached (i.e. was lower than the standard expected) and that the breach had caused the injury alleged. A civil action for battery is also a possible tort if a patient is treated without consent.

The courts

The court with jurisdiction over EU law is the European Court of Justice (ECJ). This settles legal disputes involving Community legislation and its judgments are binding on each member state. Much of its work now involves giving preliminary rulings on questions referred by the courts of the member states.

In addition, under the auspices of the Council of Europe, there is the European Court of Human Rights (ECHR), which developed separately, before the European Court of Justice, to enforce the European Convention on Human Rights. This Convention was agreed in 1949 as a direct result of the human rights' atrocities of the Second World War. The UK was a founder member but was the last of the original signatories to enact the convention into domestic law. This was principally because the English common law conventions were held to embody adequate safeguards for human rights. Until 1998, any individual who wished to claim that their human rights had been violated had to complain for redress to the European Court of Human Rights. When the UK enacted the Convention in the Human Rights Act 1998, UK citizens then acquired the right to seek redress in the UK courts first, although the European Court of Human Rights remains an option if the complainant does not receive satisfaction in the UK.

The structure of the Courts in England and Wales is shown in Table 1.2.

A strict hierarchical system of courts means that the lowest possible tier of the court system will first make a judgment on the particular facts of that case. This judgment becomes a precedent – or case law – for dealing with any similar cases, unless there are some significant facts that distinguish them from the first case. However, a higher court can disagree with the findings

Table 1.2 The courts in England and Wales	
Criminal Division	**Civil Division**
House of Lords Hears appeals from the Court of Appeal and sometimes direct from the Divisional Court	House of Lords Hears appeals from the Court of Appeal and sometimes direct from the High Court
Court of Appeal Criminal Division Hears appeals from the Crown Court	Court of Appeal Civil Division Hears appeals from High Court and County Court
Queen's Bench Division (Divisional Court)	High Court Queen's Bench Division hears negligence cases (other divisions for family law and chancery – commercial matters)
Crown Court Hears cases committed to this court, and appeals, from the magistrate's court Has greater powers of sentencing than lower court	
Magistrates Court (Bench of lay Magistrates) May sometimes sit with a stipendiary or circuit judge)	County Court Can deal with actions involving small sums of money (£5–10k)

of a lower court and overturn them. More detail on the British legal system may be found in the further reading listed below.

Examples of European legislation affecting pharmacy, pharmacists and medicines are given below; further details may also be found in the reading list. Full details of British legislation appear in subsequent chapters of this book.

Examples of European law

Most of the current UK law which applies to pharmacy practice derives from European legislation in the form of 'directives' although 'regulations' have been made concerning the marketing authorisation of medicinal products (see p. 9). The first set of digits refers to the year of enactment, the second set refers to the number of this legal instrument within that year. All retain either the EC (European Commission) or the EEC suffix.

Free movement of pharmacists

The Pharmacy Directives concerned with the free movement of pharmacists, namely Directive 85/432/EEC, which dealt with the education and training of the pharmacist, and Directive 85/433/EEC, dealing with a pharmacist's right to establishment within the member states, were revoked in 2005 and a consolidation directive exbracing all the health professions was introduced, namely Council Directive 2005/36/EC. Each member state is obliged to recognise, without impediment, the list of degrees (or equivalent) laid down in the Directives. Registration as a pharmacist in the UK is recognised. The competent authorities within the member states deal with the procedure and those authorities in the UK are the Royal Pharmaceutical Society of Great Britain (RPSGB) and its equivalent in Northern Ireland. The new Directive 2005/36/EC also recognises a new category of registrant, namely a visiting practitioner who wants to provide services in the UK on a temporary or occasional basis.

In order for a pharmacist to move freely throughout the Community s/he must produce evidence from his/her own competent authority to the corresponding one in the host member state that s/he:

1   is a national of a member state of the Community or treated as such;
2   a   possesses a university degree (or equivalent) which was obtained following a course of study of not less than five years, at least four years of which comprised theoretical and practical training in a university, together with at least six months in-service training in a community or hospital pharmacy; or
    b   has for at least three consecutive years during the previous five years been effectively and lawfully engaged in regulated pharmaceutical

activity, e.g. a community pharmacy, hospital pharmacy, etc. This is known as the *acquired rights* provision for those who cannot comply with point 2a above;

3   is in good physical and mental health; and

4   is of good character.

The pharmacy degrees in the UK together with the preregistration year and the 'A'-level at university entrance are considered to be equivalent to the total five-year requirement.

Directive 2005/36/EC has been implemented in Great Britain by means of the European Qualifications (Health and Social Care Professions) Regulations 2007 (SI 2007 No. 3101) and in the bye-laws of the RPSGB. Pharmacists seeking free movement should contact the Society.

Production and distribution of medicinal products for human use

Council Regulation 2309/93/EEC lays down Community procedures for the authorisation and supervision of medicinal products for human and veterinary use and established the European Agency for the Evaluation of Medicinal Products. Directive 2001/83/EC, which in 2001 consolidated all the earlier Council Directives, states that the primary purpose of controls on the production and distribution of medicinal products is to safeguard public health. This consolidation has also required consequential amendments to the Medicines Act and the SIs in the UK, achieved by The Medicines (Codification Amendments Etc) Regulations 2002 No. 236. The Directive defines a medicinal product and establishes that before a medicine can be put on the market it must possess a licence or marketing authorisation which had been granted on the basis of safety, quality and efficacy. In addition, the Directive covers the labelling of medicines. Comission Directive 2003/94/EC lays down the principles and guidelines of *Good Manufacturing Practice* (GMP) which is applicable to all activities which require a licence under Council Directive 2001/83/EC. Good Manufacturing Practice means the part of quality assurance which ensures that products are consistently produced and controlled in accordance with the quality of standards appropriate to their intended use, the principles and guidelines of which are specified in Commission Directive 2003/94/EC. The Council Directive 65.65/EEC and its amending Directives were revoked by and consolidated in Council Directive 2001/83/EC. Council Regulation 2309/93/EEC, Council Directive 2001/83/EC and Commission Directive 2003/94 have been implemented in the UK under the provisions of the Medicines Act (see Chapters 2 and 3).

In 2004, the EU completed its review of legislation regulating medicinal products and in April 2004 published Council Directive 2004/27/EC, which amended Council Directive 2001/83/EC and Council Directive 2003/63/EC.

Member states were obliged to amend their legislation to comply with the amending directive by October 2005 and this was achieved in SI 2005 No. 2759 and SI 2005 No. 2789 The amendments include changes to data exclusivity and generic products (see p. 33).

Council Regulation 2309/93/EC provides for marketing authorisations via the centralised procedures, the establishment of the European Agency for the Evaluation of Medicinal Products together with the setting up of a Committee for Veterinary Medicinal Products. The name of the European Agency for the Evaluation of Medicinal Products was changed to the European Medicines Agency by Council Regulation 2004/726/EC.

Analytical, toxicological and clinical standards for medicines for human use

Council Directive 2001/83/EC set up standards and protocols for the analysis, and toxicological and pharmacological tests which had to be applied to medicinal products. Clinical trials are now controlled under Council Directive 2000/21/EC.

High-technology medicinal products for human and animal use

Directive 93/41/EEC set up procedures to deal with applications for marketing authorisations involving high-technology medicinal products, in particular those derived from biotechnology.

Homoeopathic medicinal products

Council Directive 2001/83/EC is concerned with the authorisation for marketing and the labelling of homoeopathic medicinal products for human use. It also provides for a special simplified registration procedure for those traditional homoeopathic medicinal products which are placed on the market without therapeutic indications in a pharmaceutical form and dosage which do not present a risk to the public. Directive 92/74/EEC relates to homoeopathic medicinal products for veterinary use. For UK legislation implementing both these Directives see Chapter 3.

In March 2004, the European Union issued the Directive on Traditional Herbal Medicinal Products (Council Directive 2004/24/EC) to regulate herbal products. Member states were required to have a simplified registration scheme in force by October 2005. Directive 2004/24/EC is based on long-standing use of the product and no clinical trial evidence will be required. All herbal products already on the market can remain so for seven years (see Chapter 11).

Advertising, labelling and leaflets

Council Directive 2001/83/EC deals with the labelling of medicinal products and the availability of package leaflets aimed at the public. It requires that 'information supplied to users should provide a high degree of consumer protection in order that medicinal products may be used correctly on the basis of full and comprehensible information'. This was implemented in the UK on 1 January 1994 (see Chapter 15).

Council Directive 2001/83/EC deals with the advertising of medicinal products for human use both to the general public and to health professionals. It also deals with the question of hospitality related to sales promotion, samples, medical representatives, etc. (see Chapter 4).

Wholesale distribution

Council Directive 2001/83/EC covers the control of wholesale distribution of medicinal products for human use in the EC. It requires that such distribution should be subject to the possession of an authorisation to engage in the activity as a wholesaler in medicinal products and lays down the conditions for such an authorisation. Such activity is subject to licensing in the UK (see Chapter 9).

Colouring of medicinal products

Directive 78/25/EEC controls the colouring agents which can, and those which cannot, be added to medicinal products.

Production of medicinal products for animal use

Directive 2001/82/ECC as amended by 2004/28/EC provides that no veterinary medicinal product may be placed on the market of a member state unless a marketing authorisation has been granted by the competent authorities of that member state in accordance with these directives or in accordance with Regulation EC/726/2004.

Directive 91/412/EEC introduced a legal requirement for a manufacturer of medicinal products for animal use to comply with the principles and guidelines of Good Manufacturing Practice.

Regulation 90/2377/EEC lays down procedures to establish maximum residue limits for animal medicines in foodstuffs of animal origin.

Controlled drugs

Council Directive 92/109/EEC applies to the manufacture and trade in scheduled substances within the EU and is implemented in the UK by the Controlled

Drugs (Substances Useful for Manufacture) (Intra-Community Trade) Regulations 1993 as amended. It requires the person who manufactures or trades in these substances to be licensed and restricts the persons to whom supplies may be made. The 1993 UK Regulations treat the provisions of Council Directive 92/109/EEC as if they were requirements of regulations made under section 13 of the 1990 Act.

Council Regulation 90/3677/EEC controls the import, export, recording and labelling of scheduled substances and the power to enter business premises to obtain evidence of irregularities. Records must be kept for two years. It also requires member states to adopt measures to enable them to obtain information on any orders for, or activities in, scheduled substances. There is a list of scheduled substances.

Data protection

Council Directive 95/46/EEC extends data protection to all data maintained manually and affects the way in which patient medication records are stored. This Directive was implemented in the UK by way of the Data Protection Act 1998, which came into force on 1 March 2000. All data, both electronic and manual, are now controlled under the 1998 Act (see p. 279).

Human rights

The Human Rights Act 1998 applies to public authorities such as the NHS or local authorities, but it also extends to 'private bodies exercising public functions'. So private contractors dispensing NHS prescriptions would be included. A full account of how the NHS is affected by the Act can be found on the Department of Health website. Since the Act came into force, all UK laws must be interpreted to respect and protect the human rights of all UK citizens. Human rights go beyond common law, for example they recognise a right to privacy that does not exist in the common law.

Human rights law departs from legal convention in the UK in three main ways:

1   Precedent will not necessarily bind judgments in human rights cases. The courts are expected to reflect concepts of human rights at the time of consideration rather than at the time of the complaint and thus will reflect present day attitudes and conditions.
2   Statutes will be interpreted as to intention rather than 'as written'. This is a major departure from UK conventions on interpretation of statutes.
3   The UK courts can challenge and over-rule statute if not compatible with human rights; in other words, the judges may challenge Parliament in this area.

Key human rights in relation to healthcare practice

Article 2 `right to life'

The right to life is really a right not to be deprived of life save in very special circumstances. The judicial sanction of capital punishment is not a special circumstance. It should be noted that this 'right' is not a right to unlimited healthcare in an effort to preserve life nor a right to death. Such rights may be cited in cases of assisted suicide or euthanasia and there are debates regarding issues such as assisted conception, contraception and abortion. Debate can also arise over resource allocation and equity in availability of treatment to all patients.

Article 3 `Right to prohibition of torture or inhuman or degrading treatment or punishment'

Article 3 does not cover issues that have obvious relevance for healthcare but some cases have asserted that aggressive treatment in terminal care or in some treatments of the mentally handicapped are close to being inhuman.

Article 5 `right to liberty'

The right to liberty is particularly relevant to the treatment of those with mental disorder, and the use of 'sectioning' and compulsory treatment is very relevant to consent to treatment.

Article 6 `right to a fair trial'

The right to a fair trial is mostly relevant to disciplinary processes and such principles as the right to know what one is charged with, time to prepare defence, right to a defence, etc. In addition any hearing has to be within a reasonable time, without delay, and there is a right not to incriminate oneself. Pharmacy's processes (e.g. the Disciplinary Committee procedures) do not appear yet to be fully compliant.

Article 8 `right for respect for private and family life'

Human rights issues may arise in the treatment of trans-sexuals and the right to practise particular forms of sexuality. This right has also been cited in relation to use of medical records in court. Article 8 is very relevant to issues of privacy in medical care, restrictions on disclosure of confidential information, and so on.

Article 9 `right to freedom of thought, conscience and religion'

Issues may arise where treatment is contrary to religious or cultural beliefs and practices. There also may be an issue for a 24-hour health service and religious restrictions on working at certain times or days.

Further reading

Anon (2008) Judicial Review. Beware of the time limits. *Pharm J* 281: (October).
Louis J-V (1990) *The Community Legal Order*. Luxembourg: Office for Official Publications of
    the European Communities.
Rules Governing Medicinal Products for Human Use in the European Community, vol. I.
    London: The Stationery Office.
Rules Governing Medicinal Products for Animal Use in the European Community, vol. Va.
    London: The Stationery Office.

Textbooks on law

Beale HL *et al*. eds (2004) *Chitty on Contracts*, 29th edn. London: Sweet & Maxwell.
Dugdate AM *et al*. eds (2002) *Clerk & Lindsell on Torts*, 18th edn. London: Sweet & Maxwell.
Smith JC (2002) *Smith & Hogan Criminal Law*, 10th edn. London: Butterworths.
Wade ECS, Bradley EW (1996) *Constitutional and Administrative Law*, 11th edn. London:
    Longman.

Websites

Legislation: www.opsi.gov.uk
EU legislation: http://euralex.europa.eu/en/index.htm

2

Medicines Act 1968
Scope and administration

European Community Council Directives and Regulations together with the Medicines Act 1968 (from now on referred to as the Act) regulate the manufacture, distribution and importation of (a) medicines for human use, (b) medicines for administration to animals, and (c) medicated animal feeding stuffs. At present, their application to products for export is limited (see Chapter 3). The Health Ministers of the UK are responsible for the administration of the Act and they have the benefit of advice from a Medicines Commission.

In October 2005, all the provisions in the Medicines Act 1968 relating to veterinary medicinal products, including medicated feeding stuffs and additives, were replaced by a new veterinary medicinal products regulation (see p. 157).

Medicinal products placed on the market in the UK require a marketing authorisation, formerly called a product licence. Similarly the manufacture, wholesaling, importation and distribution of medicines are controlled through a licensing system operated by the Ministers and enforced by the *Medicines Healthcare Regulatory Authority* (MHRA; formed from the merger of the Medicines and Healthcare products Regulatory Agency and the Medical Devices Agency; see Chapter 3). Since the removal of Crown immunity in April 1991, manufacturing units in NHS hospitals are also within the licensing system and are subject to the oversight of the MHRA and its inspectorate. The animal medicines legislation is monitored by the Veterinary Medicines Directorate of the Department of Environment, Food and Rural Affairs (DEFRA).

The Act also deals with the registration of retail pharmacies and provides that medicines may be supplied to the public only from pharmacies, except those medicines which can with reasonable safety be sold without the supervision of a pharmacist. The Minister can make regulations relating to the labelling of medicines, the containers in which they are supplied and the manner in which their sale is promoted, whether by advertisement or oral representation.

In Great Britain, the Royal Pharmaceutical Society of Great Britain (RPSGB, referred to here as the Society) has duties of enforcement in connection with pharmacies and the retail distribution of medicines. Other enforcement duties may be given to the Society and to local authorities, as the appropriate Minister may decide (see p. 21).

Preparation of the *British Pharmacopoeia* and other books of standards also falls within the scope of the Act.

Medicinal product

The term used is not medicine but relevant medicinal product, which means a medicinal product for human use to which provisions of the 2001 Directive and Directive 2004/27/EC applies. It is newly defined in Council Directive 2004/27/EC as:

1 Any substance or combination of substances presented as having properties for treating or preventing disease in human beings.
2 Any substance or combination of substances which may be used in or administered to human beings either with a view to restoring, correcting, or modifying physiological functions by exerting a pharmacological, immunological or metabolic action or to making a medical diagnosis.

A new provision has been added to Article 2 of Directive 2001/83/EC as amended which states, 'In cases of doubt, where, taking into account all its characteristics, a product may fall within the definition of a product covered by other Community legislation the provisions of this Directive shall apply' (2004/27/EC).

Taken together these provisions are intended to ensure that where doubt exists over whether a product – those on the 'borderline' between, for example, medicines and medical devices, medicines and cosmetics, medicines and food supplements, etc. – should be regulated under medicines or other sectoral legislation, the stricter medicines regulatory regime should apply. This is a broader definition than that in the Medicines Act and can be defined as being a medicinal product (a) by presentation and (b) by function.

The term a *medicinal product* to which Chapters of the 2001 Directive apply includes all medicinal products for human use except those prepared on the basis of a magistral or official formula, medicinal products intended for research, or intermediate products intended for further processing by an authorised manufacturer (Council Directive 2001/83/EC, as amended).

Magistral means any medicinal product prepared in a pharmacy in accordance with a prescription for an individual patient.

Official formula means any medicinal product which is prepared in accordance with the prescriptions of a pharmacopoeia and is intended to be supplied directly to the patients served by the pharmacy in question.

Ingredient may be the sole active ingredient present in a medicinal product.

Hospital includes a clinic, nursing home or similar institution.

Animal includes any bird, fish or reptile.

Medicinal purpose means one or more of the following: (a) treating or preventing disease; (b) diagnosing disease or ascertaining the existence, degree or extent of a physiological condition; (c) contraception; (d) inducing anaesthesia; (e) otherwise preventing or interfering with the normal operation of a physiological function [s.130(2)].

Administer means administer to a human being or an animal, whether orally, by injection or by introduction into the body in any other way, or by external application, a substance or article either in its existing state or after it has been dissolved or dispersed in, or diluted or mixed with, some other substance used as a vehicle [s.130(9)].

By ministerial order (s.104), the Act, or specified parts of the Act, can be applied to any article or substance which is not a medicinal product but is made wholly or partly for a medicinal purpose. In the past, Orders have been made in respect of surgical ligatures and sutures, dental filling substances, contact lenses and associated substances, and intrauterine contraceptive devices. However, since 1994, these substances have been considered to be medical devices rather than medicines and are now controlled under the Medical Devices Regulations (SI 2002 No. 618, as amended) made under the Consumer Protection Act 1987 (see p. 50).

An order may also be made (s.105) in respect of any substance which (a) is used as an ingredient in the manufacture of a medicinal product, or (b) is capable of causing danger to the health of the community or to the health of animals if used without proper safeguards. The order may specify which parts of the Act are to apply. Some substances used as ingredients in the manufacture of medicinal products, and certain other substances, have been controlled by orders of this kind (SIs 1971 No. 1200, 1973 No. 367 and 1985 No. 1403) (see Appendix 1).

Orders can also be made under the European Communities Act 1972, for example the Medicines for Human Use (Marketing Authorisations, etc.) Regulations 1994 (SI 1994 No. 3144 as amended).

Certain things are specifically declared not to be medicinal products (s.130). These include:

1   Substances or articles manufactured for administration to human beings or animals in the course of the manufacturer's business, or in a laboratory on behalf of the manufacturer, solely by way of a test for ascertaining

what effects they have, and in circumstances where the manufacturer has no knowledge that the effects are likely to be beneficial.

2 Substances and articles as may be specified in a ministerial order. Chemical substances used to sterilise animals which are neither domestic nor held in captivity are not medicinal products (SI 1986 No. 2177).

Breathing gases for human use in conditions in which respiration is adversely affected by abnormal atmospheric pressure or otherwise are not medicinal products when they are not administered for the treatment or diagnosis of disease. This exemption applies to oxygen, air or any mixture of both, or of either or both with any inert gas or gases or with nitrogen (SI 1977 No. 1488).

An animal feeding stuff into which a medicinal product has been incorporated is also classed as a medicinal product. Special provisions relate to such feeding stuffs (s.130).

Administration

The Medicines Act extends to Scotland and Northern Ireland, and the terms the *Health Ministers* and the *Agricultural Ministers* include the relevant Ministers of those countries (s.1), as well as those for England and Wales. All these Ministers, taken together, comprise the Ministers who act jointly in certain matters, e.g. the appointment of the Medicines Commission (s.2). These Ministers also comprise the licensing authority (s.6), but these licensing functions are carried out by either the MHRA or the *European Agency for the Evaluation of Medicinal Products* (now know as the *European Medicines Agency*).

The MHRA is the licensing authority for the decentralised system (i.e. mutual recognition and national procedures) for market authorisations under the terms of the Council Directives (see Chapter 3). It is also the licensing authority for all other licences required under the Act (e.g. manufacturers, wholesale dealers, etc.) and is also the enforcement authority for these matters in the UK.

The European Medicines Agency, established under EC Council Regulation 2004/726/C, is the licensing authority for the centralised procedures for market authorisations under the terms of the EC Council Directives (see Chapter 3).

The *Veterinary Medicines Directorate* is the organisation for animal medicines equivalent to the MHRA.

Before exercising any power to make orders or regulations, the Ministers must, except in certain cases of emergency, consult in advance organisations which appear to them (the Ministers) to represent interests likely to be affected (s.129). In relation to medicines appropriate Ministers means the Health Ministers.

In SI 2005 No. 1094, the Medicines Commission was replaced by the Commission on Human Medicines, a body appointed by the Health Ministers to advise them on the administration of the Act and on any matters relating to medicinal products. It is a body corporate which must have at least eight members. The chairman is appointed by the Ministers from amongst the members of the Commission.

The Commission is required to make recommendations to the Ministers about the numbers of committees required under section 4 of the Act (appropriate committees) and about their functions and membership. These committees may be set up by the Ministers for any purpose in connection with the execution of the Act.

The Commission has the duty to:

- give advice with respect to safety, quality or efficacy of medicinal products;
- promote the collection and investigation of information relating to adverse reactions; for the purpose of such advice to be given; and
- undertake the functions under section 4 of the Act except in so far as those functions are for the time being assigned to a section 4 committee.

Two section 4 committees still function: the Veterinary Products Committee (SI 1970 No. 1304) and the British Pharmacopoeia Committee (SIs 1970 No. 1256 and 1982 No. 1335).

Administrative provisions relating to the Medicines Commission and the section 4 committees are in Schedule 1A to the Act and in regulations made thereunder (SI 2005 No. 1094). Section 4 committees are appointed by the Ministers. The Commission may appoint its own ad hoc committees or expert advisory groups (Schedule 1A) However, the Commission must appoint three expert advisory groups namely:

Biologicals Expert Advisory Group: to advise on the safety, quality and efficacy of medicinal products of biological or bio-technological origin including vaccines

Chemistry, Pharmacy and Standards Expert Advisory Group: to advise on the quality and quality in relation to safety and efficacy of medicinal products which are subject of an application for product licence under the Act

Pharmacovigilance Expert Advisory Group: to advise on pharmacovigilance and other issues relating to medicinal products

It can also appoint such other expert advisory groups as it considers appropriate.

Ministers can extend the functions of the Commission and can vary or terminate any of the Commission's functions, subject to the approval of a resolution of both Houses of Parliament. Annual reports about the work of the Medicines Commission and its committees and of the committees set up under section 4 of the Act must be submitted to the Ministers.

There are lay and patient representatives at all levels and no members will be allowed to hold personal company interests or represent the pharmaceutical industry.

Proposed changes in the draft Pharmacy Order 2009 (published December 2008)

Proposals for further change to the regulation of pharmacy appear in the draft Pharmacy Order 2009, which was published as this book went to press. The proposals were open to consultation until 9 March 2009 and were expected to be implemented in the second quarter of 2010. The draft Pharmacy Order includes transitional arrangements to ensure smooth transfer of functions from the RPSGB to the General Pharmaceutical Council (GPhC). Many of the major changes from regulation under the Pharmacy Act 1954 to regulation under the Pharmacists and Pharmacy Technicians Act 2007 remain in place and these are detailed in the text below, but relevant changes proposed in the draft Pharmacy Order 2009 include:

- bringing the inspectorate under the GPhC (transferred from the Medicines Act 1968 and removing from the Poisons Act 1972 (Chapters 22 and 24);
- new powers to set standards 'as the GPhC Council consider necessary' for safe and effective practice within pharmacy premises and to exercise new sanctions for failure to meet such standards (Chapters 22 and 24)

Enforcement

The primary duty of enforcing the Act rests with the appropriate Minister in England and Wales [s.108(1)], the Secretary of State in Scotland [s.109(1)] and the Minister of Health and Social Services in Northern Ireland [s.110(1)]. There are provisions for these Ministers to delegate many of their functions to other authorities, but licensing requirements and those provisions which affect hospitals or the premises of practitioners are solely the responsibility of the Ministers. In England, Wales and Scotland, arrangements can be made or directions given whereby local food and drug authorities and/or the RPSGB can have certain duties or exercise certain powers, concurrently with the Ministers [s.108(2)]. In Scotland, these enforcement authorities cannot themselves institute proceedings (s.109).

Role of the Royal Pharmaceutical Society of Great Britain

The Society is responsible under this Act for the maintenance of the Register of Pharmacy Premises (see Chapter 5) and for disciplinary control over bodies corporate and representatives of pharmacists carrying on retail pharmacy businesses (see Chapter 22).

The Society, concurrently with the Minister, is also required to enforce in Great Britain [ss.108(6) and 109(2)] the provisions relating to:

1   Sale and supply of medicinal products not on a General Sale List (s.52).
2   Sale, supply or administration of medicinal products on prescription only (s.58).
3   Regulations restricting sale, supply or administration of certain medicinal products except with the authority of specially certified practitioners (s.60).
4   Regulations restricting sale or supply of medicinal products to persons in a specified class (s.61).
5   Annual return of premises to the registrar (s.77).
6   Restrictions on use of titles, descriptions and emblems (s.78).
7   Regulations imposing further restrictions on titles [s.79(2)].

The appropriate Minister *must* arrange for the Society, and/or Food and Drug Authorities (as designated in s.198 of the Local Government Act 1972) to have a power, or a duty, to enforce in connection with retail sale, supply, etc. of medicinal products provisions relating to:

8   Prohibition of sale, supply or importation of medicinal products specified by order (s.62) (see Chapter 14).
9   Sale and supply and offer of sale or supply of adulterated medicinal products (s.63).
10 Sale of medicinal products not of the nature or quality demanded (s.64).
11 Compliance with standards specified in monographs in certain publications (s.65).
12 Regulations relating to labelling and marking of containers and packages [s.85(3), (4) and (5)].
13 Regulations relating to requirements for containers [s.87(2)].
14 Regulations relating to distinctive colours, shapes and marking of medicinal products [s.88(3)].
15 Regulations relating to display of information on automatic machines [s.89(2)].

16 Regulations relating to leaflets to be supplied with medicinal products [s.86(2) and (3)].

17 False or misleading representations or advertisements (s.93).

18 Advertisements requiring consent of product licence holder (s.94).

19 Regulations relating to issue of advertisements (s.95).

Such arrangements for enforcement have been made with the Society relating to 9 to 13. Enforcement by the Society in respect of 17, 18 and 19 is limited to premises, ships, aircraft, vehicles or places where retail sales take place, and to the display of advertisements in close proximity to automatic machines.

The Society and the Food and Drug Authorities may be given a power or duty to enforce provisions relating to:

20 Sale of medicinal products on General Sale List (s.53).

21 Sale of medicinal products from automatic machines (s.54).

22 Regulations relating to premises where medicinal products are prepared or dispensed and to dealings in medicinal products including the supervision, storage, safekeeping, record-keeping, disposal, supply as samples or precautions to be taken before sale, and to the construction etc. of automatic machines (s.66).

The Society has been given the power and is under a duty to enforce sections 53, 54 and 66 in respect of registered pharmacies and of premises where certain exempted veterinary drugs are sold (see Chapter 13). Food and Drug Authorities have a power and are under a duty to enforce these sections in respect of all other premises (SI 1980 No. 1923).

An enforcement authority must give 28 days' notice to the Minister before instituting proceedings under any of the sections in 8 to 22 above.

County councils have a duty to enforce the provisions of the Act relating to the proper labelling and description of medicated animal feeding stuffs (ss.90 and 108). These authorities also have a duty to enforce any order made under section 62(1) prohibiting the sale, supply or importation of any specified animal feeding stuffs. The council of any county district which is not a Food and Drug Authority and the overseers of the Inner Temple and the Middle Temple may be required to enforce the regulations made under section 66 (see 22 above).

Inspection and sampling

A right of entry and a right to inspect, take samples and seize goods and documents is given (ss.111 and 112) to any person duly authorised in writing by an enforcement authority in order to ascertain whether there has been a contravention of the Act. The right to inspect extends to any substance or article appearing to be a medicinal product; to any plant or equipment used to manufacture or assemble medicinal products; and to any labels, leaflets, containers or packages. An authorised person, having produced his/her credentials if required to do so, is empowered:

1   to enter any premises, stall or place other than any vehicle or home-going ship, to ascertain whether there has been a contravention of the Act, or generally for the purposes of performing the functions of the enforcement authority; and to enter any ship, aircraft or hover-vehicle to ascertain whether there is in it any article or substance imported in contravention of the Act;
2   to take a sample (by purchase or otherwise) of any medicinal product sold or supplied or any substance to be used in the manufacture of a medicinal product;
3   to require the production of any books or documents relating to the business;
4   to take copies of any entry in any such book or document; and
5   to seize and detain any substance or articles or any document which he has reasonable cause to believe may be required for proceedings under the Act (the person from whom the seizure is made must be informed).

A person duly authorised in writing by the licensing authority (i.e. an inspector of the Medicines and Healthcare products Regulatory Agency of the Department of Health) may exercise these rights in respect of the business of any applicant for a licence or certificate under Part II of the Act in order to verify any statement made in the application.

Twenty-four hours' notice must be given to the occupier if it is intended to enter any premises used only as a private dwelling house. In cases of urgency, or where refusal is anticipated, or where the giving of notice will defeat the object of entry, or where the premises are unoccupied, a justice of the peace may issue a warrant authorising entry, by force if necessary. Any person entering any property in the exercise of a right of entry may take with him/her such other persons and such equipment as may be necessary. On vacating any unoccupied property entered in pursuance of a warrant, s/he must leave it as effectively secured as s/he found it.

It is an offence wilfully to obstruct a duly authorised person, or wilfully to fail to comply with any proper request made by him/her or, without reasonable cause, to fail to give him/her any assistance or information s/he may reasonably require within his/her functions under the Act. It is also an offence to give such a person false information (s.112).

A person who has exercised a right of entry and discloses to any other person, except in the performance of his/her duty, information about any manufacturing process or trade secret obtained by him/her in the premises, commits an offence. It is similarly an offence for any person to disclose any information obtained by him/her in pursuance of the Acts (s.118).

A detailed procedure is set out in Schedule 3 for dealing with samples taken by a *sampling officer* (i.e. a person authorised by the relevant enforcement authority) either for any purpose in connection with that authority's functions under the Act or to ascertain whether there has been a contravention of the Act.

A sample must be divided forthwith into three parts, two being retained by the sampling officer and the third given to the vendor or dealer in the manner prescribed in the Schedule, according to the circumstances. One of the parts retained by the sampling officer may be submitted for analysis to a public analyst, or to a laboratory with which an arrangement has been made by the enforcement authority with the approval of the Minister.

A certificate, in the prescribed form, specifying the result of the analysis must be issued by the person having control of the laboratory, or by the public analyst carrying out the analysis. The certificate must be signed by the person issuing it and, in any proceedings, a document purporting to be such a certificate shall be sufficient evidence of the facts stated in the document unless the other party requires that the person who issued the certificates shall be called as a witness. The second part of the sample retained by the sampling officer must be produced as evidence and, if required by either party or at the direction of the court, must be submitted to the Government Chemist for analysis. The prescribed forms of certificates of analysis are in SI 1977 No. 1399.

A sampling officer must pay the value of a sample if it is demanded by the person from whom it is taken; there is provision for arbitration about the value in case of a dispute. The taking of a sample by a sampling officer has effect as though it were a sale of a medicinal product and the provisions of section 64 of the Act relating to the protection of purchasers apply (see Chapter 14).

Where a substance or article has been seized by a person exercising a right of seizure (referred to as an authorised officer) (s.113), s/he must either treat it as a sample, or set aside part of it as a sample, if requested to do so within 21 days by the person entitled to be informed of the seizure. This does not apply if the nature of the substance is such that it is not reasonably practicable to do either of these things. A substance or article treated as a sample under these provisions is subject to the procedure of division, analysis, etc., set out in Schedule 3 as described above.

Any person, other than a person authorised by an enforcement authority, who has purchased a medicinal product may submit a sample of it for analysis to the public analyst for the area where it was purchased, subject to the analyst's right to demand payment of the prescribed fee in advance. The public analyst must analyse the sample as soon as is practicable and issue a certificate in the form prescribed (s.115).

There are special enforcement and sampling provisions relating to animal feeding stuffs (s.117). The Agriculture Minister may by regulation modify, for animal feeding stuffs, the ordinary sampling procedure. These regulations may prescribe a method of analysis to be used in analysing samples of feeding stuffs and provide that the results of analysis by other methods shall not be admissible in evidence. The Agriculture Minister may by order specify the discrepancy which will be tolerated between the amount of medicinal product present in an animal feeding stuff and the amount declared on the label. Deficiencies or excesses within the prescribed limits are not regarded as contraventions of the Act.

Legal proceedings

Where a contravention is due to the default of another person, that person may be charged and convicted, whether or not proceedings are taken against the person committing the contravention. A person charged with an offence who proves to the satisfaction of the court (a) that s/he exercised all due diligence to prevent the contravention and (b) that it was due to the act or default of another person shall, subject to certain procedural requirements, be acquitted of the offence (s.121).

When an offence is committed by a body corporate, any director, manager, company secretary or other similar officer may be proceeded against, as well as the body corporate, if it is proved that the offence was committed with his/her consent and connivance, or was attributable to his/her neglect. It is specifically provided that the superintendent pharmacist of a pharmacy company (whether or not a member of the board), and any pharmacist in personal control of a pharmacy and acting under his/her direction, shall be regarded as officers for this purpose (s.124).

Medicinal products and animal feeding stuffs proved to have been found on a vehicle from which those goods are sold are presumed to have been offered for sale, unless the contrary is proved (s.126). This presumption applies when the offences concern the offering for sale of: (a) a medicated animal feeding stuff without the authority of a product licence, animal test certificate, or a veterinary direction (s.40); or (b) a medicinal product contrary to the restriction on retail sales (ss.52 and 53); or (c) an adulterated medicinal product [s.63(b)]. There is also a presumption in respect of the possession of medicinal products or medicated animal feeding stuffs (or leaflets referring to them) on premises at which the person charged carries on a business including the supply of those goods.

When the offence concerns adulteration [s.63(b)], false or misleading labels or leaflets (ss.85 and 86), requirements as to containers (s.87) or requirements as to marking of medicinal products (s.88), a person is presumed, unless the contrary is proved, to have had medicinal products in his/her possession for the purpose of sale or supply. Warranty can be pleaded as a defence to a charge of contravening any of these sections, or of sections 64 and 65.

These relate to sales made to the prejudice of the purchaser (s.64) or failure to comply with standards specified in official monographs (s.65).

Subject to certain formalities, a defendant can rely on warranty if s/he proves:

1 that s/he purchased the substance or article as one which could lawfully be sold, supplied or offered for sale and with a written warranty to that effect;
2 that at the time of the alleged offence s/he had no reason to believe that it was otherwise; and
3 that the substance or article was then in the same state as when s/he purchased it (s.122).

A defendant who is the servant of the person who purchased under warranty can rely on the same defence as his/her employer, and a name or description entered in an invoice is deemed to be written warranty that the article described can be sold under that description.

It is an offence for a person to give a false warranty unless s/he can prove that at the time s/he gave it s/he had reason to believe that the statement of description was accurate. It is also an offence wilfully to apply to any article or substance (a) a warranty or (b) a certificate of analysis issued under the Act (see p. 24), if that warranty or certificate relates to a different substance or article.

Any document purporting to be an authorised copy of the *British Pharmacopoeia*, or a compendium or a list of names as described in Part VII of the Act or of an amendment thereto, shall be received in evidence as being a true copy of the subject matter contained therein and shall be evidence of the date on which it came into operation (s.102).

The validity of licences and licensing decisions is considered under licensing (Chapter 3), and certificates issued by the registrar relating to the premises are dealt with under pharmacies (see Chapter 4).

Summary

- The legal sources for the marketing authorisations of medicinal products and the licensing of manufacturers, wholesalers, and other distributors of medicines are the European Directives and the United Kingdom Medicines Act 1968.
- The advisory structure for the Ministers is a Medicines Commission and several statutory committees including the Committee on the Safety of Medicines.
- The two licensing authorities, the Medicines and Healthcare products Regulatory Agency and the European Medicines Agency, deal with the decentralised and centralised licensing procedures for medicinal products.

- The definition of a medicinal product is set out in Council Directive 2001/83/EC.
- Certain substances (e.g. surgical ligatures and sutures, dental fillings, contact lenses and intrauterine devices) are no longer controlled under the Medicines Act but come under the Medical Devices Regulations made under the Consumer Protection Act.
- The enforcement of the Act and regulations fall upon the Medicines and Healthcare products Regulatory Agency and the Royal Pharmaceutical Society of Great Britain.
- The powers of the inspectors are laid down and stringent conditions relate to the taking of samples within a sampling procedure.
- Those liable to commit offences under the Act are listed together with any defences that can be raised.

Further reading

Rules Governing Medicinal Products for Human Use in the European Community, vol. I. London: The Stationery Office.

Website

http://ec.europa.eu/enterprise/pharmaceuticals/eudralex/vol2_en.htm

3

Medicines Act 1968
The licensing system

Licensing requirements are set out in EC Council Directives and Regulations and in the Medicines Act, which provide for marketing authorisations, manufacturers' licences, wholesale dealers' licences, clinical trial certificates and animal test certificates. The licensing system applies to medicinal products and to substances incorporated in animal feeding stuffs for a medicinal purpose. (Retailers of licensed products, unless responsible for the composition of the products they sell, do not require any licences, but medicinal products which are not on a General Sale List may be sold or supplied by retail, subject to certain exemptions, only from registered pharmacies; see Chapter 6.)

Without the appropriate marketing authorisation, licence or certificate, it is not lawful for any person, in the course of a business carried on by him/her, to manufacture, sell, supply, export or import into the UK any of these products unless some exemption is provided in the Act or regulations.

In this chapter, the provisions of the Directives and the Act and its statutory instruments (SIs) are collated and summarised under appropriate headings. The SIs mentioned are those in force on 3 December 2008. Explanatory leaflets are available from the Medicines Healthcare Regulatory Authority (MHRA) in the case of human medicines and the Veterinary Medicines Directorate of the Department for Environment, Food and Rural Affairs for medicines for animal use.

Issue of licences

Market authorisations and licences are issued by the licensing authorities, that is, MHRA or the European Medicines Agency (see also Council Regulation 26/2004/EC), who may grant, refuse, review, suspend, revoke or vary them (ss.20 and 28 and SI 1994 No. 3144 as amended). They expire at the end of five years or such shorter period as is specified in the marketing authorisation/licence. If a marketing authorisation/licence, subsequent to its issue, contravenes any European Community obligation, a notice terminating it may be served on the holder (s.24 and SI 1994 No. 3144 as amended). The authority must send copies of licences to the appropriate section 4 Committees (see p. 19). When an application for a marketing authorisation/licence is refused, the licensing authority must state the reasons for refusal in a notice served on the applicant. Refusal may not be based on any ground relating to the price of a product, and the licensing authority must consult the appropriate committee, that is the Committee on the Safety of Medicines or the Veterinary Products Committee, before refusing an application on grounds of safety, quality or efficacy (s.20).

Marketing authorisations for human medicines

The ECC issued proposals for a two-tiered system for obtaining marketing authorisations and this system was implemented in 1994, thus replacing earlier product licences with marketing authorisations. The system comprises a centralised system and a national (member state) system. The centralised licensing system is administered by the European Agency for the Evaluation of Medicinal Products and is used for new active substances and certain high-technology and biotechnology products. The centralised procedure is set out in Regulation 2004/726//EC, which has direct effect on member states without any separate implementation by a member state.

The decentralised system, also known as the mutual recognition procedure, is for the other products and involves MHRA; its marketing authorisations may be recognised by the other member states. Council Directive 2001/83/EEC together with the other European Pharmaceutical Directives, implemented by UK regulations (SI 1994 No. 3144 as amended by SI 2002 No. 236 and SI 2005 No. 2754), establish the procedures for the decentralised system. The regulations implement the Pharmaceutical Directives concerned by cross-reference to the Directives themselves, rather than setting out the details in full.

No medicinal product may be placed on the market of a member state and no such product can be distributed by way of wholesale dealing unless a marketing authorisation has been issued by the relevant Medicines and Healthcare products Regulatory Agency or the European Agency for the Evaluation of Medicinal Products. Medicinal products include immunological products, medicinal products based on human blood or blood constituents and medicinal products based on radioisotopes (radiopharmaceuticals). However, these provisions do not apply to whole human blood, plasma or blood cells of human origin, nor to a radiopharmaceutical in which the radionuclide is in a sealed source. Homoeopathic medicinal products are dealt with separately (see p. 34).

Proprietary medicinal product means any ready prepared medicinal product placed on the market in the UK under a special name and in a special pack (Council Directive 2001/83/EC, Art.1 and 2).

Radiopharmaceutical means a medicinal product which, when ready for use, contains one or more radionuclides included for a medicinal purpose (SI 1992 No. 604).

Blood product means any industrially prepared medicinal product for human use derived from human blood or blood plasma and includes albumin, coagulating factors and immunoglobulins of human origin but does not include whole blood, human plasma or blood cells of human origin (SI 1992 No. 755).

The holder of a marketing authorisation for a medicinal product may: (a) sell, supply or export the product; (b) procure its sale, supply or exportation; (c) procure its manufacture or assembly, in accordance with the marketing authorisation.

In dealing with an application for a marketing authorisation, the licensing authority must give particular consideration to the safety, quality and efficacy of the products (s.19). Considerations of safety are taken to include the extent to which the product:

1   if used without proper safeguards, is capable of causing danger to the health of the community, or of causing danger to the health of animals generally or of one or more species of animals; or
2   if administered to an animal, may be harmful to the animal or may induce disease in other animals or may leave a residue in the carcass or product of the animal which may be harmful to human beings; or
3   may interfere with the treatment, prevention or diagnosis of disease; or
4   may be harmful to the person administering it or (in the case of an instrument, apparatus or appliance) the person operating it (s.132).

When considering the *efficacy* of a product, the licensing authority must not take into account any question of the superior efficacy of another product (s.19), or refuse to grant a licence on any grounds relating to price (s.20).

For imported products, the licensing authority must have particular regard to the methods, standards and conditions of manufacture. The applicant may be required to produce one or more of the following:

1   an undertaking by the manufacturer that s/he will permit inspection by the licensing authority;
2   an undertaking by, or on behalf of, the manufacturer that s/he will comply with prescribed conditions (SI 1977 No. 1038, as amended by SI 1992 No. 2845); and/or

3   a declaration by or on behalf of the manufacturer that the product
has been manufactured in accordance with the law of the country
where it was manufactured (s.19).

An application for a marketing authorisation for a medicinal product for
human use in either of the procedures must be accompanied by the particulars
set out in Council Directive 2001/83/EEC (see website p. 51). Article 11 sets
out the details of the Summary of Product Characteristics.

Summary of Product Characteristics means the information required to
accompany any application for a marketing authorisation under Council
Directive 2001/83/EEC (Art.11).

Apart from the Summary of Product Characteristics, the particulars
required to be given in a full application include the kind of activity to be
undertaken (e.g. selling, procuring manufacture, etc.); the pharmaceutical
form of the product; its composition, physical characteristics and medicinal use; method of manufacture and assembly; quality control procedures; containers and labelling; reports of experimental and biological
studies and of clinical trials and studies; any adverse reactions; and,
where the product is made abroad, documentary evidence of authorisation relating to manufacture, assembly, etc. Special additional conditions
apply for applications concerning immunological products, radiopharmaceuticals and medicinal products derived from human blood or human
plasma.

Abridged applications are permitted where the relevant data have been
submitted in an earlier application, or data about the kind of product in
question are well documented. (Renewal applications for licenses and certificates are dealt with in SI 1994 No. 3144 as amended.)

Standard conditions and obligations for marketing authorisations are
prescribed in the relevant EC directives. These provisions are incorporated
in the marketing authorisation unless the applicant desires that any of them
shall be excluded or modified in respect of his/her product and his/her request
is granted.

Revocation, suspension or variation

There is provision in the regulations for the marketing authorisation to be
revoked, suspended or varied. The licensing authority may impose an urgency
safety restriction on the holder of a marketing authorisation. Where this
occurs, the holder shall implement the restriction within a specified period
and apply to vary the authorisation so as to make the safety restriction
immediately and in any event within 15 days (SI 2003 No. 2321).

Variations are also covered by Regulation No. 1084/2003/EC and Council
Directive 2003/63/EC.

Generic products

A product is defined as a generic medicinal product when it has:

- the same qualitative and quantitative composition in active substances; and
- the same pharmaceutical form as the reference medicinal product; and
- whose bioequivalence with the reference product has been demonstrated by appropriate bioavailability studies.

There has to be a balance struck between allowing a person applying for a marketing authorisation for a follow-on product (e.g. a generic product) to be able to use the safety and efficacy data which has been used by the original innovator against the need for such an applicant being forced to repeat that data for the product when that information is already with the licensing authority.

This balance is achieved by allowing a follow-on competitor to rely on the data for the original product only after the passage of a 'data exclusivity period'. The procedure under which a generic product can rely on the innovator's data after the end of data exclusivity period is known as an 'abridged procedure'.

The existing 'data exclusivity periods' under Council Directive 2001/83/EC vary from 6 to 10 years across the EU and continued to apply until November 2005 after which the amending Directive 2004/27/EC took effect. This harmonises the exclusivity period across the EU and is known as the 8 + 2 + 1 rule. The data can be used after 8 years but the product cannot be marketed for a further 2 years. An extra year's protection can be added if the original product had therapeutic indications which were of 'significant benefit' over other remedies (SI 2005 No. 2759).

Borderline products

Where the licensing authority are of the opinion that a product is a relevant medicinal product, they may by notice in writing serve on any person who has placed the product on the market informing him/her that the product is a relevant medicinal product and needs to be licensed together with the reasons why they are so minded. Statutory provisions provide for initial representations to be made to the licensing authority and, if necessary, for further representations to be made to an independent review body. Once a final determination has been made, the licensing authority may serve notice requiring the person not to put the product on the market or to stop marketing it from a date specified. Detail procedures are set out in the legislation (SI 2000 No. 292).

Immunity from liability for unauthorised medicinal products (SI 2005 No. 2759)

Where, in response to the suspected or confirmed spread of pathogenic agents, toxins, chemical agents or nuclear radiation which may cause harm to humans, the licensing authority may recommend or require the use of:

- a medicinal product which is not subject to a UK or EC marketing authorisation, or
- a medicinal product which is subject to such an authorisation but is used for a therapeutic indication which is not included in the Summary of Product Characteristics,

the holder of the marketing authorisation, a manufacturer of the product, an officer, servant or employee of the holder or manufacturer, or a health professional shall not be liable to any civil liability for any loss or damage resulting from the use of the product in accordance with the recommendation or requirement. A *'health professional'* means a doctor, pharmacist, dentist, nurse, optometrist, persons registered under the Health Professional Order, an osteopath and a chiropractor.

Registration certificates for homoeopathic medicines for human use

Homoeopathic Medicinal Products to which the 2001 Directive applies means a medicinal product (which may contain a number of principles) prepared from products, substances or compositions called homoeopathic stocks in accordance with a homoeopathic manufacturing procedure described by the *European Pharmacopoeia* or, in the absence thereof, by any pharmacopoeia used officially in a member state other than one prepared with a magistral or officinal formula (Council Directive 2001/83/EC amended by 2004/27/EC).

There is an Advisory Board on the Registration of Homoeopathic Products (SI 1995 No. 309 as amended by SI 2002 No. 236, SI 2005 No. 2753 and SI 2006 No. 2386), which gives advice with respect to the safety and quality of any Homoeopathic product in respect of which a certificate of registration has been granted or which is the subject of any application for such a certificate.

Certificate of Registration means a certificate granted under the Medicines (Homoeopathic Medicinal Products for Human Use) Regulations 1994 (SI 1994 No. 105, as amended by SI 2002 No. 236, SI 2005 No. 2753 and SI 2006 No. 2386).

In the case of a homoeopathic medicinal product, a marketing authorisation is not required provided that a certificate of registration has been granted (SI 1994 No. 276).

Applications for a certificate of registration under the simplified procedure for a homoeopathic medicinal product must be made in the manner prescribed in the regulations (SI 1994 No. 105, as amended by SI 2005 No. 2753). The application must be in writing, in English and include the particulars required by Council Directives 2001/83/EC and 2004/27/EC. Fees and standard variations are covered by SI 1998 No. 574.

Every holder of a certificate of registration must comply with all the obligations set in Council Directive 2001/83/EC, including record keeping, to facilitate withdrawal and recall.

The Medicines for Human Use (National Rules for Homoeopathic Products) Regulations 2006 (SI 1952) introduced the concept of a national Homoeopathic product. A *national homoeopathic product* means a homoeopathic medicines product which does not satisfy the conditions of the 2001 Directive and is indicated for the relief or treatment of minor symptoms or minor conditions in humans. Symptoms or conditions are minor 'if they ordinarily and with reasonable safety be relieved or treated without the supervision or intervention of a doctor'. The application for the grant of a UK marketing authorisation for a national homoeopathic product is required to be made in accordance of Schedule A of the regulations including safety and efficacy data. The holder of the marketing authorisation must keep the data up to date and supply any information which entails amendment to the information.

Registration of traditional herbal medicinal products

The Directive on Traditional Herbal Medicines (Directive 2004/24/EC) required each member state to put in place a simplified national registration scheme for traditional herbal medicinal products This simplified scheme consists of certain regulatory features which are specific to these products and also bring such medicines within the scope of Directive 2001/83/EC and makes changes relating to applications for registration and renewals, patient leaflets and labelling (including the Braille requirement within five years), advertising pharmacovigilance, importation and distribution, and enforcement. These provisions together with obligations imposed upon the holders of traditional herbal medicinal products registration, are laid down in the Medicines (Traditional Herbal Medicinal Products for Human Use) Regulations (SI 2005 No. 2750 regulations 5–10 and Schedule 2). Enforcement of the Regulations in England rests with the Secretary for State for Health, in Wales with the National Assembly of Wales, and in Scotland with the Scottish Ministers.

Product licences (parallel importing)

The importation from a member state of the ECC of a medicinal product which is a version of one already the subject of a UK marketing authorisation is known as parallel importing.

A modified form of licence application may be considered for such a product, subject to the following conditions:

1 the product to be imported must be a *proprietary medicinal product* (as defined in Art.1 of Council Directive 2001/83/EC) which is not a vaccine, toxin, serum or based on human blood; a blood constituent; a radioactive isotope; or homoeopathic product as specified in the Directive;

2 it must be covered by a currently valid market authorisation granted by the regulatory body of a member state;

3 it must have no different therapeutic effect from the product covered by the UK licence; and

4 it must be made by, or under licence to, the UK manufacturer, or by a member of the same group of companies.

A licence granted in these circumstances is known as a *Product Licence (Parallel Import)* (PL(PI)).

These requirements apply to the parallel importing of medicines for human use and are taken from an administrative document issued by the Department of Health and Social Security (MAL2/PI). Comparable requirements for veterinary medicines appear in the Medicines (Veterinary Drugs) (Exemption from Licences) (Importation) Order 1986 (SI 1986 No. 228).

Manufacturer's licence

A manufacturer's licence is required by a person who, in the course of a business carried on by him/her, manufactures or assembles a medicinal product (s.8). The medicinal product to be manufactured or assembled must be the subject of a marketing authorisation unless some exemption is provided in the Act or regulations. The manufacturer must hold a marketing authorisation or be acting to the order of the marketing authorisation holder (s.23).

Manufacture includes any process carried out in the course of making the product, but does not include dissolving or dispensing the product in, or diluting or mixing it with, some other substances used as a vehicle for administration.

Assemble means the enclosing of the products (with or without other medicinal products of the same description) in a container which is labelled before the product is sold or supplied or, where the product (with or without medicinal products of the same description) is already enclosed in a container in which it is to be sold or supplied, labelling the container before the product is sold or supplied in it (s.132). *Assembly* has a corresponding meaning.

A licence is not required for the manufacture of chemicals and other substances used in the manufacture of ingredients of medicinal products. Nor is a licence required for the manufacture of ingredients supplied in bulk to other manufacturers (see definition of *medicinal products*, p. 16). A manufacturer's licence covering assembly must be held for breaking bulk supplies of a medicinal product if it involves the enclosure of the product in different containers or labelling the containers.

In dealing with applications for manufacturer's licences, the licensing authority must, in particular, take into consideration:

1 the operations proposed to be carried out in pursuance of the licence;
2 the premises in which those operations are to be carried out;
3 the equipment which is or will be available on those premises for carrying out those operations;
4 the qualifications of the persons under whose supervision those operations will be carried out; and
5 the arrangements made or to be made for ensuring the safe-keeping of, and the maintenance of adequate records in respect of, medicinal products manufactured or assembled in pursuance of the licence [s.19(5)].

N.B. Comission Directive 2003/94/EC lays down the principles and guidelines of *Good Manufacturing Practic* which is applicable to all activities which require a licence under Council Directive 2001/83/EC.

Good Manufacturing Practice means the part of quality assurance which ensures that products are consistently produced and controlled in accordance with the quality of standards appropriate to their intended use, the principles and guidelines of which are specified in Commission Directive 2003/94/EC (SI 2004 No. 1678).

Applications must be made in the manner prescribed in the regulations (SI 1971 No. 974 and SI 1977 No. 1052, as amended) indicating whether the licence is to relate to manufacturing or assembly or to both, and giving the particulars mentioned in 1 to 5 above. The applicant must describe the products to be manufactured or assembled and give details of any manufacturing operations to be carried out. The qualifications of the production manager and of the person in charge of quality control must be given, and the name and function of the person to whom they are responsible. Where relevant, the qualifications of the person in charge of animals, and of the person responsible for the culture of any living tissue, must also be given.

At least one 'qualified person' is required to be nominated whose responsibilities are set out in the regulations. A *qualified person* means a person who satisfies the provisions of the 2001 Directive with respect to qualification and experience.

The standard provisions for a manufacturer's licence are incorporated in every licence unless the applicant has successfully applied for any to be excluded or modified (s.47). Renewal applications are dealt with in SI 1974 No. 832, as amended.

Wholesale dealer's licence

Council Directive 2001/83/EC requires a wholesale dealer's licence to be held by any person who, in the course of a business carried on by him/her:

1 sells, or offers for sale, any medicinal products by way of wholesale dealing; or
2 distributes, otherwise than by way of sale, any medicinal product, ready made veterinary drug or industrially produced medicinal product other than a veterinary drug which has been imported but was not consigned from a member state of the EU (s.8 and SIs 1977 No. 1050, 1983 No. 1724 and 1992 No. 604).

No person may distribute by way of wholesale any medicinal product which is subject to Directive 2001/83/EC (proprietary and generic medicinal products) except in accordance with a wholesale dealer's licence and from premises specified in that licence. The latter provision does not apply to whole human blood, plasma or blood cells of human origin, a radiopharmaceutical in which the radionuclide is in a sealed source, or a homoeopathic product. Neither does it apply to veterinary drugs which are immunological products, radiopharmaceuticals, homoeopathic, additives for animal feeding stuffs or a product specially prepared for a veterinary surgeon for an animal or herd under his/her care.

A wholesale dealer's licence is also required for exportation of any medicinal product which is subject to the 2001 Directive (proprietary and generic medicinal products) if it is to be exported to a member state of the EU (SI 1993 No. 834).

No licence under 2 is required by a person who provides facilities solely for the transport of the medicinal product, or who, in the course of his/her business as an import agent, imports a medicinal product solely to the order of another person who intends to distribute it (SI 1990 No. 566). Neither is a licence required by the holder of a marketing authorisation or by a person who has assembled the product to the order of the marketing authorisation holder and where the product has not left the premises of the manufacturer or assembler until the sale of the product (SI 1990 No. 566).

Distribution of a medicinal product by way of wholesale dealing means:

1 selling or supplying it; or
2 procuring, holding or exporting it for the purposes of sale or supply to a person who receives it for the purposes of:

a   selling or supplying it; or

b   administering it, or causing it to be administered, to one or more human beings in the course of a business carried on by that person.

The term *business* includes a professional practice and any activity carried on by a body of persons, whether corporate or unincorporated (s.132). Consequently, all sales that are made to practitioners (whether medical or dental) for use in their practices constitute sales by way of wholesale dealing. The provision of services under the NHS is treated as the carrying on of a business by the appropriate Minister, Secretary of State or Ministry [s.131(5)].

Sales made by the manufacturer of a product are excluded from the definition of wholesale dealing so that s/he does not require a licence in order to sell his/her own products (s.131). A further concession is provided (SI 1972 No. 640) in respect of wholesale sales made by a marketing authorisation holder who is not also the manufacturer, or by a person assembling to his/her order. Provided that such products do not leave the premises of the licensed manufacturer or licensed assembler until the actual sale, no wholesale dealer's licence is required.

The activities of a group of retailers or practitioners who buy medicinal products in bulk and divide the stock amongst themselves for resale does not normally require a licence. If the group has a separate legal identity of its own, or if purchases are made by it collectively for resale to members of the group, a wholesale dealer's licence may be necessary (see also Exemptions for pharmacists below).

In dealing with an application for a wholesale dealer's licence, the licensing authority must, in particular, take into consideration:

1   the premises on which medicinal products of the description to which the application relates will be stored;

2   the equipment which is or will be available for storing medicinal products on those premises;

3   the equipment and facilities which are or will be available for distributing medicinal products from those premises; and

4   the arrangements made or to be made for securing the safe-keeping of, and the manufacture of adequate records in respect of, medicinal products stored on or distributed from those premises [s.19(6)].

Applications must be made in the manner prescribed in the regulations (SIs 1971 No. 974 and 1977 No. 1052) and state the classes of medicinal products which are the subject of the application and the uses for which they are intended, together with the particulars mentioned above. The applicant must also give the name and address and qualifications of the responsible person, details of an emergency plan for the recall of products and details for keeping records by way of invoices, on computer or in any other form relating to all products received or despatched (SI 1993 No. 832).

The standard provisions for wholesale dealer's licences are incorporated in every licence unless the applicant has successfully applied for any to be excluded or modified (s.47 and SI 1971 No. 972, as amended).

Fees

Holders of marketing authorisations, manufacturers' licences and wholesale dealer's licences have to pay a fee in connection with the holding of authorisations/licences in respect of each licence period. Such fees are prescribed in regulations made under the Medicines Act 1971, for human medicines (SI 1995 No. 1116, as amended), for animal medicines (SI 1997 No. 1469 as amended) and for homoeopathic medicines (SI 1996 No. 482, as amended).

Clinical trial and animal test certificates

A *clinical trial* is an investigation or series of investigations consisting of the administration of one or more medicinal products, where there is evidence that they may be beneficial to a patient or patients, by one or more doctors or dentists for the purpose of ascertaining what effects, beneficial or harmful, the products have (s.31). (For circumstances in which the administration of a substance does not constitute a clinical trial or bring the substance within the definition of a medicinal product, see Chapter 2.) For the manufacture or assembly of a medicinal product to be used only for the purpose of a clinical trial, a manufacturer's licence or a marketing authorisation is not required (s.35).

There is a comparable definition for *medicinal test on animals* (s.32). The provisions relating to clinical trials and medicinal tests on animals are in sections 31 to 39 of the Act. No person may, in the course of a business carried on by him/her, (a) sell or supply, or (b) procure the sale or supply of, or (c) procure the manufacture of or assemble for the purpose of sale or supply a medicinal product for the purpose of a clinical trial or a medicinal test on animals unless s/he is, or acts to the order of, the holder of a marketing authorisation which authorises the clinical trial, or unless a clinical trial certificate or an animal test certificate, as appropriate, has been issued and is in force, and the trial or test is to be carried out in accordance with it.

Exemptions for clinical trials

Clinical trials are controlled by procedures under Council Directive 2001/20/ EC. A marketing authorisation or clinical trial certificate is not required for the sale, supply, manufacture or assembly of a medicinal product for the purpose of a clinical trial provided that the conditions imposed by the exempting orders are met (SI 2004 No. 1031 as amended by SI 2005 No. 2754, SI 2005 No. 2759 and SI 2006 No. 1928). Notification of the supplier's intention must be sent to the licensing authority. The notice must be accompanied by particulars of the trial and summaries of pharmaceutical data and of reports made and tests performed as specified in Schedule 1 to the Order (SI 2004 No. 1031 as amended by SI 2006 No. 1928). There is provision for termination of the exemption in certain circumstances, usually on the grounds of safety and for appeals to a person appointed (SI 2005 No. 2754). EC Council Directive 2005/28/EEC, which is implemented by SI 2006 No. 1928, lay downs the principles and detailed guidelines for good clinical practice as regards investigational medicinal products for human use.

A certificate is not required if the product to be the subject of the clinical trial is covered by a marketing authorisation and the conditions set out in SI 2004 No. 1031 are met.

Similar conditions that are applicable to licensed products to be used in medicinal tests on animals are in SI 1977 No. 161. The principal requirements are that the product is to be used strictly in accordance with the marketing authorisation and that the licensing authority is notified of any adverse reactions or effects.

A doctor or dentist wanting to have a product manufactured or imported for use in a clinical trial does not need a certificate if certain conditions are met. The products must have been manufactured or imported specially for the trial and only for administration to the practitioner's own patients. The trial must not have been arranged by, or at the request of, a third party [s.31(5) and (6) and SI 1972 No. 1200]. A similar exemption applies where a product is specially manufactured for a veterinarian to use in a medicinal test on animals [s.33(2) and (3)].

When practitioners' prescriptions are dispensed in a registered pharmacy, hospital or health centre under the supervision of a pharmacist, there is no need for any certificate [ss.31(7) and 33(4)].

Exemptions for Tests on Animal licences or Animal Test Certificates are not required for the sale, supply or administration of veterinary drugs (not including immunological drugs) for the purposes of medicinal tests on animals subject to the conditions set out in SI 1986 No. 1180.

Exemptions for imports

No marketing authorisation is required for the importation of a medicinal product:

1   by any person for administration to him/herself or to any person or persons who are members of his/her household; or

2   where it is specially imported by or to the order of a doctor or dentist
    (ss.9 and 13) for the purposes described in the section Exemptions
    for practitioners (below); or
3   intended for re-export (below).

No exemptions exist for the veterinary surgeon, who may not import unlicensed veterinary medicines.

Marketing authorisations are not required for imported medicinal products which are to be exported in the form in which they were imported (see Exemptions for exports, below).

Exemptions for exports

The application of the licensing system to exports is postponed until a *special appointed day* at some time in the future (s.48). The result is that, although a 'manufacturer's licence must be held in order to manufacture medicinal products for export, no marketing authorisations are required, except for certain products, the purity and potency of which cannot be adequately tested by chemical means. Those which are for human use are listed in SI 1971 No. 1198, namely, antigens, antitoxins, antisera, sera, toxins or vaccines. Those which are veterinary products are listed in SI 1971 No. 1309, namely, antigens, antisera, antitoxins, corticotrophin, heparin, hyaluronidase, insulin, plasma, preparations of pituitary (posterior lobe), sera, toxins, vaccines and other medicinal products or substances derived from animals.

Marketing authorisations are not required for imported medicinal products which are to be exported in the form in which they were imported and are either:

1   not assembled in a way different from the way in which they were
    assembled on being imported; or
2   assembled in a way different from the way they were assembled on being
    imported but, the assembler, being the holder of a manufacturer's licence
    and having supplied the licensing authority with required information,
    has been notified that s/he may import the product (s.13 and SIs 1971
    No. 1326 and 1977 No. 640).

This exemption for re-exported products does not apply to the veterinary products listed in SI 1971 No. 1309, which are set out in the paragraph above.

Exemptions for practitioners

A doctor, dentist or veterinarian does not require a licence of any kind in respect of medicinal products specially prepared by him/her for administration to a particular patient (Sch.1 to SI 1994 No. 3144). The exemption extends to the preparation of a medicinal product at the request of another practitioner for administration to one of his/her patients or to an animal or herd under his/her care.

There is no exemption from licensing for veterinary surgeons or veterinary practitioners in respect of any vaccine for administration to poultry, but there is exemption in respect of a vaccine for administration to an animal (other than poultry) provided it is an autogenous vaccine. Any plasma or serum specially prepared for administration to one or more animals in the herd from which it is derived is also exempt from licensing [s.9(3)].

A practitioner may hold a stock of medicinal products for the purposes described above without the need to hold marketing authorisations. The total stock of such products which may be held by him/her must not exceed 5 litres of fluids and 2.5 kg of solids (SI 1994 No. 3144), and they must have been procured from a person holding an appropriate manufacturer's licence (SIs 1971 No. 1450 and 1972 No. 1200). (See also 'Special' dispensing, manufacturing and assembly exemptions, below.)

A doctor or dentist does not require any licence for any medicinal product specially imported by him/her or to his/her order for administration to a particular patient of his/hers or at the request of another doctor or dentist for administration to one of his/her patients (ss.9 and 13). There is a similar exemption from licensing for medicinal products imported by a hospital, wholesaler or retail pharmacy business provided the sale or supply is to a doctor or dentist for administration to a particular patient of his/hers. This exemption from licensing is subject to the requirements of SI 1994 No. 3144, namely, notification to the licensing authority, maintenance of written records including adverse drug reactions (for five years) and certain other conditions.

Exemptions for nurses and midwives

A registered nurse or a registered midwife is not required to have a manufacturer's licence in order to assemble medicinal products in the course of his/her profession (s.11).

Exemptions for pharmacists

The exemptions from licensing for pharmacists are contained in section 10 of the Act, to which a number of subsections were added by SI 1971 No. 1445 and SI 2005 No. 765.

Subject to the work being done by or under the supervision of a pharmacist, no licence of any kind is required for any of the following activities being carried out in a registered pharmacy or a care home service. *Care home service* means that given in the Regulation of Care (Scotland) Act 2001.

1 Preparing or dispensing a medicinal product in accordance with a prescription given by a practitioner (including a supplementary prescriber), or preparing a stock of medicinal products for this purpose. The stock of medicinal products may be procured from a manufacturer holding the appropriate special licence (see 'Special' dispensing, manufacturing and assembly exemptions below). This exemption also applies to hospitals and health centres [s.10(1) and (4) and SI 1972 No. 1200]. In respect of vaccines, sera and plasma for administration to animals, the exemption from licensing for pharmacists is subject to the same limitation which applies to veterinarians (see Exemptions for practitioners, above).

2 Preparing or dispensing a medicinal product in accordance with a specification furnished by the person to whom the product is to be sold for administration to that person, or to a person under his/her care, or an animal or herd under his/her control, or preparing a stock of medicinal products for these purposes [s.10(3)]. This exemption does not cover any vaccine, plasma or serum for animal use.

3 Preparing or dispensing a medicinal product for administration to a person when the pharmacist is requested to do so by or on behalf of that person in accordance with the pharmacist's own judgement as to the treatment required, and that person is present in the pharmacy at the time of the request (*counter prescribing*); a stock of medicinal products prepared in a registered pharmacy in accordance with 1 and 2 above and under this paragraph may be sold or supplied from any other registered pharmacy forming part of the same retail pharmacy business.

4 Preparing a medicinal product or a stock of medicinal products, not to the order of another person, but with a view to retail sale or supply, provided that the sale or supply is made from the registered pharmacy where it was prepared and the product is not the subject of an advertisement [s.10(5)]. In this connection, *advertisement* does not include words appearing on the product or its container or package or the display of the product itself, but it does include a show-card [s.10(8)].

5 Assembling a medicinal product [s.10(1)]. This exemption also applies to hospitals and health centres. When medicinal products are assembled in a registered pharmacy for retail sale or supply, they may not be the subject of any advertisement and may only be sold or supplied at the registered pharmacy where they are assembled or at some other registered pharmacy forming part of the same retail pharmacy business (SI 1971 No. 1445).

6 Wholesale dealing, where such dealing constitutes no more than an inconsiderable part of the business carried on at that pharmacy. This covers occasional sales to practitioners or to other pharmacists (SI 1971 No. 1445) (see p. 131).

A retail pharmacist who is responsible for the composition of a medicinal product which s/he intends to sell or supply in the course of his/her business must hold a marketing authorisation if his/her activities fall outside the exemptions set out above. S/he must also have a manufacturer's licence or arrange for the product to be made by a manufacturer who has an appropriate licence.

Exemptions for chiropodists etc.

A person who is either a member of a registering body or customarily administers medicinal products to human beings in the course of a business in the field of osteopathy, chiropody, naturopathy or other similar field does not require a manufacturer's licence to assemble medicinal products for human use which are on general sale. The product must be for administration to a particular person who has requested the naturopath etc. to use his/her own judgement as to the treatment required. Exemption is obtained by notification to the licensing authority (SI 1979 No. 1114).

Exemptions for herbal remedies

A *herbal remedy* is a medicinal product consisting of a substance produced by subjecting a plant or plants to drying, crushing or any other process, or of a mixture whose sole ingredients are two or more substances so produced, or of a mixture whose sole ingredients are one or more substances so produced and water or some other inert substances (s.132).

No marketing authorisation/licence is required for the sale, supply, manufacture or assembly of any such herbal remedy in the course of a business in which the person carrying on the business sells or supplies the remedy for administration to a particular person after being requested by or on behalf of that person, and in that person's presence, to use his/her own judgement as to the treatment required. The person carrying on the business must be the occupier of the premises where the manufacture or assembly takes place and must be able to close them so as to exclude the public [s.12(1)].

No marketing authorisation/licence is required for the sale, supply, manufacture or assembly of those herbal remedies where the process to which the plant or plants are subjected consists only of drying, crushing or comminuting and the remedy is sold or supplied under a designation which only specifies the plant or plants and the process and does not apply any other name to the remedy; and without any written recommendation (whether by means of a labelled container or package or a leaflet or in any other way) as to the use of the remedy [s.12(2)]. This exemption does not extend to imported products.

Presumably, unless a herbal product is sold or supplied for a medicinal purpose, it is not even a medicinal product; no doubt there will be circumstances in which herbs of this kind will be sold for other than medicinal purposes.

Exemptions for wholesale dealing in confectionery

No wholesale dealer's licence is required for the sale, or offer for sale by way of wholesale dealing, of a medicinal product, other than a veterinary drug, which is for sale as confectionery if the marketing authorisation in respect of the medicinal product provides that the exemption shall apply, and if the medicinal product is not sold or offered for sale accompanied by or having in relation to it any particulars in writing specifying that product's curative or remedial function in relation to a disease specified, other than in relation to the relief of symptoms of coughs, colds or nasal congestion (SI 1975 No. 762).

Exemptions for foods and cosmetics

It is provided by Orders (SIs 1971 No. 1410 and 1973 No. 2079) that licensing provisions do not apply to anything done in relation to a medicinal product which is wholly or mainly for use by being administered to one or more human beings and which is for sale, or is to be for sale, either for oral administration as a food or for external use as a cosmetic.

The definition of *food* includes beverages, confectionery, ingredients in the preparation of foods and advertised dietary supplements which contain added vitamins.

Vitamins are any of the following: vitamins A, B_1, B_2, B_6, C, D and E, biotin, nicotinamide, nicotinic acid, pantothenic acid and its salts, bioflavonoids, inositol, choline, *p*-aminobenzoic acid, cyanocobalamin or folic acid.

Vitamin preparation means any medicinal product, the active ingredients of which consist only of vitamins, or vitamins and mineral salts, that is, salts of any one or more of the following: iron, iodine, calcium, phosphorus, fluorine, copper, potassium, manganese, magnesium or zinc.

A *cosmetic* is defined as 'any substance or preparation intended to be applied to the various surfaces of the human body including epidermis, pilary system and hair, nails, lips and external genital organs, or the teeth and buccal mucosa, wholly or mainly for the purpose of perfuming them, cleansing them, protecting them, caring for them or keeping them in condition, modifying their appearance (whether for aesthetic purposes or otherwise) or combating body odours or normal body perspiration'.

This general exemption from licensing requirements does not apply if the food or cosmetic is sold with some particulars, in writing, specifying the product's curative or remedial function in relation to a specified disease, or the use of the product for such curative or remedial purposes. A marketing authorisation is required for any product promoted to practitioners. In addition, *no exemption* applies to the following.

1   Cosmetics for external use containing any antibiotic; or hexachlorophane (but not if less than 0.1 per cent and labelled with a statutory caution); or any hormone in excess of 0.004 per cent weight in weight (w/w) or resorcinol in excess of 1 per cent w/w.

2   Any *vitamin preparation* for oral administration as a food in relation to which there are no written particulars or directions as to dosage.

3   Any *vitamin preparation* for oral administration as a food in relation to which there are written particulars or directions specifying a recommended daily dosage for adults involving a daily intake in excess of: vitamin A, 2500 iu or antirachitic activity 250 iu; or folic acid, 25 micrograms; cyanocobalamin, 5 micrograms.

4   Any medicinal product for oral administration as a food, not being a *vitamin preparation*, to which one or more of the ingredients, vitamin A or D, folic acid or cyanocobalamin has been added, and in relation to which product there are written particulars or directions as to recommended use of that substance which involves a daily intake in excess of the quantities and ingredients specified in 3.

5   Any medicinal product not covered by 2, 3 or 4 above which is to be sold with, accompanied by or having in relation to it any particulars in writing specifying the dosage relevant to that product's medicinal properties.

Exemption from marketing authorisations or licensing does not exempt a medicinal product from any labelling requirements which may be made under the Act (see Chapter 15).

Whether or not a substance or article is a medicinal product depends upon the purpose for which it is sold or supplied (see Chapter 2). Some substances have both medicinal and non-medicinal uses. Although the exemptions for foods and cosmetics cover a wide field, borderline cases will inevitably occur where there is doubt as to the status of a product. A legally binding decision can only be given in the courts, but enquiries can be made of the MHRA about the status of any product which is being promoted in a particular way. It is quite possible that a slight alteration in wording of a label may alter the standing of a product under the Act.

Certain examples have been mentioned in the Department of Health's leaflet MAL8. On the one hand, anti-smoking preparations which create an unpleasant taste in the mouth when the person taking them smokes tobacco, and tablets and cachets sucked in order to freshen the breath, are not considered to be medicinal products. On the other hand, hair restorers, whether to be taken orally or applied externally, and insect repellents for external application to cats and dogs, are regarded as medicinal products.

Exemptions for ingredients

Ingredients used in pharmacies, in hospitals or in businesses where herbal remedies are sold and those used by practitioners, are medicinal products (s.130), but they are exempted from licensing requirements (SI 1974 No. 1150) provided particulars of the activity have been notified to the licensing authority by the manufacturer or supplier. The exemption may, in the interest of safety, be withdrawn by the licensing authority. Certain substances which are not themselves medicinal products but may be used as ingredients are subject to licensing. They are listed in SIs 1971 No. 1200 and 1985 No. 1403 (see Appendix 1).

`Special' dispensing, manufacturing and assembly exemptions

In order *to fulfil special needs*, Council Directive 2001/83EC and SI 1994 No. 3144 (Sch.1) enable a *special* dispensing or manufacturing service to be provided in response to a bona fide unsolicited order, formulated in accordance with the specification of a doctor or dentist and for use by his/her individual patients on his/her direct personal responsibility without the need for the manufacturer to hold a marketing authorisation for the medicinal product concerned. The conditions which apply are as follows.

1 The medicinal product must be supplied to a doctor or dentist or for use in a pharmacy, hospital or health centre under the supervision of a pharmacist.
2 The medicinal product must not be the subject of any advertisement or representation. However, the service provided may be advertised.
3 Manufacture or assembly must be carried out under the supervision of such staff and such precautions must be taken as are adequate to ensure that the product is of the character required by, and meets the specifications of, the doctor or dentist who requires it.
4 Written records as to the manufacture/assembly must be maintained and available to the licensing authority.
5 The medicinal product is manufactured/assembled by the holder of a manufacturer's licence.
6 The medicinal product is distributed by way of wholesale dealing by the holder of a wholesale dealer's licence.

Medicinal products to which these special licensing provisions apply and the circumstances in which they may be supplied are given as follows.

1   Products supplied to a doctor or dentist for administration to a particular patient (but there is a limit on the amount of stock which may be held by a doctor or dentist) (see p. 42).
2   Products, or stocks of products, supplied to retail pharmacists, hospitals or health centres for dispensing, or with a view to dispensing, practitioners' prescriptions.
3   Products, or stocks of products, supplied to retail pharmacists for administration to particular persons in accordance with the pharmacist's own judgement, or in accordance with the specification of a customer for administration to him/herself or a person under his/her care.
4   Herbal remedies supplied to a retailer for administration to a particular person in accordance with the retailer's own judgement.
5   Products (not being Prescription Only or Pharmacy Only Products) supplied to a person for administration to him/herself or a member of his/her household.
6   Products (not being Prescription Only Products) for sale or supply to a person exclusively for use by him/her in the course of his/her business for administration to human beings, but not by way of sale (e.g. a special formula for use in a first-aid room). These products must be prepared under the supervision of a pharmacist.
7   Products supplied to licensed wholesale dealers for supply in the circumstances specified in 1 to 6 above.

Hospitals

On 1 April 1991, by virtue of the National Health Service and Community Care Act 1990, all NHS hospitals lost their Crown immunity and became liable to the licensing provisions of the Medicines Act. The type of activities relating to manufacture, assembly and wholesaling varies considerably from one hospital to another and whether any particular licence is required depends on the individual activity. Certain exemptions exist where an activity takes place under the supervision of a pharmacist either in a registered pharmacy (see p. 43) or in a hospital (s.10). The MRHA issued in 1992 a document entitled *Guidance to the NHS on the Licensing Requirements of the Medicines Act 1968*. Hospital pharmacists requiring further details should contact the Medicines Control Agency.

Export certificates

The licensing authority may, on the application of an exporter of medicinal products, issue to him/her a certificate containing such statements relating to the products as the authority considers appropriate, having regard to any requirements (whether having the force of law or not) which have effect in the country to which the products are to be exported and to the provisions of the Medicines Act, and to any licence granted or other things done by virtue of the Act (s.50).

Medical devices

Medical devices include such items as intrauterine devices and diaphragms, dental fillings, contact lens care products, non-medicated dressings, sutures and ligatures. These are no longer controlled under the Medicines Act but under consumer protection legislation (The Medical Devices Regulations 2002, SI 2002 No. 618 as amended by SIs 2003 No. 1697 and 2007 No. 400).

A *device* means a medical device, that is to say an instrument, apparatus, appliance, material or other article, whether used alone or in combination, together with any software necessary for its proper application which:

1   is intended by the manufacturer to be used for human beings for the purpose of:
    a   diagnosis, prevention, monitoring, treatment or alleviation of disease;
    b   diagnosis, monitoring, treatment or alleviation of or compensation for an injury or handicap;
    c   investigation, replacement or modification of the anatomy or of any physiological process; or
    d   control of contraception; and

2   does not achieve its principal intended action in or on the human body by pharmacological, immunological or metabolic means, even if it is assisted in its function by such means, even if it is intended to administer a medicinal product as defined in Council Directive 2001/83/EC or incorporates as an integral part of a substance which, if used separately, would be a medicinal product and which is liable to act upon the body with action ancillary to that of the device.

Such devices must comply with the regulations with regard to the essential requirements set out in Council Directive 93/42/EEC, as amended, with specific labelling. The former Medical Devices Agency, now merged with the former Medicines Control Agency to form the MHRA (see Chapter 2), administers and enforces the legislation. Manufacturers have to be registered and fees are payable (SI 1995 No. 449, as amended).

Summary

- All dealings in medicinal products are subject to a licensing system unless specifically exempted. Marketing authorisations or licences are needed to *place a medicine on the market*, to manufacture, wholesale or distribute medicinal products. Certification is needed for human and animal clinical trials.

- The national (decentralised) marketing authorisations are administered by the Medicines and Healthcare Regulatory Agency and the centralised system by the European Medicines Agency.
- A simplified system of licensing (*certification*) applies to homoeopathic products.
- Stringent requirements, set out in a Guide to Good Manufacturing Practice, apply to manufacturing licences and introduce the concept of a *qualified person*. Similar conditions apply to wholesale dealer's licences which have a *responsible person*.
- Clinical trials are subject to certification by the licensing authority unless specifically exempted.
- Certain exemptions from licensing exist for doctors, nurses, pharmacists, other health professionals and hospitals.
- No licences are required for certain activities carried out in a pharmacy under the supervision of a pharmacist.
- Certain products are exempt from licensing, e.g. herbal remedies, confectionery, food, cosmetics and vitamins.
- Provisions are made for *special* dispensing or manufacturing services.
- Medical devices, e.g. dental fillings, contact lenses, intrauterine devices, are now controlled under consumer protection legislation.

Further reading

MAL Advisory Leaflets. London: Medicines Control Agency.

Royal Pharmaceutical Society of Great Britain, European Industrial Pharmacists Group. *Code of Practice for Qualified Persons*. London: Royal Pharmaceutical Society of Great Britain.

Rules and Guidance for Pharmaceutical Manufacturers (GMP) (1997). London: The Stationery Office.

Rules Governing Medicinal Products in European Union, vol. 1: *Pharmaceutical Legislation, Human Medicinal Products*. London: The Stationery Office.

Websites

www.mhra.gsi.gov.uk
http://ec.europa.eu/enterprise/pharmaceuticals/eudralex/vol2_en.htm

4

Medicines Act 1968
Sales promotion of medicinal products

Advertisements and representations

Control of medicines advertising in the UK is based on a system of self-regulation underpinned by statutory powers under EU and UK law.

The Medicines (Advertising) Regulations 1994 (SI 1994 No. 1932, as amended by SI 1999 No. 267 and SI 2002 No. 236) and the Medicines (Monitoring of Advertising) Regulations 1994 (SI 1994 No. 1933, as amended by SI 2002 No. 236) implement Council Directive 2001/83/EC and both sets of regulations supplement the existing controls under the Medicines Act (Part VI) and ensure that a relevant medicinal product is only promoted in accordance with its marketing authorisation.

A distinction is drawn between *advertisements* and *representations* in the Act (see below). In the regulations governing the advertising of relevant medicinal products (SI 1994 No. 1932), the definition of *advertisement* includes a *representation* (see p. 55) but does not include reference material, factual informative statements or announcements, a trade catalogue or a price list provided there is no product claim (c.f. s.92 of the Act).

In the regulations, the word *representation* has the same meaning as in the Act, except it does not include the making of a factual, informative statement or announcement which includes no product claim.

Advertisement includes every form of advertising, whether in a publication; by the display of any notice; by means of any catalogue, price list, letter (whether circular or addressed to a particular person) or other document; by words inscribed on any article; by the exhibition of a photograph or a cinematograph film; by way of sound recording, sound broadcasting or television; or in any other way (s.92).

Representation means any statement or undertaking (whether constituting a condition or a warranty or not) which consists of spoken words other than words broadcast by way of sound recording, sound broadcasting or television, or forming part of a sound recording or embodied in a cinematograph film soundtrack [s.92(5)].

Words spoken, other than by way of sound or television broadcasting, or as part of a sound recording or film soundtrack, do not fall within the definition of advertisement. Similarly, unless provided for in regulations made under section 95, neither the sale or supply of a medicinal product in a labelled container, nor the inclusion of a leaflet relating to a specific medicinal product, constitute the issue of an advertisement (s.92).

Sound recording has the meaning assigned to it by section 12 of the Copyright Act 1956, that is 'the aggregate of the sounds embodied in, and capable of being reproduced by means of, a record of any description, other than a soundtrack associated with a cinematograph film'.

To ensure that adequate information is given about medicinal products, to promote safety in relation to them and to prevent the giving of misleading information about them, the appropriate Minister may impose by regulation any requirements which may be necessary or expedient. They may concern the form of any advertisement and the particulars contained therein and, in the case of television or cinematograph film advertisements, their duration and manner of exhibition may be controlled. Advertisements of particular kinds, as specified in the regulations, may be prohibited, either totally or subject to some exceptions [s.95(3)].

Control of advertisements and representations

No commercially interested party, and no person acting on his/her behalf, may issue an advertisement relating to a medicinal product without the consent of the holder of the marketing authorisation (s.94). The licensing authority may obtain up to 12 copies of any advertisement (including any data sheet) relating to medicinal products by serving a notice on the person who issued it or caused it to be issued (s.97).

The appropriate Ministers may, by regulation, prohibit the issue of advertisements (s.95):

1 relating to medicinal products of a specific description or class;
2 likely to lead to the use of any medicinal product, or any other substance or article, for the purpose of treating or preventing a specified disease, or diagnosing a specified disease, or ascertaining the existence, degree or extent of a specified physiological condition, or permanently or temporarily preventing or otherwise interfering with the normal operation of a specified physiological function, or artificially inducing a specified condition of mind or body;
3 likely to lead to the use of a particular class of medicinal products, or other substances or articles, for the purposes set out in b below;
4 relating to medicinal products and containing a specified word or phrase which, in the opinion of the Minister, is likely to mislead the public as to

the nature or effects of the products, or as to any condition of mind or body in connection with which the products might be used.

The regulations may also extend the prohibitions mentioned in 2, 3 and 4 above to cover any representations made:

a   in connection with the sale or supply or offer for sale or supply of a medicinal product or other substance or article to which the regulations apply; or
b   for the purpose of inducing any person to buy the medicinal product, substance or article from a retailer; or,
c   to a practitioner, or a patient or client, for the purpose of inducing the practitioner to prescribe medicinal products of a specified description.

Regulations relating to advertisements for medicinal products for human use addressed to doctors or dentists and the public are in SI 1994 No. 1932. Other regulations (SI 1979 No. 1760) specify particulars which must be included in advertisements in the form of information sheets and sent to pharmacists and opticians about substances and fluids for use with contact lenses or blanks.

Advertising in general

Definitions

Certain terms used in advertising are further defined in SI 1994 No. 1932 in relation to *relevant* medicinal products as follows.

Advertisement has the meaning as in section 92 of the Act (see p. 53), except that in relation to a relevant medicinal product (see p. 183): (a) provided that it makes no product claim, reference material, a factual informative statement or announcement, a trade catalogue or price list shall not be taken to be an advertisement, and (b) an advertisement includes a representation, and for the purposes of this representation has the meaning as in section 92 of the Act (see p. 53) except that it does not include the making of a factual informative statement or announcement which includes no product claim.

Essential information compatible with the Summary of Product Characteristics means essential information compatible with the Summary of Product Characteristics as set out in Title VIII of the 2001 Directive.

Promotional aid means a non-monetary gift made for a promotional purpose by a commercially interested party.

Reference material includes entries which are in the form of, and limited to, a brief description of a medicinal product, its uses and any relevant contra-indications and warnings appearing without charge in a publication consisting wholly or mainly of such entries where the publication is sent or delivered to persons qualified to prescribe or supply relevant medicinal products by a person who is not a commercially interested party.

General principles

1 No person may issue an advertisement for a relevant medicinal product unless that product has a marketing authorisation. This general regulation does not apply to registered homoeopathic medicinal products (SI 1994 No. 1932).
2 No person shall issue an advertisement relating to a relevant medicinal product unless that advertisement:
   a complies with the particulars listed in the Summary of Product Characteristics, and
   b encourages the rational use of that product by presenting it objectively and without exaggerating its properties (SI 1999 No. 267).
3 No person shall issue a misleading advertisement relating to a relevant medicinal product (SI 1999 No. 267).
4 No person shall issue an advertisement which is likely to lead to the use of a relevant medicinal product or substance or article for the purpose of inducing an abortion in women (SI 1994 No. 1932).

Duties of holders of marketing authorisations

Any person who holds a marketing authorisation (reg.4), a traditional herbal registration or a certificate of registration must:

1 establish a scientific service to compile and collate all information, whether received from medical sales representatives employed by him/her or from any other source relating to that product;
2 ensure that, in relation to any such product which sales representatives promote, those medical sales representatives are given adequate training and have sufficient scientific knowledge to enable them to provide information which is as precise and as complete as possible about that product;
3 keep available for Health Ministers, or communicate to them within such period as may be specified in a notice served by them on him/her, a sample of any advertisement for which s/he is responsible relating to that product, together with a statement indicating the persons to whom the advertisement is addressed, the method of dissemination and the date of its first dissemination (SI 1999 No. 267); and
4 supply, within the period specified in a notice served by the Health Ministers on him/her, any information and assistance requested by them

in order to carry out their functions under the regulations or the Monitoring of Advertising Regulations (SI 1999 No. 267).

Advertising to persons qualified to prescribe or supply

Persons qualified to prescribe or supply includes persons, and employees of such persons, who in the course of their profession or in the course of a business may lawfully prescribe, sell by retail or supply in circumstances corresponding to retail sale relevant medicinal products.

The regulations (SI 1994 No. 1932, as amended by SIs 1999 No. 267 and 2002 No. 236) implement Council Directive 2001/83/EC in connection with the control of advertising to persons who are qualified to prescribe or supply. The regulations do not relate to advertisements aimed at veterinary surgeons or veterinary practitioners.

No person may issue an advertisement relating to a relevant medicinal product and aimed at persons qualified to prescribe or supply unless the advertisement (reg.14 and Sch.2):

1   contains essential information compatible with the Summary of Product Characteristics (SPC); and
2   contains the following particulars:
    a   the licence number of the product;
    b   the name and address of the marketing authorisation holder which relates to the product or the business name and address of his/her business that is responsible for its sale or supply;
    c   the classification of the product, i.e. Prescription Only, Pharmacy Only, or General Sale List;
    d   the name of the product and a list of active ingredients using the common name placed immediately adjacent to the most prominent display of the name;
    e   the indications as within the terms of the licence;
    f   a succinct statement of the entries in the SPC or where there is no SPC the data sheet, relating to side effects, precautions and relevant contra-indications;
    g   a succinct statement of the entries in the SPC, or where there is no SPC the data sheet, relating to the dosage and method of use relevant to the indications shown. The method of administration should also be shown where this is not obvious;
    h   a warning issued by the licensing authority under Part II of the Act which is required to be included;
    i   the cost, excluding VAT, of either a specified package of the product, or a specified quantity or recommended daily dose, calculated by reference to any specified package of the product, except that the cost

may be omitted in the case of an advertisement inserted in a publication which is printed in the United Kingdom but with a circulation outside the United Kingdom of more than 15 per cent of its total circulation;

j   the particulars in paragraphs f, g and h above shall be printed in a clear and legible manner and be placed in such a position in the advertisement that their relationship to the claims and indications for the product can readily be appreciated by the reader.

Abbreviated advertisements

Abbreviated advertisement means an advertisement, other than a loose insert, which does not exceed in size an area of $420\,cm^2$, in a publication sent or delivered wholly or mainly to persons qualified to prescribe or supply relevant medicinal products. No person may issue such an advertisement unless it:

1   contains essential information compatible with the Summary of Product Characteristics; and,
2   the following particulars:
    a   the name of the medicinal product and a list of the active ingredients using the common name placed immediately adjacent to the most prominent display of the name;
    b   the name and address of the marketing authorisation holder or the business name and address of the part of the business responsible for the sale or supply;
    c   the classification of the products, i.e. Prescription Only, Pharmacy Only, or General Sale List;
    d   a form of words which clearly indicates that further information is available on request to the licence holder or in the Summary of Product Characteristics or, if there is no SPC, the data sheet, relating to the product; and
    e   any warning issued in relation to the product by the licensing authority.

Audio-visual advertisements

No person may issue in a programme service or video recording any advertisement unless the advertisement:

1   contains essential information compatible with the Summary of Product Characteristics;
2   contains the following particulars:

a   the licence number of the product,

b   the name and address of the marketing authorisation holder which
relates to the product or the business name and address of his/her
business that is responsible for its sale or supply;

c   the classification of the product, i.e. Prescription Only, Pharmacy
Only, or General Sale List;

d   the name of the product and a list of active ingredients using the
common name placed immediately adjacent to the most prominent
mention or display of the name;

e   the indications as within the terms of the licence;

f   a succinct statement of the entries in the SPC or, where there is no
SPC, the data sheet relating to side-effects, precautions and relevant
contraindications;

g   a succinct statement of the entries in the SPC or, where there is no
SPC, the data sheet relating to the dosage and method of use relevant
to the indications shown; the method of administration should also
be shown where this is not obvious; and

h   a warning issued by the licensing authority under Part II of the Act,
which is required to be included.

Promotional aids

The requirements set out above in relation to advertisements, abbreviated advertisements and audio-visual advertisements do not apply to promotional aids if:

1   the advertisement consists solely of the name of the product or the
international non proprietary name or the trademark (or in the case of a
registered homoeopathic medicinal product the scientific name of the
stock or stocks) (SI 2005 No. 2787); and

2   the advertisement is intended solely as a reminder.

Written material accompanying promotions

No person may send or deliver to prescribers or suppliers of medicinal products as part of a promotion any written material unless it:

1   contains essential information compatible with the Summary of Product
Characteristics;

2   contains the classification of the product, i.e. Prescription Only,
Pharmacy Only, or General Sale List;

3   states the date on which it was drawn up or last revised.

Any such written material shall be accurate, up-to-date, verifiable and
complete and not state any quotation, table or other illustrative matter taken

from a medical journal or other scientific work unless it is accurately reproduced and the precise source is indicated.

Free samples

A person may supply a sample only:

1   to a person qualified to prescribe medicinal products;
2   if the sample is not a narcotic or a psychotropic substance; and subject to the following:
    a   the sample is supplied on an exceptional basis only;
    b   a limited number only of samples of each product may be supplied in one year to one recipient;
    c   samples supplied may only be in response to a written request, signed and dated from the recipient;
    d   suppliers of samples must maintain an adequate system of control and accountability;
    e   every sample shall be no bigger than the smallest presentation available for sale in the United Kingdom;
    f   every sample must be marked 'free medical sample – not for resale' or bear a similar description;
    g   every sample must be accompanied by a copy of the SPC or, where there is no SPC, a copy of the data sheet.

Medical sales representatives

All sales representatives promoting medicinal products to prescribers or suppliers of medicines must give to all persons they visit a copy of the SPC or, in the absence of a SPC, a copy of the data sheet. Such representatives must report all information which they receive from prescribers, including any adverse drug reactions, to the scientific service established under the regulations.

Inducements and hospitality

When products are being promoted to health professionals, no person may supply, offer or promise any gift, pecuniary advantage or benefit in kind unless it is inexpensive and relevant to the practice of medicine or pharmacy.

Hospitality, including the payment of travelling or accommodation expenses, may be offered at events for purely professional or scientific purposes to persons qualified to prescribe or supply relevant medicinal products provided that:

- such hospitality is strictly limited to the main scientific objective of the event; and
- it is offered only to health professionals.

No person shall offer hospitality (including the payment of travelling or accommodation expenses) at a meeting or event held for the promotion of relevant medicinal products unless:

- such hospitality is strictly limited to the main purpose of the meeting or event; and,
- the person to whom it is offered is a health professional.

It is an offence for a health professional to solicit or accept any gift, pecuniary advantage, benefit in kind, hospitality or sponsorship prohibited by the regulations (amended by SI 2005 No. 2787).

Advertisements directed to the public

The regulations dealing with advertisements which are directed to the public, relating to medicinal products for human use (SI 1994 No. 1932, as amended), impose a range of prohibitions, restrictions and requirements, which are set out below.

No advertisement may be issued which is likely to lead to the use of a relevant medicinal product:

1 which is a Controlled Drug which is listed in Schedules I, II or IV of the Narcotic Drugs Convention or Schedules I–IV of the Psychotropic Substances Convention (reg.8);
2 which is for human use and is a Prescription Only Medicine (reg.7);
3 or any other medicinal product, substance or article for the purpose of inducing an abortion in women (reg.6).

Prohibition of certain material in advertisements

No person shall issue an advertisement relating to a relevant medicinal product which contains any material which (reg.9):

1 gives the impression that a medical consultation or surgical operation is unnecessary, in particular by offering a telephone number;
2 suggests that the effects of taking the medicinal product are guaranteed, are unaccompanied by side effects or are better than, or equivalent to, those of another identifiable treatment or medicinal product;
3 suggests that health can be enhanced by taking the medicinal product;
4 suggests that health could be affected by not taking the product;
5 is directed exclusively or principally at children;

6   refers to a recommendation by scientists, health professionals or persons who are neither of the foregoing but who, because of their celebrity, could encourage the consumption of medicinal products;

7   suggests that the medicinal product is a foodstuff, cosmetic or other consumer product;

8   suggests that the safety and efficacy of the medicinal product is due to the fact that it is natural;

9   might, by a description or detailed representation of a case history, lead to erroneous self-diagnosis;

10   refers, in improper, alarming or misleading terms, pictorial representations of changes in the human body caused by disease or injury, or of the action of a medicinal product on the human body or parts thereof.

Form and contents of advertisements

No person shall issue an advertisement relating to a relevant medicinal product unless that advertisement (reg.10):

1   is set out in such a way that it is clear that the message is an advertisement and so that the product is clearly identified as a medicinal product; and

2   excluding advertisements for homoeopathic medicinal products, includes the following:

    a   the name of the medicinal product;

    b   if it contains only one active ingredient, the common name of the medicinal product;

    c   the information necessary for correct use of the product; and

    d   an express and legible invitation to read carefully the instructions on the leaflet contained within the package or on the label, as the case may be.

These provisions do not apply if the advertisement relates to a relevant medicinal product which is on a promotional aid, if the advertisement consists solely of the name of the product or the international non-proprietary name or the trademark (or in the case of a registered homoeopathic medicinal product the scientific name of the stock or stocks) or its invented name and the advertisement is solely intended as a reminder (amended by SI 2005 No. 2787).

Vaccination campaigns

The regulations as set out above do not apply to any advertisement which is part of a vaccination campaign relating to a relevant medicinal product provided that such a campaign has been approved by the Health Ministers (reg.11).

Sales or supplies for promotional purposes

No person who:

1 is the holder of a marketing authorisation, traditional herbal registration or certificate of registration, or
2 carries on a business which consists wholly or partly of the manufacturing, or of selling and supplying of relevant medicinal products

shall, for a promotional purpose (whether a promotional purpose of his/her own or of a third party), sell or supply relevant medicinal products to any member of the public (SI 1999 No. 267).

Advertisements for registered homoeopathic products

An advertisement relating to homoeopathic medicinal products may not mention any specific therapeutic indications and may only contain the following details:

1 the scientific name of the stock(s) followed by the degree of dilution, making use of the pharmacopoeia symbols used in relation to the homoeopathic procedure described for that stock(s);
2 the name and address of the holder of the certificate of registration and, where different, the name and address of the manufacturer;
3 the method of administration and, if necessary, the route;
4 the expiry date of the product stating the month and year;
5 the pharmaceutical form;
6 the contents of the sales presentation;
7 any special storage precautions;
8 any special warnings;
9 the manufacturer's batch number;
10 the registration number allotted by the licensing authority preceded by the letters *HR* in capital letters (reg.22);
11 the words homoeopathic product without approved therapeutic indications;
12 a warning advising the user to consult a doctor if the symptoms persist during the use of the product.

Advertisements for traditional herbal medicinal products (SI 2005 No. 2787)

No person may issue an advertisement for such products that are marketed in the UK under a traditional herbal registration unless it contains the statement *'Traditional herbal medicinal product for use in'*, followed by a statement of one or more therapeutic indications for the product consistent with the terms of the traditional herbal registration for that product, followed by *'exclusively based on long standing use'*

Monitoring of advertising

Monitoring of advertising is governed by the Medicines (Monitoring of Advertising) Regulations 1994 (SI 1994 No. 1933, as amended by SI 1999 No. 267). However, the existing voluntary control under the Medicines Act is encouraged and the existing Codes of Advertising Practice administered by the Association of the British Pharmaceutical Industry (for Prescription Only Medicines) and by the Proprietary Association of Great Britain (for over-the-counter medicines) will continue.

Complaints, in the first instance, will be referred to the appropriate self-regulatory body, but the Minister has the power of civil injunction. A person holding a marketing authorisation will be required to issue corrective statements if their advertising is found to be in breach of the regulations.

In the amending regulations (SI 1999 No. 267), a schedule has been introduced relating to the scrutiny of certain published or proposed advertisements. The schedule gives the Health Ministers powers for determining whether or not certain advertisements, proposed or published, breach the advertising regulations. There is an opportunity for representations to be made to an Independent Review Panel before the Health Ministers determine the case and breaches of notices issued by the Health Ministers create an offence. Details of the operation of the Review Panel are available from the Medicines Control Agency.

Prohibition of representations

No representation may be made by a commercially interested party which is likely to lead to the use of a medicinal product or, where relevant, any other substance or article for any of the diseases for which advertisements are prohibited (see p. 61) if the representation:

1   is made in connection with the sale or supply, or offer for sale or supply, of that product, substance or article;
2   is made to any person for the purpose of inducing him/her to purchase from a retailer that product, substance or article;
3   is made, in connection with medicinal products, to the patient of a doctor or dentist for the purpose of inducing him/her to request the doctor or dentist to prescribe medicinal products of that description.

The prohibition on representations does not apply to any representation:

a   made by a pharmacist who sells or supplies a medicinal product when
     dispensing a prescription given by a doctor or dentist, or when using his/
     her own judgement as to the treatment required by a person, i.e. counter
     prescribing; or
b   made by a state registered chiropodist (see p. 114) in relation to a
     medicinal product which s/he supplied to his/her patient for the purpose
     of treatment by being administered to the surface of the foot; or
c   made by a registered nurse or certified midwife to a patient in relation to a
     medicinal product.

Exceptions for labels and leaflets

None of the prohibitions, restrictions and requirements imposed by the regulations applies to any labelled container or package of a medicinal product or
any other substance or article or any leaflet supplied with such product where
that product is prepared or dispensed with a view to administration to a
person in accordance with the prescription of a doctor or dentist (SI 1978
No. 41).

The prohibitions on advertising imposed under the current regulations
do not apply to labelled containers or packages of medicinal products or
to leaflets supplied, or intended to be supplied, with medicinal products
which:

1   are herbal remedies which are not restricted under the Herbal
     Remedies Order (SI 1977 No. 2130) (see p. 144); or
2   are homoeopathic preparations with licences of right; or
3   are 'counter prescribed' by a pharmacist in a registered pharmacy
     (see p. 44).

These exceptions are subject to the condition that certain words or phrases
are not included in labels or leaflets except in so far as it is necessary to explain
the contraindications or precautions or the action to be taken in the event of
overdosage of the medicinal products. The words and phrases are:

- amenorrhoea
- angina
- atherosclerosis
- erysipelas
- gallstones
- multiple sclerosis
- osteoarthritis
- phlebitis
- thrombosis
- ulcer (except when used in the phrase 'aphthous ulcer' or 'mouth
  ulcer').

There is a further condition for herbal, biochemic and anthroposophic remedies, namely that every container and package of these medicinal products must be labelled with appropriate particulars and warning thus:

a   'A herbal remedy for (name of disease)', or as appropriate, 'A biochemic remedy for', or 'An anthroposophic remedy for'.

b   'Warning. If you think you have (name of disease, as above) consult a registered medical practitioner before taking this product. If you are already receiving treatment, tell your doctor that you are also taking this product.'

The name of the product may be used in the warning instead of the words *this product* and the warning must be within a rectangle within which there shall be no other matter of any kind.

Summary

- The regulations prohibit the advertising to the public of Controlled Drugs and Prescription Only Medicines.
- Requirements as to the information on medicinal products which has to be given to persons qualified to prescribe or supply medicines includes essential information compatible with the Summary of Product Characteristics. This may be given by way of written information accompanying promotions, or by promotion by medical representatives.
- A limited number only of free samples may be supplied to a person qualified to prescribe relevant medicinal products. The samples may only be supplied in response to a written request and suppliers must maintain an adequate system of control.
- No person who is the holder of a marketing authorisation or who carries on a business which consists of the manufacturing, or of selling or supplying medicinal products shall, for promotional purposes, sell or supply medicinal products to any member of the public.
- Hospitality given to persons qualified to prescribe or supply medicines must be reasonable in level and subordinate to the main objective of meetings held solely for scientific or professional purposes. No person may supply or promise any gift, pecuniary advantage or benefit in kind unless it is inexpensive and relevant to the practice of medicine or pharmacy.
- Conditions are set out for the advertising of homoeopathic medicinal products and for traditional herbal medicinal products
- Monitoring of advertising is to be undertaken by self-regulatory bodies but there are also legal provisions involving the Health Ministers.

Further reading

Association of the British Pharmaceutical Industry (2009) *Medicines Compendium*. London: Datapharm Communications Ltd.

MHRA. *Advertising and Promotion of Medicines in the UK*. London: Medicines and Health Care Regulatory Authority Updating Service.

MHRA (May/June 1999) *MAIL 113*. London: Medicines and Health Care Regulatory Authority Updating Service.

PAGB. *Best Practice Guidelines*. London: Proprietary Association of Great Britain.

5

Medicines Act 1968
Retail pharmacy businesses

The Health Act 2006 (s.28–s.30) amended sections 70–72 of the Medicines Act and replaced personal control with a requirement that each registered pharmacy is to have a responsible pharmacist in charge of the business where this relates to the sale or supply of medicines and other conditions for registration. A new section, 72A, placed a statutory duty on the responsible pharmacist to ensure the safe and effective running of a pharmacy. It also sets out how the responsible pharmacist exercises this duty. He must:

- establish, maintain and review pharmacy procedures that set out how activities are to be carried out in the pharmacy; and
- maintain a record at the pharmacy of the pharmacist who is in charge of the pharmacy on any date and at any time.

The Medicines (Pharmacies) (Responsible Pharmacist)Regulations 2008 No. 2789 setting out the responsible pharmacist's duties, etc have been published but do not come into force until 1 October 2009. These are set out in Appendix 3.

A retail pharmacy business means a business (not being a professional practice carried on by a practitioner) which consists of or includes the retail sale of medicinal products other than medicinal products on a General Sale List (whether medicinal products on such a list are sold in the course of that business or not) (s.132). Such a business may, subject to certain conditions, lawfully be conducted by (s.69):

1 a pharmacist, or a partnership where each partner is a pharmacist, or, in Scotland, a partnership where one or more partners is a pharmacist; or

2 a body corporate where the business so far as concerns the keeping, preparing and dispensing of medicinal products other than medicinal products on a General Sale List, is under the management of a superintendent who is a pharmacist, and who does not act in a similar capacity for any other body corporate; or

3   a representative of a deceased, bankrupt or mentally ill pharmacist, whose name, together with the names and address of the representative, has been notified to the registrar [s.72(2)].

With regard to item 3, the following apply.

1   In relation to a pharmacist who has died, 'representative' means his/her executor or administrator and, for a period of three months from the date of his/her death, if s/he has died leaving no executor who is entitled and willing to carry on the business, includes any person beneficially interested in his/her estate. The representative of a deceased pharmacist may carry on the business for a period of up to five years from the date of his/her death. Should s/he cease to be a representative before the expiry of five years, on completing the distribution of the deceased pharmacist's estate, his/her authority lawfully to carry on the pharmacy business would also come to an end.
2   Where a pharmacist is adjudged bankrupt or, in Scotland, sequestration of his/her estate is awarded, the trustee in bankruptcy or in the sequestration is the pharmacist's representative. S/he may carry on the pharmacist's business for a period of three years from the date on which s/he is adjudged bankrupt or the date of the award of sequestration, as the case may be.
3   Where a pharmacist enters into a composition or scheme or deed of arrangement with his/her creditors, or in Scotland makes a trust deed for behoof of his/her creditors, or a composition contract, then the trustee appointed under any such arrangement is the pharmacist's representative. S/he may carry on the business for a period of three years from the date on which s/he became entitled to do so.
4   Where a receiver is appointed for a pharmacist under Part VIII of the Mental Health Act 1959 or, in Scotland, a curator bonis or judicial factor is appointed for him/her on the grounds that s/he suffers from some mental disorder, or in Northern Ireland a committee, receiver or guardian is appointed in his/her case under the Lunacy Regulation (Ireland) Act 1871, then that person is the pharmacist's representative. S/he may carry on the business for three years from the date of his/her appointment.

A person lawfully conducting a retail pharmacy business as the representative of a pharmacist may take or use in connection with that business any title, emblem or description which the pharmacist him/herself could have used [s.78(8)] (see p. 76).

The Health Ministers may, by order, add to, revoke or vary any of these conditions relating to the carrying on of retail pharmacy business, or provide for alternative or modified conditions. Such an order must receive the approval of each House of Parliament (s.73).

There are certain conditions applying to all premises where the business is carried on and medicinal products, other than medicinal products on a General Sale List, are sold by retail. The original concept of personal control of the sale of medicines was revoked by s.28 of the Heath Act 2006. The amended conditions are set out below. The effect of these is that in every pharmacy business a responsible pharmacist must be in charge of each pharmacy premises where medicinal products are sold.

1   *Business carried on by a pharmacist or partners*
    a   A responsible pharmacist must be in charge of the business so far as it concerns the retail sale or supply of medicinal products (whether they are on the General Sale List or not).
    b   A notice should be conspicuously displayed at those premises stating the name of the responsible pharmacist, his/her registration number and the fact that s/he is for the time being in charge of the business.
    c   The responsible pharmacist must be the person carrying on the business; if it is carried on by a partnership, one of the partners who is a pharmacist or another pharmacist be the responsible pharmacist.
    d   In relation to a pharmacy that has only been registered for less than three years, the responsible pharmacist may not be a European Economic Area (EEA) certified pharmacist.

2   *Business carried on by a body corporate*
    a   A retail pharmacy business so far as concerns the keeping, preparing and dispensing of medicinal products other than medicinal products on the General Sale list must be under the management of a superintendent for each set of premises where the business is carried on and medicinal products are sold by retail.
    b   A responsible pharmacist must be in charge of the business so far as it concerns the retail sale or supply of medicinal products (whether they are on the General Sale List or not).
    c   A notice should be conspicuously displayed at those premises stating the name of the responsible pharmacist, his/her registration number and the fact that s/he is, for the time being, in charge of the business.
    d   The responsible pharmacist must be the superintendent or a manager subject to the directions of the superintendent and who is a pharmacist.
    e   In relation to a pharmacy that has only been registered for less than three years, the responsible pharmacist may not be an EEA certified pharmacist.
    f   The superintendent must be a pharmacist, and a statement signed by him/her and on behalf of the body corporate specifying his/her name and stating whether s/he is a member of the board or not must be sent to the registrar.

3   *Business carried on by a representative in case of death or disability*
    a   The name and address of the representative pharmacist and the name of the pharmacist represented must be notified to the Registrar in case of death or disability where the business is carried on and medicinal products are sold or supplied by retail.
    b   A responsible pharmacist must be in charge of the business so far as it concerns the retail sale or supply of medicinal products (whether they are on the General Sale List or not).
    c   A notice must be conspicuously displayed at those premises stating the name of the responsible pharmacist, his/her registration number, and the fact that s/he is, for the time being, in charge of the business.

The responsible pharmacist

The Health Act introduced a new section into the Medicines Act 1968 (s.72A) namely the concept of the responsible pharmacist. His duties are listed as:

a   To ensure the safe and effective running of the pharmacy business at the premises in question as far as its concerns the retail sale or supply of medicinal products whether they are on the General Sale List or not.
b   A person may not be a responsible pharmacist in respect of more than one set of pharmacy premises at the same time except under specified circumstances set out in regulations.
c   The responsible pharmacist must establish, maintain and keep under review procedures designed to secure the safe and effective running of the business.
d   The responsible pharmacist must make a record of who is the responsible pharmacist present at any day and time and such other information set out in regulations.
e   It is the responsible pharmacist's duty to ensure that proper records are keep and preserved as set down in regulations.
f   The Health Minster may make further provisions in regulations.
g   The regulations may make provisions relating to the absence from the pharmacy, supervision in the absence of another pharmacist, the form in which records may be kept and the qualifications of the responsible pharmacist.

The owner of a pharmacy business who complies with appropriate conditions described above is a person lawfully conducting a retail pharmacy business. Registration of the premises, which is dealt with below, is essential, as the retail activities controlled under the Medicines Act 1968 and the Poisons Act 1972 must take place at registered pharmacies.

*Proposed changes in the draft Pharmacy Order 2009
(published December 2008)*

Proposals for further change to the regulation of pharmacy appear in the draft Pharmacy Order 2009, which was published as this book went to press. The proposals were open to consultation until 9 March 2009 and were expected to be implemented in the second quarter of 2010. The draft Pharmacy Order includes transitional arrangements to ensure smooth transfer of functions from the Royal Pharmaceutical Society of Great Britain (RPSGB) to the General Pharmaceutical Council (GPhC). Many of the major changes from regulation under the Pharmacy Act 1954 to regulation under the Pharmacists and Pharmacy Technicians Act 2007 remain in place and these are detailed in the text below, but relevant changes proposed in the draft Pharmacy Order 2009 include bringing the maintenance of the register of premises under the GPhC (transferred from the Medicines Act 1968 Chapters 22 and 24).

Registration of pharmacy premises

The registrar is the Registrar of the RPSGB or, where appropriate, the Pharmaceutical Society of Northern Ireland (s.69). It is the registrar's duty to keep the register of pharmacy premises and, subject to the provisions described later, to enter in the register, on payment of the prescribed fee, any premises in respect of which application is made [s.75(1)]. A document purporting to be a certificate signed by the registrar and stating that, on a specified date, specified premises were, or were not, entered in the register shall be admissible in any proceedings as evidence (and, in Scotland, shall be sufficient evidence) that those premises were, or were not, entered in the register on that date [s.76(7)].

Registered pharmacy means premises entered for the time being in the register [s.74(1)]. Where a business which concerns the retail sale or supply of medicinal products is carried on in one or more separate or distinct parts of a building, each part is taken to be separate premises [s.69(2)]. A departmental store, for example, might have a department which is a registered pharmacy and a separate department (which is not a pharmacy) where General Sale List medicines are sold.

Registration of pharmacy premises must be effected in a prescribed manner [s.75(2) and SI 1973 No. 1822 as amended]. An application must be in writing and be given or sent to the registrar with the prescribed fee. It must be made and signed by or on behalf of the person carrying on, or who intends to carry on, a retail pharmacy business at the premises to which the application relates. A separate application must be made in respect of each premises and each application must contain, or be accompanied by, the following particulars:

1   The name of the person carrying on, or intending to carry on, a retail pharmacy business and his/her private residential address. In the case of a partnership, the names and such addresses of all the partners must be given. In the case of a body corporate, the registered name and address of the registered office of the body must be given. Where a business is being carried on by a representative of a pharmacist and the business is under the personal control of a pharmacist, the name of the pharmacist in personal control and the number of his/her certificate of registration must be given.

2   The business name where a person or a partnership or body corporate is carrying on or intends to carry on such a business under a business name which is different from the name of the person or of the partners or of the corporate body.

3   The name of the pharmacist or, if more than one, the names of all the pharmacists under whose personal control the business is, or is to be, carried on at all the premises to which the application relates, and in the case of a body corporate the name of the superintendent under whose management the business is, or is to be, carried on, and the number of the certificate of each such pharmacist and, as the case may be, superintendent.

4   The full postal address of the premises to which the application relates.

5   Where the application for registration relates to premises in respect of which there has been a change of ownership of the business, the name and address of the immediate former owner of that business and the date of such change of ownership.

6   The date or intended date of the commencement of the business.

7   A brief description of the premises including the internal layout of the premises as regards the areas where medicinal products are or are intended to be sold or supplied, prepared, dispensed or stored together with:

    a   a statement showing whether or not there are arrangements so as to enable supervision to be exercised by a pharmacist of any dispensing and sale of medicinal products at one and the same time; and

    b   a sketch plan, drawn to scale, showing the areas and the layouts to which this paragraph relates.

The registrar must notify the appropriate Ministers (in England and Wales, the Minister of Health; in Northern Ireland, the Minister of Health and Social Services; in Scotland, the Secretary of State) whenever an application is made. S/he may not enter the premises in the register until two months from that date, unless the Minister otherwise consents [s.75(3)]. Premises are not to be entered in the register unless the registrar is reasonably satisfied that the applicant is a person lawfully conducting a retail pharmacy business or will be so at the time of commencement of business [s.75(7)].

If it appears to the Minister that in a material respect the premises do not comply with the requirements of section 66 regulations (see p. 77), s/he must within the two-month period serve on the applicant a notice stating his/her reasons for proposing to certify that the premises are unsuitable for registration. A copy of the notice must be served on the registrar, who may not then enter the premises in the register unless the Minister, after hearing the applicant, directs otherwise [s.75(4)]. An applicant may, within 28 days of receiving a notice from the Minister, submit written representations or seek to be heard by a person appointed by the Minister. Following this procedure the Minister must either:

1 send to the registrar a certificate that the premises are unsuitable for registration and notify the applicant that s/he has done so, stating his/her reasons if so requested; or
2 notify the applicant and the registrar that s/he has determined not to issue a certificate and the registrar must forthwith enter the premises in the register [s.75(5) and (6)].

Change of ownership

Where a change occurs in the ownership of a registered pharmacy, the registration becomes void at the end of the period of 28 days from the date on which the change occurs. If it occurs on the death of the person carrying on the business, that is on the death of a pharmacist owner or, in the case of a partnership, one of the partners, the period is three months from the date of the death [s.76(3)].

When the registration of pharmacy premises becomes void following a change of ownership, an application for restoration to the register may be made by the new owner. The registrar must restore the premises to the register if s/he is reasonably satisfied that the new owner is a person lawfully conducting a retail pharmacy business or will be so at the time s/he commences business at the premises. A fee equal to a retention fee must be paid by the new owner, but only if the retention fee for the year has not already been paid [s.76(5)]. No description of the premises or sketch plan need be submitted.

Premises retention fees

A retention fee is payable annually in respect of any premises entered in the register for each year subsequent to the year in which they were registered [s.76(1)]. In this context, year means a period of 12 months beginning on such date as the Council (i.e. the Council of the RPSGB) may from time to time determine [s.74(3)]. The Council has decided that the registration year shall commence on the first day of January.

In January each year, every person who carries on a retail pharmacy business must send to the registrar a list of all premises at which his/her business, so far as it consists of the retail sale of medicinal products, is carried on. S/he must also state the name of the pharmacist in charge of each pharmacy. This means, in effect, that the owner of a pharmacy or pharmacies must inform the registrar each January of all the addresses of businesses where s/he sells medicinal products of any kind, and pay retention fees in respect of those which are registered pharmacies (s.77).

The Council may direct the registrar to remove any premises from the register if the person carrying on the retail pharmacy business fails to pay a retention fee within two months from the date on which a demand for it has been made to him/her in the prescribed manner. If, before the end of the year, or whatever period is permitted by the Council in any particular case, the retention fee is paid, together with any prescribed sum by way of penalty, the registrar must restore the premises to the register. If the Council so directs, the restoration shall be deemed to have had effect as from the date on which the premises were removed from the register [s.76(2)]. (For Northern Ireland, any reference to the Council in this section should be construed as a reference to the Minister of Health and Social Services for Northern Ireland.)

The Health Ministers are responsible for making any regulations relating to the registration of pharmacies [s.76(6)]. Any fees received by the registrar may be used for the purposes of the RPSGB [s.76(8)].

Titles, descriptions and emblems

No person may, in connection with any business, use any title, description or emblem likely to suggest that s/he possesses any qualification with respect to the sale, manufacture or assembly of medicinal products which s/he does not in fact possess; or that any person employed in the business possesses any such qualification which that person does not in fact possess [s.78(6)].

Furthermore, the use of certain titles and descriptions is specifically restricted as follows:

1   The description pharmacy may only be used in respect of a registered pharmacy or the pharmaceutical department of a hospital or a health centre. It may not be used in connection with any business, other than a pharmacy, which consists of or includes the retail sale of any goods, or the supply of any goods in circumstances corresponding to retail sale [s.78(4)]. Its use in connection with a business carried on at any premises shall be taken as likely to suggest that the person carrying on the business (where that person is not a body corporate) is a pharmacist,

and that any other person under whose personal control the business (so far as concerns the retail sale of medicinal products or the supply of such products in circumstances corresponding to retail sale) is carried on at those premises, is also a pharmacist.

2   The titles *Pharmaceutical Chemist, Pharmaceutist, Pharmacist, Member of the Pharmaceutical Society* or *Fellow of the Pharmaceutical Society* may only be taken or used by pharmacists [s.78(5)]. These titles may not be used at any premises connected with a business which includes the retail sale or supply of any goods unless those premises are a registered pharmacy or a hospital or health centre [s.78(5)].

3   The titles *Chemist and Druggist, Druggist, Dispensing Chemist* or *Dispensing Druggist* may only be taken or used by a person lawfully conducting a retail pharmacy business [s.78(2)]. The taking or using of the title *Chemist* is also restricted to a person lawfully conducting a retail pharmacy business, but only in connection with the sale of any goods by retail or the supply of any goods in circumstances corresponding to retail sale [s.78(2)].

Where the person lawfully conducting the retail pharmacy business is a body corporate, these titles may only be used if the pharmacist who is superintendent is also a member of the board of the body corporate [s.78(3)].

None of these titles may be used at any premises connected with a business which includes the retail sale or supply of any goods unless those premises are a registered pharmacy [s.78(3)].

The Health Ministers may by order, and after consultation with the Council of the RPSGB, impose further restrictions or requirements with respect to the use of titles, descriptions and emblems. The Ministers may also provide that existing restrictions shall cease to have effect or be subject to specified exceptions. Regulations for these purposes must be approved by resolution of each House of Parliament (s.79).

Accommodation, storage, records, equipment, etc.

The appropriate Ministers have wide powers under the Act (s.66) to make regulations with respect to any of the following matters, although at the time this book closed for press such regulations had been made only in relation to 9 and 10 below (see p. 100):

1   the manner in which, or persons under whose supervision, medicinal products may be prepared or may be dispensed;

2   the amount of space to be provided in any premises for preparing or dispensing medicinal products, the separation of any such space from the remainder of the premises, and the facilities to be provided in any premises for such persons;

3   the amount of space to be provided in any premises for the sale or supply of medicinal products;
4   the accommodation (including the amount of space) to be provided in any premises for members of the public to whom medicinal products are sold or supplied or for whom medicinal products are being prepared or assembled;
5   the amount of space to be provided in any premises for the storage of medicinal products;
6   the safekeeping of medicinal products;
7   the disposal of medicinal products which have become unusable or otherwise unwanted;
8   precautions to be observed before medicinal products are sold or supplied;
9   the keeping of records relating to the sale or supply of medicinal products;
10   the supply of medicinal products distributed as samples;
11   sanitation, cleanliness, temperature, humidity or other factors relating to the risks of deterioration or contamination in connection with the manufacture, storage, transportation, sale or supply of medicinal products;
12   the construction, location and the use of automatic machines for the sale of medicinal products.

The Ministers can also prescribe requirements in respect of:

a   the construction, layout, drainage, equipment, maintenance, ventilation, lighting and water supply of premises at or from which medicinal products are manufactured, stored, transported, sold or supplied;
b   the disposal of refuse at or from any such premises; and
c   any apparatus, equipment, furnishings or utensils used at any such premises.

Disqualification of a retail pharmacy owner

It is an offence to contravene any of the regulations made under section 66 (s.67). Any person who is convicted of such an offence may, by order of the court, be disqualified from using the premises concerned for the purposes of a retail pharmacy business for a period not exceeding two years (s.68).

Summary

- Retail businesses which sell medicines not on a General Sale List must be registered as pharmacies. They may be owned by a pharmacist, a partnership, a body corporate or a representative of a deceased pharmacist. The new concept of the responsible pharmacist was introduced as a new section in the Medicines Act 1968 (s.72A)

- Detailed requirements relating to the premises, together with a fee, must be forwarded to the RPSGB in order for registration to take place.
- Certain titles may only be used by pharmacists, e.g. pharmacist, pharmaceutical chemist, Member of the Pharmaceutical Society.
- A body corporate may use the title dispensing chemist, chemist and druggist or chemist only if the superintendent is a member of the board, otherwise the body corporate may only use the title pharmacy in connection with its pharmacy premises.
- Ministers, by way of regulations, may impose a large range of conditions relating to premises from which medicines are sold.

6

Medicines Act 1968
Pharmacy Medicines

Part III of the Act is concerned with the regulation of dealings with medicinal products. The basic principle, set out in section 52, is that medicinal products may be sold or supplied by retail only from registered pharmacies, unless they are products included in a General Sale List (see Chapter 7) or subject to some other exemption under the Act.

Section 52 provides that medicinal products, which are not included in a General Sale List, shall not be sold, offered or exposed for sale by retail, or supplied in circumstances corresponding to retail sale by any person in the course of a business carried on by him/her unless:

1   that person is, in respect of that business, a person lawfully conducting a retail pharmacy business;
2   the product is sold, offered or exposed for sale, or supplied on premises which are a registered pharmacy; and
3   that person, or, if the transaction is carried out on his/her behalf by another person, then that other person is, or acts under the supervision of, a pharmacist.

N.B. A retail pharmacy business must be under the control of a responsible pharmacist so far as it concerns the sale of medicinal products including products on a General Sale List (ss.27–29 Health Act 2006, see p. 69). The meaning of *supervision* has been considered by the High Court and the Statutory Committee (see Chapters 22 and 28).

The question of interpretation of supervision was under consideration by the Department of Health when this book went to print in December 2008).

Selling by retail or retail sale includes all those sales which do not fall within the definition of selling by way of wholesale dealing [s.131(3)]. Supplying in circumstances corresponding to retail sale has a comparable meaning [s.131(4)]. Retail sale or supply, therefore, comprises all those sales or supplies of medicinal products made in the course of a business to a person who buys (or receives) them for the purpose other than that of (a) selling or supplying them or (b) administering them or causing them to be administered to one or more human beings in the course of a business carried on by him/her.

The requirements of section 52 apply to sales and supplies made in 'the course of a business'. The provision of services under the NHS is treated as the carrying on of a business [s.131(5)]. However, the dispensing of a medicinal product on a NHS prescription is not a sale but a 'supply in circumstances corresponding to retail sale' (*Appleby* v. *Sleep* [1968] 2 All ER 265) (see p. 448).

Pharmacy medicine defined

Certain medicinal products may only be sold or supplied from pharmacies in accordance with a prescription given by an appropriate practitioner. These products, called *Prescription Only Medicines* (POMs) are specified in a 'Prescription Only' order (SI 1997 No. 1830, as amended; see p. 93). Any medicinal product which is not a POM or a medicinal product on a General Sale List is a *Pharmacy Medicine* (P) (SI 1980 No. 1924, as amended). There is no definitive list of Pharmacy Medicines, as the total in the class cannot be determined. It comprises all those medicines which are not in a 'Prescription Only' or 'General Sale List', and includes all medicines made in a pharmacy for retail sale under the exemptions from licensing granted to retail pharmacists (see p. 43).

Some General Sale List medicines, when presented in packs exceeding specified quantities, may only be sold or supplied from pharmacies. They are designated Pharmacy Medicines (SI 1980 No. 1923, as amended) although there is no legal requirement for supervision by a pharmacist (see Retail pack sizes of certain products, p. 87).

Some POMs when presented in packs **not** exceeding specified quantities may only be sold or supplied from pharmacies (see Retail pack sizes of certain products, p. 94).

Exemptions in cases involving another's default

The restrictions imposed by section 52 of the Act shall not apply to the sale, offer or exposure for sale or supply of a medicinal product by a person who, having exercised all due diligence, believes on reasonable grounds that the product is a medicinal product on a General Sale List or subject to a temporary exemption but which due to the act or default of another person is not such a medicinal product, if and so long as the conditions applying to the sale of medicinal products on a General Sale List are fulfilled (SI 1980 No. 1924) (see Chapter 7).

Temporary exemptions

Where the product licence, or a variation of a product licence, provides for the sale or supply of a medicinal product without the supervision of a pharmacist, it may be sold under General Sale List conditions despite the fact that it is not included in the current General Sale List. This temporary exemption is for two years from the date of the grant of the licence, or for one year from the date of a variation in a licence (SI 1980 No. 1924). It appears that the General Sale List should be updated each year.

The conditions under which General Sale List medicines may be sold are described in Chapter 7.

Collection and delivery arrangements – exemption

A *collection and delivery arrangement* means any arrangement whereby a person is enabled to take or send a prescription given by a doctor or dentist to premises other than a registered pharmacy and to collect or have collected on his/her behalf from such premises a medicinal product prepared or dispensed in accordance with such prescription at a registered pharmacy by or under the supervision of a pharmacist if such premises at which the medicinal product is supplied are capable of being closed so as to exclude the public (SI 1978 No. 1421).

When an arrangement of this kind is used by a person lawfully conducting a retail pharmacy business, the supply of dispensed medicines for human use at the non-pharmacy premises without the supervision of a pharmacist is rendered lawful by an exemption provided in SI 1978 No. 1421.

Summary

- Pharmacy Medicines comprise all medicinal products which are not on the General Sale List, are not on the Prescription Only List or are exempt in some form or other from the latter.
- The legislation requires that retail sales or supplies of Pharmacy Medicines have to be made by a person conducting a retail pharmacy business, at a registered pharmacy, and by, or under the supervision of, a pharmacist.
- The conditions under which Pharmacy Medicines must be sold do not apply where there is a collection and delivery arrangement in place.

Further reading

Royal Pharmaceutical Society of Great Britain (published annually) *Medicines, Ethics and Practice*. London: Royal Pharmaceutical Society of Great Britain.

7

Medicines Act 1968
General Sale Medicines

General Sale Medicines are those which in the opinion of the appropriate Minister can with reasonable safety be sold or supplied otherwise than by or under the supervision of a pharmacist (s.51). Medicines for human use are listed in SI 1984 No. 769, as amended. Veterinary drugs are listed in SI 1984 No. 768 as amended.

The question of interpretation of supervision was under consideration by the Department of Health when this book went to print in December 2008.

Conditions applying to retail sale or supply of General Sale List medicinal products for human use

General Sale List medicinal products for human use may only be sold by retail, offered or exposed for sale by retail, or supplied in circumstances corresponding to retail sale either at registered pharmacies or in circumstances where the following conditions are fulfilled:

1 the place at which the medicinal product is sold, offered, exposed or supplied must be premises at which the person carrying on the business in question is the occupier and which s/he is able to close so as to exclude the public;
2 the medicinal product must have been made up for sale in a container elsewhere than at the place at which it is sold, offered, exposed for sale or supplied, and the container must not have been opened since the product was made up for sale in it;
3 the business, so far as concerns the sale or supply of medicinal products, must be carried on in accordance with such conditions as may be prescribed (s.53).

The restriction in 1 as to premises does not apply to foods and cosmetics that are medicinal products (SI 1980 No. 1924).

General Sale List Medicines for human use

The classes of medicinal product on general sale for administration to human beings are set out SI 1984 No. 769, as amended by SI 2002 No. 933. Appended to each of Schedules 1 and 2 are two lists of products, namely Table A (those for internal and external use) and Table B (those for external use only). Where a product contains a substance listed in one of the tables it must satisfy any stated specification as to maximum strength (ms), use, pharmaceutical form or route of administration. Similarly, products for internal use (Table A) must satisfy any specification as to maximum dose (md) or maximum daily dose (mdd). Containers and packages must be labelled with the required information given in the specification. The classes include:

1   medicinal products in respect of which a marketing authorisation has been granted, which in the marketing authorisation are classified as General Sale List medicines;

2   medicinal products in respect of which no marketing authorisation has been granted, other than products subject of a licence of right, which fall within a class specified in Schedule 1 of the regulations;

3   medicinal products which are products the subject of a licence of right and which fall within a class specified in Schedule 2 of the regulations;

4   licence of right products containing one or more of the following:
    a   haemoglobin or the following parts of animals, namely bone, brain, genitals, horn, prostate and spleen but not extracts from such parts;
    b   glycerine extracts of bone marrow;
    c   bovine blood derivatives; and
    d   substances of vegetable origin and extracts of such substances used in the United Kingdom as food;

5   aqueous and alcoholic extracts, spirits, syrups and liquid suspensions derived from the substances in 1 above;

6   excipients (that is substances which do not contribute directly to the pharmacological action of the medicinal product otherwise than by regulation of the release of the active ingredient);

7   medicinal products for human use which are for sale or supply either for oral administration as food or external use as a cosmetic, other than products which are eye drops, or eye ointments or which contain either:
    a   vitamin A, vitamin A acetate, or vitamin A palmitate with a mdd equivalent to more than 7500 iu vitamin A or 2250 micrograms retinol; or
    b   vitamin D with a mdd of more than 400 iu of antirachitic activity.

Automatic machines

Medicinal products which are on a General Sale List (other than veterinary drugs) may be sold from automatic machines. Such machines must be located in premises which the occupier is able to close so as to exclude the public (s.66 and SI 1980 No. 1923).

Retail pack sizes of certain products

Limits are imposed on the pack sizes of certain General Sale List products when they are sold or supplied by retail from businesses other than pharmacies. If sold outside the limits laid down, the medicinal products concerned are classed as *Pharmacy Medicine* or *Prescription Only Medicines*. The limits for general sale are as follows.

Aloxiprin

Medicines for human use containing aloxiprin may only be presented for sale in separate and individual containers or packages containing not more than (a) 30 tablets (effervescent tablets), (b) 16 capsules or tablets (non-effervescent), or (c) 10 sachets (powders or granules) (s.53) (SI 1980 No. 1923, as amended).

Aspirin and paracetamol

Medicines for human use containing aspirin or paracetamol may only be presented for sale in separate and individual containers or packages containing not more than (a) 16 capsules or tablets (non-effervescent) (SI 1999 No. 644), (b) 10 sachets (powder or granules), (c) 30 tablets containing not more than 325 mg (effervescent tablets), (d) 20 tablets where the amount of aspirin exceeds 325 mg but does not exceed 500 mg (effervescent tablets) (SI 1994 No. 2411).

In the case of tablets that are not effervescent, are enteric coated and contain aspirin only, the amount of aspirin in each tablet must not exceed 75 mg and the package must contain not more than 28 tablets (SI 2001 No. 3849).

Effervescent, in relation to a tablet, means containing not less than 75 per cent by weight of the tablet as ingredients included wholly or mainly for the purpose of releasing carbon dioxide when the tablet is dissolved or dispersed in water.

In the case of liquid preparations of paracetamol (SI 1997 No. 2045):

a   which are intended for persons over 12 years, not more than 160 mL;
b   which are intended for persons less than 12 years, individual doses of not more than 5 mL and no greater quantity than 20 doses.

Bisacodyl

Tablets for human use containing bisacodyl may only be presented for sale in a separate and individual container or package containing not more than 40 tablets (SI 2005 No. 1520).

Ibuprofen

Medicines for human use containing ibuprofen may only be presented in the following terms (SI 2001 No. 1124):

1 in the case of tablets, capsules, powder or granules for internal use for the treatment of rheumatic or muscular pain, backache, neuralgia, migraine, dental pain, dysmenorrhoea, feverishness, or symptoms of colds and influenza: ms 200 mg, md 400 mg and mdd 1200 mg in individual containers or packages containing not more than 16 tablets or capsules for use for adults and children over 12 years;
2 in liquid preparations for internal use: ms 2 per cent for the treatment of rheumatic and muscle pain, headache, dental pain, feverishness, or symptoms of colds and influenza for use in children under 12 years; ms 200 mg and mdd 800 mg;
3 in the case of liquid preparations: the individual unit doses must not exceed 5 mL each and a maximum of 20 unit doses;
4 if for external use: ms 5 per cent, md 125 mg, mdd 500 mg and individual container package containing not more than 2.5 g for rheumatic pain, muscular aches and pains, swellings such as sprains, sprains and sports injuries; in the case of a topical product, not more than 2.5 g ibuprofen (SI 2001 No. 4111).

Clotrimazole

A medicinal product for topical use containing clotrimazole may only be presented for sale in separate and individual containers or packages containing not more than 500 mg clotrimazole (SI 1995 No. 3215).

Sodium picosulphate

Medicines for human use containing sodium picosulphate may only be presented for sale in separate and individual containers or packages containing not more than 60 mL (SI 1997 No. 2045).

Loperamide hydrochloride

Medicines for human use containing loperamide hydrochloride may only be presented for sale in separate and individual containers or packages containing not more than six tablets or capsules (SI 1997 No. 2045).

Mepyramine maleate

Medicines for human use containing mepyramine maleate may only be presented for sale in separate and individual containers or packages containing not more than 20 g with a maximum strength of 2 per cent for the symptomatic relief of insect stings and bites and nettle stings, in adults and in children aged 2 and over (SI 2000 No. 1070).

Ranitidine hydrochloride

Medicines for human use containing ranitidine hydrochloride may only be presented for sale in separate and individual containers or packages containing not more than 12 tablets ms 75 mg (SI 1999 No. 2510).

Cetirizine hydrochloride

Cetirizine hydrochloride may only be presented for sale in ms 10 mg tablet form for the symptomatic relief of perennial rhinitis, seasonal allergic rhinitis and idiopathic chronic urticaria in adults and children aged 12 and over, in a individual container or package containing not more than seven tablets (SI 2001 No. 4111).

Loratadine

Loratadine may only be presented for sale in ms 10 mg tablet form for the symptomatic relief of perennial rhinitis, seasonal allergic rhinitis and idiopathic chronic urticaria in adults and children aged 12 and over, in a individual container or package containing not more than seven tablets (SI 2001 No. 4111).

Products not to be on general sale

The General Sale List Orders relating to medicinal products for human use (SI 1984 No. 769) and for veterinary drugs (SI 1984 No. 768) specify certain classes of products which are not to be on general sale. They are:

1   Medicinal products for human use or veterinary drugs promoted, recommended, or marketed:
    a   for use as eye drops or eye ointments;
    b   for administration by parenteral injection; or
    c   for use as anthelmintics, except veterinary drugs consisting or containing dichlorophen, diethylcarbamazine citrate, piperazine adipate, piperazine calcium adipate, piperazine citrate, piperazine dihydrochloride, piperazine hydrate or piperazine phosphate.

2 Medicines for human use promoted, recommended or marketed:
   a for use as enemas (SI 1985 No. 1540);
   b for use wholly or mainly for irrigation of wounds or of the bladder, vagina, or rectum (SI 1985 No. 1540); or
   c for administration wholly or mainly to children, being a preparation of aloxiprin or aspirin (SI 1987 No. 910).

Summary

- Medicines which in the opinion of the Minister can with reasonable safety be sold other than by or under the supervision of a pharmacist are listed as General Sale List medicines for both human and animal use. They may only be sold from closable premises and in their original packs.
- Certain medicines may be sold other than by or under the supervision of a pharmacist subject to certain pack sizes. These include aspirin, aloxiprin, bisacodyl, ibuprofen, topical clotrimazole and ranitidine hydrochloride.
- Certain medicines cannot be on general sale. These include eye drops and ointments, most anthelmintics, parenterals, those medicines promoted as enemas or for use as irrigations, and aspirin for children.

Further reading

Royal Pharmaceutical Society of Great Britain (published annually) *Medicines, Ethics and Practice*. London: Royal Pharmaceutical Society of Great Britain.

8

Medicines Act 1968
Prescription Only Medicines

A *Prescription Only Medicine* (POM) means a medicinal product which may only be sold or supplied by retail in accordance with a prescription given by an *appropriate practitioner* (s.58). In the Prescription Only Medicines Order for Human Use (SI 1997 No. 1830), doctors, dentists, veterinary surgeons and veterinary practitioners are designated as appropriate practitioners.

The Medicinal Products: Prescription by Nurses Etc. Act 1992 provides that registered nurses, midwives and health visitors who are of such a description and who comply with certain conditions are considered to be appropriate practitioners. Also classed as appropriate practitioners are community practitioner nurse prescribers, nurse independent prescribers, pharmacist independent prescribers (SI 2006 No. 915), optometrist independent prescribers (SI 2008 No. 1161) and an EEA health practitioner (SI 2008 No. 1692). The medicines which they may prescribe are listed in the regulations (SI 1997 No. 1830, SI 2002 No. 549 and SI No. 915).

An *EEA practitioner* means a doctor or dentist who is lawfully engaged in medical/dental practice in a relevant European state.

A *community practitioner nurse prescriber* means:

a a person who is registered nurse or registered midwife; and
b against whose name in the professional register there is an annotation that s/he is qualified to order drugs, medicines and appliances from the *Nurse Prescribers' Formulary for Community Practitioners* in the current edition of the *British National Formulary* (SI 2006 No. 915).

A *nurse independent prescriber* means:

a a person who is registered nurse or registered midwife; and
b against whose name is recorded in the professional register an annotation signifying that s/he is qualified to order drugs, medicines and appliances as a nurse independent prescriber or a nurse independent/ supplementary prescriber (SI 2008 No. 464).

A nurse independent prescriber may give a prescription for Prescription Only Medicines that are not Controlled Drugs, or, if that medicinal product is for parenteral administration, may administer the product or give directions for the administration of the product, or, if a Controlled Drug, may give a prescription for those listed in Schedule 3A (SI 2006 No. 915). If the Schedule specifies as to the use, route of administration or pharmaceutical form then it must be administered in accordance with those specific conditions. The latter conditions need not be complied with if the nurse independent prescriber is also a supplementary prescriber and is acting in accordance with the terms of a clinical management plan (SI 2003 No. 696).

A *pharmacist independent prescriber* means a pharmacist against whose name is recorded in the relevant register that s/he is qualified to order drugs (but not Controlled Drugs), medicines and appliances as a pharmacist independent prescriber.

An *optometrist independent prescriber* means an optometrist against whose name is recorded in the relevant register that s/he is qualified to order drugs (but not Controlled Drugs or parenteral drugs), medicines and appliances as a optometrist independent prescriber.

In 2003, a supplementary prescriber was added to the list of appropriate practitioners in the Health and Social Care Act 2001. A supplementary prescriber may give a prescription for a medicinal product listed in Article 3B to the regulations or if that medicinal product is for parenteral administration may administer the product or give directions for the administration of the product in accordance with the terms of a clinical management plan (SI 2003 No. 696). Particulars to be contained in a clinical management plan are set out in the regulations.

A *supplementary prescriber* means:

a   a first level nurse; or
b   a pharmacist; or
c   registered midwife; or
d   in relation to a person whose name is registered in the part of the register maintained by the Health Professions Council in pursuant of the Health Professions Order 2001 relating to (SI 2005 No. 765):
   i   chiropodists and podiatrists;
   ii   physiotherapists; or
   iii radiographers; diagnostic or therapeutic; or
e   an optometrist registered under the Opticians Act 1989 (SI 2005 No. 1507),

against whose name is recorded in the relevant statutory register an annotation signifying that s/he is qualified to order drugs, medicines and appliances as a supplementary prescriber.

The specified conditions for community practitioner nurse prescribers and supplementary prescribers do not apply in relation to the prescribing and administration of medicines where it is in accordance with the directions of another person who is an appropriate practitioner.

Prescription Only Medicines for human use

The criteria to be applied in specifying which medicinal products are to be Prescription Only are laid down in regulations (SI 2002 No. 549) implementing Council Directive 2001/83/EEC (the Human Medicines Directive).

The Prescription Only Medicines which are not for animal use are listed in SI 1997 No. 1830, as amended by SI 2002 No. 549 and SI 2003 No. 696. Unless exempt they are:

1 Medicinal products in respect of which a marketing authorisation has been granted, which in the marketing authorisation are classified as being Prescription Only Medicines.
2 Medicinal products in respect of which no marketing authorisation has been granted, consisting of or containing a substance in Schedule 1 to the regulations.
3 Medicinal products that are Controlled Drugs unless a marketing authorisation has been granted in respect of that medicinal product in which the product is classified as being a Pharmacy Only or on a General Sale List (see Exempted Controlled Drugs, p. 95).
4 Medicinal products for human use classified as subject to medical prescription granted by marketing authorisations granted under Council Regulation 2309/93.
5 Medicinal products that are for parenteral administration whether or not they include any substance included in the Prescription Only List. *Parenteral administration* means administration by breach of the skin or mucous membrane.
6 Cyanogenetic substances other than preparations for external use.
7 Medicinal products that on administration emit radiation, or contain or generate any substance which emits radiation, in order that radiation may be used.
8 Medicinal products in respect of which a marketing authorisation has been granted consisting of or containing aloxiprin, aspirin or paracetamol in the form of non-effervescent tablets or capsules which in the marketing authorisation are as being Pharmacy Only or General Sale List medicines (SI 2003 No. 696).
9 Ephedrine, its salts and pseudoephedrine (see Exemption on p. 95).

Exemptions from Prescription Only

1 Medicinal products exempt due to conditions

A medicinal product is exempt if it is listed in Column 1 of Schedule 1 and there is:

a   an entry in Columns 2, 3, 4 or 5 of that Schedule which contains a condition and that condition is satisfied; or

b   more than one such condition which applies where that substance is used in that product and each of those conditions are satisfied.

The conditions are that the medicinal product is:

i   a particular strength;

ii   a particular pharmaceutical form;

iii the route of administration specified in the schedule; and

iv   in or from containers or packages labelled to show doses not exceeding the maximum dose (md), or the maximum daily doses (mdd), or both as specified in the Schedule.

All these exempted medicinal products will be *Pharmacy Medicines*. *Maximum strength* (ms) means either:

a   the maximum quantity of a substance by weight or volume contained in a dosage unit of a medicinal product; or

b   the maximum percentage of a Prescription Only Medicine substance contained in a medicinal product calculated in terms of weight in weight (w/w), weight in volume (w/v), volume in weight (v/w) or volume in volume (v/v) and if the maximum percentage calculated in those ways differ, the higher or highest percentage.

Maximum dose (md) means the maximum quantity of a substance contained in the amount of a medicinal product for internal use which it is recommended should be taken or administered at any one time.

Maximum daily dose (mdd) means the maximum quantity of a substance contained in the amount of a medicinal product which it is recommended should be taken or administered in any period of 24 hours.

2 Retail pack sizes of certain products

Some Prescription Only Medicines when presented in packs **not** exceeding specified quantities, may only be sold or supplied from pharmacies. These are as follows.

a   *Aspirin* where if the pack size for non-effervescent tablets or capsules does not exceed 32 and the ms 500 mg then the product is a Pharmacy Medicine. The total quantity sold to a person at any one time must not exceed 100.

b   *Aspirin* where if the pack size for non-effervescent tablets or capsules does not exceed 100 and the ms 75 mg then the product is a Pharmacy Medicine.
c   *Paracetamol* where if the pack size for non-effervescent tablets or capsules does not exceed 32 and the ms 120 mg (for children under 12) or ms 500 mg (for adults or children over 12), then the product is a Pharmacy Medicine. The total quantity sold to a person at any one time must not exceed 100 (SI 1997 No. 2044).

Aspirin and paracetamol in preparations other than non-effervescent tablets and capsules are also Pharmacy Medicines.

3 New medicinal products

Where a marketing authorisation has been issued in respect of a new medicinal product restricting it to Prescription Only use, that restriction will normally apply for five years from the date of the granting of the licence. Normally, it is intended that the Prescription Only Order will be updated to include the product before the expiry of the five-year period.

4 High dilution products

There is an exemption for high dilution products diluted to at least one part per million (×6). These now include certain high diluted products which are not for parenteral administration and include aconite, arsenic trioxide, *belladonna herb*, *ignatia bean* and *nux vomica* seed (SI 2003 No. 696 as amended).

5 Ephedrine, its salts and pseudoephedrine

Ephedrine, its salts and pseudoephedrine are exempt if the following conditions are applied (wording is from the statute): the product must not be sold or supplied at the same time as another medicinal product that consists of or contains:

i   in the case of pseudoephedrine salts, ephedrine base or salts
ii   in the case of ephedrine base or salts, pseudoephedrine salts
and must not in total contain more than:
iii   in the case of pseudoephedrine salts, 720 mg pseudoephedrine salts
iv   in the case of ephedrine, 180 mg ephedrine base or salts.

6 Exempted Controlled Drugs

Maximum strengths for exempted Controlled Drugs are specified in Part 2 of Schedule 1 to the Prescription Only order for certain Controlled Drugs. A medicinal product containing only one of those substances not in excess of the maximum strength is a *Pharmacy Medicine*, provided it is not a veterinary medicinal product and does not contain any other substances at a strength which would render the product a Prescription Only Medicine, and it is sold, supplied or administered (see also p. 93):

Table 8.1 Exempt Controlled Drugs

Substance	Maximum strength	Maximum dose
Codeine, its salts	Equivalent of 1.5% codeine monohydrate base	Equivalent of 20 mg codeine monohydrate base
Dihydrocodeine, its salt	Equivalent of 1.5% dihydrocodeine base	Equivalent of 10 mg dihydrocodeine base
Ethylmorphine, its salts	Equivalent of 0.2% ethylmorphine base	Equivalent of 7.5 mg ethylmorphine base
Morphine, its salts		
(1) Liquid	Equivalent of 0.02% anhydrous morphine base	Equivalent of 3 mg anhydrous morphine base
(2) Solid	Equivalent of 0.04% and 300 micrograms anhydrous morphine base	Equivalent of 3 mg anhydrous morphine base
Pholcodine, its salts	Equivalent of 1.5% pholcodine monohydrate base	Equivalent of 20 mg pholcodine monohydrate base

a   in the pharmaceutical form specified in the order; and
b   in or from containers or packages labelled to show a dose not exceeding a
     maximum dose as specified in the order.

This exemption applies to the six Controlled Drugs set out in Table 8.1.
Subject to the limitations as to maximum strength, maximum dosage and
pharmaceutical form given in the table, these are Pharmacy Medicines.

Administration of Prescription Only Medicines

The Act provides that no person shall administer a Prescription Only Medicine,
otherwise than to him/herself, unless s/he is a practitioner or is acting in
accordance with the direction of a practitioner [s.58(2)(b)]. However, certain
injectable products may be administered by way of parenteral injection to
human beings for the purpose of saving life in an emergency. They are set
out in Box 8.1.

Radioactive medicinal products

Radioactive substance means any substance that contains one or more radionuclides of which the activity or concentration cannot be disregarded as far as
radiation protection is concerned (SI 1978 No. 1006).

Only a doctor or dentist holding an appropriate certificate issued by the
Health Minister or a person acting under the directions of such a doctor or
dentist may lawfully administer a radioactive substance.

> **Box 8.1** *Injectable products which may be administered by way of parenteral injection to human beings for the purpose of saving life in an emergency*
>
> Adrenaline (epinephrine) injection (1 in 1000)
> Atropine sulphate injection
> Atropine sulphate and obidoxime injection
> Atropine sulphate and pralidoxime chloride injection
> Atropine sulphate, pralidoxime mesilate and avizafone injection
> Antiserum
>
> Chlorphenamine injection
>
> Dicobalt edetate injection
>
> Glucagon injection
> Glucose injection 50%
>
> Hydrocortisone injection
>
> Naloxone hydrochloride
>
> Pralidoxime mesilate injection
> Pralidoxime chloride injection
> Promethazine hydrochloride injection
>
> Snake venom
> Sodium thiosulphate injection
> Sodium nitrite injection
> Sterile pralidoxime

A *radioactive medicinal product* means a medicinal product which is, contains or generates a radioactive substance and which is, contains or generates that substance in order, when administered, to utilise the radiation emitted therefrom.

Certain other conditions are laid down in the regulations (SI 1978 No. 1006, amended by SIs 1995 No. 2147; 2005 No. 2754; 2006 No. 2407; 2006 No. 2806). The current regulations concerning the control of administration of radioactive substances are SIs 2006 No. 2806 and 2006 No. 2807.

Smallpox vaccine

The restrictions imposed by the Medicines Act do not apply to the administration of smallpox vaccine for the purposes of providing protection in the event of a suspected or confirmed case of smallpox where the vaccine is administered to members of, or persons working for, Her Majesty's Forces

(SI 2004 No. 2693). The vaccines must be supplied by, or on behalf of, the Secretary of State, Scottish Ministers, the National Assembly of Wales, the Department of Health, Social Services and Public Safety or an NHS Body.

NHS Body means the Common Services Agency, a strategic health authority, health authority or special health authority, a primary care trust, a local health board, an NHS trust or an NHS foundation trust.

Prescriptions

A Prescription Only Medicine may only be sold or supplied in accordance with a prescription given by appropriate practitioners [s.58(a)]. To meet that requirement, certain conditions must be satisfied (SI 1997 No. 1830). The prescription:

a   shall be signed in ink with his own name by the appropriate practitioner giving it;

b   shall, without prejudice to subparagraph a, be written in ink or otherwise so as to be indelible, unless it is a health prescription which is not for a Controlled Drug specified in Schedule 1, 2 or 3 to the Misuse of Drugs Regulations, in which case it may be written by means of carbon paper or similar material;

c   shall contain the following particulars:
   i   the address of the appropriate practitioner giving it;
   ii the appropriate date (see below);
   iii such particulars as indicate whether the practitioner giving it is a doctor, a dentist, a supplementary prescriber, a community practitioner nurse prescriber, a pharmacist independent prescriber, a nurse independent prescriber or a optometrist independent prescriber, and
   iv where the practitioner giving it is a doctor, dentist, a supplementary prescriber, a community practitioner nurse prescriber, a pharmacist independent prescriber, a nurse independent prescriber or an optometrist independent prescriber, the name, address and the age, if under 12, of the person for whose treatment it is given;

d   shall not be dispensed after the end of the period of six months from the appropriate date, unless it is a repeatable prescription in which case it shall not be dispensed for the first time after the end of that period nor otherwise than in accordance with the directions contained in the repeatable prescription; and

e   in the case of a repeatable prescription that does not specify the number of times it may be dispensed, shall not be dispensed on more than two occasions unless it is a prescription for oral contraceptives in which case it may be dispensed six times before the end of the period of six months from the appropriate date.

The prescription, as an alternative to fulfilling the conditions a–e specified above, may fulfil the following conditions unless the prescription is for a Controlled Drug or is given by a veterinary surgeon or veterinary practitioner:

a   is created in an electronic form;
b   is signed with an advanced electronic signature; and
c   is transferred to the person by whom it is dispensed as an electronic communication (including where it is so transferred through one or more intermediaries).

Advanced electronic signature means an electronic signature which is:

a   uniquely linked to the signatory;
b   capable of identifying the signatory;
c   created using means that the signatory can maintain under his control; and
d   linked to the data to which it relates in such a manner that any subsequent change of the data is detectable.

Electronic communication means a communication transmitted (whether from one person to another, from one device to another or from a person to a device or vice versa):

a   by means of a telecommunication system (within the meaning of the Telecommunications Act 1984); or
b   by other means but in a electronic form.

Repeatable prescription means a prescription which contains a direction that it may be dispensed more than once.

Health prescription means a prescription issued by a doctor, a dentist, a supplementary prescriber, a community practitioner nurse prescriber, a pharmacist prescriber, a nurse independent prescriber under or by virtue of:

1   in England and Wales, the National Health Service Act 1977;
2   in Scotland, the National Health Service (Scotland) Act 1978; and
3   in Northern Ireland, the Health and Personal Social Services (Northern Ireland) Order 1972.

The *appropriate date* is the date on which the prescription was signed by the practitioner, or, in the case of a health prescription only, the date indicated by him/her as being the date before which it shall not be dispensed. Where a health prescription bears both dates, the later of those dates is the appropriate one.

Due diligence clause

Where a prescription given by an appropriate practitioner does not fulfill a required condition, the sale or supply is not rendered unlawful if the person making the sale or supply, having exercised all due diligence, believes on reasonable grounds that that condition is fulfilled in relation to that sale or supply.

This due diligence clause also applies to the supply made by a pharmacist in accordance with a prescription given by another pharmacist, a registered nurse or a registered midwife *who is not a appropriate practitioner* where the pharmacist believes that that person is such a practitioner (SI 2003 No. 696 and SI 2005 No. 765).

Forgeries

Similarly, the sale or supply by a pharmacist is not rendered unlawful if made against a forged prescription provided the pharmacist has exercised all due diligence and believes on reasonable grounds that the prescription is genuine.

Pharmacy records

Every person lawfully conducting a retail pharmacy business is required to keep a record in respect of every sale or supply of a Prescription Only Medicine, unless:

1 it is a sale or supply in pursuance of a health prescription or a prescription for oral contraceptives; or
2 a separate record of the sale or supply is made in accordance with regulation 19 of the Misuse of Drugs Regulations (see p. 233) or regulation 19 of the Misuse of Drugs (Northern Ireland) Regulations 1974; or
3 the sale or supply is to a person employed or engaged in connection with a scheme for testing the quality and checking the amount of drugs and appliances supplied under the National Health Service legislation of England and Wales, or Scotland, or Northern Ireland; or
4 in Scotland, the sale or supply is to a doctor of drugs or appliances which, under the National Health Service, the doctor is entitled or required to supply; or
5 in Northern Ireland, the sale or supply is in response to an order for a doctor of medicinal products which are drugs required by him/her under the National Health Service for immediate administration or in other similar cases (SI 1980 No. 1923).

For records of wholesale transactions in Prescription Only Medicines, see Chapter 10.

An entry must be a written or computerised record kept for the purpose in respect of each sale or supply (SI 1997 No. 1831). The entry must be made on the day the sale or supply takes place or, if that is not reasonably practicable, on the following day.

For an emergency supply made on the undertaking of a doctor, a dentist, a community practitioner nurse prescriber, a pharmacist independent prescriber, a nurse independent prescriber, a supplementary prescriber or an optometrist independent prescriber to furnish a prescription within 72 hours, the recording of (a) the date of the prescription and (b) the date on which the prescription is received may be made on the day that the prescription is received (SI 1980 No. 1923).

Particulars of prescriptions to be recorded

The particulars to be recorded in the case of a sale or supply of a Prescription Only Medicine in pursuance of a prescription are:

1 the date on which the medicine was sold or supplied;
2 the name, quantity and, except where it is apparent from the name, the pharmaceutical form and strength of the medicine;
3 the date on the prescription and the name and address of the appropriate practitioner, community practitioner nurse prescriber, independent nurse, pharmacist or optometrist prescriber giving it;
4 the name and address of the person for whom or for whose animal, as the case may be, the medicine was prescribed.

For second and subsequent supplies made on a repeat prescription it is sufficient to record the date of supply and a reference to the entry in the register relating to the first supply.

Additional particulars must be recorded in the case of emergency supplies to patients (see below).

Preservation of pharmacy records

The Prescription Only record must be preserved by the owner of the retail pharmacy business for a period of two years from the date of the last entry in the record. A prescription must be retained for two years from the date on which the Prescription Only Medicine was sold or supplied, or, for a repeat prescription, the date on which the medicine was supplied for the last time (see also Chapter 17).

Labelling of dispensed medicines

See p. 188.

Exemptions for hospitals, clinics, etc.

The restrictions imposed by the Medicines Act do not apply to the sale or supply of a Prescription Only Medicine in the course of the business of a hospital where the medicine is sold or supplied for the purpose of being administered (whether in the hospital or elsewhere) to a particular person in accordance with directions satisfying the following conditions:

a   the directions are in writing;
b   the directions relate to the particular person to whom the medicine is to be administered;
c   the directions are given by a person (other than a veterinary surgeon or veterinary practitioner) who is an appropriate practitioner in relation to that medicine.

Such directions may be given by a community practitioner nurse prescriber or a pharmacist, a nurse, an otomotrist independent prescriber or a supplementary prescriber *only* where s/he complies with any condition as to the cases or circumstances in which s/he may give a prescription for that medicine, as if the directions were a prescription. The exemption applies not withstanding the written directions do not satisfy the requirements for a prescription given (SI 2004 No. 2; see p. 98).

Exemptions for persons conducting retail pharmacy businesses

In the Act, and in the orders made under the Act, there are specific exemptions for persons lawfully conducting retail pharmacy businesses from the conditions or restrictions on the retail sale and supply of Prescription Only Medicine (SI 1997 No. 1830) and from the supply and administration of Prescription Only Medicines (SI 2000 No. 1917). Exemptions from control for other persons are to be found in Chapter 9.

In an emergency, a person lawfully conducting a retail pharmacy business can sell or supply a Prescription Only Medicine if and so long as certain conditions are satisfied. There are two kinds of emergency supply (those made at the request of a doctor, and those made at the request of a patient) and different conditions apply to them.

Exemption for emergency supply made at the request of a doctor or an independent prescriber

The conditions that apply for emergency supply made at the request of a doctor or an independent prescriber are:

1 that the pharmacist by or under whose supervision the Prescription Only Medicine is to be sold or supplied is satisfied that the sale or supply has been requested by a doctor, a supplementary prescriber, a community practitioner nurse prescriber, a pharmacist prescriber, a nurse independent prescriber or an optometrist independent prescriber who by reason of an emergency is unable to furnish a prescription immediately;

2 that the doctor, supplementary prescriber, community practitioner nurse prescriber, pharmacist prescriber, nurse independent prescriber or optometrist independent prescriber has undertaken to furnish the person lawfully conducting the retail pharmacy business with a prescription within 72 hours;

3 that the Prescription Only Medicine is sold or supplied in accordance with the directions of the doctor, supplementary prescriber, community practitioner nurse prescriber, pharmacist independent prescriber, nurse independent prescriber or optometrist independent prescriber requesting it;

4 that the Prescription Only Medicine is not a Controlled Drug specified in Schedule 1, 2 or 3 of the Misuse of Drugs Regulations (see Appendix 6);

5 that an entry is made in the Prescription Only Register (see above) stating:
   a the date on which the medicine was sold or supplied;
   b the name, quantity and, except where it is apparent from the name, the pharmaceutical form and strength of the medicine;
   c the name and address of the person for whom the Prescription Only Medicine was supplied;
   d the date on which the prescription was received and the name and address of the practitioner giving it;
   e the date on the prescription (SI 1997 No. 1830 as amended).

Exemption for emergency supply made at the request of a patient

The conditions that apply for emergency supply made at the request of a patient are:

1 that the pharmacist by or under whose supervision the Prescription Only Medicine is to be sold or supplied has interviewed the person requesting the medicine and has satisfied him/herself:
   a that there is an immediate need for the Prescription Only Medicine requested to be sold or supplied and that it is impracticable in the circumstances to obtain a prescription without undue delay;
   b that treatment with the Prescription Only Medicine requested has on a previous occasion been prescribed by a doctor, supplementary prescriber, community practitioner nurse prescriber, pharmacist prescriber or nurse independent prescriber for the person requesting it; and

c   as to the dose which in the circumstances it would be appropriate for that person to take;

2   that no greater quantity of the Prescription Only Medicine in question than will provide five days' treatment is sold or supplied except that there may be sold or supplied, where the medicine in question is:

a   a preparation of insulin, an aerosol dispenser for the relief of asthma, an ointment or cream which has been made up for sale in a container elsewhere than at the place of sale or supply, the smallest pack that the pharmacist has available for sale or supply;

b   an oral contraceptive a quantity sufficient for a full cycle;

c   an antibiotic for oral administration in liquid form, the smallest quantity that will provide a full course of treatment;

3   that the pharmacist by or under whose supervision the medicine is sold or supplied ensures that an entry in the Prescription Only Register is made (see above) stating:

a   the date on which the Prescription Only Medicine was sold or supplied;

b   the name, quantity and, except where it is apparent from the name, the pharmaceutical form and strength of the medicine;

c   the name and address of the person requiring the medicine; and

d   the nature of the emergency;

4   that the container or package of the medicine is labelled with:

a   the date on which the Prescription Only Medicine was sold or supplied;

b   the name, quantity and, except where it is apparent from the name, the pharmaceutical form and strength of the Prescription Only Medicine;

c   the name of the person requiring the Prescription Only Medicine;

d   the name and address of the registered pharmacy from which the Prescription Only Medicine was sold or supplied; and

e   the words 'Emergency Supply';

5   that the Prescription Only Medicine:

a   is not a Controlled Drug specified in Schedule 1, 2 or 3 of the Misuse of Drugs Regulations (see Appendix 6); or

b   does not contain one or more of the substances listed in Box 8.2.

The question of interpretation **supervision** was under consideration by the Department of Health when this book went to print in December 2008.

An emergency sale or supply is permitted of a Prescription Only Medicine which consists of or contains phenobarbital or phenobarbital sodium provided that it is for use in the treatment of epilepsy and does not contain any of the other substances listed above or any substances in Schedule 1, 2 or 3 of the Misuse of Drugs Regulations.

Box 8.2 *Substances one or more of which may **not** be contained in a Prescription Only Medicine supplied at the request of a patient (SI 1997 No. 1830, as amended)*

Ammonium bromide

Calcium bromide
Calcium bromidolactobionate

Embutramide

Fencamfamin hydrochloride
Fluanisone

Hexobarbital
Hexobarbital sodium
Hydrobromic acid

Meclofenoxate hydrochloride
Methohexital sodium

Pemoline
Piracetam
Potassium bromide
Prolintane hydrochloride

Sodium bromide
Strychnine hydrochloride

Tacrine hydrochloride
Thiopental sodium

Exemption for persons conducting a retail pharmacy pharmacies under a Patient Group Direction

Patient Group Direction (PGD) (SI 2000 No. 1917 as amended) means:

1 a written direction relating to the supply and administration of a description or class of Prescription Only Medicines; or
2 a written direction relating to the administration of a description or class of Prescription Only Medicines, and which in case 1 or 2:
   a is signed by a doctor or dentist, and by a pharmacist; and
   b relates to supply and administration, or to administration only, to persons generally (subject to any exclusions which may be set out in the Direction).

The restrictions on retail sale, supply or administration of Prescription Only Medicines do not apply to the sale or supply or administration of any such medicine by a person lawfully conducting a retail pharmacy business where the medicine is sold, supplied or is administered by such a person subject to an arrangement made with:

a   the Common Services Agency, a health authority, a special health authority, an NHS trust, or a primary care trust; or

b   a police force in England, Wales or Scotland, police service in Northern Ireland or a prison service; or

c   Her Majesty's forces; or

d   a person pursuant to an arrangement made with the authority or person carrying on the business of an independent hospital, independent clinic or independent medical agency.

Where the medicine is sold or supplied for the purpose of being administered or is administered to a particular person in accordance with a PGD, and where the following conditions are satisfied, the PGD must:

1   relate to the supply, or the administration, of a description or class of Prescription Only Medicine by a person lawfully conducting a retail pharmacy business who supplies or administers such a medicine;

2   have effect at the time at which the medicine is supplied or is administered;

3   contain the particulars specified in Schedule 7 to the regulations; if the PGD is for administration only, any restrictions on quantity may be omitted;

4   be signed on behalf of, and with whom an arrangement is made:

    i   for authority a, usually a doctor (or dentist) **and** a pharmacist;

    ii   in the case of a force under b, by or on behalf of the person designated for that force or service, e.g. Chief Constable, Prison Governor or Prison Management Board in Scotland or Northern Ireland;

    iii   in case of c, the Surgeon General or Medical Director General or chief executive at the Ministry of Defence;

    iv   for authority d, by or on behalf of the relevant provider or if there is a relevant manager for the establishment, the relevant manager;

5   at the time at which the medicine is supplied or administered the medicine has a marketing authorisation or a homoeopathic certificate of registration (SI 2000 No. 1917 as amended);

6   where the medicine is administered by the person lawfully conducting a retail pharmacy business, the individual who administers the medicine belongs to one of the classes specified in the Order (see Appendix 6) and is designated in writing on behalf of the body with which an arrangement has been made (added by SI 2000 No. 2899).

N.B. As far as pharmacies are concerned there is no provision to use PGDs to permit the supply or administration of Pharmacy Medicines and General Sale List medicines.

Exemptions from Prescription Only for certain persons, including persons who supply under Patient Group Directions

See Chapter 9.

Summary

- Appropriate practitioners for the purpose of prescribing Prescription Only Medicines are doctors, dentists, veterinary surgeons, community practitioner nurse prescribers, nurse independent prescribers, pharmacist independent prescribers (SI 2006 No. 915), optometrist independent prescribers (SI 2008 No. 1161) and EEA health practitioners (SI 2008 No. 1692). The medicines may be prescribe from a limited list.
- Certain medicines are Prescription Only by description or class including Controlled Drugs (some are exempt due to maximum strength or maximum dose), parenterals and cyanogenetic substances.
- Certain Prescription Only Medicines are exempt, depending on strength, daily dosage, specified condition for use, etc. (e.g. cimetidine).
- Certain Prescription Only Medicines may be administered in an emergency, e.g. adrenaline (epinephrine) injection.
- Detailed prescription requirements are laid down, including name and address of patient, signature and address of doctor, date, age of patient if under 12, etc.
- Detailed record requirements are imposed for Prescription Only Medicines except those on a health prescription or oral contraceptives.
- Prescription Only Medicines, except Controlled Drugs, may be supplied at the request of a doctor, supplementary prescriber, community practitioner nurse prescriber, pharmacist prescriber, nurse independent prescriber or optometrist independent prescriber, who by reason of any emergency is unable to furnish a prescription immediately.
- Prescription Only Medicines, except Controlled Drugs, may be supplied at the request of a patient if the pharmacist has interviewed the patient, is satisfied that there is an immediate need, it is impracticable to obtain a prescription without undue delay and the medicine has been prescribed before by a doctor, supplementary prescriber, community practitioner nurse prescriber, pharmacist prescriber or nurse independent prescriber. Detailed quantity, labelling and record conditions apply.
- Under certain conditions, Prescription Only Medicines may be supplied under Patient Group Directions.

Further reading

Royal Pharmaceutical Society of Great Britain (published annually) *Medicines, Ethics and Practice*. London: Royal Pharmaceutical Society of Great Britain. (Lists of Prescription Only Medicines are included.)

9

Medicines Act 1968
Retail sale and supply: exemptions from controls for other persons

In the Act, and in orders made under the Act, there are specified exemptions for certain classes of person from the conditions or restrictions on retail sale and/or supply which apply to medicines on a General Sale List (s.53), Pharmacy Medicines (s.52) and Prescription Only Medicines (s.58). Exemption from the restriction on the administration of Prescription Only Medicines for parenteral use is also conferred on certain persons (SI 1997 No. 1830, as amended).

The classes of person and the body exempted, the medicinal products to which the exemptions apply and the conditions (if any) which attach to the retail sale, supply or administration by these exempted persons are described in this chapter.

The sale of a Prescription Only Medicine or a Pharmacy Medicine to any of these persons in accordance with the exemptions granted to them is a sale by way of wholesale dealing (SI 1980 No. 1923, amended by SI 2000 No. 1918). The persons who may engage in wholesale dealing, the extent to which it may be carried on at retail pharmacy businesses and the records to be kept in respect of wholesale transactions are described in Chapter 10.

Hospitals and health centres

The restrictions on the sale, offer for sale, or supply of any medicinal products (not being Prescription Only Medicine) do not apply when the sale, offer for sale or supply is in the course of the business of a hospital or health centre for the purpose of being administered (whether in the hospital or health centre or elsewhere) in accordance with the directions of a doctor or dentist (s.55).

The restrictions on the sale, offer for sale or supply of any other medicinal products (not being Prescription Only Medicines) do not apply when the sale, offer for sale or supply is in the course of the business of a hospital or health centre for the purpose of being administered (whether in the hospital or health centre or elsewhere) to a particular person in accordance with the written directions of a supplementary prescriber or a nurse prescriber relating to that person (SI 2004 No. 1).

National Health Service bodies: medicines supplied under a Patient Group Direction

1   The restrictions on retail sale or supply of Prescription Only Medicines do not apply to the supply of any such medicine, by:
    a   the Common Services Agency;
    b   a strategic health authority, health authority or special health authority;
    c   an NHS trust; or NHS foundation trust, or
    d   a primary care trust; or
    e   a person, other than an excepted person, subject to an arrangement made with one of the bodies in a–d for the supply of Prescription Only Medicines where the medicine is supplied for the purpose of being administered to a particular person in accordance with the written directions of a doctor or dentist relating to that person. The written directions need not satisfy the requirements for a prescription given in the Prescription Only Order (SI 2000 No. 1917) (see p. 98).

Excepted person means: a doctor, a dentist, or a person lawfully conducting a retail pharmacy business.

2   The restrictions on retail sale or supply of Prescription Only Medicines do not apply to the supply, or as the case may be, the administration of any such medicine by:
    a   the Common Services Agency;
    b   a strategic health authority, health authority or special health authority;
    c   an NHS trust; or NHS foundation trust, or
    d   a primary care trust; or
    e   a person, other than an excepted person, subject to an arrangement made with one of the persons in a–d above for the supply, or, the administration of Prescription Only Medicines where the medicine is supplied for the purpose of being administered or, as the case may be, is administered, to a particular person in accordance with a Patient Group Direction (PGD) and where the following conditions are satisfied:
        i   the PGD relates to the supply, or the administration, of a description or class of Prescription Only Medicine by the person who supplies or administers a Prescription Only Medicine;
        ii   the PGD has effect at the time at which the medicine is supplied or is administered;

iii the PGD contains the particulars specified in the regulations; if the PGD is for administration only any restrictions on quantity may be omitted;

iv the PGD is signed on behalf of the person specified in a–d above (the *authorising person*) by a doctor (or dentist) **and** a pharmacist;

v the individual who supplies or administers the medicine belongs to a class of health professionals (Schedule 7) and is designated in writing on behalf of the authorising body for the purpose of supply or administration under the PGD;

vi at the time at which the medicine is supplied or administered the medicine has a marketing authorisation, a homoeopathic certificate of registration (SI 2000 No. 1917), or a traditional herbal registration (SI 2005 No. 2750).

For definition of *Patient Group Direction,* see p. 105.

N.B. The particulars required in the PGD iii and the list of designated health professionals v are set out in the regulations.

An *excepted person* means a doctor, dentist, or person lawfully conducting a retail pharmacy.

Similar provisions apply to permit the supply or administration of Pharmacy medicines and General Sale List medicines by means of PGDs (SI 2000 No. 1919).

Doctors, dentists and veterinarians

The restrictions on retail sale or supply do not apply to the sale, offer for sale or supply of any medicinal products:

1 by a doctor or dentist to a patient of his/hers, or to a person under whose care such a patient is; or

2 by a veterinary surgeon or veterinary practitioner for administration by him/her or under his/her direction to an animal or herd under his/her care (ss.55 and 58).

For interpretation of *patient of his/hers* see Chapter 28.

Unorthodox practitioners

Persons who at 11 February 1982 were customarily administering medicinal products to human beings by parenteral administration in the course of a business in the field of osteopathy, naturopathy, acupuncture or other similar field (except chiropody) may *administer* Prescription Only Medicines which are only so classified because they are for parenteral use and provided they do not contain an ingredient which would otherwise make them Prescription Only. The person administering the medicine must, at the request of the person to whom it is to be administered, use his/her own judgement as to the treatment required (SI 1997 No. 1830).

Midwives

Sale or supply

The restrictions on retail sale or supply do not apply to the supply or sale (but not offer for sale) of certain medicinal products by a registered midwife in the course of his/her professional practice. The medicinal products to which this exemption applies (SI 1997 No. 1830) are:

1   all medicinal products that are not Prescription Only Medicines;
2   Prescription Only Medicines containing any of the following substances but no other Prescription Only Medicine:
   • chloral hydrate
   • ergometrine maleate (only when contained in a medicinal product which is not for parenteral administration)
   • pentazocine hydrochloride
   • phytomenadione (SI 1998 No. 2081)
   • triclofos sodium.

Administration

Registered midwives may also administer parenterally in the course of their professional practice Prescription Only Medicines containing any of the following substances (SI 1997 No. 1830 as amended):

   • diamorphine (SI 2004 No. 2)
   • ergometrine maleate
   • lidocaine
   • lidocaine hydrochloride
   • morphine (SI 2004 No. 2)
   • naloxone hydrochloride
   • oxytocin, natural and synthetic
   • pentazocine lactate
   • pethidine hydrochloride
   • phytomenadione
   • promazine hydrochloride.

Additionally lidocaine, lidocaine hydrochoride and promazine hydrochloride may only be administered by a midwife while attending a woman in childbirth.

Midwives may also supply or administer Prescription Only Medicines, Pharmacy Medicines and General Sale List medicines under PGDs (see p. 118).

Registered nurses

The restrictions on retail supply or sale do not apply to the supply or sale (but not offer for sale) by a registered nurse in the course of his/her professional practice of any medicinal product specified in an order made by the Health Ministers (s.55). No such order has yet been made. *Registered nurse* does not include enrolled nurses (see Chapter 25).

Nurse practitioners may prescribe, but not sell or supply, a limited list of Prescription Only Medicines (see p. 118).

Registered nurses may also supply or administer Prescription Only Medicines, Pharmacy Medicines and General Sale List medicines under PGDs (see p. 118).

Optometrists

The designation of ophthalmic optician was changed to optometrist in 2005 (SI 2005 No. 848).

Registered optometrist means a person whose name in entered in the register of optometrists maintained under section 7a of the Opticians Act 1989 (SI 2005 No. 1507).

Additional supply optometrist means a person who is registered as an optometrist and against whose name particulars of the additional supply speciality has been entered in the register.

The restrictions on retail supply or sale do not apply to the sale or supply of certain medicinal products (those in 3 and 4 below) by registered optometrists provided they are only in the course of their professional practice and only in an emergency. The medicinal products to which this exemption applies are:

1 all medicinal products on a General Sale List;
2 all Pharmacy Medicines;
3 Prescription Only Medicines that are either:
   a   eye drops containing not more than 0.5 per cent chloramphenicol; or
   b   eye ointments containing not more than 1.0 per cent chloramphenicol;
4 Medicines which are Prescription Only by reason only that they contain any of the following substances:
   • cyclopentolate hydrochloride
   • fusidic Acid (SI 2005 No. 765)
   • physostigmine sulphate
   • pilocarpine nitrate (SI 2005 No. 3324)
   • tropicamide.

Supplies of these Prescription Only Medicines may be obtained by opticians for use in their practice from a retail pharmacy business subject to the presentation of an order signed by a registered optometrist (SI 1997 No. 1830).

Optometrists may also *purchase* for use in their practice (but not for sale or supply) medicines which are Prescription Only by reason only that they contain any one or more of the following substances (SI 1980 No. 1923):

- amethocaine hydrochloride
- lidocaine hydrochloride
- oxybuprocaine hydrochloride
- proxymetacaine hydrochloride.

Registered optometrists may also supply or administer, Prescription Only Medicines, Pharmacy Medicines, and General Sale List medicines under PGDs (see p. 118).

An *optometrist independent prescriber* is a registered optometrist whose name is annotated in the relevant register as qualified to order drugs and medicines.

Additional supply optometrists may sell or supply the following Prescription Only Medicines in the course of their professional practice and in an emergency

- acetylcysteine
- atropine sulphate
- azelastine hydrochloride
- diclofenac sodium
- emedastine
- homatropine hydrobromide
- ketotifen
- levocabastine
- lodoxamide
- nedocromil sodium
- olopatadine
- pilocarpine hydrochloride
- polymyxin B/bacitracin
- polymyxin B/trimethoprim
- sodium cromoglicate.

Persons lawfully conducting a retail pharmacy may sell these items on the presentation of a signed order from an additional supply optometrist.

Chiropodists

Sale or supply

The restrictions on retail sale or supply do not apply to the sale or supply of certain medicinal products by state registered chiropodists provided:

1 the sale or supply is made in the course of their professional practice; and
2 the product has been made up for sale or supply in a container elsewhere than at the place at which it is sold or supplied.

The medicinal products to which this exemption applies are:

1 medicinal products for external human use that are on a General Sale List; and
2 any of the following *Pharmacy Medicines* for external use only: ointment of heparinoid and hyaluronidase, potassium permanganate crystals or solution, and products containing, as their only active ingredients, any of the following substances, at a strength, in the case of each substance, not exceeding that specified in relation to that substance (SI 1982 No. 27):

- 9.0 per cent borotannic complex
- 10.0 per cent buclosamide
- 3.0 per cent chlorquinaldol
- 1.0 per cent clotrimazole
- 10.0 per cent crotamiton
- 5.0 per cent diamthazole hydrochloride
- 1.0 per cent econazole nitrate
- 1.0 per cent fenticlor
- 10.0 per cent glutaraldehyde
- 0.4 per cent hydrargaphen
- 2.0 per cent mepyramine maleate
- 2.0 per cent miconazole nitrate
- 2.0 per cent phenoxypropan-2-ol
- 20.0 per cent podophyllum resin
- 10.0 per cent polynoxylin
- 70.0 per cent pyrogallol
- 70.0 per cent salicylic acid
- 0.1 per cent thiomersal
- ibuprofen; other than preparations of ibuprofen which are Prescription Only Medicines and in an amount sufficient for three days' treatment where the md [maximum dose] is 400 mg, the mdd [maximum daily dose] 1200 mg and the maximum pack is 3600 mg (SI 1998 No. 107).

Registered chiropodists against whose names are recorded in the relevant register annotations signifying that they are qualified to use the following medicines may sell or supply any of them in the course of their professional practice:

- Co-dydramol 10/500 tablets: the quantity sold or supplied to a person at any one time not to exceed an amount sufficient for three days' treatment to a maximum of 24 tablets;

- amorolfine HCl cream: the maximum strength of amorolfine not to exceed 0.25 per cent w/w;
- amorolfine HCl lacquer: the maximum strength of amorolfine not to exceed 5 per cent w/v;
- topical hydrocortisone the maximum strength of hydrocortisone in the medicinal product not to exceed 1 per cent w/w;
- amoxicillin;
- erythromycin;
- flucoxacillin;
- tioconazole 28%; or
- silver sulfadiazine (SI 2006 No. 2807).

Administration

Registered chiropodists against whose names are recorded in the relevant register annotations signifying that they are qualified to use the following medicines may administer the following substances (SI 2006 No. 2807):

- adrenaline (epinephrine)
- bupivacaine hydrochloride
- bupivacaine hydrochloride with adrenaline (epinephrine) where the maximum strength of the adrenaline does not exceed 1 mg in 200 ml of bupivacaine hydrochloride
- levobupivacaine hydrochloride
- lidocaine hydrochloride
- lidocaine hydrochloride with adrenaline (epinephrine) where the maximum strength of the adrenaline does not exceed 1 mg in 200 ml of lidocaine hydrochloride
- mepivacaine hydrochoride (SI 1998 No. 2081)
- methylprednisolone
- prilocaine hydrochloride
- ropivicaine hydrochoride (SI 2006 No. 2807).

Registered chiropodists may also supply or administer Prescription Only Medicines, Pharmacy Medicines, and General Sale List medicines under PGDs (see p. 118).

Ambulance paramedics

Persons who hold a certificate of proficiency in ambulance paramedic skills issued by, or with the approval of, the Secretary of State may parenterally administer (but not sell or supply) the following Prescription Only Medicines:

1 diazepam 5 mg per mL emulsion for injection;

2 succinylated gelatin (modified fluid gelatin) 4 per cent intravenous infusion;

3 medicines containing ergometrine maleate 500 micrograms/mL with oxytocin 5 iu/mL but no other active ingredient;

4 Prescription Only Medicines containing one or more of the following substances, but no other active ingredient:
- adrenaline (epinephrine) acid tartrate
- amiodarone
- anhydrous glucose
- benzylpenicillin
- bretylium tosylate
- compound sodium lactate intravenous infusion (Hartmann's solution)
- ergometrine maleate
- furosemide
- glucose
- heparin sodium
- lidocaine hydrochloride
- metoclopramide
- morphine sulphate
- nalbuphine hydrochloride
- naloxone hydrochloride
- polygeline
- reteplase (SI 2004 No. 1189)
- sodium bicarbonate
- sodium chloride
- streptokinase
- tenecteplase (SI 2004 No. 1189).

The administration may only be for the immediate, necessary treatment of sick or injured persons. In the case of a Prescription Only Medicine containing heparin sodium, it may only be used for cannula flushing (SI 1997 No. 1830).

Individuals who hold a certificate of proficiency in ambulance paramedic skills issued by the Secretary of State or individuals who are state registered paramedics may also supply or administer Prescription Only Medicines, Pharmacy Medicines, and General Sale List medicines under PGDs (see below under Health Professionals).

Operators under the Ionising Radiation (Medical Exposure) Regulations 2000 (IRME)

The restriction imposed on administration by section 58(2)(b) of the Medicines Act does not apply to a radioactive medicinal product, administration of which results in a medical exposure, or any other Prescription Only Medicine if it is being administered in connection with a medical exposure where the following provisions apply:

1   the radioactive medicinal substance or Prescription Only Medicine is administered by an operator acting in accordance with the procedures and protocols laid down in the IRME regulations;
2   the administration has been authorised by a IRME practitioner;
3   an IRME certificate has been granted pursuant to the Medicines (Administration of Radioactive Substances) Regulations 1978 as amended;
4   the radioactive medicinal substance or Prescription Only Medicine is not a controlled drug; and
5   in the case of a Prescription Only Medicine that is not a radioactive medicinal product, it is specified in the IRME regulations.

For definition of a radioactive medicinal product, see p. 96.

Health professionals who supply or administer Prescription Only Medicines under a Patient Group Direction in order to assist doctors or dentists in providing National Health Service primary medical and dental services

For the definition of a *Patient Group Direction*, see p. 105.

Primary Medical (Dental) Services means the provision of general medical (dental) services under the National Health Service Act 1977, or the performance of personal medical (dental) services in connection with a pilot scheme under the National Health Service (Primary Care) Act 1997.

The restrictions on retail sale or supply of a medicinal product do not apply to the supply by any of the following individuals listed in Schedule 7 to the regulations. These include registered pharmacists, nurses and midwives, health visitors, optometrists, chiropodists, ambulance paramedics, orthoptists, physiotherapists and radiographers where the individual supplies or administers a medicine in order to assist a doctor or dentist in the provision of NHS primary medical (or dental) service. The medicine is supplied in accordance with a PGD and the following conditions apply.

1   The PGD relates to the supply, or the administration of a description or class of medicine in order to assist the doctor or dentist in question in the provision of National Health Service primary medical (dental) services.
2   The PGD has effect at the time at which the medicine is supplied or is administered.
3   The PGD contains the particulars specified in the regulations. If the PGD is for administration only, any restrictions on quantity may be omitted.

4   The PGD is signed by the doctor or dentist in question and, on behalf of the health authority, by a doctor **and** a pharmacist.
5   The health professional who supplies or administers the medicine is designated in writing by the doctor or dentist in question.
6   At the time at which the medicine is supplied or administered, the medicine has a marketing authorisation or a homoeopathic certificate of registration (SI 2000 No. 1917).

Similar provisions apply to permit the supply or administration of Pharmacy Medicines and General Sale List medicines by means of PGDs (SI 2000 No. 1919 as amended).

Dietitians, occupational therapists, orthoptists and prosthetists, and speech and language therapists were added by SI 2004 No. 1190.

Independent hospitals, clinics and agencies which supply medicines under a Patient Group Direction

For the definition of a *Patient Group Direction*, see p. 105. This grouping of suppliers is covered further on p. 110.

The restrictions on the supply or sale of a medicinal product do not apply in the course of a business of an independent hospital, independent clinic or independent medical agency where the product is supplied sold under a PGD and the following conditions apply.

1   The PGD relates to the supply or sale of a description or class of medicine.
2   The PGD has effect at the time at which the medicine is supplied or sold.
3   The PGD contains the particulars specified in the regulations. If the PGD is for administration only any restrictions on quantity may be omitted.
4   The PGD is signed by the registered provider or the relevant manager.
5   The person who supplies the medicine is designated in writing on behalf of the registered provider or relevant manager.
6   At the time at which the medicine is supplied, the medicine has a marketing authorisation, a homoeopathic certificate of registration (SI 2003 No. 697 and SI 2007 No. 2178), or a traditional herbal registration (SI 2005 No. 2750).

Police, prison and armed forces supply of medicines under a Patient Group Direction

For the definition of a *Patient Group Direction*, see p. 105. This grouping of suppliers is covered further on p. 106.

The restrictions on the supply of a medicinal product does not apply to the supply of a medicinal product by an individual belonging to the police, the prison service or the armed forces where it is supplied for the purpose of being administered in accordance with a PGD and the following conditions apply.

1 The PGD relates to the supply of a description or class of medicine.
2 The PGD has effect at the time at which the medicine is supplied.
3 The PGD contains the particulars specified in the regulations. If the PGD is for administration only any restrictions on quantity may be omitted.
4 The PGD is signed by the registered provider or the relevant manager.
5 The person who supplies the medicine is designated in writing on behalf of the chief constable, prison governor, surgeon general, medical director general or chief executive of the Ministry of Defence as the case may be.
6 At the time at which the medicine is supplied the medicine has a marketing authorisation, a homoeopathic certificate of registration (SI 2003 No. 697), or a traditional herbal resitration (SI 2005 No. 2750).

Prison officer means an officer of a prison, young offenders institution, remand centre, juvenile justice centre, young offender centre or secure training centre and includes a prison custody officer. Prisoner is similarly defined as any person over 16 years of age detained in legal custody as a result of court orders, in similar institutions.

All prison officers may supply, only so far as is necessary for the treatment of prisoners, medicinal products on a General Sale List (SI 2005 No. 766).

Persons authorised to be sold cyanide salts under the Poisons Act 1972

Pharmacists may sell amyl nitrite to such persons who would include a person or institution concerned with scientific education or research, a person who requires the article for the purpose of his/her trade or business, and a person who requires the article for the purpose of enabling him/her to comply with any requirements made by or in pursuance of any enactment with respect to the medical treatment of persons employed by that person in any trade or business carried on by him/her (see also p. 123). The sale or supply must only be so far as it is necessary to enable an antidote to be available to persons at risk of cyanide poisoning (SI 1997 No. 1830).

Manufacturers of products for treatment of the hair and scalp

The holder of a manufacturer's licence for a medicinal product which is for external use in the treatment of hair and scalp conditions may sell or supply the product free from the statutory restrictions or conditions applicable to retail sales provided that:

1 the licence in question contains a provision that the licence holder shall only manufacture the medicinal product for a particular person after being requested by or on behalf of that person and in that person's presence to use his/her own judgement as to the treatment required; and

2 the sale or supply is made only upon receipt of such a request.

The medicinal products to which this exemption applies are:

1 medicinal products on a General Sale List which are for human external use; and

2 Pharmacy Medicines which are for external use in the treatment of hair and scalp conditions and which contain any of the following substances:
   - not more than 5 per cent of boric acid
   - isopropyl myristate or lauryl sulphate
   - not more than 0.004 per cent oestrogens
   - not more than 1 per cent resorcin
   - not more than 3 per cent salicylic acid
   - not more than 0.2 per cent sodium pyrithione or zinc pyrithione (SI 1980 No. 1924).

Public analysts, sampling officers and other such persons

The restrictions on retail sale or supply do not apply to persons who sell or supply any medicinal product to any of the following:

1 a public analyst appointed under section 27 of the Food Safety Act 1990 or Article 36 of the Food (Northern Ireland) Order 1989;

2 an authorised officer within the meaning of section 5(6) of the Food Safety Act 1990;

3 a sampling officer within the meaning of Article 38(1) of the Food (Northern Ireland) Order 1989;

4 a person duly authorised by an enforcement authority under sections 111 and 112 of the Act;

5 a sampling officer within the meaning of Schedule 3 to the Act (see p. 24).

The sale or supply is subject to the presentation of an order signed by or on behalf of the analyst, authorised officer, sampling officer or enforcement officer, as the case may be. It must state the status of the person signing it and the amount of the Prescription Only Medicine required and shall be only in connection with the exercise by those persons of their statutory functions (SI 1997 No. 1830).

National Health Service drug testing

The restrictions on retail sale or supply do not apply to persons who sell or supply any medicinal product to any person employed or engaged in connection with the scheme for testing the quality and amount of the drugs, preparations and appliances supplied under the National Health Service Act

1977, the National Health Service (Scotland) Act 1978 and the Health and Personal Social Services (Northern Ireland) Order 1972 or any subordinate legislation made under those Acts or that Order (SIs 1980 No. 1924 and 1983 No. 1830).

The sale or supply must be for the purpose of the relevant scheme and is subject to the presentation of an order signed on behalf of the person so employed or engaged stating:

1 the status of the person signing it;
2 the amount of the medicinal product required.

Owners and masters of ships

The restrictions on supply (but not sale) of any medicinal product do not apply when the supply is made by the owner or the master of a ship which does not carry a doctor on board as part of her complement. An owner or master may also administer Prescription Only Medicines that are for parenteral administration. The supply or administration shall be only so far as is necessary for the treatment of persons on the ship (SI 1997 No. 1830).

Offshore installations

Persons employed as qualified first-aid personnel on offshore installations may:

1 supply any medicinal product; and
2 administer all parenteral Prescription Only Medicines

only so far as is necessary for the treatment of persons on the installation (SI 1997 No. 1830).

British Standards Institution

The restrictions on the retail sale or supply do not apply to persons who sell or supply any Prescription Only Medicine, any Pharmacy Medicine or any medicinal product on a General Sale List to the British Standards Institution. The British Standard Institution itself cannot sell, supply or administer medicinal products.

The sale or supply shall only be for the purpose of testing containers of medicinal products or determining the standards for such containers and is subject to the presentation of an order signed on behalf of the British Standards Institution stating the status of the person signing it and the amount of the medicinal product required (SIs 1980 No. 1924 and 1997 No. 1830).

Statutory requirements as to medical treatment

The restrictions on retail supply (but not sale) of medicinal products do not apply to supplies made by persons requiring medicinal products for the purpose of enabling them, in the course of any business carried on by them, to comply with any requirements made by or in pursuance of any enactment with respect to the medical treatment of employees. The exemption extends to the Prescription Only Medicines and the Pharmacy Medicines specified in the relevant enactment and to medicinal products on a General Sale List.

The supply shall be:

1 for the purpose of enabling them to comply with any requirements made by or in pursuance of any such enactment; and
2 subject to such conditions and in such circumstances as may be specified in the relevant enactments (SIs 1980 No. 1924 and 1997 No. 1830).

Persons employed or engaged in the lawful drug treatment services

Persons employed or engaged in the lawful drug treatment services may supply ampoules of sterile water for injection containing not more than 2 mL of sterile water.

Licences and group authorities

The restrictions on the supply of Prescription Only Medicines do not apply to persons authorised by licences granted under regulation 5 of the Misuse of Drugs Regulations 1973 to supply the Controlled Drugs specified in the licence.

The supply shall be subject to such conditions and in such circumstances and to such an extent as may be specified in the licence.

Similarly, the restrictions on the administration of Prescription Only Medicines do not apply to persons who are authorised as members of a group by a group authority granted under regulations 8(3) or 9(3) of the Misuse of Drugs Regulations 1985. The exemption is limited to the administration of Controlled Drugs that are specified in the group authority and is subject to such conditions and in such circumstances and to such an extent as may be specified in the group authority (SI 1997 No. 1830).

Royal National Lifeboat Institution

The restrictions on the retail supply of any medicinal product do not apply to supply by the Royal National Lifeboat Institution or certificated first-aiders of the Institution. The supply of any Prescription Only Medicine shall be only so far as it is necessary for the treatment of sick or injured persons in the exercise of the functions of the Institution (SI 1997 No. 1830).

British Red Cross Society and other such organisations

The restrictions on the retail supply of Pharmacy Medicines and all medicinal products on a General Sale List (but *not* Prescription Only Medicines) do not apply to supply by the bodies specified below and their certificated first-aid and certificated nursing members. In all cases the supply shall be only so far as it is necessary for the treatment of sick or injured persons. The bodies concerned (SI 1980 No. 1924) are:

- British Red Cross Society
- St John Ambulance Association and Brigade
- St Andrew's Ambulance Association
- Order of Malta Ambulance Corps.

Dental schemes

Pharmacy Medicines that are for use in the prevention of dental caries and consist of or contain sodium fluoride (see below) may be supplied, in the course of 'pre-school dental schemes', by health authorities and, in the course of 'school dental schemes', by persons carrying on the business of a school providing full-time education.

A *pre-school dental scheme* means a scheme supervised by a doctor or dentist in which medicinal products are supplied to parents or guardians of children under five years for use by such children for the purpose of preventing dental caries. The supplies must be made by a registered nurse or an enrolled nurse.

A *school dental scheme* means a scheme supervised by a doctor or dentist in which medicinal products are supplied at a school to pupils of that school for the purpose of preventing dental caries. A supply may also be made to a child under 16 years of age with the consent of the parent or guardian of that child (SI 1980 No. 1924).

N.B. The following are the Pharmacy Medicines affected:

1 preparations of sodium fluoride for use in the prevention of dental caries in the form of:
   a tablets or drops (maximum daily dose 2.2 mg);
   b mouth rinses containing not more than 0.2 per cent (other than those for daily use);
   c mouth rinses for daily use (containing not more than 0.05 per cent);
   d dentifrices containing not more than 0.33 per cent.

Other medicinal products containing sodium fluoride are Prescription Only Medicines and may not be sold, supplied or administered.

Mountain rescue teams

Persons who hold a certificate from the Mountain Rescue Council or from the Northern Ireland Mountain Rescue Co-ordinating Committee may supply Prescription Only Medicines as far as is necessary for the treatment of sick or injured persons. The supply must be in the course of mountain rescue services and in response to an order in writing signed by a doctor (SI 2006 No. 2807).

Occupational health schemes

Pharmacy Medicines and Prescription Only Medicines may be supplied by a person operating an *occupational health scheme*, that is, a scheme in which persons, in the course of a business carried on by them, provide facilities for their employees for the treatment or prevention of disease.

The supply must be made in the course of the scheme. The medicinal products may be supplied to the person operating the scheme in response to an order in writing signed by a doctor, a registered nurse or an enrolled nurse.

The individual supplying or administering the medicines in the course of the scheme, if not a doctor, must be:

1 a registered nurse or an enrolled nurse; and
2 where the medicinal product in question is a Prescription Only Medicine, acting in accordance with the written instructions of a doctor as to the circumstances in which Prescription Only Medicines of the description in question are to be used in the course of the occupational health scheme (SIs 1980 No. 1924 and 1997 No. 1830).

Aircraft commanders

The commander of an aircraft or the operator, that is, the person for the time being having the management of the aircraft, may supply certain medicinal products but only so far as is necessary for the immediate treatment of sick or injured persons on the aircraft. S/he may supply any medicinal products on a General Sale List, any Pharmacy Medicine and Prescription Only Medicines which are *not* for parenteral administration and which have been sold or supplied to him/her in response to an order in writing signed by a doctor. The supply of those Prescription Only Medicines by the commander or operator shall be in accordance with the written instructions of a doctor as to the circumstances in which Prescription Only Medicines of the description in question are to be used on the aircraft (SIs 1980 No. 1924 and 1997 No. 1830).

In addition, the commander or operator of an aircraft may administer Prescription Only Medicines for parenteral use which have been sold or supplied to him/her in response to an order in writing signed by a doctor. The administration shall be only so far as is necessary for the immediate treatment of sick or injured person on the aircraft and shall be in accordance with the written instructions of a doctor as to the circumstances in which Prescription Only Medicines of the description in question are to be used on the aircraft (SI 1997 No. 1830).

Universities, higher education institutions or institutions concerned with research

The restrictions on retail sale or supply do not apply to persons selling or supplying any medicinal product to a university, an institution concerned with higher education or an institution concerned with research but only for the purposes of the education or research with which the institution is concerned. The sale or supply is subject to the presentation of an order signed by the principal of the institution for education or research or the appropriate head of department in charge of a specified course of research (SIs 1980 No. 1924 and 1997 No. 1830). The order must state:

1   the name of the institution for which the medicinal product is required;
2   the purpose for which it is required; and
3   the total quantity required.

Sales by licence holders

The restrictions on sale or supply do not apply to holders of marketing authorisations and holders of manufacturing licences who sell or supply medicinal products referred to in the licences to pharmacists so as to enable them to prepare an entry relating to the medicinal product in question in a tablet or capsule identification guide or similar publication. No greater quantity than is reasonably necessary for that purpose may be supplied (SI 1997 No. 1830).

Veterinary drugs

The exemptions which apply to the retail sale or supply of certain veterinary drugs are dealt with in Chapter 13.

Foot and mouth disease vaccine

Specified government officers and other persons including contractors, volunteers and employees are exempt from the general restrictions of the Medicines

Act in relation to Pharmacy Only and Prescription Only Medicines in certain conditions (SI 2004 No. 2779). Those conditions are when they supply foot and mouth disease vaccine as part of the government's responses to an outbreak in the UK of foot and mouth disease and complying with specified EEC measures laid down in Council Directive 2003/85/EC.

Summary

- Doctors and dentists may sell or supply all medicines to their own patients.
- Veterinary practitioners and veterinary surgeons may sell or supply all medicines for administration by them, or under their direction to an animal or herd under their care.
- For the purposes of their professional practice, midwives have a list of medicines which can be sold or supplied by them and another list of medicines which they may administer.
- In the course of their professional practice, and only in an emergency, optometrists have a list of medicines which they may sell or supply to their patients. They may also purchase for use in their practice, but not for sale or supply, a limited list of Prescription Only Medicines.
- In the course of their professional practice, chiropodists may sell or supply to their patients any General Sale List medicine for external use and a limited list of Pharmacy Medicines. Chiropodists holding a certificate of competence in the use of analgesics may administer, in their practice, a named list of local parenteral analgesics.
- Persons who hold a certificate of proficiency in ambulance paramedic skills may parenterally administer certain medicines for the immediate, necessary treatment of the sick or injured.
- Other categories of activities also have limited lists of medicines which they may sell or supply. These include dental and occupational health schemes, owners and masters of ships, offshore installations, the Royal National Lifeboat Institution, public analysts, aircraft commanders, universities and the British Red Cross.
- NHS bodies and certain health professionals can supply medicines under Patient Group Directions. These include registered nurses and midwives, registered health visitors, registered optometrists, state registered chiropodists, state registered ambulance paramedics, registered orthoptists, registered physiotherapists and registered radiographers.
- Independent hospitals, clinics and medical agencies together with the police service, prison service and Her Majesty's Armed Forces can supply and administer under Patient Group Directions.

10

Medicines Act 1968
Wholesale dealing

Regulations (SI 1980 No. 1923, as amended) made under the Act (s.61) control the sale of medicinal products by way of wholesale dealing, that is, the sale of medicinal products to a person for the purpose of (a) selling or supplying them, or (b) administering them to human beings in the course of a business (see p. 38). Sales of medicinal products by way of wholesale dealing can be made as set out below by:

1 the holder of a marketing authorisation; or
2 a person carrying on a business which consists (wholly or partly) of manufacturing medicinal products or of selling them by way of wholesale dealing. The sales must be made in the course of the business. (Retail pharmacy owners, who are not licensed as wholesalers, may sell by way of wholesale dealing provided the sales constitute no more than an inconsiderable part of the business; see p. 45.)

A person making sales by way of wholesale dealing

A person making sales by way of wholesale dealing must possess a wholesale dealer's licence (see p. 38). Such sales must be from a specified place and the licence holder must (SI 1993 No. 833):

1 keep records, which may be in the form of invoices or on computer or in any other form, giving the following information in respect of such products which have been received or despatched:
   a the date of receipt and of despatch;
   b the name of the products;
   c the quantity of the products received or despatched; and
   d the name and address of the person from whom, or to whom, the products are sold or supplied as appropriate;
2 have at all times at his/her disposal the services of a person – a *responsible person* – who possesses in the opinion of the licensing authority:

a   knowledge of the activities to be carried out and of the procedures to be performed under the licence; and

b   experience in those activities and procedures which is adequate for those purposes;

3   obtain supplies of medicinal products only from:

a   any person who is the holder of a manufacturer's licence or a wholesale dealer's licence which relates to those products; or

b   any person who holds an authorisation granted by the competent authority of a member state other than the UK authorising the manufacture of such products or the distribution by way of wholesale dealing of such products;

4   institute an emergency plan which ensures effective implementation of any recall from the market.

The functions of the *responsible person* shall be to ensure that the conditions under which the licence has been granted have been, and are being, complied with and that the quality of the products is maintained in accordance with the requirements of the appropriate marketing authorisation.

Pharmacy Medicines by wholesale dealing

Pharmacy Medicines may be sold by way of wholesale dealing to (SI 1980 No. 1923 as amended):

1   practitioners;

2   any person lawfully conducting a retail pharmacy business;

3   authorities or persons carrying on the business of an independent hospital, independent clinic, independent medical agency or a hospital or health centre which is not an independent hospital or clinic (SI 2003 No. 698);

4   holders of wholesale dealer's licences, or persons to whom the requirements to hold a wholesale dealer's licence do not apply by virtue of an exemption conferred by or under the Act;

5   Ministers of the Crown and government departments and officers thereof;

6   a NHS trust established under the National Health Service and Community Care Act 1990 or the National Health Service (Scotland) Act 1978;

7   the Common Services Agency in Scotland;

8   any person who requires Pharmacy Medicines for the purpose of administering them to human beings in the course of a business where the medicines are for the purpose of being so administered;

9   any person who may sell or supply, in circumstances corresponding to retail sale, Pharmacy Medicines as specified in an exemption order

(SI 1980 No. 1924, as amended) (see Chapter 9), certain herbal remedies (s.56 and SI 1977 No. 2130) (see Chapter 12) or veterinary drugs (see Chapter 13);

10 a person other than an exempted person who carries on a business consisting (wholly or partly) of the supply or administration of medicinal products for the purpose of assisting the provision of healthcare by or on behalf of the police force in the UK, a prison service or Her Majesty's Forces (SI 2003/698).

Prescription Only Medicines by wholesale dealing

Prescription Only Medicines may be sold by way of wholesale dealing to the same persons and authorities as in 1, 2, 3, 4, 5, 6 and 7 for Pharmacy Medicines above, plus:

11 any person who is the subject of an exemption in Schedule 3 to the Prescription Only Order (SI 1997 No. 1830) but only in respect of the medicinal products covered by the exemption (see Chapter 9);

12 registered optometrists: there are certain Prescription Only Medicines which optometrists are entitled to supply to their patients or use in their practice (see p. 113);

13 any person selling or supplying by retail, or administering, unit preparations of Prescription Only Medicines (other than Controlled Drugs) diluted to one part in a million (6×) having been requested by or on behalf of the particular person and in that person's presence to use their own judgement as to the treatment required (see also Chapter 11).

Wholesale dealing from a pharmacy

A pharmacist may supply medicines by way of wholesale dealing provided that the sales constitute no more than an inconsiderable part of the business carried on at that pharmacy [s.10(7)] (see also p. 38). This figure is generally accepted as not more than 5 per cent of the turnover in medicinal products; above that figure, a wholesale dealer's licence would be required.

If the pharmacist does not possess a wholesale dealer's licence, then the only records required to be kept are a copy of the order or invoice relating to the supply or an entry made in the Prescription Only Register by the owner of the retail pharmacy business (SI 1980 No. 1923). Orders or invoices (and all orders required as a condition in connection with any exempted sale of a Prescription Only Medicine; see Chapter 9) must be kept for two years from the date of the sale or supply.

If the pharmacist does possess a wholesale dealer's licence, then all the provisions of such a possession apply (see above).

Wholesale dealing of veterinary products

See Chapter 13.

Summary

- Normally, a person who sells medicines by way of wholesale dealing requires a wholesale dealer's licence which requires special premises, records to be kept and the appointment of a responsible person whose functions are to ensure that the conditions of the licence are being complied with and that the quality of the products is maintained in accordance with the requirements of the appropriate marketing authorisation.
- A pharmacist may supply medicines by way of wholesale dealing (e.g. to a doctor) provided the sales constitute no more than an inconsiderable part of the business carried on at that pharmacy [s.10(7)] (see also p. 38). This value is generally accepted as not more than 5 per cent of the turnover in medicinal products.

11

Medicines Act 1968
Sale and supply of homoeopathic medicines for human use

Most homoeopathic medicines for human use are subject to licensing procedures but, provided certain conditions are met, a simplified system of certification is permitted under regulations made under EC Council Directive 2001/83/EEC and 2004/27/EC (see p. 34). A further scheme for national homoeopathic medicines is also available under SI 2006 No. 1952 (see p. 35). A similar scheme is in force regarding the registration of veterinary homoeopathic medicines under EC Council Directive 2001/82/EEC as amended by SI 2005 No. 2753.

Medicinal products at high dilutions (homoeopathic medicines)

Medicinal products at high dilutions are prepared from 'unit preparations'. *Unit preparation* means 'a preparation, including a mother tincture, prepared by a process of solution, extraction or trituration with a view to being diluted tenfold or one hundredfold, either once or repeatedly, in an inert diluent, and then used either in this diluted form or, where applicable, by impregnating tablets, granules, powders or other inert substances' (SI 1997 No. 1830 as amended).

Homoeopathic medicines for human use: licensing

See p. 34.

Homoeopathic medicines for which general sale is permitted

If the seller complies with the conditions which apply to the sale or supply of products in the General Sale List (s.53) (see p. 85), then s/he may sell by retail, offer or expose for sale or supply certain medicinal products which consist of one or more unit preparations diluted to the extent specified and for the use specified, but not any Controlled Drug or product for parenteral administration (SI 1980 No. 1924).

Products for internal or external use

1   Any substance where the unit preparation has been diluted to at least one part in a million million (6c).
2   Any substance in Part II of Schedule 2 to the Pharmacy and General Sale Exemption Order (SI 1980 No. 1924), where the unit preparation has been diluted to at least one part in a million (6×). These substances are listed in Box 11.1.

Box 11.1 *Substances in Part II of Schedule 2 to SI 1980 No. 1924 where the unit preparation has been diluted to at least one part in a million (6×)*

Adonis vernalis
Agaricus bulbosus
Agaricus muscarius
Agnus castus
Ailanthus glandulosa
Alum
Amethyst
Ammonium iodide
Amygdalae amarae
Apatite
Apocynum androsaemifolium
Apocynum cannabinum
Argentite
Argentum chloride
Argentum iodide
Arnica
Artemisia cina
Aspidium anthelmintica
Aspidium filix-mas
Aurum sulphide

Balsamum copaivae
Balsamum peruvianum

Barium citrate
Barium sulphate
Bismuth metal
Bismuth subgallate
Bismuth subnitrate
Boletus laricis
Bovista

Cade oil
Calcium fluoride
Cantharis
Carduus marianus
Cedar wood oil
Cerium oxalicum
Chalcocite
Chalcopyrite
Chelidonium majus
Chenopodium oil
Colocynthis
Convallaria majalis
Copper silicate, Nat.
Crotalus horridus
Cucumis melo

Box 11.1 (continued)

Cucurbita

Datura stramonium

Derris

Diamond

Ephedra vulgaris

Ferric acetate

Ferrous iodide

Ferrous oxalate

Ferrous sulphide

Formic acid

Gall

Gelsemium sempervirens

Gneiss

Granatum (pomegranate bark)

Hamamelis virginiana

Hepar sulfuris

Hyoscyamus niger

Iris florentine

Jaborandi

Juniperus sabina

Kaolinite

Lachmanthus tinctoria

Lapis albus

Lycopodium

Magnesium

Magnesium acetate

Magnesium chloride

Magnetite

Manganese acetate

Nicotiana tabacum

Nicotiana tabacum oil

Oleander

Opuntia vulgaris

Oxalic acid

Petroleum

Phellandrum acquaticum

Pix liquida

Platinum

Platinum chloride

Potassium hydroxide

Potassium silicate

Pyrethrum

Pyrolusite

Ranunculus acris

Ranunculus bulbosus

Ranunculus flammula

Ranunculus repens

Ranunculus sceleratus

Rhodium oxynitrate

Rhododendron chrysanthemum

Rhus toxicodendron

Salicylic acid

Scrophularia aquatica

Sodium aluminium chloride

Sodium aurochloride

Sodium hypochlorite

Sodium nitrate

Squill

Stannum metal

Staphisagria

Sulphur iodide

Tamus communis

Tannic acid

Terebinthinae oleum

Theridion

Topaz

Uric acid

Zinc hypophosphite

Zinc isovalerate

3   Any substance in Table A of Schedule 2 to the General Sale List
     Order (ingredients of licences of right) (SI 1984 No. 769), where
     the unit preparation has been diluted to at least one part in
     ten (1×).
4   Any substance in Part III of Schedule 2 to the Pharmacy and General Sale
     Exemption Order (SI 1980 No. 1924), where the unit preparation has
     been diluted to at least one part in ten (1×). The substances are listed in
     Box 11.2.

Box 11.2 Substances in Part III of Schedule 2 to SI 1980 No. 1924, where
the unit preparation has been diluted to at least one part in ten (1×)

Abies excelsa	Calcium metal
Abies nigra	Calcium chloride
Abies nobilis	Calcium oxide
Acalypha indica	Calcium sulphate
Agate	Castoreum
Alisma plantago aquaticum	Ceanothus americanus
Alstonia scholaris	Cedron
Aluminium	Cerato (*Ceratostigma willmottiana*)
Amber (Succinum)	
Ambra grisea	Cherry plum (*Prunus cerasifera*)
Ammonium phosphate	
Angostura vera	Chestnut, Red and Sweet
Anthoxanthum	Cholesterinum
Apis mellifera	Chrysolite
Aqua marina	Cistus canadensis
Aqua mellis	Clematis erecta
Aralia racemosa	Conchae vera
Aranea diadema	Conchiolinum
Arum maculatum	Corallium rubrum
Arum triphyllum	Crab apple
Asarum	Crocus sativus
Asperula odorata	Erbium
Astacus fluviatilis	Erigeron canadense
Auric chloride	
Badiaga	Fuligo
Beech (*Fagus sylvestris*)	Genista tinctoria
Bellis perennis	Geum urbanum
Berberis aquifolium	Glycogen
Borago officinalis	Gnaphalium leontropodium
Butyric acid	Gold

Box 11.2 (continued)

Gorse (*Ulex europocus*)
Graphites
Gratiola officinalis
Gymnocladus (American coffee tree)

Haematoxylon campechianum
Hecla lava (Ash from Mount Hecla)
Hedeoma pulegioidies
Hedera helix
Heliotrope
Heracleum spondylium
Herniaria
Hornbeam (*Carpinus betulus*)

Iberis amara
Impatiens
Iris germanica
Iris pseudacorus

Jacaranda procera
Jatropha curcas
Juncus communis
Justicia adhatoda

Lamium album
Laurocerasus
Laurus nobilis oil
Ledum palustre
Lilium tigrinum
Lonicera caprifolium
Lysimachia vulgaris

Magnesium phosphate
Magnesite
Magnolia
Marum verum
Melilotus officinalis
Menispermum canadense
Mephitis putorius
Mercurialis perennis
Mimulus (*Mimullis guttatus*)

Moschus
Myrica gale
Myrtus communis

Ocimum basilicum
Olive
Oxalis acetosella

Pangamic acid
Paullinia cupana
Penthorum sedoides
Pollen (mixed)
Polygonatum multiflorum
Polygonum aviculare
Polypodium vulgare
Primula vulgaris
Prunella vulgaris
Ptelea trifoliata

Ratanhia
Robinia pseudoacacia
Rubia tinctorum
Rumex acetosella

Sal marina
Sarcolactic acid
Sarracenia purpurea
Scleranthus (*Scleranthus annus*)
Silica
Silphium laciniatum
Sodium benzoate
Spongia marina
Star of Bethlehem (*Ornithogalum umbellatum*)

Ulmus campestris

Vine

Walnut (*Juglerus regia*)
Water violet (*Hottonia palustris*)
Wild oat
Wild rose

Products for external use only

1 Any substance in Table B of Schedule 2 to the General Sale List Order (ingredients of licences of right) (SI 1984 No. 769) where the unit preparation has been diluted to at least one part in ten (1×).

2 Any substance in Part IV of Schedule 2 to the Pharmacy and General Sale Exemption Order (SI 1980 No. 1924), where the unit preparation has been diluted to at least one in part in ten (1×). The substances are listed in Box 11.3.

Box 11.3 *Products for external use only listed in Part IV of Schedule 2 to SI 1980 No. 1924 where the unit preparation has been diluted to at least one part in ten (1×)*

Adonis vernalis
Agaricus bulbosus
Agaricus muscarius
Agnus castus
Ailanthus glandulosa
Alum
Amethyst
Ammonium iodide
Amygdalae amarae
Apatite
Apocynum androsaemifolium
Apocynum cannabinum
Argentite
Argentum chloride
Argentum iodide
Artemisia cina
Aspidium anthelmintica
Aspidium filix-mas
Aurum sulphide
Balsamum copaivae
Balsamum peruvianum
Barium citrate
Barium sulphate
Bismuth metal
Bismuth subgallate
Bismuth subnitrite
Boletus laricus
Bovista

Cade oil
Calcium fluoride
Carduus marianus
Cedar wood oil
Cerium oxalicum
Chalcocite
Chalcopyrite
Chelidonium majus
Chenopodium oil
Colocynthis
Convallaria majalis
Copper silicate, Nat.
Crotalus horridus
Cucumis melo
Cucurbita
Datura stramonium
Derris
Diamond
Ephedra vulgaris
Ferric acetate
Ferrous iodide
Ferrous oxalate
Ferrous sulphide
Formic acid
Gall
Gelsemium sempervirens
Gneiss

Box 11.3 (continued)

Hamamelis virginiana
Hepar sulfuris
Hyoscyamus niger

Iris florentine

Jaborandi
Juniperus sabina

Kaolinite

Lachmanthus tinctoria
Lapis albus
Lycopodium

Magnesium
Magnesium acetate
Magnesium chloride
Magnetite
Manganese acetate

Nicotiana tabacum
Nicotiana tabacum oil

Oleander
Opuntia vulgaris
Oxalic acid

Petroleum
Phellandrium aquaticum
Pix liquida
Platinum
Platinum chloride
Potassium hydroxide

Potassium silicate
Pyrethrum
Pyrolusite

Ranunculus acris
Ranunculus bulbosus
Ranunculus flammula
Ranunculus repens
Ranunculus sceleratus
Rhodium oxynitrate
Rhododendron chrysanthemum
Rhus toxicodendron

Salicylic acid
Scrophularia aquatica
Sodium aluminium chloride
Sodium auro-chloride
Sodium hypochlorite
Sodium nitrate
Squill
Stannum metal
Sulphur iodide

Tannic acid
Terebinthinae oleum
Topaz

Uric acid

Zinc hypophosphite
Zinc isovalerate

Homoeopathic medicines for treatment according to the judgement of the seller

If the person selling the product is requested by or on behalf of a particular person and in that person's presence to use their own judgement as to the treatment required then they may sell by retail, offer or expose for sale or supply certain medicinal products (other than excluded products) which are registered or consist solely of one or more unit preparations diluted to the extent specified and for the use specified. The substances to which this exemption applies and which are subject to section 53 of the Act (see p. 85) are listed below.

Products for internal or external use

1 Any substance, where the unit preparation has been diluted to at least one part in a million (6×).

2 Any substance listed in Part I of Schedule 2 to the Pharmacy and General Sale Exemption Order (SI 1980 No. 1924) where the unit preparation has been diluted to at least one part in a thousand (3×). The substances are listed in Box 11.4.

3 Any substance in Table A of Schedule 2 to the General Sale List Order (SI 1984 No. 769) (ingredients of licence of right products), where the unit preparation has been diluted to at least one part in ten (1×).

4 Any substance in Part III of Schedule 2 to the Pharmacy and General Sale Exemptions Order (SI 1980 No. 1924), where the unit preparation has been diluted to at least one part in ten (1×). The substances are listed in Boxes 11.1, 11.2 and 11.3.

5 Any **registered** homoeopathic medicinal product for human use other than an excluded product (SI 1998 No. 2368).

Excluded products include Controlled Drugs, Prescription Only Medicines and any in a class specified in Schedule 3 of the main order (SI 1984 No. 769), that is, medicines for use as anthelmintics, for parenteral administration or for use as eye drops or eye ointments.

Box 11.4 *Substances listed in Part I of Schedule 2 to SI 1980 No. 1924, where the unit preparation has been diluted to at least one part in a thousand (3×)*

Agaricus muscarius	Cina
Ailanthus glandulosa	Colocynthis
Apocynum cannabinum	Convallaria majalis
Aurum iodatum	
	Gelsemium sempervirens
Belladonna	
Bismuth subgallate	Hyoscyamus niger
Bryonia alba dioica	
	Lycopodium
Calcium fluoride	
Cantharis	Manganese acetate
Cerium oxalicum	
Chelidonium majus	Ranunculus bulbosus
Chenopodium oil	
	Terebinthinae oleum

Products for external use only

The substances and unit dilutions for external use are the same as those for homoeopathic medicines for which general sale is permitted.

Summary

- Most homoeopathic medicines are on the General Sale List and may be sold from any retail shop which is closable to the public.
- Certain listed homoeopathic medicines may be sold if the seller is requested by a customer to use the seller's own judgement as to the treatment required. There are certain excluded categories.

Further reading

MHRA. *MAL Advisory Leaflets*. London: Medicines and Healthcare Regulatory Authority.

12

Medicines Act 1968
Herbal medicines

In March 2004, the European Community issued a Directive on Traditional Herbal Medicinal Products (2004/24/EC), which amended Council Directive 2001/83/EC as far as herbals products were concerned. The provisions of the Directives were implemented in the UK on 30 October 2005 by means of The Medicines (Traditional Herbal Medicinal Products for Human Use) Regulations 2005 (SI 2005 No. 2750).

A Herbal Medicines Advisory Committee has been established (SI 2005 No. 2791) to give advice:

1 with respect to safety, quality and efficacy in relation to human use of herbal medicinal products, other than any product:
   a in respect of which a marketing authorisation, product licence or certificate of registration has been granted; or
   b which is the subject of an application for such an authorisation, licence or certificate;
2 with respect to safety, quality and efficacy in relation to human use of any herbal medicinal product:
   a in respect of which a marketing authorisation, product licence of certificate of registration has been granted; or
   b which is the subject of an application for such an authorisation, licence or certificate where the Health Minister or the licensing authority request such advice or provide the committee with information relating to that product;
   c in relation to the sale, supply, manufacture or assembly of medicinal products under section 12 of the Act, which provides exemptions from the requirements to have a product, manufacturing or wholesale dealing licences for herbal remedies which are sold under consultation, and for remedies which are not industrially produced and are sold without any written recommendations for their use.

A traditional herbal medicinal product means a herbal medicinal product that fulfils the conditions laid down in Article 16a(1) of Directive 2004/27EC. The conditions laid down are that a simplified registration procedure is established for the product (see p. 35) which fulfils the following criteria. The product:

1   has indications exclusively appropriate to traditional herbal medicinal products which, by virtue of its composition and purpose, is intended and designed for use without the supervision of a medical practitioner for diagnostic purposes or for prescription or monitoring of treatment;
2   is exclusively for administration in accordance with a specified strength and posology;
3   is an oral, external and/or an inhalation preparation;
4   has a period of traditional use which has elapsed; the period of traditional use is 30 years, including 15 years within the European Community, preceeding the date of application for registration;
5   has data on the traditional use sufficient to prove that the product is not harmful in the specified conditions of use and the pharmacological effects or efficacy of the product are plausible on the basis of long-standing use and experience.

Subject to several exceptions, no traditional herbal medicinal products may be placed on the market or distributed by way of wholesale dealing unless a traditional herbal registration in respect of the product has been granted.

A *traditional herbal registration* means a registration by the licensing authority in accordance with the regulations (SI 2005 No. 2750) (see p. 35).

Exception from registration

The regulations regarding registration (see p. 35) do not apply to a traditional herbal medicinal product under the following conditions.

1   It is supplied in response to a bona fide unsolicited order formulated in accordance with the specification of a doctor, dentist or supplementary prescriber and for use by his/her individual patients on his/her direct responsibility. However the supply is subject to the following conditions, namely the supply is made to a doctor, dentist or supplementary prescriber or for use in a registered pharmacy, a hospital or health centre under the supervision of a pharmacist. There must be no advertising of any sort to the public; the manufacture must be undertaken under the supervision of such staff and such precautions to ensure that the product is of the character required by the specification, subject to a manufacturer's licence, and written records of the manufacture must be kept.

2   It is prepared by a doctor or to his/her order for administration to one of his/her patients or other patients in a doctors' group practice and consists of procuring the manufacture of a stock of the product.

3   It is prepared in a pharmacy, a hospital or health centre and is done there under the supervision of a pharmacist and consists of procuring the manufacture of a stock of the product with a view to dispensing it against a prescription given by a doctor, dentist or supplementary prescriber.

4   It is sold or supplied to a person exclusively for use by him/her in the course of a business carried on by him/her for the purposes of being administered or causing it to be administered to one or more human beings otherwise than by selling it. The product must be prepared by or under the supervision of a pharmacist and manufactured by the holder of a manufacturer's licence.

All persons who sell or supply traditional herbal medicinal products in accordance with the exceptions 1 to 4 above must maintain and keep records for a period of 5 years. S/he must also notify the licensing authority of any suspected adverse reaction which is a serious reaction and make available for inspection at all reasonable times the records kept. The records must show:

a   the source from which the person obtained the product;
b   the person to whom, and the date on which, the sale or supply was made;
c   the quantity of each sale or supply;
d   the batch number of the batch of the product from which the sale or supply was made; and
e   details of any suspected adverse reaction to the product so sold or supplied of which s/he is aware.

Labelling of dispensed traditional herbal medicinal products

Dispensed traditional herbal medicinal products means a traditional herbal medicinal product prepared or dispensed in accordance with a prescription given by a practitioner. Where such a product is dispensed, the container of that product must be labelled to show the following particulars:

1   the name of the person to whom the product is to be administered;
2   the name and address of the person who sells or supplies the product;
3   the date of dispensing;
4   where prescribed by a practitioner:
    a   the name of the product or its common name;
    b   the directions for use; and
    c   any precautions relating to its use;
    d   where a pharmacist, in the exercise of his/her professional skill and judgement, is of the opinion that any of such particulars are

inappropriate and has taken steps as in all the circumstances are reasonably practical to consult with the practitioner but has been unable to do so, particulars of the same kind as those requested by the practitioner as appear to the pharmacist to be appropriate.

Where the container of a dispensed product is enclosed in a package immediately enclosing the container the particulars set out in 1–4 above may be omitted from the container if that package is labelled to show those particulars.

Where a number of containers or packages of such products all of the same description are enclosed in a package, item 4 above shall be deemed to have been complied with if such particulars are shown on either one or more such containers or packages as the case may be.

Traditional herbal medicinal products not on a General Sale List

Such traditional herbal medicinal products not on a General Sale List must be labelled to show the capital letter 'P' within a rectangle within which there is no other matter of any kind.

Exemptions from labelling

1 Any package in the form of a transparent wrapping or cover provided the container is labelled and clearly visible.
2 Any package in the form of wrapping paper, paper bag or similar covering need not be labelled provided the enclosed container is labelled accordingly.
3 Any container which is for export.
4 Any container which is an ampoule or other container of not more than 10 mL normal capacity which is enclosed in a package which is labelled accordingly.
5 Any package in the form of a wrapper consisting of paper, plastic, metal foil, or other strip material or in the form of a bubble enclosing one or more dosage units and such a container is enclosed in a package which is labelled accordingly.
6 Packages in themselves in the form of a bubble or blister, or a sheet or strip of like packages, and required to be labelled 'P', the requirement shall be met if the letter is displayed at frequent intervals on the strip or sheet.

Transitional provisions

The provisions of the above regulations do not apply until 30 April 2011 to herbal medicinal products which were on the market in the UK on 30 April 2004 without a marketing authorisation.

Under the present law, a *herbal remedy* is a medicinal product consisting of a substance produced by subjecting a plant or plants to drying, crushing or any other process, or of a mixture whose sole ingredients are two or more substances so produced, or of a mixture whose sole ingredients are one or more substances so produced and water or some other inert substance (s.132).

Exemption from licensing

Subject to the limitations described in this chapter, herbal remedies are exempted from licensing requirements by section 12 of the Act, which describes remedies of two classes:

1   Any herbal remedy which is manufactured or assembled on premises of which the person carrying on the business is the occupier and which s/he is able to close so as to exclude the public, and the person carrying on the business sells or supplies the remedy for administration to a particular person after being requested by or on behalf of that person and in that person's presence to use his/her own judgement as to the treatment required.

For convenience these can be described as 'herbal practitioner's remedies', although that term is not used in the statute.

2   Any herbal remedy where the process to which the plant or plants are subjected in producing the remedy consists only of drying, crushing or comminuting, and the remedy is, or is to be, sold or supplied:
    a   under a designation which only specifies the plant or plants and the process and does not apply any other name to the remedy; and
    b   without any written recommendation (whether by means of a labelled container or package or a leaflet or in any other way) as to the use of the remedy (see also p. 45).

Exemptions from controls on retail sale

There is an exemption for herbal remedies in section 56 of the Act from the restrictions on retail sale and supply of medicinal products in sections 52 and 53 (see Chapters 6 and 7). The exemption, which extends to both classes 1 and 2 described above, applies to anything done at premises of which the person carrying on the business in question is the occupier and which s/he is able to close so as to exclude the public (s.56).

This general exemption is modified by the Herbal Remedies Order (SI 1977 No. 2130) so that there is no exemption (except as below) from the restriction on retail sale or supply for herbal remedies:

1   that are not on the General Sale List;
2   that are not exempted from licensing as in 2 above; or

3 that are exempted from licensing as in 2 above but contain one or more of the substances listed in Part I or Part II of the Schedule to the Herbal Remedies Order (see Exemption of 'herbal practitioners', below).

The effect of this is that any shopkeeper can sell:

a any herbal remedy on the General Sale List; or
b any herbal remedy which is exempted from licensing as in 1 above, except those in Part I and Part II of the Schedule.

Further exemption for shopkeepers

The order further modifies the controls on retail sale so that any person can, subject to certain conditions, sell or supply by retail any herbal remedy included under 1, 2 or 3 above where the process to which the plant or plants are subjected consists of drying, crushing or comminuting with or without any subsequent process of tabletting, pill-making, compressing or diluting with water but not any other process.

The conditions are that:

4 the herbal remedy does not contain a substance listed in Part I or Part II of the Schedule (see below);
5 the seller (or supplier) of the herbal remedy either:
 a has notified the enforcement authority in the UK in writing that s/he is selling or supplying or intending to sell or supply herbal remedies included in 1, 2 or 3 in the section above, which are prepared by the limited processes described in the opening paragraph of this chapter; or
 b has a manufacturer's licence granted under Part II of the Act in respect of that remedy.

Exemption of 'herbal practitioners'

In addition to the exemptions already described, SI 1977 No. 2130 provides further exemptions for herbal remedies, prepared by any process, from the controls on retail sale or supply provided:

1 the herbal remedy concerned does not contain:
 a any substance included in Part I of the Schedule to the order; or
 b any substance in Part III of the order, except for internal remedies, when sold or supplied in or from containers or packages labelled to show a dosage not exceeding that specified, or for external remedies, when sold or supplied with the strength of the substance not exceeding the percentage specified;

2   the person selling or supplying the herbal remedy (a herbal practitioner):

   a   has been requested by or on behalf of a particular person and in that person's presence to use his/her own judgement as to the treatment required; and

   b   has notified the enforcement authority in writing that s/he is selling or supplying or intends to sell or supply from the premises specified in the notice herbal remedies as in 1, 2 or 3 in the section above on Exemptions from Controls on Retail Sale.

A person (*herbal practitioner*) selling or supplying herbal remedies to which the exemption described in this section applies may be required to furnish to the enforcement authority a list of the substances contained in those herbal remedies. The exemption will not apply if the herbal practitioner fails to furnish the list within the time specified in the notice served upon him/her by the enforcement authority.

Enforcement authority

The term *enforcement authority* includes the Secretaries of State and the Royal Pharmaceutical Society of Great Britain (RPSGB).

Schedule to the Herbal Remedies Order

The Schedule to the Medicines (Retail Sale or Supply of Herbal Remedies) Order 1977 (SI 1977 No. 2130) is in three parts, reflecting the different degrees of control over the retail sale or supply of the substances in each part.

Part I

The substances in this part (Table 12.1) may only be sold by retail at registered pharmacies and by or under the supervision of a pharmacist.

Part II

The list of substances in this part is the same as that in Part III. They may only be sold by retail from registered pharmacies and by or under the supervision of a pharmacist except when the conditions under Part III are met (see below).

Part III

Persons who comply with the requirements set out on page 152 (commonly known as *herbal practitioners*) can sell or supply by retail herbal remedies containing any of the substances listed in Table 12.2 subject to the maximum dosages and strengths indicated.

Table 12.1 Substances in Part I of the Schedule to SI 1977 No. 2130

Common name	Botanical name
Areca	Areca catechu
Canadian hemp	Apocynum cannabinum
Catha	Catha edulis
Chenopodium	Chenopodium ambrosioides var. anthelminticum
Crotalaria fulva	Crotalaria berberoana
Crotalaria spect.	Crotalaria spectabilis
Cucurbita	Cucurbita maxima
Duboisia	Duboisia leichardtii, D. myoporoides
Elaterium	Ecballium elaterium
Embelia	Embelia ribes, E. robusta
Erysimum	Erysimum canescens
Holarrhena	Holarrhena antidysenterica
Kamala	Mallotus philippinensis
Kousso	Brayera anthelmintica
Male fern	Dryopteris filix mas
Mistletoe berry	Viscum album
Poison ivy	Rhus radicans
Pomegranate bark	Punica granatum
Santonica	Artemisia cina
Savin	Juniperus sabina
Scopolia	Scopolia carniolica, Scopolia japonica
Stavesacre seeds	Delphinium staphisagria
Strophanthus	Strophanthus courmonti, S. emini, S. gratus, S. hispidus, S. kombe, S. nicholsoni, S. sarmentosus
Slippery elm bark (whole or unpowdered)	Ulmus fulva, U. rubra
Yohimbe bark	Pausinystalia yohimbe

Table 12.2 Substances in Part III of the Schedule to SI 1977 No. 2130

Common name	Column 1 Substance/botanical name	Column 2 Maximum dose (md) and maximum daily dose (mdd)	Column 3 Percentage
Aconite	Aconitum balrourii		
	Aconitum chasmanthum		
	Aconitum deinorrhizum		
	Aconitum lycoctonum		
	Aconitum napellus		
	Aconitum spicatum		
	Aconitum stoerkianum		
	Aconitum uncinatum var. japonicum		1.3%
Adoni vernalis	Adonis vernalis	100 mg (md)	
		300 mg (mdd)	
Belladonna herb	Atropa acuminata	150 mg (mdd)	
	Atropa belladonna	50 mg (md)	
Belladonna root	Atropa acuminata	90 mg (mdd)	
	Atropa belladonna	30 mg (md)	
Celandine	Chelidonium majus	2 g (md)	
		6 g (mdd)	
Cinchona bark	Cinchona calisaya	250 mg (md)	
	Cinchona ledgerana	750 mg (mdd)	
	Cinchona micrantha		
	Cinchona officinalis		
	Cinchona succirubra		
Colchicum corm	Colchicum autimnale	100 mg (md)	

(continued overleaf)

Table 12.2 *(continued)*

		300 mg (mdd)	
Conium leaf	*Conium maculatum*		7%
Conium fruits	*Conium maculatum*		7%
Convallaria	*Convallaria majalis*	150 mg (md)	
		450 mg (mdd)	
Ephedra	*Ephedra distachya*		
	Ephedra equisetina		
	Ephedra gerardiana	1800 mg (mdd)	
	Ephedra sinica		
Gelsemium	*Gelsemium sempervirens*	25 mg (md)	
		75 mg (mdd)	
Hyoscyamus	*Hyoscyamus albus*	300 mg (mdd)	
	Hyoscyamus muticus		
	Hyoscyamus niger	100 mg (md)	
Jaborandi	*Pilocarpus jaborandi*		5%
	Pilocarpus microphyllus		
Lobelia	*Lobelia inflata*	200 mg (md)	
		600 mg (mdd)	
Poison Oak	*Rhus toxicodendron*		10%
Quebracho	*Aspidosperma quebrachoblanco*	50 mg (md)	
		150 mg (mdd)	
Ragwort	*Senecio jacobaea*		10%
Stramonium	*Datura innoxia*	150 mg (mdd)	
	Datura stramonium	50 mg (md)	

Banned herbal remedies

Aristolochia

The various forms of *Aristolochia* were made Prescription Only Medicines on 13 January 1997. Since then the sale, supply and importation of medicinal products consisting or containing a plant belonging to the species of the genus *Aristolochia* or belonging to any of the species *Akebia quinata*, *Akebia trifoliata*, *Clematis armandi*, *Clematis montana*, *Cocculus laurifolius*, *Cocculus orbiculatus*, *Cocculus trilobus* and *Stephania tetrandra*, or consisting of or containing an extract from such a plant, are prohibited. The ban was extended in SI 2001 No. 1841.

The prohibition relating to *Aristolochia* does not apply to the importation from an EEA state if the product originates in a EEA state or originates from outside the EEA but is in free circulation in member states and is being, or is to be exported to a third country or to an EEA state other than the UK (SI 2008 No. 548), or possesses a traditional herbal registration (SI 2005 No. 2750).

Mu Tong and Fangji

The sale, supply and importation of medicinal products is prohibited where, at the time of the sale, supply or importation, the label on the container or package, or any document accompanying the product indicates in any language that the product consists of or contains Mu Tong or Fangji or that the product consists of or contains *Akebia quinata*, *Akebia trifoliata*, *Clematis armandi*, *Clematis montana*, *Cocculus laurifolius*, *Cocculus orbiculatus*, *Cocculus trilobus* and *Stephania tetrandra*, or an extract from such a plant.

The prohibition relating to Mu Tong and Fangii does not apply to the importation from an EEA state if the product originates in a EEA state or originates from outside the EEA but is in free circulation in member states and is being, or is to be, exported to a third country or to an EEA state other than the UK (SI 2008 No. 548), or possesses a traditional herbal registration (SI 2005 No. 2750).

Kava-kava

The sale, supply and importation of any medicinal product for human use which consists or contains a plant or part of a plant belonging to the species *Piper methysticum* (known as kava-kava) or an extract from such a plant is prohibited.

The prohibition relating to *Piper methysticum* does not apply to the importation from an EEA state if the product originates in a EEA state or originates from outside the EEA but is in free circulation in member states and is being, or is to be, exported to a third country or to an EEA state other than the UK (SI 2008 No. 548), or possesses a traditional herbal registration (SI 2005 No. 2750).

Senecio

This sale, supply and importation of any medicinal product for human use which consists or contains a plant belonging to the species *Senecio* or an extract from such a plant is prohibited.

The prohibition relating to *Senecio* does not apply where the product is:

a   for external use only and not a teething preparation, throat spray or pastilles, throat lozenge or tablet, nasal spray, inhalation or drops;

b   sold or supplied to public analyst, a sampling officer, an enforcement officer or a food safety officer;

c   imported from an EEA state if the product originates in a EEA state or originates from outside the EEA but is in free circulation in member states and is being, or is to be, exported to a third country or to an EEA state other than the UK;

d   the subject of a product licence, a marketing authorisation, a certificate of registration as a homoeopathic substance or a traditional herbal registration (SI 2008 No. 548).

Summary

- There is a Herbal Medicines Advisory Committee established to deal with the safety and quality of herbal products other than products which possess a marketing authorisation, product licence or certificate of registration.
- Ordinary shopkeepers can sell herbal remedies on the General Sale List and herbal remedies which are merely dried, crushed or comminuted without any written recommendation, but this excludes those in the Schedule to the Herbal Remedies Order.
- Shopkeepers who have a manufacturer's licence, or choose to notify the enforcement authority, can sell dried, crushed and comminuted herbs which have also been subjected to certain other limited processes, but not those in the Schedule to the Herbal Remedies Order.
- Herbal practitioners can sell herbal remedies of the kind described above which shopkeepers can sell and also those remedies containing substances in and subject to the requirements of Part III of the Schedule to the Herbal Remedies Order.
- Herbal remedies containing substances in Part I or Part II of the Schedule to the Herbal Remedies Order may only be sold from pharmacies.

- There is a simple registration procedure established for traditional herbal medicinal products.
- Certain herbals have been banned, e.g. *Aristolochia*, Mu Tong, Fangji, *Piper methysticum* (kava-kava) and *Senecio*.

Further reading

Barnes J, Anderson LA, Phillipson JD (2007) *Herbal Medicines 3rd edn.* London: Pharmaceutical Press.

13

Veterinary medicinal products

The earlier Veterinary Medicines Regulations have had all their provisions relating to veterinary medicinal products under the Medicines Act 1968 replaced by annual Veterinary Regulations. The current ones being the Veterinary Medicines Regulations 2008 (SI 2008 No. 2297). The Department of Environment, Food and Rural Affairs (DEFRA) proposes to update these regulations annually. There is a Veterinary Products Committee which provides scientific advice on any aspect of veterinary medicinal products requested by the Secretary of State or DEFRA and will carry out functions specified in these Veterinary Regulations. The following provisions now apply.

Annual Veterinary Regulations

A *veterinary medicinal product* means:

1   any substance or combination of substances presented as having properties for treating or preventing disease in animals; or
2   any substances or combination of substances which may be used in, or administered to, animals with a view to restoring, correcting or modifying physiological functions by exerting a pharmacological, immunological or metabolic action or by making a medical diagnosis (Directive 2001/82/EC amended by Directive 2004/28/EC, together known as the 'amending directive').

In addition:

3   'animal' means all animals, other than man, and includes birds, reptiles, fish, molluscs, crustacea and bees';
4   'horse' means all species of Equidae and a horse is a food-producing animal unless it has been declared not intended for slaughter for human consumption in accordance with various 'passport' regulations.

Offences

It is an offence:

1   to place a veterinary medicinal product upon the market unless that product has a marketing authorisation granted by the Secretary of State;

2   to administer a veterinary medicinal products to an animal unless;

   a   the product has a marketing authorisation authorising its administration in the UK; and

   b   it is administered in accordance with Schedule 4 to the Regulations;

3   to supply a veterinary medicinal product that has passed its expiry date;

4   to supply a medicinal product authorised for human use for administration to an animal other than in accordance with a prescription given by a veterinary surgeon for administration under the cascade (see below).

The Veterinary Regulations do not apply to:

1   inactivated immunological veterinary medicinal products that are manufactured from pathogens or antigens obtained from an animal and used for the treatment of that animal or other animals on the same site; and

2   veterinary medicinal products based on radioactive isotopes.

As with human medicines, there are three types of marketing authorisation systems, centralised, decentralised and national, with full data being required. The centralised procedure is obligatory for high-technology products and growth promoters (as defined in EU Regulation 726/2004) and is optional for other innovatory veterinary medicines. The decentralised scheme is available where the applicant wishes to license a product for more than one state, and the national scheme where registration is only required in one state. An application for a marketing authorisation for a medicinal product for animal use in any of the procedures must be accompanied by the particulars set out in Council Directive 2001/82/EEC and are similar to those for human medicines. The Committee for Veterinary Medicinal Products, established under Council Directive, gives advice to the Commission and to the national authorities.

Registration certificates for homoeopathic veterinary medicinal products

No person may market a veterinary homoeopathic medicine for animals unless the product is registered in accordance with the provisions of EC Council Directive 2001/83/EC. Regulations set out a simplified procedure for veterinary homoeopathic products similar to that for human medicines (SI 2005 No. 2745).

Council Regulation 2377/90/EEC lays down the procedures for the evaluation of the safety of residues and the establishment of maximum residue limits (MRLs) in foodstuffs. Provisions for the renewal of applications are set out in SI 1994 No. 3142.

Standard conditions for marketing authorisations are prescribed in the relevant EC directives. These provisions are incorporated in the marketing authorisation unless the applicant desires that any of them shall be excluded or modified in respect of his/her product and his/her request is granted.

Classes of veterinary medicinal product

All veterinary medicinal products, fall into one of three categories, namely:

1 those on a General Sale List;
2 those on a Prescription Only List, POM-V or POM-VS; and
3 those medicines for non-food producing animals (e.g. pets) (NFA-VPS).

In the regulations, there are four classes of veterinary medicinal products together with authorised suppliers namely:

POM-V: Prescription Only Medicines prescribed by a veterinarian;
POM-VPS: Prescription Only Medicines prescribed by a veterinarian, pharmacist or suitably qualified person (SQP);
NFA-VPS: non-food animal medicines prescribed by a veterinarian, pharmacist or SQP;
AVM-GSL: Authorised Veterinary Medicines on the General Sale list.

Records of prescriptions must be kept for five years and retailers will have to audit stock annually.

Wholesale supply of veterinary medicinal products

1 Only a holder of a marketing authorisation, the holder of a manufacturing authorisation or the holder of a wholesale dealers authorisation may supply veterinary medicinal product by wholesale or be in possess of it for that purpose.
2 They may only supply to a person who may supply veterinary medicinal products either by wholesale or retail.
3 If supply is made to SQPs, the supply must be made to them on that person's approved premises.
4 A wholesale dealer may break open any package (other than the immediate package of a veterinary product).
5 It is irrelevant whether or not the supply is for profit.

6   This last paragraph does not apply if a retailer supplies another retailer and the amount supplied does not exceed five per cent of the turnover of the supplying retailer.

Retail supply of veterinary medicinal products

Retail supply means any supply other than to or from the holder of a wholesale authorisation and whether or not for payment.

1   POM-V products may only be supplied by a veterinary surgeon or a pharmacist and must be supplied in accordance with a prescription from a veterinary surgeon.
2   POM-VPS products may only be supplied by a veterinarian, pharmacist or a SQP and must be in accordance with a prescription from one of those persons.
3   NFA-VPS products may be supplied without a prescription but may only be supplied if prescribed by a veterinarian, a pharmacist or a SQP.
4   AVM-GSL products have no supply restrictions.

Any person supplying in accordance with 1–4 above must:

a   advise on the safe administration of the product;
b   advise as necessary any warnings or contraindications on the label or package to allow the product;
c   be satisfied that the person who will use the product is competent to use it safely and intends to use it for a use for which it was intended.

Prescription Only Medicines for animal use

Prescription Only medicinal products for animal use are listed in SI 1991 No. 1392. They are:

1   Those veterinary medicinal products containing one or more substances listed in Part I of Schedule 1 to the Order. Maximum strengths are shown in the Schedule for certain substances. A veterinary medicinal product containing such a substance at or below the maximum strength and complying with any other specification in the Schedule as to use, pharmaceutical form or route of administration is not a Prescription Only Medicine.
2   Veterinary medicinal products that are Controlled Drugs.
3   Veterinary medicinal products for parenteral administration. But any parenteral preparation which contains a substance in Schedule 2 to the Order is not a Prescription Only Medicine provided that substance does not exceed any specified maximum strength and the preparation is sold or supplied for the purpose stated in the Schedule. These are:

- lidocaine
- lidocaine hydrochloride
- procaine hydrochloride.

4 Medicinal products which are veterinary medicinal products by reason of their having been sold or supplied for the administration to animals and which prior to such sale or supply were Prescription Only Medicines as defined in the Prescription Only Medicines (Human Use) Order (SI 1997 No. 1830).

Prescription requirements

A veterinary surgeon who prescribes a veterinary medicinal product classified as POM-V must first carry out a clinical assessment of the animal and the animal must be under his/her care; failure to do so is an offence. It is an offence to prescribe more than the minimum amount of the product required for the treatment.

A prescription may be oral or written but if classified as POM-V or POM-VPS, it may only be supplied by the person who has prescribed it under a written prescription that complies with the conditions below or in the case of POM-VPS a SQP under certain conditions (see p. 167).

The person supplying the product may only supply the product specified on the prescription, must ensure the supply is only made to the person named on the prescription and must take reasonable steps to ensure that the prescription has been written and signed by a person entitled to prescribe it.

A written prescription must be in ink or other indelible format and must include:

a the name, address, and telephone number of the person prescribing the product;
b the qualifications enabling the person to prescribe the product;
c the name and address of the owner or keeper;
d the identity (including the species) of the animal or group of animals;
e the premises at which the animals are kept if this is different from the address of the owner or keeper;
f the date of the prescription;
g the signature or other authentication of the person prescribing the product;
h the name and amount of the product prescribed;
i the dosage and administration instructions;
j any necessary warnings;
k the withdrawal period if relevant; and
l if it is prescribed under the cascade, a statement to that effect.

A prescription for a Controlled Drug is valid for 28 days and for any other drug is valid for six months. If the prescription is a repeatable one that does not specify the number of times the product may be supplied, the prescription may only be repeated once.

The cascade

If there is no authorised veterinary product in the UK for a condition, the veterinary surgeon responsible for the animal may, to avoid unacceptable suffering, treat the animal concerned under the following cascade in the following order:

1 a veterinary product authorised in the UK for use with another animal species or for another condition in the same species; or
2 if and only if there is no such product that is suitable, either
  a a medicinal product authorised in the UK for human use; or
  b a veterinary product not authorised in the UK but authorised in another member state of the EC for use with any animal species (if for food-producing animal must be for a food-producing species; or
3 if and only if there is no such product that is suitable, a veterinary product prepared extemporaneously by a pharmacist, a veterinary surgeon or a person holding manufacturing authorisation authorising the manufacture of that type of product.

A veterinary medicinal product for use under the cascade must be prescribed by a veterinary surgeon and may only be supplied by a veterinary surgeon or a pharmacist.

Unless the veterinary surgeon supplies, and administers it to the animal himself, the person supplying must label the product with the following information:

1 the name and address of the pharmacy or veterinary surgery supplying the product;
2 the name of the veterinary surgeon who prescribed it;
3 the name and address of the animal owner;
4 the identification of the animal or group of animals;
5 the date of supply;
6 the expiry date of the product, if applicable;
7 the name or description of the product, which should include at least the name and quantity of the active ingredients;
8 the dosage and administration instructions;
9 any special storage precautions;
10 any necessary warnings for the user, target species, administration or disposal of the product;

11   the identity (including the species) of the animal or group of animals;
12   the withdrawal period, if relevant; and
13   the words 'Keep out of reach of children' and 'For animal treatment only'.

Supply by veterinary surgeons

A veterinary surgeon supplying veterinary products (other than AVM-GSL) must be present when the product is handed over unless s/he authorises each transaction individually before the product is supplied and s/he is satisfied that the person handing it over is competent to do so. A veterinary surgeon may open any package containing a veterinary product,

A veterinary surgeon who supplies veterinary products from any practice premises not registered with the Royal College of Veterinary Surgeons under these regulations as a veterinary practice where veterinary medicines are stored or supplied is guilty of an offence. This provision came into effect as and from 1 April 2009.

Supply by pharmacists

A pharmacist may only supply a veterinary product which is classified POM-V, POM-VPS or NFA-VPS from premises registered as a pharmacy. From 1 April 2009, a pharmacist may also supply veterinary products from a registered veterinary practice premises.

In the case of products classified as POM-VPS or NFA-VPS supplied from premises registered as a listed merchant, a pharmacist may:

- supply veterinary product prepared in a pharmacy in accordance with the prescriptions of a pharmacopoeia and supplied to the end use;
- supply a homoeopathic remedy prepared extemporaneously in a pharmacy provided it is supplied to the end-user; and
- can break open any package containing a veterinary medicinal product other than the immediate package.

A pharmacist supplying veterinary products (except AVM-GSL) must be present when the product is handed over unless s/he authorises each transaction individually and is satisfied that the person handing over the product is competent so to do.

Supply by suitably qualified persons

A *suitably qualified person* (SQP) is a person who has passed an examination approved by a body and is registered with such a body by the Secretary of State. Such a body is the Animal Medicines Training Regulatory Authority.

The Secretary of State must be satisfied that the body:

1 has in place a system for ensuring that the person applying for registration has had adequate training as an SQP registration;
2 has adequate standards in deciding whether to register a SQP;
3 maintains a programme of continuing professional development; and
4 operates an adequate appeal system if it intends to register a person as an SQP.

The supply of veterinary products permitted to be supplied by a suitably qualified person must take place from premises approved by the Secretary of State as being suitable for the storage and supply of such products and the suitably qualified person must be present at each supply of such products. An SQP can supply from a registered pharmacy or, from 1st April 2009, from a registered veterinary practice premises. A SQP may break open any package (other than an immediate package) containing a veterinary product.

The SQP who supplies POM-VPS or NFA-VPS products must:

a hand over or dispatch the product personally;
b ensure that when the product is handed over or dispatched s/he is in a position to intervene; or
c check that the product allocated for supply is in conformity with a prescription and satisfy himself/herself that the person handing over the product is competent so to do.

The list of registered suitably qualified persons and the premises approved for sales by the Secretary of State is available on the DEFRA website (see p. 176).

The Secretary of State has the power to remove the approval of SQP premises. An SQP who considers that his/her registered premises no longer complies with its approval conditions must notify the Secretary of State or else s/he commits an offence under the regulations.

Code of good practice

The Secretary of State has issued a Code of Practice for suitable qualified persons and has recognised the Animal Medicines Training Regulatory Authority, whose duty it is to ensure that SQPs registered with it comply with that Code of Practice. The Code of Practice sets out the standards which SQPs are expected to meet and supplements the principal legal requirements with other provisions relating to personnel, sale and storage arrangements and standards of premises. The Code is available on the DFRA website (see p. 176).

Records of receipt and supply for Prescription Only veterinary products

Any veterinary surgeon, pharmacists or SQP who sells or receives veterinary medicinal products by retail intended for administration to animals whose flesh or products are intended for human consumption (POM-V and POM-VPS) and/or in respect of which a withdrawal period must be observed must keep a record.

Similarly any person who sells any other veterinary medicinal products by retail intended for administration to such animals, unless the products are on a General Sale List must keep records.

For each incoming and outgoing transaction a record must be kept of the:

1 date of transaction;
2 identity of the product;
3 the batch number (except that, in the case of a product for a non-food-producing animal, this need only be recorded on the date s/he receives the batch or the date s/he starts to use it);
4 quantity;
5 name and address of supplier or recipient; and
6 if there is a written prescription, the name and address of the person who wrote the the prescription and a copy of the prescription.

When s/he starts to use the product, s/he must record the batch number and the date. All records must be durable but may be kept by electronic means. They must be kept for five years and be made available on request to any person having a duty of enforcement.

Records and storage by wholesalers

A registered wholesaler must keep detailed records of all incoming and out-going sales including disposal for at least three years. These must include the:

1 date and nature of the transaction;
2 identity of the product;
3 manufacturer's batch number;
4 expiry date;
5 quantity;
6 name and address of supplier or recipient.

The wholesale premises must be weatherproof, secure and lockable; clean; and free from contaminants. The holder of the authorisation must have the services of technically competent staff and an effective recall system The authorisation, which may cover more than one site, must list the type of products dealt with, where they are stored, the name and address of the person holding the authorisation, the address of the premises and the name of the qualified person under the Guide to Good Distribution Practice.

Annual audit

At least once a year, every person entitled to supply veterinary products on prescription must carry out a detailed audit and incoming and outgoing products must be reconciled with products currently held stock, any discrepancies being recorded.

Veterinary products on the General Sale List

The medicinal products permitted for general sale as veterinary medicines are set out in Schedule 1 to SI 1984 No. 768 as follows.

1   Those listed in Table A (substances for internal and external use) or Table B (substances for external use only). Where a product contains an ingredient which is listed in Table A or B it must comply with specifications in the table as to maximum strength (ms), maximum dose (md), maximum daily dose (mdd), use, pharmaceutical form or route of administration and be labelled accordingly.
2   Excipients.
3   Substances of animal origin (including extracts of such substances) used in the UK as a human or animal food.
4   Substances of vegetable origin (including extracts and residues of such substances) used in the UK as a human or animal food.
5   Grit in veterinary drugs for birds.

Veterinary medicines

For veterinary drugs the quantities permitted in individual containers or packages are listed in Table 13.1. Packs containing more than these quantities may only be sold or supplied from pharmacies and must be labelled P (SI 1981 No. 1791).

Labelling requirements for veterinary medicinal products

The labelling requirements for veterinary medicinal products are in Schedule 1 of the Veterinary Regulations 2008 (SI 2008 No. 2297). These regulations implement Council Directive 81/851/EEC, as amended.

It is an offence not to label such products under the new regulations. All labels and leaflets must be in English but may contain other languages provided they give the same information in all languages. The regulations require

Table 13.1 Quantities permitted in individual containers or packages for veterinary drugs

Drug	Amount
Aminonitrothiazole	100 mL of solution or 50 capsules
Aspirin	25 tablets or 25 sachets of powder
Bromhexine hydrochloride	20 g
Paracetamol	25 tablets
Phenylephrine hydrochloride	15 mL
Potassium chlorate	30 mL

the following information to appear in legible characters on the immediate packaging:

1 the name, strength and pharmaceutical form of the veterinary medicinal product;
2 name and strength of each active substance, and of any excipient, if this is required under the Summary of Product Characteristics;
3 route of administration (if not immediately apparent);
4 batch number;
5 expiry date;
6 the words 'for animal treatment only' and if appropriate 'to be supplied only on a veterinary prescription';
7 the contents by weight, volume or number of dose units;
8 the marketing authorisation number;
9 the name and address of the market authorisation holder or if there is a distributor authorised in the marketing authorisation, the distributor;
10 suitably labelled space to record discard date (if relevant);
11 target species;
12 the distribution category;
13 the words 'keep out of reach of children';
14 storage instructions;
15 the in-use shelf-life (if appropriate);
16 for food-producing species, the withdrawal period for each species or animal product concerned;
17 any warning specified in the marketing authorisation;
18 disposal advice;
19 full indications;
20 dosage instructions;
21 contraindications;
22 further information required by the marketing authorisation;

23   if the product is one where the dose needs to be specified for the
      animal being treated, a space for this.

If all these are on the immediate package, there is no necessity for any out-
packaging or a package leaflet.

If it is not reasonably practicable to have all the above information on the
immediate package, then the immediate package must have at least the following information:

1   name, strength, and pharmaceutical form of the veterinary medicinal
     product;
2   name and proportion of each active substance, and of any excipient
     if knowledge of excipient is needed for safety reasons;
3   route of administration (if not immediately apparent);
4   batch number;
5   expiry date;
6   the words 'for animal treatment only' and, if appropriate, 'To be supplied
     only on veterinary prescription';
7   the words 'keep the container in the outer carton'.

In this case of reduced labelling, the full information must be on an outer
packaging and if this is not practicable then in a leaflet accompany the
product. The leaflet must contain all the information 1–23 as above except
the expiry date and the batch number.

Labelling of ampoules

For containers such as ampoules or other unit dose forms, where the container
cannot bear legibly the required information, the following information must
be shown on the immediate package:

1   the name of the veterinary medicinal product;
2   the name and strength of the active ingredient;
3   the batch number;
4   route of administration, if not immediately apparent;
5   the expiry date;
6   the words 'for animal treatment only' or, if appropriate, 'to be supplied
     only on a veterinary prescription'.

Small containers other than ampoules

For small immediate packaging containing a single dose, other than ampoules,
on which it is impossible to give the required information the immediate
package must be labelled with the batch number and the expiry date.

Advertising of veterinary products

It is an offence to advertise a veterinary medicinal product which is misleading or carries a claim not in the Summary of Product Characteristics. It is also an offence to advertise a human medicine for administration to animals, including a price list of or including human medicines, to a veterinary surgeon or veterinary practice. However, a wholesaler may send a list of human medicines with prices to a veterinary surgeon provided the list has been requested by the veterinary surgeon, who has specified the type of human medicines s/he intends to use and the list states that the products do not have a marketing authorisation as a veterinary product and that they are for use only under the cascade.

Advertising of Prescription Only Medicines

This covers both those classified as POM-V and those classified as POM-VPS. It is an offence to advertise veterinary medicinal products that are available on a veterinary prescription only or contain psychotropic drugs or narcotics.

In the case of POM-V medicines, the prohibition does not apply to price lists or to advertisements aimed at veterinary surgeons, veterinary nurses, pharmacists or professional keepers of animals.

In the case of POM-VPS medicines, the prohibition does not apply to price lists or to advertisements aimed at veterinary surgeons, pharmacists, registered SQPs, other veterinary healthcare professionals, professional keepers of animals or owners or keepers of horses.

Exemptions for small pet animals

These exemptions apply solely to aquarium fish, cage birds, ferrets, homing pigeons, rabbits, small rodents and terrarium animals. A veterinary product intended solely for one of these categories of pets may be placed on the market, imported or administered without a marketing authorisation provided it complies with the conditions of Schedule 6 to the regulations (SI 2007 No. 2539). The conditions include the following.

1   The Secretary of State may approve the active substance in a veterinary medicinal product manufactured in accordance with the Schedule. A limited number of specific active ingredients are listed in the Schedule. The Secretary of State may not grant approval if the active substance requires veterinary control.
2   The product must not be an antibiotic.
3   The product must not contain narcotic or psychotropic drug.

4   The product is not for treatments or pathological processes that require precise prior diagnosis or the use of which may cause effects that impede or interfere with subsequent or therapeutic measures.

5   The product must comply with detailed labelling requirements set down in the Schedule.

Sale of sheep dips

The regulations apply to any veterinary medicinal product that is a sheep dip of any type. The sale must be to a person who holds, or to a person acting on behalf of a person who holds, a *Certificate of Competence in the Safe Use of Sheep Dips*; this means the certificate issued:

- in England, Wales and Northern Ireland, by the National Proficiency Tests Council or by the National Proficiency Tests Council part of the City and Guilds Group; or
- in Scotland, by one of those organisations or the Scottish Skills Testing Service;

and showing that Parts 1 and 2 of the assessment referred to in the certificate have been satisfactorily completed. The supplier must keep a record of the certificate number as soon as is reasonably practicable and retain it for three years from the date of the sale.

If the active ingredient is an organophosphorus compound, the supplier must give to the buyer:

- a double-sided laminated notice, at least A4 in size, meeting the specification set out in the regulations as to advice on sheep dipping; and
- two pairs of gloves, either as described in the notice or providing demonstrably superior protection to the user against exposure to the dip than would be provided by the gloves described.

The notice must be at least A4 size with laminated cover and must tell the reader:

1   to read and act in accordance with instructions;
2   that sheep dip is absorbed through the skin and always to wear the recommended protective clothing including gloves and always to have a spare set of clothing;
3   to always wash protective clothing before taking it off; and
4   in a diagram, the recommended protective clothing.

It is an offence to use sheep dip unless it is done by or under the supervison of a person who holds a Certificate of Competence in the Safe Use of Sheep Dips.

Veterinary surgeons and veterinary wholesalers

A set of regulations concerning supply and prescribing of veterinary medicinal products has been issued by the Department of Trade and Industry under competition law (SI 2005 2751).

The regulations prohibit the veterinary surgeon from charging a client a fee for a prescription during the relevant period (defined as three years). It is also unlawful for him/her to discriminate between a client to whom s/he provides a prescription and a client to whom s/he does not as far as fees are concerned.

It is unlawful for a manufacturer or wholesaler to discriminate unreasonably between veterinary surgeons and pharmacists in:

- the price that they charge for the supply of veterinary medicinal products;
- any discount or rebate in connection with such a supply; or
- any other terms or conditions upon which they supply.

A manufacturer must at intervals of not more than three months notify in writing the relevant veterinary surgeon and pharmacist of the net price at which s/he supplies veterinary medicinal products. Net price means the list price less any discount and should state whether it includes VAT.

Summary

- Veterinary surgeons and practitioners may sell or supply any medicinal product for administration by them, or under their direction, to an animal or herd under their care.
- There are four classes of veterinary medicinal products with several classes of sellers:
  - POM-V products may only be supplied by a veterinary surgeon or a pharmacist and must be supplied in accordance with a prescription from a veterinary surgeon;
  - POM-VPS products may only be supplied by a veterinarian, pharmacist or a suitably qualified person and must be in accordance with a prescription from one of those persons;
  - NFA-VPS products are non-food and may be supplied without a prescription but may only be supplied by prescribed by a veterinarian, a pharmacist or a suitably qualified person;
  - AVM-GSL products are authorised on the General Sale List and there are no supply restrictions.
- There are detailed rules governing each class of veterinary medicinal products concerned with the questions of prescribing, supplying, labelling and advertising.
- There are rules concerning supply by veterinary surgeons, pharmacists, suitably qualified persons and wholesalers.

- Details are laid down for the registration, and training of suitably qualified persons and the premises from which they may supply veterinary medicinal products.
- There is a code of practice for suitably qualified persons and for saddlers.
- There are controls over the supply of sheep dips.

Further reading

Kayne S, Jepson M (2000) *Veterinary Pharmacy*. London: Pharmaceutical Press.

Rules Governing Medicinal Products in the European Union, vol. 5: *Pharmaceutical Legislation, Veterinary Medicinal Products*. London: The Stationery Office.

Veterinary Medicines Directorate. *MAVIS Advisory Leaflets*. London: Veterinary Medicines Directorate.

Websites

DEFRA: www.defra.gov.uk

14

Medicines Act 1968
Prohibitions for protection
of the purchaser

A prohibition, either total or limited in some way, on the sale, supply or importation of specified classes of medicinal product or of particular medicinal products may be imposed by order of the appropriate Ministers if it appears to them necessary to do so in the interest of safety. Before making such an order, the Ministers are required to consult the appropriate committee (or the Medicines Commission) and to consider representations made by other organisations who have been consulted. These requirements may be waived if, in the opinion of the Ministers, it is essential to make the order with immediate effect to avoid serious danger to health, whether of human beings or of animals. An order made without consultation is effective for three months only but may be renewed (s.62).

Any person who, otherwise than for performing or exercising a statutory duty or power, is in possession of such a medicinal product, knowing or having reasonable cause to suspect that it was sold, supplied or imported in contravention of the order, is guilty of an offence (s.67) (see also p. 21).

Section 62 Orders

Bal Chivan Chamcho

The sale, supply or importation of Bal Chivan Chamcho is prohibited. It is a baby tonic in the form of a dark brown aromatic solid substance affixed to a spoon-shaped metal appliance (SI 1977 No. 670 as amended). The prohibition does not apply to importation from a member state of the EU or if it originated in a state within the EEA. Neither does the prohibition apply to the sale or supply to a public analyst, a sampling officer or a person duly authorised by an enforcement authority under the Act.

Four other section 62 banning orders have been made in relation to herbal medicines, namely *Aristolochia*, Mu Tong and Fangji, kava-kava and *Senecio* (see p. 153).

Non-medicinal antimicrobial substances

There are a number of antimicrobial substances which have medicinal and non-medicinal uses (e.g. sulphanilamide, streptomycin and certain other antibiotics). For medicinal purposes, they are classed as Prescription Only Medicine. When used for non-medicinal purposes, they are also within the control of the Medicines Act by virtue of an order made under section 105 (see p. 17). Further orders under section 62 (SIs 1977 No. 2131 and 1992 No. 2684) prohibit the sale or supply of these substances when used for non-medicinal purposes except for certain purposes. The list of substances and the exceptions to the prohibition on sale are set out in Appendices 1 and 2.

Stilbenes and thyrostatic substances

Regulations (SI 1982 No. 626) made under the European Communities Act 1972 prohibit the administration to farm animals of stilbenes and thyrostatic substances or of medicinal products or animal feeding stuffs containing them. Administration is not prohibited if prior steps are taken to ensure that the animals and their products are unavailable for animal or human consumption.

Chloroform

The sale or supply of medicinal products for human use which consist of or contain chloroform is prohibited (SI 1979 No. 382) subject to the following exceptions. A sale or supply made:

1 by a doctor or dentist to a patient of his/hers, where the medicinal product has been specially prepared by that doctor or dentist for administration to that particular patient;
2 by a doctor or dentist who has specially prepared the medicinal product at the request of another doctor or dentist for administration to a particular patient of that other doctor or dentist;
3 from a pharmacy or hospital where the medicinal product has been specially prepared in accordance with a prescription given by a doctor or dentist for a particular patient;
4 to a hospital, a doctor or a dentist for use as an anaesthetic;
5 to a person who buys it for the purpose of reselling it to a hospital, a doctor or a dentist for use as an anaesthetic;

6   where the medicinal product contains chloroform in a proportion of
    not more than 0.5 per cent (w/w) or (v/v);
7   where the medicinal product is solely for use in dental surgery;
8   where the medicinal product is solely for use by being applied to the
    external surface of the body which for the purpose of this order does
    not include any part of the mouth, teeth or mucous membranes;
9   where the medicinal product is for export; or
10 where the medicinal product is sold for use as an ingredient in the
    preparation of a substance or article in a pharmacy, a hospital or by a
    doctor or dentist.

For the purposes of sale or supply (but not of importation) of medicines
for human use, the exemption limits for chloroform given in the Prescription
Only and General Sale List orders are over-ridden by this order. The practical effect is that only products falling within items 6 and 8 above may be
sold by retail to the general public. But for the purposes of record keeping,
the exemption levels in the Prescription Only order still apply, so that
records are required to be kept only of sales or supplies of products for
internal use which contain more than 5 per cent of chloroform w/w or v/v as
appropriate.

Adulteration of medicinal products

It is an offence:

1   to add any substance to, or abstract any substance from, a medicinal
    product so as to affect injuriously the composition of the product, with
    intent that the product shall be sold or supplied in that state; or
2   to sell or supply, or offer or expose for sale or supply, or have in
    possession for the purpose of sale or supply, any medicinal product
    whose composition has been injuriously affected by the addition or
    abstraction of any substance (s.63).

It is also an offence to sell (or supply on a practitioner's prescription) to the
prejudice of the purchaser (or patient) any medicinal product which is not of
the nature or quality demanded by the purchaser (or specified in the prescription) (s.64).

There is no offence if the medicinal product contains some extraneous
matter, the presence of which is proved to be an inevitable consequence of the
process of manufacture, nor is it an offence where:

1   a substance has been added to, or abstracted from, the medicinal
    product which did not injuriously affect the composition of the
    product and was not carried out fraudulently; and

2   the product was sold having attached to it, or to a container or package in which it was sold, a conspicuous notice of adequate size and legibly printed specifying the substance added or abstracted.

False or misleading advertisements or representations

An advertisement or representation (whether it contains an accurate statement of the composition of medicinal products of the description or not) is taken to be false or misleading if (but only if) it falsely describes the medicinal products to which it relates, or is likely to mislead as to the nature or quality of medicinal products of that description or as to their uses or effects (s.93).

A document, advertisement or representation is taken to be likely to mislead as to the uses or effects of medicinal products of a particular description if it is likely to mislead as to any of the following matters:

1   any purposes for which medicinal products of that description can with reasonably safety be used;
2   any purposes for which such products cannot be so used;
3   any effects which such products when used (or when used in any particular way referred to in the document, advertisement or representation) produce or are intended to produce [s.130(10)].

Medicinal products are 'of the same description' if (but only if) they are manufactured to the same specifications, and they are, or are to be, sold, supplied, imported or exported in the same pharmaceutical form [s.130(8)].

The purposes for which medicinal products of any description may be recommended for use are limited to those specified in the licence relating to them. Any recommendation that they may be used for purposes other than those specified is an *unauthorised recommendation* [s.93(1) and (10)].

Any commercially interested party, or other person acting at that party's request or with their consent, who issues or causes to be issued a false or misleading advertisement or one containing an unauthorised recommendation relating to medicinal products of any description is guilty of an offence (s.93). It is also an offence [s.93(3)] to make, in the course of a relevant business, a false or misleading representation or one which amounts to an unauthorised recommendation:

1   in connection with the sale or offer for sale of a medicinal product;
2   to a practitioner, or to a patient or a client, for the purpose of inducing the practitioner to prescribe medicinal products of a particular description; or
3   to a person for the purpose of inducing him/her to purchase medicinal products of a particular description from a retailer.

A *relevant business* is one which consists of or includes the sale or supply of medicinal products [s.92(4)].

Summary

- The sale or supply of some medicinal products is either prohibited (e.g. Bal Chivan Chamcho) or prohibited subject to exceptions (e.g. stilbenes and thyrostatic substances, non-medicinal antimicrobials and chloroform).
- It is an offence to adulterate, by way of addition or abstraction, a medicinal product or to sell, supply or possess an adulterated product.
- It is an offence to sell or supply to the prejudice of the purchaser (or patient) any medicinal product which is not of the nature or quality demanded by the purchaser (or specified on a prescription).
- An advertisement is false or misleading if it falsely describes the medicinal product to which it relates or is likely to mislead as to the nature and quality of the product or to its use.

15

Medicines Act 1968
Containers, packages and identification

Regulations and penalties

Regulations may be made as the appropriate Ministers consider expedient or necessary for promoting the safety of medicinal products and for securing (a) that such products are correctly described and readily identifiable, and (b) that any appropriate warning or information or instruction is given, and that false or other misleading information is not given. These regulations may apply to:

1 the labelling of containers [s.85(1)];
2 the labelling of packages [s.85(1)];
3 the display of distinctive marks on containers and packages [s.85(1)];
4 leaflets [s.86(1)];
5 colour or shape [s.88(1)];
6 distinctive marks to be displayed on such products [s.88(1)]; and
7 information to be displayed on automatic machines (s.89).

For the same purposes and also for preserving the quality of the products, regulations may prohibit the sale of medicinal products in containers which do not comply with specified requirements, in particular as to the strength, shape or pattern of the containers or of the materials of which they are made (s.87).

It is an offence for any person in the course of a business carried on by him/her to sell or supply, or have in their possession for the purpose of sale or supply, any medicinal product or any leaflet relating to medicinal products in such circumstances as to contravene any requirements which may be imposed by these regulations [ss.85(3) and 86(2)].

The sale of a medicinal product without it being enclosed in a container is regarded as a contravention of the regulations concerning the labelling of containers [s.85(4)].

It is an offence for any person in the course of a business carried on by him/her to supply a product to which the provisions of Council Directive 2001/83/EC applies, unless:

1   a leaflet is enclosed in, or supplied with, the container or package; or
2   the container or package itself contains the particulars which a leaflet
    relating to the product is required by the regulations to contain and
    does so in the manner required (SI 1994 No. 276).

It is also an offence for a person in the course of a business carried on by
him/her to sell or supply or have in their possession for the purpose of sale or
supply a medicinal product in a container or package which is labelled or
marked in such a way, or supplied with a leaflet so that the container, package
or leaflet falsely describes the product, or is likely to mislead as to the nature or
quality of the product or as to its uses or the effects of medicinal products of
that description [ss.85(5) and 86(3)].

Any person contravening the labelling regulations (see below) is liable on
summary conviction to a fine of up to £5000 and, on conviction or indictment,
to a fine or to imprisonment for a term not exceeding two years or to both.

Definitions

The terms defined here are those used in the Act and regulations in connection
with labelling which are not explained elsewhere in the text.

Appropriate non-proprietary name means, briefly:

1   any name, or abbreviation or suitable inversion of such name, at the
    head of a monograph in a 'specified publication' (see below);
2   where the product is not described in a monograph, the British
    approved name;
3   where there is no monograph name or British approved name, the
    international non-proprietary name (INN); or
4   where there is no monograph name, British approved name or INN,
    the accepted scientific name or other name descriptive of the true nature
    of the product (SI 1976 No. 1726 as amended by SI 2002 No. 236).

Appropriate quantitative particulars means the quantity of each active
ingredient (or that part of the active molecule responsible for the therapeutic
or pharmacological activity) identified by its appropriate INN and expressed
in terms of weight, volume, capacity or for certain products, in units of
activity or as a percentage. The quantity to be shown is:

1   the quantity in each dosage unit (for pastilles and lozenges only, it can be
    shown as a percentage); or
2   if there is no dosage unit, the quantity of each active ingredient in the
    container; or
3   if the product contains any active ingredient which cannot be definitively
    characterised, the quantity of the ingredient present in the highest
    proportion other than diluents, excipients, etc.

The quantity of antimicrobial preservative added to a biological medicinal product must be stated. That applies to antigens, toxins, antitoxins, sera, antisera and vaccines.

The quantity can be expressed in terms of the dilution of the unit preparation for a *homoeopathic product* (that is, a product prepared in accordance with the methods of homoeopathic medicine or similar system which is sold or supplied as a homoeopathic product and is so described by the person who sells or supplies it) (SI 1976 No. 1726 as amended by SI 2002 No. 236).

Strength in relation to a relevant medicinal product means the content of active ingredient in that product expressed quantitatively per dosage unit, per unit volume or by weight, according to the dosage form.

Dosage unit means:

1 where the medicinal product is in the form of a tablet or capsule or is an article in some other similar pharmaceutical form, that tablet, capsule or other similar article; or
2 where the medicinal product is not in the aforesaid form, that quantity of the medicinal product which is used as the unit by reference to which the dose of the medicinal product is measured (SI 1976 No. 1726 as amended by SI 2002 No. 236).

Quantity means, where the quantity is not the exact quantity, the quantity which is as near the exact quantity as is reasonably practicable or which differs from the exact quantity only to such extent as is reasonably necessary in the circumstances having regard to the nature of the medicinal product in question (SI 1976 No. 1726 as amended by SI 2002 No. 236).

A *container*, in relation to a medicinal product, means the bottle, jar, box, packet or other receptacle which contains or is to contain it, not being a capsule, cachet or other article in which the product is or is to be administered; and where any such receptacle is or is to be contained in another such receptacle, it includes the inner receptacle but not the outer (s.132).

It should be noted that a capsule, cachet or other article in which a medicinal product is to be administered is not normally a container, but if the capsule, etc., is not to be administered, then it is a container.

A *package*, in relation to any medicinal products, means any box, packet or other article in which one or more containers of the products are to be enclosed, and where any such box, package or other article is, or is to be itself, enclosed in one or more other boxes, packets or other articles, includes each of the boxes, packets or other articles in question (s.132).

In effect, the inner receptacle which actually contains the medicinal products is a container; every outer receptacle is a package.

Labelling, in relation to a container or package of medicinal products, means affixing to or otherwise displaying on it a notice describing or otherwise relating to the contents (s.132).

Expiry date means the date after which, or the month and year after the end of which, the medicinal product should not be used or the date before which or the month and year before the beginning of which, the medicinal product should be used (SI 1977 No. 996).

External use means:

1   in relation to medicinal products for use by being administered to human beings, application to the skin, hair, teeth, mucosa of the mouth, throat, nose, ear, eye, vagina or anal canal; or
2   in relation to veterinary drugs, application to the skin, hair, fur, feathers, scales, hoof, horn, ear, eye, mouth, or mucosa of the throat or prepuce;

in either case when a local action only is necessary and extensive systemic absorption is unlikely to occur. References to *medicinal products for external use* shall be read accordingly, except that in relation to 1 above the references shall not include throat sprays, throat pastilles, throat lozenges, throat tablets, nasal sprays, nasal inhalations or teething preparations (SI 1997 No. 1830 as amended).

Proprietary medicinal product means a ready prepared medicinal product placed on the market in the UK under a special name and in a special pack (SI 1992 No. 604).

Ready made veterinary drug means a ready prepared veterinary drug placed on the market in the UK in a pharmaceutical form in which it may be used without further processing, not being a drug placed on the market under a special name and in a special pack.

Specified publication means the *European Pharmacopoeia,* the *British Pharmacopoeia,* the *British Pharmaceutical Codex,* the *British Veterinary Codex* (or other official compendia which may in the future be produced under the Medicines Act) and the list of British approved names (Medicines Act, s.100).

Labelling regulations

The regulations apply at all stages of distribution, except where otherwise stated. Medicinal products which are Controlled Drugs must also be labelled in accordance with the Misuse of Drugs Regulations 1985 (see p. 236).

Regulations implementing Council Directive 2001/83/EC have been issued dealing with *relevant medicinal products* (SI 1992 No. 3273 as amended) (see the definition, below). Regulations dealing with homoeopathic medicinal products (SI 1994 No. 104) have also been issued.

Labelling of relevant medicinal products

Relevant medicinal product means a product to which the provisions of Council Directive 2001/83/EC applies in respect of which a marketing authorisation is granted or renewed. Thus, all medicinal products for human use are included except those prepared on the basis of magistral (see p. 16) or official formula, those intended for research or development trials, or intermediate products intended for further processing.

General labelling provisions for relevant medicinal products for human use

All labelling of containers and packages must be:

1   legible;
2   comprehensible;
3   indelible; and
4   either in the English language only or in English and in one or more other languages provided that the same particulars appear in all the languages used.

Where the holder of a marketing authorisation for a relevant medicinal product proposes to alter the labelling relating to it in any respect, s/he must notify the licensing authority and, unless the licensing authority has notified him/her that it does not approve the alterations, s/he may, after a period of 90 days from the date of notification by him/her, supply the product with the altered labelling (SI 1992 No. 3273 as amended).

Standard labelling requirements for relevant medicinal products for human use

The standard requirements for the labelling of containers and packages of relevant medicinal products are set out in Council Directive 2001/83/EC and SI 1992 No. 3273, as amended. There are modifications for small containers and blister packs (see p. 185).

The standard requirements are as follows.

1   The name of the medicinal product, followed by the common name where the medicinal product contains only one active ingredient and if its name is an invented name; where a medicinal product is available in several pharmaceutical forms and/or several strengths, the pharmaceutical form and/or strength (baby, child or adult as appropriate) must be included in the name of the medicinal product.

Common name means the international non-proprietary name or, if one does not exist, the usual common name.

Strength in this context means the suitability of the product for a baby, child or adult.

2   A statement of the active ingredients expressed qualitatively and quantitatively per dosage unit or according to the form of administration for a given volume or weight, using their common names.

3   The pharmaceutical form of the product and the contents by weight, by volume or by number of doses of the product.

4   A list of those excipients known to have a recognised action or effect and included in the guidelines published in pursuant to Article 12. However, if the product is injectable or a topical or eye preparation, all excipients must be stated.

5   The method and, if necessary, the route of administration.

6   A special warning that the medicinal product must be stored out of the reach of children.

7   Any special warning if this is necessary for the medicinal product concerned.

8   The expiry date in clear terms (month/year).

9   Special storage precautions, if any.

10 Special precautions for disposal of unused medicinal products, if appropriate, or waste materials derived from such products.

11 The name and address of the holder of the marketing authorisation.

12 The marketing authorisation number.

13 The manufacturer's batch number.

14 In the case of self-medication, instructions on the use of the medicinal product.

The outer packaging may be labelled to show symbols or pictograms designed to clarify certain information mentioned in 1 to 14 above and other information compatible with the Summary of Product Characteristics which is useful for health education, to the exclusion of any element of a promotional nature.

In addition, member states of the EU may require certain additional labelling, for example the price of the product, the reimbursement conditions and the classification, e.g. Prescription Only Medicine (POM).

Summary of Product Characteristics means the information required to accompany any application for a marketing authorisation under Council Directive 2001/83.EC.

Small containers for relevant medicinal products for human use

Where the container of a relevant medicinal product is *not* a blister pack but is too small to include all the standard particulars for relevant medicinal products it must be labelled with:

1 the name of the medicinal product as laid down in standard labelling (see p. 183);
2 the contents of the product by weight, by volume or by unit;
3 the method, and if necessary the route, of administration;
4 the expiry date; and
5 the batch number.

Blister packs for relevant medicinal products for human use

Where the container of a relevant medicinal product is a blister pack and is enclosed within a package which complies with the standard labelling (see above), the container must be labelled with:

1 the name of the medicinal product as laid down in standard labelling (see p. 183);
2 the expiry date;
3 the name of the holder of the marketing authorisation;
4 the batch number.

Standard labelling requirements for containers and packages for radiopharmaceuticals for human use

Containers and packages for radiopharmaceuticals must be labelled with the standard particulars for relevant medicinal products (see p. 183) together with the following additional particulars:

1 the container and package must be labelled in accordance with the current edition of the Regulations for the Safe Transport of Radioactive Materials;
2 the labelling on the shielding must explain in full the codings used on the vial and shall indicate where necessary, for a given time and date, the amount of radioactivity per dose or per vial and the number of capsules, or for liquids the number of millilitres in the container; and
3 the vial shall be labelled to show:
   a the name or code of the medicinal product, including the name or chemical symbol of the radionuclide;
   b the international symbol for radioactivity;

c   the name of the manufacturer;

d   the amount of radioactivity as specified in 2 above.

Labelling of relevant General Sale List medicinal products

All relevant medicinal products for human use on a General Sale List when sold or supplied by retail must be labelled as follows (SI 1994 No. 3144, Sch.5 as amended). If the product contains:

1   aloxiprin, aspirin or paracetamol, with the words *'If symptoms persist, consult your doctor'* and, except where the product is for external use only, the recommended dosage; in addition, the following words must appear on the container and package *'Do not give to children under 16 years, unless on the advice of a doctor'* (SI 2003/1618).

2   aloxiprin, with the words *'Contains an aspirin derivative'*;

3   aspirin, except where the product is for external use only or where the name of the product includes the word *'aspirin'* and appears on the container or package, the words *'contains aspirin'*;

4   paracetamol, except where the name of the product includes the word *'paracetamol'* and appears on the container or package, the words *'Contains paracetamol'*;

5   paracetamol, the words *'Do not exceed the stated dose'* (these words must appear adjacent to either the directions for use or the recommended dosage);

6   paracetamol, unless it is wholly or mainly intended for children who are 12 years old or younger (i.e. it is a product for children 12 and over), the words *'Do not take with any other paracetamol containing products'* and

    a   if a package leaflet accompanying the product displays the words *'Immediate medical advice should be sought in the event of overdose, even if you feel well, because of the risk of delayed, serious liver damage'*, the words *'Immediate medical advice should be sought in the case of overdose, even if you feel well'* must be added to the label; or

    b   if no package leaflet accompanies the product or the package leaflet does not display the words *'Immediate medical advice should be sought in the event of overdose, even if you feel well, because of the risk of delayed, serious liver damage'* then those words must be added to the label (SI 1998 No. 3105);

7   paracetamol, and is wholly or mainly intended for children who are 12 years old or younger, the words *'Do not give with any other paracetamol containing products'* and

a   if a package leaflet accompanying the product displays the words *'Immediate medical advice should be sought in the event of overdose, even if the child seems well, because of the risk of delayed, serious liver damage'*, the words *'Immediate medical advice should be sought in the case of overdose, even if the child seems well'* must be added to the label; or

b   if no package leaflet accompanies the product or the package leaflet does not display the words *'Immediate medical advice should be sought in the event of overdose, even if the child seems well, because of the risk of delayed, serious liver damage'* then those words must be added to the label (SI 1998 No. 3105).

Where more than one of the phrases in 2, 3 and 4 above apply they may be combined, for example, *'contains aspirin, an aspirin derivative and paracetamol'*. Those phrases must be within a rectangle in which there is no other matter and must be in a prominent position.

On those General Sale List medicines which are subject to pack size provisions (see p. 87), the larger pack sizes must be labelled with a 'P' within a rectangle in which there is no other matter.

Labelling of relevant medicinal products for pharmacy sale only

All medicinal products for pharmacy sale only when sold or supplied by retail must be labelled as follows (SI 1994 No. 3144, Sch.5 as amended SI 2002 No. 236):

1   With the capital letter 'P' in a rectangle containing no other matter; this also applies:
    a   to sales of pharmacy medicines by way of wholesale dealing; and
    b   to General Sale List Medicines in pack sizes restricted to pharmacy sale (SI 1994 No. 3144 as amended SI 2002 No. 236).

2   If containing aspirin, aloxiprin or paracetamol, labelled in the manner described above for medicinal products on a General Sale List.

3   If for human use and exempt from Prescription Only control by reason of the proportion or level in such a product of the Prescription Only substance, with the words *'Warning, do not exceed the stated dose'*. (This does not apply to products for external use or products containing any of the substances set out in 5 below.)

4   If for the treatment of asthma or other conditions associated with bronchial spasm or contains ephedrine or any of its salts, with the words *'Warning. Asthmatics should consult their doctor before using this product'*. (This does not apply to products for external use.)

5   If the product contains an antihistamine or any of its salts or molecular compounds, with the words *'Warning. May cause drowsiness. If affected do not drive or operate machinery. Avoid alcoholic drink'*. (This does not apply to products for external use or where the marketing authorisation contains no warning to the sedating effect of the product in use.)

6   If the product is an embrocation, liniment, lotion, liquid antiseptic or other liquid preparation or gel and is for external application, with the words *'For external use only'*.

7   If the product contains hexachlorophane, either with the words *'Not to be used for babies'* or a warning that the product is not to be administered except on medical advice to a child under two years.

The relevant warning phrase or phrases described under Labelling of relevant General Sale List medicinal products and Labelling of relevant medicinal products for pharmacy sale only above must be in a rectangle within which there is no other matter. That does not apply to the phrases *'Do not exceed the stated dose'* or *'If symptoms persist consult your doctor'* on the labels or products for human use required to be labelled because of their aspirin, aloxiprin or paracetamol content.

Labelling of relevant Prescription Only Medicines

The container and package of every medicinal product included in a Prescription Only list must be labelled to show:

1   The capital letters 'POM' within a rectangle within which there shall be no other matter of any kind. That requirement applies to wholesale transactions (which include sales to doctors or dentists) but does not apply to dispensed medicines.

2   If the product is an embrocation, liniment, lotion, liquid antiseptic or other liquid preparation or gel and is for external application, with the words *'For external use only'*.

3   If the product contains hexachlorophane, either with the words *'Not to be used for babies'* or a warning that the product is not to be administered except on medical advice to a child under two years.

Labelling of relevant dispensed medicinal products

The standard labelling requirements do not apply to dispensed medicines.

A *dispensed relevant medicinal product* means a relevant medicinal product prepared or dispensed in accordance with a prescription given by a practitioner.

The container of a dispensed relevant medicinal product must be labelled to show the following particulars:

1 the name of the person to whom the medicine is to be administered;

2 the name and address of the person who sells or supplies the relevant medicinal product;

3 the date of dispensing; and

4 where the product has been prescribed by a practitioner such of the following particulars as s/he may request:

   a the name of the product or its common name;

   b directions for use of the product;

   c precautions relating to the use of the product; or where a pharmacist in the exercise of his/her professional skill and judgement is of the opinion that any of such particulars are inappropriate and has taken all reasonable steps to consult with the practitioner and has been unable to do so, particulars of a same kind as those requested by the practitioner which the pharmacist considers appropriate;

5 the words 'Keep out of the reach of children' or words of direction bearing a similar meaning; and

6 the phrase 'For external use only' if the product is not on a General Sale List and is an embrocation, liniment, lotion, liquid antiseptic or other liquid preparation or gel and is for external use only.

A container need not be labelled if it is enclosed in a package which is labelled with the required particulars.

Labelling of medicinal products exempt from product marketing authorisations

The following classes of medicinal product, exempt from marketing authorisations (product licences) by various orders made under the Medicines Act, are subject to modified labelling requirements.

Foods and cosmetics

Certain medicinal products which are foods are exempt from marketing authorisations (product licences) by the Foods and Cosmetics Order (SI 1971 No. 1410) and the labelling particulars (see above) which apply to these products are:

1 name of product (container and package);

2 description of pharmaceutical form (package only);

3 appropriate quantitative particulars (container only);

4 quantity (container and package);

5   any special handling and storage requirements (container and package); and

6   expiry date (container only).

The labels of the container and of the package must also bear the name and address of the manufacturer or the person responsible for its composition or the person who first sells or supplies it as a medicinal product.

These labelling requirements do not apply to any product which is subject to the Labelling of Food Regulations. There are no labelling requirements for cosmetics.

Special and transitional cases

'Special' dispensing and manufacturing services provided by manufacturers for practitioners, pharmacists and others are the subject of two orders (SIs 1971 No. 1450 and 1972 No. 1200) under the Medicines Act which provide exemptions from marketing authorisations (see Chapter 3). These orders also extend to certain other special cases. The label of the container of medicinal products affected, and the packages immediately enclosing them, must show the following labelling particulars:

1   name of the product;
2   pharmaceutical form (package only);
3   appropriate quantitative particulars;
4   quantity;
5   any special handling and storage requirements;
6   batch reference; and
7   manufacturer's licence number, or name and address.

The package must also bear the name and address of the manufacturer, or of the person responsible for the composition of the product, or of the person who first sells or supplies it as a medicinal product.

Other exempt medicinal products

Apart from the orders mentioned under Foods and cosmetics and Special and transitional cases above, the Medicines Act provides other exemptions from marketing authorisation (product licence) requirements for certain medicinal products.

The following requirements apply, for example, to medicinal products which are prepared in a registered pharmacy for retail sale from that pharmacy and which are not advertised. (Such products are familiarly known as 'chemist's nostrums'.)

The label of the container of such a medicinal product and the package immediately enclosing it must show the following labelling particulars:

1 name of the product;
2 pharmaceutical form (package only);
3 appropriate quantitative particulars;
4 quantity;
5 directions for use;
6 any special handling and storage requirements; and
7 expiry date (if relevant).

The label of the container and the package must also show the name and address of the seller.

Ingredient medicinal products

The label of the container and of the package of ingredients which are to be used in the preparation of medicinal products must show the following labelling particulars:

1 name of the product (i.e. ingredient);
2 pharmaceutical form;
3 appropriate quantitative particulars;
4 quantity;
5 any special handling and storage requirements;
6 expiry date (if relevant);
7 marketing authorisation number (or the name and address of the holder of the marketing authorisation);
8 batch reference;
9 manufacturer's licence number, or name and address; and
10 particulars required by the marketing authorisation.

Contract manufacture or assembly

Where a medicinal product is supplied solely for the purpose of assembly and the supply is between persons concerned in the manufacture or assembly of the product, the package immediately enclosing the container must be labelled to show:

1 name of the product;
2 name and address of the person supplying the product;
3 marketing authorisation number (if any); and
4 batch reference.

The person taken to be concerned in the manufacture or assembly of a medicinal product is (a) the marketing authorisation holder or, if there is no authorisation, the person responsible for the composition of the product, or (b) the person who manufactures or assembles the product to the order of the authorisation holder etc. or to the order of the Crown.

Those are the only requirements which apply to stocks held in the manufacturing process.

Delivery and storage

The labelling particulars required for delivery and storage must appear on the outer package, that is to say, the package enclosing the package immediately enclosing the container. The required labelling particulars are:

1 any special handling and storage particulars;
2 the expiry date of the product; and
3 the manufacturer's batch number.

Clinical trials

Where a medicinal product is for administration in a clinical trial, the labelling on the container and package must sufficiently identify the clinical trial, the product (if more than one product is supplied in the course of the trial) and such designation as will identify the person to whom the product is to be administered. It must also show the name and address of the premises where the clinical trial is to be carried out (or the name and address of the product licence holder) and particulars required to be stated on the labels by the product licence or clinical trial certificate.

Standard labelling requirements for containers and packages of homoeopathic products for human use

All containers and packages for homoeopathic products must be labelled clearly and make reference to their homoeopathic nature by clear use of the words *homoeopathic medicinal product*. In addition, they must carry the following particulars and no others (SI 1994 No. 104):

1 the scientific name of the stock or stocks followed by the degree of dilution, making use of the symbols of the pharmacopoeia used in relation to the homoeopathic manufacturing procedure described therein for that stock or stocks;
2 the name and address of the holder of the certificate of registration and, where different, the name and address of the manufacturer;
3 the method of administration and, if necessary, route;
4 the expiry date of the product in clear terms, stating the month and year;
5 the pharmaceutical form;
6 the contents of the sales representation;
7 any special storage precautions;
8 any special warning necessary for the product concerned;
9 the manufacturer's batch number;

10   the registration number allocated by the licensing authority preceded by the letters 'HR' in capital letters;

11   the words 'Homoeopathic medicinal product without approved therapeutic indications'; and

12   a warning advising the user to consult a doctor if the symptoms persist during the use of the product.

Surgical materials

Certain surgical materials (for example, ligatures and sutures) are medicinal products by virtue of the Medicines (Surgical Materials) Order 1971 (SI 1971 No. 1267). The label of the container of such a product and the package immediately enclosing it must show the following labelling particulars:

1   name of the product;
2   description of the pharmaceutical form;
3   directions for use;
4   contraindications, warnings and precautions (if any);
5   any special handling and storage requirements;
6   expiry date where relevant;
7   name and address of the holder of the marketing authorisation;
8   marketing authorisation number;
9   batch reference;
10   manufacturer's licence number, or name and address; and
11   particulars required by the marketing authorisation (product licence).

The label must also show the nature and origin of the article or substance and the quantity of the product in the container expressed in terms of weight or volume or length.

Labelling of animal medicines

See p. 166.

Labelling of small containers for animal medicinal products

See p. 168.

Leaflets

Medicinal products which are relevant medicinal products for human use

All leaflets included in the package or container of any relevant medicinal product (see p. 183) must comply with section 7(1) of SI 1994 No. 3144 and contain the particulars as set out in Council Directive 2001/83/EC as amended.

All particulars must be drawn up in accordance:

1 with the Summary of Product Characteristics, if there is one;
2 if there is no Summary of Product Characteristics, with the data sheet, if there is one;
3 if there is no Summary of Product Characteristics and no data sheet, with the information which would be required to accompany an application for a product licence under Council Directive 65/65/EEC.

The particulars must be written in clear and understandable terms for the patient, and be clearly legible in the language of the member state where the product was placed on the market. Other languages may be used provided that the same particulars appear in all the languages used.

The particulars which must be included are as follows.

1 For identification of the medicinal product:
   a the name of the product, followed by the common name if the product contains only one active ingredient and if its name is an invented name; where a medicinal product is available in several pharmaceutical forms and/or several strengths, the pharmaceutical form and/or strength (for example, baby, child, adult) must be included in the name of the product;
   b a full statement of the active ingredients and excipients expressed qualitatively and a statement of the active ingredients expressed quantitatively, using their common names, in the case of each presentation of the medicinal product;
   c the pharmaceutical form and the contents by weight, by volume or by number of doses of the product, in the case of each presentation of the product;
   d the pharmacotherapeutic group, or type of activity, in terms easily comprehensible for the patient;
   e the name and address of the holder of the marketing authorisation and of the manufacturer.
2 The therapeutic indications.
3 A list of information which is necessary before taking the medicinal product, as follows:
   a contraindications;
   b appropriate precautions for use;
   c forms of interaction with other medicinal products and other forms of interaction (e.g. with alcohol, tobacco and foodstuffs) which may affect the action of the medicinal product;

    d   special warnings, which:

        i   take into account the particular condition of certain categories of users (e.g. children, pregnant or breastfeeding women, the elderly, and persons with specific pathological conditions);

        ii   mention, if appropriate, potential effects on the ability to drive vehicles or operate machinery;

        iii   give details of those excipients, knowledge of which is important for the safe and effective use of the medicinal product.

4   The necessary and usual instructions for proper use, in particular:

    a   dosage;

    b   method and, if necessary, route of administration;

    c   the frequency of administration, specifying, if necessary, the time at which the medicinal product may or must be administered;

    d   and, where the nature of the product makes it appropriate:

        i   the duration of treatment, where it should be limited;

        ii   the action to be taken in the case of an overdose (e.g. symptoms and emergency procedures);

        iii   the course of action to be taken where one or more doses have not been taken;

        iv   indication, if necessary, of the risk of withdrawal effects.

5   A description of the undesirable effects which can occur with normal use of the medicinal product and, if necessary, the action to be taken in such a case, together with an express invitation to the patient to communicate any undesirable effect which is not mentioned in the leaflet to his/her doctor or pharmacist.

6   A reference to the expiry date indicated on the label with:

    a   a warning against using the product after this date;

    b   where appropriate, special storage precautions;

    c   if necessary, a warning against certain visible signs of deterioration.

7   The date upon which the leaflet was last revised.

The licensing authority may decide that certain therapeutic indications need not be included in a leaflet where the dissemination of such information might have serious disadvantages for the patient.

A leaflet for a relevant medicinal product may include:

1   a symbol or pictogram designed to clarify the particulars set out in 1 to 7 above;

2   other information compatible with the Summary of Product Characteristics which is useful for health education, to the exclusion of any element of a promotional nature.

Paracetamol

Where a package leaflet is included in the packaging of a relevant medicinal product containing paracetamol, unless the product is wholly or mainly intended for children who are 12 years old or younger (i.e. where the product is intended for children 12 and over), the leaflet shall display the words *'Immediate medical advice should be sought in the event of overdose, even if you feel well, because of the risk of delayed, serious liver damage'*.

Where a package leaflet is included in the packaging of a relevant medicinal product containing paracetamol, and the product is wholly or mainly intended for children who are 12 years old **or younger,** the leaflet shall display the words *'Immediate medical advice should be sought in the event of overdose, even if the child seems well, because of the risk of delayed, serious liver damage'* (SI 1998 No. 3105).

Aspirin

Where in accordance with the relevant Community provisions a package leaflet is included in the packaging of a relevant medicinal product containing aspirin or aloxiprin, the leaflet must display the words *'There is a possible association between aspirin and Reye's syndrome when given to children. Reye's syndrome is a very rare disease, which can be fatal. For this reason aspirin should not be given to children aged under 16 years, unless on the advice of a doctor'* (SI 2003 No. 1618).

Radiopharmaceuticals and radiopharmaceutical-associated products

A leaflet enclosed with a radiopharmaceutical or radiopharmaceutical-associated product must in addition to containing particulars required in the regulations (SI 1994 No. 3144) contain:

1   details of any precautions to be taken by the user and the patient during the preparation and administration of the product; and
2   details of any special precautions to be taken in respect of the disposal of the container and its unused contents.

Homoeopathic medicinal products

Any leaflet enclosed in or supplied with the packaging of a homoeopathic product which is placed on the market in accordance with a certificate of registration must bear the words *'homoeopathic medicinal product'*. In addition the leaflet must carry the following particulars and no others (SI 1994 No. 104):

1   the scientific name of the stock or stocks followed by the degree of dilution, making use of the symbols of the pharmacopoeia used in relation to the homoeopathic manufacturing procedure described therein for that stock or stocks;
2   the name and address of the holder of the certificate of registration and, where different, the name and address of the manufacturer;
3   the method of administration and, if necessary, route;
4   the expiry date of the product in clear terms, stating the month and year;
5   the pharmaceutical form;
6   the contents of the sales representation;
7   any special storage precautions;
8   any special warning necessary for the product concerned;
9   the manufacturer's batch number;
10 the registration number allocated by the licensing authority preceded by the capital letters 'HR';
11 the words 'Homoeopathic medicinal product without approved therapeutic indications'; and
12 a warning advising the user to consult a doctor if the symptoms persist during the use of the product.

Child safety regulations

It is an offence to sell or supply relevant medicinal products otherwise than in containers that are both opaque, or dark tinted, and child resistant (The Medicines [Child Safety] Regulations SI 2003 No. 2317 amended by SI 2005 No. 1520 and SI 2008 No. 1162).

For the purpose of these regulations, *relevant medicinal products* means medicinal products for human use consisting of, or containing, aspirin, para-cetamol or more than 24 mg of elemental iron, which are in the form of tablets, capsules, pills, lozenges, pastilles, suppositories or oral liquids, except for:

1   effervescent tablets containing not more than 25 per cent of aspirin or paracetamol by weight
2   medicinal products in sachets or other sealed containers which hold only one unit of dose
3   medicinal products that are not intended for retail sale by a retail pharmacy or supplied in pursuance of a prescription
4   for export.

Containers that are not-reclosable are child resistant if they have been evaluated in accordance with, and comply with:

1   British Standard BS 8404 published by the British Standard Institution on 21 December 2001; or

2 any equivalent or higher specification for non-reclosable child-resistant packaging recognised for use in the EEA.

Containers that are reclosable are child resistant if they have been evaluated in accordance with and comply with:

1 British Standard BS 28317 published by the British Standard Institution on 15 February 1993; or
2 any equivalent or higher specification for reclosable child-resistant packaging recognised for use in the EEA.

The regulations do not apply to products which are (a) for export or not intended for retail sale; (b) sold or supplied from a registered pharmacy under the supervision of a pharmacist on the prescription of an appropriate practitioner or supplementary prescriber (which are subject to voluntary controls under the Society's Code of Ethics) or at the request of a person (not a child) who specifically request the non-use of a child-resistant container; (c) sold or supplied by a doctor, dentist, supplementary prescriber, pharmacist, nurse or optometrist independent prescriber to a patient of theirs or to the patient's carer or to another prescriber for a particular patient; or (d) sold or supplied for administration in accordance with the directions of a prescriber at a hospital or health centre.

These products, for aspirin and paracetamol, when for administration exclusively to children must be white and the contents of each container or pack of unit packages must not exceed 25. This does not apply to the sale or supply of a medicinal product containing either paracetamol in oral liquid dosage form or more than 24 mg elemental iron.

Use of fluted bottles

A liquid medicinal product which is for external use (for definition see p. 186) must be sold or supplied in a bottle the outer surface of which is fluted vertically with ribs or grooves recognisable by touch if the product contains any of the substances listed below (SI 1978 No. 40). This requirement applies to the following substances subject to the exemptions shown:

- aconite, alkaloids of
- adrenaline (epinephrine), its salts
- amino-alcohols esterified with benzoic acid, phenylacetic acid, phenylpropionic acid, cinnamic acid or the derivatives of these acids; their salts
- p-aminobenzenesulphonamide, its salts; derivatives of
- p-aminobenzenesulphonamide having any of the hydrogen atoms of the p-amino group or of the sulphonamide group substituted by another radical; their salts

- *p*-aminobenzoic acid, esters of; their salts
- ammonia except in medicinal products containing less than 5 per cent weight in weight of ammonia
- arsenical substances, the following: arsenic sulphides, arsenates, arsenites; halides of arsenic; oxides of arsenic; organic compounds of arsenic
- atropine, its salts
- cantharidin, cantharidates
- carbachol
- chloral, its addition and its condensation products other than alpha-chloralose; their molecular compounds
- chloroform except in medicinal products containing less than 1 per cent volume in volume of chloroform
- cocaine, its salts
- creosote obtained from wood except in medicinal products containing less than 50 per cent volume in volume of creosote obtained from wood
- croton, oil of
- demecarium bromide
- dyflos
- ecothiopate iodide
- ephedrine, its salts; except in medicinal products containing less than the equivalent of 1 per cent weight in volume of ephedrine
- ethylmorphine, its salts
- homatropine, its salts
- hydrofluoric acid, alkali metal bifluorides, potassium fluoride, sodium fluoride, sodium silicofluoride; except in mouth washes containing not more than 0.05 per cent weight in volume of sodium fluoride
- hyoscine, its salts
- hyoscyamine, its salts
- lead acetates except in medicinal products containing lead acetates equivalent to not more than 2.2 per cent weight in volume of lead calculated as elemental lead
- mercury, oxides of; nitrates of mercury; mercuric ammonium chloride; mercuric chloride; mercuric iodide, potassium mercuric iodide; organic compounds of mercury; mercuric oxycyanide; mercuric thiocyanate: except in medicinal products containing not more than 0.01 per cent weight in volume of sodium ethylmercurithiosalicylate as a preservative
- nitric acid, except in medicinal products containing less than 9 per cent weight in weight of nitric acid
- opium
- phenols (any member of the series of phenols of which the first member is phenol and of which the molecular composition varies from member to

member by one atom of carbon and two atoms of hydrogen); compounds of phenol with a metal except in:

— medicinal products containing one or more of the following: butylated hydroxytoluene, carvacrol, creosote obtained from coal tar, essential oils in which phenols occur naturally, tar (coal or wood, crude or refined), tert-butylcresol, p-tert-butylphenol p-tert-pentylphenol, p-(1,1,3,3-tetramethylbutyl) phenol, thymol

— mouth washes containing less than 2.5 per cent weight in volume of phenols

— any liquid disinfectant or antiseptics not containing phenol and containing less than 2.5 per cent weight in volume of other phenols

— other medicinal products containing less than 1 per cent weight in volume of phenols

- physostigmine, its salts
- picric acid; except in medicinal products containing less than 5 per cent weight in volume of picric acid
- pilocarpine, its salts; except in medicinal products containing less than the equivalent of 0.025 per cent weight in volume of pilocarpine
- podophyllum resin; except in medicinal products containing not more than 1.5 per cent weight in weight of podophyllum resin
- solanaceous alkaloids not otherwise included in the Schedule.

Other exceptions to fluted bottle requirements

The fluted bottle requirements do not apply where:

1 medicinal products are contained in bottles with a capacity greater than 1.14 litres;
2 a medicinal product is a Prescription Only Medicine containing a listed substance (fluted bottle requirements do apply to dispensed medicinal products or any other retail sale or supply);
3 medicinal products are packed for export for use solely outside the UK;
4 medicinal products are sold or supplied solely for the purpose of scientific education, research or analysis;
5 eye or ear drops are sold or supplied in a plastic container; or
6 where the product licence, clinical trial certificate or animal test certificate otherwise provides.

Summary

- There are detailed labelling requirements for relevant medicinal products for human use, which includes all medicines which have been granted, or had renewed, marketing authorisations (product licences) since

January 1994. These do not include those medicines dispensed against a prescription or official formula, or for research or trials.

- There are specific labelling requirements for relevant medicinal products for human use containing aloxiprin, aspirin and paracetamol, and additional requirements for Prescription Only Medicines.
- There are additional warning labels for paracetamol.
- There are modified labelling provisions for relevant medicinal products for human use which are in small containers, blister packs, homoeopathic products and for radiopharmaceuticals.
- Abbreviated labelling provisions exist for medicines dispensed against a prescription given by a practitioner.
- There are separate labelling requirements for ingredients, food and cosmetics, contract manufacture and assembly, chemist's nostrums, import and export, surgical materials and clinical trials.
- Every container or package of relevant medicinal products must contain a patient leaflet. Detailed requirements exist for the contents of these leaflets.
- Special leaflets provisions exist for homoeopathic medicinal products.
- Special requirements apply to the sale of medicinal products in unit-dose form which contain aspirin or paracetamol. These products must be packed in child-resistant containers, i.e. opaque reclosable resistant containers or bubble/blister packs.
- There is a list of liquid medicinal products which are for external use that must be sold in bottles the outer surface of which is fluted with ribs or grooves recognisable by touch. These 'fluted' bottle requirements do not apply where medicinal products are contained in bottles greater than 1.14 litres, for export, for analysis or clinical trial, or which are eye or ear drops.

16

Medicines Act 1968
Pharmacopoeias and other publications

European Pharmacopoeia

The *European Pharmacopoeia* is published under the direction of the Council of Europe (Partial Agreement) in accordance with the Convention on the Elaboration of a European Pharmacopoeia held in 1964.

In 1973, the standards in the *European Pharmacopoeia*, together with any amendments or alterations published in the *Gazette*, took precedence over the standards in other publications. The Health Ministers may publish amendments to the *British Pharmacopoeia* when necessary to give effect to the Convention but, should a difference exist at any time between the two pharmacopoeias, the standard of the *European Pharmacopoeia* would prevail (s.102).

A name is taken to be an approved synonym for a name at the head of a monograph in the *European Pharmacopoeia* if, by a notice published in the *Gazette* and not subsequently withdrawn, it is declared to be approved by the Medicines Commission as a synonym for that name [s.65(8)].

British Pharmacopoeia, compendia and other publications

Until 1970, the *British Pharmacopoeia* was compiled by the General Medical Council under the Medical Act 1956 when the copyright was assigned to Her Majesty (Medicines Act, s.98). A committee set up under section 4 of the Act, known as the British Pharmacopoeia Commission, has been established to prepare new editions of the *British Pharmacopoeia* and any amendments to such editions.

The *British Pharmacopoeia* comprises *relevant information*, that is, information consisting of descriptions of, standards for, notes or other matters relating to:

1   substances and articles (whether medicinal products or not) which are or may be used in the practice of medicine (other than veterinary medicine), surgery other than veterinary surgery, dentistry and midwifery; and

2   substances and articles used in the manufacture of substances and articles listed under 1.

In addition to the *British Pharmacopoeia*, compendia containing other relevant information may be published (s.99). Information relating to substances and articles used in veterinary medicine and surgery (whether veterinary drugs or not) is published in a separate compendium, the *British Pharmacopoeia (Veterinary)*.

The British Pharmacopoeia Commission is authorised to prepare lists of suitable names (British Approved Names) for substances and articles for placing at the head of monographs in the *British Pharmacopoeia* or in the compendia (s.100 and SI 1970 No. 1256). The publication of any such lists supersedes any previously published list.

If the Medicines Commission so recommends, the *British Pharmacopoeia*, the compendia and the lists of names must be published and made available for sale to the public by the appropriate Ministers. Every copy must specify the date from which it is to take effect, and notice must be given in the *Gazette* not less than 21 days before that date (s.102). The Agriculture Ministers are responsible for the veterinary publication and the Health Ministers for the others (s.99).

Apart from the *British Pharmacopoeia* and the compendia, other publications containing relevant information may be prepared at the discretion of the Medicines Commission (s.101). These may be journals published periodically and made available to the public.

British Pharmaceutical Codex and British Veterinary Codex

The *British Pharmaceutical Codex*, prepared and published by the Royal Pharmaceutical Society of Great Britain (RPSGB), first appeared in 1907. Successive editions were published, the last being in 1973. The requirements for drugs and dressings in the *British Pharmaceutical Codex* have provided legally recognised standards which continue to be official standards under the Medicines Act. No analytical standards have been given in any codex published by the RPSGB since 1973.

The *British Veterinary Codex*, also prepared and published by the RPSGB, has similarly provided standards for medicines in veterinary use, which are now official standards under the Medicines Act.

The Medicines Commission has recommended that there should be only one source of published standard for medicines, namely the *British Pharmacopoeia*.

Compliance with official standards

It is unlawful for any person, in the course of a business carried on by him/her, (a) to sell a medicinal product which has been demanded by the purchaser by, or by express reference to, a particular name; or (b) to sell or supply a medicinal product in pursuance of a prescription given by a practitioner in which the product required is described by, or by express reference, to a particular name; or (c) to sell or supply a medicinal product which, in the course of the business, has been offered or exposed for sale by, or by express reference to, a particular name; if that name is at the head of the relevant monograph in a specified publication, or is an approved synonym for such a name, and the product does not comply with the standard specified in that monograph (ss.65 and 67).

It is also an offence if the name in question is the name of an active ingredient of the product and, in so far as the product consists of that ingredient, it does not comply with the standard specified.

The publications to which these requirements extend are the *European Pharmacopoeia*, the *British Pharmacopoeia*, the *British Pharmaceutical Codex*, the *British Veterinary Codex* and any compendium published under Part VII of the Act.

For the purpose of complying with official standards the *relevant monograph* is ascertained as follows.

1   If a particular edition of a particular publication is specified together with the name of the medicinal product, then the relevant monograph is (a) the monograph (if any) headed by that name in that edition of the publication; or (b) if there is no such monograph in that edition, the *appropriate current monograph* (if any) headed by that name.

2   If a particular publication, but not a particular edition, is specified, together with the name of the medicinal product, then the relevant monograph is (a) the monograph (if any) headed by that name in the current edition of the specified publication; or (b) if there is no such monograph in the current edition of the publication, the *appropriate current monograph* headed by that name; or (c) if there is no *appropriate current monograph*, then the monograph headed by that name in the latest edition of the specified publication which contained a monograph so headed.

3   If no publication is specified together with the name of the medicinal product, the relevant monograph is *the appropriate current monograph*, if any [s.65(4)].

Appropriate current monograph, in relation to a particular name, means the monograph (if any) headed by that name, or by a name for which it is an approved synonym, in the current edition of (a) the *European Pharmacopoeia*, or (b) the *British Pharmacopoeia*, or (c) a compendium published under section 99 of the Act, or (d) the *British Pharmaceutical Codex* or the *British Veterinary Codex*, taken in that order of precedence.

Current means current at the time when the medicinal product in question is demanded, described in a prescription, or offered or exposed for sale; and the current edition of a publication is the one in force at that time, together with any amendments, alterations or deletions. If the reference is to an edition previous to the current edition, it must be taken as it was immediately before the time when it was superseded by a subsequent edition of that publication. Any monograph shall be construed in accordance with any general monograph, notice, appendix, note or other explanatory material applicable to the monograph which is contained in the relevant edition of the publication [s.65(5) and (6)].

Specifications in licences

When reference is made in a licence or certificate (Part II of the Act) to a publication specified in the Act, but no particular edition is mentioned, then it is to be construed as the current edition, that is, with any amendment, alteration or deletion made up to the date of issue of the licence or certificate (s.103). The publications specified are those mentioned above, that is the *European Pharmacopoeia*, the *British Pharmacopoeia*, the *British Pharmaceutical Codex*, the *British Veterinary Codex*, and compendia prepared under section 99 of the Act, and the lists of names prepared under section 100 of the Act, together with the *British National Formulary* and the *Dental Practitioners' Formulary*.

These two formularies are published jointly by the British Medical Association and the RPSGB. The *British National Formulary* is a standard formulary, with notes on drugs and other information for medical practitioners and pharmacists, which is recognised for use in the NHS. The *Dental Practitioners' Formulary* similarly provides standard formulae, notes and information relating to dental treatment pharmacopoeias and other publications.

Summary

- The *British Pharmacopoeia* comprises information consisting of descriptions and standards for substances and articles which may be used in medicine other than veterinary medicine together with substances and articles used in the manufacture of medicinal products.
- The *European Pharmacopoeia*, where appropriate, takes precedence over the standards in other publications.
- It is an offence to sell, supply or dispense a medicinal product of a particular name if that name is at the head of a monograph in a pharmacopoeia, and the product does not comply with the standard specified in that monograph.

17

Misuse of Drugs Act 1971

The Misuse of Drugs Act 1971 came into operation on 1 July 1973 [SI 1973 No. 795 (C.20)]. It consolidates and extends previous legislation and controls the export, import, production, supply and possession of dangerous or otherwise harmful drugs. The Act is also designed to deal with the control and treatment of addicts and to promote education and research relating to drug dependence. It extends to Northern Ireland (s.38).

In relation to drugs, the Act is largely restrictive in its terms although it does provide for licences to be issued for importation and exportation (s.3). Apart from that, the general effect is to render unlawful all activities in the drugs which are controlled under the Act, except as provided in the regulations made under the Act. The extent to which these regulations relax the restrictions is dealt with later in this chapter.

Advisory Council on Misuse of Drugs

The *Advisory Council on Misuse of Drugs* (s.1) was formally established from 1 February 1972 [SI 1971 No. 2120 (C.57)], replacing the former Advisory Committee on Drug Dependence which had no statutory authority. It advises the Ministers, that is, the Secretary of State for the Home Affairs Department, and the Ministers responsible for Health and Education in England, Wales, Scotland and Northern Ireland.

The Advisory Council consists of not fewer than 20 members appointed by the Secretary of State after consultation with such organisations as s/he considers appropriate, including at least one person appearing to the Secretary of State to have wide and recent experience in each of the following:

1 the practice of medicine (other than veterinary medicine);
2 the practice of dentistry;
3 the practice of veterinary medicine;
4 the practice of pharmacy;
5 the pharmaceutical industry;
6 chemistry other than pharmaceutical chemistry;

together with persons appearing to the Secretary of State to have wide and recent experience of social problems connected with the misuse of drugs (Sch.1 to the Act). The Secretary of State appoints one of the members of the Advisory Council to be Chairman, and the Council may appoint committees and include on them persons who are not members of the Council.

The Advisory Council is required to keep under review the situation in the UK with respect to drugs which are being, or appear to them likely to be, misused (s.1). If it considers that misuse could cause harmful effects which might constitute a social problem, it has a duty to advise the Ministers on the action to be taken. In particular it must advise on measures:

1   to restrict the availability of such drugs or to supervise the arrangements for their supply;
2   to enable persons affected by the misuse of such drugs to obtain proper advice, and to secure the provision of proper facilities and services for the treatment, rehabilitation and aftercare of such persons;
3   to promote co-operation between the various professional and community services which, in the opinion of the Council, have a part to play in dealing with social problems connected with the misuse of such drugs;
4   to educate the public (and in particular the young) in the dangers of abusing such drugs, and to give publicity to those dangers; and,
5   to promote research into, or otherwise to obtain information about, any matter which in the opinion of the Council is of relevance for the purpose of preventing the misuse of such drugs or dealing with any social problem connected with their misuse. The Secretary of State has authority to conduct or assist in conducting such research (s.32).

The Advisory Council also has a duty to advise on any matter relating to drug dependence or misuse of drugs which any of the Ministers may refer to it. In particular, the Advisory Council is required to advise the Secretary of State on communications relating to the control of any dangerous or otherwise harmful drug received from any authority established under a treaty, convention or other agreement to which HM Government is a party. Before any regulations are made under the Act, the Advisory Council must be consulted [s.31(3)].

Class A, class B and class C drugs

The drugs subject to control are listed in Schedule 2 to the Act and the term *Controlled Drug* means any substance or product so listed. The Schedule is divided into three parts or classes largely on the basis of decreasing order of harmfulness: Part I (class A); Part II (class B); and Part III (class C). This division into three classes is solely for the purpose of determining penalties for offences under the Act (s.25) (see Appendix 5).

Changes may be made to the list of Controlled Drugs subject to consultation with the Advisory Council. Amendment is made by an Order in Council which must be approved by an affirmative resolution of each House of Parliament (s.2).

It should be noted that the classification of Controlled Drugs for purposes of the regimes of control which must be applied to drugs when used for lawful purposes appears in the Schedules to the Misuse of Drugs Regulations 2001. This classification is of importance to practitioners and pharmacists in their daily work and is set out in Appendix 6.

Restrictions and exemptions

The importation or exportation of Controlled Drugs is prohibited, except in accordance with a licence issued by the Secretary of State or when permitted by regulations (s.3). Certain activities are specifically declared to be unlawful:

1   producing a Controlled Drug (s.4);
2   supplying or offering to supply a Controlled Drug to another person (s.4);
3   possessing a Controlled Drug (s.5);
4   cultivating any plant of the genus *Cannabis* (s.6).

Producing a Controlled Drug means producing it by manufacture, cultivation or any other method, and *supplying* includes distribution (s.37). For the purposes of the Act, the things which a person has in his/her possession are taken to include anything subject to his/her control which is in the custody of another (s.37). *Cannabis* (except in the expression *cannabis resin*) means any plant of the genus *Cannabis* or any part of any such plant (by whatever name designated) except that it does not include cannabis resin or any of the following products after separation from the rest of the plant, namely:

1   mature stalk of any such plant;
2   fibre produced from mature stalk of any such plant; and
3   seed of any such plant (Criminal Law Act 1977, s.52).

Exemptions from these controls may be authorised by the Secretary of State. S/he may:

1   by regulations, exempt any specified Controlled Drug from any of the restrictions on import, export, production, supply or possession (s.7);
2   by regulations, make it lawful for persons to produce, supply or possess Controlled Drugs to the extent which s/he thinks fit (s.7);
3   permit by licence or other authority any of the activities in 2 and prescribe any conditions to be complied with (s.7).

The Secretary of State must exercise his/her powers to make regulations so as to secure appropriate exemptions for the possession, supply, manufacture or compounding of Controlled Drugs by practitioners, pharmacists and persons lawfully conducting retail pharmacy businesses, and for prescribing and administration by practitioners (s.7). The term *practitioner* (except in the specific expression 'veterinary practitioner') means a doctor, dentist, veterinary practitioner or veterinary surgeon (s.37).

If the Secretary of State considers that it is in the public interest for a drug to be used only for the purposes of research or other special purposes, s/he may make an order to that effect. It is then unlawful for a practitioner, pharmacist or a person lawfully conducting a retail pharmacy business to do anything in relation to that drug except under licence. In this connection *doing* things includes having things in one's possession. When making an order of this kind, the Secretary of State must act on the recommendation of the Advisory Council or after consulting that Council (s.7). Licence fees are prescribed in SI 1986 No. 416, as amended.

The 2001 Regulations (SI 2001 No. 3998) list 'exempted' products, which means a preparation or other product consists of one or more parts any of which contains a Controlled Drug where:

1   the preparation or other product is not designed for administration
    of the Controlled Drug to a human being or animal;
2   the Controlled Drug in any component part is packaged in such a form
    or in combination with other active or inert substances in such a
    manner that it cannot be recovered by readily applicable means or in a
    yield which constitutes a risk to health;
3   no one component part of the product or combination contains more
    than 1 mg of the Controlled Drug or 1 microgram in the case of
    lysergide or any other N-alkyl derivative of lysergamide.

Other exemptions will apply, for example to *in vitro* diagnostic devices or kits used by laboratories for the detection of drugs of misuse or for clinical diagnosis, or other products containing very small quantities of Controlled Drugs (e.g. radioactive research compounds). The provisions of the Act will apply to the possession of a stock of Controlled Drugs for the purpose of producing kits and other exempted products. The safe custody regulations will also apply to any stock of Schedule 1 and 2 Controlled Drugs and stocks of buprenorphine, diethylpropion, flunitrazepam and temazepam held for the propose of manufacture of the exempted products.

Supply of articles for administering or preparing Controlled Drugs

The following persons:

- a practitioner,
- a pharmacist,

- a person employed or engaged in the lawful provision of drug treatment services, and acting in their capacity as such

may supply or offer to supply the following articles namely:

- a swab,
- utensils for the preparation of a controlled drug,
- citric acid,
- a filter, and
- ampoules of Water for Injection

only when supplied or offered for supply in accordance with the Medicines Act and its regulations

Provisions for preventing misuse

The Secretary of State may make such regulations as appear to him/her necessary or expedient for preventing the misuse of Controlled Drugs (s.10). In particular s/he may make provisions that:

1 require precautions to be taken for the safe custody of Controlled Drugs;
2 impose requirements as to the documentation of transactions involving Controlled Drugs, and require copies of documents relating to such transactions to be furnished to the prescribed authority;
3 require the keeping of records and the furnishing of information with respect to Controlled Drugs and in such circumstances and in such manner as may be prescribed;
4 provide for the inspection of any precautions taken or records kept in pursuance of regulations under this section;
5 relate to the packaging and labelling of Controlled Drugs;
6 regulate the transport of Controlled Drugs and the methods used for destroying or otherwise disposing of such drugs when no longer required;
7 regulate the issue of prescriptions containing Controlled Drugs and the supply of Controlled Drugs on prescriptions, and require persons issuing or dispensing prescriptions containing such drugs to furnish to the prescribed authority such information relating to those prescriptions as may be prescribed;
8 require any doctor who attends a person who s/he considers, or has reasonable grounds to suspect, is addicted (within the meaning of the regulations) to Controlled Drugs of any description to furnish to the prescribed authority such particulars with respect to that person as may be prescribed;
9 prohibit any doctor from administering, supplying and authorising the administration and supply to persons so addicted, and from prescribing for such persons, such Controlled Drugs as may be prescribed, except and

in accordance with the terms of a licence issued by the Secretary of State in pursuance of the regulations.

In addition to making regulations about safe custody, the Secretary of State may also, by notice in writing, require the occupier of any premises where Controlled Drugs are kept to take further precautions as specified in the notice (s.11).

Information concerning misuse

Doctors, pharmacists and persons lawfully conducting retail pharmacy businesses in any area may be called upon to give particulars of the quantities of any dangerous or otherwise harmful drugs (not necessarily controlled under the Act) which have been prescribed, administered or supplied over a particular period of time. The Secretary of State may call for this information if it appears to him/her that a social problem exists in that area caused by a drug or drugs.

A notice in writing may be served on the persons concerned specifying the period, and requiring particulars of the drug to be furnished in such a manner and within such time as set out in the notice. Pharmacists may be required to give the names and addresses of the prescribing doctors but may not be required to identify the patients concerned. It is an offence to fail, without reasonable excuse, to give the information required or to give false information (s.17).

Prohibitions on possession, prescribing and supply

Directions following convictions

Where a pharmacist or practitioner has been guilty of any offence under the Act or of any offence under the Customs and Excise Act 1952 or the Customs and Excise Management Act 1979 relating to the unlawful importation or exportation of Controlled Drugs, the Secretary of State may make a direction in respect of him/her. If s/he is a practitioner, the direction will prohibit him/her from having in his/her possession, prescribing, administering, manufacturing, compounding and supplying, and from authorising the administration and supply of, the Controlled Drugs specified in the direction. If s/he is a pharmacist. the direction will prohibit him/her from having in his/her possession, manufacturing, compounding and supplying and from supervising and controlling the manufacture, compounding and supply of the Controlled Drugs specified in the direction (s.12).

A copy of any such direction given by the Secretary of State must be served on the person to whom it applies and notice of it must be published in the London, Edinburgh and Belfast *Gazettes*. A direction takes effect when a copy has been served on the person concerned and it is then an offence for him/her to contravene it. The Secretary of State may cancel or suspend any direction which s/he has given. S/he may also bring a suspended direction into force again by cancelling its suspension (ss.12, 13 and 16).

Conviction for an offence under the Act committed by a pharmacist or other person who is a director, officer or employee of a body corporate carrying on a retail pharmacy business renders that body liable to disqualification under Part IV of the Medicines Act 1968 (s.80) and consequent removal of its premises from the register of pharmacies (see Chapter 24).

Prohibitions affecting doctors

If a doctor contravenes the regulations relating to notification of addicts or the prescribing of Controlled Drugs for addicts, s/he does not commit any offence under the Act. The Secretary of State may, however, make a direction prohibiting him/her from prescribing, administering or supplying, or authorising the administration or supply of, the Controlled Drugs specified in the direction. The doctor commits an offence if s/he contravenes that direction (s.13).

Irresponsible prescribing

If the Secretary of State is of the opinion that a practitioner has been prescribing, administering or supplying, or authorising the administration or supply of, any Controlled Drugs in an irresponsible manner, s/he may give a direction in respect of the practitioner concerned prohibiting him/her from prescribing, administering and supplying or authorising the administration and supply of the Controlled Drugs specified in the direction (s.13).

Tribunals, advisory bodies and professional panels

Before s/he gives a direction prohibiting a doctor or other practitioner from prescribing, administering or supplying Controlled Drugs, the Secretary of State must, except when the direction is based on a conviction, follow the procedure set out in the Act (ss.14, 15 and 16). S/he must refer the case to a *tribunal* consisting of four members of the practitioner's profession and with a lawyer as chairman (Sch.3). The procedure to be followed before tribunals is in SI 1974 No. 85 (L.1) and, for Scotland, SI 1975 No. 459 (s.59). If, as a result of the tribunal's finding that the practitioner has been responsible for the contravention or conduct alleged, the Secretary of State then proposes to make a direction, the practitioner must be informed and given the opportunity to make representations in writing within 28 days. If the practitioner so does, then the case must be referred to an *advisory body* of three appointed persons, one being a member of the practitioner's profession. After receiving the advice of that body, the Secretary of State may (a) advise that no further proceedings be taken; (b) refer the case back to the same, or another, tribunal; or (c) give a direction under section 13 as described above (s.14).

In a case of irresponsible prescribing, if the Secretary of State considers circumstances require that a direction be given with the minimum of delay, s/he may refer the matter to a *professional panel* consisting of three members of the practitioner's profession appointed by the Secretary of State. The panel must afford the practitioner an opportunity to appear before it and, after considering the circumstances of the case, must report to the Secretary of State whether or not it believes there are reasonable grounds for thinking that there has been conduct as alleged. If the panel considers there are such grounds, the Secretary of State may give a direction at once which is effective for a period of six weeks. S/he must also refer the case at once to a tribunal, in accordance with the procedures outlined above. The period of operation of the temporary direction may be extended from time to time by a further 28 days if the tribunal consents. After the tribunal, or the advisory body as appropriate, has considered the case, the Secretary of State may, if s/he thinks fit, make a permanent direction, if that is the advice given to him/her. If no such direction is given, the temporary prohibition will cease (s.15).

Offences, penalties and enforcement

Schedule 4 to the Act is a tabulated summary of offences under the Act and the penalties applicable to them. The level of penalty for offences which concern a Controlled Drug varies according to the class (A, B or C) into which the drug falls, the generally more harmful drugs attracting greater penalties.

The occupier or manager of any premises commits an offence if s/he knowingly permits or suffers any of the following to take place on the premises:

1 producing or supplying, or attempting to produce or supply, or offering to supply any Controlled Drug in contravention of the Act;
2 preparing opium for smoking;
3 smoking cannabis, cannabis resin or prepared opium (s.8).

It is an offence for any person to:

1 smoke or otherwise use prepared opium; or
2 frequent a place used for the purpose of opium smoking; or
3 have in his/her possession:
   a any pipes or other utensils made or adapted for use in connection with the smoking of opium, being pipes or utensils which have been used by him/her or with his/her knowledge and permission in that connection or which s/he intends to use or permit others to use in that connection; or

b   any utensils which have been used by him/her or with his/her
       knowledge and permission in connection with the preparation of
       opium for smoking (s.9).

Other offences are described in some detail in Schedule 4. Those relating to
contravention of regulations or of conditions of any licence, or of directions
relating to safe custody of Controlled Drugs, are of special concern to practising pharmacists (ss.11 and 18).

A person commits an offence if in the UK s/he assists in or induces the
commission in any place outside the UK of an offence punishable under the
provisions of a corresponding law in force in that place (s.20).

Corresponding law means a law stated, in a certificate purporting to be
issued by or on behalf of the government of a country outside the UK, to be a
law providing for the control and regulation in that country of the production,
supply, use, export and import of:

1   drugs and other substances in accordance with the provisions of the
       Single Convention on Narcotic Drugs signed at New York on 30 March
       1961; or
2   dangerous or otherwise harmful drugs in pursuance of any treaty,
       convention or other agreement or arrangement to which the government
       of that country and of the UK are parties (ss.20 and 36).

The unlawful import and export of Controlled Drugs is an offence under
the Customs and Excise Management Act 1979, which provides penalties for
improper importation or exportation or for fraudulent evasion of any prohibition or restriction affecting Controlled Drugs.

Attempting to commit an offence under any provision of the Act or
inciting or attempting to incite another to commit such an offence are also
offences. They attract the same penalty as the substantive offences (ss.19
and 25).

Where any offence under the Act committed by a body corporate is proved
to have been committed with the consent or connivance of, or to be attributable to any neglect on the part of, any director, manager, secretary or other
similar officer of the body corporate, or any person purporting to act in any
such capacity, s/he, as well as the body corporate, is guilty of the offence and is
liable to be proceeded against accordingly (s.21).

Proof that the accused neither knew of nor suspected, nor had reason to
suspect, the existence of some fact which it is necessary for the prosecution to
prove, is a defence in connection with the offences of production, supply or
possession of Controlled Drugs, cultivation of cannabis or possession of
opium pipes and utensils. When it is necessary, in connection with any
offence, to prove that a substance or product is a Controlled Drug, the accused
may prove that s/he believed it to be a different Controlled Drug. This, in

itself, will not constitute a defence unless there could have been no offence had the drug been of that description (s.28).

It is also a defence for a person accused of unlawful possession of a Controlled Drug to prove that s/he took possession of it to prevent another person committing an offence, and that s/he took steps to destroy it as soon as possible, or that s/he took possession of the drug to hand it over to some authorised person as soon as possible (s.5).

A constable, or other person authorised by the Secretary of State, has power to enter any premises used for the production and supply of Controlled Drugs and inspect books and documents and any stocks of drugs. An inspector of the Royal Pharmaceutical Society of Great Britain (RPSGB) is authorised by the Secretary of State to inspect books and documents. It is an offence to conceal any such books, documents or stock.

A constable may also, on the authority of a warrant, enter any premises named in the warrant, by force if necessary, and search them and any person found therein, seizing any Controlled Drug or any document relevant to the transaction, if s/he has reasonable grounds to consider that an offence under the Act has been committed (s.23).

A constable may arrest a person who has committed an offence under the Act, or whom s/he suspects has committed an offence, if that person's name and address are unknown to him/her or cannot be ascertained, or if s/he suspects the name and address are false, or if s/he has reasonable cause to think that the person may abscond unless arrested (s.24). S/he may detain for the purposes of search any person whom s/he has reasonable grounds to suspect is in unlawful possession of a Controlled Drug. S/he may also stop and search any vehicle or vessel for the same reason, and may seize anything which appears to be evidence of an offence under the Act (s.23).

It is an offence intentionally to obstruct a person exercising their powers of examination or search. Failure to produce any book or document without reasonable excuse is also an offence, and proof of the reasonableness of the excuse rests with the person offering it as a defence (s.23).

Upon a conviction, anything relating to the offence may be forfeited and destroyed or otherwise dealt with by order of the court, subject to any person claiming to be the owner showing cause why the order should not be made (s.27). The Drug Trafficking Offences Act 1986 provides for the confiscation of the proceeds of drug trafficking received by convicted persons.

Scheduled substances: precursors

Scheduled substances means those substances which are useful for the manufacture of Controlled Drugs.

Council Regulation 90/3677/EEC controls the import, export, recording and labelling of scheduled substances and the power to enter business premises to obtain evidence of irregularities. Records must be kept for two years. It also requires member states to adopt measures to enable them to obtain information on any orders for, or activities in, scheduled substances. There is a list of scheduled substances.

The EC regulation was implemented by the Criminal Justice (International Co-operation) Act 1990 (s.12), which created the offences of manufacturing or supplying scheduled substances knowing or suspecting they are to be used in or for the unlawful production of a Controlled Drug. Regulations made under the 1990 Act (s.13) enable the other requirements of the EC regulation to be investigated and enforced (SI 2008 No. 296).

Council Directive 92/109/EEC, which is complementary to the above EC regulation, applies to the manufacture and trade in scheduled substances within the EU and is implemented in the UK by the Controlled Drugs (Substances Useful for Manufacture) (Intra-Community Trade) Regulations SI 1993 No. 2166 as amended by SI 2004 No. 850. It requires the person who manufactures or trades in these substances to be licensed and restricts the persons to whom supplies may be made. The 1993 UK regulations as amended treat the provisions of Council Directive 92/109/EEC as if they were requirements of regulations made under section 13 of the 1990 Act.

Powers of the Secretary of State

The power of the Secretary of State to make regulations is exercised by statutory instruments (ss.7, 10, 22 and 31). Regulations may make provision for different cases and circumstances and for different Controlled Drugs and different classes of person. The opinion, consent or approval of a prescribed authority or of any person may also be made material to a regulation, for example the approval of a chief officer of police is required in connection with certain safekeeping requirements for drugs (s.31). Any licence or other authority issued by the Secretary of State for the purposes of the Act may be made subject to such conditions as s/he thinks proper and may be modified or revoked at any time (s.30).

The application of any provision of the Act which creates an offence, and those provisions of the Customs and Excise Management Act 1979 which apply to the importation and exportation of Controlled Drugs (see p. 219), may, in prescribed cases, be excluded by regulation. Similarly, any provision of the Act or any regulation or order made under it may, by regulation, be made applicable to servants and agents of the Crown (s.22).

Most of the regulations are designed to render lawful various activities in connection with Controlled Drugs which would otherwise be unlawful under the Act. For example, they are necessary to enable doctors, pharmacists and others to prescribe, administer, manufacture, compound or supply Controlled

Drugs as appropriate to their particular capacities. They also govern such matters as the safekeeping of Controlled Drugs and their destruction, the notification of addicts and the supply of Controlled Drugs to addicts.

Regimes of control

The drugs controlled under the Act are classified in the Misuse of Drugs Regulations 2001 (SI 2001 No. 3998, as amended) into five schedules in descending order of control, the most stringent controls applying to drugs in Schedule 1. All the schedules are set out fully in Appendix 6 and the controls applying to each are outlined below.

Schedule 1

Schedule 1 lists Controlled Drugs which may not be used for medicinal purposes, their production and possession being limited, in the public interest, to purposes of research or other special purposes. Certain limited classes of person have a general authority to possess these drugs in the course of their duties, for example constables or carriers (reg.6). Other persons may only produce, supply or possess the drugs within the authority of a licence issued by the Secretary of State. The requirements of the Misuse of Drugs Regulations relating to (a) documentation, (b) keeping of records, (c) preservation of records, (d) supply on prescription, (e) marking of containers and (f) procedure for destruction apply in full to these drugs in Schedule 1.

Schedule 2

Schedule 2 includes the opiates (such as heroin, morphine and methadone) and the major stimulants (such as the amphetamines). A licence is needed to import or export drugs in this schedule, but they may be manufactured or compounded by a practitioner, or a pharmacist, or a person lawfully conducting a retail pharmacy business acting in their capacity as such, or a person holding an appropriate licence. A pharmacist may supply a Schedule 2 drug to a patient (or the owner of an animal) only on the authority of a prescription in the required form issued by an appropriate practitioner (regs.15 and 16).

The drugs may only be administered to a patient by a doctor or dentist, or by any person acting in accordance with the directions of a doctor or dentist (reg.7). Requirements as to safe custody in pharmacies and control over destruction apply to these drugs, and the provisions relating to the marking of containers and the keeping of records must also be observed (regs.18 and 19). A list of persons who may lawfully possess or supply them is given under the heading Possession and supply (p. 225 below).

Schedule 3

Schedule 3 includes the barbiturates (except quinalbarbital, which is a Schedule 2 Controlled Drug) and a number of minor stimulant drugs, such as benzphetamine, and other drugs which are not thought likely to be so harmful when misused as the drugs in Schedule 2. The controls which apply to Schedule 2 also apply to drugs in Schedule 3, except that:

1 they may also be manufactured by persons authorised in writing by the Secretary of State;
2 there is a difference in the classes of person who may possess and supply them;
3 the requirements as to destruction do not apply to retail dealers; and
4 entries in the register of Controlled Drugs need not be made in respect of these drugs but invoices or like records must be kept for a period of two years (see p. 237).

Schedule 4, Part I

Part I of Schedule 4 contains the benzodiazepine tranquillisers. The restrictions applicable to Schedule 3 drugs apply to these drugs with the relaxations as for Schedule 4, Part I drugs at 1, 2, 3, 4 and 5 below. There is no restriction on imports and exports.

Schedule 4, Part II

Part II of Schedule 4 contains the anabolic and androgenic steroids and derivatives, together with an andrenoceptor stimulant and polypeptide hormones. The restrictions applicable to Schedule 3 drugs apply to them with the following relaxations:

1 there is no restriction on the possession of any Schedule 4, Part II drug when contained in a medicinal product;
2 prescription and labelling requirements under the Misuse of Drugs Act do not apply, but the provisions of the Medicines Act do apply;
3 records need not be kept by retailers;
4 destruction requirements apply only to importers, exporters and manufacturers;
5 there are no safe custody requirements;
6 there is no restriction on imports or exports *provided* they are imported or exported:
   a in the form of a medicinal product; *and*
   b by a person for administration to him/herself.

Schedule 5

Schedule 5 specifies those preparations of certain Controlled Drugs for which there is only negligible risk of abuse. There is no restriction on the import, export, possession or administration of these preparations, and safe custody requirements do not apply to them. A practitioner or pharmacist, acting in his/her capacity as such, or a person holding an appropriate licence, may manufacture or compound any of them.

No record in the register of Controlled Drugs need be made in respect of Schedule 3, 4 or 5 drugs obtained by a retail dealer, but the invoice, or a copy of it, must be kept for two years. Producers and wholesale dealers must retain invoices of quantities obtained and supplied [reg.24(1)]. No authority is required to destroy these drugs, and there are no special labelling requirements, though Medicines Act labelling requirements apply. A *retail dealer* is defined as a person lawfully conducting a retail pharmacy business or a pharmacist engaged in supplying drugs to the public at a NHS health centre.

Poppy-straw

Poppy-straw, which includes poppy heads, is listed as a Controlled Drug in Schedule 2 to the Act, where it is defined as '*all parts, except the seeds, of the opium poppy, after mowing*'. It is not included in any of the schedules to the regulations. Although a licence is required to import or export poppy-straw, its production, possession and supply are free from control (reg.4). *Concentrate of poppy-straw*, which means the material produced when poppy-straw has entered into a process for the concentration of its alkaloids, is included in Schedule 1 to the regulations to which apply the stringent controls described above.

Import and export

Controlled Drugs may only be imported or exported in accordance with the terms and conditions of a licence issued by the Secretary of State (s.3 of the Act) but drugs in Schedules 4 (Part II) and 5 are exempted from this requirement (reg.4). Drugs in Schedule 4, Part I are subject to certain restrictions (see p. 219). Unlawful import or export is an offence under the Customs and Excise Management Act 1979 (see p. 215).

The 2001 regulations includes the exemption that in the case of drugs included in Part II of Schedule 4 in the form of medicinal products imported or exported by any person for administration to himself.

Possession and supply

It is unlawful for any person to be in possession of a Controlled Drug unless:

1 s/he holds an appropriate licence from or is registered by the Secretary of State (reg.10); or,
2 s/he is a member of a class specified in the regulations and is acting in his/her capacity as a member of that class (regs.6 and 10); or
3 the regulations provide that possession of that drug or group of drugs is not unlawful.

Possession of poppy-straw or drugs in Schedule 5 and medicinal products in Schedule 4 are not controlled (reg.4).

The classes of person who may possess or supply Controlled Drugs are given in Table 17.1, with an indication of the range of drugs they may possess and/or supply. A person authorised to supply may supply only those persons authorised to possess, and such supply is subject to any provisions of the Medicines Act 1968 which apply to the drug being supplied.

	Class of person	Possession	Supply
1	A person holding an appropriate licence from the Home Office	S1 S2 S3 S4 S5	S1 S2 S3 S4 S5
2	A constable when acting in the course of his/her duty	S1 S2 S3 S4 S5	S1 S2 S3 S4 S5
3	A person engaged in the business of a carrier when acting in the course of that business	S1 S2 S3 S4 S5	S1 S2 S3 S4 S5
4	A person engaged in the business of a postal operator when acting in the course of that business (SI 2003 No. 1653)	S1 S2 S3 S4 S5	S1 S2 S3 S4 S5
5	An officer of Customs and Excise when acting in the course of his/her duty as such	S1 S2 S3 S4 S5	S1 S2 S3 S4 S5
6	A person engaged in the work of any laboratory to which the drug has been sent for forensic examination when acting in the course of his/her duty as a person so engaged	S1 S2 S3 S4 S5	S1 S2 S3 S4 S5

Table 17.1 Possession and supply of Controlled Drugs

(continued overleaf)

Table 17.1 *(continued)*

	Class of person	Possession	Supply
1–6	[The supply of any Controlled Drug by any person in categories 1–6 above may only be to a person who may lawfully possess that drug]		
7	A person engaged in conveying the drug to a person authorised by the regulations to have it in his/her possession (see under Requisitions p. 228)	S1 S2 S3 S4 S5	S1 S2 S3 S4 S5
8	A person possessing a drug for administration in accordance with the directions of a practitioner (for example, on a prescription) [The Home Office take the view that it is unlawful for a doctor to possess a Controlled Drug on the strength of a prescription issued by him/herself and naming him/herself as patient (*Pharm J* 8 October 1977 p. 328)]	S2 S3 S4 S5	
9	A person authorised under a group authority	S2 S3 S4 S5	S2 S3 S4 S5
10	A practitioner	S2 S3 S4 S5	S2 S3 S4 S5
11	A pharmacist	S2 S3 S4 S5	S2 S3 S4 S5
12	A person lawfully conducting a retail pharmacy business	S2 S3 S4 S5	S2 S3 S4 S5
13	The person in charge or acting person in charge of a hospital or care home which is wholly or mainly maintained by a public authority out of public funds or by a charity or by voluntary subscriptions (c.f. 24 below) may not supply if there is a pharmacist responsible for dispensing and supply of drugs	S2 S3 S4 S5	S2 S3 S4 S5
14	The senior or acting senior registered nurse for the time being in charge of a ward, theatre or other department in a hospital or care home as in 13, in the case of drugs supplied to	S2 S3 S4 S5	S2 S3 S4 S5

Table 17.1 (continued)		
	Class of person	Possession	Supply
	him/her by a person responsible for the dispensing and supply of medicines at the hospital or care home (c.f. 25 below). *Senior or acting senior registered nurse* includes any male nurse occupying a similar position. Supply subject to direction by doctor or dentist		
15	A person who is in charge of a laboratory, the recognised activities of which consist in, or include, the conduct of scientific education or research and which is attached to a university, university college or a hospital as described in 13 or to any other institution approved for the purpose by the Secretary of State (c.f. 26 below)	S2 S3 S4 S5	S2 S3 S4 S5
16	A public analyst appointed under section 89 of the Food and Drugs Act 1955 or section 27 of the Food and Drugs (Scotland) Act 1956	S2 S3 S4 S5	S2 S3 S4 S5
17	A sampling officer within the meaning of the Food and Drugs Act 1955 or the Food and Drugs (Scotland) Act 1956	S2 S3 S4 S5	S2 S3 S4 S5
18	A sampling officer within the meaning of Schedule 3 to the Medicines Act 1968	S2 S3 S4 S5	S2 S3 S4 S5
19	A person employed or engaged in connection with a scheme for testing the quality or amount of the drugs, preparations and appliances supplied under the National Health Service Act 1946 or the National Health Service (Scotland) Act 1947 and the regulations made thereunder	S2 S3 S4 S5	S2 S3 S4 S5
20	A person authorised by the Royal Pharmaceutical Society of Great Britain for the purposes of sections 108 and 109 of the Medicines Act 1968	S2 S3 S4 S5	S2 S3 S4 S5

(continued overleaf)

Table 17.1 *(continued)*

	Class of person	Possession	Supply
21	The owner or master of a ship (which is not carrying a doctor) for the purposes of complying with the Health and Safety at Work, etc. Act 1974 or the Merchant Shipping Acts. *Master of ship* includes every person (except a pilot) having command or charge of any ship	S2 S3 S4 S5	S2 S3 S4 S5
22	The master of a foreign ship in port in Great Britain possessing drugs as necessary for the equipment of his/her ship and authorised by the local medical officer of health	S2 S3 S4 S5	
23	The installation manager of an offshore installation possessing drugs for the purpose of compliance with the Health and Safety at Work etc. Act 1974, or the Mineral Workings (Off-Shore Installations) Act 1971. S/he may supply to (a) any person who may lawfully supply the drug; (b) any person on the installation whether employed there or not; (c) any constable for destruction	S2 S3 S4 S5	S2 S3 S4 S5
24	The person in charge or acting person in charge of a hospital or care home (c.f. 13 above). May not supply if there is a pharmacist responsible for dispensing and supply of drugs	S3 S4 S5	S3 S4 S5
25	The senior or acting senior registered nurse for the time being in charge of a ward, theatre or other department in a hospital or care home in the case of drugs supplied to him/her by a person responsible for the dispensing and supply of medicines at the hospital or care home (c.f. 14 above). Supply subject to direction by doctor or dentist	S3 S4 S5	S3 S4 S5
26	A person in charge of a laboratory the recognised activities of which	S3 S4 S5	S3 S4 S5

Table 17.1 *(continued)*

	Class of person	Possession	Supply
	consist in, or include, the conduct of scientific education or research (c.f. 15 above)		
27	A person whose name is entered in a register maintained by the Home Office relating to Schedule 3 drugs	S3 S4 S5	S3 S4
28	A person authorised in writing by the Secretary of State	S5	S5
29	Registered practising midwives (see supply to midwives and administration, p. 227) [reg.11]. Any Controlled Drug s/he may lawfully administer under the Medicines Act Regulations	see p. 227	see p. 227
30	A person licensed under the Wildlife and Countryside Act 1981	S2 S3	S2 S3
31	A registered nurse (SI 2003 No. 2429)	A registered nurse may possess in accordance with a Patient Group Direction any drug specified in Schedule 4 and 5 to a person who can lawfully possess that drug except anabolic steroids or any preparation for injection	A registered nurse may supply in accordance with a Patient Group Direction any drug specified in Schedule 4 and 5 to a person who can lawfully possess that drug except anabolic steroids or any preparation for injection
32	A registered nurse (SI 2003 No. 2429)	A registered nurse may possess in accordance with a Patient Group Direction diamorphine for the treatment of cardiac pain to a person admitted as a patient to a coronary care unit or an accident and emergency department of a hospital	A registered nurse may supply in accordance with a Patient Group Direction diamorphine for the treatment of cardiac pain to a person admitted as a patient to a coronary care unit or an accident and emergency department of a hospital
33	A supplementary prescriber (SI 2005 No. 271		May administer a Controlled Drug when acting in accordance with the terms of a clinical management plan without the directions of a doctor or dentist

(continued overleaf)

Table 17.1 (continued)

	Class of person	Possession	Supply
34	Nurse independent prescriber (SI 2005 No. 2864 and SI 2006 No. 986)	Only prescribe: (a) morphine and oxycodone for use in palliative care or (b) diazepam, lorazepam, midazolam for use in palliative care or treatment of tonic–clonic seizures (c) codeine phosphate, dihydrocodeine tartrate or co-phenotrope (d) chlorodiazepoxide HCL or diazepam for the treatment of initial or acute withdrawal symptoms caused by alcohol withdrawal from person habituated to it (e) buprenorphine or fentanyl for transdermal use in palliative care (f) diamorphine or morphine for pain relief in respect of suspected infarction or for relief of acute or severe pain after trauma	May supply/administer (a) diamorphine, morphine and oxycodine for use in palliative care (b) codeine phosphate, dihydrocodeine tartrate or co-phenotrope (c) fentanyl for transdermal use in palliative care (d) diamorphine or morphine for pain relief in respect of suspected infarction or for relief of acute or severe pain after trauma

Standard operating procedures

All healthcare providers including retail pharmacies must have up-to-date standard operating procedures (SOPs) in place that cover the following:

1 who has access to Controlled Drugs;
2 where Controlled Drugs are stored;
3 security in relation to the storage and transportation of Controlled Drugs, as required by the legislation;
4 disposal and destruction of Controlled Drugs;
5 record keeping, including:
  a maintaining relevant Controlled Drug registers under the legislation; and
  b maintaining a record of Controlled Drugs specified in Schedule 2 to the Misuse of Drugs Regulation SI 2001 as amended and that have been returned from patients together with details of name and address of patient and method and date of destruction (see also p. 237);

6 who is to be alerted if complications arise which may include details of when and how the relevant accountable officer should be informed of incidents.

The Department of Health has issued guidelines giving more detailed advice that may need to be covered by standard operating procedures (www.dh.gov.uk).

Other general authorities to possess and supply include:

1 any person who is lawfully in possession of a Controlled Drug may supply that drug to the person from whom s/he obtained it;

2 any person who is in possession of a Schedule 2, 3, 4 or 5 drug which has been supplied for him/her by, or on the prescription of, a practitioner may supply that drug to any doctor, dentist or pharmacist *for the purpose of destruction*;

3 any person who is in lawful possession of a Schedule 2, 3, 4 or 5 drug which has been supplied by, or on the prescription of, a veterinary surgeon or veterinary practitioner for the treatment of animals may supply that drug to any veterinary surgeon, veterinary practitioner or pharmacist *for the purpose of destruction*;

4 any of the following persons may supply or administer a specified controlled drug under a patient group direction:

    a   a person who holds a certificate of proficiency in ambulance paramedic skills issued by, or with the approval of, the Secretary of State or a person who is a state registered paramedic;

    b   a registered health visitor;

    c   a registered midwife;

    d   a registered optometrist;

    e   a state registered chiropodist;

    f   a person who is registered in the Register of Orthoptists under the Health Professions Council;

    g   a person who is registered in the Register of Physiotherapists under the Health Professions Council; or

    h   a person who is registered in the Register of Radiographers under the Health Professions Council.

Midwives and pethidine

A registered midwife who has, in accordance with the Nurses, Midwives and Health Visitors Act 1997, notified to the local supervising authority his/her intention to practise may, as far as is necessary for the practice of his/her profession or employment as a midwife, possess and administer any Controlled Drug which the Medicines Act 1968 permits him/her to administer. Supplies may only be made to him/her, or possessed by him/her, on the authority of a *midwife's supply order*, that is, an order in writing specifying the name and occupation of the midwife obtaining the Controlled Drug, the purpose for which it is required and the total quantity to be obtained (reg.11). It must be signed by the *appropriate medical officer*, which means:

1 a doctor who is for the time being authorised in writing for the purpose of regulation 11 by the local supervising authority for the region or area in which the Controlled Drug was, or is to be, obtained; or
2 a person appointed by that authority to exercise supervision over certified midwives within their area, e.g. a non-medical supervisor of midwives.

A midwife may surrender any stocks of Controlled Drugs in his/her possession which are no longer required by him/her to a doctor falling within category 1 above (reg.11) or to the person from whom s/he obtained them (reg.6).

The midwife must, on each occasion on which s/he obtains a supply of a Controlled Drug, enter in a book kept by him/her solely for this purpose, (a) the date, and (b) the name and address of the person from whom the drug was obtained, the amount obtained and the form in which it was obtained. When administering any Controlled Drug to a patient, s/he must enter in the same book as soon as practicable the name and address of the patient, the amount administered and the form in which it was administered (reg.21).

A midwife's supply order must be retained for two years by the pharmacist who supplies the Controlled Drug and s/he must make an appropriate entry in his/her Controlled Drugs register (regs.19 and 22).

Requisitions

Standard requisition forms are now produced by the NHS but there is no legal requirement for them to be used. If a non-standard requisition form is used, all the legal requirements must be complied with. The requisition must be signed by the recipient, state his/her name, address and profession or occupation, and must specify the total quantity of the drug and the purpose for which it is required.

A requisition in writing must be obtained by a supplier before s/he delivers any Controlled Drug except those in Schedules 4 and 5, poppy-straw or any drug in Schedule 3 contained in or comprising a preparation which (a) is required for use as a buffering agent in chemical analysis, (b) has present both a substance in the Schedule and a salt of that substance, and (c) is pre-mixed in a kit [reg.14(7)]. A *supplier*, in this context, means any person who is not a practitioner supplying such a Controlled Drug, otherwise than on prescription, or by way of administration, to any of the following *recipients*:

1 a practitioner;
2 the person in charge or acting person in charge of a hospital or care home;

3   a person who is in charge of a laboratory;
4   the owner of a ship, or the master of a ship which does not carry a doctor among the seamen employed in it;
5   the installation manager of an off-shore installation;
6   the master of a foreign ship in a port in Great Britain [reg.14(4)];
7   a supplementary prescriber;
8   a senior or acting senior registered nurse in charge of a ward, department or care home who obtains supply from the hospital; the requisition must be maintained in the dispensary and a copy left with the nurse;
9   an operating department practitioner, who can obtain from the pharmacy in his/her hospital.

The recipient must mark the requisition with the suppliers name and address, keep a copy for two years and send the original documents to the National Health Agency This also applies to the non-standard forms.

A *wholesale dealer*, that is, a person who carries on the business of selling drugs to persons who buy to sell again, when supplying a pharmacist does not require a requisition. The supplier must be reasonably satisfied that the signature is that of the person purporting to have signed the requisition and that s/he is engaged in the profession or occupation stated [reg.14(2)].

Where a supplier, who is not a practitioner, supplies a Controlled Drug for which a requisition is required, s/he may not supply it to any person sent on behalf of the recipient to collect the drug unless that person (a) is authorised to have the drug in his/her possession otherwise than as a messenger; or (b) produces to the supplier a statement in writing signed by the recipient to the effect that s/he is empowered by the recipient to receive the drug on his/her behalf, and the supplier is reasonably satisfied that the document is genuine [reg.14(1)].

Where a recipient is a practitioner who represents that s/he urgently requires a Controlled Drug for the purpose of his/her profession, the supplier, if s/he is reasonably satisfied that the practitioner requires the drug and is by reason of some emergency unable to furnish a written requisition, may deliver the drug on an undertaking by the practitioner to furnish a written requisition within the next 24 hours. Failure to do so is an offence on the part of the practitioner [reg.14(2)].

A requisition furnished by the master of a foreign ship must contain a statement signed by the proper officer of the port health authority or, in Scotland, the medical officer designated under section 14 of the National Health Service (Scotland) Act 1978 by the health board within whose jurisdiction the ship is, that the quantity of drug to be supplied is the quantity necessary for the equipment of the ship [reg.14(5)].

A requisition furnished by the matron or acting matron of a hospital or care home must also be signed by a doctor or a dentist employed or engaged in that hospital or care home [reg.14(5)].

A senior or acting senior registered nurse for the time being in charge of any ward, theatre or other department of a hospital or care home who obtains a supply of a Controlled Drug from the person responsible for dispensing and supplying medicines at that hospital or care home must furnish a requisition in writing signed by him/her which specifies the total quantity of the drug required. S/he must retain a copy or note of the requisition. The person responsible for the dispensing and supply of medicines must mark the requisition in such a manner as to show that it has been complied with and must retain the requisition in the dispensary [reg.14(6)].

Prescriptions for Controlled Drugs

Prescription means a prescription used by a doctor for the medical treatment of a single individual, by a dentist for the dental treatment of a single individual, a nurse independent prescriber for the medical treatment of a single individual or by a veterinary surgeon or veterinary practitioner for the purposes of animal treatment.

No prescription requirements are laid down for any Controlled Drug in Schedules 4 or 5 to the regulations except for temazepam.

A person shall not issue a prescription other than a health prescription or a veterinary prescription for temazepam unless it is written on a prescription form provide by a primary care trust or equivalent body for the purpose of private prescribing and it specifies the identification number and address of the person issuing it (SI 2006 No. 1450). In the case of other Controlled Drugs (i.e. those in Schedules 2 and 3), a prescription must not be issued unless it complies with the following requirements:

1 be written so as to be indelible, be dated and be signed by the person issuing it with his/her usual signature and dated by him/her (it is unlikely that a carbon copy, even one bearing an original signature would be sufficient to satisfy the indelibility requirement) (SI 2005 No. 2864);

2 except in the case of a health prescription, it must specify the address of the person issuing it;

3 it must have written thereon, if issued by a dentist, the words '*for dental treatment only*' and, if issued by a veterinary surgeon or a veterinary practitioner, a declaration that the Controlled Drug prescribed is for an animal under his/her care;

4 it must specify the name and address of the person for whose treatment it is issued or, if it is issued by a veterinary surgeon or veterinary practitioner, the name and address of the person to whom the Controlled Drug prescribed is to be delivered;

5 it must specify the dose to be taken, and

   a   in the case of a prescription containing a Controlled Drug which is a preparation, it must specify the form and, where appropriate, the strength of the preparation, and either the total quantity (in both words and figures) of the preparation or the number (in both words and figures) of dosage units, as appropriate, to be supplied;

b   in any other case, it must specify the total quantity (in both words and figures) of the Controlled Drug to be supplied;

6   in the case of a prescription for a total quantity intended to be dispensed by instalments, it must contain a direction specifying the amount of the instalments of the total amount which must be dispensed and the intervals to be observed when dispensing [reg.15(1)].

A prescription issued for the treatment of a patient in a hospital or care home and written on the patient's bed card or case sheet need not specify the address of the patient [reg.15(3)].

When a drug is administered from stock held in the ward, the prescription requirements do not apply.

A Controlled Drug, except those in Schedules 4 and 5, must not be supplied by any person on a prescription (Regulation 15):

1   unless the prescription complies with the provisions set out above;
2   unless the prescriber's address on the prescription is within the UK;
3   unless the supplier is either acquainted with the prescriber's signature, and has no reason to suppose that it is not genuine, or has taken reasonably sufficient steps to satisfy him/herself that it is genuine;
4   before the date specified on the prescription;
5   later than 28 days after the date specified on the prescription unless it is an instalment prescription (see below) (SI 2006 No. 1450).

Prescriptions (other than those for drugs in Schs.4 or 5) which contain a direction that specified instalments of the total amount may be supplied at stated intervals must not be supplied otherwise than in accordance with the directions:

1   the first instalment must be supplied not later than 13 weeks after the date specified in the prescription;
2   the prescription must be marked with the date at the time when each instalment is supplied;
3   the prescription must be retained for two years after the supply of the last instalment;
4   repeat prescriptions as such are not provided for, in that the total quantity of drug prescribed must be stated on the prescription [regs.16(4) and 23(3)].

A pharmacist may supply a Controlled Drug if the prescription contains minor typographical errors or spelling mistakes or if it does not comply with the provisions of regulation 15 provided that:

1   having exercised all due diligence s/he is satisfied on reasonable grounds that the prescription is genuine;

2 having exercised all due diligence s/he is satisfied on reasonable grounds that the supply of the drug is in accordance with the intention of the person issuing the prescription;

3 s/he amends the prescription in ink or otherwise indelibly to correct the minor errors or mistakes or so that the prescription complies with the Regulation 15 requirements;

4 s/he marks the prescription so that the amendment s/he has made is attributable to her/him;

5 items 1–4 above apply if the total quantity or number of doses is specified in either words or figures but not if both words and figures are missing.

A person supplying temazepam in accordance with an electronic prescription shall at the time of supply enter on the form by electronic means the date on which the drug was supplied [16(3) of the 2001 Regulations].

A person who is asked to supply a controlled drug specified in Schedule 2 must first ascertain whether the person collecting the drug is the patient, the patient's representative or a healthcare professional acting in his/her professional capacity (SI 2006 No. 1450; reg.6):

1 where the person is the patient or the patient's representative, s/he may
  a request evidence of identity, or
  b refuse to supply if he is not satisfied as to identity;

2 where the person is a healthcare professional, s/he may
  a request the identity of the person,
  b obtain that person's name and address, or
  c supply even if not satisfied as to identity.

A copy of every prescription other than a health or veterinary prescription must be sent to the relevant NHS service agency (SI 2006 No. 1450).

Nothing in the regulations relating to prescriptions (regs.15 and 16) has effect in relation to prescriptions issued for the purposes of a scheme for testing the quality and amount of the drugs, preparations and appliances supplied under the NHS, or to any prescriptions issued to sampling officers under the Food and Drugs (Scotland) Act 1956 or the Medicines Act 1968 (reg.17).

A person is not in lawful possession of a drug if s/he obtained it on a prescription which s/he obtained from the prescriber (a) by making a false statement or declaration, or (b) by not disclosing to the doctor that s/he was being supplied with a Controlled Drug by or on the prescription of another doctor [reg.10(2)].

Marking of containers

The container in which a Controlled Drug, other than a preparation, is supplied must be plainly marked with the amount of drug contained in it. If the drug is a preparation made up into tablets, capsules or other dosage units, the container must be marked with the amount of Controlled Drug(s) in each dosage unit and the number of dosage units in it. For any other kind of preparation, the container must be marked with the total amount of the preparation in it and the percentage of Controlled Drug(s) in the preparation [reg.18(1)]. These requirements do not apply to (a) poppy-straw, (b) Controlled Drugs in Schedules 4 and 5, (c) Controlled Drugs supplied on the prescription of a practitioner or for administration in a clinical trial or a medicinal test on animals, or (d) any Schedule 3 drug in a preparation used as a buffering agent in chemical analysis or which has present in it both a substance in that Schedule and a salt of that substance or is pre-mixed in a kit (reg.18(2), as amended).

Registers and records

There is no statutory format for the register provided the following information is recorded. However the National Pharmacy Association does produce a register which complies with the requirements. Samples of registers are shown in Figures 17.1, 17.2 and 17.3.

Register means either a bound book, which does not include any form of loose-leaf register or card index, or a computerised system which is in accordance with best practice guidlines endorsed by the Secretary of State under the National Health Service Act 1977 (SI 2005 No. 2864) (see also www.rpsgb.org).

Minimum information regarding Controlled Drugs obtained to be recorded

An entry in a register of Controlled Drugs must be made in respect of every quantity of any drug in Schedules 1 and 2 which is obtained or supplied (whether by way of administration or otherwise), the name and address of

Date on which supply received	Name and address of person or firm from whom obtained	Amount obtained	Form in which obtained

Figure 17.1 Examples of possible entry formats for receiving Controlled Drugs.

Date on which transaction was effected	Name and address of person or firm supplied	Particulars as to licence or authority of person or firm supplied to be in possession	Amount supplied	Form in which supplied

Figure 17.2   Entries to be made in case of supply of Controlled Drugs.

Persons collecting Schedule 2 Controlled Drugs (patient/patient's representative/health care professional, and if health care professional name and address	Was proof of identity requested of patient or patient's representative (Yes/No)	Was proof of identity of person collecting provided (Yes/No)

Figure 17.3   Entries to be made on collection of Controlled Drugs.

the supplier and the date received. This requirement applies to any person authorised to supply those drugs except a senior or acting senior registered nurse for the time being in charge of a ward, theatre or other department in a hospital or care home, or a person licensed to supply by the Secretary of State if the licence does not require a register to be kept (reg.19).

Minimum information to be recorded of drug supplies

The following information must be recorded:

1   date supplied;
2   name and address of person supplied;
3   quantity of drug supplied;
4   person collecting Schedule 2 drug, for example patient/representative or name and address of healthcare professional collecting (see below);

5   proof of identity of person collecting Controlled Drugs requested or obtained (Yes/No).

In the case of a drug on the schedules supplied on a prescription, an entry should be made as to whether the person who has collected the drug was the patient, the patient's representative or a healthcare professional acting on behalf of the patient (SI 2006 No. 4150) and:

a   if the person who collected the drugs was a healthcare professional acting of behalf of the patient, that person's name and address; or

b   if the person who collected the drugs was the patient or the patient's representative, whether evidence of identity was requested of that person and whether evidence of identity was provided by that person.

Nothing prevents the use of the register to record additional information to that required or allowed under these provisions.

Entries in the register must be made in chronological sequence in the form specified in Schedule 6 to the regulations, as illustrated.

A separate register or separate part of the register must be used in respect of each class of drugs. A separate page shall be used in respect of each strength and form of that drug and the head of each such page shall specify the class of the drug, its strength and form (SI 2007 No. 2154).

Dexamphetamine, for example, may be entered under amphetamine, but a separate part of the register is required for methylamphetamine. Separate sections can be used, if desired, in respect of different drugs or different strengths of a drug falling within the same class (reg.19).

The class of drugs recorded must be specified at the head of each page of the register and entries must be made on the day of the transaction or the following day. No cancellation, obliteration or alteration of any entry may be made, and corrections must be by way of marginal notes or footnotes, which must be dated. Every entry and every correction of such an entry must be in ink or be otherwise indelible or shall be in a computerised form in which every entry is attributable and capable of being audited and which is in accordance with best practice guidelines endorsed by the Secretary of State (SI 2005 No. 2864).

A register must not be used for any other purpose and must be kept at the premises to which it relates, and where the register is in a computerised form, it must be accessible from those premises. A separate register must be kept in respect of each set of premises of the business. There may only be one such register for each premises unless the Secretary of State has approved the keeping of separate registers in different departments (reg.20).

Where a supply is made to a member of the crew of a ship or a person on an off-shore installation, an entry, specifying the drug, in the official log book or installation log book is a sufficient record. These books are required to be kept under the Merchant Shipping Acts. In the case of a ship which is not required to carry an official log book, a report signed by the master of the ship is sufficient if it is delivered as soon as may be to the superintendent of a mercantile marine office.

For record-keeping requirements for midwives, see page 228.

Return of Controlled Drugs from patients

A pharmacist or practitioner need not legally record any prescribed drug returned to him/her for destruction, but good pharmaceutical practice would suggest that an entry is made in the drugs register giving the date of receipt; quantity, strength and name of the Controlled Drug; name and address of person who returned the stock; and the date of destruction (see also p. 237). Standard operating procedures should be available for these returns from patients and relate to the above information and details of storage and destruction.

Running balances

At present there is no legal requirement to keep running balances. However it is strongly recommended that they be kept in accordance with a standard operating procedure pending future legislation.

Furnishing of information

Particulars of stocks, receipts and supplies of Controlled Drugs must be furnished on request to any person authorised in writing by the Secretary of State. The register, the stocks of drugs and other relevant books and documents must also be produced if requested (reg.25). If records are held in a computerised form, a copy of the computerised form must be supplied if requested (SI 2005 No. 2864). Inspectors of the RPSGB are authorised for this purpose in relation to registered pharmacies. Those required to furnish information are:

1 practitioners;
2 wholesale dealers;
3 retail dealers;
4 persons in charge of hospitals, care homes or laboratories;
5 persons authorised under the Act or regulations to produce, import or export any Controlled Drug;
6 persons authorised under regulation 9(4) (a) to supply drugs in Schedules 3 and 4.

Professional *personal records* relating to the physical or mental health of an individual are exempt.

Preservation of records

All registers and midwives' record books must be preserved for two years from the date on which the last entry is made therein. Every requisition, order or prescription (other than a health prescription) on which a Controlled Drug is supplied must be preserved for two years from the date on which the last delivery is made (reg.23).

For Controlled Drugs in Schedules 3 and 5 to the regulations, it is sufficient if every invoice is preserved for two years from the date on which it is issued. Producers and wholesalers must keep invoices in respect of Schedule 3 and 5 drugs obtained or supplied by them, and retail dealers must keep invoices in respect of the drugs they obtain. Copies of invoices (e.g. on microfilm) may be retained in place of the original document (reg.24).

Destruction of Controlled Drugs

Persons who are required to keep records in respect of Controlled Drugs in Schedules 1, 2, 3 or 4 may only destroy them in the presence of a person authorised by the Secretary of State either personally or as a member of a class. Among the classes of authorised persons for this purpose are police officers, inspectors of the Home Office and of the RPSGB and, for stock kept in a hospital, the regional pharmaceutical officer or the senior administrative officer employed on duties connected with the administration of the hospital concerned (see Role of accountable officers, below). An accountable officer cannot be an authorised person.

Particulars of the date of destruction and the quantity destroyed must be entered in the register of Controlled Drugs and signed by the authorised person in whose presence the drug was destroyed. The authorised person may take a sample of the drug which is to be destroyed, and destruction must be carried out according to his/her directions.

A pharmacist or practitioner may destroy prescribed drugs returned by a patient or the patient's representative without legally being required to make any record and without the presence of an authorised person (but see Registers and records, p. 233).

The master of a ship or installation manager of an off-shore installation may not destroy any surplus drugs but may dispose of them to a constable or to a person who is lawfully entitled to supply them (i.e. to any pharmacist or licensed dealer who could have supplied them to him/her) (reg.26).

Accountable officers

The Controlled Drugs (Supervision of Management and Use) Regulations SI 2006 No. 3148 made under the Health Act 2006 introduced the concept of an accountable officer as the final amendment to the legislation following the Shipman report.

Accountable officer means a fit, proper and suitable experienced person appointed or nominated by a designated body to ensure the safe, appropriate and effective management and use of Controlled Drugs within organisations subject to their oversight.

A designated body (i.e. a trust or heath board) must nominate or appoint an accountable officer who is responsible to its registered manager and is not involved in the management or use of Controlled Drugs themselves. The accountable officer must have regard to:

1   best practice, and establish and operate, or ensure that his designated body establishes and operates, the safe management and use of Controlled Drugs by his designated body;
2   ensuring that a body or person acting on behalf or providing services under arrangements made with his designated body establishes and operates appropriate arrangements for securing the safe management and use of Controlled Drugs;
3   ensuring that his designated body or those providing services have up-to-date standard operating procedures in place in relation to the management and use of Controlled Drugs; such standard operating procedures must comply with the statutory requirements (see p. 226);
4   ensuring adequate destruction and disposal of Controlled Drugs and appoint authorised persons for this;
5   ensuring monitoring and auditing of Controlled Drugs;
6   ensuring adequate training of persons handling Controlled Drugs;
7   ensuring the monitoring and audit and use of Controlled Drugs by individuals and ensure their performance;
8   maintaining a record of concerns regarding individuals;
9   sharing information with trusts, RPSGB, police, etc.

Accountable officers have the right of assess, carry out periodic inspections of premises, investigate concerns and take action if there are well-founded concerns. Accountable offers must make annual reports to their designated body, always act to protect the safety of patients and the general public, and are immune from civil action when sharing information if disclosure is made in good faith.

Addicts

There are separate regulations relating to addicts and the supply of certain Controlled Drugs to them (SI 1997 No. 1001). A person is regarded as being addicted to a drug 'if, and only if, s/he has, as a result of repeated administration, become so dependent on a drug that s/he has an overpowering desire for the administration of it to be continued'. The expression drug in this context means those specified in the regulations namely:

1 cocaine, dextromoramide, diamorphine, dipipanone, hydrocodone, hydromorphone, levorphanol, methadone, morphine, opium, oxycodone, pethidine, phenazocine and piritramide;

2 any stereoisomeric form of a substance specified in item 1 above, except dextrorphan;

3 any ester or ether of a substance specified in items 1 or 2 above not being a substance for the time being specified in Part II of Schedule 2 to the Misuse of Drugs Act 1971 (see Appendix 6);

4 any salt of a substance specified in any of items 1 to 3 above;

5 any preparation or other product containing a substance or product specified in any of items 1 to 4 above.

Except for the treatment of organic injury or disease or unless s/he is licensed so to do by the Secretary of State, no doctor may administer or authorise the supply of cocaine, diamorphine or dipipanone, or the salts of any of these, to an addicted person (SI 1997 No. 1001).

There is provision for addicts to receive daily supplies of cocaine, heroin, dextromoramide, dipipanone, methadone and pethidine on special prescription forms [FP(10) HP] issued by drug addiction clinics. There is also provision for supplies of all Schedule 2 Controlled Drugs for the treatment of addiction to be issued by general medical practitioners on special prescription forms [FP(10) MDA or in Scotland GP10]. These are administrative arrangements made under the NHS and do not form part of the Misuse of Drugs Regulations.

Safe custody of Controlled Drugs

The regulations relating to safe custody (SI 1973 No. 798, as amended) apply to all Controlled Drugs except:

1 any drug in Schedules 4 and 5;

2 any liquid preparations, apart from injections, which contain any of the following:
   a amphetamine
   b benzphetamine
   c chlorphentermine
   d fenethylline
   e mephentermine
   f methaqualone
   g methylamphetamine
   h methylphenidate

    i   phendimetrazine
    j   phenmetrazine
    k   pipradol
    l   any stereoisomeric form of a substance specified in a to k above; and any salt of a substance specified in a to l above;

3   any of the following:
    a   cathine
    b   ethchlorvynol
    c   ethinamate
    d   mazindol
    e   meprobamate
    f   methylphenobarbitone
    g   methyprylone
    h   pentazocine
    i   phentermine
    j   any 5,5-disubstituted barbituric acid
    k   any stereoisomeric form of a substance specified in a to j above
    l   any salt of a substance specified in a to k above; and any preparation or other product containing a substance or product specified in a to l above;

The premises to which the safe custody requirements apply are:

1   any premises occupied by a retail dealer (see p. 220) for the purposes of his/her business;
2   any care home within the meaning of Part VI of the Public Health Act 1936 or the Care Homes Registration (Scotland) Act 1938;
3   any residential or other establishment provided under or by virtue of section 59 of the Social Work (Scotland) Act 1968;
4   any mental care home within the meaning of Part III of the Mental Health Act 1959;
5   any private hospital within the meaning of the Mental Health (Scotland) Act 1960.

The occupier and every person concerned in the management of any of these premises must ensure that all Controlled Drugs (except those mentioned above) are, so far as circumstances permit, kept in a locked safe, cabinet or room which is so constructed and maintained as to prevent unauthorised access to the drugs (see also p. 211).

This requirement does not apply in respect of any Controlled Drug which is for the time being constantly under the direct personal supervision of (a) a pharmacist in the premises of a retail dealer (e.g. when dispensing prescriptions), or (b) the person in charge of the premises or any member of his/her

Table 17.2 Summary of the Misuse of Drugs Regulations

	Schedule 1	Schedule 2	Schedule 3	Schedule 4 Part I & II	Schedule 5
Administration	By licence only	To a patient by a doctor or dentist or by any person acting in accordance with the directions of a doctor or dentist	As for Schedule 2	As for Schedule 2	No restriction
Import and export	By licence only	By licence only	By licence only	No restriction when contained in a medicinal product [Part I] No restriction [Part II]	No restriction
Possession	By licence only	See under Possession and supply (p. 221)	See under Possession and supply (p. 221)	No restriction	No restriction
Supply	By licence only	See under Possession and supply (p. 221)	See under Possession and supply (p. 221)	See under Possession and supply (p. 000)	See under Possession and supply (p. 000)
Emergency supply permitted	No	No	No, except phenobarbital for epilepsy	Yes	Yes
Production	By licence only	Licence holders, pharmacists, practitioners and owners of pharmacies	Licence holders, authorised persons, pharmacists practitioners and owners of pharmacies	Licence holders, authorised persons, pharmacists, practitioners and owners of pharmacies	Licence holders, pharmacists, practitioners and owners of pharmacies
Prescription requirements	By licensed person only	Yes	Yes except temazepam	Do not apply	Do not apply

Table 17.2 (continued)

	Schedule 1	Schedule 2	Schedule 3	Schedule 4 Part I & II	Schedule 5
Hand-written	No	No	No	No	No
Records in register	Yes	Yes	No register, but records to be kept by licensed and authorised persons Invoices to be kept by retail dealers, wholesalers, hospitals, care homes and laboratories	No register, but licensed producers and authorised suppliers must keep records of imports and exports	No register, but licensed producers, wholesalers, and retail dealers must keep invoices
Labelling requirements	Yes	Yes	Yes	No	No
Destruction requirements	Yes	Yes, but do not apply to drugs returned by patients	Apply only to imports, exports, and licensed manufacturers	Apply only to imports, exports, and licensed manufacturers	Do not apply
Safe custody required	Yes except quinalbarbital	Yes (except certain liquids, quinalbarbital and temazepam) (see p. 239)	No (except temazepam buprenorphine and diethylpropion (see p. 239)	No	No
Requisition requirements	Yes	Yes	No	No	No

staff designated by him/her for the purpose in the case of other premises to which the regulations apply.

The relevant requirements which apply to safes, cabinets and rooms where Controlled Drugs are kept are in Schedule 2 to the regulations.

The owner of a pharmacy may, as an alternative, elect to apply to the police for a certificate that his/her safes, cabinets or rooms provide an adequate degree of security. Applications must be made in writing. After inspection by the police, and if the degree of security is found to be adequate, a certificate, renewable annually, may be issued. The certificate will specify conditions to be observed and may be cancelled if there is a breach of any condition, or if the occupier has refused entry to a police officer, or if there has been any change of circumstances lowering the degree of security.

Quite apart from these special requirements, which affect only certain classes of premises, a person having possession of any Controlled Drug to which the safe custody regulations apply must ensure that, as far as circumstances permit, it is kept in a locked receptacle which can be opened only by him/her or by a person authorised by him/her. This requirement does not apply to a carrier in the course of his/her business or to a person engaged in the business of the Post Office when acting in the course of that business, or to a person to whom the drug has been supplied on the prescription of a practitioner for his/her own treatment or that of another person or an animal.

Summary

Table 17.2 summarises the Misuse of Drugs Regulations.

Further reading

National Prescribing Centre (2007) A Guide to Good Practice in the Management of Controlled Drugs in Primary Care, England, 2nd edn. Liverpool: National Prescribing Centre.

18

Poisons and pesticides

The Poisons Act 1972 and the Poison Rules made under it are concerned with the sale of poisons. Unlike the Medicines Act 1968, the Poisons Act does not extend to Northern Ireland.

A *poison* means a non-medicinal poison (Rule 2) and is defined in the Act (s.11) as a substance which is included in Part I or Part II of the Poisons List made under the Act and which is neither a medicinal product as defined under section 130 of the Medicines Act 1968 nor a substance which is treated as a medicinal product by virtue of an order made under section 104 or 105 of the Medicines Act (see Chapter 2). In line with the Medicines Act, the other definitions include *the board* (s.11); this means, in relation to a body corporate, persons controlling the body by whatever name it is called (e.g. the management committee of a co-operative society). The Act also follows the definitions of the Medicines Act for 'persons lawfully conducting a retail pharmacy business' and a 'registered pharmacy' (see Chapter 5). A more restricted meaning is given to 'sale by way of wholesale dealing'; in relation to poisons, this means sale to a person who buys for the purpose of selling again (see Medicines Act definition, p. 38).

Meaning of poison

Three cases concerned the interpretation of certain sections of the Pharmacy Act 1868 (now repealed). It was held by the High Court that a compound containing a poison, as well as the actual poison, was subject to the Act. The principal point at issue was the meaning of the word *poison* as used in that Act and similarly used in the current Poison Act 1972. Further detail of these earlier cases can be found *in Pharmacy Law and Ethics*, 8th edition.

Poisons Board

The Act (s.1) provides for the continuation of an advisory committee first established under the Pharmacy and Poisons Act 1933 called the Poisons Board. It consists of at least 16 members and the Secretary of State has powers to appoint up to three additional members if s/he thinks fit. The board must include five persons appointed by the Royal Pharmaceutical Society of Great Britain (RPSGB), one of whom is required to be engaged in the manufacture for sale by wholesale dealing of pharmaceutical preparations. Members of the Poisons Board hold office for three years and the Secretary of State appoints one of the members as the chairman. The quorum is 11 and the Board has power to appoint replacements for casual vacancies. The Board makes its own regulations as to procedure, subject to the approval of the Secretary of State (s.1).

Poisons List

The Poisons List is a list of substances treated as poisons for the purposes of the Act (s.2) and is set out in a Poisons List Order, as amended (SI 1982 No. 218) (see Appendix 7). After consultation with, or on the recommendations of, the Poisons Board, the Secretary of State may amend or vary this list. This list is divided into two parts.

> *Part I* consists of poisons the sale of which is restricted to persons lawfully conducting a retail pharmacy business (subsequently referred to as Part I poisons).
>
> *Part II* consists of poisons which may only be sold either by a person lawfully conducting a retail pharmacy business or by a person whose name is entered in a local authority's list (subsequently referred to as Part II poisons). Except where provision is made to the contrary an unqualified reference to a poison includes a substance containing that poison.

N.B. Some substances in the Poisons List also have medicinal uses (e.g. arsenic, strychnine). When sold as medicinal products, they are controlled under the Medicines Act 1968 but when sold for non-medicinal purposes they are subject to the Poisons Act 1972.

Local authorities' lists

Every local authority is obliged to keep a list of the names and business addresses of persons, *listed sellers*, who are entitled to sell Part II poisons and must enter on the list all those persons who make application. A local authority has power (a) to refuse to enter a name if in its opinion the person is not fit to be on the list, and (b) to remove a name for non-payment of the prescribed fee. A person aggrieved by such a decision can appeal to the Crown Court or, in Scotland, to the Sheriff (s.5).

A local authority's list, which is open to inspection without fee, must include particulars of the premises and of the names of the persons listed (Sch.9 and Rule 24, see Appendix 8).

The Act provides for the payment of reasonable fees as determined by the authority for a person making application for his/her name to be included on the list, and also for further annual payments of fees for having his/her name retained on the list [s.6(2), as amended].

If a person whose name is on a local authority's list is convicted of any offence which in the opinion of the Court renders him/her unfit to have his/her name so listed, the Court may, as part of the sentence, order his/her name to be removed and disqualified from being on the list for a specified period. Any person whose name is on a local authority list may not use in connection with his/her business any title, emblem or description reasonably calculated to suggest that s/he is entitled to sell any poisons which s/he is not entitled to sell (s.6).

Local authority means (a) in relation to England and Wales, the council of a county or London borough or the Common Council of the City of London; and (b) in relation to Scotland, the council of a region or island area [s.11(2), as amended].

Proposed changes in the draft Pharmacy Order 2009 (published December 2008)

Proposals for further change to the regulation of pharmacy appear in the draft Pharmacy Order 2009, which was published as this book went to press. The proposals were open to consultation until 9 March 2009 and were expected to be implemented in the second quarter of 2010. The draft Pharmacy Order includes transitional arrangements to ensure smooth transfer of functions from the RPSGB to the General Pharmaceutical Council (GPhC). Many of the major changes from regulation under the Pharmacy Act 1954 to regulation under the Pharmacists and Pharmacy Technicians Act 2007 remain in place and these are detailed in the text below, but relevant changes proposed in the draft Pharmacy Order 2009 include bringing the inspectorate under the GPhC (transferred from the Medicines Act 1968 and removing from the Poisons Act 1972; see Chapter 2).

Inspection and enforcement

It is the duty of the RPSGB to take reasonable steps by means of inspection and otherwise to enforce the provisions of the Poisons Act and its Rules. To do this, the Society must appoint as many inspectors as the Privy Council may direct. Nineteen have been appointed. Only a pharmacist can be appointed as an inspector, and every such appointment is subject to the approval of the Privy Council.

An inspector appointed by the RPSGB, to ensure compliance by pharmacists and persons carrying on retail businesses, has (a) power at all reasonable times to enter any registered pharmacy and (b) power to enter any premises in which s/he has reasonable cause to suspect that a breach of the law has been committed in respect of any Part I poison. Whether in a retail pharmacy business or any other premises, an inspector has power to make such examination and inquiry and do any other thing, including the taking of samples, as is necessary to ascertain that the Act and the rules are being complied with. (The RPSGB's inspectors also have other duties under the Medicines Act 1968 and the Misuse of Drugs Act 1971; see pp. 22 and 214.)

It is the duty of every local authority, by means of inspection and otherwise, to take all reasonable steps to secure compliance with the provisions of the Poisons Act and its rules, as far as they concern Part II poisons, (a) by persons not being persons conducting a retail pharmacy business, and (b) by any persons lawfully conducting a retail pharmacy business in so far as that business is carried on at premises which are not a registered pharmacy. Each local authority must appoint inspectors for these purposes.

An inspector appointed by the RPSGB may, with the consent of the RPSGB, also be appointed by a local authority to be an inspector for the purposes of this section of the Act (s.9).

For the purposes of enforcement, an inspector appointed by a local authority has power at all reasonable times to enter any premises on the local authority's list and any premises where s/he has reasonable cause to suspect that a breach of the law has been committed in respect of any Part II poison (s.9). An inspector appointed by a local authority has power, with the consent of the authority, to institute proceedings before a court of summary jurisdiction, and to take any proceedings instituted by him/her, notwithstanding that s/he is not of counsel or a solicitor.

It is an offence for any person wilfully to delay or obstruct an inspector, to refuse to allow a sample to be taken, or to fail without reasonable excuse to give any information which the Poisons Act requires him/her to give to an inspector (s.9). It is specifically provided that nothing in the Poisons Act authorises an inspector to enter or inspect the premises of a doctor, a dentist, a veterinary surgeon or a veterinary practitioner unless those premises are a shop (s.9).

A document purporting to be a certificate sent by a public analyst appointed under section 89 of the Food and Drugs Act 1955 or section 27 of the Food and Drugs (Scotland) Act 1956 or a person appointed by the Secretary of State (in Scotland the Lord Advocate) to make analyses for the purposes of the Poisons Act is admissible in any proceedings under the Act as evidence of the matters stated therein, and either party may require the person who has signed the certificate to be called as a witness (s.8).

Penalties and legal proceedings

Any person who contravenes or fails to comply with the Poisons Act, or any of the provisions made under the Poisons Rules, is liable on summary conviction to a fine not exceeding £2500, and for continuing offences to a further fine not exceeding £200 for every day subsequent to the day on which s/he is convicted of the offence (s.8 and the Criminal Law Act 1977). For the misuse of titles (s.6) and obstruction of an inspector (s.9) the maximum fine is £500.

In the case of proceedings against a person under the Poisons Act or rules for or in connection with the sale, exposure for sale or supply of a poison effected by an employee, it is not a defence that the employee acted without the authority of the employer and any material fact known to the employee is deemed to have been known to the employer (s.8).

Information in respect of any offence under the Poisons Act or Rules must be laid within 12 months of the commission of the offence. There is an additional provision that the Secretary of State may institute proceedings within a period of three months after the date on which evidence sufficient in his/her opinion to justify a prosecution for an offence comes to his/her knowledge (s.8).

The Poison Rules

The Poisons Act (s.7) provides that the Secretary of State may, after consultation with or on the recommendation of the Poisons Board, make rules (see Appendix 8) in respect of any of the following:

1 the sale, whether wholesale or retail, or the supply of poisons by or to any persons or classes of person and in particular but without prejudice to the generality of the foregoing provisions:
   a for regulating or restricting the sale or supply of poisons by persons whose names are entered in a local authority's list and for prohibiting the sale of any specified poison or class of poisons by any class of such persons; and
   b for dispensing with or relaxing with respect to any poisons of this Act relating to the sale of poisons;
2 the storage and labelling of poisons (but see pp. 252 and 253);
3 the containers in which poisons may be sold or supplied;
4 the addition to poisons of specified ingredients for the purpose of rendering them readily distinguishable as poisons;
5 the compounding of poisons, and the supply of poisons on and in accordance with a prescription duly given by a doctor, a dentist, a veterinary surgeon or a veterinary practitioner;
6 the period for which any books required to be kept for the purpose of this Act are to be preserved;

7   the period for which any certificate for the purchase of a poison given under section 3 of the Act (see Appendix 8) is to remain in force;

8   for prescribing anything which is by the Act to be prescribed by rules.

The Secretary of State may issue to the Poisons Board a direction that, before recommending rules under 1a, 2, 3 and 4 above, the Board must first consult a body representative of persons engaged in the manufacture of poisons or preparations containing poisons.

The power to make rules or orders under the Act is exercised by Statutory Instrument. The current rules are set out in the Poison Rules 1982 (SI 1982 No. 218, as amended) (see Appendix 8). Apart from their general classification into Part I or Part II poisons, poisons may, in addition, be divided into classes by their inclusion in certain Schedules to the Poison Rules.

There are eight Schedules to the rules and they are described, briefly, below. More detailed reference is made later in this volume (see also Appendix 8).

Schedule 1: A list of poisons to which special restrictions apply relating to storage, conditions of sale, and keeping of sales records.

Schedule 4: A list of articles exempted from control as poisons (Rule 8). It is in two groups. Group I comprises classes of article which contain poisons but are totally exempt (e.g. builders' materials). Group II lists exemptions for certain poisons when in specified articles or substances (e.g. paraquat in pellet form containing not more than 5 per cent of salts of paraquat calculated as paraquat ion).

Schedule 5: Some Part II poisons may be sold by listed sellers only in certain forms. The details are given in this Schedule, which also specifies certain poisons which may be sold by a person duly authorised, in England or Wales, by DEFRA, only to persons engaged in the trade or business of agriculture or horticulture and for the purpose of that trade or business. In any other circumstances the sale of poisons in this Schedule is restricted to pharmacies.

Schedule 8: Form of application for inclusion in local authority's list of sellers of Part II poisons.

Schedule 9: Form of the list kept by a local authority of listed sellers of Part II poisons.

Schedule 10: Form of certificate for the purchase of a poison.

Schedule 11: Form of entry to be made in the poisons book on sale of a Schedule 1 poison.

Schedule 12: Restriction of sale and supply of strychnine and other substances. Forms of authority required for certain of these poisons.

N.B. Schedules 2, 3, 6 and 7 were deleted by the Poisons Rules (Amendment) Order 1985 (SI 1985 No. 1077). Packaging and labelling of poisons is now controlled under the Chemicals (Hazard Information and Packaging) Regulations 1994, as amended (see Chapter 20).

Sale and supply of poisons

General requirements

Except in certain circumstances (see Sales Exempted by the Poisons Act, p. 261) it is unlawful for a person to sell any substance which is a Part I poison unless:

1 s/he is a person lawfully conducting a retail pharmacy business;
2 the sale is effected on the premises which are a registered pharmacy; and
3 the sale is effected by or under the supervision of a pharmacist (s.3).

It is unlawful for a person to sell any substance which is a Part II poison unless:

1 s/he is a person lawfully conducting a retail pharmacy business and the sale is effected on premises which are a registered pharmacy; or
2 his/her name is entered in a local authority list in respect of the premises on which the poison is sold (s.3).

As sales of poisons must be effected on registered or listed premises, it is not lawful for sales to take place from door to door, although a sale through the post from registered or listed premises would appear to be lawful.

The conditions required for persons lawfully to conduct 'a retail pharmacy business' have been described in Chapter 5. Such persons may sell at a registered pharmacy any poison whether it is in Part I or Part II of the Poisons List. The sale of a Part I poison from retail premises must be made by or under the supervision of a registered pharmacist (s.3). Each sale, if not made by the pharmacist personally, must be effected under his/her supervision in the sense that s/he should be in a position to intervene to prevent the sale.

The opinion was expressed in the High Court (*Roberts* v. *Littlewoods Mail Order Stores* [1943] KB 269, see Chapter 27) that supervision could not be said to have been exercised if the pharmacist were in another part of the building from that at which the sales were effected. The sale, by a person lawfully conducting a retail pharmacy business, of a poison included in Schedule 1 (see p. 253) must be effected by or under the supervision of a pharmacist even though it may be a Part II poison (Rule 9).

Listed sellers may not sell any Part II poison which has, since being obtained by them, been subject to any form of manipulation, treatment or processing as a result of which the poison has been exposed, and in the case of any poison included in Schedule 1, unless the sale is effected by him/herself or by a responsible deputy (Rule 10).

A *responsible deputy* means a person nominated as a deputy on the listed seller's form of application or any person substituted, by notice in writing to the local authority, for the person originally nominated. Not more than two deputies can be nominated at the same time in respect of one set of premises (Rule 10).

A listed seller may not sell (Rule 10):

1 any poison included in the first column of Part A of Schedule 5 (see p. 500) unless the article or substance is in the form specified in the second column of that Part;
2 any poison included in Part B of Schedule 5 (see p. 503) unless the purchaser is engaged in the trade or business of agriculture, horticulture or forestry and requires the poison for the purposes of that trade or business.

Containers

Rule 20 of the rules which set out provision for containers has been repealed (SI 1992 No. 2293). Provision for containers which have to bear tactile danger warnings are contained in the Chemicals (Hazard Information and Packaging for Supply) Regulations 1994 (see Chapter 20).

Storage of poisons

When a poison is included in Schedule 1 (see p. 495), it must be stored in any retail shop or premises used in connection with a retail shop:

1 in a cupboard or drawer reserved solely for the storage of poisons; or
2 in a part of the premises which is partitioned off or otherwise separated from the remainder of the premises and to which customers are not permitted to have access; or
3 on a shelf reserved solely for the storage of poisons and no food is kept directly under the shelf.

Schedule 1 poisons used in agriculture, horticulture or forestry must not be stored on any shelf, or in any part of the premises where food is kept, or in any cupboard or drawer unless the cupboard or drawer is reserved solely for the storage of poisons to be used in agriculture, horticulture or forestry (Rule 21).

Labelling of hydrogen cyanide

It is an offence to sell or supply any compressed hydrogen cyanide unless the container is labelled with the words 'Warning: this container holds poisonous gas and should only be opened and used by persons having expert knowledge of the precautions to be taken in its use' (Rule 18). This does not apply to sale or supply of compressed hydrogen cyanide to be exported to purchasers outside the UK (Rule 18).

Labelling and packaging of poisons which are `chemicals'

Substances in the Poisons List are also subject to the Chemicals (Hazard Information and Packaging for Supply) Regulations 1994, as amended, and must be labelled and packed in accordance with those regulations (see Chapter 20). The provisions of the Poisons Act and rules relating to labelling, containers and storage do not apply to these substances except:

1 the special warning label for compressed hydrogen cyanide (see above); and
2 the storage requirements for poisons on retail premises (see above).

Schedule 1 Poisons

Sales of poisons included in Schedule 1 to the Poisons Rules are subject to requirements additional to those applying to Part I and Part II poisons.

Knowledge of the seller

The purchaser of a Schedule 1 poison must be either:

1 certified in writing in the prescribed manner, by a person authorised in the Poisons Rules to give such a certificate, to be a person to whom the poison may properly be sold; or
2 known by the seller, or by a pharmacist employed by him/her at the premises where the sale is effected, to be a person to whom the poison may properly be sold (s.3).

Any householder is a person authorised to give a certificate as in 1 above (Rule 25). If the householder giving the certificate is not known to the seller to be a responsible person of good character, then the certificate is required to be endorsed by a police officer in charge of a police station. N.B. The police officer certifies that the householder, not the purchaser, is a responsible person of good character. The form of the certificate is laid down in Schedule 10 (see p. 506) and the certificate has to be retained by the seller (Rule 25).

For certain sales or supplies of Schedule 1 poisons, the requirement of knowledge of the purchaser by the seller is deemed to be satisfied if the purchaser is known by the person in charge of the premises in which the poison is sold, or of the department of the business in which the sale is effected, to be a person to whom the poison may properly be sold or supplied. This relaxation applies to:

1   sales of Part II, Schedule 1 poisons made by listed sellers (Rule 5);
2   supplies of commercial samples of Schedule 1 poisons (Rule 6); and
3   sales of Schedule 1 poisons exempted under section 4 of the Act (Rule 6)
     (see also p. 255).

Records

The seller must not deliver a Schedule 1 poison until s/he has made, or
caused to be made, the required entry in the poisons book and the purchaser has signed it (s.3). The entries must be made in the manner and
form prescribed in Schedule 11 (Rule 26, and see p. 506). The particulars
to be recorded are the:

1   date of the sale;
2   name and quantity of the poison supplied;
3   purchaser's name and address and their business trade or occupation;
4   purpose for which the poison is stated to be required;
5   date of certificate (if any); and
6   name and address of persons giving certificate (if any).

The poisons book must be retained for two years from the date on which
the last entry was made (Rule 27). A signed order may be accepted in lieu of
the purchaser's signature in certain circumstances (see below).

Signed orders

A person who requires a Schedule 1 poison for the purpose of their trade,
business or profession may give the seller a signed order in lieu of his/her
signature in the poisons book (Rule 6). The seller must obtain, before
completion of the sale, the order in writing signed by the purchaser
stating:

1   their name and address;
2   their trade, business or profession;
3   the purpose for which the poison is required; and
4   the total quantity of the poison to be purchased.

The seller must be reasonably satisfied that the signature is that of the
person purporting to have signed the order and that that person carries on the
trade, business or profession stated in the order being one in which the poison
is used. The seller must make the entry in the poison book before delivery. S/he
must include the words *signed order* in place of the signature and add a
reference number by which the order can be identified.

When a person represents that s/he urgently requires a poison for his/her
trade, business or profession, the seller may, if s/he is reasonably satisfied

that there is an emergency and the purchaser is unable to supply a signed order before delivery, supply the poison on an undertaking by the purchaser that the purchaser will supply a signed order within 72 hours. Failure to comply with an undertaking or the making of false statements in order to obtain Schedule 1 poisons without a signed order are contravention's of the Poison Rules (Rule 6).

Exemptions from Schedule 1 requirements

The requirements described above as to the knowledge of the purchaser by the seller and entry in the poisons book with signature of the purchaser or supplier of a signed order do not apply to:

1 the sale of poisons to be exported to purchasers outside the UK;
2 the sale of any article by its manufacturer, or by a person carrying on a business in the course of which poisons are regularly sold by way of wholesale dealing if:
   a the article is sold or supplied to a person carrying on a business in the course of which poisons are regularly sold or regularly used in the manufacture of other articles; and
   b the seller or supplier is reasonably satisfied that the purchaser requires the article for the purpose of that business (Rule 6);
3 the sale of nicotine, which is a Part II, Schedule 1 poison, in the form of agricultural or horticultural insecticides consisting of nicotine dusts containing not more than 4 per cent w/w of nicotine (Rule 5);
4 the sale of articles containing barium carbonate or zinc phosphide and prepared for the destruction of rats or mice (Rule 7).

Schedule 1 poisons subject to additional restrictions (Rule 12)

All the Schedule 1 poisons mentioned below are subject to additional restrictions on sale or supply. They may only be sold or supplied:

1 by way of wholesale dealing; or
2 or export to purchasers outside the UK; or
3 to persons or institutions concerned with scientific education or research or chemical analysis for the purpose of that education research or analysis; or
4 in the circumstances described below under the name of each particular poison.

Since September 2006, *strychnine* no longer has approval from the Pesticide Safety Directorate for purchase or use for mole control. There is, however, provision for the supply for the purpose of killing foxes in an infected area under the Rabies (Control) Order.

Strychnine may be sold:

a   for the purposes of 1, 2 and 3 above; or
b   to an officer of the Department of Environment, Food and Rural Affairs (DEFRA) or, in Scotland, of the Department of Agriculture and Fisheries who produces a written authority in the form set out in Part III of Schedule 12 (see p. 509) authorising the purchase by that officer for killing foxes in an infected area within the meaning of the Rabies (Control) Order 1974. The quantity must not exceed that stated in the authority and must be supplied within four weeks of the date of the written authority.

N.B. Since 1991, strychnine has also been controlled under the Control of Pesticides Regulations 1986 and may only be supplied to holders of an Authority to Purchase issued in England by DEFRA, in Wales by a person authorised by the National Assembly and in Scotland by the Secretary of State. It must be labelled in an approved manner, supplied only in the original sealed package(s) and only in units of 2 grams or multiples thereof. Quantities of more than 8 grams may only be supplied to providers of a commercial service. These conditions are *in addition* to the possession of a strychnine permit under the Poisons Rules (see p. 509).

Fluoroacetic acid, its salts or fluoroacetamide may be sold for the purposes of 1, 2 and 3 above, or to a person producing a certificate in form 'A' or form 'B' as provided in Schedule 12 (see p. 510). The quantity must not exceed that specified and must be sold or supplied within three months of the date on the certificate. The certificates must specify the quantity, certify that the substance is to be used as a rodenticide and identify the place where it is to be used, which may be:

a   ships or sewers as indicated in the certificate; or
b   such drains as are identified in the certificate, being drains which are in restricted areas and wholly enclosed and to which all means of access are kept closed when not in use; or
c   such warehouses as are identified in the certificate which are in residential dock areas and to which all means of access are kept securely locked or barred when not in use.

Only the proper officer of a local authority or port health authority may issue Form 'A' to employees of the authority for the purpose of purchasing rodenticide for use in a, b or c above, or Form 'B' to persons carrying on the business of pest control for the purpose of rodenticide for use in a and b above. For the purpose of rodenticide for use in a and b above, Form 'B' may also be issued by a person duly authorised by DEFRA in England, a person authorised by Scottish Ministers (Scotland) or by a person authorised by the National Assembly in Wales.

Salts of thallium, potassium and sodium arsenites, the cyanides of calcium, potassium and sodium, and *zinc phosphide* are also included in Schedule 12 but like strychnine are no longer approved by the Pesticides Safety Directorate.

Calcium, potassium and sodium cyanides and *sodium and potassium arsenites* may only be sold in any of the circumstances described in section 4 of the Act (Rule 14; see Sales exempted by the Poisons Act, below).

Wholesale dealing

See Sales Exempted by the Poisons Act, category 1 below.

Sales exempted by the Poisons Act

Section 4 of the Poisons Act exempts certain categories of sales of poisons from the provisions of the Act, except as provided by the Poisons Rules. The principal effect is that sales of poisons falling within these categories are not required to be made from pharmacies or the premises of listed sellers and, for Part I poisons, the supervision of a pharmacist is not required. Except as indicated, the provisions as to labelling (p. 253), containers (p. 252) and Schedule 1 poisons (p. 253) do apply to these exempted sales (Rules 4, 6 and 2).

The exempted categories are as follows.

1   Sales of poisons by way of wholesale dealing, that is, sales made to a person who buys for the purpose of selling again.

N.B. 'Wholesale dealing' has a wider meaning in the Medicines Act 1968 (see p. 38). A wholesaler who sells a Part I poison to a shopkeeper must have reasonable grounds for believing that the purchaser is a person lawfully conducting a retail pharmacy business. If not, then the wholesaler must obtain a statement signed by the purchaser, or a person authorised by the purchaser, to the effect that the purchaser does not intend to sell the poison on any premises used for or in connection with his/her retail business (rule 11).

2   Sales of poisons to be exported to purchasers outside the UK.
3   The sale of an article to a doctor, dentist, veterinary surgeon or veterinary practitioner for the purposes of his/her profession.
4   The sale of an article for use in connection with any hospital, infirmary or dispensary or similar institution approved by an order of the Secretary of State.
5   The sale of an article by a person carrying on a business, in the course of which poisons are regularly sold either by way of wholesale dealing or for use by purchasers in their trade or business to:

a a government department or an officer of the Crown requiring the article for the public service, or any local authority requiring the article in connection with the exercise of any statutory powers; or

b a person or institution concerned with scientific education or research, if the article is required for the purposes of that education or research; or

c a person who requires the article for the purpose of enabling him/her to comply with any requirements made by or in pursuance of any enactment with respect to the medical treatment of persons employed by that person in any trade or business carried on by him/her; or

d a person who requires the article for the purpose of his/her trade or business.

A person can be said to be carrying on a business if s/he engages in full-time, or part-time commercial activity with a view to profit. A sale of cyanide to a commercial fruit grower for killing wasps would be a *trade or business* sale but a sale for the same purpose to a householder for garden use would not. Sales in circumstances exempted by section 4 are the only sales of cyanides which are lawful (see p. 257), so a sale made to a householder would be unlawful.

Automatic machines

It is unlawful for a poison to be exposed for sale in, or to be offered for sale by means of, an automatic machine (s.3) (see Automatic machines p. 87).

Controls on pesticides

The Food and Environment Protection Act 1985 is concerned, amongst other matters, with the reduction of pollution of the environment by pesticides. Subject to certain exemptions, the Control of Pesticide Regulations 1986 (SI 1986 No. 1510, as amended) prohibit the advertisement, sale, supply, storage and use of pesticides unless in accordance with an approval and consent given by DEFRA. Any breach of the regulations may result in seizure and disposal of the offending pesticide and any material treated with it, and an order for remedial action.

Pesticide is defined as 'products used for the control of rats and mice, flies and other garden pests; cyanide, strychnine, wood and masonry treatments; and pesticides used in public health maintenance'. Additional restrictions are placed on 'pesticides approved for agricultural use'. These apply to all crop protection products such as herbicides, fungicides and insecticides, plus some soil sterilants and fumigants. The regulations and consents are supplemented by two codes of practice: one dealing with sale, supply and storage and the other covering use.

Failure on the part of any person to follow the guidance given in the codes does not of itself render that person liable to proceedings, but such failure is admissible in evidence in any criminal proceedings brought under the Act.

Anyone stocking in excess of 200 litres or 200 kg of 'pesticides approved for agricultural use' must comply with the parts of the code dealing with the physical construction, design and maintenance of sites used for the storage of any pesticide. A person in charge of a store or a salesperson who advises on the use of these products must be in possession of the appropriate DEFRA certificate.

Anyone offering a commercial service for the use of pesticides must possess DEFRA certification, and any persons using pesticides must be instructed as to such matters as storage and transport on the farm, application techniques and disposal and record keeping.

The effect of all these provisions is to impose the following obligations upon anyone selling, supplying or storing pesticides:

1 they and their staff must be provided with such instructions and guidance as is necessary to enable them to be competent for the duties they are called upon to perform;
2 all reasonable precautions must be taken, especially with regard to storage and transport, to protect the health of human beings and creatures, and to safeguard the environment; and
3 the pesticide must be sold or supplied in the container supplied by the manufacturer of the pesticide and under the label approved by DEFRA.

Summary

- The Poisons Board advises the Secretary of State as to which substances should be in the Poisons List.
- The Poisons List is divided into two parts. Poisons in Part I may be sold only by authorised sellers of poisons (i.e. from retail pharmacies by or under the supervision of a pharmacist) whereas Part II poisons can be sold from retail pharmacies and other shopkeepers who are listed with the local authority.
- There are eight active Schedules. Schedule 1 contains poisons to which special restrictions apply relating to sale, storage and the keeping of records. The seller must have special knowledge of the purchaser and record the transaction and obtain the purchaser's signature in a 'poisons register'. Special provisions are made for signed orders in lieu of the purchaser's signature and for storage of poisons (away from the public).

- Special conditions apply to the sale of strychnine. It may only be sold by way of wholesale, or to persons or institutions concerned with education or research, for export, or to a person who has obtained a written authority from the appropriate agricultural authority in England, Scotland or Wales. It is no longer approved for killing moles. The form of the written authority is set out in Schedule 12.
- Sodium and potassium arsenites, thallium, zinc phosphide, and the cyanides are no longer approved by the Pesticide Safety Directorate.
- Pesticides are controlled under the Control of Pesticides Regulations 1986 and a Pesticides Safety Directorate supplemented by two codes of practice; one dealing with sale, supply and storage and the other covering use.

Further reading

Royal Pharmaceutical Society of Great Britain (annual publication) *Medicines, Ethics and Practice*. London: Royal Pharmaceutical Society of Great Britain. (Lists of poisons are included.)

Websites

Department for Environment, Food and Rural Affairs: http://www.defra.gov.uk
Pesticides Safety Directorate: http://www.pesticides.gov.uk/home.asp

19

Alcohol and denatured alcohol

The law relating to alcohol and denatured alcohol is contained mainly in the Customs and Excise Management Act 1979, the Alcoholic Liquor Duties Act 1979 and the Denatured Alcohol Regulations 2005 No. 1524.

The term *alcohol* means 'alcohol of any description and includes all liquor mixed with alcohol and all mixtures, compounds or preparations made with alcohol but does not include denatured alcohol'.

Intoxicating liquor means alcohol, wine, beer, cider and any other fermented, distilled or spirituous liquor, but (apart from cider) does not include any liquor for the sale of which, by wholesale, no excise licence is required.

Retail sales of intoxicating liquor

Intoxicating liquor may be sold only by a person holding an appropriate justice's licence granted in England and Wales by licensing justices or in Scotland by a licensing court. The justices have an absolute discretion in the granting of such licences.

The justice's licence may be granted to authorise sales for consumption either on or off the premises. Sales of intoxicating liquor may be made only during permitted hours and these hours are usually fixed by the licensing justice. The holder of a licence requires to have painted on or affixed to his/ her premises in a conspicuous place his/her name and, after the name, the word 'licensed', followed by words sufficient to express the business for which the licence is granted.

The maximum quantity of intoxicating liquor which may be sold by retail to any one person is nine litres or one case for alcohol, wine or made wine, and 21 litres or two cases for beer or cider.

N.B. A licence is not required for the sale by retail of alcohol made up in a medicine by a pharmacist or a sale to a trader for the purpose of that trade.

Alcohol duty

Alcohol and all goods containing alcohol imported into the UK are liable to a customs duty, and all alcohol made in the UK by a licensed distiller are liable to an excise duty (Customs and Excise Management Act 1979). Exemption from Customs and Excise duty exists for alcohol used in making denatured alcohol (see below).

A *reduced rate of duty* is payable if any person can prove to the Commissioner of Customs and Excise that s/he has used alcohol, upon which the full duty has been paid, solely for the purpose of manufacturing or preparing any article recognised by the Commissioner as being used for medical or scientific purposes. This concession is granted subject to any conditions which the Commissioner may impose by means of regulations. The guidelines have been made and are contained in the Alcohol Regulations 1952 (SI 1952 No. 2229, as amended) (see below).

A person wishing to claim repayment of a portion of the duty must comply with the following (as set out in Part VIII of the regulations): s/he must not *receive* at his/her premises any alcohol except (a) alcohol accompanied by a permit or certificate; or (b) alcohol which, if not required to be accompanied by a permit or certificate on removal, are accompanied by an invoice or similar document containing particulars of the alcohol and the duty paid, and the name and address of the supplier (reg.63).

A claimant must *store* separately (a) alcohol recovered from alcohol in respect of which s/he has or intends to make a claim; (b) any other recovered alcohol; (c) any other alcohol (reg.65). S/he is not allowed to mix alcohol recovered from alcohol, in respect of which s/he has or intends to make a claim, with any other alcohol except for use in the manufacture or preparation of a medicine which is recognised as such by the Commissioners, or for scientific purposes (reg.65). On each container in which s/he stores alcohol or recovered alcohol, the claimant must permanently and legibly mark the capacity of the container. Each container has to be stored to give convenient access to a Customs and Excise officer (reg.64).

The claimant is required to keep a *stock book* in an approved form (reg.66) and is required to make immediate entries in respect of:

1 alcohol received at the premises, brought back into stock for use or recovered on the premises;
2 alcohol or recovered alcohol intended to be delivered from, or to be used on, the premises; and
3 any article made with alcohol (reg.67).

The pharmacist both in retail and hospital is mainly concerned with alcohol other than recovered alcohol. Separate accounts must be kept for alcohol and recovered alcohol in a stock book. Specimen stock-book rulings are illustrated in Figures 19.1 and 19.2.

Date	Permit No.	Name and address of supplier	Quantity received	Strength o.p.

Figure 19.1 Alcohol received.

Repayment of duty not claimed plus sales			Repayment of duty claimed				
Date	Quantity	Strength	Date	Quantity	Strength	Recognised article made	
						Name	Quantity

Figure 19.2 Alcohol used or sold.

If a person uses alcohol in the *manufacture or preparation of any recognised medicine* (e.g. homoeopathic medicine), entries must be made in a stock book recording:

1 all alcohol received at his/her premises;
2 all alcohol and mixtures brought back into stock for use in the manufacture or preparation of a recognised medicinal article, being alcohol or mixtures previously entered in the stock book as having been used and in respect of which s/he has in accordance with the Alcoholic Liquor Duties Act 1979 refunded any duty repaid;
3 all alcohol delivered from his/her premises;
4 all alcohol used on his/her premises, the purposes for which they are used and the quantities used for each purpose;
5 the name and quantity of each recognised medical article made;

6   the name and quantity of any other article made;

7   any other use of the alcohol (reg.66).

Separate particulars are required for alcohol used for scientific purposes (reg.66).

It is an offence for a claimant to cancel, obliterate or, except with the permission of a Customs and Excise officer, alter any entry in the book (reg.68). The book must be left on the premises while in use and for 12 months following the final entry, together with all books, invoices and other trade documents containing any information on which entries in the book are based. The claimant must at all reasonable times allow an officer to inspect the book, invoices and documents, and take extracts therefrom or make entries in the book (reg.69). Unless the Commissioners permit otherwise, the claimant, if not a rectifier, must take stock and balance the account of alcohol in his/her stock book at the end of each month (reg.70) or when required to do so by an officer.

A claimant must not deliver from his/her premises or use for any purpose other than manufacture or preparation of a recognised medicinal article or for a scientific purpose any alcohol in respect of which s/he has made or intends to make a claim (reg.71). Claims for recovery of duty must be made on the approval form obtainable from a Customs and Excise officer. The claim must be signed by the claimant or a person duly authorised by the claimant, and must be made within three months of the date on which the alcohol was used. Claims cannot be made more frequently than twice a month in respect of alcohol used on any one set of premises (reg.73).

When in doubt concerning any provisions of the alcohol regulations, pharmacists are advised to consult the local officer of Customs and Excise.

Denatured alcohol

Denatured alcohol is alcohol which is mixed with other substances in accordance with regulations made by the Commissioners under the Alcoholic Liquor Duties Act 1979.

There are three types of denatured alcohol but the pharmacist is generally concerned only with two, namely completely denatured alcohol (CDA; formerly mineralised methylated spirits) and industrial denatured alcohol (IDA; formerly industrial methylated spirits).

The regulations giving particulars for the supply, receipt, sale, storage, etc. of all types of denatured alcohol are to be found in the Denatured Alcohol Regulations 2005 (SI 2005 No. 1524), although the provisions for licensing and inspection are to be found in the Act itself. In addition, the Commissioners issue notices for guidance and these can be obtained from local Customs and Excise offices. No person may methylate, or wholesale, denatured alcohol of *any type* unless they hold a licence as a methylator from the Commissioners authorising them to do so.

The local Customs and Excise officer may enter and inspect in the daytime the premises of any person authorised by the regulations to receive alcohol, and may inspect and examine any of the alcohol stored there. The local officer is empowered to take samples of alcohol and any goods containing denatured alcohol, provided a reasonable price is paid for the sample.

It is unlawful:

1   to prepare, attempt to prepare or sell any alcohol for use as a beverage or mixed with a beverage;
2   to use alcohol in the preparation of any article capable of being used as a beverage or as a medicine for internal use;
3   to sell or possess any such article;
4   to purify or attempt to purify any alcohol, or recover or attempt to recover the alcohol therein, by means of distillation, condensation or in any other manner unless permitted to do so by the Commissioners.

Nothing in the statute prevents the use of alcohol in the making for external use only of any article sold or supplied in accordance with regulations.

If required to do so by the Commissioners the retailer must keep an account, in a prescribed form, of his/her stock of alcohol (reg.27). The retailer is required to keep alcohol under proper control or under the control of a responsible person appointed by the retailer and held under lock or otherwise stored to the satisfaction of the local officer.

On the closure or transfer of a business, or on the death of the retailer, the stock of alcohol must be disposed of in an approved manner and within a reasonable time to the satisfaction of the Commissioners (reg.26).

Industrial denatured alcohol (formerly industrial methylated spirits)

The regulations require that industrial denatured alcohol must consist of 95 parts by volume of alcohol together with 5 parts by volume of wood naphtha (reg.15). The formulation of denatured alcohol that is supplied must be approved by the UK or an EU member state.

A person lawfully conducting a retail pharmacy business cannot receive industrial denatured alcohol for sale by him/her or for export unless s/he has made application to the proper officer in the required form which is available from the local office of Customs and Excise, and has supplied such information as may be required. The proper officer may make the certificate of authority subject to conditions (reg.25) and restrict it to the receipt of denatured alcohol for certain purposes only. Pharmacists *must* comply with the conditions of the certificate. The certificate of authority may be revoked or varied for any reasonable cause at any time (reg.24). The authorised uses for which industrial denatured alcohol may be sold are set out in HM Customs and Excise Notice No. 473 dated July 2005.

The proper officer may authorise a pharmacist to receive industrial denatured alcohol and:

1 use to make any article approved by the proper officer;
2 dispense it, or articles made from it, on a prescription; and
3 sell or supply it, other than on a prescription, for medical or scientific purposes.

Sales of industrial denatured alcohol may be made:

1 to any person authorised to receive it in any quantity not exceeding 20 litres provided that a written statement is received from the user that s/he is authorised to receive it;
2 in any quantity not exceeding 3 litres to a doctor, dentist, nurse, chiropodist, veterinary surgeon or any other person entitled by law to provide medical or veterinary services in the UK, provided that a written order signed by such a person is received;
3 of not more than 20 litres to persons outside the UK; and
4 for medical or veterinary purposes on a prescription or order of a medical practitioner, dentist or veterinary surgeon or practitioner.

Similarly, a pharmacist may supply or sell articles:

1 which have been manufactured by that pharmacist using industrial denatured alcohol in accordance with the conditions imposed in the certificate of authority; or
2 which are so manufactured in accordance with the certificate of authority and are sold or supplied on a prescription.

Industrial denatured alcohol must be purchased from an authorised methylator in quantities of not less than 20 litres. Alternatively, not more than 20 litres at a time can be obtained from an authorised user (e.g. a wholesale chemist).

An authorised user, such as a pharmacist, must keep records of his dealings with industrial denatured alcohol in accordance with any conditions imposed by the regulations or a proper officer, who must be allowed to inspect such records at any reasonable time. An annual return of all industrial denatured alcohol received and used or supplied must be made to the proper officer on request. Records must be kept for two years.

All stocks must be kept under lock and key under the control of the pharmacist. The local Customs and Excise may require a pharmacist to comply with special storage requirements.

Received or set aside as a separate stock for sale			Sold		
Date	Whence received	Quantity	Date	Whether sold on requisition or for use of a doctor etc., on written order	Quantity

Figure 19.3 Specimen form of account for guidance of pharmacists when selling industrial denatured spirits other than on prescription.

All bottles and other containers in which industrial denatured alcohol or articles containing it are supplied must be labelled in accordance with the Chemicals (Hazard Information and Packaging for Supply) Regulations (see Chapter 20). If supplied or dispensed for medical use, it must also be labelled '*For external use, not to be taken*', or words to the same effect.

A specimen form of account is shown in Figure 19.3.

Completely denatured alcohol (formerly mineralised methylated spirits)

The regulations require that completely denatured alcohol must consist of 90 parts by volume of alcohol together with 9.5 parts by volume of wood naphtha and 0.5 part of crude pyridine. To every 1000 litres of the mixture must be added 3.75 litres of petroleum oil and not less than 1.5 grams by weight of powdered aniline dye (methyl violet).

Completely denatured alcohol can be purchased from a methylator or, in small quantities, from a wholesaler. No restrictions are placed on the retailing of completely denatured alcohol in England and Wales. The weekend restrictions on sale were removed by the Regulatory Reform (Sunday Trading) Order 2004 (SI 2004 No. 470). The local officer of Customs and Excise visits the premises to satisfy him/herself as to the suitability of the premises for the storage of completely denatured alcohol.

Scotland: sale of completely denatured alcohol and surgical alcohol

For many years there were additional restrictions on the retail sale of methylated alcohol and surgical alcohol in Scotland. These included the need for sellers to register, keep records and additional labelling requirements. These restrictions were removed in 1998 by the Deregulation (Methylated Alcohol Sale by Retail) (Scotland) Regulations [SI 1998 No. 1602 (S. 87)].

The 2005 regulations now apply to Scotland and are similar to those in England and Wales. However it remains an offence to sell completely denatured alcohol in Scotland to a person under 14 years of age.

Summary

- The law relating to denatured alcohol and the rules regarding the duty on products are outlined.
- The term denatured alcohol includes alcohol of any description including liquors mixed with spirits and all mixes with spirits but not industrial spirits.
- Intoxicating liquor comprises any fermented, distilled or spirituous liquor but (apart from cider) does not include any liquor that does not require a licence for wholesale.
- There are three types of denatured alcohol but the pharmacist is generally concerned with two: completely denatured alcohol and industrial denatured alcohol; there are specific regulations for these alcohols governing the supply, receipt, sale, storage, etc. of all types of denatured alcohol.

Further reading

Website

HM Revenue and Customs: www.hmrc.gov.uk

20

Dangerous substances and consumer protection

The way in which certain chemicals are classified, packaged and labelled is now controlled under the Chemical (Hazard Information and Packaging for Supply) Regulations 2002 (SI 2002 No. 1689, as amended). They are known collectively as the CHIP Regulations. The regulations, made under the Health and Safety at Work etc. Act 1974 and the European Communities Act 1972, implement within Great Britain the European Community Directives regulating and controlling the classification, packaging and labelling of dangerous substances (Council Directive 99/43/EEC, as amended, and Council Directive 96/769/EEC).

Chemicals classified under the CHIP Regulations as being harmful to health are also subject to control under the Control of Substances Hazardous to Health Regulations 1999 (the COSHH Regulations; see p. 276).

Definitions

Substances dangerous to supply means a substance listed in Part 1 of an approved supply list.

Approved supply list means the list approved by the Health and Safety Commission entitled *Information Approved for the Classification and Labelling of Substances and Preparations Dangerous for Supply*, 6th edition (SI 2000 No. 2381).

Preparations means mixtures or solutions of two or more substances and *preparation dangerous to supply* means a preparation which is in one or more categories of danger in Schedule 1 to the CHIP Regulations 2002 (SI 2002 No. 1689 as amended).

Supply, in relation to a substance or preparation, means supply by way of:

1   sale or offer for sale;
2   commercial sample; or
3   transfer from a factory, warehouse or other place of work and its curtilage to another place of work whether or not in the same ownership.

Application of the regulations and exceptions

The CHIP Regulations apply to the classification, packaging and labelling of any substance or preparation which is dangerous for supply except:

1   a substance which is either:
    a   a medicinal product; or
    b   a substance specified in an order made under sections 104 or 105 of the Medicines Act 1968;
2   Controlled Drugs;
3   animal feeding stuffs;
4   cosmetic products;
5   pesticides approved under the Food and Environmental Act 1985 (N.B. a preparation intended for use as a pesticide is classified as dangerous to supply and must comply with the regulations unless it is approved under the 1985 Act);
6   radioactive substances;
7   substances and preparations intended for use as food;
8   substances intended for export to a country which is not a member state of the European Union;
9   munitions, including fireworks;
10 waste materials;
11 substances and preparations which are dangerous by reason that they contain disease-producing microorganisms;
12 a substance transferred from a factory, warehouse or other place of work to another place of work in the same ownership and in the immediate vicinity;
13 a substance to which the Notification of New Substances Regulations 1982 apply and is labelled in accordance with such regulations;
14 a substance imported and still under Customs control.

Most of the substances controlled as dangerous substances in the approved supply list are chemicals and only a few are likely to be encountered in pharmacy. A selection of the substances taken from the approved supply list is given in Appendix 9. It comprises:

1   those dangerous substances which are also controlled by the Poisons Act 1972 (see Chapter 18);
2   other dangerous substances which may be held in stock in a pharmacy.

A pharmacy dealing with a request for any chemical not shown in Appendix 9 should refer to the approved supply list and regulations, or seek advice from the Royal Pharmaceutical Society of Great Britain (RPSGB). It should be borne in mind that substances sold as medicinal products or pesticides are not subject to the labelling requirements of the CHIP Regulations 2002 as amended.

Inspection and enforcement

The provisions are enforced as if they were health and safety regulations made under the Health and Safety at Work Etc. Act 1974.

Where a dangerous substance is supplied in or from a registered pharmacy, the enforcing authority is the RPSGB. The enforcing authority in relation to supplies made in any shop, market stall or other retail outlet is the local weights and measures authority and in all other cases the Health and Safety Executive.

Classification

Substances or preparations which are dangerous to supply have to be classified by the manufacturer. The manufacturer must decide what kind of danger the chemical presents and allocate to it a phrase describing the general nature of the risk attached to it (a *risk phrase*).

Each substance or preparation is classified in the approved list as to its category of danger:

1 *physicochemical properties*: explosive, extremely flammable, highly flammable or flammable, and oxidising;
2 *health effects*: very toxic, toxic, harmful, irritant, corrosive, sensitising, carcinogenic, mutagenic and toxic for reproduction;
3 dangerous to the environment.

All substances and preparations which are classified as carcinogenic, mutagenic or toxic for reproduction, together with certain solvents (e.g. chloroform and carbon tetrachloride) have to be labelled '*Restricted for professional users*' and therefore cannot be sold to the general public.

Pharmacists will normally not have to classify dangerous substances or preparations as this will have been done by the supplier. However, if a pharmacist still produces preparations to his/her own formulation then s/he will have to classify the dangers.

Each classification of danger will carry with it indications of danger, particular risks and safety precautions which will be required when such substances or preparations are labelled and sold.

Indications of danger

There are 10 categories of indications of danger. Each category has its own symbol which must be in black on an orange/yellow background. The symbols are shown in Appendix 9 and are:

1   explosive: an exploding bomb;
2   extremely flammable, highly flammable: a flame;
3   very toxic, toxic: a skull and cross-bones;
4   corrosive: a hand and a piece of metal being dissolved by liquid dropping
     from two test tubes;
5   oxidising: a flame over a circle;
6   irritant, harmful: a St Andrew's cross;
7   dangerous to the environment: a tree and a fish.

Indications of particular risks

Each dangerous substance or preparation is classified in the approved
list as to the indications of particular risks with which the receptacle
must be labelled. These include, for example: *'reacts violently with
water'*, *'irritating to the eyes'*, *'harmful if swallowed'*, *'explosive when
mixed with a combustible material'*, *'sensitising'*, *'carcinogenic'*, etc.
(see Appendix 9).

Indications of safety precautions required

Each dangerous substance or preparation is classified in the approved list as
to the indication of safety precautions with which the receptacle must
be labelled. These include, for example, *'keep out of the reach of children'*,
'wear suitable protective clothing', *'never add water to this product'*, (see
Appendix 9).

Packaging

It is unlawful to supply any person with a substance or preparation dangerous
to supply unless it is in a receptacle which is designed, constructed, maintained
and closed so as to prevent its escape when subjected to the stresses and strains
of normal handling. This does not prevent the fitting of a suitable safety device
(reg.8).

When the receptacle is fitted with a replaceable closure, the latter must be
so designed so that the receptacle can be repeatedly reclosed without the
contents escaping.

The packaging must be made of materials which are neither adversely
affected by the substance nor liable in conjunction with that substance to
produce another substance which is a risk to the health and safety of the public
(reg.8).

Receptacle means a vessel or the innermost layer of packaging which is in
contact with the substance and which is liable to be individually handled when
the substance is used and includes any closure or fastener.

Package means the package in which a substance or preparation is supplied and which is liable to be individually handled during the course of the supply and includes the receptacle containing the substance or preparation and any other packaging associated with it and any pallet or other device which enables more than one receptacle containing a substance or preparation to be handled as a unit, but does not include:

1   a freight container (other than a tank container), a skip, a vehicle or other article of transport equipment; or

2   in the case of supply by way of retail, any wrapping such as a paper or plastic bag into which the package is placed when presented to the purchaser.

Child-resistant closures

Child-resistant closures must be used on certain products when sold to the general public. These substances or preparations include those that are classified as *toxic, very toxic* or *corrosive*, and methanol above 3 per cent.

Tactile danger warnings

In order to aid the blind and partially sighted, a tactile danger warning (EN ISO 11683) (SI 2000 No. 2381), such as a raised triangle, must be used on packaging when products classified as *harmful, highly flammable, extremely flammable, toxic, very toxic* and *corrosive* are sold to the general public.

Labelling for supply

Labelling for supply must be in English, unless supply is to another member state of the EEC, when it has to be in the language of that state. It must be clearly and indelibly marked on a part of the package reserved for that purpose and securely fixed with its entire surface in contact with the package. Where it is impracticable to attach a label in this way, because the package is an awkward shape or is too small, then it may be attached in some other appropriate manner.

The colour and nature of the markings on the label must be such that the symbols required (see below) stand out from the background so as to be readily noticeable and the wording be of such a size and spacing as to be easily read.

The package must be labelled so that the particulars can be read horizontally when the package is set down normally.

The dimensions of the label must be in accordance with Table 20.1.

Any symbol required to be shown must be printed in black on an orange/ yellow background and its size, including the orange/yellow background,

Table 20.1 Label dimensions for supply	
Capacity of package	*Dimensions of label*
(a) 3 litres or less	If possible at least 52 mm × 74 mm
(b) Exceeding 3 litres but not exceeding 50 litres	At least 74 mm × 105 mm
(c) Exceeding 50 litres but not exceeding 500 litres	At least 105 mm × 148 mm
(d) Exceeding 500 litres	At least 148 mm × 210 mm

must be at least equal to one-tenth of the area of a label and in any case shall not be less than $100 \, mm^2$.

Where because of the size of the label it is not reasonably practicable to provide safety phrases on the label, that information may be given on a separate label or on a sheet accompanying the package.

No *dangerous substance* (e.g. a chemical) may be supplied unless it is in a package which clearly shows the following particulars:

1   the name and full address and telephone number of a person in a member state who is responsible for supplying the substance, whether s/he is the importer, manufacturer or distributor;
2   the name of the substance;
3   the following particulars:
    a   the indication(s) of danger and the corresponding symbol(s) (if any);
    b   the risk phrases (set out in full);
    c   the safety phrases (set out in full);
    d   the EEC number and, in the case of a substance dangerous for supply which is listed in Part 1 of the approved supply list, the words *EC label* or *EEC label*;
4   for certain substances which are specified in Schedule 2 to the regulations and which are classified as carcinogenic, mutagenic or toxic for reproduction, the label '*restricted for professional users*' or '*for use in industrial installations only*'.

N.B. The risk and safety phrases need not be shown on packages of 125 mL or less except if the substance is classified as *flammable, highly flammable, oxidising* or *irritant*.

No *dangerous preparation* (e.g. a mixture of substances) may be supplied unless it is in a package which clearly shows the following particulars:

1   the name and full address and telephone number of a person in a member state who is responsible for supplying the preparation whether s/he is he importer, manufacturer, or distributor;
2   the trade name or other designation of the preparation;

Completely Denatured Alcohol	
	Highly flammable Toxic by inhalation and if swallowed Keep locked up and out of reach of children Keep container tightly closed Keep away from sources of ignition - no smoking
	Avoid contact with skin In case of accident or if you feel unwell, seek medical advice immediately and show label where possible
EEC 250 659 6	
Tel: 0101 1111	**A.N.Other MRPharmS** **1 High Street** **Blanktown** 500 ml

Figure 20.1 Example of a label.

3 the following particulars:
  a the identification of the constituents of the preparation which result in the preparation being classified as dangerous to supply;
  b the indication(s) of danger and the corresponding symbol(s) (if any);
  c the risk phrases (set out in full);
  d the safety phrases (set out in full);
  e in the case of a preparation intended for sale to the public, the nominal quantity;
4 for certain preparations which are specified in Schedule 2 to the regulations and which are classified as carcinogenic, mutagenic or toxic for reproduction, the label *'restricted for professional users'* or *'for use in industrial installations only'*.

Figure 20.1 is an example of such a label.

Data sheets

Safety data sheets have to be provided when substances and preparations which are subject to the regulations are supplied for the first time in connection with work, for example a supply to a doctor for use in his/her practice, to a health centre or to factories. This is to ensure that the recipient can take any necessary precautions relating to the protection of health and safety at work and relating to the protection of the environment.

The supplier must ensure that the data sheet is kept up to date and revise it in line with any new health or safety information. A revised data sheet must be supplied to a customer who has received a supply within the last 12 months.

Data sheets do not have to be given when supplies are made to the general public for private use.

The data sheet must contain the following headings: identification of the substance/preparation, composition/information on the product, supplier's name, hazard identification, first-aid measures, fire-fighting measures, accidental release measures, handling and storage, exposure controls and personal protection, and physical and chemical properties.

Control of substances hazardous to health

The Control of Substances Hazardous to Health Regulations 1999 (SI 1999 No. 437), (the COSHH Regulations) are made under the Health and Safety at Work Act and impose duties on employers to protect employees and other persons who may be exposed to substances hazardous to health and impose certain duties on employees concerning their own protection in the work place. The regulations implement a number of European Directives and are consistent particularly with Council Directive 80/1107/EEC, which provides for protection of workers from risks related to exposure from chemical, physical and biological agents.

The regulations apply to any place of work including hospital or community pharmacies, pharmaceutical laboratories or administrative offices. They cover virtually any substance (except those subject to specific legislation such as asbestos, ionising radiation) but are particularly relevant to pesticides, chemicals, harmful microorganisms and medicines. Persons consuming medicines are not covered by the regulations.

The COSHH Regulations require that an assessment of risk is made of substances used and procedures operated in the workplace.

Risk means the likelihood of harm in the actual circumstances of use and depends on, for example, how the substance is used, who is using it, how much substance is involved, how long the exposure and what precautions are taken. A high-level hazard could arise from mishandling a low-risk substance, for example licking the fingers while handling metallic mercury. The level of hazard is usually greater following ingestion and becomes progressively less through inhalation to skin contamination from leakage and spillage.

Every employer must ensure that the exposure of their employees to substances hazardous to health is either prevented or, where this is not reasonably practicable, is adequately controlled. *Substances hazardous to health* are those as defined in the CHIP Regulations 2002 (see p. 269).

Every employer must not carry out work which is liable to expose his/her employees to any hazardous substance unless s/he has made a suitable and sufficient assessment of the risks created by that work and the steps needed to avoid risk as set out in the regulations. Where employees are exposed to risk, the employer must ensure that they are under suitable health surveillance.

Manufacturers of substances which may be hazardous to health must provide full details (e.g. labels, leaflets, data sheets, instruction manuals) of the precautions to be taken when handling the substance.

Employers must take measures to train and inform staff of the dangers, to prevent or minimise exposure where possible and, if necessary, to monitor exposure and implement a health surveillance programme for all those exposed. Risk can be reduced by avoiding the substance altogether, using a safer substance or the same substance in a safer form, by enclosing the process and extracting the by-products, by improving ventilation or hygiene facilities, by instituting safer handling procedures or by introducing personal protective equipment such as gloves, masks and respirators. In cases of difficulty, advice should be sought from the local area office of the Health and Safety Executive or from the local authority environmental health officer.

Summary

- The Chemical (Hazard Information and Packaging for Supply) Regulations 2002 (CHIP Regulations), as amended, require that all substances and preparations defined as dangerous to supply must be classified, usually by the supplier, as to the kind of danger the chemical presents and be allocated a phrase describing the general nature of the risk.
- All substances and preparations defined as dangerous to supply must be supplied in packages which comply with the standards set out in the regulations, including child-resistant closures and tactile warnings.
- All packages must be labelled with the appropriate symbols of danger, the relevant risk phrases and safety precautions.
- The Control of Substances Hazardous to Health Regulations 1999 (COSHH Regulations) impose duties on employers to protect employees and other persons who may be exposed to substances hazardous to health and impose certain duties on employees concerning their own protection in the workplace.
- Employers must take measures to train and inform staff of the dangers, to prevent or minimise exposure where possible and, if necessary, to monitor exposure and implement a health surveillance programme for all those exposed.

Further reading

COSHH (1998) *The New Brief Guide for Employers*, INDG 136 (rev). London: Health and Safety Executive.

Health and Safety Executive (2000) *The Complete Idiot's Guide to CHIP*. London: HSE Books.
Health and Safety Executive (2002) *CHIP for Everyone*. London: HSE Books.
Royal Pharmaceutical Society of Great Britain (annual publication) *Medicines, Ethics and Practice*. London: Royal Pharmaceutical Society of Great Britain.

Websites

Health and Safety Executive: www.hse.gov.uk/chip
e-mail contact HSE Guidelines: hse.infoline@natbrit.com

21

Miscellaneous legislation affecting pharmacy

The principal statutes concerning medicines, Controlled Drugs, poisons, spirits and dangerous substances have been explained in Chapters 2 to 20. There remain several enactments, and other measures, which are relevant to pharmacy. Some are of general application; others may apply only to one of the branches of pharmacy practice. This chapter comprises notes on some relevant statutes and regulations. The law outlined is that applying in England and Wales, but similar provisions apply in Scotland. The notes are grouped under appropriate subject headings, as follows:

- data protection and freedom of information
- pharmacy ownership
- employment and anti-discrimination law
- consumer protection law
- health and safety law
- environmental law
- merchant shipping: medical scales
- jury service.

Data protection and freedom of information

Data Protection Act 1998

The Data Protection Act 1998 regulates the 'processing' of 'personal data'. *Personal data* means any information whereby a living individual can be identified. *Processing* means virtually any activity such as obtaining, recording or holding the data; carrying out operations or sets of operations on the data; organisation, adaptation or alteration of the data; retrieval; consultation or use of the data; and alignment, combination, blocking, erasure or destruction of the data. Unlike the earlier Act of 1984, which applied only to 'computerised' data, the 1998 Act additionally covers paper records and filing systems and, indeed, any storage system structured so that data relating to a living individual can be retrieved.

The person to whom the data relates is called the *data subject*. The person who determines how and for what purposes the personal data is processed is called the *data controller*; anyone else who actually processes the data is called a *data processor* (s.1). The 1998 Act also imposes additional controls on *sensitive personal data*, which includes any information, including opinion, relating to the physical or mental health or condition of the data subject (s.2).

The Act is administered by the Information Commissioner (formerly Data Protection Registrar, then Commissioner) who maintains a register of *registrable particulars* notified by data controllers, who pay an annual fee (s.18). Data controllers must comply with the eight *data protection principles* set out in the Act (Sch.1). These principles have the force of law. Briefly, the principles require that personal data shall be:

1 obtained and processed fairly and lawfully and shall not be processed at all unless certain conditions are met (see below);
2 obtained and processed for, or in ways compatible with, one or more lawful purpose;
3 adequate, relevant and not excessive in relation to that purpose or purposes;
4 accurate and kept up to date;
5 kept for no longer than necessary;
6 processed in accordance with the rights of data subjects under the Act (see below);
7 protected against unauthorised or unlawful processing and against accidental loss, destruction or damage; and
8 not transferred (with certain exceptions) outside the EEA unless the recipient country operates the same controls on data protection as applies within the EEA.

The Information Commissioner may refuse to register notification if s/he considers that these principles will be contravened (s.22). Processing personal data without notification is a criminal offence (s.21).

The Act imposes conditions which must be met even before processing of personal data can be contemplated (see principle 1 above). Generally, no personal data may be processed at all unless either the data subject has given consent or one of a series of other conditions has been met. These include 'the need to pursue the legitimate interests of the controller' *provided* these are not prejudicial to the interests of the data subject (Sch.2). This condition should be applicable to all uses of personal data in pharmacy practice. In addition, where the data are also *sensitive* personal data, either *explicit consent* must be obtained from the data subject or such consent may not be needed if the processing is 'necessary for medical purposes' and is undertaken by:

1   a health professional, or
2   a person who in the circumstances owes a duty of confidentiality which is equivalent to that which would arise if that person were a health professional.

Medical purposes includes the purposes of preventative medicine, medical diagnosis, medical research, the provision of care and treatment and the management of healthcare services (Sch.3).

Therefore, virtually all personal data used in pharmacy practice are 'sensitive' but 'explicit consent' (which implies a written explanation, a consent form and a decision freely made in appreciation of all its consequences) is not deemed necessary for patient medication records at least, provided **all** personnel who may process such data are bound by the health professional's duty of confidentiality. The definition of *health professional* in the Act includes pharmacists (s.69).

The Act sets out explicit rights of data subjects and others (see principle 6 above). Data controllers must, on receipt of a written request accompanied by a fee:

1   inform the data subject if personal data are being processed;
2   give data subjects a description of the data which are being processed, for what purposes and to whom the data will be disclosed; and
3   provide data subjects with that information in an intelligible form within 40 days of the request (s.7).

Data subjects also have a right to prevent processing of their data for marketing purposes (s.11) and to be notified if 'automated' decisions are taken in relation to, for example, work performance, creditworthiness, reliability or conduct (s.12). Rights are also conferred to allow data subjects to claim compensation from the data controller for failure to comply with any of the requirements of the Act or to fail to rectify, block, erase or destroy any inaccurate data (s.14).

There are exemptions allowing the data controller to exclude information relating to an individual other than the data subject, to allow some latitude where provision of copy records is very difficult or impossible to achieve, to protect trade secrets (s.8) and to withhold data if they are likely to cause substantial damage or distress to the data subject or any other person (s.10). Regulations made under section 7 also allow data controllers to decline to disclose data if this would be likely to cause serious harm to the physical or mental health or condition of the data subject or any other person. Information should not normally be disclosed without data subject consent unless it has been established that the data subject is incapable of managing his/her own affairs and the person requesting disclosure has been appointed by a court to manage those affairs (SI 2000 No. 413).

Parents, guardians or carers may seek disclosure of information about data subjects other than themselves for whom they undertake parental or carer responsibility. If the data subject is a child or anyone else who is likely to understand fully his or her rights to confidentiality, then consent should be established if at all possible. The maximum fee for arranging access to automated health records is £10, although £50 is the maximum if paper records are included (SI 2000 No. 191).

A further condition for the processing (which includes disclosure) of sensitive personal data is in accordance with circumstances specified by the Secretary of State (para.10, Sch.3 of the Act). This could, therefore, include disclosure where it is necessary for the prevention or detection of crime or for protecting the public against dishonesty, malpractice, incompetence or mismanagement where seeking the consent of the data subject would prejudice those purposes (SI 2000 No. 417).

Additional controls (SI 2003 No. 2426) over the processing of personal data electronically introduced two new rules for email marketing: all marketing messages must disclose the sender's identity and provide a valid address for opt-out requests and unsolicited messages, and, in most circumstances, require prior consent from the recipient.

In 2007, a detailed Code of Practice on information security management was introduced for NHS providers of healthcare, as part of their *information governance* arrangements. This Code applies to both managed NHS services and contractors who provide services for the NHS and covers all forms of patient health records, administrative information, X-rays, photographs, digital media such as DVDs and removable memory sticks, networked computer records and email, text and other message types.

Access to health records

Most of the provisions of the Access to Health Records Act 1990 are now within the Data Protection Act 1998, but the 1990 Act continues to provide that a personal representative of a deceased person or anyone who has a claim arising out of a patient's death can also claim access to 'sensitive personal data' maintained in health records.

Generally speaking, the requirements of data protection legislation do not apply to any information which relates to a data subject who has died (but see above) nor to data which have been 'anonymised' (i.e. have been detached from any details or any links whatsoever which could identify a living individual). A series of legal cases have been brought to clarify the limits on the use of anonymised data when derived from patient medication records held by community pharmacists. Details are given in Chapter 27 (p. 450).

Freedom of Information Act 2000

The Freedom of Information Act 2000 seeks to promote the openness and accountability of public authorities. Whereas the Data Protection Act is concerned to protect the privacy of individuals and their personal data, the Freedom of Information Act gives people the right to seek information from public authorities about how they carry out their duties, why they make the decisions they do and how they spend public money. Public authorities would include NHS trusts and primary care trusts. Such trusts must adopt and maintain a publication scheme, setting out details of information it will routinely make available, how the information can be obtained and whether there is any charge for it. Each trust must comply, normally within 28 days, with requests for the information that it holds unless an exemption from disclosure applies. Exemptions include personal data covered by the Data Protection Act (see above), information provided to the public authority in confidence and some limited protection from disclosure which may jeopardise commercial interests. From 1st January 2009, pharmacies providing NHS services were required to adopt a model publication scheme approved by the Information Commissioner.

Pharmacy ownership

A full explanation has been given in Chapter 5 of the controls applied by the Medicines Act 1968 to the conduct of 'retail pharmacy businesses'. As such, a business can be owned by an individual pharmacist, a partnership of pharmacists or a body corporate (i.e. a company); it is desirable that the legal status of partnerships and companies should be understood. Only a brief explanation can be given here and any pharmacist contemplating ownership should seek advice from a suitably specialised lawyer or from the business law pages of the Department for Business, Enterprise and Regulatory Reform (BERR; formerly the Department of Trade and Industry) website.

Partnerships

A partnership is defined in the Partnership Act 1890 as the relationship which exists between persons carrying on a business in common with a view of profit. In contrast to a company (see below), a partnership, or *firm*, is simply a number of individuals each of whom has a responsibility for the affairs and the liabilities of the firm as a whole.

In England and Wales, a partnership (firm) does not have a legal status of its own as does a company. This means that the private assets of each partner can be called upon to satisfy any of the firm's debts. All the partners are liable for any debts incurred by one partner acting on behalf of the firm.

In Scotland, a partnership has a status similar to that of a body corporate (i.e. it *is a legal person distinct from the partners of whom it is composed*). It is for this reason that in a partnership owning a retail pharmacy in England and Wales, all the partners must be pharmacists, whereas in a Scottish partnership only one partner need be a pharmacist (Chapter 5).

A partnership can arise in either of two ways: by express agreement or by implied agreement between two or more persons. A partnership can be implied if two or more persons work together in such a way as to fall within the definition as set out in the Act. Generally, if they share in the management of the business and share the profits, then the law will recognise them as partners.

When a partnership is formed to run a retail pharmacy, it is invariably a partnership of express agreement, and the conditions of the partnership are set out in a partnership contract or articles. The articles can be altered at any time with the consent of all the partners, whether this is express or implied. The only exception is where the articles restrict the right to vary (e.g. that no change may be made for two years).

A partnership can be formed where one of the partners may limit their responsibility for the firm's debts, leaving the other partners to share the unlimited liability. This partner is often referred to as a *sleeping partner*, as he takes no part in the management of the firm. Partnerships of this type are not common and are governed by the Limited Partnerships Act 1907. If a person wishes to limit their liability in this way today, they are more likely to invest in a limited company. Once again, it is stressed that before contemplating forming a partnership, pharmacists should take legal advice and have any partnership contract drawn up by a solicitor.

The Limited Liability Partnership Act 2000 allowed the creation of Limited Liability Partnerships (LLPs) within England, Scotland and Wales to retain the organisational flexibility and tax treatment of a partnership but also derive benefit from the separate legal personality of a company with limited liability. LLPs must register and submit annual accounts to Companies House.

Companies

A company – or corporation aggregate – is a body of persons combined or incorporated for some common purpose. The most common example is a registered trading company, that is, a company which has been incorporated under the relevant Companies Act. The notes given here can only outline the general principles of company law, with some special reference to certain aspects which particularly affect pharmacy businesses. Incorporation as a company enables a group of people to act and to trade in the same way as an individual owner. It also enables them to trade with limited liability to the individual shareholder. Once incorporated, a company is *a legal person* and quite distinct from its members. It can own property, employ persons and be a creditor or debtor just like a human being. This is the fundamental principle of company law.

The promoters of a company must file (electronic submission became permitted in 2006) the following documents with the Register of Companies:

1 memorandum of association;
2 articles of association;
3 list of directors and name of secretary;
4 statement of the nominal share capital;
5 notice of the address of the registered office; and
6 declarations by a solicitor or a person named in the articles as a director or secretary that all the requirements of the Companies Acts in respect of registration have been complied with.

If all the documents are in order, the registrar will issue a certificate of incorporation which is conclusive evidence that the company has been registered and that the requirements of the Act have been complied with.

There are at least three types of company: a public company, a private limited company and a private unlimited company. Most pharmacists will be concerned with the private company, whether limited or not.

A *private company* needs only one director but if there is a sole director, s/he cannot also be the company secretary. Shares and debentures in a private company cannot be offered to the public.

An *unlimited company* is one where there is no limit on the members' liability to contribute to the assets in order to satisfy the company's debts.

Memorandum of association

The memorandum of association regulates the external affairs of the company and must include five clauses, namely those relating to the name, registered office, objects, liability and capital of the company. It must be signed by each subscriber.

The name of a private limited company must end with the word *limited*. For a public limited company, the last words must be *public limited company* or *plc*.

There is a general freedom of choice of the company name, but a company cannot be registered under the Act by a name which includes, otherwise than at the end of its name, the word *limited, unlimited* or *public limited company* or the Welsh equivalents (e.g. *cfyngedig*). Where *cfyngedig* is used, the fact that the company is a limited company must be stated in English and in legible characters on all official company stationery and publications, and in a notice conspicuously displayed in every place where the company's business is carried on.

No name may be used which the registrar considers offensive or which, if used, would constitute a criminal offence. In the latter category would fall a retail company which is not conducting a retail pharmacy business and which wished to use the title *chemist*.

Certain words and expressions may only be used in company or business names with the approval of the Secretary of State or other relevant body specified in regulations (SI 1981 No. 1685, as amended). For the word *chemist* the Royal Pharmaceutical Society of Great Britain (RPSGB) is the relevant body, but, when *chemist* or *chemistry* is used in an industrial sense, it is the Royal Society of Chemistry. Similarly, for the word *apothecary* the relevant body in England and Wales is the Worshipful Society of Apothecaries and in Scotland, the RPSGB.

Articles of association

The articles regulate the internal affairs of the company (i.e. the rights of share-holders and the manner in which the business of the company is conducted). A model set of articles is set out in regulations made under the Act. It may be used by a company as it is or adapted as required. If no articles are submitted with the application for registration, the statutory ones will apply. The articles of a company are freely alterable by special resolution, subject to certain safeguards.

The legal effect of the memorandum and articles is that they bind the company and its members as if they had been signed and sealed by each individual member and contained covenants on the part of each member to observe all the provisions of the memorandum and articles.

Directors

The first directors of a company are usually appointed in accordance with the articles; if not they are appointed by the original subscribers to the company. Subsequent appointments are usually governed by a procedure laid down in the articles. It must be stressed that a pharmacist becoming a director should be fully aware of the contents of the memorandum and articles of association of the company s/he joins. Directors must exercise their powers as directors for the benefit of the company. A director has a duty to the company to exercise such skill and care as s/he possesses. If appointed in a specific capacity calling for a particular skill (e.g. a pharmacist who is a director of a body corporate), s/he must exercise that skill in a reasonable manner for the benefit of the company. Directors are not bound to give continuing and unremitting attention to the company's affairs and are justified in trusting the officers of the company to perform their duties honestly.

A pharmacist who becomes superintendent chemist (pharmacist) of a company will almost invariably be appointed a director, and a knowledge of the powers and duties of directors is essential. For example, if a company fails to make its annual return then the company and/or any of its officers or directors is liable to a default fine. A pharmacist who resigns as a superintendent chemist should ensure that s/he also resigns as a director. Instances have occurred where a pharmacist, some years after having resigned as a superintendent chemist, has been prosecuted for failing to make an annual return as s/he had remained a director of the company.

Business Names Act 1985

A *business name* is a name used by a business which is other than (a) for a sole trader, his/her surname; (b) for a partnership, the surnames or corporate names of all members of the partnership, or (c) for a corporate business, the names of the company concerned. Certain additions are permitted (e.g. forenames or initials).

Where a business name is used, the true name(s) and address(es) of the owner(s) must appear on all business stationery and that information must be prominently displayed at the business premises. The use of certain types of business name require the written approval of the Secretary of State and regulations may specify certain words or expressions which may only be used with the approval of a government department or some other relevant body.

Employment and anti-discrimination law

Knowledge of employment law is important to pharmacists both in their capacity as employer and as employee. Employment rights derive from two main areas: those created by Acts of Parliament (statutory employment rights) and those created by decisions of courts over time (common law rights; Chapter 1).

Statutory employment rights

Employment rights cover rights such as equal pay; sick pay; the right not to be unlawfully discriminated against on the grounds of sex or marital status, sexual orientation, race, disability, religion or belief, age, trade union membership, or part-time or fixed term status; not to suffer a detriment for making a protected disclosure in the public interest ('whistle blowing'); and not to be dismissed unfairly. Employees have also been granted rights to a written statement of the terms of employment, of the reasons for dismissal, to minimum disciplinary procedures, to be accompanied at a disciplinary hearing, to an itemised pay statement, for time off for public duties, for time off for antenatal care, for time off for care of dependants, to a minimum wage, to a minimum period of notice for termination of employment, to maternity leave and pay, to paternity leave and pay, to request flexible working and entitlement to rest breaks and restrictions on weekly working time. This list is not exhaustive.

The rights are enforceable by employees in the Employment Tribunal. Some rights require the employee to have a qualifying period of service before they be enforced in the Employment Tribunal. The compensation that can be awarded by the tribunal is sometimes subject to a statutory minimum or a statutory cap depending on the nature of the claim. However, in other claims, the tribunal considers what is just and equitable in all the circumstances having regard to the loss sustained by the employee.

In the context of employment law, *disability* means 'a physical or mental impairment which has a substantial and long-term adverse effect on a person's ability to carry out normal day-to-day activities'. *Day-to-day activities* involve mobility; manual dexterity; physical co-ordination; ability to lift, carry or move ordinary objects; speech, hearing or eyesight; memory; or ability to concentrate, learn, understand or perceive physical danger. Therefore, the definition includes those with hearing or visual impairment, those with learning disabilities or mental illness and those with long-term illnesses such as severe arthritis, human immunodeficiency virus infection, multiple sclerosis and muscular dystrophy. Certain conditions are excluded, notably addiction to alcohol, nicotine or non-therapeutic drugs.

Common law rights

In the employment context, the principal common law claim is where an employee claims that the employer has acted in breach of the contract of employment. Employment Tribunals can deal with breach of contract claims where the breach has arisen or is outstanding on the termination of the employment. There is a limit of £25 000 on the awards a tribunal can make in these circumstances. Alternatively, employees can make claims either in the County Court or High Court (Chapter 1), depending on the amount of damages claimed and other certain criteria applied by the courts.

European law

Sometimes, UK national law is in conflict with EU legislation. In these instances, the case may be referred to the European Court of Justice (Chapter 1), the decisions of which will be binding on UK courts and tribunals. Decisions of the European Court of Justice may also result in amendments to national law.

Further information on this complex and fast changing area of law can be obtained at the websites at the end of this chapter.

Vicarious liability

The term *vicarious liability* in this context signifies the liability which an employer may incur to a customer for damage caused by an employee in the course of his/her employment. This in legal terms is the relationship between *master* and *servant* and means that the 'master' cannot only order or require *what* must be done but also *how* it shall be done.

All employee pharmacists should have a contract of employment, but in many areas pharmacists themselves will decide *how* a task should be performed and this will often be a matter for the pharmacist's own professional judgement. Therefore, if an employee pharmacist makes a mistake or is so careless as to cause *damage* (e.g. injury, fear, anxiety, etc.) to a patient or customer, the employer would probably be liable. However, if the act or omission fell into the realm of professional judgement, the pharmacist may also incur additional personal liability and might be accountable to the RPSGB and/or to his/her employer to justify his/her actions. This is why pharmacists are advised to carry their own professional indemnity insurance or ensure that they practise only in an establishment which is covered by such insurance (see p. 368).

Access to goods, facilities and services

The Equality Act 2006 established the Commission for Equality and Human Rights (CEHR), which has combined the activities of the Equal Opportunities Commission and the Commission for Racial Equality and, from April 2009, the Disability Rights Commission. The Act makes discrimination on many grounds unlawful (sex or marital status, sexual orientation, race, disability, religion or belief, and age) in the provision of goods, facilities or services; the disposal or management of premises; education; and the exercise of public functions. Provision of NHS services, either directly or under contract, is a public service. The Act further creates a duty on public authorities, such as NHS bodies, to promote equality of opportunity between men and women, to prohibit sex discrimination in the exercise of public functions and to promote understanding of the Human Rights Act. Earlier legislation also creates a duty on NHS bodies to prepare and publish a gender equality scheme in accordance with a detailed code of practice.

Vetting of healthcare workers

Legislation designed to protect children and vulnerable adults from abuse has meant that persons working in either health or social care are now subject to several vetting processes before employment. These include criminal record checks with the Criminal Records Bureau to preclude or possibly constrain the employment of those with relevant convictions. From 2008, the Criminal Records Bureau will be working with Independent Safeguarding Authority (the new name for the Independent Barring Board established under the Safeguarding Vulnerable Adults Act 2006) to assess who should be barred from working in posts which involve close contact with, or substantial access to, children and vulnerable adults.

Consumer protection law

Detailed information on consumer protection law may be found on the Department for Business, Enterprise and Regulatory Reform website (given at the end of this chapter); a review of all such law was announced in 2008. All retailers are subject to controls on price, description and the safety of the goods they sell. The majority of the law in this area is enforced by the local authority, usually the trading standards department. In some cities, those duties may be shared with the local environmental health officer. The general principle of most of this law is that it makes it a criminal offence to mislead consumers as to the description, price or safety of goods and services. The majority of the criminal offences in this area are strict liability offences, coupled to a defence of due diligence. It is, therefore, vitally important that processes and procedures are in place so that a pharmacist can show that s/he took reasonable steps and precautions to check that descriptions of goods and services were accurate or that the goods s/he sold were safe. The following points should be specifically noted.

Trades Descriptions Act 1968

The Trades Descriptions Act makes it an offence to falsely describe goods or services in the course of a trade or business. The law is wide enough to cover all forms of description and it should be noted that the retailer is to some extent in double jeopardy as there is an offence for supplying goods to which a false description has been applied as well as an offence of applying a false description to goods. Particular care needs to be taken where verbal descriptions are being applied to goods, as the individual becomes personally liable for those descriptions should they subsequently prove to be inaccurate. With regard to services, it is an offence to knowingly make a false statement.

Consumer Protection Act 1987

Product liability

The Consumer Protection Act 1987 creates liability without fault on the part of the producer for damage caused by a defect in their product. Four classes of person may face liability for a defective product: the manufacturer, the importer, the person who holds themselves out as the manufacturer or, in the event of none of the former being identified, the person supplying the product to the victim. The first three groups have a primary liability; the supplier has a secondary liability based upon their inability to identify a primary producer. When medicines might be the subject of an action in the courts (there have been very few cases under the Act), the primary producer will normally be the product licence holder. The supplying pharmacist should, therefore, ensure that s/he has adequate systems and records to ensure that the licence holder or manufacturer can always be identified with some certainty. Liability probably does not arise from repackaging licensed medicines or from supplying them against a prescription, provided the source is known.

The supplying pharmacist will carry full liability for 'own branded' goods in which the pharmacy's name and address are affixed to containers of medicines made up elsewhere and not so identified. The supplying pharmacist also carries full liability when s/he prepares his/her own remedies for a patient under section 10 of the Medicines Act (see p. 43). In these circumstances, it is advisable to maintain full manufacturing records so that the producer of the ingredients can always be identified. Claims may be made for up to three years after the 'relevant date' – when the victim became aware of the facts – subject to a maximum of 10 years from the date of putting the product into circulation.

Price control

Customers' rights on pricing are protected in two areas of consumer protection law: controls on misleading price indications and requirements to display price, and in certain circumstances unit price, in close proximity to the goods. It is an offence to give a misleading price indication and it is, therefore, important for any pharmacist involved in retailing to be aware of the Code of Practice for Traders on Price Indications. This code provides guidance to retailers on what constitutes 'misleading' and how 'offer' prices can be constructed. A second obligation is simply a requirement to display a price in such a way that customers see it without having to ask in close proximity to all goods available for sale. If those goods are required to be sold by weight or measure, then there is an obligation to give a unit price (cost per kilogram or litre) as well as the actual selling price. Unit price controls do not apply to medicines. Within pharmacies, cosmetics, toiletries and food supplements are the items most likely to be affected. Unit price controls apply only in larger stores (over 280 m²). Details of the controls are complicated and subject to change. Advice on price indications should, therefore, be sought from the local trading standards department.

Safety of goods

Consumer protection law also creates an obligation to provide customers with goods that are safe. Any reasonably foreseeable risks arising out of the goods should have been dealt with by the manufacturer and addressed either by changing the design of the goods to make them safer or by issuing warnings or instructions that deal with the issue. Where local authorities find unsafe goods, as well as prosecuting they can also serve enforcement notices requiring that the products are removed from the marketplace.

Weights and Measures Act 1985

The Weights and Measures Act 1985 and the regulations made under it control the manner in which goods should be weighed, measured and retailed. They also control the way quality indications should be given on the packaging. The legislation lays down specific construction criteria for equipment and measures and sets down the accuracy tests that the equipment must pass if it is to be used for selling goods. The regulations also set out a detailed regime for the packaging of goods, and those pharmacists involved in packing bulk goods should consult the Code of Practice for Guidance of Packers available from The Stationery Office as well as seeking guidance from the local trading standards department. The selling of goods deficient in weight or volume is a strict liability offence but defences are available.

Competition Act 1998

The Competition Act 1998 reflects a worldwide trend to open up markets, stimulate competition and establish transparent and fair marketing arrangements. It seeks to do this by outlawing agreements between businesses and decisions taken by businesses on concerted practices that affect trade in the UK or Europe. Those decisions are not allowed to have as their object or effect the prevention, distortion or restriction of competition within the UK. An example of such a practice would be people acting together directly or indirectly to fix the purchase or selling process. The rules not only affect retailers but also trade associations or any other group of persons acting together in a way as to distort competition. The fines under the Competition Act can be very high, as the maximum ceiling on the fine is 10 per cent of company turnover.

In pharmacy, the advent of the Competition Act led to the abolition of *resale price maintenance* on the price at which medicines available over the counter could be supplied (*Pharm J* 16 August 1997 p. 236; 25 October 1997 p. 676). This Act has also affected the profession's Code of Ethics. The rules of trade associations and professional bodies are covered by the anti-competitive prohibitions in the Act, unless they are specifically exempted in Schedule 4. For historical reasons, pharmacy was not included in Schedule 4 (although some other health professions were) and the Code of Ethics for pharmacy must comply with the provisions of the Act. Prior to 2002, the Codes of Ethics contained several restraints, in the public interest, on the promotion and supply of medicines but there are none in the 2007 Code of Ethics (see Chapter 23).

Websites providing detailed information on trading and other retail law are given at the end of this chapter.

Health and safety law

Health and Safety at Work Act 1974 and other related Acts

The Health and Safety at Work Act 1974 is extremely broad and basically sets out the requirements for a 'duty of care' for everyone in the workplace, including the protection of the health and safety of the public against the risks to health arising from work activities. It, therefore, applies to employers, employees, owners/occupiers of premises, suppliers and the self-employed. The Act provides a framework for other health and safety legislation. Detailed requirements are set out in specific regulations; an example being the Workplace (Health, Safety and Welfare) Regulations 1992 (SI 1992 No. 3004). These regulations are themselves supported by an Approved Code of Practice that expands the requirements contained within individual regulations by providing detailed interpretation and guidance. Approved Codes of Practice are the main working documents for those with health and safety responsibilities.

Employers have a duty of care under the Health and Safety at Work etc. Act, together with its associated regulations, to ensure, so far as is reasonably practicable, the health, safety and welfare of employees while they are at work. The main areas covered are:

- safe plant and machinery (work equipment) and safe operating procedures;
- safe use, handling and storage and transport of articles and substances;
- provision of information, instruction, training and supervision;
- provision and maintenance of a safe place of work with safe means of access and egress; and
- for an employer with more than four employees, provision of a written policy for health and safety and details of the arrangements for carrying out the requirements of the policy.

Employers, including the self-employed (e.g. a locum pharmacist), and owners/occupiers have a similar duty to safeguard the health and safety of others who are not employees but who may be affected by his/her business activities. 'Others' include customers, visitors and the general public. Employees themselves also have a duty under the Act to take reasonable care for their own health and safety and for that of anyone else who may be affected by what they (employees) do or fail to do. There is also a duty to co-operate with their employer on health and safety issues.

Enforcement of health and safety requirements is undertaken by inspectors from the Health and Safety Executive for 'industrial premises' or by officers from the local authorities for 'retail premises'. Both regulatory groups have the powers to inspect, investigate cases of non-compliance, warn and issue 'improvement notices' or 'prohibition notices' as well as prosecute offenders.

It is beyond the scope of this book to provide much detail about health and safety legislation. However, it is important to raise the awareness of *risk assessment* as the basic 'tool' for identifying and managing risk. Areas where risks might arise in pharmacy practice include:

- work equipment (Provision and Use of Work Equipment Regulations);
- substances (COSHH Regulations; Chapter 20); and
- manual handling (Manual Handling Operations Regulations).

To manage health and safety risks, it is necessary to identify the risks. The risk-assessment process achieves this by examining the workplace itself and work activities (tasks). Hazards (things with the potential to cause harm) are noted and the associated consequences (severity) of each hazard ranked should the harm be inflicted. For each hazardous situation, the types of person at risk are also identified. An assessment is also made of the likelihood of the harm actually occurring, again ranked according to likelihood. An assessment of the risk is then made for each situation based on the equation:

Risk = Consequence × Likelihood for each category of persons at risk

The basic principles of risk assessment are detailed in a Health and Safety Executive Approved Code of Practice *Management of Health and Safety at Work Regulations 1999*, to which reference should be made. Persons compiling risk assessments must be trained and have sufficient knowledge and experience of the process such that they are able to demonstrate their competence to the persons at risk depending upon the assessment and any regulatory inspector. Consideration should always be given to engaging suitable experts to do this work for anything other than situations where there are low consequences from workplace hazards. A key outcome of risk assessment is to require the identification and implementation of control measures to reduce risks to as low a level as is reasonably practicable. Control measures may range from hardware (e.g. guards for machinery) to procedural matters (e.g. operating procedures) to personal protective equipment (e.g. gloves/goggles). Risk can be eliminated only if a hazard is eliminated. Substituting something less hazardous (e.g. less-toxic cleaning materials) can reduce risk.

Regulatory inspectors would expect to see 'suitable and sufficient' risk assessments during any visit. It is important to review risk assessments and other health and safety arrangements periodically, or in the event of an accident or even a 'near miss', to see if the assessment and control measures are still valid and whether they can be improved to reduce risks to health and safety further. All such assessments should be discussed with employees who are 'at risk'.

Websites providing detailed information on health and safety law are given at the end of this chapter.

Environmental law

The Department for Environment, Food and Rural Affairs (DEFRA) is the government department responsible for a vast range of public services and controls such air quality, noise pollution, litter, energy and chemicals. This section provides an overview of two areas that are relevant to pharmacy practice: controls on waste and the protection of animals and birds; controls on pesticides are covered in Chapter 18. UK legislation on waste disposal derives largely from European Directives and is both complex and subject to change. Readers are directed to the DEFRA, RPSGB and Pharmaceutical Services Negotiating Committee (PSNC) websites (see list at the end of the chapter) for up-to-date information.

Controls on waste

The Environmental Protection Act 1990 introduced a *duty of care* which applies to all persons who import, produce, carry, keep, treat or dispose of controlled waste. This, therefore, applies to pharmacists, who necessarily handle waste or unwanted medicines in the course of their practice. The duty of care lies on all holders of waste at every stage in its history, such that a pharmacist having held controlled waste may only pass it on to an *authorised person*, such as a registered carrier, a licensed waste manager or a waste collection or regulation authority. Further, s/he must transfer with the waste such a written description of the waste – a consignment note – as will enable others to avoid committing an offence under the Act.

Controlled waste includes household, industrial and commercial waste of any kind, whether conventionally thought of as polluting or not. The Controlled Waste Regulations 1992 (SI 1992 No. 588) define *clinical waste* as, amongst other things, 'waste arising from...pharmaceutical or similar practice', and further describes clinical waste which arises from a private dwelling or residential home as *household waste*, as distinct from that from any other source, such as a nursing home, which is classified as *industrial waste*. This is significant because the local waste collection authority has a duty to collect household waste, albeit for a fee, but producers of industrial waste are more likely to have to use private contractors for this purpose. It is unlawful to deposit controlled waste in, or to keep it on, any land or knowingly cause or permit such waste to be deposited unless a waste management licence authorising the deposit is in force under the Environmental Protection Act 1990. The Water Resources Act

1991 prohibits a person from causing or knowingly permitting any noxious poisonous or polluting matter to enter any controlled inland waters.

The special restrictions on the destruction of Controlled Drugs under the Misuse of Drugs Act 1971 were considered in Chapter 17. Controlled Drugs, whether stock or returned by patients, are subject to the same considerations described above for other returned medicines and advice, so disposal via the sewage system does not comply with the Water Resources Act. Further, the Misuse of Drugs Act requires that Controlled Drugs be denatured in such a way as to render the drug irretrievable. Technically, this denaturing would be regarded as waste treatment and would require a licence under waste management legislation (see below); however, the relevant authorities have agreed that, provided pharmacy contractors use specially designed controlled drug denaturing kits, no licence will be required.

Under the Waste Management Licensing Regulations 1994 (SI No. 1056), businesses must hold a licence to store waste other than their own, pending disposal. This would include medicines returned by patients but pharmacies are exempted from the need for a licence provided the total quantity of returned medicines does not exceed $5\,m^3$ at any time and is stored for no longer than six months (these conditions vary in Scotland). This exemption must be registered individually with the local Environment Agency Office. Where medicines are returned by patients or care homes in blister packs, then these must remain in their blisters for disposal – 'de-blistering' is also regarded as waste treatment under the law. 'Sharps' – mostly used needles and syringes, but also including broken glass – are collected from households by the local authority. Medical practices have an exemption which allows them to accept back sharps from patients but this does not extend to pharmacies. However, the Environment Agency has indicated that needle-exchange schemes may continue to operate from pharmacies.

The Hazardous Waste (England and Wales) Regulations 2005 SI No. 894 essentially replaced earlier Special Waste Regulations (1996). They have the effect of removing Prescription Only Medicines from their former classification of special waste and include only two categories, cytotoxic and cytostatic medicines, as being *hazardous waste*. There is an exemption from the need to notify the Environment Agency where pharmacies produce hazardous waste themselves, but such waste must be kept separate from non-hazardous waste. This can cause difficulties with quantities of patient-returned medicines and guidance is available on how best to examine and segregate hazardous waste from returned medicines from patients to avoid a breach of the law.

Controls to protect animals and birds

Pesticides

Information on legislation relating to pesticides is in Chapter 18.

Animals in research

The Animal (Scientific Procedures) Act 1986 makes provision for the protection of animals used for experimental or scientific procedures. A *protected animal* for the purposes of the Act means *any living vertebrate other than a human*. Any experimental or other scientific procedure applied to a protected animal which may have the effect of causing that animal pain, suffering, distress or lasting harm is known as a *regulated procedure*. The Act provides for a system of (a) personal licences, (b) project licences and (c) scientific establishment licences. Before issuing any licence, the Secretary of State must consult one of the inspectors appointed under the Act (s.9). The breeding and sale of animals for experimental purposes is also controlled.

The Act specifies the type of programmes for which project licences may be issued including, amongst other things, the prevention, diagnosis or treatment of disease; certain educational purposes; and forensic enquiries. Projects may only be carried out by licensed persons on licensed scientific establishments. The Act deals specifically with humane methods of killing experimental animals. The Animals Procedures Committee has the duty of advising the Secretary of State on matters concerned with the Act. S/he may consult the Committee on the question of licences and on the preparation of codes of practice. Proposals were published in 2008 to amend the supporting European Directive to update arrangements for animal experimentation.

Wild animals and farm livestock

Where under the Animal (Cruel Poisons) Act 1962, the Secretary of State has specified that a poison cannot be used for destroying animals without causing undue suffering and that other suitable methods of destroying them exist, s/he may, by regulations, prohibit or restrict the use of that poison for destroying animals or animals of a particular description.

Regulations have been made (SI 1963 No. 1278) which prohibit the use of yellow phosphorus and red squill for the destruction of animals. The regulations also prohibit the use of strychnine for killing any animals including moles. The supply of these substances for prohibited purposes could constitute aiding and abetting an offence under the Act.

NB Where the Minister believes or suspects that rabies exists in any area, s/he may by an order made under the Rabies Act 1974 declare that area to be an *infected area* for purposes connected with the control and eradication of that disease. S/he may also take steps to secure destruction of foxes in an *infected area* and an officer of DEFRA and any person authorised in writing by the Minister may enter any land for the purpose of carrying out such destruction. Where the Minister exercises this power, methods of destruction may be used (e.g. the use of strychnine) which would apart from these provisions be unlawful [Rabies (Control) Order 1974 (SI 1974 No. 2212)]. For restrictions on the sale of strychnine under poisons legislation, see Chapter 18.

The Protection of Animals Act 1911 provides that it is unlawful wilfully to administer, or cause or procure to be administered, to any animal a poisonous or injurious drug or substance. Similarly, it is unlawful to sell or offer or expose for sale any grain or seed which has been rendered poisonous except for *bona fide* use in agriculture. It is also an offence to place upon any land or in any building any poison or any fluid or edible matter (not being seed or grain) which has been rendered poisonous.

It is a defence to prove that the poison was placed for the purpose of destroying insects and other invertebrates where it is found necessary in the interest of public health or agriculture, or to preserve other animals, and that adequate precautions have been taken to prevent injury to dogs, cats, other domestic animals and wild birds [Protection of Animals (Amendment) Act 1927].

A defence also exists where a person uses poisonous gas in a rabbit hole or places in a rabbit hole a substance which by evaporation or any contact with moisture generates poisonous gas (e.g. Cymag; Prevention of Damage by Rabbits Act 1939). These defences are not valid where the poison concerned is prohibited by the Animal (Cruel Poisons) Act 1962 (see above). It is also a defence under the Wildlife and Countryside Act 1981 to prove that what was done was performed in accordance with a licence granted under that Act.

In relation to wildlife, the Wildlife and Countryside Act 1981 prohibits certain methods of killing or taking of wild birds and wild animals including the laying of 'any poisonous, poisoned or stupefying substance'. The prohibition does not apply to anything done under or in accordance with the terms of a licence granted by the appropriate authority. The appropriate authority varies according to the purpose of the licence (e.g. if the licence is issued for the purpose of preventing the spread of disease, then the appropriate authority is the Agriculture Minister). Such a licence may be issued by Agriculture Ministers for the killing or taking of certain wild birds (e.g. feral pigeons, house sparrows, etc.), using the chemical alpha-chloralose. Alpha-chloralose can be sold to local authorities and to *bona fide* pest control companies who have had issued to them by the Agriculture Minister a licence which allows them to compound and use their own bait. Farmers have been known to make approaches to pharmacists for supplies of alpha-chloralose; although the pharmacist may lawfully supply this chemical under poison legislation, a supply made for the purpose of stupefying birds could be an offence under the Wildlife and Countryside Act 1981. Pharmacists receiving requests for alpha-chloralose or stupefying bait should, before supplying, contact the RPSGB for further details.

Merchant shipping: medical scales

The Merchant Shipping and Fishing Vessels (Medical Stores) Regulations 1995 (SI 1995 No. 1802, as amended), implement Council Directive 92/29/EEC and make for the minimum safety and health requirements for improved medical treatment so far as the Directive relates to the carriage of medicines and other medical stores. They cover the carrying of appropriate medical stores on board ships, including fishing vessels. A *ship* in this context means a UK ship other than pleasure vessels used for non-commercial purposes and not manned by professional crews and ships employed in inland navigation.

The master of any ship which does not carry a doctor is required to make arrangements for securing medical attention on board ship to be given by himself or by some other person appointed by him/her for the purpose. There are minimum requirements for the medicines and medical stores to be carried before a ship may put to sea and the *scale of medicines* to be carried depends upon whether or not there is a duly qualified medical practitioner in the ship's complement.

The various scales are provided for in the 1995 regulations and in Merchant Shipping Notices M.1607 and M.1608. The regulations also specify requirements for the packaging, labelling and storage of medicines and other medical items (e.g. disinfectants).

The containers must be labelled amongst other things, with:

1   the name of the medicine, in English, as indicated in the respective scale;
2   the expiry date, where appropriate;
3   any storage requirements;
4   name and address of supplier, product licence number and batch number; and
5   any further information required by the notices.

The containers of capsules and tablets must be capable of reclosure so as to prevent the ingress of moisture.

A ship in the UK may be detained if a person empowered under the Act to inspect the medical stores is not satisfied that the required stores are being carried.

Orders made under the Misuse of Drugs Act 1971 and the Medicines Act 1968 permit the owner or master of a ship which does not carry a doctor as part of its complement to obtain certain Controlled Drugs (see p. 224) and any other Prescription Only Medicines (see p. 118) which are necessary for the treatment of persons on the ship. The medical scales issued under the Merchant Shipping Act are minimum requirements only.

Jury service

All persons normally resident in the UK and aged between 18 and 70 who are registered as parliamentary or local government electors are, with very few exceptions, liable for jury service. Schedule 33 (under s.321 of the Criminal Justice Act 2003) sets out the exemptions, which are broadly persons who are mentally disordered; persons who are or have been subject to certain detention, custody, prison or court martial sentences; and, as a discretionary exemption, persons who are needed for military service at the material time. Pharmacists have no occupational exemption. Details of what jury service entails and the payment and expenses arrangements can be found on the Court Service website at the end of this chapter.

In Scotland, pharmacists may be eligible for exemption from jury service. Exemption is not automatic and the pharmacist who wishes to be excused must give written notice to the clerk of the court from whom the citation is received, indicating his/her right and desire to be so excused. Details can be found on the Scottish Courts website at the end of the chapter.

Summary

- This chapter outlines enactments and other measures which can be relevant to pharmacy. Some are of general application and others may apply only to one of the branches of pharmacy practice.
- The law covering being an owner, an employer or an employee is outlined as is the law relating to running a retail business and health and safety issues.
- There are controls on disposal of waste, on supply of pesticides and to protect animals and birds.
- The carriage of appropriate medical stores on board ships to fulfil minimum safety and health requirements for medical treatment where a ship does not carry a doctor is covered by scales that specify the medicines to be included.
- Data protection and freedom of information legislation covers virtually all personal data used in pharmacy practice. Under the legislation, health professionals, including pharmacists, have a duty of confidentiality.

Further reading

Austen N, Hawkins A (2007) Get your Company Act together. *Pharmacy Today*, April, pp. 26–27.

Connelly D (2002) Disability awareness: what the new rules mean for community pharmacies. *Pharm J* 269:389–390.

Davies J (2005) In good company. *Chemist and Druggist*, 26 November, p. 38.

Day C (2007) To err can be expensive. *Pharmacy Magazine*, July, p. 49.

Department of Health (2007) *Information Security Management: NHS Code of Practice*. London: The Stationery Office.

Edwards G (2007) They've got to go. *Pharmacy Today*, June, pp. 22–23.

Exten-Wright J, Stansfield T (2008) Employing overseas workers. *Chemist and Druggist*, 8 November, pp. 35–37.

Muir J (2002) Sometimes things go wrong: the concept of unfair dismissal. *Pharm J* 268:445–447.

Richman C, Castensson S (2008) Impact of waste pharmaceuticals: an environmental hazard or 'greenwash'? *Pharm J* 280:335–337.

Rosenbloom K *et al.* (2005) The Disability Discrimination Act. *Pharm J* 275:747–750.

Royal Pharmaceutical Society of Great Britain (2006) Changes to the return and storage of waste medicines in Scotland. *Law Ethics Bull* 277:675.

Wakeman R (2007) Clean up your act. *Pharmacy Today*, June, pp. 6–7.

Websites

Access to all government websites: http://www.direct.gov.uk/en/index.htm

Advisory, Conciliation and Arbitration Service: http://www.acas.gov.uk

Chemist and Druggist: http://www.chemistanddruggist.co.uk

Community pharmacists: http://www.rpsgb.org/pdfs/hazwastecommphguid.pdf

Consumer Regulations: http://www.crw.gov.uk

Department for Business, Enterprise and Regulatory Reform: http://www.berr.gov.uk/

Department for Environment, Food and Rural Affairs: http://www.defra.gov.uk

Equality and Human Rights Commission: http://www.equalityhumanrights.com/en/Pages/default.aspx

Health and Safety Executive: http://www.hse.gov.uk

Hospital pharmacists: http://www.rpsgb.org/pdfs/hazwastehospphguid.pdf

Independent Safeguarding Authority: http://www.isa-gov.org.uk/

Information on disposal of waste: Royal Pharmaceutical Society of Great Britain, Interim guidance on the Hazardous Waste Regulations 2005 (modified 2006): www.rpsgb.org (and then use search engine for waste disposal)

Jury service: http://www.courtservice.gov.uk

Jury service in Scotland: http://www.scotcourts.gov.uk

Leaflets and guidance on disposal of hazardous waste are also available from the National Pharmacy Association: http://www.npa.org.uk

Local Authority Circulars Subject Index: http://www.hse.gov.uk/lau/lacs/index.htm

Office of Fair Trading: http://www.oft.gov.uk

Office of the Information Commissioner: http://www.informationcommissioner.gov.uk

Pharmaceutical Journal: http://www.pjonline.com

Pharmaceutical Services Negotiating Committee (2005): http://www.psnc.org.uk/publications_detail.php/191/disposal_of_unwanted_medicines

Proposals to update animal experimentation legislation: http://scienceandresearch.homeoffice.gov.uk/animal-research/legislation/

Trading Standards Departments: http://www.tradingstandards.gov.uk

22

Pharmacy regulation and leadership

After more than 50 years of operation, the Pharmacy Act of 1954 was replaced on 30 March 2007 by new primary legislation: the Pharmacists and Pharmacy Technicians Order 2007 (P&PT Order 2007). This gave wider and more flexible powers to the Royal Pharmaceutical Society of Great Britain (RPSGB, referred to here as the Society) to discipline pharmacists and, ultimately, a new group of regulated pharmacy support staff, pharmacy technicians. However, in February 2007, a Government White Paper set out its intention to separate the functions of the Society and to create, from 2010, a new pharmacy regulator, the General Pharmaceutical Council (GPhC), subject to parliamentary approval. Further, the White Paper invited the profession itself to establish a distinct professional leadership body if it so chose. By the end of 2008, the Society had published a new Code of Ethics and Professional Standards (see Chapter 23) and was already operating new disciplinary procedures (see Chapter 24). During 2009, the Society will undergo a gradual drawing apart of its former combined functions so that:

- The Society's regulatory and disciplinary functions, including the setting of educational standards, will pass to the GPhC in 2010 and will be extended to registered pharmacy technicians. The Society's law enforcement powers under various sections of the Medicines Act 1968 (Chapters 2–16), the Misuse of Drugs Act (Chapter 17) and the Poisons Act 1972 (Chapter 18), together with its inspectorate will pass to the GPhC, which will also maintain the register of pharmacy premises.
- The remaining functions of the Society are likely to pass to a new body, also established in 2010, representing the wider body of pharmacists and others associated with pharmacy, to influence and develop pharmacy policy and practice with government and the GPhC, as well as offering a range of membership benefits. This body will be constituted under an amended Royal Charter, modified from those which underpinned many of the powers of the former Society.

*Proposed changes in the draft Pharmacy Order 2009
(published December 2008)*

Proposals for further change to the regulation of pharmacy appear in the draft Pharmacy Order 2009, which was published as this book went to press. The proposals were open to consultation until 9 March 2009 and were expected to be implemented in the second quarter of 2010. The draft Pharmacy Order includes transitional arrangements to ensure smooth transfer of functions from the RPSGB to the GPhC. Many of the major changes from regulation under the Pharmacy Act 1954 to regulation under the Pharmacists and Pharmacy Technicians Act 2007 remain in place and these are detailed in the text below, but important changes proposed in the draft Pharmacy Order 2009 include:

- establishment of roles, functions and powers of the new regulator for pharmacy: the GPhC;
- power to include pharmacy in Northern Ireland under the GPhC (subject to a decision by Northern Ireland Ministers);
- extension of regulation by the GPhC to pharmacy technicians in Scotland;
- extension of statutory duty of GPhC towards the public and other stakeholders and to include co-operation and co-ordination between other regulators and employers;
- establishment, as a minimum, of parity of membership between lay and professional members of the GPhC Council and their independent appointment;
- addition of statutory duty to provide regular strategic plans to relevant governments and report on arrangements to address equality and diversity;
- creation of provision for temporary registration in emergency situations;
- abolition of the non-practising register;
- creation of single register in three parts: pharmacists, pharmacy technicians and pharmacy premises;
- power to modify registration fees where appropriate;
- establishment of provisions for the implementation of continued professional development criteria and assessment of portfolios;
- introduction of measures into undergraduate and preregistration training to ensure fitness to practise and patient safety;
- establishment of provisions to require certain information from education providers and for the appointment of 'visitors' to accredit quality;

- movement of the inspectorate to be under the GPhC (transferred from the Medicines Act 1968 and removing from the Poisons Act 1972 (Chapter 18);
- movement of the maintenance of the register of premises to be under the GPhC (transferred from the Medicines Act 1968 Chapter 5);
- creation of new powers to set standards 'as the GPhC Council consider necessary' for safe and effective practice within pharmacy premises and to exercise new sanctions for failure to meet such standards (Chapter 24);
- reduction in the number of statutory committees under Fitness to Practise Procedures; mandatory five year duration for erasure from the register (Chapter 24);
- extension of the remit of the Appeals Committee to include accreditation (Chapter 24);
- power to extend the role of the Office of the Health Professions Adjudicator to pharmacy: likely to be 'sometime after 2010' (Chapters 24 and 25).

Because the separation of functions was not complete at the time of going to press, this chapter can only set out the law paving the way for the GPhC together with the progress made in forming a separate professional leadership body at the end of 2008. While this separation should be completed during 2010, timetables can slip, and the end of the chapter also retains details of the Society's residual remit and functions at the end of 2008.

Council for Healthcare Regulatory Excellence

External to the Society's activities, Part 2 of the NHS Reform and Health Care Professionals Act 2002 (NHS 2002 Act) provided power to set up an over-arching body to investigate and report on the performance of, and recommend changes to, a range of healthcare regulatory bodies, including the Society (see also Chapters 24 and 25). This over-arching body was originally called the Council for the Regulation of Health Care Professionals, but under the Health and Social Care Act 2008, its title was changed to the Council for Healthcare Regulatory Excellence (CHRE) and new regulations, the Council for Healthcare Regulatory Excellence (Appointment, Procedure, etc) Regulations 2008 (SI No. 2927), reformed the membership of its Council. The CHRE has powers 'to formulate principles relating to good professional self-regulation and to encourage regulatory bodies to conform to them' (s.25 NHS 2002 Act) so it takes a keen interest in the constitution and powers of the Society and all other healthcare professions. The CHRE is also empowered to receive details of all the decisions of the Society's Fitness to Practise cases (Chapter 24) and, subject to certain conditions, to refer cases to the High Court. Further details of the general activities of the CHRE are provided in Chapter 25.

Changing the regulation of pharmacy

Powers to change the regulation of the pharmacy profession were established in section 60 of the 1999 Health Act. The original order under section 60 was the P&PT Order 2007 (SI 2007 No. 289), followed at the end of 2008 by the draft Pharmacy Order 2009 made under the Health and Social Care Act 2008. The content of the P&PT Order 2007 reflected findings and recommendations set out in the *The Regulation of the Non-medical Healthcare Professions* (Foster Review) published by the Department of Health in July 2006. The P&PT Order 2007 amended the powers of the Society in four key areas:

1 changes to the Society's registers;
2 introduction of new statutory committees;
3 new 'fitness to practise' powers and procedures; and
4 extension of the regulatory regime to pharmacy technicians.

The last of these changes will not be complete until the establishment of the GPhC, although the Society has created a substantial voluntary register of pharmacy technicians who would be eligible for registration. The Society's register is now separated into Part 1 (practising) and Part 2 (non-practising) with annotation to reflect specialisms. Six new committees have been introduced; those concerned with registration and education are considered here; those concerned with Fitness to Practise are covered in Chapter 24.

The draft Pharmacy Order 2009 reflects the content of a (Royal) Command Paper (Cmmd.7013), *Trust, Assurance and Safety: the Regulation of Health Professionals in the 21st Century* published in February 2007. This document recommended that all healthcare regulatory bodies should:

- have smaller councils – 10–15 members – with equal numbers of lay and professional members;
- have faster, more transparent procedures (for fitness to practise);
- develop meaningful accountability to the public and users of the services of registrants.
- develop a 'robust, deliverable, cost effective implementation plan' for the establishment of the GPhC.

This last recommendation led to the setting up of a working party comprising the Chief Pharmaceutical Officers of England, Wales, Northern Ireland and Scotland to develop such a plan. These proposals became known as the *Carter Report* and were published in May 2007. One important outcome of this report was the creation of an 'oversight' group – known as Pharmacy Regulation and Leadership Oversight Group (PRLOG) – to manage the complex process of separating the functions of the Society without losing its regulatory effectiveness.

The account below details the Society's powers at the end of 2008; it is anticipated that a 'shadow' GPhC will be in place by mid-2009 and that a professional leadership body for pharmacy should be developed on a parallel time scale.

Legislation regulating the pharmacy profession

The primary legislation is the P&PT Order 2007 (as amended by the European Qualifications (Health and Social Care Professions) Regulations 2007 [SI 2007 No. 3101]). This is in seven parts with two schedules containing revocations of previous legislation and transitional arrangements. The contents are:

> Part 1 Preliminary provisions
> Part 2 Registration of pharmacists
> Part 3 Registration of pharmacy technicians
> Part 4 Matters common to both the Society's registers
> Part 5 Fitness to practise
> Part 6 Proceedings (related to fitness to practise)
> Part 7 Miscellaneous.

We shall deal here with Parts 1–4 and relevant items under Part 7. Chapters 23 and 24 will deal with Parts 5 and 6, and relevant items under Part 7. The P&PT Order 2007 empowers the Society's Council to make detailed rules, which are gradually replacing the bye-laws and regulations formerly made by the Society under both the 1954 Act and its Charter (see below).

Most relevant to this chapter are the Royal Pharmaceutical Society of Great Britain (RPSGB) (Registration Rules) Order of Council 2007 (the 'Registration Rules' SI 2007 No. 441), which should be read in conjunction with the Approved European Pharmacy Qualifications Order of Council 2007 (SI 2007 No. 564). The latter legislation lists (in schedules) what shall be considered 'appropriate European diplomas' for the purposes of registration in the Register of Pharmacists together with specific clauses relating to certain diplomas and certain recently established European states. Requirements regarding preregistration training are still largely set out in the bye-laws of the Society as are those related to the adjudication and reciprocity arrangements (see below). In July 2008, rules were introduced to allow pharmacists and, in due course, pharmacy technicians to pay their annual retention fee in instalments and by direct debit rather than needing to pay the full amount at the start of the calendar year – the RPSGB (Registration Amendment Rules) Order of Council 2008 (SI 2008 No. 1553).

Rules for the Registration Appeals Committee (RAC) (see below) may be found in the RPSGB (Fitness to Practise and Registration Appeals Committees and their Advisers Rules) Order of Council 2007 (the 'Committee Rules' SI 2007 No. 561). Rules relating to Fitness to Practise may be found in the RPSGB (Fitness to Practise and Disqualification etc. Rules) Order of Council 2007 (the 'Procedure Rules' SI 2007 No. 442). Where relevant to registration matters, these are mentioned below, but fitness to practise matters are discussed more fully in Chapter 24. At the time of writing, the Society continues to maintain the register of pharmacy owners and premises under the Medicines Act 1968 (see Chapter 5) and power to disqualify owners and remove premises is retained in the P&PT Order 2007 (see Chapter 24).

At the time of writing, 'Education Rules' to implement the remaining aspects of sections 13–15 of the P&PT Order 2007 had not been made and a consultation on the relationship between continued professional development (CPD) and fitness to practise was issued in November 2008. 'Education Rules' are expected to be made under the draft Pharmacy Order 2009 when it comes into force.

The role of the Society and its Council

The P&PT Order 2007 extends to the whole of Great Britain, that is, England, Scotland and Wales. It provides for two registers of *registrants*: pharmacists (a change from the former term, pharmaceutical chemists, in the 1954 Act) and pharmacy technicians. It also allows for two parts to each register: practising (Part 1) and non-practising (Part 2) – marked with the letters 'P' for practising or 'NP' for non-practising (bye-law XXI 3rd Schedule). The definition of *practising* (s.3 [2]) is

> For the purposes of this Order, a person practises as a pharmacist or a pharmacy technician if, whilst working in the capacity of or holding himself out as a pharmacist or pharmacy technician, he undertakes any work or gives any advice in relation to the dispensing or use of medicines, the science of medicines, the practice of pharmacy or the provision of health care.

The Society is given general duties (s.4) to protect and promote the health and safety of the public, having proper regard to the interests of those who use or need pharmacy services and the registrants themselves. The Society must co-operate with other health or social care regulators and with educators and employers of registrants. The Privy Council (s.5) may vary the size and composition of the Society's Council but it may not comprise more than 35 members, in which registered pharmacists may constitute a majority (this will not apply to the GPhC). The Privy Council must ensure that at least one person who lives or works wholly or mainly in each of England, Scotland and Wales is on the Council. Members of Council must be on Part 1 (practising) of their respective registers and they must declare and accept publication of their private interests.

The Council is required (s.6) to publish an annual report on its Fitness to Practise activities (see Chapter 24) and its accounts and may publish guidance to those non-pharmacists who provide services in connection with registrants (s.6[6]). The Society is required (s.7) to have six statutory committees – meaning committees set up under statute law. They are the:

- Education Committee
- Registration Appeals Committee
- Continuing Professional Development Committee
- Investigating Committee
- Disciplinary committee
- Health Committee.

The last three are concerned with fitness to practise and will be covered in Chapter 24. The Council must make rules to cover the size and composition of these committees; the appointment of their members; the quorum at meetings; their procedures, education and training of committee members; collection and declaration of members' interests; and provisions to pay committee members (s.8). Before making these rules, the Council must consult with the NHS primary care organisations in England, Wales and Scotland (not Scotland for pharmacy technicians) and must ensure the rules are consistent with the obligations of the UK regarding the EU (s.66). Finally the Council must appoint a 'fit and proper' person to be the Registrar (and may appoint a Deputy Registrar) to carry out the functions assigned to the Registrar within the P&PT Order 2007.

Entitlement to register as a pharmacist

Conditions for registration of pharmacists appear in Part 2 of the P&PT Order 2007 with almost identical provisions for pharmacy technicians in Part 3. We have already referred to the two parts to each register: Part 1 for practising pharmacists (or pharmacy technicians) and Part 2 for non-practising pharmacists (or pharmacy technicians). Entitlement to registration (s.11) depends upon the applicant satisfying the Registrar that:

1   s/he is appropriately qualified;
2   his/her fitness to practise is not impaired;
3   before registration, where necessary, s/he has met such requirements as to additional education, training or experience as are appropriate to the case; and
4   after registration, s/he meets such requirements as to continuing professional development as are appropriate to the case;
5   s/he has paid any prescribed registration fee;
6   s/he has not given an undertaking not to practise.

Rule 6 of the Registration Rules set out in detail the form of an application to register. These include the need for countersignature of the application by a practising pharmacist who is in 'good standing' with the Society, evidence of identity and a validated photograph of the applicant, evidence of date of birth and evidence about physical and mental health. Information about the gender, ethnicity and disabilities of applicants is collected voluntarily for monitoring purposes. When making a decision about an applicant's 'good character', the Registrar shall have regard to the Society's Good Character Assessment Framework (see Box 22.1), published by the Council under s.45(1) of the P&PT Order 2007. This section also provides statutory force to the Society's Code of Ethics and supplementary documents (see Chapter 23).

A person is 'appropriately qualified' (s.12) if s/he has a qualification awarded in Great Britain that has been approved by the Society, or is an 'exempt person' (meaning being in possession of an approved European qualification set out in SI 2007 No. 564, see above) or has gone through the adjudicating process (see below). The Registrar may require evidence of an adequate standard of proficiency in the knowledge and use of English (not applicable to exempt persons).

Box 22.1   Definition of good character

For the purposes of the Society's registration procedures, good character is defined as 'the absence that a person has committed (and/or has any disposition towards) conduct or behaviour that is inconsistent with Standards of Conduct published by the Society, or the exercise of the pharmacy profession'.

Source: *The Assessment of Good Character and Health Framework*, RPSGB March 2007.

Education and training

The Society is required (s.13) to oversee all stages of the education, training and acquisition of experience of pharmacists and prospective pharmacists including pre- and post-registration and specialist training and training for those seeking restoration to the registers. In particular, the Society shall (s.14) determine the nature and assessment of the knowledge and skills needed and shall accredit degrees for appropriate qualification in Great Britain to practise (the MPharm). The Society shall also determine all aspects of the preregistration training year, including providers; premises; approval of tutors, courses and programmes; arrangements for assessment; appointment of examiners; and the setting of relevant fees (s.15).

The Society must also (s.14) oversee providers, tutors and assessment of postgraduate training if it leads to an approved qualification and the arrangements for adjudication on the acceptability of overseas (non-EU) qualifications (see below). After registration, the Society has powers to prescribe the amount and type of CPD that registrants must undertake to stay on the register, or is necessary for those who have specialist annotations in the registers (see below), as well as the education and training needed to address fitness to practise matters or to move back from non-practising to practising parts of the registers. In connection with the above functions, the Society may (s.15) approve training premises, providers and programmes, charge fees and approve examiners for additional preregistration training or postgraduate training. The Society can enter into arrangements with other bodies to carry out the above functions (s.16).

Application to register

The Council (s.17) may make registration rules (see Rule 6 of the Registration Rules above) that prescribe the form and manner in which applicants may apply to be added to the registers and what information will be needed, including:

1   the name under which the applicant intends to practise;
2   his or her home address; and
3   information to determine whether the applicant's fitness to practise is impaired.

Failure to comply with the rules may constitute misconduct sufficient to warrant referral to the fitness to practise procedures (see Chapter 24). The Registrar may refuse to register an applicant if s/he fails to comply with the rules (s.18) but the applicant has the right of appeal to the RAC (see below). Under Rule 37 of the Fitness to Practise and Disqualification etc. Rules, the Registrar may also 'seek advice' from the Health Committee or the Disciplinary Committee when relevant.

In section 19, it is made clear that if a person is on the Register of Pharmacists, s/he is also a member of the Society – at the time of writing it is not clear how this provision will apply when the Society splits its functions. Section 20 creates offences carrying fines for anyone falsely representing that they are on the Society's Register of Pharmacists, using the title 'registered pharmacist' when they are not registered or practising when they are not on Part 1 of the Register of Pharmacists. Pharmacists may also not allow anyone else to use their certificate of registration.

Registration of pharmacy technicians

Generally Part 3 (s.21 to 29) of the P&PT Order 2007 mirrors the provisions above in relation to the Register of Pharmacy Technicians but it will not come into force until the establishment of the GPhC, expected in 2010. There are a few differences however to note.

- Amendments are awaited to extend the application of the P&PT Order 2007 to pharmacy technicians in Scotland. This will be commenced under the proposed Healthcare and Associated Professions (Miscellaneous Amendments) Order 2009 and taken forward under the Pharmacy Order 2009.
- Qualifications for pharmacy technicians in Europe are covered by Council Directive 92/52/EEC implemented by the European Communities (Recognition of Professional Qualifications) (Second General System) Regulations 2002 (SI 2002 No. 2934 as amended by the P&PT Order 2007).
- No reference is made to postgraduate training for pharmacy technicians.
- There is a two year transitional period, after Part 3 of the Order comes into force, before 'pharmacy technician' becomes a restricted title.
- No mention is made of registration as a pharmacy technician conferring membership of the Society (but this may be considered in the formation of the new professional body (see below).

The European Qualifications (Health and Social Care Professions) (Amendment) Regulations 2008 (SI 2008 No. 462) have amended the earlier European Qualifications (Health and Social Care Professions) Regulations 2007 (SI 2007 No. 3101) to defer regulation of European pharmacy technicians until s.21 of the P&PT Order 2007 is brought into force.

The Registers of Pharmacists and Pharmacy Technicians

Part 4 of the P&PT Order 2007 covers 'matters common to both of the Society's registers'. The Council may make rules (s.30) covering the form of these registers; the Registration Rules (SI 2007 No. 441) require (Rule 5) the following to be in the register,

- the registrant's title (including fellowship of the Society);
- the name under which the registrant is known professionally (*registered name*);
- the registrant's registration number;
- the registrant's home address (*registered address*);
- the date of first, and any subsequent, registration; and
- any specialisations approved by Council in accordance with rules made under the P&PT Order 2007 (see below).

The Registrar must maintain the register, which may be in electronic form (Rule 4), in a secure manner which guards against falsification, although at least one hard copy must be kept. S/he may also disclose all of this information (except home address) to an employer of a registrant, or any other person, if he considers it to be in the public interest to do so. For the first time (s.31), the registers may denote 'specialisations' by an annotation; the Registration Rules make provision for only two annotations at the time of writing (Rule 9): either for *pharmacist independent prescriber* (IP) or for *pharmacist supplementary prescriber* (SP). The Registrar must publish the registers from time to time, limiting reference to the address to a city, town or district only. Registrants whose registration is suspended are not regarded as being on the register for this purpose. Rule 4 also requires that the registrant's entry is annotated, where applicable, with details of fitness to practise matters (see Chapter 24). Section 30 makes similar provisions regarding CPD matters but these were not in force at the time of writing.

Certificates of registration (s.32) are issued free of charge on first registration; further certificates may be issued, on payment of a fee, if the Registrar is satisfied that one of three circumstances apply:

1 the original certificate, and any further certificate has been lost or destroyed;
2 there has been a change to registrant's name; or
3 the registrant is moving to a different part of the register.

The Registrar can require return of a certificate if it incorrect.

Removal from the registers

Registrants must (s.33) notify to the Registrar any changes of name or address and may be removed from the register if they fail to do so after reasonable notice. It should be noted that under Rule 3 of the Registration Rules, this notice may be given by electronic mail. If the notification is sent by post and the registrant has moved without telling the Registrar, then the Registrar may remove him or her from the register after two months (and two notifications). If removed in these circumstances, the registrant has the right to appeal to the RAC (see below). The Registrar is obliged to keep the Society's registers up to date and correct (s.34) and remove the names of any registrants who have died. Section 35 allows the Registrar to implement any orders from the Fitness to Practise Committee that may affect registration. The Council may make rules (s.36) to cover moving from one part of a register to another and, under s.27, the rules may also cover voluntary removal. Before voluntary removal can take place, the Registrar must be satisfied that there are no outstanding fitness to practise allegations or procedures to be dealt with before effecting such removal. Under Rule 10 of the Registration Rules, a registrant who is also a superintendent pharmacist must declare this on his or her application for voluntary removal.

Moving to different parts of the registers

Section 35 allows the Council to make rules in connection with moving from the practising (Part 1) to the non-practising (Part 2) parts of the registers, or vice-versa. The rules may cover the information required from the applicant, including fitness to practise matters and whether any, and if so what, additional education or training is required (as determined by the Continuing Professional Development Committee) if moving from non-practising to practising. Rule 8 of the Registration Rules requires the registrant to complete a declaration that s/he will adhere to the 'standards' – meaning those set out in the Code of Ethics and the related guidance (see Chapters 23 and 24) – but no rules regarding training had been made at the time of writing.

Retention on the registers

The P&PT Order 2007 introduces two new conditions for remaining on the practising (Part 1) sections of the registers: the possession of *professional indemnity arrangements* (s.38) and the undertaking of *CPD* (s.39). At the time of writing, only the first of these conditions was in force; the second, along with processes for revalidation, are expected to become mandatory after regulation passes to the GPhC. A practising registrant must 'have in force in relation to him an adequate and appropriate indemnity arrangement which provides cover in respect of liabilities which may be incurred in carrying out work as a pharmacist or pharmacy technician'. Indemnity arrangements may comprise an insurance policy, arrangements made for indemnifying a person (such as vicarious liability insurance held by an employer) or a combination of both. Generally, employees will be covered for injury to third parties (patients) through their employer but many will choose to supplement this with their own insurance against personal risks;

self-employed practising pharmacists or pharmacy technicians must carry their own insurance. The Society has made it an ethical requirement (since 2007) that registered pharmacists make a declaration, with their annual retention application, to the effect that they are undertaking CPD.

Restoration to the registers

Section 41 prescribes the provisions that will apply for restoration to the register in a range of circumstances such as failing to comply with registration rules, fraudulently procured registration, fitness to practise matters, failure to comply with requirements regarding indemnity or simple non-payment of fees. Rule 12 of the Registration Rules requires that in certain circumstances including within 12 months of voluntary removal, an applicant may be restored to the register if s/he completes declarations concerning fitness to practise (and eventually CPD). Further detail of the conditions for restoration in this case is given in Rule 11 of the Procedure Rules. Rule 15 of the Registration Rules lays down a three-stage process in connection with removal for fraudulent or incorrect entries in the registers.

Fees

Under section 40, the Council may make rules with respect to charging fees in connection with applications to register, being retained on one of the Society's registers, retention of annotation in the registers, moving from one part of the registers to another, applications for voluntary removal and the issuing of further registration certificates. These fees may be waived at the discretion of the Registrar and registrants may be removed from the registers for failure to pay the appropriate fees. Before setting the fees, the Council must consult 'such registrants or classes of registrants' as it consider appropriate. Rule 7 of the Registration Rules requires a registrant wishing to retain his or her entry on the registers to notify the Registrar if they have not received an application for retention by 10 December in any year. Retention fees should be paid by 1 January in the following year. If the fee is not paid, the Registrar must 'serve' (by post or electronic mail) a final demand and may remove the registrant from the register two months after the final demand has been served. The fees are published in the *Pharmaceutical Journal* before and after consultation and on the Society's website.

The Registration Appeals Committee

For the first time, the Society is required by the P&PT Order 2007 to have formal structures and processes for appealing against registration decisions. Section 42 sets out the decisions that are appealable. Decisions to refuse registration or retention because of failure to pay fees or comply with the rules are not appealable. Appeals may however include:

- removal because of failures on the part of the Society to carry out its duty to notify decisions promptly;
- decisions concerning requirements to undergo aptitude tests to show that an applicant is 'appropriate qualified';
- decisions to refuse annotations for specialisations;
- decisions to remove a registrant because of fraudulent procurement of registration;
- failure to have indemnity arrangements; or
- failure to disclose fitness to practise matters before registration.

Appeals against appealable registration decisions (s.43) must be made to the RAC within 28 days of the decision (with certain exceptions).

Provisions for the composition and appointment of members of the RAC (and the Fitness to Practise Committee, see Chapter 24) and the functions of advisers (legal, clinical and specialist) appear in the Fitness to Practise and Registration Appeals Committee and their Advisers Rules (the Committee Rules). These define a 'lay member' as someone who is not a registrant or associated with one: a 'professional member' is a practising pharmacist or pharmacy technician. The RAC shall consist of:

- a legally qualified lay member who is the chair;
- a legally qualified lay member who is the deputy chair;
- three other lay members; and
- five professional members.

Members of each committee do not normally sit all together; rather they constitute a panel from which members are drawn as appropriate to a case, subject to a quorum (minimum number).

The RAC may dismiss the appeal, allow the appeal and quash the decision appealed against, substitute another decision or instruct the Registrar to dispose of the case in some other way. The appellant is entitled to receive reasons for the RAC decision and, if the appeal is not allowed, s/he has the right to appeal, again within 28 days of the RAC decision, to the relevant court (s.44). The detailed procedures for the RAC are to be found in Part 5 (Rules 18–35) of the Registration Rules. These include provision for case management meetings to be held to establish the grounds for the appeal and give preliminary rulings on questions of law and admissibility of evidence. The RAC may seek advice from clinical or specialist advisers (see Chapter 24); representation by a lawyer or defence organisation or trade union is permitted and the decision will be reached on the civil standard of proof (balance of probabilities; see Chapter 1). The RAC may reach a decision based on submitted papers only unless a hearing is requested by the appellant, in which case it will usually be held in public. The RAC may order an appellant to pay costs or expenses. Examples of some RAC cases are given in Chapter 24.

The Education and Continuing Professional Development Committees

The draft Pharmacy Order 2009 makes it clear that the establishment of the statutory Education and Continuing Professional Development Committees under the P&PT Order 2007 will not proceed but their functions will be part of the general duties placed upon the GPhC.

Preregistration training

Sections 13–15 of the P&PT Order 2007 and bye-law XX mean that any person applying to be a registered pharmacist must produce to the Registrar of the Society a declaration that, subsequent to passing the final degree examination, the applicant has passed a registration examination and has satisfactorily undergone a period of approved preregistration training, performed under the supervision of a pharmacist preregistration tutor, of not less than 52 weeks in an approved site, usually one or more of the following:

- a community pharmacy;
- the pharmaceutical department of a hospital;
- a pharmaceutical industrial establishment;
- a school of pharmacy; and/or
- a registered pharmacy selling only agricultural and veterinary products.

Approval of preregistration training sites is normally given for five years and preregistration tutors must meet certain competences. Detailed conditions are set out in the bye-laws and on the Society's website. Most of the bye-laws will be replaced by 'Education Rules' made under the P&PT Order 2007 or subsequent Orders.

Registration from other countries

Reciprocal registration

Section 11 of the P&PT Order 2007 requires the Registrar to recognise a certificate confirming membership, good standing and registration (as a pharmaceutical chemist) from the Pharmaceutical Society of Northern

Ireland as an appropriate qualification for entry on to the British register. The applicant must provide solicitor-certified copies of birth and marriage certificates, a health declaration and a passport-sized photograph. Under section 12, the Society also accredits courses leading to registration in Northern Ireland. Earlier reciprocal agreements with New Zealand, Australia and South Africa terminated at the end of June 2006.

European pharmacists

A person who is a national of a member state of the EEA, is entitled to practise as a pharmacist there and is in good standing with the relevant professional authority may apply for admission to the British Register. The procedures and necessary documentation are available on the Society's website. The Society cannot require evidence of English language competency from EEA nationals wishing to register (because if it did so it would have to apply the same requirement to 'home' applicants as well). However, it is made clear that potential EEA registrants must comply with Principle 7 of the Code of Ethics, in particular paragraph 7.1, which requires 'sufficient language competence' for any work undertaken as a pharmacist.

From October 2007, in common with provisions for the professions of doctor, nurse, dental practitioner, veterinary surgeon, midwife and architect, pharmacists registered in the EEA or Switzerland may provide 'temporary and occasional' professional services cross-border subject to certain limited conditions (the European Communities (Recognition of Professional Qualifications) Regulations 2007 SI 2007 No. 2781).

Overseas pharmacists

Sections 12–16 of the P&PT Order 2007, particularly 14(f), (g) and (h), allow a person with a degree or diploma in pharmacy granted by a university or body outside the UK or Europe to apply for registration in Great Britain. The details appear in section XIX of the bye-laws, which will in due course be replaced by 'Education Rules'. Such a person must produce evidence that s/he holds a degree or diploma in pharmacy granted by a university or body of comparable academic status in a country outside the UK; that s/he is registered or qualified to be registered in that country; and that s/he is of good character and in good health, both mentally and physically. S/he must then satisfy an adjudicating committee appointed by the Council of the Society as to the content and standard of the course and examination in pharmacy that s/he has taken, and as to his/her knowledge of pharmacy as practised in the UK.

If English is not his/her mother tongue, s/he must demonstrate his/her knowledge of the English language. S/he will also be required by the adjudicating committee to the registration examination and s/he must complete a period of employment in the practice of pharmacy in Great Britain under conditions laid down by the committee. Further details of the conditions are set out in bye-law XIX and on the Society's website.

A new professional body for pharmacy

The paper *Trust, Assurance and Safety: the Regulation of Health Professionals in the 21st Century* (Cmmd.7013) asserted that, as well as the GPhC, the pharmacy profession 'will need a strong and clear voice to assume the critical responsibility of undertaking a role akin to that played by a Royal College, supporting clinical excellence in the profession'. Subsequently, a section of the Carter Report (also see above) focused on what this 'body akin to a Royal College' might look like and what its functions might be. Considerable protest and resistance followed from pharmacists, who objected to a quasi-governmental group expressing any view at all on how the profession might wish to constitute its leadership and development body. The Society, therefore, commissioned an independent inquiry under the chairmanship of Nigel Clarke, who published his report in April 2008. A key recommendation, which was implemented, was to set up a Transitional Committee – called 'Transcom' – to further develop the delivery of a new professional body.

Accordingly, Transcom met for the first time in July 2008, with the key objective of producing a prospectus for the new professional body by the end of 2008 so that potential members could make an informed choice about membership. One important distinction between the existing RPSGB (which was a registration and regulatory body as well as a professional body) and a new professional body is that membership of the latter will be voluntary. A Transcom prospectus was published on 28 November 2008 and consultation on its content closed on 9 January 2009. The new professional body will be underpinned by a modified Royal Charter (see below).

Royal Charter

In 2004, the Society was granted a 'new' Charter (an authority directly from the monarch to take certain powers) to clarify the remit of its representational role. The 2004 Charter is legally a supplemental charter since it retains the incorporation aspect of the 1843 Charter while replacing all the provisions of the 1953 Charter. At the time of writing, the RPSGB was the professional body for pharmacy (but see details of forthcoming separation at the beginning of this chapter). The Society was founded in 1841 and incorporated by Royal

Charter in 1843. A Supplemental Charter was granted in 1953. These Charters are revoked by the Supplemental Charter of 2004 (see above) except in so far as the 1843 Charter incorporated the Society, authorised it to have a common seal and to sue and be sued.

Objects of the Charter

The main objects (in short) of the current Supplemental Charter are:

1   to advance knowledge of, and education in, pharmacy and its application;
2   to safeguard, maintain the honour and promote the interests of the members in their exercise of the profession of pharmacy;
3   to promote and protect the health and well-being of the public; and
4   to maintain and develop the science and practice of pharmacy.

The Charter also provides powers to:

1   promote public understanding of pharmacy;
2   maintain any charitable or benevolent trusts for distressed members or dependants or students of the Society;
3   to undertake any functions designed to maintain fitness to practise;
4   to undertake any function relating to the control and licensing of premises used in connection with pharmacy;
5   to maintain registers of members;
6   to maintain registers of premises;
7   to fix fees for any non-statutory services provided by the Society;
8   to set and enforce standards of education and to hold examinations;
9   to award fellowships and other distinctions;
10 to establish and maintain museum collections;
11 to undertake, encourage, fund or commission research and its publication;
12 to co-operate with other relevant bodies and authorities;
13 to engage and pay staff and run pension schemes;
14 to acquire, dispose of or mortgage property;
15 to take out liability insurance for the Society;
16 to indemnify members of Council in respect of any liability arising from the performance of their duties in good faith;
17 to receive income, legacies or gifts and to borrow money;
18 to invest money;
19 to carry on trade in furtherance of Charter objects;
20 to do anything else lawful to promote the attainment of the Charter objects; and
21 to set terms of office for Council members.

Charter powers

The Charter goes on to control how the income and property of the Society may be used, to limit membership of the Society to registered pharmacists in Great Britain, to require an Annual General Meeting to be held, to make arrangements to recognise the devolved powers and responsibilities for health in Scotland and Wales, and to establish the branch structure for members of the Society. Control, direction and management of the policies and affairs of the Society are vested in the Council, which is constituted as follows:

1   seventeen elected registered pharmacists, of which one place each is reserved for members from Scotland and Wales;
2   one registered pharmacist appointed by the universities (schools of pharmacy);
3   two pharmacy technicians; and
4   ten persons appointed by the Privy Council.

No places on the Council are to be reserved for sectoral pharmacy practice representation. The election and appointment processes are laid down in the Charter regulations. The Council may then exercise all powers and functions of the Society except where a Special Resolution is required. The Council itself is subject to a code of governance and a conduct panel. Council members can be suspended or removed from office following breach of this code. Transcripts of recent Council meetings are available on the Society's website; from 2005 this will be extended to agendas and other relevant papers.

The Supplemental Charter gives the Council power to make regulations for all or any of the purposes for which regulations may, by the express provisions of the Charter, be made and such other regulations as seem to the Council to be necessary for the management and regulation of the affairs and property of the Society and its chartered objects. The Charter requires that there shall be a president, who is a registered pharmacist, and other officers as laid down by regulations. Although many of the powers of the Society are contained in the 2004 Charter, additional powers and duties have been conferred and/or imposed by various Acts of Parliament. One of the principal duties under statute is that the Council of the Society must appoint 'a fit and proper person' as the Registrar (Pharmacy Act 1954, s.1). It is the duty of the Registrar to maintain the Register of Pharmaceutical Chemists under the Pharmacy Act 1954 (s.2) and the Register of Premises (registered pharmacies) under the Medicines Act 1968 (s.75).

Organisation of the Society

The Council has full power to manage the Society's affairs but needs a special resolution to amend, add to or revoke any of the Supplemental Charter provisions. A special resolution means a resolution of the Council confirmed, in accordance with regulations, either at a duly convened general meeting of members of the Society by not less than a two-thirds majority of the votes of the members present (or by proxy), or by ballot of the membership. The Council has a duty to manage the Society's affairs and, subject to the provision of the regulations, has power to regulate the conduct of proceedings at meetings of the Council and its committees and subcommittees. In anticipation of separation into the regulator (GPhC) and the professional body, the Society restructured its organisation in July 2008 and may well do so again in future years. At the time of writing, the expected functions of the regulator were delegated to the office of the Deputy Registrar, with subdivisions into fitness to practice and three sections for education: education development, registration and accreditation. The expected functions of the future professional body were carried out within Directorates of Professional Services, Publishing, Policy and Communications, Finance and Resources, alongside three national pharmacy boards for England, Scotland and Wales. The Directorate of Professional Services included supporting (not regulatory) activities in education and standards, in practice, in leadership and marketing of membership services. The following sections are largely taken from the Society's website – more information is available on the website.

The national pharmacy boards

The Society has always been involved in shaping and influencing policy and since devolution this has been necessary in three administrations – the UK Parliament, the Scottish Parliament and the Welsh assembly. In 2005 the English, Scottish and Welsh Pharmacy Boards were established for this purpose. Their remit in each country is to:

- provide strategic leadership and support for pharmacy practice;
- assist development of council policy and its implementation and implement and develop national policy;
- promote the science and practice of pharmacy and its contribution to health;
- provide professional advice to the relevant government and its agencies, NHS bodies and other health and social care organisations;
- support the Society's branches; and
- support pharmacists in their professional roles.

Branches and regions of the Society

The Society has around 130 local branches, which provide a local focus for professional and educational matters and hold regular meetings on a wide range of scientific and current affairs topics. There are also 11 regions in

England, which act as a link between the branches and the Society's Council, and co-ordinate larger-scale public-relations activities.

Membership and special interest groups

The Society has membership groups for community pharmacists, hospital pharmacists, industrial pharmacists and veterinary pharmacists. There is also a special interest group for academic staff. The groups hold meetings on topics of interest within their own fields and provide a source of advice to the Society's council on specialised matters.

Fellows and honorary members and fellows of the Society

Fellowship of the Society is awarded to members who have made a distinguished contribution to the profession. The Society's Panel of Fellows is empowered to confer fellowship on members of not less than 12 years' standing who have made an outstanding original contribution to the advancement of pharmaceutical knowledge or have attained distinction in the science, practice, profession or history of pharmacy. The Society may also confer honorary membership or fellowship on non-pharmacists who have made a distinguished contribution to the profession.

Students

In 1978, the Society formed a section of the Society entitled 'The British Pharmaceutical Students Association', membership of which was open to all pharmaceutical students. Membership is also open to those members of the Society who have been registered initially for not more than 12 months. The Association, which is jointly financed by the Society, is recognised by the Council to be the representative body for the students. The Association is administered, in accordance with its constitution, by an elected executive.

Support for pharmacists

The Benevolent Fund (renamed Pharmacist Support in 2008) is an organisation working for pharmacists and their families in time of need. Its role includes the offer of grants and financial assistance to cover a range of circumstances. In addition, the Listening Friends scheme offers free listening services to pharmacists suffering from stress. The service is entirely confidential and anonymous and provides the opportunity to talk to a pharmacist trained to offer support regarding the particular pressures that apply to pharmacy. The service is not restricted to work-related problems but offers support for all causes of stress such as ill-health, family issues and bereavement.

Specialist advice services regarding benefits, debt and employment law are also available and are provided confidentially and completely free of charge.

Summary

- The role of the Society is undergoing significant change to separate out the regulatory role of the General Pharmaceutical Council (GPhC) and a leadership role for a new professional body. Both are expected to be established in shadow form during 2009.
- At the end of 2008, the Society derived its powers from two Royal Charters, 1843 and 2004, and the Pharmacists and Pharmacy Technicians Order 2007 (P&PT Order 2007).
- The P&PT Order 2007 and the bye-laws specify requirements for preregistration training, registration and retention on the registers and make provisions for fellowship and honorary membership of the Society.
- The P&PT Order 2007 and the bye-laws allow, subject to detailed conditions, for admission to the register of pharmacists from other countries.
- Arrangements for regulation of pharmacy technicians will be completed following the implementation of the expected Pharmacy Order 2009.
- The expected Pharmacy Order 2009 will complete the separation by establishing the GPhC.
- The Society exercises its powers through rules made under the order and regulations, or bye-laws made under the Charter.
- The Council comprises 17 elected registered pharmacists, 1 registered pharmacist appointed by the Schools of Pharmacy, 2 pharmacy technicians and 10 persons appointed by the Privy Council.
- A president and other officers of the Council must be appointed annually; the Council also appoints a Registrar to maintain the Register of Pharmacists and the Register of Pharmacies and carry out fitness to practise duties.
- Three national boards (English, Scottish, Welsh) shape and influence pharmacy policy in Great Britain.
- Members of the Society are assigned to 136 geographical branches, falling within 12 regions.
- There are membership groups for pharmacists in agricultural and veterinary, hospital, industrial and community pharmacy practice.
- The Society has a section for membership of students.
- The Society offers support for pharmacists experiencing difficulties in all areas of their lives and a help-line for alcohol, drug or stress-related problems.

Further reading

Department of Health (2006) *The Regulation of the Non-medical Healthcare Professions.* [The Foster Review] London: The Stationery Office.

Department of Health (2007) *Report of the Working Party on Professional Regulation and Leadership in Pharmacy.* [The Carter Report] London: The Stationery Office.

Department of Health (2007) *Trust, Assurance and Safety: The Regulation of Health Professionals in the 21st Century* [Cmmd.7013] London: The Stationery Office.

Fyfield C, John DN, Edwards R, Tweddell S, Wilson K.(2006) The RPSGB's fitness to practise and professional discipline procedures: what would schools of pharmacy find useful as a resource for teaching and facilitating learning?. *Int J Pharm Pract* 14: B114–B115.

Fyfield C, John DN, Edwards R, Tweddell S, Wilson K. (2007) Different approaches to teaching law and ethics in UK undergraduate pharmacy degrees. *Pharm Educ* 7: 288–289.

Royal Pharmaceutical Society of Great Britain (2008) *Report of the Independent Inquiry into a Professional Body for Pharmacy.* [The Clarke Report; commissioned by the Royal Pharmaceutical Society of Great Britain] London: Royal Pharmaceutical Society of Great Britain.

Websites

Association of Pharmacy Technicians UK: www.aptuk.org
Council for Healthcare Regulatory Excellence: www.chre.org.uk
Department of Health: www.dh.gov.uk
Pharmacist support: www.pharmacistsupport.org
Pharmacy Regulation and Leadership Oversight Group: www.dh.gov.uk/en/Managingyourorganisation/Humanresourcesandtraining/Modernisingprofessionalregulation/Pharmacyprofessionalregulation/DH_081562
The Clarke Inquiry website: www.theclarkeinquiry.com/
The Transcom website: www.transitionalcommittee.com/

23

Professional conduct

From its inception, this book has only made reference to ethics in relation to the Society's Code of Ethics and its application to professional conduct or misconduct. A wider exposition of pharmacy ethics, its underpinning moral philosophy and how it interfaces with statute and case law is beyond the scope of this book. However, interested readers are referred to the relevant reading material at the end of the chapter for this area. In addition, the concept of good professional conduct and misconduct is now embodied in the wider disciplinary term 'impaired fitness to practise' which is the basis for all disciplinary referrals within the profession (see Chapter 24) and indeed all other health professions. While at the time of writing, these disciplinary referrals are administered by the Royal Pharmaceutical Society of Great Britain (RPSGB, referred to here as the Society), from 2010 they will fall under the remit of the General Pharmaceutical Council (GPhC) (subject to parliamentary approval; see Chapter 22).

The term 'profession' was formerly applied only to the church, the law and medicine – the three 'learned' professions. The meaning of the term is now broader, as is apparent from the definition in the Oxford English Dictionary: 'a vocation in which a professed knowledge of some department of learning is used in its application to the affairs of others, or in the practice of an art founded upon it'. In modern usage, it seems that almost all occupations that require some measure of intellectual training can be described as professions. However, an organised profession requires more than the mere existence of an intellectual discipline. The essence of professionalism is the relationship of trust which exists between the practitioner and the person who receives his/her advice or services. The recipient, relying entirely on the knowledge of the practitioner, must be able to have complete trust in his/her services and the impartiality of his/her advice. It follows that there must be an established minimum standard of knowledge for practitioners, and that there must be agreement amongst them about standards of behaviour in their professional work. This means that there must be a body which determines the standard of education and establishes the code of conduct, and that this body must be representative of practitioners and be subject to their collective control.

The profession of pharmacy

If the characteristics described are accepted as the elements of a profession, then pharmacy meets the essential requirements, which are four in number.

An intellectual discipline and a standard of knowledge. Pharmacy is of ancient origin. In Great Britain, it was never clearly separated from medicine until the formation of the Pharmaceutical Society of Great Britain in 1841. Membership of the Society was, from the first, by examination, but it was not until the Pharmacy Act 1868 that all newcomers to the profession who wished to practise were required to pass a qualifying examination, whether or not they intended to become members of the Society. Today a university degree in pharmacy followed by a period of practical training is required before registration as a pharmaceutical chemist (Chapter 22).

A representative body of practitioners. The professional body for pharmacy is currently the Society, but from 2010 the registration and regulatory functions are expected to come under the GPhC and all registered pharmacists (and registered pharmacy technicians) will be regulated by the GPhC. The GPhC then will be the regulatory body of registered pharmacists and technicians but the proposed new professional body is also likely to have these and others associated with pharmacy in its membership. Collectively, therefore, these two bodies together should develop the profession's code of ethics to be properly representative not just of the views of pharmacists and pharmacy technicians, but also of those who support and use pharmacy services (for more information on the splitting of the Society's functions, see Chapter 22). One clear difference between the former Society and the GPhC is that the GPhC governing body will comprise publicly appointed individuals, not elected representatives from the profession.

Standards of conduct. There are accepted standards of conduct known throughout the profession. These have been expressed in the Society's Code of Ethics, a document which represents the collective views of *members* of the Society and which has been approved at a general meeting of *members*. In 2007, the Code of Ethics was rewritten using input from many who were external to the profession, such as members of the public and patients, academic experts in healthcare law and ethics, and practising lawyers. This anticipated the transfer of enforcement of the Code to a public protection regulator, the GPhC. The Code of Ethics now has statutory force, constituting the 'guidance as to the standards of conduct, practice and performance expected of registrants' required under article 45 (and Rule 2 of the Procedure Rules) of the Pharmacists and Pharmacy Technicians Order 2007. At the time of writing, the Council of the Society, through its Investigating Committee, interprets the Code and gives guidance on any matter concerning professional conduct. The Disciplinary Committee of the Society – formerly the Statutory Committee – takes into account the Code of Ethics when considering professional conduct but is not bound by it (see Chapter 24).

Service and advice. Pharmacists have traditionally been mainly concerned with the supply to the public of medicines, either in response to a prescription or other authority or sold over the counter. In these supplies, the pharmacist should give whatever advice is necessary in the interest of the patient or customer. Increasingly, pharmacists are also concerned with the provision of services specifically to improve health and the management and use of medicines, usually accompanied by advice or recommendations, intervention and support for patients and fellow health professionals.

The existence of a body of independent private practitioners has been held to be essential if an occupation is truly to be regarded as a profession. The argument is that only the relationship between an independent practitioner and his/her client is a fully professional one, and an employed practitioner must inevitably be subject to external pressures, either consciously or unconsciously, according to the conditions of his/her employment. No pharmacist, whether employed in public service or in the service of a body corporate engaged in retail pharmacy, would accept that his/her standards or his/her judgement are in any way affected by the fact that s/he is an employee. Indeed, some might argue that a pharmacist in public service is free from some of the commercial pressures which may influence the judgement of the independent practitioner. Even so, there is some force in the argument that the existence of a number of independent practitioners is indispensable for the full development of the profession.

Trade and profession

There is a deep-rooted feeling that trading and professional activities are incompatible. Yet what is the difference between making a living from selling one's professional services and making a living from the buying and selling of goods? The professional person might have some difficulty in explaining his/her objections to commerce without casting doubts on the integrity of the tradesperson. Although there is an element of snobbery in it, there is undoubtedly a difference between the trading outlook and the professional outlook. The tradesperson, however honest, is principally concerned with the profitability of his/her business. His/her main object is to achieve as large a financial return as possible. S/he holds his/her customers to be the best judges of what they want and s/he seeks to satisfy their demands. The old common law maxim applicable to trade was 'let the buyer beware'.

Professional people working in their special field of knowledge where their advice is crucial must often be the judges of what is best for their clients or customers, although patients are increasingly encouraged to take part in and exercise choice over healthcare decisions. If professionals do this according to the standards of their profession, then the advice they give must, at times, be to the practitioners' own financial disadvantage. It is recognition of this essential trust by the public which confers any special status the professional person may have.

Some pharmacists, such as those who work in hospitals or in teaching, do not engage in trade, although within the context of the NHS (Chapter 26) they are increasingly involved in marketing their services and operating within budgets and business constraints similar to those applied in retailing. However, the majority of pharmacists in retail pharmacy businesses practise pharmacy in a trading environment. In addition to the supply of medicines and the provision of other professional services, they sell many other goods. Theirs is a trading profession, a description applied by Lord Wilberforce in the Dickson case (see below and Chapter 27).

Not surprisingly, pharmacists are often misunderstood in their attempts to apply professional principles in a commercial world. If it is hard for the proprietor pharmacist, it is even harder for the employed superintendent pharmacist of a company or other body corporate which is controlled by non-pharmacist directors or shareholders. The fact that the control of the pharmacy is given by statute to the pharmacist is sometimes found irksome to the owners, and the restrictions pharmacists place on ordinary commercial practices because of their profession are not understood. For this reason, the Society has found it necessary to incorporate in the Code of Ethics statements setting out the personal responsibilities of a superintendent pharmacist and for other pharmacists or pharmacy technicians in positions of authority. It is also worth noting that the 2007 Order provides power in section 6(6) to provide guidance 'to registrants, employers and such other persons as it considers appropriate in respect of the standards for the education, training, supervision and performance of persons who are not registrants but who provide services in connection with those provided by registrants'. No such guidance has yet been published.

The Dickson case

The conflict between professional and commercial methods in pharmacy has its origin in the economic need for most pharmacists to engage in ordinary trade as well as pharmacy, together with the fact that any corporate body which complies with certain requirements has the legal right to establish a retail pharmacy business (Chapter 5). As might be expected, the Society, as the professional body at that time, has throughout its history resisted any pressures of the commercial world that have appeared to be adverse to the profession. The Dickson case is the best example of a clash of this kind and is discussed in more detail in Chapter 27. However, the advent of competition law (Chapter 21), now limits the extent to which the Society can impose ethical constraints on commercial activities, for example, on the promotion and supply of medicines.

Professional ethics and law

Ethics is the science of morals, or moral philosophy. The principles, written or unwritten, that are accepted in any profession as the basis for proper behaviour are the ethics of the profession. Rules of law and rules of ethics are commonly held to differ because law is enforced by the state while ethical rules are only morally binding. However, law and ethics are not opposites. The law itself has a basis in ethics; in general it reflects the moral standards of the community. Criminal law comprises those rules of conduct which the community (through parliament) has decided must be observed on pain of a penalty, such as a fine or imprisonment. Criminal law, therefore, includes the Medicines, Poisons and Misuse of Drugs Acts, where transgression may result in prosecution.

Other parliamentary legislation creates administrative law, which gives power to public bodies to regulate certain activities carried out on behalf of the public. The NHS Terms of Service is an example. A breach may result in an administrative sanction following investigation under the NHS complaints procedures (Chapter 26).

Moral obligations are also recognised by the state through common law, which essentially enshrines certain duties which individuals owe to one another. Breach of these duties may result in action through the civil law courts to seek compensation for a 'civil wrong'. The most familiar of these is probably an action alleging negligence on the part of a health practitioner. Negligence is just one of a range of torts, or civil wrongs, and is discussed in more detail later in this chapter (see p. 337). Other torts which might arise in pharmacy practice are breach of confidentiality and defamation.

Pharmacists, as they become integrated into the healthcare team, will increasingly come into possession of sensitive information and will be expected to observe strict confidentiality over the use and disclosure of such information and refrain from using it in ways which may lower the standing of the subject in the eyes of the community (i.e. defamation).

However, the state does not attempt to enforce every rule of social behaviour, nor does it interfere in those matters which are by common consent left to the consciences of individuals (e.g. religious observance) and in those standards which are agreed amongst a profession provided they can be seen to be necessary for the further protection of the public.

Codes of ethics

Ever since the foundation of the Society in 1841, there has been concern about the need to maintain and improve standards of conduct in pharmacy. The advantage of having a written code was recognised, but nothing positive emerged until the changes made by the Pharmacy and Poisons Act 1933 gave the Society wider authority, including the power to take disciplinary action and to remove names from the Register of Pharmaceutical Chemists. A proposal for a code of ethics made by the Teesside branch of the Society in 1937 was widely discussed, but it was found difficult to strike the right balance between a general description of good behaviour and the expression of specified principles in clear-cut terms. The document which was finally accepted by the profession was the first attempt at a written code. An amended version of this 'Statement upon Matters of Professional Conduct' was later published in the *Pharmaceutical Journal* (17 June 1944).

Other amendments led to the publication of revised versions in 1953, 1964, 1970, 1984, 1992 and 2002. In each case, a revised code was presented to the membership for approval and ratification at the Annual General Meetings in May. In the latter part of 2006, the Society undertook a six month review, involving consultations (*Pharm J* 11 November 2006 p. 589; 20 January 2007 p. 82) with the membership and the wider public on proposals for the content and structure of a new Code of Ethics, which, unlike earlier versions, aimed to be a statement on the values, attitudes and behaviours expected of pharmacy professionals. Revision of supporting Professional Standards and Guidance was completed in July. The final Code (the 2007 Code) and supporting documents came into operation in August 2007 and applies to both pharmacists and pharmacy technicians.

The 2007 Code of Ethics

For ease of reference a brief overview of the Code of Ethics is given below; where reference to pharmacist/s is made, this also applies to pharmacy technicians. The full text appears on the Society's website and in the current copy of the Society's *Medicines, Ethics and Practice Guide*. The 2007 Code of Ethics comprises seven principles which are all of equal status and importance, together with a series of statements to amplify the scope of the principle. There are additional standards and guidance that expand on some of the principles and others that cover special areas of practice. The principles are mandatory and constitute the statutory standards expected by the pharmacy regulator. They are intended to apply to all areas of professional pharmacy practice, and to general conduct expected of pharmacy professionals in ordinary life. Some of the concepts implicit in the principles, such as respect, autonomy and consent, are new to pharmacy and readers may wish to consult a series of three explanatory articles by Joy Wingfield that appeared in the *Pharmaceutical Journal* in late 2007 (see Further reading).

1 Make the care of patients your first concern

This principle is at the centre of professional practice, even when this does not involve direct contact with patients. The amplifying statements include the need to provide a proper standard of practice and care; to promote health and safeguard patients, especially those who are vulnerable; to assess an individual's needs and provide suitable treatment and care; to ensure clinical appropriateness of medicines; to encourage effective use of medicines; to ensure quality of products for patients; to maintain accurate, legible and adequate records; to ensure proper facilities, equipment and materials; and to undertake regular reviews and audits and minimise risks to patient and public safety.

2 Exercise your professional judgement in the interests of patients and the public

This principle reflects the need to balance the requirements of individuals with society as a whole and to manage competing priorities and obligations in professional life. The amplifying statements include the need to act in the best interests of individual patients and public; not to allow judgement to be impaired by personal or commercial interests; to make the best use of resources available; to be prepared to challenge the judgement of colleagues and, in emergency, to take action to provide care and reduce risks, taking into account one's own competence and other options.

3 Show respect for others

A fundamental quality of professional healthcare is the demonstration of respect for the dignity, views and rights of others. This quality is amplified in statements covering the need to respect the culture, values and beliefs of others; to treat others politely and considerately; to ensure one's views do not prejudice treatment; to ensure that, if one's religious or moral beliefs prevent you from providing a particular professional service, the relevant persons or authorities are informed of this and patients are referred to alternative providers; to respect and protect the dignity and privacy of others; to get consent for the provision of care and use of related information; to use information only for the purpose for which it was sought; to ensure privacy for consultations; to maintain proper professional boundaries and take special care when dealing with vulnerable individuals.

4 Encourage patients to participate in decisions about their care

A fundamental trend across all of healthcare is the need to involve patients in their care and to avoid paternalistic attitudes where the health professional decides what is best for the patient without any reference to them. This principle requires that, when possible, pharmacists work in partnership with patients, their carers and other healthcare professionals to manage the patient's treatment and care. Further statements make it clear that pharmacists must listen and try to communicate effectively with patients and carers, share information with patients and carers, respect a patient's right to refuse treatment and consider what stops individuals from obtaining or taking their treatment.

5 Develop your professional knowledge and competence

This principle is well established, reflecting the requirement that all pharmacists must ensure that their knowledge, skills and performance are of a high quality, up to date and relevant to their field of practice. Additional statements make it clear that pharmacists must seek to keep up to date, recognise their limits of competence, maintain evidence of competence, respond well to criticism and appraisal, practise only when fit to do so and report themselves if there are concerns about their continuing competence.

6 Be honest and trustworthy

Patients, colleagues and the public at large place their trust in pharmacists. They must behave in a way that justifies this trust and maintains the reputation of their profession. Amplifying statements under this principle include the need to act with honesty and integrity; not to abuse one's position; to avoid conflicts of interest; to be accurate and impartial; to comply with standards; and honour commitments.

7 Take responsibility for your working practices

This principle aims to recognise that pharmacists increasingly work in teams to deliver healthcare and operate within organisations that have performance and commercial goals that may come into conflict with individual healthcare decisions. The supporting statements include the need to train others and ensure competence and training of those to whom pharmacists delegate work; not to agree to unreasonable conditions of work and to raise concerns if there are problems; to carry indemnity insurance; and to respond to complaints and co-operate with investigations.

Professional standards and guidance documents

The Code of Ethics is designed to be a 'stand-alone' document, intended to cover present and future pharmacy practice. It is 'principle based' and allows for the likelihood that certain areas of practice or professional responsibilities will still require more detailed standards and guidance than is provided in the Code itself. The supporting standards and guidance are, therefore, likely to change fairly often and indeed, since their original publication, consultation during 2008 has considered further amendments, included changes to anticipate a possible influenza pandemic and to allow the de-blistering of blister-packed medicines in certain circumstances. The Professional Standards and Guidance documents are available on the Society's website and in the current edition of the Society's *Medicines, Ethics and Practice Guide*.

At the time of writing, additional documents cover:

- pharmacists and technicians in positions of authority;
- patient consent;
- patient confidentiality;
- the sale and supply of medicines;
- advertising medicines and professional services;
- internet pharmacy services; and
- pharmacist prescribers.

Clinical governance

Since 1999, following publication of the UK Government's White Paper *A First Class Service*, the concept of clinical governance has been applied to all healthcare provision, especially by those within or contracted to the NHS (Chapter 26). The concept essentially makes all health professionals and their staff accountable for their standards of patient care. Clinical governance requires a continuous commitment to measuring and improving those standards. As the quality of patient care to be expected becomes more transparent, then the expectations of 'a reasonably competent practitioner', as used in determining negligence and Disciplinary Committee cases, will become higher. Clinical governance is a topic that could fall within the remit of the new pharmacy regulator, the GPhC, and the new professional body. Guidance at the time of writing appeared on the Society's website under 'registration and support' in the functions of the Society and under its own heading in the 'registration and protecting the public' sections, which are likely to pass to the GPhC. The Society's guidance on clinical governance also appears in the 'improving pharmacy practice' pages of the current edition of the Society's *Medicines, Ethics and Practice Guide*.

Continuing professional development and revalidation

All healthcare professionals are now expected to undertake and document their CPD and since 2007 pharmacists have been required to complete a declaration to this effect when applying to be retained on the registers each year (see Chapter 22). Consultation on the preparation of statutory rules covering CPD took place at the end of 2008 (*Pharm J* 8 November 2008, p. s1–s4 [centre pullout]).When the GPhC is established, CPD will become mandatory for those on the registers. Guidance on CPD at the time of writing appeared on the Society's website under 'registration and support' in the functions of the Society and under its own heading in the 'registration and protecting the public' sections, which are likely to pass to the GPhC. The Society's guidance on CPD also appears in the 'improving pharmacy practice' pages of the current edition of the Society's *Medicines, Ethics and Practice Guide*. Failure to undertake and document participation in CPD could jeopardise the registration status of a pharmacist and be considered a breach of duty of care in both professional disciplinary cases and litigation. In due course, in common with all other healthcare professionals, this will be extended to a process of *revalidation* of competence for pharmacists. Work progressed during 2008 on how revalidation should be introduced into pharmacy but was not completed at the time of writing.

Professional discipline

Prior to the implementation of the Pharmacists and Pharmacy Technicians Order 2007 (P&PT Order 2007), the criteria for reference to the Society's then Statutory Committee were allegations of misconduct or the acquisition of a criminal conviction (see Chapter 24). The inability of a pharmacist to carry out his/her duties because of a mental or physical disability did not normally amount to an allegation of misconduct. In the P&PT Order 2007, however, it was made clear that anything which might impair the pharmacist's 'fitness to practise' should be investigated and consideration given to whether it should be referred to the Society's Disciplinary Committee (replacing the Statutory Committee) or to a newly established Health Committee. This change considerably widened the scope of regulatory scrutiny to allow early investigation of competence or health problems, rather than having to wait until failing performance caused some obvious harm to patients or breach of the law or Code of Ethics.

A significant issue has become apparent in how the Society (and its successor regulator, the GPhC) should deal with dispensing errors. In the past, in most cases considered by the Statutory Committee, there had always been some additional factor above and beyond the simple error, such as an indifference to the consequences or evidence of repeated errors, which led to an allegation of misconduct. As the Society implemented the P&PT Order 2007, its wider remit (coupled with an increased number of complaints from patients) resulted in a significant increase in disciplinary workload. The Society has sought to address this by introducing transparent criteria for the factors which might result in the referral of a dispensing error to the Disciplinary Committee or might result in a warning from the Infringements Committee (see Chapter 24).

Criminal negligence

There are two concepts of negligence in law: 'gross negligence manslaughter' which falls under the criminal law and the civil tort of negligence, which is part of civil law (see Chapter 1 for a discussion of types of law). Until 2000, a pharmacist was unlikely to be charged with criminal sanctions in respect of a death arising from a dispensing error. However, this position has changed following charges of manslaughter brought in that year (the Peppermint Water case) against a pharmacist and a preregistration graduate who failed to prevent a fatal dispensing error when preparing a mixture for an infant. The mixture was erroneously compounded using concentrated instead of double-strength chloroform water. When the case came to court, the Crown prosecution service agreed to drop the charges of manslaughter and to substitute prosecutions under section 64 of the Medicines Act (see Chapter 2 p. 21) for supplying a medicine not of the nature and quality demanded (*Pharm J* 4 March 2000 p. 356; 11 March 2000 pp. 389–392; 18 March 2000 p. 427). Since that time, it has become increasingly common for pharmacists and their staff to be involved in Coroner's inquests following deaths associated with medication and to be at risk of charges of criminal negligence if their failings may have led directly to the death.

In addition, the Corporate Manslaughter and Corporate Homicide Act 2007 came into force in 2008 and may mean that manslaughter charges will be laid against managers and directors of large companies or NHS bodies, such as hospital trusts and primary care organisations, if death occurs through major failures in management arrangements, such as staffing, training or resources.

Professional or clinical negligence

A pharmacist is more likely, however, to be faced with an action for negligence in the civil courts. The essence of the tort of negligence is that there is on the part of the defendant a legal duty of care which s/he has failed to meet, as a result of which the plaintiff has suffered damage. The duty to take care was described in the case of *Donoghue* v. *Stephenson* [1932] AC 562 at 580 thus:

> You must take reasonable care to avoid acts or omissions which you can reasonably foresee would be likely to injure your neighbour. Who, then, in law is my neighbour? The answer seems to be...persons who are so closely and directly affected by my act that I ought reasonably to have them in contemplation as being so affected when I am directing my mind to the acts or omissions which are called in question.

The law imposes a duty to take care in a variety of circumstances. As sellers of goods, community pharmacists have a duty to take reasonable care to warn customers of any potential dangers arising from them. Quite apart from this general duty on all vendors of goods, there is a special relationship between pharmacists and their customers in respect of transactions involving pharmaceutical knowledge. Reliance is placed upon the special skill and knowledge of the pharmacist when selling, dispensing or prescribing medicinal products. The law would expect him/her to exercise that degree of competence which the average member of the profession is required to possess. This is known as the 'duty of care'. A pharmacist occupying a special position in any branch of pharmacy would be expected to have a degree of ability commensurate with that position. Pharmacists consistently, and with good reason, press for recognition as experts upon drugs and medicines, and for the right to take a greater part in the health services. Every right has its correlative duty, and pharmacists, as they achieve greater recognition, must expect the law to require from them a higher degree of skill. It is probable that they will, as a consequence, be more liable to actions for professional negligence.

Four High Court decisions illustrate this point well. A woman who suffered gangrene in both feet, requiring extensive surgery, as a result of receiving an overdose of Migril (ergotamine tartrate, cyclizine hydrochloride and caffeine citrate) prescribed for migraine was awarded £100 000 damages (The Migril Case *Pharm J* 20 February 1982 p. 205). The owner of the pharmacy, who admitted negligence, was held liable for 45 per cent of the damages awarded. The judge, Mr Justice Stuart-Smith, in making the award said that the pharmacist owed a duty to the patient to ensure that drugs were correctly prescribed and that the pharmacist should have spotted the doctor's error and queried the prescription with the prescriber.

It is clear from the judgment that a pharmacist must not be deterred in querying prescriptions with the prescriber by any adverse response on the part of the prescriber, who may resent his/her decisions being questioned. The legal and professional responsibility of the pharmacist to verify and question prescriptions has been highlighted and established by this case.

In another case in 1988, a patient visited his doctor for his regular prescription for inhalers and tablets. At the same time, he was prescribed Amoxil (amoxicillin) for a chest infection. When he took the prescription to the pharmacy, the pharmacist misread Amoxil as Daonil (glibenclamide) and the patient suffered irreversible brain damage.

Mr Justice Auld in awarding £139 000 damages (75 per cent against the pharmacist; 25 per cent against the doctor) said that even assuming that the prescription was unclear, the pharmacist should have been alerted to the fact that Daonil was being recommended in the wrong dosage and quantity. He should also have noticed that the man who collected the drugs did not claim exemption from paying for the Daonil, although diabetics were entitled to free drugs. It was not enough for pharmacists to blindly dispense drugs without giving thought to what they were doing. Giving the decision in the High Court, Mr Justice Auld held that a doctor had a duty to his/her patient to write a prescription sufficiently legibly so as to reduce the likelihood of it being misread by a busy or careless pharmacist. But the pharmacist, in turn, was under a duty to give some thought to the prescriptions s/he was dispensing. If there was an ambiguity in the prescription, s/he should not dispense a drug without first satisfying him/herself that it was the correct one (The Amoxil/Daonil case *Pharm J* 26 March 1988 p. 404).

The apportioning of liability is now an accepted principle in dispensing negligence cases, as demonstrated in two more recent cases. In a settlement in the High Court in Manchester on 28 February 2000, the claim arose from a negligently written prescription, in November 1999, for Epilim (sodium valproate) 500 mg tablets where the strength, and hence the dosage and administration instructions, were incorrect. The pharmacy's professional indemnity insurer agreed to pay 25 per cent of the settlement (£225 000 plus costs) for the pharmacist's failure to detect and correct the error. The prescribing doctor was held liable for the remaining 75 per cent of the compensation paid to the patient (The Epilim Case *Chemist and Druggist* 4 March 2000 p. 5).

In 2006, despite patient medication records showing a series of previous supplies of dexamethasone 0.5 mg, a pharmacist dispensed a prescription that had incorrectly been written for dexamethasone 4 mg. This error was compounded when the patient returned home to America and her physician continued to prescribe 4 mg tablets for her, based on the label on her supply made in the UK. She suffered severely from Cushing's syndrome which led to the loss of her business and personal difficulties. In this case, more than £1m of compensation was awarded (for legal reasons this was not actually paid) and was apportioned between the UK doctor and the employer of the pharmacist (the Horton/Lloyds case *Pharm J* 18 November 2006 p. 595; 17 March 2007 p. 302; see also Chapter 27).

Summary

- Pharmacy is regarded as a profession because its members are bound by regulated standards of education and a code of conduct – the Code of Ethics.
- Most pharmacists are engaged in trading in goods as well as the provision of services and advice; this has led to the development of detailed guidance on how to avoid conflict between these two areas.
- Pharmacists' activities are subject to criminal law, administrative law, civil law and the Society's Code of Ethics.
- The Code of Ethics comprises seven key principles and supporting professional standards and guidance.

- Several legal cases now demonstrate the duty of care owed by pharmacists to their clients.

Further reading

Reissner D (2008) Fatal distraction. *Chemist and Druggist*, 29th March, p. 15 [available at http:// www.chemistanddruggist.co.uk].

Rodgers R, John D (2006) Paternalism to professional judgement: the history of the Code of Ethics. *Pharm J* 276: 721.

Royal Pharmaceutical Society of Great Britain (annual publication) *Medicines, Ethics and Practice*. London: Royal Pharmaceutical Society of Great Britain.

Wingfield J (2007) Consent: the heart of patient respect. *Pharm J* 279: 411–414.

Wingfield J (2007) New emphasis in the Code of Ethics. *Pharm J* 279: 237–240.

Wingfield J (2007) When confidences should be kept and what constitutes an exception. *Pharm J* 279: 533–536.

Wingfield J, Badcott D (2007) *Pharmacy Ethics and Decision Making*. London: Pharmaceutical Press.

Website

The Royal Pharmaceutical Society of Great Britain site carries information on all the functions and organisation of the Society, how it assures pharmacists' competence and fitness to practice, its services to members and continuing news about pharmacy policy and practice: http://www.rpsgb.org.uk This site will be subject to constant revision as the role of the Society splits during 2009 into a regulator (the GPhC) and a new professional body and should be consulted directly on a regular basis for the latest position.

24

Fitness to practise

On 30 March 2007, new primary legislation, the Pharmacists and Pharmacy Technicians Order 2007 (P&PT Order SI 2007 No. 289) replaced the Pharmacy Act 1954. This Order also replaced the previous regulations (made in 1984, see earlier editions of this book) which set out the disciplinary processes of the Royal Pharmaceutical Society of Great Britain (RPSGB; referred to here as the Society) in relation to pharmacists. Disciplinary processes relating to bodies corporate remain unchanged in the Medicines Act 1968 (ss.80 to 83). The new Order also extended disciplinary powers to a new group of regulated pharmacy support staff, pharmacy technicians. However, also in early 2007, a UK Government White Paper set out its intention to separate the functions of the Society and to create, from 2010, a new pharmacy regulator, the General Pharmaceutical Council (GPhC). Statutory powers to regulate registered pharmacy technicians will not come into force until the GPhC (or its 'shadow' body) is established (mid-2009 to 2010). The account below covers the disciplinary processes in place at the end of 2008 as administered by the Society. From mid-2009, disciplinary powers, now called Fitness to Practise (FTP), will pass to the new regulator, the GPhC (subject to parliamentary approval). For a fuller account of the separation of the Society's functions, see Chapter 22.

Proposed changes in the draft Pharmacy Order 2009 (published December 2008)

Proposals for further change to the regulation of pharmacy appear in the draft Pharmacy Order 2009, which was published as this book went to press. The proposals were open to consultation until 9 March 2009 and were expected to be implemented in the second quarter of 2010. The draft Pharmacy Order includes transitional arrangements to ensure smooth transfer of functions from the RPSGB to the GPhC. Many of the major changes from regulation under the Pharmacy Act 1954 to regulation under the P&PT Order 2007 remain in place and these are detailed in the text below, but important changes proposed in the draft Pharmacy Order 2009 include:

- merging the role of the Disciplinary and Health Committees into a single statutory Fitness to Practise Committee;
- implementing a mandatory five year duration for erasure from the register;
- widening the remit of the Appeals Committee to include accreditation; and
- creating the power to extend the role of the Office of the Health Professions Adjudicator to pharmacy – likely to be 'sometime after 2010' (Chapter 25).

A full list of proposed changes appears in Chapter 22.

The Council for Healthcare Regulatory Excellence

Set up under Part 2 of the National Health Service Act 2002 (NHS Act 2002) and consolidated under the Health and Social Care Act 2008, the Council for Healthcare Regulatory Excellence (CHRE; see also Chapters 22, 25 and 26) is empowered to receive details of all the decisions of the Society's disciplinary cases and it may then, if it considers that any decision is 'unduly lenient' or 'should not have been made' and 'that it would be desirable for the protection of members of the public' (NHS Act 2002, s.29), refer the case to the High Court.

Since the CHRE was established, three decisions from the former Statutory Committee were referred back for reconsideration (*Pharm J* 10 September 2005 p. 300). In addition, one case from the Society's disciplinary processes has been referred to the High Court but the outcome was still unknown at the time of writing. This case concerned a pharmacist who, following the discovery of £2000 cash at her place of work, faced allegations of taking the money home, subsequently failing to inform her colleagues or employers of its location and initially failing to admit to investigators that the money was taken home. The Society's then Statutory Committee issued a reprimand against the pharmacist, determining that her actions in the case were not to be characterised as dishonest. The Chairman found that the pharmacist 'had been an extremely foolish woman, but not a dishonest one' (*Pharm J* 1 December 2007 p. 609). In August 2008, however, the pharmacist concerned accepted a consent order from the High Court to transfer to the non-practising register for a period of 12 months.

Legislation regulating fitness to practise

The first four parts of the P&PT Order 2007 have been considered in Chapter 22. Here we consider:

Part 5 Fitness to practise
Part 6 Proceedings
Part 7 Miscellaneous (where relevant to fitness to practise).

The P&PT Order 2007 provides authority for the Society's Council to make Rules (replacing the Society's former bye-laws) as follows:

- RPSGB (Fitness to Practise and Disqualification etc. Rules) Order of Council 2007 (SI 2007 No. 442), which essentially covers procedures and conduct of hearings (the Procedure Rules 2007);
- RPSGB (Fitness to Practise and Registration Appeals Committee and their Advisers Rules) Order of Council 2007 (SI 2007 No. 561), which is concerned with the composition of the committees, appointment and removal of committee members and functions of legal, clinical and specialist advisers to the committees (the Committee Rules 2007).

Transitional arrangements

Because there were already disciplinary cases in the 'pipeline' for consideration by the Society's Statutory Committee (established under the Pharmacy Act 1954), transitional operations (s.69 Schedule 2 of the P&PT Order 2007) were applied during 2007. Allegations from the Infringements Committee (predecessor of the Investigating Committee) referred to the Statutory Committee before 30 March 2007 continued to be heard under the old regulations and procedures. Allegations that had not been so referred and any new allegations considered by the investigating committee after 30 March 2007 were referred to either the new Disciplinary Committee or the new Health Committee. The last new case before the old Statutory Committee was heard on 13 December 2007 (*Pharm J* 5/12 January 2008 p. 4) although some of its residual orders and activities may continue until early 2009.

Fitness to practise processes

Under the Pharmacy Act 1954, a single disciplinary body – the Statutory Committee – considered cases of 'misconduct' by a pharmacist 'such as to render him or her unfit to be on the register'. In common with changes applied across the whole of the healthcare professions (see Chapter 25), the P&PT Order 2007 introduces the term 'fitness to practise', which has a rather wider scope (although it still includes misconduct). When the

GPhC is established, the concept will also be extended to registered pharmacy technicians. Moreover, the P&PT Order 2007 extends the concept to include impaired FTP through health reasons and allows a rapid response to such allegations through the imposition of an *interim order* suspending a pharmacist's registration. Again, consistent with regulatory changes across the whole of healthcare, the P&PT Order 2007 and its associated Rules also specifies detailed FTP structures, procedures and sanctions.

For the first time (s.45 and Rule 2 of the Procedure Rules), the Code of Ethics and its related guidance is the statutory benchmark for 'the standards of conduct, practice and performance expected of registrants' (see also Chapter 23). The Council is expected to keep the Code under review and to vary or withdraw parts of it, or more usually the subsidiary standards and guidance, when appropriate. Significant powers are given to assist the Society in discharging its duties in relation to FTP (s.46). The Society (and its Council, staff or committees) can require relevant information or documents to be provided to it by anyone, including other pharmacists and 'any other person', if the FTP of a registrant is in question. If a person fails to provide such information or documents, then the Society may seek a court order to force disclosure. Further if the Society considers it to be in the public interest, it may publish information about the FTP of any pharmacist or group of pharmacists (s.47).

The P&PT Order 2007 establishes three statutory (meaning set up by statute law) committees involved in the Society's FTP processes, collectively called the FTP Committees:

- the Investigating Committee
- the Disciplinary Committee
- the Health Committee.

The composition of the FTP Committees (and the Registration Appeals Committee – see Chapter 22) and common provisions relating to meetings, the appointment and removal of committee members, their training and competencies and the functions of advisers (legal, clinical and specialist) are set out in the Committee Rules 2007. These define a 'lay member' as someone who is not a registrant or associated with one: a 'professional member' is a practising pharmacist or pharmacy technician. Members are appointed through a public appointment process. Each member is appointed for four years and is allowed two terms of office. All members must undertake training in legal process and jurisprudence. Members of each FTP do not normally sit all together; rather they constitute a panel from which members are drawn as appropriate to a case, subject to a quorum (minimum number). Detailed provisions regarding remit and jurisdiction, production of evidence, standard and burden of proof, order of proceedings, award of costs, etc. for the FTP committees appear in the Procedure Rules 2007.

Impaired fitness to practise

Section 48 of the P&PT Order 2007 says that a person's FTP shall be regarded as 'impaired' if a series of conditions are met. These conditions include

- misconduct
- adverse physical or mental health
- a criminal conviction
- certain orders under Scottish criminal law
- certain social security offences
- a police caution
- a finding of impaired FTP by another health or social care regulator
- deficient professional performance (which includes competence)
- failure to comply with a professional performance requirement.

Procedures to assess professional performance (*revalidation*) were not in place at the time of writing. Misconduct is defined as:

> The demonstration towards a patient or customer, or a prospective patient or customer, by a pharmacist or pharmacy technician of attitudes or behaviour from which that person can reasonably expect to be protected.

An allegation or information that a registrant's FTP might be impaired is first considered by the Registrar (s.49). The allegation or information may relate to matters arising anywhere in the world and at any time in the past. The Registrar decides, firstly, whether the complaint is of such seriousness and urgency as to warrant immediate reference to the Disciplinary or Health Committees for an *interim order* (see below); if not, the matter passes to the Investigating Committee but only if certain criteria are met.

In its *Guidance on making complaints* the Society states that it does not deal with claims for compensation, employment or contractual issues or complaints about non-medicinal products such as faulty hair sprays. The Registrar will then consider Rule 9 of the Procedure Rules and will not refer, unless he considers there is a risk to the public or it is in the public interest, if:

- the allegation is more than five years old;
- the complainant is anonymous;
- the identity of the registrant against whom the allegation is made is unknown; or
- the allegation is of a type that fall outside the Council's published 'threshold criteria'.

In March 2007, the Council approved *threshold criteria* that would allow more minor cases to be dealt with through advice and guidance by the Society's inspectorate, rather than by referral to the Investigating Committee (see below);

the criteria were expressed separately for single one-off dispensing errors and for cases other than single one-off dispensing errors (Box 24.1). Further clarification on *non-referral criteria* was published in August 2008 (Box 24.2). Following the outcome of consultation at the end of 2008, early failure to comply with CPD standards are also likely to be dealt with initially without referral to Investigating Committee. The criteria are intended to ensure that only the more serious cases are referred to the Investigating Committee. Once a decision has been made to refer a case to the Investigating Committee, the Registrar must seek details of any person who employs the registrant, with a view to notifying them of the case and will notify the relevant government health minister. The Registrar may seek a court order to force disclosure if the registrant fails to provide details of employment within 14 days.

Box 24.1 *Threshold criteria for referral to the Investigating Committee*

For all cases

Cases are not likely to be referred to the Investigating Committee **unless** one or more of the following statements are true:

- there is potential for, or evidence that moderate or severe harm or death was caused by the incident (the definitions of these are from the National Patient Safety Agency definitions for grading patient safety incidents);
- there is evidence that there was a deliberate attempt to cause harm to patients or the public;
- there is evidence of ill health or substance abuse by the pharmacist;
- there is evidence that the individual departed from agreed safe protocols or standard operating procedures and in doing so took an unacceptable risk;
- there are no systems to learn from the incident in the pharmacy;
- no attempt has been made to learn from the incident;
- the Society has previously given advice that would have prevented the incident had it been implemented;
- there has been an attempt to cover up;
- there has been a failure to co-operate with an investigation carried out by the Society's inspector or other investigatory body;
- there is evidence of other misconduct that would form the basis of a complaint; and/or
- there is a failure to apologise/provide an explanation to the patient/ representative.

Box 24.1 (Continued)

In addition, for single one-off dispensing errors

- There has been a failure to make a dispensing error log (if aware of the error).

For cases other than single one-off dispensing errors

The following statements are also considered in this second group:

- there is a demonstration of 'misconduct' as defined in the legislation;
- there has been an intention to mislead the public or the public has been involved;
- there are Controlled Drugs involved (excluding single one-off dispensing errors and simple book-keeping cases); and/or
- there is evidence that the case meets the referral criteria (to the Disciplinary Committee) set out in http://www.rpsgb.org/pdfs/ftpicreferralcriteria.pdf.

Source: www.rpsgb.org under Protecting the Public > investigating committee.

Box 24.2 Categories of cases that could be considered for non-referral to the Investigating Committee

These categories are subject to the published threshold criteria (Box 24.1).

Employment issues
Minor NHS terms of service breaches
Commercial/customer service complaints
Failure to supply a patient information leaflet with a medicine
Attitude and behaviour issues
Emergency supply issues
Advertising breaches
Police notification of use of restricted tittles
Fixed penalty Road Traffic Act offences
Failure to display a registration certificate
Failure to dispense a prescription for an abusive/aggressive patient
Simple book-keeping cases
Cases involving inadequate standard operating procedures
Cases involving Pharmacy Medicines on self selection

(continued overleaf)

Box 24.2 (Continued)

Cases involving a failure to supply an over-the-counter medicine

Cases involving disputes over pharmacy contracts

Cases where the Society has received external legal advice that the facts, if established, are not capable of amounting to impairment of fitness to practise or that there is no prospect that sufficient evidence can be obtained to prove impairment of fitness to practise

Cases against superintendents, owners or partners where there is no evidence that the individual concerned (i) has been directly involved in any misconduct, (ii) has omitted to fulfil a specific legal or ethical obligation, or (iii) has failed to supervise others or failed to take appropriate action in response to the misconduct of others under his or her supervision (including joint owners, fellow partners and staff)

Failure to comply with CPD requirements*

Sources: *Pharm J* 2 August 2008 p. 143; *Pharm J* 8 November 2008 s1–s4, subject to consultation.

The Investigating Committee

The function of the Investigating Committee is set out in section 50 of the P&PT Order 2007 and its detailed operation is covered by Part 3 of the Society's Procedure Rules 2007. The Investigating Committee may decide that a case before it need not be referred to the Health or Disciplinary Committee (see below), may issue a warning or advice to the registrant and/or others or may seek undertakings as to future conduct. Alternatively, the Investigating Committee should refer to the Health or Disciplinary Committee (or both) as appropriate. If the Investigating Committee considers that the Society should bring a prosecution (under s.65 of the P&PT Order 2007 or under s.108 of the Medicines Act), then it will notify the Registrar to this effect. In addition, the Investigating Committee will consider whether 'disqualification cases' (involving companies that own pharmacies) should be referred to the Disciplinary Committee (see below).

The Investigating Committee shall consist of:

- a lay member who is the chair;
- a lay member who is the deputy chair;
- three other lay members; and
- five professional members.

The Investigating Committee meets in private and considers cases on documents alone. It can consider written representations from the registrant and require further inquiries to be made. If it considers that the registrant's health is an issue, it can require the registrant to be medically examined. The Investigating

Committee has to be satisfied that there is a 'real prospect' that the relevant committee will find impaired FTP before referring to either the Health or Disciplinary Committee. The registrant should be sent the decision of the Investigating Committee, with reasons and appropriate legal advice, within 10 days. The Investigating Committee can ask for the case to be 'fast tracked' to the Disciplinary Committee (Rule 18 of the Procedure Rules) and can recommend that the Disciplinary Committee or the Health Committee consider an immediate interim order. Under Rule 6 of the Procedure Rules, the Investigating Committee must provide an annual report to the Council. In conjunction with advice from the other FTP committees, the report will include trends, patterns and learning points from the cases, details of the numbers of FTP and disqualification allegations which were disposed of by means of warnings and undertakings and reasons why they were not referred to the other FTP committees.

The Health Committee

Section 51 of the P&PT Order 2007 sets out the function of the Health Committee and its detailed operation is covered by Part 4 of the Society's Procedure Rules 2007. Cases can reach the Health Committee via the Investigating Committee, direct from the Registrar or transferred from the Disciplinary Committee. The Health Committee may find that the registrant's FTP is not impaired but may nevertheless issue warning or advice to them or any other involved person; it may also publish its finding that the registrant's FTP is not impaired. If the Health Committee considers that the registrant's FTP is impaired, it may issue warnings or advice as above, suspend the registrant for up to 12 months, allow the registrant to continue to practise under conditions for up to three years or refer him/her to the Disciplinary Committee. A suspension may be extended on review for a further 12 months; if it has been in force continuously for two years, it may be extended indefinitely or terminated, subject to review or further conditions. The Health Committee cannot order the removal of a registrant's name from the register.

The Health Committee shall consist of:

- a lay member who is the chair;
- two lay members who are deputy chairs;
- four other lay members; and
- six professional members.

The Registrar must notify the registrant of any such decisions, with reasons and details of a right of appeal (see below). The Health Committee meets in private unless the Committee, having obtained legal and clinical advice, is satisfied that the public interest in holding the inquiry in public outweighs the interest of the registrant or a third party in maintaining their privacy. Special provisions (Rule 47 of the Procedure Rules) may be operated by the Health and Disciplinary Committees in the case of vulnerable witnesses or allegations of a sexual nature.

The Disciplinary Committee

The Disciplinary Committee may consider two types of case:

- FTP cases involving a registrant, and
- Disqualification cases under Part 4 of the Medicines Act 1968.

Fitness to practise cases

Section 52 of the P&PT Order 2007 sets out the function of the Disciplinary Committee and its detailed operation is covered by Part 4 of the Society's Procedure Rules 2007. Cases can reach the Disciplinary Committee via the Investigating Committee, direct from the Registrar or transferred from the Health Committee. The Disciplinary Committee may find that the registrant's FTP is not impaired but may nevertheless issue a warning or advice to them or any other involved person; it may also publish its finding that the registrant's FTP is not impaired. If the Disciplinary Committee considers that the registrant's FTP is impaired, it may offer warnings or advice as above, suspend the registrant for up to 12 months or allow him/her to continue to practise under conditions for up to three years. A suspension may be extended on review for a further 12 months; if it has been in force continuously for two years, it may be extended indefinitely or terminated, subject to review or further conditions. The Disciplinary Committee can give a direction that a registrant's name be removed from the register (i.e. 'struck off'). In this case, no application for restoration to the register can be considered by the Disciplinary Committee until the expiry of a period of five years from the date on which the name was removed.

The Disciplinary Committee shall consist of:

- a legally qualified lay member who is the chair;
- three legally qualified lay members who are deputy chairs;
- six other lay members; and
- nine professional members.

Decisions made by the Disciplinary Committee are made in three stages (Rule 35 Procedure Rules):

1 findings of fact using the civil standard of proof (on the balance of probabilities – see Chapter 1)
2 In FTP cases, findings on whether the registrant's FTP is impaired
3 Consideration of the appropriate sanction.

The Registrar must notify the registrant of the final determination, with reasons and details of a right of appeal (see below). The Disciplinary

Committee meets in public (which may include news media), unless the Committee is satisfied that the interests of the registrant or a third party in maintaining their privacy outweighs the public interest in holding all or part of the hearing in public. The Committee members retire in private to make their decisions but the full determination is delivered in public.

Disqualification cases

Under Section 80 of the Medicines Act 1968, the former Statutory Committee could consider cases against a body corporate (or company) that conducts a retail pharmacy business. This power has continued under Part 5 of Schedule 2 to the P&PT Order 2007. Such cases, after consideration by the Investigating Committee, are now passed to the Disciplinary Committee.

A 'disqualification' allegation may arise when:

- a company is convicted of an offence under the Medicines Act or the Misuse of Drugs Act; or
- any member of the board or any officer of or person employed by that body is convicted of an offence or has been guilty of misconduct, and the offence or misconduct is such as in the opinion of the (Disciplinary Committee) renders him, or would if he were a pharmacist render him, unfit to be on the register.

The Disciplinary Committee considers such cases in the three stages set out under fitness to practise cases but stage 2 becomes whether the second of the above conditions is proven. If the allegation is found proved, then the Disciplinary Committee may direct the Registrar to remove any or all of the company's pharmacies from the register and disqualify the company from lawfully running a pharmacy business.

Professional performance assessments

Section 53 of the P&PT Order 2007 allows the Council to make rules whereby the Registrar or the Disciplinary Committee may order 'an assessment of the standard of a registrant's professional performance by an individual assessor or an assessment team'. No such rules had been made at the time of writing.

Interim orders

Where the Health or Disciplinary Committee is 'satisfied that it is necessary for the protection of members of the public or is otherwise in the public interest, or is in the interests of the registrant', it may make an interim order suspending the registrant from the register for up to 18 months or making his or her practise subject to conditions (s.54). The registrant is entitled to attend the hearing, to be represented and to bring witnesses. The order must be reviewed within six months, and every three months or earlier if the registrant requests it or new evidence is available. The Council may apply to the High Court to extend the interim order beyond 18 months and the registrant may apply to the High Court to terminate, revoke or vary the conditions or period of time specified in the original order. The interim order is made pending further investigations or a full hearing; these will still follow.

Indicative sanctions guidance

Both the Health and Disciplinary Committees have produced guidance (under Rules 7 and 8 of the Procedure Rules) on sanctions to assist those who appear before the committees. The sanctions available are already covered under each committee above, but the guidance goes on to clarify the purpose of the sanctions as threefold:

- the protection of the public;
- the maintenance of public confidence in the profession; and
- the maintenance of proper standards.

The guidance stresses that the role of the Health and Disciplinary Committees is not to punish a registrant twice for the same offence. In particular, the Health and Disciplinary Committees are required to weigh the interests of the registrant against the need for public protection. In making its decision, the committees have issued lists of 'aggravating features' and 'mitigating features' which they will take into account when reaching their decisions (see Box 24.3). In addition the guidance gives examples of the types of case where each particular sanction might be most appropriate.

Box 24.3 Extract from Indicative Sanctions Guidance: aggravating and mitigating features used by the Disciplinary Committee when deciding sanctions

Aggravating features include:

- dishonesty
- vulnerable victim
- sexual misconduct in relation to professional duties
- previous convictions or findings of misconduct by the Disciplinary Committee or its predecessor, the Statutory Committee
- failure to comply with or disregard of previous warnings issued by any current or previous Fitness to Practise (FTP) Committee of the Society

Box 24.3 (Continued)

- failure to co-operate or comply with assessment of professional performance
- failure to co-operate with investigation into allegation
- breach of confidentiality
- potential harm
- no steps taken to prevent actual harm
- actions premeditated
- abuse of trust or position
- blatant disregard for system of registration
- blatant disregard of established or generally accepted guidelines, or standards and guidance published by the Society
- lack of insight
- concealment of wrongdoing or failure to respond to complaint by patient
- breach of any written undertakings previously given to a FTP Committee
- disregard of written or oral advice given by a Society's inspector
- misconduct or deficient professional performance committed by person in charge on pharmacy premises.

Mitigating features include:

- repayment of any misappropriated funds
- ill health at the time of misconduct/in which the professional performance was deficient
- single isolated incident in a long and unblemished career
- open and frank admission at an early stage, demonstrating insight into misconduct or deficient professional performance
- no potential harm
- steps taken to prevent actual harm.

Neither of these lists is exhaustive.

Source: www.rpsgb.org.uk.

General procedures of the Fitness to Practise Committees

A simplified flowchart of the FTP procedures is provided in Figure 24.1. Full details of the procedures of all the FTP Committees are set out in the Procedure Rules 2007.

Hearings before the Health or Disciplinary Committees follow a process very like proceedings in court. Rules specify clear steps to be taken prior to the

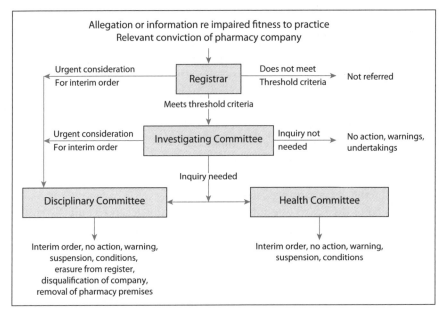

Figure 24.1   Simplified flowchart of RPSGB fitness to practise procedures.

hearing, including a timetable for exchange of evidence between the registrant (or representative) and the Society and sufficient notice of the allegation to be heard (no less than 28 days before the date of the hearing). The Chairman of the Health or Disciplinary Committee may issue specific '*practice directions*' (Rule 26 of the Procedure Rules) of general application to the proceedings of the committee.

The registrant may be represented (Rule 43) by a solicitor or counsel or a representative from his or her trade union or defence organisation. S/he may also be accompanied and advised by a 'supporter' but that person may not be associated with the Society or be a witness in the case, and may only address the committee with the permission of the chair. The registrant does not have to attend the hearing but the case may then be heard in his or her absence. Both 'sides' may call witnesses, who have to give evidence on oath. Witnesses may not be heard, however, if they have not provided a signed witness statement at least seven days before the hearing.

Sections 61 and 62 of the P&PT Order 2007 make provision for the Council to appoint *legal advisers* (in addition to the legally qualified chairman and deputies of the Disciplinary Committee) and *clinical and other specialist advisers* to assist the Health and Disciplinary Committees in their deliberations. Rule 29 of the Procedures Rules allows a clinical adviser to advise on health-related issues. Other specialist advisers may be appointed to advise on issues falling within their speciality; these are most likely to be needed in professional performance assessments, for which arrangements were not in place at the time of writing.

The P&PT Order 2007 provides power (s.59) for the Council to make rules covering the 'award of, and in respect of the assessment of, *costs* or expenses' against either party to a hearing, but not in respect of the making of an interim order. When considering costs, the Committee will have regard to Rule 48 of the Procedure Rules and to a person's ability to pay. All hearings of the Health or Disciplinary Committee must be recorded electronically or in writing and parties to the hearing may obtain transcripts, on payment of a fee.

Appeals

Sections 56–58 of the P&PT Order 2007 are concerned with appeals. Only certain decisions are appealable.

1   The Registrar's decision to refuse an application for restoration for reasons relating to FTP.
2   A decision of the Health Committee to suspend registration or set conditions for practise, or variations or extensions of conditions.
3   A decision of the Disciplinary Committee to:
    a   remove a person from the register; or
    b   to suspend registration or set conditions for practise, or variations or extensions of conditions.
4   A decision of the Disciplinary Committee to give a direction for conditional registration.
5   A decision of the Disciplinary Committee that no further applications for restoration may be made.

Appeals may be made within 28 days to the relevant court, which may dismiss the appeal, quash the decision, quash or substitute an alternative form of direction or refer the case back to the Registrar or relevant FTP committee with directions for disposal of the case. Directions and decisions do not take effect until the appeal period has expired or the appeal case has been finally disposed of, is abandoned or fails. However, if the Health or Disciplinary Committee believes that the public or the registrant is at risk, it may direct immediate suspension.

Availability of information about the Fitness to Practise Committees and their determinations

The Society's website now carries copious information about the operation of its FTP activities; at the time of writing this was under 'protecting the public' at www.rpsgb.org. During 2009, this information is likely to move to the website for the GPhC when established. Notices of inquiry and the decisions (determinations) of the Health and Disciplinary Committees and interim orders are available. Short reports of most cases were also carried in the *Pharmaceutical Journal* until early 2008. In September 2008, the Society published its first *Fitness to Practise Annual Report*, for 2007, as required by Section 6(1) of the P&PT Order 2007. The report is required to contain statistical information and descriptions of the Society's FTP processes, together with the Council's observations on the report. The report is submitted to the Privy Council, which then lays a copy before each House of Parliament.

The work of the Fitness to Practise Committees

Interim orders

All interim orders from both the Health and Disciplinary Committees are posted on the Society's website and appear in the official pages of the *Pharmaceutical Journal*. However, there is very little background information or reasons given as to why the interim order has been made. The first interim order was rather notorious, involving an Australian pharmacist Samuel Edwin Ashby, who attacked an official of the Society with an iron bar at his hearing before the then Statutory Committee (*Pharm J* 28 October 2006 p. 503; 1 March 2008 p. 239), when his name was ordered to be removed from the register. This order, made on 18 April 2007 under the authority of the Disciplinary Committee merely says that Mr Ashby's registration is suspended for 18 months and the order is subject to review after six months. Mr Ashby appealed the original ruling, which meant he could legally continue to practise until his appeal was heard, although the Society took the unusual step of giving publicity to the case shortly after the initial ruling. The interim order was made as soon as the powers to make such orders under the P&PT Order came into force on 30 March 2007.

Other Disciplinary Committee interim orders are usually for suspension for 12 or 18 months, with occasional conditions such as moving on to the non-practising register and not returning to practise until the case is heard in full by the Committee. Interim orders under the authority of the Health Committee are also largely for suspension for 12 or 18 months, although some have specified further requirements such as return of registration certificates, provision of medical reports before applying to be on the practising register and working restrictions, as set out under Health Committee determinations below.

Cases before the Health Committee

Determinations made by the Health Committee are posted on the Society's website and appear in the official pages of the *Pharmaceutical Journal*. Rather fewer of these are made than under the Disciplinary Committee and the details of the hearing normally remain confidential. The determinations specify a variety of conditions upon registration for a specific period such as:

- to notify all employers, prospective employers and agents of the matters under consideration in the case;
- not to work as a superintendent pharmacist, a responsible pharmacist (see Chapter 5) or single-handed practitioner;
- not to undertake any pharmacy practice as a locum;
- not to undertake on-call duties, weekend work, out of hours work or extended hours;
- to remain on the non-practising part of the register;
- to allow exchange of regular progress reports with the Society; or
- to inform in writing the Society's FTP Directorate before undertaking any position in the UK or elsewhere for which registration is required.

Cases before the Disciplinary Committee

The notice of inquiry, a determination notice and the full determination of the Disciplinary Committee are posted on the Society's website. Shortened versions of the notice of inquiry and the determination notice appear in the *Pharmaceutical Journal* together with short reports appearing some time after the determinations are made. Transcripts are prepared of the Disciplinary Committee hearings and these are available (on payment of a fee) to the parties concerned in the hearing; they may also be made available for research purposes on request. Between its first new case (Iqbal; 13 July 2007) and August 2008, the Committee considered around a dozen new cases, all of which demonstrated features that have appeared frequently in the cases before the former Statutory Committee such as NHS fraud, Inland Revenue fraud, theft and unlawful supply of Controlled Drugs. In cases concerning such dishonesty, the chairman often made reference to the words of the Privy Council in an earlier appeal case as follows:

> For professional persons, a finding of dishonesty lies at the top end of the spectrum of the gravity of misconduct.

It is likely, therefore, that future cases involving dishonesty will often result in a 'striking off' order unless there are significant mitigating features. It is less clear what the position of the Disciplinary Committee is likely to be when dispensing errors are concerned. In the case of Iqbal (13 July 2007), a single error was not considered to be sufficient to order removal from the register but unrelated convictions for falsifying applications for an NHS contract led nevertheless to a striking off (*Pharm J* 16 February 2008 p. 195). A series of errors for a single patient (Mason 10 September 2007) led to a reprimand, and series of errors for different patients led to forced retirement from practice for one senior pharmacist (Ferrigno 23 January 2008).

The Disciplinary Committee used its powers to award costs – around £20 000 against the Society – in relation to unsupported allegations against two of three pharmacist brothers. The Society had alleged that all three were guilty of misconduct because the third brother incorrectly endorsed a number of NHS prescriptions, but did not have an answer when asked what exactly they were alleged to have done wrong (*Pharm J* 1 March 2008 p. 235).

Applications for restoration to the registers

It should be noted that restoration following removal for reasons other than those of FTP would be considered by the Registration Appeals Committee (see Chapter 22). Following removal for FTP matters, the procedure is governed by Rule 11 of the Procedure Rules. In the first of these (Kantaria 17 April 2007), concerning a pharmacist who was struck off following a conviction for NHS fraud, the chairman set out a number of conditions that the Committee would take into account before reaching a judgment as to whether suitability to be restored to the register had been demonstrated.

- The seriousness of the original offence or misconduct, the degree of insight shown by the applicant of the gravity of the original offence or misconduct.
- Whether the applicant has made real efforts to demonstrate suitability to be restored to the register, including attempts to keep up to date in terms of knowledge and skills and with development of practice.
- Whether public confidence in the profession would be maintained if the applicant were to be restored to the register.
- The length of time that has elapsed since removal from the register and/or any previous application for restoration.
- The conduct of the applicant since removal from the register and any previous application for restoration.
- Testimonials, character references in support of the application and any representation from patients or victims affected by the original offence or misconduct.

This application to restore was refused on the grounds of failure to demonstrate the necessary degree of insight into the offences. In a subsequent case (Sheikh 14 May 2007), a restoration was allowed on the grounds of adequate insight and genuine contrition. In a third (Singh 12 July 2007), the Committee allowed restoration on the basis of evidence identifying a change in the pharmacist's attitude and character but required him to undertake a Return to Practice course and work under supervision for the first six months.

The former Statutory Committee

The final transfer of business from the former Statutory Committee (established under the Pharmacy Act 1954) was expected to be completed early in 2009. Details of its constitution, jurisdiction and remit will, therefore, now only be found in earlier editions of this book. Unlike civil case law (see Chapter 1), the decisions of professional regulators are not binding on subsequent similar cases – they do not set precedents. Nevertheless, decided cases are instructive as to the scope of inquiries heard and likely outcome as well as helping pharmacy students and others to understand what conduct is expected of pharmacists. The following account is more of an overview than in previous editions of this work and to keep the text manageable we have arbitrarily deleted full details of most cases prior to 1990 and have reduced appeals and judicial reviews to a table. Interested readers will find more information in previous editions. The types of case before the new Disciplinary Committee have remained very similar and a few examples have been added where relevant.

The three purposes of the Statutory Committee were set out by the Chairman in 1990 (*Pharm J* 14 April 1990 p. 488):

> The protection of the public; next comes the honour and dignity of the profession and the third dimension is the best interest of the pharmacist.

Criminal convictions

In the past, the majority of Statutory Committee inquiries arose following criminal convictions relating to pharmaceutical matters such as lack of supervision. In more recent years, inquiries have more often followed convictions for theft or fraud. Inquiries are also held relating to other criminal offences, not all of which are connected with a pharmacist's professional work, for example motoring offences, theft, receiving stolen goods, forgery, indecent assault and other sexual offences, offences against the Misuse of Drugs Act or the Food and Drugs Act, procuring abortion, firearms offences and labelling offences under the Medicines Act 1968. The appeal case of Harari (see earlier editions) supported a striking off for unlawful eviction and intimidation. Other cases have included trading unlawfully in written-off cars, making false statements to collect insurance monies (*Pharm J* 7 August 1993 p. 189), making untrue endorsements on passport applications (*Pharm J* 13 December 1997 p. 965), impersonating a general practitioner (*Pharm J* 29 June 1991 p. 811), paedophilia (*Pharm J* 15 August 1998 p. 234), false imprisonment and assault (*Pharm J* 27 November 1999 p. 853), breaching the terms of a community service order (*Pharm J* 2 November 2002 p. 660), possession and distribution of indecent photographs (*Pharm J* 21/28 December 2002 p. 891), indecent assault (*Pharm J* 24 July 2004 p. 130), the sending of offensive letters to the editor of the *Pharmaceutical Journal* (*Pharm J* 22 February 2003 p. 285), threats and abuse to a wholesaler (*Pharm J* 26 February 2005 p. 252), assault (*Pharm J* 28 January 2006 p. 116) and smuggling orchids (*Chemist and Druggist* 23 August 2008, p. 8).

Many Statutory Committee cases, however, dealt directly with a pharmacist's professional and legal responsibilities and were related to his/her professional work.

The jurisdiction of the Committee also applied to offences committed outside the UK such as drug offences committed in Canada (*Pharm J* 1 December 1984 p. 695) and convictions under Jersey's state law (*Pharm J* 3 December 1988 p. 727). Moreover, there is no time limit which removes the possibility of inquiry; in 1999, a pharmacist was removed from the register by the Committee in relation to child abuse offences which were committed 20 years previously (*Pharm J* 10 July 1999 p. 51).

Professional practice

The Statutory Committee has regarded the Code of Ethics as reflecting standards of professional practice but is not bound by it. In a 1987 case (*Pharm J* 21 November 1987 p. 633), the chairman began his judgment thus:

> (The Code represents) in clear terms the views of the most senior members of the profession and they have been approved by the profession as a whole, they are expressed in terms which are easy to understand and this Committee attaches great importance to them.

Notwithstanding the above, there is no specific reference in any Code of Ethics suggesting that it is wrong to be in charge of a pharmacy when drunk or to make a dispensing error. Such things are self-evident and implicit in the duty of pharmacists to have in mind at all times their responsibilities to the general public, although many of these responsibilities have now been made explicit in the Code of Ethics. Several new professional 'charges' anticipated matters which are now part of the Registration Rules (see Chapter 22) or the Procedure Rules (see above). They included a reprimand for failure to co-operate with an inquiry (*Pharm J* 18 March 2006 p. 332), a reprimand for a pharmacist who had poor English and little grasp of his responsibilities as a superintendent (*Pharm J* 19 February 2005 p. 218), reprimands for false completion of FTP declarations to two primary care trusts (*Pharm J* 9 February 2008 p. 156) and a striking off for persistent failure to carry professional indemnity insurance (*Pharm J* 18/24 December 2004 p. 895).

In 2005, an inquiry into the actions of the pharmacist in 1993 who had been named in the notorious Shipman Inquiry (see Chapter 25) ended with a ruling of 'no case to answer' (*Pharm J* 26 March 2005 pp. 374–375). Though not necessarily related, the Statutory Committee declined to hear a case concerning events more than eight years old (*Pharm J* 9 September 2006 p. 319) and then declared that it would not consider any cases where the events were more than four years previous (*Pharm J* 14 October 2006 p. 461). The P&PT Order 2007 has now set the 'time-bar' for cases at five years (see above).

Applications for restoration to the register

The advent of a Health Committee under the P&PT Order 2007 has provided a means for dealing with the rehabilitation of an offending pharmacist without recourse to disciplinary action. In the past, the Chairman noted that, albeit reluctantly, the Statutory Committee had to act as a Health Committee (*Pharm J* 26 June 2004 p. 823). So the Committee has played this part by imposing certain conditions on the respondent pharmacist before consideration would be given to an application for restoration to the register. For example, a pharmacist who had a 'history of heavy and chaotic drinking' was strongly recommended to continue to receive counselling and support, to produce a report on his conduct, a psychiatric assessment and a clear prognosis of his ability to refrain from excessive consumption of alcohol before restoration to the register might be considered (*Pharm J* 3 July 2004 p. 33). In a similar case, the conditions included submission to blood tests to ensure freedom from alcohol or drugs and an agreement to work only in situations where the pharmacist was not in sole charge of the pharmacy at any time (*Pharm J* 24 April 2004 p. 525).

Restoration to the register generally depends upon some evidence of rehabilitation (*Pharm J* 14 February 2004 p. 201) or commitment to improved practice (*Pharm J* 22 February 2003 p. 286). Applications may be rejected if there is little evidence of 'genuine regret' for wrongdoing (*Pharm J* 5 April 2003 p. 494), very serious convictions for drug dealing (*Pharm J* 20 May 2006 p. 608), 'premature' application (*Pharm J* 25 March 2006 p. 367), repeated deception (*Pharm J* 16 April 2005 p. 467) or may be deferred pending removal from a sex offender's register (*Pharm J* 17 September 2005 p. 354).

Initial applications to register can also be blocked. A preregistration graduate who had convictions for actual bodily harm, failed to surrender to custody and who attempted to deceive the Society in regard to details about his preregistration training was refused admittance to the register (*Pharm J* 20 July 1996 p. 91). Similarly, admittance was refused in the case of an overseas pharmacist involved in a benefit fraud (*Pharm J* 24 June 2000 p. 947) and again in 2001 (*Pharm J* 24 March 2001 p. 386). Conversely, a case involving the provision of untruthful information about preregistration training, but lacking in evidence of an intention to deceive, resulted in eventual permission to seek registration (*Pharm J* 6 September 1997 p. 367).

Cases before the Registration Appeals Committee

At the time of writing, only three appeals had been heard by the Registration Appeals Committee; full details appear on the Society's website. In the case of A A Aromolaran (29 January 2008), which was dismissed, the decision to refuse was because of doubts about the applicant's FTP. These were based on recent convictions (during the undergraduate course) involving dishonesty and deception that were considered to be relevant to the practice of pharmacy. In its decision, the Committee said that Mr Aromolaran showed 'a worrying lack of insight' into his offences, that the offences were not merely careless and there was a lack of evidence regarding his rehabilitation.

In Y Nazir (7 December 2007), the applicant had a conviction for theft from his workplace (a grocery store) acquired during undergraduate training; the appeal was allowed (i.e. the applicant was put on the register) because of the passage of time and demonstration of Mr Nazir's remorse and insight into his wrongdoing. In S Mohamed (7 December 2007), the applicant had, during her undergraduate training, received a police caution for having altered a cheque from her former employer so as to increase the sum paid to her by £1000. The appeal was allowed because the Committee accepted references that Ms Mohamed was honest, hardworking and reliable and that the offence was not premeditated and was entirely out of character.

Examples of cases before the Statutory Committee and the Disciplinary Committee

Theft of money and deception

Cases of theft or deception are always treated by the Committee very seriously on the grounds that the pharmacist is in a position of trust, both in relation to his/her employer and the NHS. The theft by an employee of three tubes of moisturiser led to a striking off because there were no significant factors in mitigation (*Pharm J* 16 April 2005 p. 466) and a locum who stole £26 000 worth of medicines from his employer and sold them to a pharmacist friend was also struck off; his friend was reprimanded (*Pharm J* 2 April 2005).

Theft of money from the NHS by deception has frequently led to erasures: for example where false declarations of exemption were made when submitting prescriptions for payment (*Pharm J* 24 November 1990 p. 702), for falsely claiming urgent dispensing fees on non-urgent prescriptions (*Pharm J* 5 March 1994 p. 323), falsely claiming extemporaneous fees (*Pharm J* 10 June 2000 p. 876), making false endorsements (*Pharm J* 3 June 2000 p. 841), claiming for prescriptions not dispensed (*Pharm J* 22 January 2000 p. 128), and withholding low-cost prescriptions and keeping the difference between the prescription charge and the actual cost price of the medicines

(*Pharm J* 3 July 2004 p. 34). A reprimand was administered for substituting medicines on a prescription without the prescriber's consent (*Pharm J* 31 October 1998 p. 698) and for falsified claims for emergency contraception supply (*Pharm J* 29 November, 2003 p. 759). Nothing much changes; the Disciplinary Committee also struck off a pharmacist for false endorsements (*Pharm J* 8 March 2008 p. 289) and reprimanded a second pharmacist for similar offences (*Pharm J* 22 March 2008 p. 347).

Theft by deception from employers also features: false locum claims (*Pharm J* 16 February 2008 p. 195), false sick pay claims (*Pharm J* 30 October 2004 p. 664) and theft by deception from wholesalers (*Pharm J* 8 December 2001 p. 834) have led to reprimands or striking off. An attempt to deceive the Society by forging a certificate of professional indemnity resulted in erasure from the register (*Pharm J* 4 December 1999 p. 896).

Theft and unlawful consumption or supply of drugs

The potential danger to the public of a pharmacist who consumes or is addicted to drugs is amply demonstrated in cases before the Statutory Committee. In a case where the pharmacist had stolen diamorphine, replaced it with tragacanth powder and abused the stolen diamorphine himself (*Pharm J* 19 August 1995 p. 246), the chairman commented:

> ...three years of dispensing in a pharmacy while taking diamorphine, with its euphoric and distorting effects, and while there was no-one to check him, correct him or monitor him, meant that there was the chance of a mistake.

Such activities clearly bring the profession into disrepute and represent a breach of trust and potential risk to the public. Nevertheless, such cases are prevalent: for example, theft and consumption of amoxicillin, salbutamol, ephedrine and Sudafed (paracetamol and pseudoephedrine hydrochloride) (*Pharm J* 14 December 2002 p. 870); of Equagesic (meprobamate, ethoheptazine citrate and aspirin) (*Pharm J* 14 December 2002 p. 871); of temazepam (*Pharm J* 22 February 2003 p. 285); of Ritalin (methylphenidate) and Dexedrine (dexamfetamine sulphate) (*Pharm J* 8 November 2003 p. 661); of dihydrocodeine tablets (*Pharm J* 3/10 January 2004 p. 38); and of 'ecstasy' (methylenedioxymethamfetamine) and cocaine (*Pharm J* 14 February 2004 p. 201). To these could be added the theft and consumption of Dexedrine, temazepam and diazepam (*Pharm J* 11 December 2004 p. 866) and driving while unfit through taking dihydrocodeine, codeine and diazepam (*Pharm J* 9 July 2005 p. 66).

Sometimes the theft is for the purpose of illegal supplies to others: for example illegal import of steroids at the employer's expense and supply to gymnasiums (*Pharm J* 18 November 2000 p. 750), theft of medicines for illegal sale (*Pharm J* 21 April 2001 p. 534), illegal sales of Rohypnol (flunitrazepam) and Distalgesic (co-proxamol) (*Pharm J* 1 November 2003 p. 629) and theft of several thousand bottles of glycerin and rosewater for export to Nigeria (*Pharm J* 6 July 2002 p. 38). The advent of medicines for erectile dysfunction, with restrictions on prescribing within the NHS, led to a series of cases concerning illegal supplies of Viagra (sildenafil) to individual patients (*Pharm J* 23 February 2003 p. 265; 7 September 2002 p. 343; 2 November 2002 p. 659; 7 December 2002 p. 829). The supply of large quantities of laxatives and diuretics to a patient with anorexia nervosa led to erasure of a pharmacist from the register (*Pharm J* 9 September 2006 p. 320). After a test purchase by the Sun newspaper, a pharmacist (Sanghvi, 3–7 March 2008) was reprimanded by the Disciplinary Committee for supplying amoxicillin in an unlabelled bottle to a reporter posing as a Kosovan refugee. The Statutory Committee struck off a pharmacist who tried to smuggle cocaine into Britain (*Pharm J* 10 December 2005 p. 728) as did the Disciplinary Committee for a pharmacist supplying mannitol for use in 'cutting' illegal supplies of cocaine (*Pharm J* 10 May 2008 p. 575).

A persistent 'misuse' of medicines involves the use of steroid creams for 'skin lightening'. Investigation by the media resulted in a complaint leading to erasures for pharmacists who unlawfully made supplies of Dermovate (clobetasol) without prescription in 1997 (*Pharm J* 12 July 1997 p. 57) and, following convictions, again in 2000 (*Pharm J* 19 February 2000 pp. 290–291).

Excessive or uncontrolled supplies of substances of abuse

The fact that the sale of certain substances is not unlawful does not permit the pharmacist to abrogate his professional responsibility as custodian of the nation's medicines, nor to ignore his/her specialised knowledge of chemicals and other harmful material. The names of many pharmacists have been erased from the register in connection with selling excessive quantities of medicines likely to be abused or for being unable to account, other than by way of sale, for large discrepancies between the amount of such medicines purchased and supplies made on prescription. A complaint of misconduct commonly follows irresponsible supply of abused medicines such as those containing codeine, morphine, methadone, ephedrine, cyclizine and antihistamines or anabolic steroids.

The distinctions between what is and is not considered to be irresponsible can be fine. Commenting on a case involving the supply, over a six-month period, of 39 000 Valoid (cyclizine hydrochloride) tablets to a single customer (*Pharm J* September 2, 2000 p. 326), the chairman commented:

> It was startling to the point of disbelief if he did not know that Valoid was [cyclizine]...[the pharmacist] had demonstrated a complete lack of expertise, the public had been put at risk, no check had been made on the customer or on the use of the tablets, and no warning had been given.

Yet another pharmacist was reprimanded by the Disciplinary Committee for regularly supplying Valoid (72 containers of 100 tablets) to a customer who claimed to represent an oil rig company (*Pharm J* 29 March 2008 p. 377).

Failure to account satisfactorily for 725 g ephedrine hydrochloride powder, 59.5 litres ephedrine hydrochloride elixir, 541.5 litres Phensedyl linctus, 1857.9 litres codeine linctus, 9432 tablets of codeine phosphate 30 mg and 5600 tablets of codeine phosphate 60 mg led to erasure from the register (*Pharm J* 28 September 1991 p. 445). The chairman declared that the pharmacist's duty of care could not be avoided even under duress and added:

> Even if those threats were made, which we do not accept, we were invited...to consider the balance of the Code of Ethics...and...the law...against the threat of violence to himself, to his children and to his livelihood...and, upon striking that balance, to determine that what he did was right and the only alternative a professional man could follow. We emphatically reject that suggestion and anything approaching that. A professional man does not see things in that way at all. It is not a question of balance. A professional man does not act illegally, neither does he deliberately act in a flagrant breach of the Code...What he does is to face up to threats and temptations as part of his professional responsibilities. It is no way for a professional man to behave, to feed secretly the addiction of drug addicts, having given in to the temptation of supplying their demands, and to allow seepage of drugs of abuse and addiction onto the street where they can be absorbed into the black market and into the wrong hands...We have decided...that Mr X, by behaving in such an utterly irresponsible way, must reasonably expect that he may have forfeited forever his right to practise as a pharmacist.

Despite these clear warnings, two pharmacists were removed from the register in 1999 for making excessive sales of codeine linctus (*Pharm J* 30 January 1999 p. 152) and similarly in relation to kaolin and morphine mixture (*Pharm J* 10 July 1999 p. 50). Regarding supply of more than the authorised instalment amount of methadone to two addicts (*Pharm J* 21 April 2001 p. 534), the chairman commented that the Committee wished it to be crystal clear that it could never be a legitimate excuse to plead intimidation in such circumstances. Pharmacies known as a 'soft touch' would attract ever greater numbers of drug abusers:

> If they (pharmacists) give way to intimidation...the whole arrangement will collapse.

Two further erasures from the Disciplinary Committee concerned pharmacists who had deliberately supplied unlawfully Controlled Drugs to those known to be addicted to the substances (*Pharm J* 3 May 2008 p. 544; 8 March 2008 p. 288).

The dangers of too close a relationship with drug misusers were again dramatically demonstrated in a case where a pharmacist had allowed her pharmacy to be used by a substantial number of recreational drug users, giving rise to drug dealing on the premises, brawls and the dumping of used needles and syringes in the vicinity. The pharmacy had been christened a 'drug den' and 'Smack Street' by local residents and had attracted drug users far beyond the local population; in short, it was 'a honey pot for illicit trading in drugs' (*Pharm J* 29 November 1997 p. 888). The chairman said that a pharmacist could not dispense a prescription simply because a doctor had written it and added that:

> The pharmacist is there to check, to monitor, to counsel, to use his informed judgement, to use experience, to sniff out mistakes. If one is asked to do something which is unlawful, or which is highly likely to be, then one should challenge it and confront the prescriber.

Controlled drug registers

Many convictions under Controlled Drugs legislation have related to inadequate record keeping (e.g. *Pharm J* 30 June 2001 p. 885; 5 April 2003 p. 495). The importance of keeping proper records was summed up in a case in 1990 when the chairman listed four important reasons (*Pharm J* 4 August 1990 p. 158).

> One is that it is essential to know where dangerous drugs are. [Secondly], where one is dealing with a drug commonly supplied to addicts, one is playing with fire if records are not kept. Such people, in order to feed their habit, frequently lie, sell part of the drugs they are given, horde drugs and forge prescriptions...it is...extremely important that records are kept right up to date, scrupulously and accurately. [Thirdly]...it is for the greater protection of the pharmacist himself that he keeps records in that fashion...his records would help to avoid any false accusations being made against him... [Fourthly] Controlled Drugs have to be locked away...sometimes those cabinets are broken into and the drugs stolen. It therefore becomes very, very important for the proper authorities to know precisely what had been in the cabinet before the commencement of their enquiries.

Commenting that the Committee was growing weary of repeating the following injunction, the chairman said (*Pharm J* 24 April 2004 p. 526):

> Pharmacists across the country should recognise how close they would come to imperilling their careers if they fail to do what the law requires,

and fail to keep the registers. . .up to date, and make the entries on the day, or the next day.

Disposal of dangerous waste

Implementation of environmental protection laws has led to a number of convictions of pharmacists. A pharmacist had cleared out stock from a pharmacy he had just acquired and caused sacks containing Prescription Only Medicines and Controlled Drugs to be left in a skip outside the premises. Issuing a reprimand, the chairman concluded that the pharmacist had made no enquiries at all about what the refuse sacks contained and thereby led the public to be exposed to dangerous substances (*Pharm J* 2 February 1991 p. 154). Irresponsible dumping by a pharmacist of waste containing potassium dichromate and other dangerous material caused a fire in the dustcart that attempted disposal (*Pharm J* 9 January 1993 p. 50); more recently, a pharmacist simply left sacks of obsolete medicines in the garden of his old house (*Pharm J* 22 January 2000 p. 129). Persistent failure to dispose of pharmaceutical waste led to a reprimand (*Pharm J* 10 December 2005 p. 729) and failure to comply with health and safety improvement notices concerning unlicensed and insecure storage of pharmaceutical waste led to a striking off for a pharmacist in 2007 (*Pharm J* 9 February 2008 p. 156).

Unsatisfactory conduct

Until the 1990s, cases which could be classified as 'unsatisfactory conduct' would principally be situations where a pharmacist's personal or professional conduct was compromised by alcoholism. Today, transgressions which reflect lack of professional competence or application of proper standards for whatever reason have become more common and they frequently arise from a course of conduct rather than a single event.

The Committee has taken a strong line with pharmacists who have been found incapable of carrying out their duties as a pharmacist through the influence of alcohol and has used its limited powers to introduce measures which approximate to both suspension from the register and the imposition of conditions before readmission. Such matters would now come before the Health and/or Disciplinary Committees, which now have appropriate powers to suspend or make practice subject to conditions (see above).

A wide variety of other forms of unsatisfactory conduct, which generally include failure to adopt safe practices, have come before the Statutory Committee and its successor. Failures in 'good housekeeping' are quite common. 'Chaotic' conditions (*Pharm J* 9 July 2005 p. 67) and 'shambolic' procedures both led to erasures from the register (*Pharm J* 19 April 2008 p. 487); inquiries also followed taking on too much work (*Pharm J*

7 September 2002 p. 344), knowingly dispensing a prescribed overdose (*Pharm J* 20 September 2003 p. 386), putting patients at risk by failing to meet appropriate standards for aseptic manufacture of cytotoxic preparations (*Pharm J* 14 December 2002 p. 870) and dispensing over-prescribed medicines in a poorly managed repeat prescription service (*Pharm J* 22 March 2008 p. 347). An unsafe and untidy monitored dosage system room (*Pharm J* 13 August 2005 p. 206) and a repeat prescription service which was a 'shambles' (*Pharm J* 13 August 2005 p. 205) both led to reprimands.

Pharmacists have been removed from the register for other unsafe practices such as using an open unlocked Controlled Drugs cabinet, the presence of unlabelled pre-packs on the dispensary shelves, the presence of plastic measures containing unidentified tablets recovered from monitored dosage system trays and an intention to re-use tablets of which the pharmacist had no knowledge of either batch number or expiry date (*Pharm J* 8 January 2000 p. 52). A reprimand was given to a pharmacist who removed expiry dates from medicines (*Pharm J* 20 September 2003 p. 387) but such behaviour led to an erasure, in another case, when accompanied by the re-use of patients' returned medicines and deliberate 'popping' of tablets from their original blister packaging (*Pharm J* 22 August 1998 p. 264).

Following three reprimands at earlier hearings, a pharmacist was erased for failure to achieve proper standards, namely failure to produce evidence of professional indemnity insurance cover, trading as a pharmacy when the premises were not registered, re-use of patient returned medicines, sale of restricted medicines in the absence of a pharmacist, lack of personal control, poor physical standards of the premises (such as stock stored in the toilet area, heavily frosted refrigerator and no segregation of waste medicines) and unacceptable practices in relation to handling medicines (such as handling tablets with bare hands and preparing food in a room used for dispensing) (*Pharm J* 27 November 1999 p. 852). Such standards might also include faulty systems for supplies of medicines to a hospice (*Pharm J* 16 June 2001 p. 813), inadequate record keeping and medicines storage (*Pharm J* 23 February 2002 p. 266) or regularly dispensing unsigned prescriptions (*Pharm J* 8 May 2004 p. 590). A reprimand was given to a pharmacist who had claimed for items not dispensed and allowed himself to be duped into giving credit to a bogus doctor (*Pharm J* 10 June 2000 p. 876) and to a pharmacist who kept a stock of blank prescription forms to fill in on behalf of prescribers (*Pharm J* 26 June 1999 p. 914); when this last practice was also linked to deliberate sale of blank forms to drug misusers, the pharmacist's name was erased from the register (*Pharm J* 24 June 2000 p. 947).

Inappropriate behaviour, including rudeness and aggression to patients, resulted in a reprimand (*Pharm J* 7 December 2002 p. 830) although refusal to accept warnings from the Council's Infringements Committee about the handling of a patient's complaint subsequently resulted in no further action

(*Pharm J* 24 April 2004 p. 525). Other 'irregularities' in professional practice which have resulted in Statutory Committee cases have included working full-time for three years while paying a part-time retention fee (*Pharm J* 3/10 January 2004 p. 37), continuing to work as a pharmacist after being struck-off (*Pharm J* 29 November 2003 p. 758) or having not paid the current retention fee (*Pharm J* 21/28 December 2002 p. 891) and a locum 'storming out' of a pharmacy, thus obliging it to be closed for three days (*Pharm J* 3/10 January 2004 p. 37). A pharmacist who dispensed out-of-date medicines and told the patient it was usable was struck off (*Pharm J* 9 September 2006 p. 321). Disparaging remarks about a competitor were a 'grubby and flip evasion of responsibility' warranting a reprimand (*Pharm J* 17 June 2006 p. 735).

Dispensing mistakes

It has been rare for dispensing errors to lead to removal from the register unless there are particularly worrying circumstances. This position has been formalised in the non-referral criteria developed for the work of the Investigating Committee (see above). However, a series of dispensing errors ultimately (after a year's adjournment) resulted in a reprimand for a pharmacist who was dispensing nearly twice the national average of prescriptions without dispensing assistance and in the knowledge that he had impaired eyesight. The chairman commented that Mr X should have backed up his practice with protocols and double-checks so that even if he had blurred vision, mistakes were picked up (*Pharm J* 5 June 1999 p. 804). Later the same year, another pharmacist was reprimanded for making dispensing errors while being grossly overworked (*Pharm J* 21 August 1999 p. 270). Any error which demonstrates lack of competence is likely to result in an inquiry. In 1992, a pharmacist who did not understand the difference between Oramorph Concentrate and Oramorph Solution supplied a medicine which was 10 times as strong as it should have been. The patient survived but the pharmacist was erased from the register (*Pharm J* 6 June 1992 p. 746).

A case in 1998 provided the opportunity for the chairman to give advice on what to do, or rather what not to do, when a dispensing mistake is discovered. A pharmacist discovered that a supply of atenolol had inadvertently been given to the wrong patient but did nothing active to try and remedy the mistake. The chairman did not accept that the pharmacist could simply expect the patient to realise the mistake and return to the pharmacy. In fact it took 28 days before the wrong recipient of the atenolol was identified (*Pharm J* 27 February 1999 p. 288). Listing all the things that could have been done when a mistake is discovered, the chairman said:

> Forget personal dignity and reputation. The patient comes first. If it needs to be disclosed to the whole world that one has made a mistake,

so be it. . .Let the profession know that this particular pharmacist. . .sat on her hands and waited for the tablets to turn up. Pharmacists should not do that; they should get on the rooftop and shout.

Poor handling of errors is likely to increase the seriousness with which such errors are viewed. A pharmacist who denied having made an error and tried to blame it on the patient's GP was roundly criticised but only reprimanded because he intended to cease practice (*Pharm J* 16 April 2005 p. 467). Criticism of the way in which errors are handled features in a number of cases (*Pharm J* 8 April 2006 p. 427; 6 May 2006 p. 548; 26 August 2006 p. 263).

Erasures are more likely if there are some aggravating circumstances pertaining to the pharmacist, such as looking unkempt 'as if he (the pharmacist) had been sleeping rough', talking to himself, failing to answer questions, appearing confused and falling asleep in the dispensary (*Pharm J* 16 June 2001 p. 812). In two further cases, the pharmacists demonstrated failure to respond to a postponed hearing pending a change in employment (*Pharm J* 24 August 2002 p. 264) or to take advice or heed warnings (*Pharm J* 2 November 2002 p. 658). Even where the consequences have been hospitalisation of a child (*Pharm J* 11 August 2001 p. 211) or death of an infant, actions have varied. No action was taken against the preregistration graduate who actually prepared the prescription in the 'Peppermint Water' case (see Chapter 23 p. 337) (*Pharm J* 11 August 2001 p. 212) and the pharmacist who supervised the preparation was reprimanded (*Pharm J* 16 February 2002 p. 228). A 20-fold dosage error in the supply of pergolide to an 80 year old patient led to a reprimand (*Pharm J* 16 September 2006 p. 353) as did the issue of a wart ointment instead of a nasal cream (*Pharm J* 27 November 2004 p. 798). 'Multiple failings', including several dispensing errors, led to a reprimand for a locum pharmacist (*Pharm J* 9 July 2005 p. 66) but a 'string' of dispensing errors (*Pharm J* 9 December 2006 p. 719) and a 'catalogue' of dispensing errors led to erasure for a husband and wife pharmacist team (*Pharm J* 19 May 2007 p. 592).

Responsibility of the superintendent pharmacist

The role of the superintendent pharmacist (see Chapters 5 and 23) has continued to feature in cases before the Statutory Committee. In particular, circumstances may arise where the duty of the superintendent can conflict with proprietors or other senior managers who are not pharmacists. In 1995, the Committee ordered the removal from the register of a superintendent pharmacist whose conduct had appalled the Committee. The non-pharmacist sole director of the company which owned the pharmacy was also arraigned. The Committee heard that the director had insisted that the superintendent pharmacist should only work for four of the eight hours a day that the pharmacy was open and that no other pharmacist had been present at other times. When the Society's inspectors made test purchases to demonstrate the absence of a pharmacist, the superintendent could not return to the unsupervised pharmacy because he was employed on a regular basis at another pharmacy.

Making reference to the Code of Ethics at that time (Guidance to Principle 6, 1992), the superintendent may carry total responsibility if, as a result of his neglect or inactivity, a director is permitted to exercise functions which are the superintendent pharmacist's own responsibility (*Pharm J* 25 February 1995 p. 255). The chairman said:

> [the superintendent pharmacist should have been] obliged to resign. He cannot lend his name to an operation to be carried on in the pharmacy in flagrant defiance of either the law or the ethics of the profession. . .It is the superintendent pharmacist who must insist on things being done as he wishes and as he requires, being informed pharmaceutically as to what is right and proper. . .The employer should not be. . .allowed to do [just] what he wishes. A superintendent pharmacist should be firm and robust with his employer and exercise his own professional integrity and insist. . .that things are done properly.

In a case involving a young female pharmacist, the chairman said she had been unable to stand up to the pressure put on her by a non-pharmacist director who was effectively in day-to-day control of the business. For two or three years, the pharmacy had been run without a pharmacist between 3.00 p.m. and 6.00 p.m. on Saturday afternoons and Ms X ought to have known such a thing was happening because it was 'her job to find out' (*Pharm J* 23 August 1997 p. 283). The chairman set out a very clear summary of the duties of a superintendent:

> A superintendent pharmacist. . .was in charge of seeing that the premises were run in a proper manner – legally, pharmaceutically and ethically. A superintendent pharmacist had to insist on things being done properly even when they may be contrary to the company's interests. Furthermore. . .a superintendent pharmacist had to take responsibility for any acts or omissions by the company or its directors which were within the scope of the superintendent's responsibilities.

Noting that Ms X became superintendent at the age of 23 or 24, the chairman commented that it was 'simply outrageous' for the *Pharmaceutical Journal* to have accepted an advertisement for a superintendent which included the words 'suitable for a newly qualified pharmacist'. Given the responsibilities set out above, the chairman considered that, having entered the role at 'a young age and in a vulnerable frame of mind', the fact that the non-pharmacist director had run the pharmacy since 1981 was pertinent to the case (*Pharm J* 23 August 1997 p. 283). In the accompanying editorial, the Editor did not agree and also questioned the fairness of the judgment in which the name of the pharmacist was erased from the register but the employing company was only reprimanded.

In more recent cases, superintendents have been erased for allowing two pharmacies to operate without a pharmacist in personal control (*Pharm J* 19 August 2000 p. 261; see also Disqualification of a company, below) and reprimanded for failing to notify the Society of their resignation (*Pharm J* 24 March 2001 p. 385), for failing to prevent returned medicines from being re-dispensed (*Pharm J* 24 March 2001 p. 385), failing to prevent excessive sales of codeine linctus (*Pharm J* 9 June 2001 p. 781), failure to ensure that a pharmacist was present at a late-opening pharmacy (*Pharm J* 2 November 2002 p. 660) and for continuing to be a superintendent even when the pharmacist lived in Jordan and was only in Britain every two or three months (*Pharm J* 22 April 2006 p. 488).

An example of the right approach by a superintendent pharmacist, and indeed by a locum pharmacist, can be found in a case reported in 2000 in which a locum went to lunch and returned to find that the director, a former pharmacist struck off three years earlier, had dispensed seven prescriptions in her absence. She immediately closed the premises, contacted the superintendent and took steps to trace all the patients involved. Several dispensing errors had been made by the non-pharmacist director. The superintendent pharmacist contacted the Society, told the non-pharmacist to leave the premises and ordered the locks on the pharmacy to be changed. The chairman congratulated the superintendent for acting in a way that was a model for all superintendent pharmacists (*Pharm J* 24 June 2000 p. 948).

Disqualification of a company

In a rare case, the Statutory Committee disqualified a limited company from owning pharmacy premises 'without limitation of time'. The company's director, a former pharmacist who had been struck off, had run the company's pharmacy business without appointing a superintendent pharmacist or having a pharmacist in charge while medicines were supplied and prescriptions dispensed (*Pharm J* 30 October 2004 p. 663).

`Quackery' or unprofessional claims

Two cases of an unprecedented nature came before the Committee in the late 1990s.

In the first, a five-day inquiry resulted in an unusual order to the superintendent of Signalysis Ltd, a company which provided 'Spagyrik Therapy'. Adjourning the case until later that year, the superintendent was advised that she would be reprimanded if she had resigned from the company by that time; if not, her name would be removed from the register. An order was also made immediately to remove from the register all the premises at which the company conducted a retail pharmacy business. Spagyrik Therapy was said to consist of a treatment of the patient's own body fluids in such a way that they became the remedy for that patient. Such activity was not accepted as a therapy either by the Medicines and Healthcare products Regulatory Agency or the Centre for Complementary Health Studies at the University of Exeter. Conducting such activity from registered pharmacy premises under the supervision of a pharmacist might lead potential customers to believe that the therapy enjoyed some recognition within the profession, which it did not (*Pharm J* 16 August 1997 p. 250).

The following year, a pharmacist who had made misleading and unprofessional claims for products which were not licensed medicines was reprimanded by the Committee. Despite a warning from the Society, the pharmacist had continued to lend her name to advertising material from a company called NutriHealth Ltd, which suggested that certain products could be 'fat eliminators', could reduce mood swings, reduce cholesterol, relieve symptoms of poor bowel function, reduce risk of bowel cancer and many similar medicinal claims. The Committee was impressed by the pharmacist's sincerity but said she had overstepped the mark (*Pharm J* 24 October 1998 p. 663):

> This profession has won the reputation that if it says something then it really is true…and these claims from a pharmacist are likely to be believed totally…We should be very careful when we appeal to the public's greed and vanity…

Supervision

At the time of writing, proposals to modify the interpretation of supervision (see Chapter 6) by amending section 52 of the Medicines Act were under discussion alongside changes to the requirement for a pharmacist to be in 'personal control' of a pharmacy (see Chapter 5). The cases below illustrate the attitude of the former Statutory Committee to supervision but this is likely to be reinterpreted in any future cases before the Disciplinary Committee or its successors.

In a case of unsupervised sales (*Pharm J* 30 August 1997 p. 322), the chairman stated that:

> …to be on the shop floor looking after the public was essential to the pharmacist's role.

In the following year, the Committee removed a pharmacist from the register for attempting to supervise by telephone from 19 miles away (*Pharm J* 2 May 1998 p. 625).

Permanent or temporary absence is equally culpable. Late arrival in the pharmacy on three occasions led to pharmacist being reprimanded (*Pharm J* 22 January 2000 p. 128). A locum pharmacist who failed to fulfil his engagement (*Pharm J* 25 May 1985 p. 662) was reprimanded in the following terms:

> We can point out that the sale of these medicines without any supervision by a pharmacist is a matter that is not only serious, but the cause of great possible and potential danger to the public.

Failure on the part of a pharmacist proprietor, about to holiday in New Zealand, to act when he knew that a locum had cancelled a booking led to the unsupervised dispensing of over 200 prescriptions and an unknown number of unsupervised sales before the inspector intervened. The pharmacist was removed from the register (*Pharm J* 1 February 1997 p. 166). Erasure in a very similar case followed failure to arrange adequate locum cover when the proprietor was on holiday in India (*Pharm J* 3 June 2000 p. 840).

Inquiries have resulted from attempts to run two pharmacies with only one pharmacist, to do without the services of a pharmacist at quiet times like Saturday afternoons (*Pharm J* 26 June 1999 p. 915), Sundays (see below) or Bank Holidays (*Pharm J* 18 February 1995 p. 221) or to leave businesses in the charge of a range of unqualified persons. In a case in 1990 (*Pharm J* 18 August 1990 p. 220), a pharmacist had paid a visit to his 'other shop' following which the chairman commented:

> ...The fact that dispensing is left to the hands of experienced staff we will not receive as mitigation. Such staff should never be regarded as a substitute for what the Act requires.

Later the same year, a pharmacy had had no regular pharmacist for seven months and sales of Pharmacy Medicines were in the hands of a 15-year-old girl (*Pharm J* 29 September 1990 p. 436). The company owning both pharmacies was disqualified following the chairman's general statement:

> The signal we send out to the profession is, 'if you cannot get proper cover then the pharmacy has to be closed'...There are no half measures.

In two cases in 1991, the chairman was even more forceful. In the first (*Pharm J* 19 January 1991 p. 89), he commented:

> Parliament does not offer a choice, such as 'I would like to run this pharmacy without proper cover, because it helps those around and in

the district'. There is no alternative – the pharmacy has to close and that is the end of the matter.

And, following an attempt to operate a partial service on a Sunday (*Pharm J* 27 July 1991 p. 136), he commented

> ...a point arose as to whether or not the shop was open...A sale can take place whether the premises are open or not...it is the opinion of the Committee that the shop was willing to take casual trade...and customers would be dealt with...as and when they came in.

The reasons for the Committee's position are clear, as stated in a case in 1991 (*Pharm J* 17 August 1991 p. 224):

> ...medicines can be ill-used, ill-advisedly, by members of the public when they are uninstructed by a pharmacist...Sales have to be under the supervision of a pharmacist, not for any fanciful notion, but because the law requires it for the safety of the public.

The chairman went on to say that the subject of supervision should be routinely discussed from time to time with such individuals to ensure the meaning of the prohibition on their activities was brought home and fully understood.

To the above list should be added the dispensing assistant (*Pharm J* 3 May 1997 p. 622) and the preregistration graduate, who does not assume the privileges or responsibilities of a pharmacist either in the sale of Pharmacy Medicines (*Pharm J* 8 October 1994 p. 496) or in dispensing (*Pharm J* 17 May 1997 p. 697) until registration. In the last case, the chairman said:

> It is very important indeed to make sure that those persons you leave behind know precisely what they can do and what they cannot do...ultimately the pharmacist is there to serve the public safely. The pharmacist should not put the public at risk for the sake of his own private profit.

A pharmacist who allowed a dispenser to dispense Prescription Only Medicines when no pharmacist was present (and failed to have indemnity cover) was struck off (*Pharm J* 3 September 2005 p. 295) and a second pharmacist who had permitted the sale of Pharmacy Medicines in similar circumstances was reprimanded by the Disciplinary Committee (*Pharm J* 28 June 2008 p. 784).

Cases before the Committee almost exclusively reflect situations where the pharmacist was simply not present, rather than any failure to ensure supervisory procedures were carried out.

Personal control of a pharmacy

The Medicines Act 1968 (s.71) requires that in each set of pharmacy premises the business must, in relation to the retail sale of drugs, be under the personal control of a pharmacist. The requirement that medicinal products not on the General Sale List must be supervised by the pharmacist is an additional provision. The more general requirement of personal control by the pharmacist extends to all medicinal products, including those on the General Sale List.

At the time of writing, regulations had been made (The Medicines (Pharmacies) (Responsible Pharmacist) Regulations 2008 SI No. 2789) to replace the term 'personal control' with the concept of a 'responsible pharmacist'. Although the regulations are not scheduled to come into force until October 2009, there have been no cases concerning personal control of a pharmacy since 2004 when the chairman provided a liberal interpretation of the meaning of 'personal control' (*Pharm J* 7 August 2004 p. 203), which is essentially reflected in the forthcoming changes to the law.

Appeals against decisions

To keep this chapter current and of a manageable size, we have summarised the appeals resulting from the Statutory Committee's deliberations in Table 24.1. Full details of the early appeals and the judicial reviews appear in earlier editions of this work.

Table 24.1 Appeals and judicial reviews of Statutory Committee decisions		
Case	*Details*	*Result*
Appeals		
Re Lawson (*Pharm J* 22 February 1941 p. 40)	Advertisements of products for sexual weakness	Appeal lost
Re Sims (*Pharm J* 3 February 1962 p. 89)	Unlawful sale of Dexedrine	Appeal lost
Re Levy and Pharmaceutics (M/C) Ltd (*Pharm J* 25 May 1968 p. 615)	Unsupervised sale of poisons	Appeal lost
Re Eyre (*Pharm J* 24 July 1976 p. 69)	Forging of NHS prescriptions	Appeal lost
Re Fletcher and Lucas (*Pharm J* July 1978 p. 93)	Excessive sales of amyl nitrite	Appeal won
Re Harari (*Pharm J* 1 May 1982 p. 509)	Assault, motoring convictions and intimidation of tenants	Appeal lost

Table 24.1 *(continued)*

Re Whitechurch (1998) 41 BLMR 46 QB	Failure to maintain professional indemnity insurance	Appeal lost
Re Korsner (*Pharm J* 30 January 1999 p. 147; 27 February 1999 p. 277)	Irregular arrangements for private patients to receive medicines on the NHS	Appeal lost
Re Zygmunt (Chemists) Ltd (*Pharm J* 4 April 1966 p. 324)	Conviction/Pharmacy and Poison Act 1933	Appeal won
Re Robinson (*Pharm J* 19 April 1975 p. 19)	Conviction/Misuse of Drugs Act 1971	Appeal lost
Re Jobson (*Pharm J* 22 November 1980 p. 589)	Conviction/Misuse of Drugs Act 1971	Appeal lost
Re Rajabali (*Pharm J* 7 February 1981 p. 136)	Misconduct/excessive sale of drugs liable to misuse	Appeal lost
Re Kuperberg (*Pharm J* 29 January 1983 p. 97)	Misconduct/excessive sale of drugs liable to misuse	Appeal lost
Re Riley (*Pharm J* 2 March 1985 p. 282)	Conviction/Theft Act 1968	Appeal won
Re Tenbrook Ltd (*Pharm J* 13 July 1985 p. 61)	Conviction/Medicines Act 1968	Appeal lost
Re Leach (unreported, July 1985)	Conviction/Misuse of Drugs Act 1971	Appeal lost
Re Patel (unreported, January 1986)	Conviction/Medicines Act 1968	Appeal lost
Re Sowood (*Pharm J* 6 December 1986 p. 754)	Conviction/Medicines Act 1968	Appeal lost
Re Smith (*Pharm J* 3 January 1987 p. 17)	Misconduct/under influence of drink	Appeal lost
Re Singh (*Pharm J* 28 March 1987 p. 416)	Convictions/Misuse of Drugs Act 1971 and others	Appeal lost
Re Parkin (*Pharm J* 2 April 1988 p. 451)	Misconduct/unsatisfactory pharmacy premises	Appeal lost
Re Shah (*Pharm J* 7 May 1988 p. 607)	Conviction/Theft Act 1968	Appeal won
Re Sabir (*Pharm J* 19 November 1988 p. 665)	Conviction/Misuse of Drugs Act 1971	Appeal lost
Re Thobani (*Pharm J* 3 February 1990 p. 122)	Offences/Theft Act 1968	Appeal lost
Re Kansal (*Pharm J* 27 July 1996 p. 111)	Offences of dishonesty	Appeal lost
Re Mistry (unreported)	Forged certificate of professional indemnity	Appeal lost

(continued overleaf)

Table 24.1 *(continued)*

Re Kuforiji (*Pharm J* 26 January 2002 p. 833-4)	Controlled Drugs offences	Appeal lost
Re Chanins (*Pharm J* 28 May 2005 p. 636)	Offensive, abusive and threatening behaviour	Appeal lost
Re AS Black and Formans (Chemists) Ltd (*Pharm J* 17 December 2005 p. 735)	Erroneous claims for prescription payment	Appeal lost but Society's procedures criticised
Re M K Shah (unreported June 2006)	Not stated in Fitness to Practise Annual Report	Not known
Re Adekaiyaoja (*Pharm J* 11 November 2006 p. 590)	Dispensing errors and incompetent practice	Not known
Judicial reviews of finding of misconduct from former Statutory Committee (not appealable)		
Re Lewis and Jeffries (*Pharm J* 1/8 January 1983 p. 13)	Advertising – found no evidence that the defence case was incorrect	Reprimands quashed
Re Sokoh (*Pharm J* 13 December 1986 p. 797)	A single dispensing error – can be misconduct	Reprimand upheld
Re Boots The Chemists (*Pharm J* 14 February 1997 p. 257	Re a collection and delivery service – found was not justified on the evidence	Reprimand quashed

Summary

- The Society's fitness to practise powers were established in the Pharmacists and Pharmacy Technicians Order 2007 (P&PT Order 2007).
- During 2009–2010, the Society's fitness to practise powers will be transferred to the General Pharmaceutical Council (GPhC) (subject to Parliamentary approval).
- At that time, registered pharmacy technicians are expected to be subject to regulation by the GPhC.
- The P&PT Order 2007 gives statutory force to the current Code of Ethics and its supporting standards and guidance.
- The P&PT Order 2007 established three Fitness to Practise Committees: the Investigating Committee, the Health Committee and the Disciplinary Committee.
- Details of the appointment, constitution, powers and procedures of these committees are laid down in Rules made under the Order.
- The Health and Disciplinary Committees may issue interim orders for immediate suspension from the register or for conditional practice.
- The Health Committee may issue warnings, impose conditions on practice or suspend registration.

- The Disciplinary Committee may issue warnings, impose conditions, suspend registration or remove a pharmacist's name from the register and may consider the fitness to practise of persons applying for admission or restoration to the register.
- The Disciplinary Committee may consider convictions against pharmacists and others in pharmacy businesses where they relate to offences under the Medicines and Misuse of Drugs Acts. For a company, the Committee may disqualify it from conducting retail pharmacies or remove any or all of their premises from the register.
- The jurisdiction of the committees extends to offences committed outside the UK and is not subject to any time limits.
- Examples of cases have been given for the former Statutory Committee and the Disciplinary Committee.
- A summary of judicial reviews and appeals from the decisions of the former Statutory Committee is provided in Table 24.1.

Further reading

Harris W (2008) First annual fitness-to-practise report. *Pharm J* 281: 278.

John DN, Angell RN, Genner S, Hussain MZ (1999) A descriptive study of reasons for appearing before, and outcomes, of Statutory Committee hearings (1990 to 1998). *Pharm J* 263: R48.

John DN, Holton JE (2004) Statutory Committee inquiries of pharmacists involving controlled drugs. *Int J Pharm Pract* 12: R60.

Rodgers RM, John DN (2005) To strike-off or not to strike-off; a descriptive study of ethics infringement cases. *Int J Pharm Pract* 13: R77.

Soothill K, Sharp D (2000) Discipline and punishment: reflections on the disciplinary procedures of the Royal Pharmaceutical Society. *Pharm J* 264: 266–267.

Websites

Council for Healthcare Regulatory Excellence: www.chre.org.uk
The Royal Pharmaceutical Society of Great Britain: www.rpsgb.org.uk

25

Organisation of other health professions

Medical scandals and convergence of regulation

During the 1990s and into the first years of the 21st century, a series of scandals, mostly involving doctors, led to a radical overhaul of the regulation of all health professions, including pharmacy. Space does not permit a full account here but the following overview is well supported by website resources covering the detailed inquiries that followed the scandals. The first of these inquiries with the greatest impact, in 2001, was the Kennedy Inquiry or to give it the full name: The Inquiry into the Management of Care of Children Receiving Complex Heart Surgery at the Bristol Royal Infirmary. As the title suggests, this inquiry investigated a flawed system at an NHS hospital, which 'led to around one-third of all the children who underwent open-heart surgery receiving less than adequate care. More children died than might have been expected in a typical (comparative) unit'. The inquiry criticised in particular the presence of a 'club culture' and the absence of any agreed means of assessing the quality of care, of standards for evaluating performance or of clarity as to who in the NHS was responsible for monitoring the quality of care This last finding led to the development of clinical governance (see p. 335) within the NHS and then in private healthcare. A second inquiry, at Alder Hey Hospital in Liverpool, set out to inquire into the removal, retention and disposal of human tissue and organs following coroners' and hospital postmortem examinations and the extent to which the Human Tissue Act 1961 had been complied with. In this inquiry, it was found that the doctors and staff at Alder Hey had failed to provide suitable advice, counselling and support necessary to affected families and showed a lamentable grasp of the modern concepts of consent and involvement of patients, parents and relatives in medical care.

To some extent, the above two inquiries pale into insignificance beside a third, the Shipman inquiry, at least in relation to the number of deaths caused. Dr Harold Shipman, by all accounts a benign, caring general practitioner with a single-handed practice in Hyde, a small town in a pleasant part of north-west

England, was eventually proven to have murdered at least 200 of his patients and more were suspected. When he was eventually imprisoned for life after nearly 30 years of practice, he hanged himself, thus taking any further information about numbers or his motives to his grave. One of the key outcomes of the Shipman Inquiry was a series of recommendations to modify the legislation regarding Controlled Drugs to limit the likelihood of such unnoticed diversion occurring again. A further series of inquiries were published into the conduct of Clifford Ayling, Richard Neale and jointly William Kerr and Michael Haslam. These revealed both appalling flaws in the professional behaviour of a few doctors and the failure of those in positions of authority or the regulator (the General Medical Council [GMC]) to detect signs of this behaviour and to take timely and effective action to protect patients from it.

The Council for Healthcare Regulatory Excellence

Largely as a result of political concern about the unsatisfactory nature of self-regulation of doctors, the government established the Council for the Regulation of Health Care Professionals under the National Health Service and Health Care Professions Act 2002. Under the Health Act 2008, this Council was officially renamed the Council for Healthcare Regulatory Excellence (CHRE). CHRE is charged with promoting the interests of patients and other members of the public in relation to the performance by the regulatory bodies of health professionals including the medical, dental, nursing, optical, chiropractic and osteopathic councils plus the Royal Pharmaceutical Society of Great Britain (RPSGB) and the Pharmaceutical Society of Northern Ireland. In essence, its role is to review and scrutinise the regulatory systems of all the health professions to set up and drive up standards and foster harmonisation of regulatory practice and outcomes. The Council may investigate, and report on the performance, of each regulatory body in its functions, and recommend to such a body changes to the way in which it performs its functions. It may refer to the High Court those bodies whose disciplinary committees appear to be too lenient in dealing with the public's complaints against health professionals.

In 2004, CHRE agreed procedures under section 27 of the 2002 Act to oblige professional regulators to change or make new rules; noted a need for cross-notification between regulators when a practitioner is removed from a professional register and suggested that greater control may be needed to manage the rise of corporate ownership within pharmacy. CHRE publishes annual reports of its activities, in particular performance reviews 'learnings' from fitness to practise cases from all the health professions. In 2008, CHRE published a report highlighting variations between regulation in the individual health professions, including several notified from the RPSGB's Statutory or Disciplinary Committees (see Chapter 24).

Legislation underpinning healthcare regulation

In June 1999, the Government enacted the Health Act 1999, which provided powers to change by order the regulation of health professions and health professionals. Many changes have since been made to the statutory regulations applying to the medical, dental, nursing and midwifery professions, together with changes regulating the smaller healthcare professions. The Health and Social Care Act 2008 builds on the powers in the 1999 Act to enable the establishment of the General Pharmaceutical Council (GPhC).

At the time of going to press a new Pharmacy Order 2009 was under consultation. Its effects are listed at the beginning of Chapter 22.

The 2008 Act also established the Office of the Health Professions Adjudicator, which will take over the adjudication function of the GMC and the General Optical Council (see below). In due course, it is expected that the adjudication function for all health professions will fall under the remit of a single adjudicator.

Various classes of professional person are mentioned in the statutes relating to poisons, medicinal products and Controlled Drugs. Pharmacists are principally concerned with supplies made to, or to the order of, medical practitioners, veterinary surgeons, dentists and nurse prescribers, and some knowledge of the statutory registration requirements of these and other related professions is desirable.

The medical profession

The Acts at present regulating the medical profession are the Medical Act 1983 as amended by Order (SI 2002 No. 3135) and the Medical (Professional Performance) Act 1995.

The General Medical Council

The GMC, which is the sole registering authority in the UK, was established by the Medical Act 1858. Its main objective is to protect, promote and maintain the health and safety of the public. The GMC shall consist of no more than 35 members. At present there are 19 elected members from the profession, two appointed members (one from the universities and one from the medical colleges) and 14 nominated (lay) members, the number of elected members exceeding the number of appointed and nominated members (SI 2002 No. 3136). The quorum is 25.

The nominated or lay members, the majority of whom must be without any registerable medical qualification, are nominated by the Privy Council. The electoral scheme for elected members is made by the GMC with the approval of the Privy Council.

The Act provides for four constituencies:

1   England, the Channel Islands, and the Isle of Man;
2   Wales;
3   Scotland; and
4   Northern Ireland.

There is provision for any of the constituencies to be divided into two or more separate constituencies. The persons qualified to elect members for any constituency are those resident in the constituency for which the election is held and who are registered medical practitioners. The universities and other bodies which appoint members to the GMC are designated in an Order in Council. Persons who are fully registered, provisionally registered or registered with limited registration are eligible for election (subject to certain restrictions for those with limited registration). The term of office for a member is four years. The GMC has power to regulate medical education and to provide advice for members of the medical profession on standards of professional conduct or on medical ethics.

The GMC must establish and maintain a system for the declaration and registration of the private interests of its members and must publish such interests in a register.

The GMC must have the following committees (SI 2002 No. 3135):

1   the Education Committee;
2   one or more Interim Orders Panels;
3   one or more Registration Decisions Panels;
4   one or more Registration Appeals Panels;
5   the Investigation Committee; and
6   one or more Fitness to Practise Panels.

The register and registration

The registrar of the GMC is appointed under Schedule 1 to the 1983 Act but the procedures for registration and the maintenance of the registers are dealt with in Part IV of the Act and the regulations made thereunder. There are two registers: the Register of Medical Practitioners and the Register of Medical Practitioners with Limited Registration. The former includes the names of those doctors who are fully registered, that is, those with UK qualifications and those doctors who hold primary European qualifications and who are nationals of an EEA member state.

Where a person satisfies the registrar that s/he holds an acceptable overseas qualification other than a primary European one and that s/he is an eligible specialist, of good character and knowledge of English, the registrar may direct that s/he be registered as a fully registered medical practitioner (s.21A).

The registrar must publish the Register of Medical Practitioners and the Register of Medical Practitioners with Limited Registration (s.34) (SI 2002 No. 2135). The register must contain each practitioner's qualifications, whether he has a licence to practise and other such directions as the Council may direct. Practitioners must pay registration fees and annual retention fees.

Appeals are provided for persons whom the registrar has decided shall not be registered as a fully registered medical practitioner. The person concerned may appeal to the Registration Appeals Panel (see below) (Schedule 3A). A further appeal is possible against a decision of the Registration Appeals Panel to a county court or in Scotland to the sheriff. Costs may be awarded.

Any reference (however expressed) to a person registered under the Medical Act or as a medical practitioner means a fully registered person registered under the 1983 Act. A prescription for a Controlled Drug or a Prescription Only Medicine may lawfully be dispensed even though the prescriber's name is in the Overseas List.

Section 60 of the Medicines Act 1968 provides that specified medicinal products may be prescribed only by a practitioner who holds a certificate issued for that purpose from the appropriate Minister (Chapter 9) and a licence from the Secretary of State is required in respect of certain Controlled Drugs (Chapter 17). Apart from these restrictions, there is no limitation on the prescribing of a fully registered practitioner, unless s/he is the subject of a direction by the Secretary of State under the Misuse of Drugs Act 1971 in respect of named Controlled Drugs (Chapter 17).

Only fully registered persons may hold certain appointments as physicians, surgeons or other medical officers (e.g. in the naval, military or air services or in the prison service), or recover in any court of law any charge made for medical or surgical advice or attendance. A certificate required by law to be from a physician, surgeon, licentiate in medicine and surgery, or other medical practitioner is not valid unless the person signing it is fully registered.

Any person who wilfully and falsely pretends to be or takes or uses the name or title of physician, doctor of medicine, licentiate in medicine and surgery, bachelor of medicine, surgeon, general practitioner (GP) or apothecary, or any name, title, addition or description implying that s/he is registered under any provision of the 1983 Act, or that s/he is recognised by law as such, commits an offence (s.49). Nothing in the Act prejudices or in any way affects the lawful occupation, trade or business of chemists and druggists, or of dentists, so far as they extend to selling, compounding and dispensing of medicines (s.54).

List of Visiting European Economic Community practitioners

An applicant can also be registered as a visiting EEC practitioner, although s/he may render medical services temporarily without first being registered.

The registrar is required to enter the names of such practitioners on a list of visiting EEC practitioners, which forms part of the Register of Medical Practitioners (s.18). Visiting EEC practitioners will be issued with certificates of registration by the GMC.

Pharmacists may lawfully supply Prescription Only Medicines and Controlled Drugs (Chapter 17) against a prescription issued by a visiting practitioner only if that practitioner is in fact registered in the UK in accordance with the Act.

Provisional registration

A person who holds a qualification which entitles him/her to be registered but has not completed the requirements as to experience is entitled to be provisionally registered. While s/he is completing these requirements, s/he is deemed to be fully registered so far as is necessary to enable him/her to be engaged in employment in a resident medical capacity in one or more approved hospitals or institutions, but not further (s.15).

The effect is that s/he may issue prescriptions for Controlled Drugs or for Prescription Only Medicines only if required to do so as part of his/her duties in that resident medical post. S/he may not order or prescribe such drugs or medicinal products in any other circumstances (e.g. for his/her own use or for the use of his/her own private patients).

Limited registration

There is also provision in the Act (ss.22–25) for the limited registration of practitioners having acceptable overseas qualifications (i.e. qualifications granted outside the UK) which are accepted by the GMC as furnishing a sufficient guarantee of possession of the knowledge and skill required for the practise of medicine under the supervision of a fully registered medical practitioner. An applicant for limited registration must, in addition to holding an acceptable overseas qualification:

1 satisfy the registrar that s/he has been selected for employment in the British Isles as a medical practitioner in one or more approved hospitals or institutions;
2 that s/he has the necessary knowledge of English;
3 that s/he is of good character; and
4 that s/he has the knowledge and skill and has acquired the experience which is necessary for practise as a medical practitioner appropriate in his/her case.

A direction for limited registration is for a specified period only; the total aggregate period in which limited registration is permitted is five years, except for doctors who have held temporary registration. In relation to employment covered by his/her limited registration and to things done or omitted to be done in the course of it, and to any other thing incidental to his/her work in that employment which may not lawfully or validly be done except by a fully registered person, a doctor holding limited registration is treated as being fully registered, but not otherwise (s.22).

S/he may, therefore, only issue prescriptions for Controlled Drugs and Prescription Only Medicines in connection with employment to which his/her limited registration relates. The names of practitioners with limited registration are not included in any published register. Any enquiries about such practitioners should be made to The Registrar, General Medical Council, 24 Gosfield Street, London W1P 8BP.

Voluntary erasure from the register

Provisions have been made for a doctor to request that his/her name be removed from, and following voluntary erasure subsequently restored to, the register. The registrar shall remove the name unless he is aware that any proceedings are pending or have been started against the doctor (SI 2003 No. 1341).

Licence to practise

The GMC has to make regulations with respect to the grant, refusal to grant and the withdrawal of a licence to practise by a licensing authority and for the revalidation of medical practitioners' continuation to remain registered. There is an appeals procedure to the Registration Appeals Panel and subsequently to the county court or, in Scotland, the sheriff.

The licensing authority means the registrar, the Registration Decisions Panel or such other committee the Council may prescribe.

Revalidation means evaluation of a medical practitioner's fitness to practise. In July 2008, a working party on Medical Revalidation – Principles and Next Steps suggests that revalidation should include patient and carer participation, be focused on raising standards rather than be a further disciplinary mechanism, include remediation and rehabilitation, be a continuing process and be introduced incrementally through piloting to ensure that it works well. These principles are likely to be applied to the revalidation of all health professionals in the future.

If a person who does not have a licence to practise holds himself/herself out as having such a licence or engages in any conduct calculated to suggest s/he has such a licence then s/he is liable on summary conviction to a fine.

The Education Committee

The composition of the Education Committee shall be such as the GMC may think fit. The Committee has to determine the extent of the knowledge and skill required for the granting of primary UK medical qualifications and secure that the instruction in universities is sufficient to equip students with such skill and knowledge. It has to determine and maintain the standard of proficiency required from students and determine patterns of experience which may be recognised as suitable for giving to those engaged in the practical training of students.

Professional conduct and fitness to practise

The functions of the GMC in respect of professional conduct and fitness to practise are performed by the following committees:

1   an Investigation Committee;
2   one or more Fitness to Practise Panels; and
3   an Interim Orders Panel.

These committees are constituted as provided by the GMC by rules made under the Medical Act 1983 (Amendment) Order 2002 No. 3135.

The Council has the power to provide advice for members of the medical profession on matters of standards of professional conduct, standards of professional performance and medical ethics. The GMC makes rules for each of these committees with respect to referral of complaints to these panels and for the procedure and evidence to be followed before the committee or the panels (Schedule 4 of SI No. 3135).

In May 2004, the GMC published a document on changes it has made to its procedures when dealing with complaints. This is available on the GMC website (see Further reading).

The Investigation Committee

Where an allegation is made against a registered medical practitioner to the effect that his/her fitness to practise is impaired, then the Investigation Committee shall investigate the allegation and decide whether or not the matter should be considered by a Fitness to Practise Panel.

A person's fitness to practise is regarded as 'impaired' by reason only of:

* misconduct;
* deficient professional performance;
* a conviction or caution in the British Isles for a criminal offence or a conviction elsewhere for an offence which, if committed in England and Wales, would constitute a criminal offence;
* adverse physical or mental health; or
* a determination by a body in the UK responsible for the regulation of a health or social care profession to the effect that his/her fitness to practise as a member of that profession is impaired.

The Investigation Committee may:

1 refer the matter to a Fitness to Practise Panel for its consideration;
2 refer the matter to a Fitness to Practise Panel or an Interim Orders Panel for their consideration to issue an order for interim suspension or interim conditional registration;
3 decide that an allegation ought not to be considered under 1 or 2 but to issue a warning letter itself; or
4 decide that an allegation ought not to be considered under 1 or 2 but to take no further notice.

In any of the circumstances above, the Registrar is informed and s/he, in turn, serves notification of the facts on the person who is subject to the allegation.

Rules made under Schedule 4 of the Act may make provision for the Registrar or any other officer of the Council to exercise the functions of the Investigation Committee either generally or in relation to such cases as may be specified in the rules.

Fitness to Practise Panel

Where any registered person's fitness to practise is found to be impaired by a Fitness to Practise Panel, the panel may:

1 except in a health case, direct that the person's name shall be erased from the register;
2 direct that his/her registration shall be suspended during a period not exceeding 12 months, as may be specified in the direction; or
3 direct that his/her registration shall be conditional on his/her compliance, during a period not exceeding three years as may be specified in the direction, with such requirements so specified as the Panel thinks fit to impose for the protection of the public or in his/her interest.

Where the Fitness to Practise Panel finds the person's fitness to practise is not impaired, it may nevertheless give him/her a warning letter regarding his/her future conduct or performance. During a period of suspension, the suspension can be extended or converted to an erasure.

In a health case, a Fitness to Practise Panel may extend a suspension indefinitely where the initial period of suspension has lasted two years. In these cases, there are provisions for review either after two years has elapsed or at the person's request. After review, a Fitness to Practise Panel may confirm its direction or direct that the suspension be terminated.

All directions are appealable within 28 days of the direction being given; appeals are to the relevant court.

The relevant court means the Court of Session in Scotland, the High Court of Justice in Northern Ireland in Northern Ireland and, in any other case, the High Court of Justice in England and Wales.

When a name has been erased from the register, a Fitness to Practise Panel may, if it thinks fit, direct that his/her name be restored but no application for restoration may be made before the expiration of five years from the date of erasure.

The Interim Orders Panel

The Interim Orders Panel was established under the Medical Act 1983 (Amendment) Order 2002 (SI 2002 No. 3135). Where the Interim Orders Panel or a Fitness to Practise Panel is satisfied that it is necessary for the protection of the public, or in the interests of the doctor, for registration of the doctor to be suspended, or made subject to conditions, the Panel may make an order suspending registration for up to 18 months or one that registration may continue conditional on compliance during a period not exceeding 18 months, with such requirements as the Panel think fit.

The Interim Orders Panel must review the order within six months of the order being made and every three months subsequently as long as the order remains in force or where new evidence becomes available.

The Interim Orders Panel may revoke the order or any condition, or vary any condition, if it is satisfied that to do so is necessary for the protection of, or in the interest of, the public or the doctor and can replace it with an interim suspension order for the remainder of the term. The Council may apply to the courts for any order to be extended and the courts may further extend an order for up to 12 months.

Disclosure of information

Regulations give power to persons authorised by the Council to require disclosure of information that would assist them in carrying out their functions in respect to fitness to practise and professional conduct.

In addition, the Council is obliged to notify specified persons when formal proceedings are initiated against a doctor in respect of his/her fitness to practise or professional conduct where they consider it in the public interest so to do. Those specified persons include the Secretary of State, Scottish Ministers, the National Assembly of Wales and any person in the UK who the Council is aware that the doctor concerned is employed by in any area of medicine (SI 2002 No. 3135).

The veterinary profession

Under a proposed major agricultural plan, the Veterinary Medicines Directorate is to undertake a review of the provisions of the Veterinary

Surgeons Act 1966. A consultation paper has been produced. No further details were available at the time of going to press.

The Council of the Royal College of Veterinary Surgeons

The Veterinary Surgeons Act 1966 is the principal statute dealing with the management of the veterinary profession in relation to registration, education and professional conduct. The Council of the Royal College of Veterinary Surgeons, the controlling body, includes 24 persons elected by the members, four appointed by the Privy Council and two appointed by each university in the UK that grants a veterinary degree recognised by the Privy Council. Degrees of Irish universities are also recognised by the Privy Council.

Veterinary surgery means the art and science of veterinary surgery and medicine and includes the diagnosis of diseases in, and injuries to, animals, including tests performed on animals for diagnostic purposes; the giving of advice based upon such diagnosis; the medical or surgical treatment of animals; and the performance of surgical operations on animals (s.27).

The Register of Veterinary Surgeons

The registrar of the college, who is appointed by the Council of the Royal College, maintains the register. It is published as often as the Council thinks fit, but in any year in which a full register is not produced, alterations to it must be published instead (s.9). It comprises four lists (s.2).

1   The *General List* of persons entitled to be registered as graduates in veterinary surgery of universities recognised by the Privy Council (s.3) or as students of other universities who have passed the examinations held by the Royal College of Veterinary Surgeons (s.4) or persons from the EU who hold recognised European qualifications (s.5a).
2   The *Commonwealth List* of persons entitled to be registered as holding some Commonwealth qualification (s.6).
3   The *Foreign List* of persons entitled to be registered as holding some foreign qualification (s.6).
4   The *Temporary List* of persons registered to practise veterinary surgery temporarily, subject to such restrictions as to place and circumstances as the Council of the Royal College may specify (e.g. persons who have passed the examinations for a degree but have not yet formally graduated, or the holders of Commonwealth or foreign qualifications not otherwise registerable). It is not lawful for a temporarily registered person to practise except in accordance with the restrictions specified in the Council's direction.

The details required for registration, and the powers to register and de-register members is set out in the Veterinary Surgeons and Veterinary Practitioners (Registration) Regulations Order of Council 2003 No. 3342.

An applicant for registration on lists 2 and 3 must satisfy the Council that s/he has the requisite knowledge and skill to practise veterinary surgery in the UK.

In addition to these lists, there is the Supplementary Register (first established under the Veterinary Surgeons Act 1948) of persons known as veterinary practitioners. The 1948 Act restricted the practice of veterinary surgery by unqualified persons as from 30 July 1949. Those persons whose principal means of livelihood, for seven out of ten years before that date, had been the diagnosing of diseases of animals were included in the Supplementary Register. Certain licensed employees of societies and institutions providing free treatment for animals were also transferred to the Supplementary Register under the 1966 Act but are subject to such restrictions as the Council of the Royal College may impose.

Professional discipline

Names may be removed from the register for crimes or 'disgraceful conduct in any professional respect'. There is a Preliminary Investigation Committee and a Disciplinary Committee. The disciplinary procedure is similar to that of the medical profession and there is provision for suspension of registration as well as complete removal from the register (ss.15 and 17). Appeals against a direction are made to the Privy Council.

Restrictions on practice and use of titles

No one may practise, or hold themselves out as practising, or being prepared to practise, veterinary surgery unless they are registered as a veterinary surgeon or are in the supplementary register as a veterinary practitioner (s.19). It is an offence for an unregistered person to use the titles 'veterinary surgeon' or 'veterinary practitioner' or any name, title, addition or description implying that s/he is qualified to practise veterinary surgery (s.20).

The Act provides some limited exceptions for students of veterinary surgery, for medical practitioners and dentists in certain circumstances, and for the carrying out of minor treatment in terms of exemption orders made under the Act. Examples include orders allowing treatment by physiotherapists at veterinarians' request, blood sampling for the brucellosis eradication scheme, vaccinations of poultry against certain diseases and the use of epidural anaesthesia (SIs 1973 No. 308; 1982 No. 1267; 1983 No. 6, as amended; 1990 No. 2217).

Exemption is also provided in Schedule 3 to the Act, as amended by SI 1988 No. 526, for the following treatments and operations to be given or carried out by unqualified persons:

1   Any minor medical treatment given to an animal by its owner, by another member of a household of which the owner is a member, or by a person in the employment of the owner.

2   Anything given, otherwise than for the reward, to an animal used in agriculture, as defined in the Agriculture Act 1947, by the owner of the animal or by a person engaged or employed in caring for animals so used.

3   The rendering in an emergency of first-aid for the purpose of saving life or relieving pain.

4   The performance by any person aged 18 or more of any of the following operations:

   a   castration of a male animal or caponising of an animal, whether by chemical means or otherwise (except the castration of a horse, pony, ass or mule; of a bull, boar or goat which has reached the age of two months; or of a ram which has reached the age of three months; the spaying of a cat or dog);
   b   the docking of the tail of a lamb;
   c   the amputation of the dew claws of a dog before its eyes are open; or
   d   the disbudding of a calf subject to certain conditions.

5   Any medical treatment or minor surgery (not involving entry into the body cavity) to a companion animal by a veterinary nurse provided the animal is under the care of a veterinary surgeon, the treatment is carried out under his/her direction and the veterinary surgeon is the employer, or acting on behalf of the employer, of the nurse (SI 1991 No. 1412).

6   Any medical treatment or any minor surgery (not involving entry into the body cavity) to any animal by a veterinary nurse if the following conditions are complied with:

   a   the animal is for the time being under the care of a veterinarian and any treatment or minor surgery is carried out under his direction;
   b   the veterinarian is the employer or acting on behalf of the employer of the veterinary nurse; or
   c   the veterinarian directing the treatment or minor surgery is satisfied that the veterinary nurse is qualified to carry out the treatment or surgery (SI 2002 No. 1479).

The dental profession

The General Dental Council

The practice of dentistry is controlled by the Dentists Act 1984 through the General Dental Council, whose constitution, as amended (SI 2002 No. 1625), comprises 15 registered dentists, four dental auxiliaries and 10 lay members appointed by the Privy Council. The functions in respect of education, registration and discipline are similar to those of the GMC.

The practice of dentistry is deemed to include the performance of any such operation and the giving of such treatment, advice or attendance as is usually performed or given by dentists, and any person who performs any operations or gives any treatment, advice or attendance on or to any person as preparatory to or for the purpose of or in connection with the fitting, insertion or fixing of dentures, artificial teeth or other dental appliances is deemed to have practised dentistry within the meaning of the Act (s.37).

The Dentists Register

The Dentists Register is required to be published each year (s.22). It is kept by the registrar appointed by the General Dental Council in the manner prescribed by the Council's regulations (ss.14 and 19). The following are entitled to be registered:

1 any person who is a graduate or licentiate in dentistry of a dental authority;
2 any person who is a national of a EU member state and holds an appropriate European diploma; and
3 any person who holds a recognised overseas diploma.

An applicant must satisfy the registrar as to his/her identity, good character and good physical and mental health. An overseas applicant under item 3 above must also satisfy the registrar that s/he has the necessary skill and knowledge, and a knowledge of English which, in the interests of him/herself and patients, is necessary for the practice of dentistry in the UK.

The holder of a recognised overseas diploma may, without meeting any additional requirements, be temporarily registered in the Dentists Register for a specified period for the purpose of practising dentistry in a specified hospital or institution. The register must include a note of the restriction.

The names of all dentists who are entitled to practise are, therefore, included in the published register and there is no provisional registration as is the case with the medical profession. It is not lawful for a temporarily registered dentist to practise except as indicated in the register.

Serious professional misconduct or conviction in the UK for a criminal offence may lead to removal of a dentist from the register. There is a Preliminary Proceedings Committee and a Disciplinary Committee. The disciplinary procedure closely resembles that of the medical profession.

Titles and descriptions

Only registered dentists and medical practitioners may use the titles dentist, dental surgeon or dental practitioner. It is an offence for other persons to use such titles. Similarly, no person, including a medical practitioner, may use the term registered dentist unless s/he is so registered (s.39). Dentists, however, have no legal right or title to be registered under the Medical Act 1983 and may not assume any title implying a right to practise medicine or general surgery (s.7).

The practice of dentistry is restricted to registered dentists and medical practitioners (s.38). It is no longer lawful for a pharmaceutical chemist to extract a tooth in the case of emergency.

The business of dentistry

A person is treated as carrying on the business of dentistry if, and only if, s/he or a partnership of which s/he is a member receives payment for services rendered in the course of the practice of dentistry by him/her or by a partner of his/hers, or by an employee of his/hers or of the partnership (s.40). A lay person cannot employ dentists for the purpose of carrying on a business of dentistry (s.41) but there is an exception for individuals who were carrying on the business of dentistry on 21 July 1955. That was the date of the introduction into parliament of the Bill for the Dentists Act 1956, which was subsequently absorbed into the Dentists Act 1984. Bodies corporate which were in the business of dentistry on that date are also exempted if the majority of the directors are dentists and all the operating staff are dentists or dental auxiliaries.

The Act provides for the establishment of classes of dental auxiliary and for regulations, made by the General Dental Council, to prescribe qualifications for such auxiliaries and the dental work they undertake. The General Dental Council may entrust to the Dental Auxiliaries Committee all matters relating to ancillary dental services, including enforcement of standards of conduct (Part V of the Act).

Nurse, midwives and health visitors

The Nurses, Midwives and Heath Visitors Act 1977 was replaced on 12 February 2002 by the Nursing and Midwifery Order 2001. This Order, which applies in the UK, establishes a body corporate to be known as the Nursing and Midwifery Council. The objective of the Council is to safeguard the health and well-being of persons using or needing the services of registered nurses and midwives.

The Nursing and Midwifery Council

The Nursing and Midwifery Council comprises 12 elected registrant members, 12 elected alternate members, who attend in the absence of the corresponding elected registrant member, and 11 lay members appointed by the Privy Council. There must be at least one registrant member and one alternate member from each part of the Nursing and Midwifery Register and at least one member from each of the national constituencies for each part of the register.

There are four statutory Practice Committees of the Council:

1   the Investigating Committee;
2   the Conduct and Competence Committee;
3   the Health Committee; and
4   the Midwifery Committee.

The Council must ensure that the standards of training meet any EU obligations of the UK and, by means of rules, establish the standards of education and training necessary to achieve standards of proficiency and the requirements for admission to, and continued participation in, such education and training, which may include requirements as to good health and good character for registration. The rules may also make provision for further training to be available to persons already registered.

The Council has power to provide advice to the professions on standards of professional conduct and has done so, for example the Code of Professional Conduct for the Nurse, Midwife and Health Visitor. The principal functions of the Council are to establish standards of education, training, conduct and performance for nurses and midwives and to ensure the maintenance of those standards. It is required, in the discharge of its functions, to have a proper regard for the interests of all groups within the professions, including those with minority representation. The powers and procedures of the Council are laid down in Part I of Schedule I to the Nursing and Midwifery Order 2001.

The register

The Council is required to establish and maintain, on a proposal from the Council, a register of qualified health professionals and must from time to time establish standards of proficiency necessary to be admitted to the different parts of the register, being standards it considers necessary for safe and effective practice. It must also prescribe requirements to be met as to evidence of good health and good character in order to satisfy the registrar that an applicant is capable of safe and effective practice as a registrant under the relevant part of the register. Before prescribing these standards and subsequently publishing them, the Council must consult the Conduct and Competence Committee.

The register is divided into such parts as the Privy Council determine, on a proposal from the Council, each part having a designated title indicative of different qualifications and different kinds of education or training; a registrant is entitled to use the title corresponding to that part of the register. The register may contain the recording in Welsh of titles, qualifications and other entries in respect of those registrants whose registered address is in Wales, together with their competence in a field of practice or at a particular level of practice.

The Council may make rules as to the format of the register, method of entries and erasures and the payment of fees. The Council must make the register available for inspection by members of the public and must publish the register in such a manner and at such times as it considers appropriate.

A person may be registered if s/he holds an approved qualification within the past five years and satisfies the registrar as to any additional education required, that s/he is capable of safe and effective practice as a nurse or midwife and that s/he has paid the prescribed fee.

On renewing registration, a nurse or midwife must satisfy the registrar as to his/her initial registration particulars and that s/he has met any prescribed requirements for continuing professional development within the prescribed time; where s/he has not practised or has practised for less than the prescribed period, a nurse or midwife must satisfy the registrar that s/he has met such requirements as to additional education and training or experience as the Council may specify.

Fitness to practise

The Council must establish and keep under review the standards of conduct, performance and ethics expected of registrants and give them guidance on these matters. It must also establish and keep under review effective arrangements to protect the public from persons whose fitness to practise is impaired. The Council has to make rules governing the procedure of the three Practice Committees.

When any allegation is made against a registrant that his/her fitness is impaired by reason of misconduct, lack of competence, a conviction or by way of physical or mental health, the Council must refer it to the Investigating Committee.

The Investigating Committee

The Investigating Committee comprises a chairman and deputy chairman plus three other members and has a quorum of three, which must include the chairman or deputy chairman (SI 2003 No. 1738). Where the Investigating Committee considers there is a case to answer, it must undertake mediation, refer the case to screeners for them to undertake mediation or refer the case to the Health Committee or to the Conduct and Competence Committee. In order to protect the public, in the public interest or in the interest of the registrant, the Investigating Committee may make an interim order suspending the registrant's registration for not more than 18 months ('interim suspension order') or make an order imposing conditions with which the registrant must comply ('interim conditions of practice order'). There is an appeal procedure to a County Court (or Sheriff in Scotland).

The Conduct and Competence Committee

The Conduct and Competence Committee comprises a chairman and deputy chairman plus six other members and has a quorum of three, which must include the chairman or deputy chairman (SI 2003 No. 1738). Where the Conduct and Competence Committee considers there is a case to answer, it must either undertake mediation itself or refer the case to screeners for them to undertake mediation. Alternatively, it may order the person's name to be struck of the register ('striking off order'), suspend registration (a 'suspension order'), issue a caution ('caution order') or impose conditions for practice (a 'conditions of practice order'). Appeals are to the High Court or Court of Session (in Scotland) or High Court in Northern Ireland.

The Health Committee

The Health Committee comprises a chairman and deputy chairman plus two other members and has a quorum of three, which must include the chairman or deputy chairman (SI 2003 No. 1738). The Health Committee has the same powers, and appeal procedures, as the Conduct and Competence Committee.

The Midwifery Committee

The majority of the members of the Midwifery Committee must be practising midwives and the chairman a member of the Council. The Midwifery Committee advises the Council on matters affecting midwifery and the Council must consult the Committee in matters affecting midwifery. The Council shall determine by rules the circumstances and procedures by means of which a midwife may be suspended from practice and any courses of instruction required to be attended by midwives. Rules may also require midwives to give notice of their intention to practise to a local supervising authority for the area in which they intend to practise. Each local supervising authority must exercise general supervision over midwives practising in their area and report back to the Council where it appears that any midwife's fitness to practise as a midwife is impaired.

Offences by unqualified persons

Except in a case of sudden or urgent necessity, or a person undergoing training with a view to becoming a midwife or doctor, it is an offence for any person other than a registered midwife or a registered medical practitioner to attend a woman in childbirth.

It is also an offence for any person, with intent to deceive, falsely to represent him/herself to be registered or to possess qualifications in nursing or midwifery. The deception may be expressly or by implication or by the assumption of any title, name or description or by any other kind of conduct.

Opticians

The Opticians Act 1989 is the statute which regulates the practice of opticians and the conduct by bodies corporate of their business as opticians.

Legislation in 2005 introduced mandatory continuing education and training for full registrants and registration for student optometrists and dispensing opticians.

The General Optical Council

The General Optical Council, established under the Act (s.1), has the general function of promoting high standards of professional education and professional conduct among opticians. Its members include elected representatives of optometrists and dispensing opticians, together with medical practitioners nominated by the College of Ophthalmologists, persons nominated by the Privy Council and the examining bodies, including the British College of Optometrists. The Council must appoint an Education Committee (s.2) and a Companies Committee to advise on matters relating to bodies corporate (s.3). The Council has an Investigation Committee (s.4) and a Disciplinary Committee (s.5). The Council has power to approve institutions for the purpose of training opticians and to approve of qualifications (s.12).

Registers of opticians

The Council is required to maintain two registers (s.7) of optometrists: namely, those engaged in the testing of sight and the fitting and supply of optical appliances and those engaged in the testing of sight only. In addition, the Council must maintain a register of dispensing opticians: persons who are engaged in the fitting and supply of optical appliances.

Those persons entitled to be included in any of the health service ophthalmic lists at the time of establishment of the General Optical Council in 1959 were entitled to be registered, as also were other persons who in 1961 satisfied the Council as to their qualifications. Subsequently, only applicants holding qualifications approved or recognised by the Council could be accepted for inclusion in the appropriate register (s.8).

The register must be published by the Council (s.11). The Council is also required to maintain and publish lists of bodies corporate carrying on businesses as optometrists or carrying on businesses as dispensing opticians (s.9). A body corporate is entitled to be included in any of the following circumstances:

1   if the majority of its directors are registered opticians;
2   if it was included in one of the NHS ophthalmic lists on 20 November 1957;
3   if the greater part of its business consists of activities other than the testing of sight and the fitting and supply of optical appliances; or
4   if it is a society registered under the Industrial and Provident Societies Act 1965.

In 3 and 4, the business of testing sight or the fitting or supply of optical appliances must be under the management of a registered optometrist or a registered optician as is appropriate.

Professional discipline

The General Optical Council has an Investigating Committee (s.4) and a Disciplinary Committee (s.5) to deal with any disciplinary case. The Disciplinary Committee may direct the removal of a name from the register or list (s.17). The name of a registered optician may be suspended or removed from the register following a conviction in the UK for any criminal offence or following a judgment of the Disciplinary Committee that s/he has been guilty of serious professional misconduct. A financial penalty can also be imposed, either on its own or together with a suspension or erasure. The name of an enrolled body corporate may be removed following a conviction of the body corporate for an offence under the Act; aiding, abetting, counselling or inciting another person to commit an offence; or following a finding of the Disciplinary Committee that the conditions for enrolment of the body corporate are no longer satisfied.

The Disciplinary Committee may also direct the suspension or erasure of a name from the list or register on grounds of fraud or error (s.19); for a contravention of any rule of the Council made under section 31 (e.g. advertising); or for carrying on a practice or business without the supervision of a registered ophthalmic or dispensing optician, as appropriate (s.17).

Offences under the Opticians Act 1989

Subject to certain exceptions, it is unlawful for any person who is not a registered medical practitioner or registered optometrist to test the sight of another person (s.24). It is also unlawful to sell any optical appliance, that is an appliance designed to correct, remedy or relieve a defect of sight, unless the sale is effected by or under the supervision of a registered medical practitioner or a registered optician (s.27). This does not apply to certain types of sale (e.g. sales to an optician, to medical practitioners, to hospitals or to government departments); neither does it apply to the sale to a person over 16 of 'reading glasses', subject to limitation on spherical power, to correct presbyopia (s.27). It is a defence to prove that an appliance was sold as an antique.

The Sale of Optical Appliances Order of Council 1984 (SI 1984 No. 1778), which is applicable to the new Act, also exempts from the supervision requirements the sale of spectacles provided such sales are made against a prescription written by a registered medical practitioner or registered optician. The exemption does not apply to the sale or supply of contact lenses or spectacles for those aged under 16 years.

It is an offence for any person or body corporate to use any of the titles optometrist, dispensing optician, registered optician or ancillary optician if that person is not registered or, in the case of a body corporate, enrolled. It is also an offence to use any name, title, addition or description falsely implying registration or enrolment (s.28).

Healthcare and associated professions

The Professions Supplementary to Medicines Act 1960 was replaced on 12 February 2002 by the Health Professions Order 2001 (SI 2002 No. 254). This Order, which applies in the UK, establishes a body corporate to be known as the Health Professions Council. The objective of the Council is to safeguard the health and well-being of persons using or needing the services of health professionals.

The Order provides a regulatory system for a number of smaller health professions: arts therapists, chiropodists, clinical scientists, dieticians, medical laboratory technicians, occupational therapists, orthoptists, paramedics, physiotherapists, prosthetists and orthotists, radiographers, and speech and language therapists.

In July 2004, several changes were made. Firstly, operating department practitioners became the thirteenth member of the smaller professions. Secondly, chiropodists changed their name to chiropodists and podiatrists and medical laboratory technicians became biomedical scientists (SI 2004 No. 2033).

The Health Professions Council

The Health Professions Council now comprises 13 elected registrant members, 13 elected alternate members, who attend in the absence of the corresponding elected registrant member, and 12 lay members appointed by the

Privy Council (SI 2002 No. 254, as amended by SI 2004 No. 2033). There are four committees of the Council:

1   the Investigating Committee;
2   the Conduct and Competence Committee;
3   the Health Committee; and
4   the Education and Training Committee.

The registers

The Council is required to establish and maintain, on a proposal from the Council, a register of qualified health professionals and must from time to time establish standards of proficiency necessary to be admitted to the different parts of the register, being standards it considers necessary for safe and effective practice. It must also prescribe requirements to be met as to evidence of good health and good character in order to satisfy the registrar that an applicant is capable of safe and effective practice as a registrant under the relevant part of the register. Before prescribing these standards and subsequently publishing them, the Council must consult the Conduct and Competence Committee.

The Register shall be divided into such parts as the Privy Council determines, on a proposal from the Council, each part having a designated title indicative of different qualifications and different kinds of education or training; a registrant is entitled to use the title corresponding to that part of the register. The register may contain the recording in Welsh of titles, qualifications and other entries in respect of those registrants whose registered address is in Wales; it also contains possession of qualifications and competence in a field of practice or at a particular level of practice.

The Council may make rules as to the format of the register, method of entries and erasures and the payment of fees. The Council must make the register available for inspection by members of the public and must publish the register in such a manner and at such times as it considers appropriate.

A person may be registered if s/he holds an approved qualification within the past five years and satisfies the registrar as to any additional education required, that s/he is capable of safe and effective practice as a health professional and that s/he has paid the prescribed fee.

On renewing registration, a health professional must satisfy the Education and Training Committee as to his/her initial registration particulars and satisfy that Committee that s/he has met any prescribed requirements for continuing professional development within the prescribed time. Where s/he has not practised, or has practised for less than the prescribed period, s/he must satisfy the Committee that s/he has met such requirements as to additional education and training or experience as the Council may specify.

The Education and Training Committee

The Council must establish the standards of education and training necessary to achieve standards of proficiency and the requirements for admission to, and continued participation in, such education and training, which may include requirements as to good health and good character for registration. The rules may also make provision for further training to be available to persons already registered.

The Committee must take appropriate steps to satisfy itself that those standards and requirements are met and advise the Council on the performance of the Council's functions in relation to standards and proficiency.

Fitness to Practise Committees

The Council must establish and keep under review the standards of conduct, performance and ethics expected of registrants and give them guidance on these matters. It must also establish and keep under review effective arrangements to protect the public from persons whose fitness to practise is impaired. The Council has to make rules governing the procedure of the three Practice Committees and must consult the Conduct and Competence Committee before establishing any standards. The Council must appoint a chairman for each of its Practice Committees and may appoint another member of the committee to act as deputy chairman in the chairman's absence.

When any allegation is made against a registrant that his/her fitness is impaired by reason of misconduct, lack of competence, a conviction or by way of physical or mental health, then the Council must refer it to the Investigating Committee.

The Investigating Committee

The Investigating Committee comprises a chairman and possibly a deputy chairman and not less than nine members and has a quorum of five, which must include the chairman (SI 2003 No. 1209). Where the Investigating Committee considers there is a case to answer, it must undertake mediation, refer the case to screeners for them to undertake mediation, refer the case to the Health Committee or refer the case to the Conduct and Competence Committee. In order to protect the public, in the public interest or in the interest of the registrant, the Investigating Committee may make an interim order suspending the registrant's registration for not more than 18 months ('interim suspension order') or make an order imposing conditions with which the registrant must comply ('interim conditions of practice order'). There is an appeal procedure to a County Court or Sheriff (in Scotland).

The Conduct and Competence Committee

The Conduct and Competence Committee comprises a chairman plus other members and has a quorum of five. A member, appointed as deputy chairman, may act in the chairman's absence (SI 2003 No. 1209). Where the Conduct and Competence Committee considers there is a case to answer, it must either undertake mediation itself or refer the case to screeners for them to undertake mediation. Alternatively, it may order the person's name to be struck of the register ('striking off order'), suspend registration (a 'suspension order'), issue a caution ('caution order') or impose conditions for practise (a 'conditions of practise order'). Appeals are to the High Court or Court of Session (in Scotland) or High Court in Northern Ireland.

The Health Committee

The Health Committee, dealing with mental or physical matters, has a similar constitution, powers and procedures as the Conduct and Competence Committee.

Titles and descriptions

A registered person is entitled to use the title state registered (e.g. state registered dietician and similarly for the other professions). It is an offence for any person to take or use, alone or in conjunction with other words, the title state registered, state or registered (e.g. state registered chiropodist, state chiropodist or registered chiropodist [and similarly for the other professions]) if s/he is not so registered, or to take or use any name, title, addition or description falsely implying, or otherwise pretending, that his/her name is on a register established under the Act (s.6).

Only registered persons may be employed by health authorities within the NHS unless they were employed in their specific capacity prior to the registration requirements applying to their profession. Apart from these restrictions, there is no prohibition on practice by unregistered persons.

Hearing aid supply

The main Hearing Aid Council Act 1968 was amended by the Hearing Aid Council (Amendment) Act 1989. The Hearing Aid Council has the general function of securing adequate standards of competence and conduct among persons engaged in dispensing hearing aids. It is required to draw up standards of competence for dispensers of hearing aids and codes of trade practice for adoption by such dispensers and by persons employing them (s.1). The Hearing Aid Extension Act 1975 extended the Act to Northern Ireland.

The Council is appointed partly from persons representing persons registered under the Act and partly from persons representing the interests of persons with impaired hearing. The Council is required to maintain for public inspection a register of dispensers of hearing aids, and a register of persons (including bodies corporate) employing such dispensers (s.2).

A dispenser of hearing aids means an individual who conducts or seeks to conduct 'oral negotiations' with a view to effecting the supply of a hearing aid, whether by him/her or another, to or for the use of a person with impaired hearing. An employer of dispensers includes any person who enters into any arrangement with an individual whereby that individual undertakes for reward or anticipation of reward to act as a dispenser with a view to promoting the supply of hearing aids by that person (s.14).

Professional discipline

The Hearing Aid Council must also establish an Investigating Committee (s.5) and a Disciplinary Committee (s.6) comparable with those under the Professions Supplementary to Medicine Act 1960. A registered person may have his/her name suspended or removed from the register for any criminal conviction or if judged by the Disciplinary Committee to be guilty of serious misconduct in connection with the dispensing of hearing aids or the training of persons to act as dispensers of hearing aids (s.7, as amended by the 1989 Act). A financial penalty may also be imposed. Appeals against a direction lie to the High Court. It is an offence for any person whose name is not in the appropriate register to act as a dispenser of hearing aids or to employ such a dispenser.

Regulation of practitioners of traditional medicines

A Department of Health steering group was set up in 2006 to prepare the ground for the regulation of practitioners of acupuncture, herbal medicine, traditional Chinese medicine and other traditional medicine systems practised in the UK such as Ayurveda, Unani Tibb, Kampo and Tibetan medicine. The steering group reported in May 2008 and recommended that these practitioners should eventually come under the remit of the Health Professions Council, although there will be considerable need for the Council to have more resources, to modify its admission criteria and to consider 'grandparenting' arrangements. Implementation of this report is likely to take a number of years.

Summary

- The Council for Healthcare Regulatory Excellence (CHRE) is charged with promoting the interests of patients and other members of the public in relation to the performance by the regulatory bodies of health professionals.

- There are registering authorities for medical, dental, nursing, optical, chiropractic and osteopathic health professionals. All have committees set up to evaluate and maintain fitness to practise among registrants.
- The Health Professions Order 2001 established the Health Professions Council, which is intended to provide a regulatory system for a number of smaller health professions and safeguard the health and well-being of persons using or needing their services.
- Eventually it is intended that practitioners of traditional medicines will come under the remit of the Health Professions Council.

Further reading

Appelbe GE, Harrison I (1994) Professional self-regulation: pharmacy and the other health professions. *Pharm J* 254: 679.
Gray C (2002) How the other professions are responding to the drivers for change. *Pharm J* 268: 154–155.
Moore W (2002) How other professions are coping with the regulatory reforms. *Pharm J* 268: 460–461.

Websites

Committee of Inquiry – independent investigation into how the NHS handled allegations about the conduct of Clifford Ayling: http://www.dh.gov.uk/en/Publicationsandstatistics/Publications/PublicationsPolicyAndGuidance/DH_4088996
Committee of inquiry to investigate how the NHS handled allegations about the performance and conduct of Richard Neale: http://www.dh.gov.uk/en/Publicationsandstatistics/Publications/PublicationsPolicyAndGuidance/DH_4088995
Council for Healthcare Regulatory Excellence: http://www.chre.org.uk/
General Dental Council: http://www.gdc-uk.org/
General Medical Council: http://www.gmc-uk.org/
General Optical Council: http://www.optical.org/
Health Professions Council: http://www.hpc-uk.org/
Learning from Bristol: the report of the public inquiry into children's heart surgery at the Bristol Royal Infirmary 1984–1995 Command Paper: CM 5207 chaired by Professor Sir Ian Kennedy, a lawyer: http://www.bristol-inquiry.org.uk/
Nursing and Midwifery Council: http://www.gnmc-uk.org/nmc/main/home.html
Royal College of Veterinary Surgeons: http://www.rcvs.org.uk
The Kerr/Haslam Inquiry, full report: http://www.dh.gov.uk/en/Publicationsandstatistics/Publications/PublicationsPolicyAndGuidance/DH_4115349
The Report of the Royal Liverpool Children's Inquiry, 2001: http://www.rlcinquiry.org.uk/
The Shipman Inquiry: http://www.the-shipman-inquiry.org.uk/home.asp

26

National Health Service law and organisation

History

The National Health Service (NHS) Act 1946 made it the duty of the Minister of Health (now the Secretary of State for Health) in England, and later the Secretary of State for Wales (SI 1968 No. 1699), to:

- promote the establishment in England and Wales of a comprehensive health service designed to secure improvement in the physical and mental health of the people of England and Wales and the prevention, diagnosis and treatment of illness;
- provide or secure the provision of services to do this; and
- provide these services free of charge unless otherwise expressly provided in any other Act.

In Scotland, a similar health service was established by the NHS (Scotland) Act 1947, the Minister responsible being the Secretary of State for Scotland.

The service was reorganised into a single management structure in England and Wales by the NHS Reorganisation Act 1973 and in Scotland by the NHS (Scotland) Act 1978. The 1978 Act for Scotland is still the basis for the NHS in Scotland although there have been a number of later amendments [notably the NHS Reform (Scotland) Act 2004]. For England and Wales, the provisions of the 1946 Act and most of the provisions of the 1973 Act, including those affecting the pharmaceutical service, were consolidated into the NHS Act 1977. The 1977 Act has been effectively replaced by the consolidated NHS Act 2006 (for England) and the NHS (Wales) Act 2006. All three Acts (for England, Scotland and Wales) retain the same duty upon the relevant government minister as set out in 1946.

In addition the NHS Act 2006 incorporated the NHS provisions in a large number of amending Acts and Regulations [set out in the NHS (Consequential Provisions) Act 2006] up to, and including, the Health Act 2006. The NHS Act 2006 is in 14 parts of which the following are relevant to pharmacy.

In Part 1, the Secretary of State or the appropriate Ministers have a duty to provide (throughout England, but the requirements are essentially the same in Wales and Scotland) the following to such an extent as they believe necessary to meet reasonable requirements:

- hospital accommodation;
- other accommodation for the purpose of any service provided under the Act;
- medical, dental, ophthalmic, nursing and ambulance services;
- facilities for the care of expectant and nursing mothers and young children;
- facilities for the prevention of illness, the care of persons suffering from illness and the aftercare of persons who have suffered from illness;
- services for the diagnosis and treatment of illness; and
- a family planning service.

The Secretary of State may direct that any of his functions be carried out by a strategic health authority, a primary care trust (PCT), an NHS trust or a special health authority by way of statutory 'Directions' (see below). Broadly the NHS is operated under NHS contracts between one health service body 'the commissioner' and another 'the provider'. These contracts are not generally enforceable at law but only through appeal to the Secretary of State. Part 2 of the NHS Act 2006 sets out the health service bodies concerned with NHS services in England (see below) and Part 3 makes it clear that local authorities and health service bodies must collaborate where needed to enable the provision of NHS services. It also includes arrangements for care trusts, which provide both health and social care to local communities.

Arrangements for the NHS contractual framework (henceforward called a contract) for community pharmacy services and local pharmaceutical services (LPS schemes) appear in Part 7 of the NHS Act 2006 and are dealt with in more detail later in this chapter (but note that the contractual framework for community pharmacy services is not a contract in law, although the LPS is a legal contract). Part 8 continues the arrangements for the Family Health Services Appeal Authority (FHSAA), which hears appeals concerning NHS pharmacy contracts and Part 9 contains the provisions for prescription fees (levies) to be paid by certain people presenting NHS prescriptions in the community. Part 10 makes a series of requirements concerning the protection of the NHS from fraud such as compulsory disclosure of documents and information. Part 12 includes details of how the public and patients will have an input into NHS planning and operation and Part 13 contains provisions enforcing controls on the maximum price of medicines (the Pharmaceutical Price Regulation Scheme [PPRS]) and other medical supplies to the NHS. This Department of Health negotiates the PPRS on behalf of the whole of the UK. Part 14 contains sections covering interpretation and defined expressions and brought the Act into force on 1 March 2007.

Other legislation affecting the National Health Service

Health Act 1999

Although the provisions of the Health Act 1999 which are directly related to the management of the NHS are now incorporated into the NHS Act 2006, there remain some other sections of the 1999 Act that are relevant to pharmacy. These include the statutory duty of quality on NHS bodies and services (*clinical governance*) and enabling powers to regulate healthcare professions, including pharmacy. Section 60 of the Health Act 1999 in particular provided power to change the regulatory and disciplinary powers of the Royal Pharmaceutical Society of Great Britain (RPSGB; see Chapters 22, 23 and 24).

Health and Social Care Act 2001

Again, most of the NHS provisions in the Health and Social Care Act 2001 have been subsumed into the NHS Act 2006, but section 63 amends the Medicines Act and adds pharmacists to the groups of health practitioners who are able to authorise a prescription for a Prescription Only Medicine (see independent and supplementary prescribing: Chapters 8 and 9).

National Health Service Reform and Health Care Professions Act 2002

As its name suggests, the NHS reforms in the National Health Service Reform and Health Care Professions Act 2002 are now in the NHS Act 2006, but the 2002 Act also provides for the establishment of the Council for the Regulation of Healthcare Professions (now called the Council for Healthcare Regulatory Excellence [CHRE]), which oversees the regulatory and disciplinary roles of all the healthcare professions (see Chapters 22, 24 and 25).

Health and Social Care (Community Health and Standards) Act 2003

Once again, a significant number of provisions relating to the NHS in this Act now appear in the NHS Act 2006. However, the 2003 Act replaced an earlier provision in the Health and Social Care Act 2001 creating the Commission for Health Improvement (CHI) with a wider body, the Commission for Health Care Audit and Inspection (CHAI or as it preferred to be called, the Healthcare Commission). In addition, a parallel inspection body for social care inspection, the Commission for Social Care Inspection (CSCI) was set up.

Health Act 2006

The Health Act 2006 became rather famous for introducing a ban on smoking in public premises but it also contained a wide range of provisions affecting the NHS and other matters. For pharmacists, the most important provisions are in Part 3. Sections 17–25 create powers to change the regulations under the Misuse of Drugs Act (see Chapter 17), following the Shipman scandal (see Chapter 25). These changes are now in place. Section 30 inserts a new section in the Medicines Act 1968 to change the requirement for a pharmacist to be in 'personal control' of a pharmacy to there being a 'responsible pharmacist' for each pharmacy. These regulations were laid in November 2008 and they are planned to come into force in October 2009 (see Chapter 5). Moreover, section 26 of the Health Act 2006 inserts further sections into the Medicines Act 1968 to change the interpretation of 'supervision' in section 10 and 52 of the 1968 Act. Consultation on these changes is expected to span 2008 and 2009.

Health and Social Care Act 2008

The Health and Social Care Act 2008 has introduced changes in two areas affecting pharmacy. Firstly, it implements the recommendations from the White Paper *Trust, Assurance and Quality – Regulation of Healthcare Professionals in the 21st Century* and establishes the General Pharmaceutical Council (see Chapters 22, 23 and 24). Secondly, the 2008 Act changes the name of the over-arching regulator for healthcare professions to the CHRE and, from April 2009, brings together the roles of CHAI (the Healthcare Commission), CSCI (see above) and the Mental Health Act Commission into the Care Quality Commission (CQC).

Further NHS Reform

In the draft legislative programme announced in May 2008, the government included proposals for further reform to take forward the recommendations in Lord Darzi's review (see below), notably the establishment of an NHS Constitution and an National Quality Board for the NHS, making PCTs more responsive to their local communities, giving greater scope for patients to shape their care and reinforcing the public health role of the NHS. A new Health Bill was announced in December 2008.

Thus the above legislation *all* forms the legal basis for the NHS in England. The NHS (Wales) Act 2006 as amended will apply to the NHS in Wales.

The National Health Service (Scotland) Act 1978 as amended will apply to NHS Scotland.

National Health Service policy and planning

Government ministers and health departments continually issue large quantities of strategic and planning documents, supplemented with guidance and procedures as to how policy should be implemented. Where changes to legislation are required, the government will issue a White Paper (in England see Chapter 1) or similar blueprints in Scotland and Wales setting out how policy goals will be secured. A full account of these is outside the scope of this book but major changes in the community pharmacy contract in England were first envisaged in September 2000 in *Pharmacy in the Future: Implementing the NHS Plan – A Programme for Pharmacy*. In July 2003, the Department of Health issued *A Vision for Pharmacy in the New NHS*, which set out 10 key roles for pharmacists in the NHS, and in June 2004 it issued the *NHS Improvement Plan*, which set out priorities for development until 2008. These were carried forward in 2006 in *Our Health, Our Care, Our Say*, and, in April 2008, a strategic plan for England, *Pharmacy in England: Building on Strengths – Delivering the Future* extended earlier measures to develop further the community pharmacy contract and to respond to a review (the Galbraith Review) of the exemptions from the control of entry restrictions to such contracts introduced in 2005 (see below). The *Pharmacy in England* paper paves the way principally for further changes in community pharmacy, namely a greater shift from dispensing to provision of clinical services, a wider range of services being made available through pharmacies and greater use of the clinical skills of pharmacists and the talents of other pharmacy staff.

The pharmacy paper was published alongside a series of documents from the Department of Health comprising the *NHS Next Stage Review* (Darzi Review). This was in several parts.

> *High Quality Care for All*: 'a new foundation for a health service that empowers staff and gives patients choice'
> *A Quality Workforce*: 'workforce proposals to free up the front line and improve our services'
> A draft NHS Constitution
> *A Primary and Community Care Strategy*: 'to give patients and the public a stronger voice, enable them to make informed decisions and have greater choice and control in managing their health and healthcare'.

For pharmacy, one key proposal in the Darzi Review is to introduce a requirement upon pharmacies to demonstrate that their services secure improvements in quality and health outcomes. In addition, two pharmacist national clinical directors (see below) were appointed in 2008 to champion pharmacy change in hospitals and in the community. A consultation document on proposals for legislative changes, principally to the NHS community pharmacy contract (see below) was published in September 2008; these changes are likely to be implemented in 2009 and beyond.

There are similar strategic documents for pharmacy in Scotland and Wales (see Further reading).

National Health Service structure in Great Britain

Like the legislation that underpins it, the structure of the NHS undergoes constant change. Although the structures and titles vary significantly in England, Wales and Scotland, all have organisations that plan and commission local health services and deliver family health practitioner services, plus organisations that provide secondary (mostly hospital) care. Reference should be made to websites at the end of the chapter for the latest information on NHS developments in each home country.

England

The Department of Health

The Department of Health has six ministers (the most senior is called the Secretary of State for Health) who work with a board of eight members to manage Department of Health business and priorities (Figure 26.1). The Board is responsible for advice to ministers, setting Department of Health standards and establishing governance frameworks. Key national clinical priorities, such as cancer and cancer networks, mental health, older people's services or diabetes services are led by national clinical directors (often termed

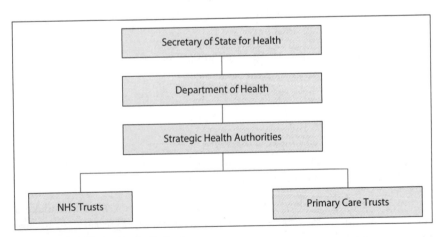

Figure 26.1 NHS structure in England.

'czars' by the media). In addition, there are six 'heads of professions', including a Chief Pharmaceutical Officer. The Department of Health works with a wide range of agencies and independent bodies to deliver its objectives: executive agencies such as the Medicines and Healthcare products Regulatory Agency (see Chapter 2 et seq.), special health authorities such as the National Patient Safety Agency, and commissions and tribunals such as the Healthcare Commission and the Family Health Services Appeal Authority. These so-called 'arm's length bodies' are constantly evolving.

The NHS Act 2006 (Chapter 1) continues the establishment of the strategic health authorities (England only; see Figure 26.1), which audit, oversee and monitor the effectiveness of the PCTs. Chapter 2 of the Act maintains the existence of the PCTs, which award and manage NHS contracts with the four family health services: medical, dental, ophthalmic and pharmacy. Chapter 3 continues arrangements for NHS trusts (hospitals) and Chapter 4 provides for special health authorities, which commission services.

Strategic health authorities

England is split into 10 strategic health authorities that manage the NHS on behalf of the Secretary of State and are responsible for:

- developing plans for improving health services in their local area;
- making sure that local health services are of a high quality and are performing well;
- increasing the capacity of local health services; and
- making sure that national priorities are integrated into local healthcare plans.

Trusts

A trust is an NHS body which is permitted, by individual orders under the NHS Acts, to assume responsibility for the ownership and management of health service bodies. A trust is run by a board, which may engage staff and set rates of pay and may borrow capital and dispose of assets. However, this freedom is constrained in that the staff remain NHS employees and the premises remain NHS property. Moreover, the Secretary of State may require that certain services are provided (e.g. accident and emergency facilities) regardless of the wishes of the trust board. Secondary care trusts are essentially providers of healthcare; their services are principally commissioned by PCTs, although this role is increasingly transferring to groups of general practitioner (GP) practices: *practice-based commissioning*.

There are several types of trust, taking legal responsibility for providing particular health services in particular localities. The most familiar perhaps are *acute trusts*, which essentially manage hospitals delivering secondary healthcare. Some acute trusts are regional or national centres for more specialised (tertiary) care or are attached to universities and train health professionals (*teaching trusts*). Acute trusts may also provide community healthcare through clinics and outpatient services, although these are increasingly being transferred to PCTs. Since April 2004, many acute trusts (around 100 by 2008) have become *foundation trusts*, with greater financial and operational freedom and accountable to the Independent Regulator of NHS Foundation Trusts (known as Monitor). There are also *ambulance trusts*, providing emergency access to healthcare, and *mental health trusts*, often working closely with local council social services to provide health and social care for people with mental health problems.

The majority of healthcare delivered in the community is controlled by PCTs, which receive some 75 per cent of the total NHS budget. Statutory instruments have formalised the membership, procedure and administration arrangements for PCTs, the composition of their executive committees and their functions [The PCT (Membership, Procedures and Administration Arrangements) Regulations 2000 SI 2000 No. 89, as amended, with Directions]. Although the statutory input of pharmacists to local health planning, lost in 1990, has not been formally replaced, the composition of the PCT executive committee is now covered by 'directions' [The PCT Executive Committees (Membership) Directions 2003] made under the authority of the Secretary of State for Health. These provide explicit authority for local community pharmacists to be eligible for inclusion on the Committee. PCTs commission services from other trusts and from NHS Direct (see below), award NHS dispensing contracts, administer the relevant conditions (the Terms of Service, see below), operate statutory disciplinary arrangements and make arrangements for persons in the PCT locality to be supplied with 'pharmaceutical services'. Pharmaceutical services are provided by community pharmacists, or their employers, who are under contract to the local PCT and are legally known as pharmacy or chemist contractors or simply chemists.

A small number of care trusts have also been established to deliver social care, mental healthcare and primary healthcare in a given locality.

Special health authorities

These are health authorities that provide a health service to the whole of England, not just to a local community. Examples include the Health Protection Agency, the National Institute for Health and Clinical Excellence (NICE), the National Patient Safety Agency, NHS Direct and the NHS Business Services Agency, which includes the Prescription Pricing Division.

NHS Direct, National Health Service walk-in centres

NHS Direct was established in 1999 as a directly funded Department of Health body; in 2007, it became an NHS trust and in 2008 it was planning to apply for foundation trust status. There is now an NHS Direct Wales and NHS 24 for Scotland. NHS Direct provides 24 hour nurse-led telephone help on health matters plus an online website and digital TV service, publishes a self-help guide and provides interactive information point terminals in public places such as surgeries, accident and emergency departments, libraries and post offices. Since 2004, PCTs have received funding to commission the telephone and other core services and many will integrate their out-of-hours arrangements with NHS Direct support.

A number of pilot NHS walk-in centres were established during 1999 and 2000; again led by nurses, these aim to improve access to primary healthcare services. Legally they are equivalent to NHS hospital outpatient units so supplies of medicines and collection of prescription charges may be made on the spot to patients who use the centres. If appropriately trained, nurse prescribers in walk-in centres may also issue NHS prescriptions. Most NHS walk-in centres also supply a range of medicines under Patient Group Directions (see Chapters 8 and 9).

Managed National Health Services and the private sector

The term 'managed service' generally implies services paid for 'out of the public purse', that is through the payment of taxes to the state. In that sense, pharmacists who work within PCTs, NHS trusts (mostly hospitals but see above), most prison health services and health services for the armed forces are working in the managed sector. Increasingly, pharmacists working for GP practices are subject to NHS management. By contrast, pharmacists in community practice are employed privately but their NHS services are subject to NHS management arrangements. The private sector (such as private hospitals run by a range of insurers and provident societies or nursing homes run by commercial agencies) is financed by shareholders and by direct payments from the service users.

Boundaries between these sectors, at least in the provision of health services, have become increasingly blurred, and management and measurement of the quality of these services is converging. Since April 1991 (removal of Crown immunity; Chapter 1), the major statutes concerning medicines (including Controlled Drugs) and related matters now apply to NHS hospitals as well to hospitals and nursing homes that are privately owned. Prison services, whether state or privately run, are expected to comply with UK law as far as is practicable, as are military health services, even when operating overseas. In addition, it is now relatively common for an NHS trust to register the hospital dispensary or pharmacy department with the RPSGB as a registered pharmacy (see Chapter 5), thus enabling it to engage in over-the-counter sales and a limited amount of wholesale dealing (licence exempted; Chapter 10).

Trusts and other public bodies are legally responsible for the activities they manage. Litigation against them is increasing and it is important that pharmacists employed in these sectors of pharmacy understand not only the legislation but also the criteria against which accepted standards of care may be judged. The common law principles of negligence (pp. 6 and 337) and professional responsibility apply to pharmacists in the managed sector and they should be aware of the differences between managerial responsibility (master/servant relationship) and professional obligations.

National Health Service directions

In addition to the requirements of primary statutes and subsidiary legislation (such as the Misuse of Drugs Act 1971 and the regulations made under it), power is also given to the Secretary of State for Health (and occasionally to strategic health authorities) to make additional 'directions'. They must be in writing and cite the relevant powers being used. They have the force of law so that a breach is a breach of statutory duty. Of particular relevance are those directions that have been addressed to PCTs to set up, amend and regulate their functions and powers regarding the contracted family health services; others have applied to NHS trusts and their complaints procedures or provisions on delayed discharge.

Circulars and official publications

The NHS is an enormous bureaucracy and vast quantities of communication are sent from the Department of Health to trusts and other NHS bodies giving guidance and instruction on how they should carry out their work. This guidance may incorporate, for example, interpretation of statute law within the managed service, policy directions, and reports of studies into matters of NHS importance, changes to financial arrangements or simply information on current topics of importance. Mechanisms include *The Month*, an 'agenda setting monthly update of key messages from the NHS Chief Executive and the leadership team' and *The Week*, 'providing need-to-know news, consultations and events' for chief executives. There are also now fairly infrequent *Health Service Circulars*, updates from the Chief Medical Officer or other heads of professions and letters to chief executives and non-executive directors of NHS bodies. Similar arrangements prevail to manage the NHS services in Wales and Scotland, but the names and form may vary. A detailed account of these internal communications is outside the scope of this book but interested readers are referred to the websites listed at the end of this chapter.

Clinical governance

Introduced by the Health Act 1999 and strengthened by subsequent NHS Acts, the concept of clinical governance is now embedded in a wide range of mechanisms for maintaining the competence of health professionals and ensuring the quality of health services provided both within the NHS and in the private sector. The scope of clinical governance is too wide to encompass here but brief details are given below of arrangements for audit and inspection, patient safety and public involvement where they are likely to have an impact on pharmacists employed by, or providing services to, the NHS.

In the first few years of the 21st century, measures have been implemented to reform, tighten and rationalise initially the processes of hospital (NHS trust) inspection and then to extend the standards to PCTs and to voluntary and private healthcare. The Healthcare Commission (see above) carries out audit and inspection of all health and social care facilities and in 2009 will be merged with the CSCI and the Mental Health Act Commission to form the CQC. The CQC will become the single, integrated regulator for health and adult social care. Under the Health and Social Care Act 2008, the CQC will have powers to register, for the first time, providers of NHS care. The CQC will have a wide range of enforcement powers to achieve compliance with registration requirements, and may require a ward or service to be closed until safety requirements are met as well as being able to suspend or de-register services where absolutely necessary. The inclusion of the functions of the Mental Health Act Commission in the remit of the CQC will strengthen the oversight of patients subject to compulsory detention for mental health reasons.

Following a consultation on the *Future Regulation of Health and Adult Social Care in England*, it has become clear that community pharmacies will **not** have to register with the CQC provided they are engaged only in 'dispensing and associated activities'. Nor will registration be required for 'diagnostic testing of the simplest kind'. However, prescribing, clinical services or services designed to promote health and well-being may become subject to registration requirements. The Healthcare Commission monitors and enforces the Standards for Better Health (see below). These will gradually be converted into registration requirements as the CQC begins to function.

Standards for Better Health

From 2005, the Healthcare Commission established a set of core and developmental standards (and outcomes) for seven domains of healthcare: safety, clinical and cost effectiveness, governance, patient focus, accessible and responsive care, care environment and amenities and public health. The *Core Standards* represent the level of quality that healthcare organisations must meet; *Developmental Standards* the level that they should aspire to and work towards. The Standards include *Criteria*, defined as ways of demonstrating compliance with, and performance relevant to, a Standard. They establish specific, objective expectations, drawing on such evidence and indicators as the Healthcare Commission may establish. *Targets* refer to defined levels of performance that are being aimed for, often with numerical and time dimensions. The purpose of a target is to provide incentives for improvement in the specific area covered by the target over a particular time frame. *Benchmarks* are used as comparators to compare performance between similar organisations or systems. The Healthcare Commission (and subsequently the CQC) uses Standards for Better Health (S4BH) to monitor performance within NHS trusts; PCTs monitor performance of community pharmacy contracts using the Community Pharmacy Assurance Framework (published by NHS Primary Care Contracting), which has cross-references to S4BH. An example of a Standard relevant to pharmacy practice is given in Box 26.1 and details of how part of the Standard has been incorporated into the framework appears in Box 26.2.

Patient safety

In 2001, the National Patient Safety Agency was established to develop and deliver a programme for healthcare providers to improve the safety and quality of care through reporting, analysing and learning from adverse incidents involving NHS patients. This process is now well advanced, with

---

Box 26.1 *Extract from Standards for Better Health*

Third Domain: Governance

Domain Outcome

Managerial and clinical leadership and accountability, as well as the organisation's culture, system and working practices ensure that probity, quality assurance, quality improvement and patient safety are central components of all the activities of the health care organisation

Core Standards	Developmental Standard
C7 Healthcare organisations	D3 Integrated governance arrangements representing best practice are in place in all healthcare organisations and across all health communities and clinical networks
a apply the principles of sound clinical and corporate governance	
b actively support all employees to promote honesty, probity, accountability and the economic, efficient and effective use of resources	
c undertake systematic risk assessment and risk management	
d ensure financial management achieves economy, efficiency, probity and accountability in the use of resources	
e challenge discrimination, promote equality and respect human rights	
f meet performance requirements	

Box 26.2 *Extract from the Community Pharmacy Assurance Framework*

Service Indicator and Terms of Service (ToS) Reference & Standards for Better Health (S4BH) Reference	Pre-visit questions	PCT comment/ explanation	Pharmacy response	PCT verification
Before providing any drugs or appliances, the pharmacist shall ask any person who make a declaration that the person named on the prescription form or repeatable prescription does not have to pay the prescriptions charges to produce satisfactory evidence of such entitlement. ToS 7 (3) & (4) S4BH C7	Does the SOP include the need to ask for proof of entitlement when checking exemption declarations?	The NHS relies on pharmacists and their staff to request proof of entitlement as part of the measures to reduce patient fraud. PCTs may monitor exemption declarations and the frequency of 'evidence not seen' endorsements. The PCT may observe prescription reception procedures during monitoring visits.	Yes	

PCT, primary care trust; SOP, standard operating procedure.

Source: Community Pharmacy Assurance Framework 2007/8, www.pcc.nhs.uk

anonymous reporting of patient safety incidents to the agency from NHS trusts and from community pharmacies. The National Patient Safety Agency also issues patient safety alerts from time to time, highlighting serious safety failures and providing instructions on how they may be best avoided.

Patient and public involvement

The 2003 Health and Social Care Act set up the Commission for Patient and Public Involvement in Health and it continues to appear in the NHS Act 2006. In addition, local groups, initially called 'patient and public involvement forums', later just 'patient forums', have been established in each trust to 'watch over the quality of local healthcare'. However, under the Local Government and Public Involvement in Health Act 2007 (Part 14) both the Commission and the forums have been phased out and *local involvement networks* (LINks), funded by local authorities to 'give citizens a stronger voice in how their health and social care services are delivered', were being established in the latter part of 2008. Providers of health services, including trusts and community pharmacies will be expected to allow reasonable access to members of LINk teams to 'enter and view and observe the carrying-on of activities' (s.225). Sections 244–247 of the NHS Act 2006 maintain the functions of local authority *overview and scrutiny committees* to oversee and question local health services on behalf of local citizens.

Patient complaints

In relation to complaints (and general advice), each trust has been required since September 2003 to set up a *'patients advice and liaison service'* (PALS) to provide information, advice and support to help patients, families and their carers to get the most out of the NHS. This may include giving advice and support on the making of complaints and referral to the Independent Complaints Advocacy Service; this service aims to secure consistent national standards and performance indicators for the handling of complaints. Since 1993, there has been a Health Service Commissioner (Ombudsman) to consider complaints about clinical matters and complaints involving practitioners. The Ombudsman can only consider complaints related to NHS care in England which have had a response from the practitioner and a final response from the Healthcare Commission. There are separate Ombudsmen for Scotland and Wales.

In December 2008, the Department of Health announced plans for a single complaints system to cover all health and adult social care services in England. These will incorporate responses to a consultation *Making Experiences Count* in 2007 and the proposals set out in *Reform of Health and Social Care Complaints: Proposed Changes to the Legislative Framework* published in February 2008. Draft regulations are expected to be published in January 2009.

Pharmaceutical Price Regulation Scheme

A voluntary regulatory scheme to allow the NHS to have access to good quality, proprietary medicines at reasonable prices while allowing a fair return for the pharmaceutical industry has been in place since 1957. In 2007, the Department of Health announced its intention to renegotiate the PPRS largely because of criticism from the Office of Fair Trading and a High Court ruling that jeopardised its operation. The current scheme applies to the whole of the UK. It is underpinned by sections 260–266 of the NHS Act 2006 (see above) and the Health Service Branded Medicines (Control of Prices and Supply of Information) Regulations 2008 (SI 2008 No. 1938) and the Health Service Medicines (Information Relating to Sales of Branded Medicines, etc) Regulations 2007 (SI 2007 No. 1320). While the bulk of the industry will continue to comply with the voluntary scheme, the legislation allows the NHS to control the prices it will pay to any company which chooses not to sign up to the voluntary agreement or fails to reach agreement. The implementing regulations will be renewed annually to comply with the requirements of Council Directive 89/105/EEC.

Prison health services

The Home Office generally administers prisons and the Home Office used to purchase health services within prisons from a variety of NHS and private providers. By 2007, responsibility for healthcare services had transferred to PCTs and is now subject to a National Partnership Agreement between the Department of Health and the Home Office for the accountability and commissioning of health services for prisoners in public sector prisons in England.

Health services in the armed forces

Health services for the armed forces are the responsibility of the Ministry of Defence. A commitment has been made to ensure that the nature and quality of healthcare services provided met the specific needs of the military population to defined standards, at least to the level of those in the NHS. This is reflected in a Concordat between the UK Health Services and the Ministry of Defence made in 2005.

The pharmacy contractual framework in England

Made initially under Part III of the NHS Act 1977, later replaced by Part 7 of the NHS Act 2006, the principal regulations covering the provision of pharmaceutical services in England are the NHS (Pharmaceutical Services) Regulations 2005 (SI 2005 No. 641) as amended. These regulations also included four exemptions from the restrictions on award of contracts (Control of Entry, see the Galbraith Review [p. 423 and below]) which had been in place since 1987. The regulations incorporate, among other things, provisions to enable any person to receive such drugs, medicines and appliances as are ordered and include the contract conditions or the Terms of Service for pharmacists – a term that also includes persons lawfully conducting a retail pharmacy business (see Chapter 5). Each PCT is required to prepare a list, the *pharmaceutical list*, of the names and addresses of all those pharmacists who have undertaken to provide pharmaceutical services in the area, together with the services provided (reg.4). In this context, 'pharmacists' includes all pharmacy contractors – including company-owned pharmacies.

Any pharmacist who wishes to be included in the list must apply to the PCT in the prescribed form. Other than for a minor relocation of an existing pharmacy, or the transfer of ownership, the application is only granted if the PCT is satisfied that a service is necessary or **expedient** to grant the application in order to provide in its neighbourhood adequate pharmaceutical services (reg.14). (Under s.129 of the NHS Act 2006, the word 'expedient' has replaced the former 'desirable' test; at the time of writing, consultation was underway to update the 2005 regulations to reflect this change in the 2006 Act.) The PCT must remove from the list the name of any pharmacist who has died or has ceased to be a pharmacist. Provision is made for representatives of a deceased chemist who comply with the provisions of the Medicines Act (s.71) (see Chapter 5) and who agree to be bound by the Terms of Service to remain on the list (reg.45). Regulations 46 to 55 set out detailed provisions for conditional inclusion, suspension or removal from the pharmaceutical list under powers now to be found in Sections 151 to 163 of the NHS Act 2006. These include disqualification because:

- the continued inclusion of the pharmacist in the list will be prejudicial to the efficiency of the pharmaceutical service (an 'efficiency case');
- the pharmacist has (whether on his own or together with another) by an act or omission, caused, or risked causing, detriment to the health service by securing or trying to secure for himself or another any financial or other benefit and knew that s/he or the other was not entitled to the benefit (a 'fraud case'); or
- the pharmacist is unsuitable to be included in the list (an 'unsuitability case'), perhaps through having convictions or concerns about fitness to practise.

Appeals against disqualification are made to the Family Health Services Appeal Authority.

Control of entry to the list

The 2005 Regulations introduced four exemptions (reg.13) from the need to satisfy the general requirement that an application for a new community pharmacy contract shall only be granted if the PCT is satisfied that it is necessary or expedient to grant the application in order to secure, in the neighbourhood, the adequate provision of pharmaceutical services (the 'necessary or expedient' test). These are in respect of:

a   premises which are in an approved retail area (essentially large out-of-town shopping centres);

b   premises which the applicant is willing to keep open at least 100 hours per week;

c   premises which are in a new one-stop primary care centre; and

d   premises at which all persons receive services otherwise than at those premises ('distance selling' or Internet pharmacies).

For premises that fall within a to c, the PCT may specify which 'directed services' (see below under Terms of Service) shall be provided from the premises. Proposals to modify these exemptions were included after the Galbraith Review in the *Pharmacy in England* White Paper (see p. 411) published in 2008.

The Drug Tariff

For the purpose of paying pharmacists for their pharmaceutical services, the Secretary of State publishes the *Drug Tariff* (reg.56), a detailed list of standards and prices for:

- the appliances, chemical reagents and drugs approved by the Secretary of State;
- the prices on the basis of which the payment for drugs and appliances ordinarily supplied is to be calculated;
- the method of calculating the payment for drugs not mentioned in the Drug Tariff;
- the method of calculating the payment for containers and medicine measures;
- the dispensing or other fees payable in respect of the supply of drugs and appliances and other supplemental services; and
- arrangements for claiming fees, allowances and remuneration for the provision of pharmaceutical services.

A reward scheme (reg.59) is in place for pharmacists who assist in the detection of forged or otherwise fraudulent prescriptions.

Terms of Service of pharmacists

The Terms of Service appear in Schedule 1 to the 2005 Pharmaceutical Services Regulations. Part 2 of the schedule defines 'essential services' as dispensing and associated services. A pharmacist is required to supply pharmaceutical services against prescriptions from health professionals written in pursuance of their functions in the UK health service. This may be against a paper prescription or, in due course, an electronically transferred prescription, which ultimately may bear the prescriber's advanced electronic signature. The pharmacist must supply any drugs except those called 'scheduled drugs' (popularly known as the Black List), which comprises medicines in certain categories that cannot be prescribed for supply against NHS prescriptions. The categories were originally indigestion remedies, laxatives, analgesics for mild to moderate pain, bitters and tonics, vitamins and the benzodiazepine tranquillisers and sedatives. The Black List is made under the NHS (General Medical Services Contracts) (Prescription of Drugs) Regulations 2004 (SI 2004 No. 629) and the list now includes many other medicines, more recently, and subject to exceptions, so-called 'lifestyle' drugs such as Viagra (sildenafil) and Propecia (finasteride). Some of the scheduled drugs can be supplied in certain circumstances; for example, Viagra can be prescribed for men suffering from certain medical conditions. A full list of the drugs affected is also to be found in Part XVIIIA and B of the *Drug Tariff*.

All supplies of medicines (and appliance where relevant) must be made with reasonable promptness. However, when a doctor, by telephone or in writing, requests the chemist to dispense a medicine (not a Controlled Drug) in a situation of urgency without a signed prescription, the chemist may dispense the medicine provided that the doctor is personally known to him/her and has undertaken to supply a signed prescription within 72 hours.

Prescription levies

The pharmacist is expected to give an estimate of the time when drugs or appliances will be ready. Pharmacy staff are required to check at the point of dispensing, where an exemption has been claimed and other than on age grounds, and whether patients have evidence of their entitlement to free prescriptions. Where the patient cannot produce satisfactory evidence, the 'evidence not seen' box on the reverse of the prescription form must be marked with an X, but the prescription need not be refused. Any fees collected by the pharmacist are later debited from the payments he subsequently receives from the pricing authorities. At the time of writing, the exemption categories were of four types (full details are to be found in Part XVI of the *Drug Tariff*):

- persons who are exempt on age grounds;
- holders of a range of exemption certificates;
- persons who receive, or are partners of someone receiving, state benefits; and
- persons receiving no-charge contraceptives.

Providing ordered drugs or appliances

The pharmacist must only supply the drugs or appliances as ordered on the prescription (para.8) but, provided they are not Controlled Drugs, the pharmacist may exercise his professional skill and knowledge to remedy deficiencies in dosage or strength and where quantity is not stated to supply treatment for up to five days. Where the drug is only available in minimum original packs (such as oral contraceptives or liquid antibiotics) or is of a special nature (such as a sterile product or an effervescent or hygroscopic product), original packs may be supplied at the discretion of the pharmacist. The supply must be under the supervision of the pharmacist (this will also be affected if and when 'supervision' under the Medicines Act is reinterpreted). The pharmacist must supply the drug in a suitable container, if needed, free of charge.

A pharmacist may refuse to provide the supply (paragraph 9):

- where he reasonably believes that the prescription is forged;
- where to supply would be contrary to the pharmacist's clinical judgement;
- where the pharmacist or others on the premises are subject to or threatened with violence;
- where the person presenting the prescription commits or threatens to commit a criminal offence; or
- where irregularities or deficiencies in a repeat dispensing service mean that a repeat supply is not appropriate.

The pharmacist must ensure that appropriate advice on use and information is given to patients about their supplies (para.10) to enable them to use the medicines appropriately. This may include advice on safe keeping and safe destruction, providing guidance about only requesting repeats of items that are actually needed and details of any items or part-items that are owed. Records must be kept of supplies made and of any clinically significant advice, interventions or referrals made. If the pharmacist undertakes a repeat dispensing service, s/he must accept appropriate training and follow the management arrangements for the scheme. If an item is refused, the prescriber must be informed; where a repeat prescription is denied, the patient must be referred back to the prescriber for further advice.

Electronic prescribing or electronic transfer of prescriptions
At the time of writing, a significant proportion of community pharmacies were able to receive 'Release 1' electronic prescriptions, which may be transmitted electronically but still require the existence of a paper form for the supply to be completed. Implementation of 'Release 2' in which the prescription is only transmitted electronically (ETP) was enabled in 17 'initial implementer PCTs' at the beginning of December 2008 by the Primary Medical Services (Electronic Prescription Authorisation) Directions 2008. Paragraph 11 of the Terms of Service require a pharmacist to inform patients whether or not s/he is participating in ETP and, if not, to inform the patient of at least two other pharmacies in the area who are. The paragraph also requires the pharmacist to record the name of the pharmacy nominated by the patient to receive his or her electronic prescription, where the patient wishes to use that service.

Other essential services
Paragraphs 12, 13 and 14 require that a pharmacist shall accept and dispose of unwanted drugs (returned from patients) in the appropriate manner. Paragraphs 15 to 17 require the pharmacist to promote public

health messages to the public as prescribed by the PCT and to undertake prescription-linked interventions, backed up by leaflets and referral if necessary, for patients who have diabetes, risk of coronary heart disease, who smoke or who are obese. Records of any clinically significant advice must be made in a form that facilitates audit and follow-up care. Paragraphs 18 and 19 set out the pharmacist's duty to provide information to users of the pharmacy about other health and social care providers and organisations ('signposting'). Paragraphs 20 and 21 set out how the pharmacist shall also provide advice and support to people caring for themselves or their families.

Hours of opening

A pharmacist shall ensure that at each premises with an NHS contract (para.22), pharmaceutical services are provided for not less than 40 hours per week unless the PCT allows a variation or the contract is under the exemption requiring 100 hours a week (see control of entry above). Unless the pharmacy is a 'distance selling' (Internet) pharmacy, a pharmacist is required to exhibit a notice showing his/her hours of contract. At times when the business is not open, the pharmacist must exhibit, where practicable legible from outside the premises, a notice based on information from the PCT, listing the addresses of the other pharmacists in the pharmaceutical list, together with the hours of opening of their premises for the supply of medicines. The pharmacist must, at the request of the PCT, submit a return giving particulars of their pharmaceutical service and the days and hours on which it is provided. Pharmacists wishing to amend their contractual hours must apply to the PCT and, if they wish to open for additional hours beyond the 40 hour core contract, they must notify the PCT at least 90 days in advance. Arrangements for Bank Holidays and Christmas are also specified; they are complex and interested readers are referred to the Pharmaceutical Services Negotiating Committee (PSNC) website for full details.

Clinical governance, fitness to practise and complaints

Regulation 26 of the Terms of Service requires that the pharmacist shall 'participate in an acceptable system of clinical governance', which must comprise a 'patient and public involvement programme'. This is met by means of a practice leaflet for the public giving information about the pharmacy services available from each premises, the undertaking of approved community pharmacy patient questionnaires, an approved complaints system, co-operation with the local patient's forum (soon to be LINks, see above) and the PCT in visits and inspections, and implementation of monitoring arrangements to ensure compliance with the Disability Discrimination Act (see Chapter 21). The pharmacy must implement at least one pharmacy-based and one multidisciplinary audit per year. It must also have in place and implement:

- a *risk management programme*, including the appointment of a clinical governance lead, procedures to manage the quality of stock and equipment, appropriate standard operating procedures, child protection procedures, incident-reporting systems, waste disposal arrangements and monitoring of compliance with health and safety legislation (see Chapter 21);
- a *clinical effectiveness programme*, including advice with repeat dispensing arrangements;
- a *staffing and management programme*, including induction and training, checking of qualifications and references and addressing poor performance for all staff; and
- a *use of information programme*, which includes regard to rights of access and confidentiality of healthcare delivery and clinical information, compliance with the NHS Code of Practice on Confidentiality and the data protection legislation (see Chapter 21).

The pharmacist must conform to the generally accepted professional standards within the pharmacy profession (reg.27) and must not give, promise or offer any person any gift or reward (whether by way of a share of or dividend on the profits of the business, or by way of discount, rebate or otherwise) as an inducement for any kind of prescriptions to be presented to a particular pharmacy (reg.28). The pharmacist (including superintendent pharmacists and other pharmacists who are directors of a pharmacy company) must notify the PCT about any convictions or adverse fitness to practise incidents as they arise. For companies, this would be to the PCT in which the registered office is situated. A satisfactory complaints procedure must comply with Part II of the NHS (Complaints) Regulations 2004 (SI 2004 No. 1768). It should also be noted here that the NHS Act 2006 (s.166) requires that a person listed in the pharmaceutical list must hold approved *indemnity cover*. This is also required in the conditions for being a practising registered pharmacist (see Chapter 22).

Information and inspection

Paragraphs 34, 35 and 36 specify information that the pharmacist must supply, with adequate notice, to the PCT, such as changes of address, the name of an employee pharmacist who is responsible for dispensing a particular prescription, name and registered office of a company that runs pharmacies, information about any contract applications and withdrawal from the pharmaceutical list. The pharmacist must allow persons authorised by the PCT to enter and inspect his/her pharmacy at any reasonable time for the purpose of ensuring compliance with the Terms of Service and auditing and monitoring of any pharmaceutical services (see also above under Standards for Better Health). This does not extend to entry of parts of the premises used solely for residential purposes, and the confidentiality of patient information should be protected.

Directed services

Paragraph 33 of the Terms of Service covers the arrangements a PCT may make for *directed services*. These may be for *advanced services* (for which a national tariff has been set) or for *enhanced services* (where the fee is agreed between the local PCT and the contractor). The key Directions implementing this paragraph are the Pharmaceutical Services (Advanced and Enhanced Services) (England) Directions 2005 (this and later amendments are available on the PSNC and Department of Health websites). These set out the conditions that apply only to the advanced service which was in place at the time of writing, namely *Medicines Use Review* (MUR) (or a prescription intervention that leads to an MUR). The best source of this detailed information is the PSNC website. In addition, the 2005 Directions list 19 services that may be the subject of arrangements for enhanced services. These include:

- monitoring and screening for patients taking anticoagulants;
- advice and support for patients in care homes;
- smoking cessation services;
- services to school staff and children;
- home delivery of medicines;
- needle and syringe exchange schemes;
- services using Patient Group Direction authorisations (see Chapter 8);
- full medication reviews; and
- minor ailment services.

Several of these are likely to become nationally required services if and when the proposals in the White Paper *Pharmacy in England* are implemented (see above).

Local pharmaceutical services

PCTs may commission any other services (LPS schemes) from pharmacies, usually services not traditionally associated with pharmacy, to address local needs. These are most commonly contracts for 'essential small pharmacies' where there is insufficient demand for a viable business without some financial support. From 2006, PCTs have been able to set their own timetables for developing and commissioning LPS schemes subject to regulations [NHS (Local Pharmaceutical Services, etc) Regulations 2006 SI 2006 No. 552].

Compliance arrangements

The monitoring of the contractual framework for community pharmacy by PCTs aims to encourage the provision of services to a high standard. PCTs, therefore, are expected not only to inspect and monitor services but also to support improvement in cases where deficiencies are identified. A Department of Health statement *Pharmacy Contract: Non-compliance and Dispute Resolution* (July 2006) provides guidance for PCTs on how to deal with non-compliance which does or does not pose a risk to the public and how to resolve disputes. However, formal action against the contractor can be taken in two ways. The PCT can convene a *Discipline Committee* to consider the matter under the NHS (Service Committee and Tribunal Regulations 1992, SI 1992 No. 664) or it can invoke procedures under the fitness to practise sections of the Terms of Service (see above). Finally sections 151 to 163 of the NHS Act provide power for a pharmacist to be nationally disqualified from being on any pharmaceutical list (see above). The PSNC and the RPSGB provide guidance for community pharmacies on the rights and limits of access by a wide range of other compliance authorities, including NHS representatives of LINks, PCTs and the counter-fraud service and non-NHS authorities such as the police, RPSGB inspectors, Healthcare Commission agents, health and safety inspectors and HM Revenue and Customs.

Local pharmaceutical committees

Local Pharmaceutical Committees (LPCs) are recognised under section 167 of the NHS Act 2006 as representative of the persons providing pharmaceutical services in the locality of one or more PCTs. Those LPCs which have adopted the model constitution promulgated by the PSNC comprise 13 pharmacists elected or appointed by contractors in accordance with the 'Model Constitution' updated in 2006). Full details are available on the PSNC website.

Each Committee appoints its own secretary and the appointment has to be notified to the PCT and to the PSNC. The term of office for members of the Committee is four years and the Committee has power of co-option for casual vacancies. A person ceases to be a member of the Committee if s/he ceases to be engaged in the section of the NHS which s/he represents. His/her seat must be declared vacant if s/he has been absent from three consecutive meetings of the Committee without reasonable cause.

The duties of an LPC include:

1 consulting with the PCT on such occasions and to such an extent as may be prescribed by the Secretary of State;
2 ensuring that the Committee conducts its affairs in accordance with accepted principles of good governance;
3 establishing effective liaison with other NHS bodies in the PCT(s) area;

4   appointing representatives to any body on which pharmaceutical representation is required;

5   advising any pharmacy contractor who needs help or assistance on NHS matters;

6   considering any complaint made by a pharmacy contractor against another pharmacy contractor carrying on a business in the area and involving any question of the efficiency of the pharmaceutical services;

7   making representations to the PCT and to the PSNC on matters of importance to pharmacy contractors;

8   making requests to the PCT(s) for such sums of money required to defray the Committee's administrative expenses from money available for remuneration of pharmacy contractors;

9   assisting in the formulations of bids for local funding;

10   ensuring transparency and equality of information and opportunity for all contractors in matters relating to the local purchasing of pharmaceutical services;

11   collaborating with the PSNC;

12   collaborating with other LPCs;

13   responding to any request from a contractor for an enquiry into irregularities in the LPC's activities; and

14   ensuring that appropriate structures such as subcommittees and resources are in place to discharge its duties in a proper manner.

The Committee must prepare an annual report and accounts, and must circulate them to the electors in the area and to the PSNC.

Pharmaceutical Services Negotiating Committee

The PSNC negotiates terms and conditions of service for pharmacy contractors. The Committee is composed of 31 persons as follows: 14 members elected on a regional basis from England, one member from Wales, five members from the board of the National Pharmaceutical Association, eight members from the Company Chemists Association and three members from the Association of Independent Multiple Pharmacies The PSNC has four subcommittees concerned with funding and contract, NHS service development, LPC and implementation support and resource development and finance. The PSNC has also set up the National Prescription Research Centre, which carries out both random or routine checking and special checks at the request of a contractor, of the pricing of prescriptions by the Prescription Pricing Division of the NHS Business Authority.

Prescription pricing

Prescription pricing is now carried out by a division of the NHS Business Authority to calculate and make payments to pharmacy and appliance contractors. It also produces prescribing and costs information for the NHS, administers a range of health benefits such as maternity and pre-payment exemption, certifies the checking of these exemptions, and produces the *Drug Tariff* (see above).

Wales

National Health Service organisation

In Wales, secondary legislation (i.e. that which is made under enabling powers set out in an Act) on health is made by the National Assembly for Wales. The Welsh Assembly then executes Assembly policies on health and social care through NHS Wales. The parent legislation for the NHS in Wales is the NHS (Wales) Act 2006; secondary implementing legislation will be made by the Assembly. In late 2008, the Health Minister for Wales announced plans to simplify the NHS structure in Wales so that single unified health delivery bodies will be responsible for delivering all healthcare services, secondary and primary, within a geographical area. These local bodies will be overseen by the National Board (Figure 26.2). The Welsh Pharmaceutical Committee was reconstituted in 2000 to provide professional advice to the National Assembly and the Welsh Government and its membership and constitution were reviewed in 2007. The Welsh Pharmaceutical Committee roles are to:

- advise the First Secretary and the Assembly Minister for Health and Social Services on pharmaceutical services in Wales;
- implement an annual work programme agreed between the Director of the Health and Social Services Department, Chief Medical Officer, Chief Pharmaceutical Adviser and the Chairman and Vice Chairman on behalf of the Committee; and
- comment and advise upon documents or issues referred to it by the Assembly.

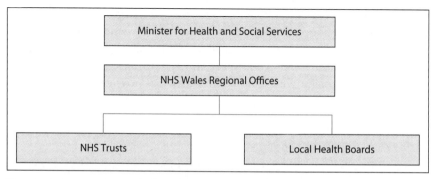

Figure 26.2 NHS structure in Wales. From April 2009, the regional offices are planned to merge to form a National Advisory Board, and NHS trusts and local health boards will merge to become local unified delivery bodies.

NHS Wales falls within the Health and Social Care Department, which has three regional offices, North Wales, Mid & West Wales and South & East Wales, which co-ordinate and manage the performance of local health boards (LHB) and NHS trusts. At the time of writing there were 21 LHBs, one unified health board and 13 NHS trusts, plus an All Wales Ambulance Trust, but these are likely to become seven unified bodies from April 2009, legislation permitting. The LHBs share common boundaries with local government authority areas to facilitate a partnership approach to planning healthcare and social care. The LHBs commission health services and are supported by the Business Service Centre, which, amongst other functions, manages payments for pharmacy contractor services. There is a place for a pharmacist on each LHB. Responsibility for inspection and investigation of health lies with Health Inspectorate Wales, an 'arm's length body' answerable directly to the Welsh Permanent Secretary. In 2005, the Welsh Assembly Government published Healthcare Standards for Wales and the Inspectorate is charged with undertaking reviews and investigations of all NHS-funded care to support continuous quality improvement. Community health councils in each local government area represent the patient's voice in healthcare and may inspect both primary and secondary care establishments.

Pharmacy organisation

Negotiation on reimbursement and national service payments are undertaken by *Community Pharmacy Wales*, which is separate from but has close links to the PSNC (see p. 430). The status of Community Pharmacy Wales as a negotiating body for Welsh pharmacy contractors was legally established in April 2004; full details of its constitution and activities are available on the relevant website at the end of this chapter. At the time of writing, Wales had adopted a community pharmacy contract that is very similar to that in England, particularly with regard to essential, advanced and enhanced service levels. However, the detailed arrangements, especially fees, may diverge from those in England; for example, Wales has dropped charges for NHS prescriptions and has not adopted either LPS schemes or the exemptions to control of entry that currently apply only in England. Other differences will emerge in the very near future and readers are advised to check the websites for Community Pharmacy Wales and NHS Wales for current information.

Scotland

National Health Service organisation

Scotland has had its own Parliament since July 1999 and it has powers to make primary legislation on healthcare. The NHS in Scotland has always operated separately from the service in England and Wales. Although the principal Act remains the NHS (Scotland) Act 1978, this has now been modified by the NHS Reform (Scotland) Act 2004. NHS Scotland policy is developed and administered through the Scottish Government Health Department via 14 territorial 'unified' NHS boards. Primary and secondary care are separate divisions within the unified NHS boards, with representation from each local authority to improve management of health and social care. In addition, there is oversight of the Board's activities by NHS Quality Improvement Scotland (QIS). At the end of 2008, plans were announced to merge QIS, the Mental Welfare Commission for Scotland and the private healthcare inspection undertaken by the Care Commission.

The functions of the NHS boards include the planning and provision of healthcare services and the management of pharmacy contracts. The Scottish Health Council monitors the performance of the NHS boards and promotes public involvement in healthcare. Each board also supports community health partnerships, which focus on planning and provision of local health services. Each community health partnership has on its committee a place for a registered pharmacist whose name is included in, or who is fully or substantially employed by a person or body whose name is included in, a pharmaceutical list prepared by an NHS board. Most NHS boards have the services of a pharmacist, called variously a 'consultant' or 'specialist' in pharmaceutical public health, who provides strategic pharmacy advice to the NHS board. The overall control of pharmaceutical services within each NHS board lies with the board's director of pharmacy. In addition all NHS boards have an area pharmaceutical committee. These committees comprise pharmacists who work in both the hospital and community sectors and are representative of the professionals working in the area.

The Practitioner Services Division of NHS National Services Scotland manages payments for pharmacy contractors. Responsibility for inspection

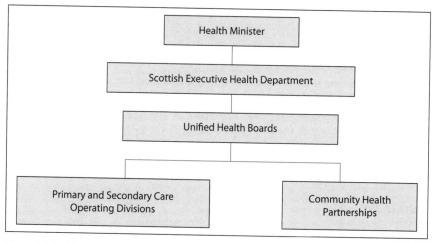

Figure 26.3 NHS structure in Scotland.

and audit of healthcare lies with the NHS Quality Improvement Scotland. The Scottish Health Council represent the patient's voice in healthcare and may inspect both primary and secondary care establishments.

Pharmacy organisation

Negotiation on remuneration and reimbursement on behalf of Scotland's community pharmacy contractors is carried out by *Community Pharmacy Scotland* (previously known as the Scottish Pharmaceutical General Council). This body negotiates nationally on behalf of 14 pharmacy contractor committees, one for each health board. The Community Pharmacy Contract in Scotland is radically different from that in either England or Wales and its scope is to be found in the Smoking, Health and Social Care (Scotland) Act 2005 (asp.13). The Scottish contract comprises services in four areas:

Minor Ailment Service (MAS). This is a scheme whereby patients who are registered with a Scottish GP and who are exempt from prescription charges (with some exceptions) may register with a community pharmacy and receive over-the-counter medicines within a formulary, free of charge, following consultation with the pharmacist.

Public Health Service (PHS). This involves community pharmacists and staff in national programmes to promote healthy lifestyles and public health interventions such as smoking cessation, chlamydia screening and supply of emergency hormonal contraception.

Acute Medication Service (AMS). This essentially is the dispensing of acute prescriptions.

Chronic Medication Service (CMS). This covers the dispensing and management of repeat prescriptions.

Details of service specification and remuneration for the last two areas had not been finalised at the time of writing.

The Terms of Service for chemists in Scotland are laid down in the NHS (Pharmaceutical Services) (Scotland) Regulations [SI 1995 No. 414 (s.28), as amended]. Amendments include adoption of procedures for the handling of complaints and the establishment of discipline committees [SIs 1996 No. 840 (s.95); 1996 No. 938 (s.103)], the adoption of point-of-dispensing checks for evidence of exemption [SI 1998 No. 3031 (s.174)] and powers to exclude from the pharmaceutical list pharmacists who are subject to fraud enquiries (SI 2004 No. 39). Arrangements for disciplinary service committees and tribunals are covered by SI 2004 No. 38.

Summary

- The statutory framework for NHS services differs between England, Scotland and Wales, although the objectives are similar.

- The NHS is a mixed market of commissioning and provision of services by a range of health service bodies, overseen by civil service departments reporting to governments.
- NHS trusts, mostly hospitals, provide NHS secondary care in England and Wales; in Scotland, the provision of secondary care comes under the acute operational divisions of the NHS boards.
- Primary care trusts in England and local health boards in Wales secure the provision of primary care, including pharmaceutical services, through contracts with local owners of pharmacies; in Scotland, this activity has passed to the primary care operational division of the NHS boards.
- In Wales, NHS trusts and local health boards are likely to merge into single NHS boards in the near future.
- NHS contracts are limited in number and impose numerous conditions on the chemist, as set out in the NHS chemists' Terms of Service.
- Specifications for the amount and conditions which apply to payments under the NHS chemists' Terms of Service are set out in the *Drug Tariff*.
- Negotiations for payments take place nationally through the Pharmaceutical Services Negotiating Committee, Community Pharmacy Wales or Community Pharmacy Scotland and locally through local pharmaceutical committees or their Welsh or Scottish equivalents.
- The public interest in the NHS is represented by patient forums and the patients' advice and liaison service (PALS) in England, community health councils in Wales and local health councils in Scotland.

Further reading

Department of Health (2008) *NHS Next Stage Review Our Vision for Primary and Community Care*. London: The Stationery Office.
Department of Health (2008) *Pharmacy in England Building on Strengths – Delivering the Future*. [Cmmd.7341] London: The Stationery Office.
Merrills J, Fisher J (1997) *Pharmacy Law and Practice*, 2nd edn. Oxford: Blackwell Scientific.
Montgomery J (2002) *Health Care Law*, 3rd edn. Oxford: Oxford University Press.
National Assembly for Wales Government (2002) *Remedies for Success: A Strategy for Pharmacy in Wales*. Cardiff: Welsh Assembly Government.
Scottish Executive (2002) *The Right Medicine: A Strategy for Pharmaceutical Care in Scotland*. Edinburgh: The Scottish Executive.

Websites

Commission for Social Care Inspection: www.csci.org.uk
Community Pharmacy Scotland: www.communitypharmacyscotland.org.uk/
Community Pharmacy Wales: www.lpc-online.org.uk/community_pharmacy_wales
Department of Health (England): www.dh.gov.uk/en/Healthcare/
    Medicinespharmacyandindustry/index.htm
Health Inspectorate Wales: www.hiw.org.uk/
Healthcare Commission: www.healthcarecommission.org.uk

National Institute for Clinical Excellence: www.nice.org.uk

National Patient Safety Agency: www.npsa.nhs.uk

NHS 24: http://www.nhs24.com/content/

NHS Choices portal: www.nhs.uk/aboutnhs/HowtheNHSworks/authoritiesandtrusts/Pages/authoritiesandtrusts.aspx

NHS Direct: www.nhsdirect.nhs.uk/

NHS Direct Wales: http://www.nhsdirect.wales.nhs.uk/

NHS Primary Care Contracting: www.pcc.nhs.uk

NHS Scotland: www.scotland.gov.uk/Topics/Health/NHS-Scotland or www.show.scot.nhs.uk/

NHS Wales: www.wales.nhs.uk/sites3/home.cfm?OrgID=452

Pharmaceutical Services Negotiating Committee: www.psnc.org.uk

Prescription Pricing Authority (England): www.ppa.org.uk

27

Legal decisions affecting pharmacy

The decisions in important cases in the courts which have directly affected pharmacy are brought together in this chapter. Although Acts of Parliament take precedence over all other law, the meaning of any statute is subject to interpretation by the courts. Consequently, most of the cases outlined here are about the meaning of terms, or of individual words, used in the statutes. Some arise from the application of a statute in particular circumstances. A few are concerned with general principles. *Jenkin* v. *The Pharmaceutical Society* and *The Pharmaceutical Society* v. *Dickson* deal with the extent of the powers of the Royal Pharmaceutical Society of Great Britain (RPSGB, referred to here as the Society) under its Charter; the authority of the Statutory Committee is considered in *Re Lawson*, while *The Pharmaceutical Society* v. *Boots Cash Chemists (Southern) Ltd* has a bearing on the law of contract.

The cases are set out individually, or in groups, under headings which indicate the subject or the point at issue. Where appropriate some explanatory comment is added. Table 27.1 lists the cases together with references to the pages on which the relevant points at issue are explained.

The meaning of `acting in accordance with the directions of a practitioner'

Roberts v. Coombs (1949)

The Penicillin Act 1947 reads:

> ...no person shall sell or otherwise supply any substance to which this Act applies or any preparation of which any such substance is an ingredient or part unless (a) he is a duly qualified medical practitioner, a registered dental practitioner or a registered veterinary surgeon, or a person acting in accordance with the directions of any such practitioner or surgeon, and the substance or preparation is sold or supplied for the purposes of treatment by or in accordance with the

Table 27.1 Decisions in important cases in the courts which have directly affected pharmacy

Topic	Cases	Where discussed (p.)
1 Meaning of acting in accordance with the directions of a practitioner	*Roberts* v. *Coombs* (1949)	437
2 Meaning of by a doctor or dentist to a patient of his	*Pharmaceutical Society* v. *Wright* (1981)	439
3 Meaning of *person*	*Pharmaceutical Society of Great Britain* v. *London and Provincial Supply Association Ltd* (1880)	440
4 Powers of the Royal Pharmaceutical Society	*Jenkin* v. *Pharmaceutical Society of Great Britain* (1921)	440
	Pharmaceutical Society of Great Britain v. *Dickson* (1968)	442
5 Meaning of sale by way of wholesale dealing	*Oxford* v. *Sanger* (1964)	443
6 Meaning of *shop*	*Greenwood* v. *Whelan* (1966)	444
7 Meaning of *supervision*	*Roberts* v. *Littlewoods Mail Order Stores Ltd* (1943)	444
	Pharmaceutical Society of Great Britain v. *Boots Cash Chemists (Southern) Ltd* (1953)	445
	R v. *Family Health Services Appeal Authority, ex parte Elmfield Drugs Ltd, Selles Dispensing Chemists Ltd, and E Moss (Chemists) Ltd* (1998)	446
8 Use of titles and descriptions	*Norris* v. *Weeks* (1970)	447
9 Meaning of *a sample*	*Mistry* v. *Norris* (1985)	447
10 Sale of Prescription Only Medicine: offence of strict liability	*Pharmaceutical Society of Great Britain* v. *Storkwain Ltd* (1986)	448
11 Is dispensing a medicine on a National Health Service prescription a *sale*?	*Appleby* v. *Sleep* (1968)	448
12 Importation of medicinal products from the European Community	*R* v. *Royal Pharmaceutical Society of Great Britain, ex parte Association of Pharmaceutical Importers and Others* (1989)	449
13 Sale of prescription data: breach of confidentiality?	*R* v. *Department of Health, ex parte Source Informatics Ltd* (2000)	450
14 Meaning of professional assessment	*Cathy Bosworth Horton* v. *Timothy Evans and Lloyds Pharmacy Ltd* (2006)	451

directions of that practitioner or surgeon; or (b) he is a registered pharmacist or an authorised seller of poisons, and the substance or preparation is sold or supplied under the authority of a prescription signed and dated by any such practitioner or surgeon as aforesaid.

A shopkeeper who was not an authorised seller sold penicillin ointment to customers who presented prescriptions signed and dated by a medical practitioner. The shopkeeper was charged with selling ointment containing penicillin contrary to section 1(1) of the Act, he not being one of the qualified persons mentioned in that subsection. The magistrates dismissed the summonses on the grounds that, although the shopkeeper was not a practitioner, he was a person acting in accordance with the directions of a duly qualified medical practitioner.

On appeal to the High Court it was held that *a person acting in accordance with any such practitioner or surgeon* was a person in the employment of a doctor or in some way actually under the direct orders of the doctor. A prescription signed and dated by a medical practitioner could be made up only by a registered pharmacist or an authorised seller of poisons.

[1949] 2 All ER 37; *Pharm J* 14 May 1949 p. 356.

Comment: The Penicillin Act 1947 was later replaced by the Therapeutic Substances Act 1956. The wording was subsequently retained in section 58(2) (b) of the Medicines Act 1968 which also repealed the 1956 Act.

The meaning of 'by a doctor or dentist to a patient of his' under the Medicines Act 1968

Pharmaceutical Society v. Wright (1981)

The Medicines Act requires that no person shall sell a Prescription Only medicinal product except in accordance with a prescription given by an appropriate practitioner. However, the Act provides that this provision does not apply to the sale or supply of a medicinal product to a patient of his/hers by a doctor or dentist who is an appropriate practitioner.

Once a week, Dr Wright ran a slimming clinic and those attending were given a medicinal product which was on the Prescription Only list. Many of the persons attending the clinic were patients of other doctors in the town and only attended the clinic, which was supervised by a nurse, for slimming purposes. The issue turned upon whether or not there was a doctor–patient relationship between the attendees and Dr Wright.

Mr Justice Bingham said:

>...if a doctor acting as such, treats or gives advice to a person and assumes responsibility for that treatment or advice, that person may very well be his patient...in determining whether the relationship does exist it is not...of primary importance whether the person is a patient

of another doctor as well nor whether the treatment or advice is given by the doctor's staff under his supervision rather than the doctor himself. Nor ...whether the relationship is a short-lived or long-lived. Nor ...need it be of primary importance whether the doctor takes less care in giving the advice or treatment than he should ...

(1981) Unreported.

Comment: In dismissing the appeal brought by the Society, Lord Donaldson, who sat with Mr Justice Bingham, said that it was for the Society to prove there was no doctor–patient relationship not for Dr Wright to prove there was.

The meaning of `person'

Pharmaceutical Society of Great Britain v. London and Provincial Supply Association Ltd (1880)

The Pharmacy Act 1868 (s.1) provided:

From and after 31 December, 1868 it shall be unlawful for any person to sell or keep open shop for retailing ...poisons ...unless such person shall be a pharmaceutical chemist, a chemist and druggist ...and be registered under this Act ...

Section 15 provided penalties for offences under section 1.

A company had sold poisons by retail from its shop. The Society took legal proceedings against the company, contending that a body corporate was a 'person' in law and that section 1 applied to it. The High Court had supported that view but the Court of Appeal had not.

On appeal to the House of Lords, it was held that in the context of the Act the word *person* in sections 1 and 15 meant a natural person and did not include a body corporate.

5 App. Cases 857; *Pharm J* 31 July 1880 p. 83.

Comment: This decision enabled a company to keep open shop for the sale of poisons provided the other conditions in the Act were met. The Poisons and Pharmacy Act 1908 and subsequent statutes took account of the decision and required a body corporate to appoint a superintendent to conduct and manage the keeping, retailing and dispensing of poisons.

Powers of the Royal Pharmaceutical Society of Great Britain

Jenkin v. Pharmaceutical Society of Great Britain (1921)

The Society's Charter of Incorporation 1843 had, as one of its objects, the protection of those who carry on the business of chemists and druggists.

In 1919, the Council of the Society took part in promoting an Industrial Council for the drug trade. The objects of the proposed body included, among others, the regulation of wages, hours and working conditions, and of production and employment. Mr Jenkin, who was a member of the Society and, prior to the case, a member of the Council of the Society, sought an injunction in the High Court (Chancery Division) to prevent the Society from sponsoring the Industrial Council on the grounds that the functions proposed were not within the scope of the Society's powers.

It was held by the High Court that a member was entitled to obtain an injunction restraining the commission of acts outside the scope of the Charter. The Society could not carry on a business of general insurance, even though limited to members, as it would not benefit members as a whole. Nor could it legalise by its Charter a combination in restraint of trade and so convert itself into a trade union as defined in the Trade Union Act 1876 (s.16).

The Court declared that it was not within the power or purposes of the Society to take part in, or expend any of its funds in the formation, establishment, maintenance or work of the Industrial Council, or to undertake or perform the following matters:

1   to regulate the hours of business of members of the Society; or
2   to regulate the wages and conditions of employment as between masters and their employees who were members of the Society; or
3   to regulate the prices at which members should sell their goods; or
4   to insure and to effect insurance of members of the Society against errors, neglect and misconduct of employees, and against fire, burglary, damage to plate glass and generally against insurable risks.

[1921] 1 Ch 392, *Pharm J* 23 October 1920 p. 386 and 30 October 1920 p. 405.

Comment: As a result of this decision a separate body, the Retail Pharmacists' Union (later called the National Pharmaceutical Association) was established to carry out various functions including those denied to the Society. No action was taken by the Society to carry on any of the other activities which had been proposed for the Industrial Council and which had not been declared to be outside the Society's powers. They were:

1   the provision and maintenance of an employment register and a register of unsatisfactory employees;
2   the auditing of accounts, the collection of debts, and the taking of stock for its members;
3   the provision and supply of information to the commercial standing of persons and firms with whom members of the Society wish to transact business; and
4   the provision of legal advice to members.

In the Supplemental Charter of 1953 (see Chapter 19), the objects of the Society were amended. The wording 'the protection of those who carry on the business of chemists and druggists' was replaced by 'to maintain the honour and safeguard and promote the interests of the members in the exercise of the profession of pharmacy'.

In the *Dickson* case (see below) reference was made to the decision in the *Jenkin* case to the change of emphasis in the chartered objects of the Society from *business* to *profession*.

Pharmaceutical Society of Great Britain v. Dickson (1968)

This was an appeal by the Society to the House of Lords against an Order of the Court of Appeal ([1967] All ER 558; *Pharm J* 4 February 1967 p. 113), which upheld a judgment of the High Court (Chancery Division) ([1966] 3 All ER 404; *Pharm J* 2 July 1966 p. 22).

The background to the case was as follows. Arising out of a recommendation of the Report on the General Practice of Pharmacy (*Pharm J* 20 April 1963) a motion was put to the Annual General Meeting of the Pharmaceutical Society in 1965 in the following terms:

New pharmacies should be situated only in premises which are physically distinct, and should be devoted solely to:

(i) professional services, as defined,
(ii) non-professional services, as defined . . .and
(iii) such other services as may be approved by the Council; and the range of services as may be approved by the Council; and the range of services in existing pharmacies, or in pharmacy departments of larger establishments should not be extended beyond the present limits except as approved by the Council.

Owing to the large attendance at the Annual General Meeting, no vote could be taken and a special general meeting to consider the recommendation was held at the Royal Albert Hall on 25 July 1965. Mr RCM Dickson (a director of Boots Pure Drug Co. Ltd) sought an injunction to restrain the holding of the meeting. He also claimed that the motion:

1   was outside the scope of the Society's powers; and
2   if implemented, would be a restraint upon trade.

Application for an injunction was refused by the High Court, an undertaking being given by the Society that the motion would not be made effective until after the judgment in the action to determine whether or not the object of the motion was within the Society's powers. At the Albert

Hall meeting, a motion supporting the recommendation was passed by 5020 votes to 1336.

The order of the High Court declared:

> That it is not within the powers, purposes or objects of the Pharmaceutical Society of Great Britain . . .to enforce or carry out or attempt to enforce or carry out the provisions of the motion . . .on the ground that the said provisions are in restraint of trade.

The Court of Appeal dismissed an appeal by the Society against the order. On further appeal to the House of Lords, the order given by the High Court was affirmed. It was held that:

1   The proposed restriction, although intended to be binding in honour only, might be a basis for disciplinary action. The courts had the power and the duty to determine its validity.
2   It was not within the powers or purposes of the Society to control selling activities which did not interfere with the proper performance of professional pharmaceutical duties. The only relevant object in the Society's Charter was 'to maintain the honour and safeguard and protect the interests of the members in their exercise of the profession of pharmacy', and the proposed rules of conduct had too slender a connection or link with that object.
3   The proposed restrictions were beyond the powers of the Society as they were in restraint of trade and had not been shown to be reasonable.

[1968] 2 All ER 686; *Pharm J* 1 June 1968 p. 651.

Comment: This decision did not affect the Society's powers to regulate professional conduct in pharmacy (see Chapter 23).

The meaning of 'sale by way of wholesale dealing'

Oxford v. Sanger (1964)

The Pharmacy and Poisons Act 1933 (s.18) provided that poisons in Part I of the Poisons List could be lawfully sold only by authorised sellers of poisons. An exemption from this requirement was given in section 20(1) of the Act in respect of sales of poisons by way of wholesale dealing. Section 29 defined *sale by way of wholesale dealing* as 'sale to a person who buys for the purposes of selling again'.

Sanger Ltd (wholesalers) had on five occasions sold Part I poisons to a retail shopkeeper who had subsequently sold the poisons (tablets) to the public by retail. The shopkeeper was not an authorised seller of poisons.

The wholesaler was charged with selling Part I poisons contrary to section 18 of the Act. It was contended for the prosecution that the company could not claim the benefit of the exemption for wholesale dealing as the poison had been sold to a shopkeeper who could not lawfully sell again. The magistrate dismissed the information, and an appeal to the High Court against that decision was also dismissed.

It was held in the High Court that the word *lawfully* could not be read into the definition of *wholesale dealing*. Section 20 did not lay any duty upon a wholesaler to ascertain that the retailer to whom he sold was lawfully entitled to resell. If it was desired to control wholesalers, it could and must be done by rule.

[1965] 1 All ER 96; *Pharm J* 12 December 1964 p. 599.

Comment: Rule 11 of the Poisons Rules made under the Poisons Act 1972 now requires wholesalers who sell Part I poisons to be satisfied that their shopkeeper customers who order such poisons are authorised sellers of poisons, or that they do not intend to sell the poisons by way of retail trade. The Medicines Act 1968 (s.61) provides for similar regulations to be made in respect of medicinal products (SI 1980 No. 1923).

The meaning of `shop'

Greenwood v. Whelan (1966)

[1967] All ER 294; *Pharm J* 3 December 1966 p. 575.

Comment: This case turned on the meaning of the word *shop* in the Pharmacy and Medicines Act 1941. In *Greenwood* v. *Whelan*, the Lord Chief Justice, referring to the Shops Act 1950, pointed out that retail trade or business could be carried out in three different ways, firstly from a shop, secondly, from a place that is not a shop, e.g. a stall, and thirdly from a barrow or itinerant van, in a way where there is no fixed place. The stall in that case, notwithstanding the regularity of the business, the permanence of the site, and the type of the structure, was a *place not being a shop*. The 1941 Act was repealed by the Medicines Act 1968 which now refers to *premises* not *shops* (s.53). Medicinal products may only be sold from premises which the occupier can 'close so as to exclude the public' (see Chapter 6).

The meaning of `supervision'

Roberts v. Littlewoods Mail Order Stores Ltd (1943)

The Pharmacy and Poisons Act 1933 (s.18) provided: '. . .it shall not be lawful for a person to sell any poison in Part I of the Poisons List unless . . .the sale is effected by, or under the supervision of, a registered pharmacist.' Similar wording is now in the Medicines Act (s.52) (see Chapter 5).

A sale of a Part I poison was made at the company's pharmacy to one of the Society's inspectors while the sole pharmacist was in a stockroom upstairs and unaware that the sale was being made by an unqualified assistant. The magistrates found that the sale, though not effected by the pharmacist, was effected sufficiently under his supervision. His actual presence was not reasonably required.

The decision was reversed in the High Court, where it was held that the sale had not been supervised. Lord Caldecote said:

> ...the man who was upstairs might have been a person who was exercising personal control of a business, but I do not think that, while he was upstairs and therefore absent, he could be a person who was supervising a particular sale. It has been suggested that a man can supervise a sale without being bodily present. I do not accept that contention ...each individual sale must be, not necessarily effected by the qualified person, but something which is shown by the evidence to be under his supervision in the sense that he must be aware of what is going on at the counter, and in a position to supervise or superintend the activities of the young woman by whom each individual sale is effected.

[1943] 1 All ER 271; *Pharm J* 30 January 1943 p. 38.

Pharmaceutical Society of Great Britain v. Boots Cash Chemists (Southern) Ltd (1953)

This was a case arising under the Pharmacy and Poisons Act 1933 (s.18) (see also *Roberts v. Littlewoods Mail Order Stores Ltd*, above). It was an appeal by the Pharmaceutical Society against a judgment of the Lord Chief Justice in the High Court.

A Boots pharmacy was arranged on a 'self-service' system. A customer could select goods, including Part I poisons, from the shelves, place them in a wire basket and take them to the cash desk. Before the cashier accepted payment, a pharmacist at the cash desk could, if he thought fit, prevent a sale. It was suggested by the Society that a purchase was completed when a customer took an article and put it in the basket so that the pharmacist could not later intervene. That suggestion had not been accepted in the High Court by the Lord Chief Justice, who had said that self-service was no different from the normal transactions in a shop. He had continued:

> ...the mere fact that a customer picks up a bottle of medicine from the shelves in this case does not amount to an acceptance of an offer to sell.

It is an offer by the customer to buy . . .By using the words the sale is effected by, or under the supervision of, a registered pharmacist, it seems to me the sale might be effected by somebody not a pharmacist. If it be under the supervision of a pharmacist, the pharmacist can say: 'You cannot have that. That contains poison'. In this case I decide . . .that there is no sale until the buyer's offer to buy is accepted by the acceptance of the money, and that takes place under the supervision of a pharmacist . . .

The Court of Appeal upheld this decision and dismissed the appeal by the Society.

[1953] 1 All ER 482; *Pharm J* 14 February 1953 p. 115.

R v. Family Health Services Appeal Authority, ex parte Elmfield Drugs Ltd, Selles Dispensing Chemists Ltd, and E Moss (Chemists) Ltd (1998)

The Pharmacy companies appealed against a judicial review judgment that three health authorities were correct in allowing dispensing contracts to doctors who intended to delegate dispensing of medicines to their staff. The case was based on the wording of section 55(1) (a) of the Medicines Act 1968 which reads:

The restrictions imposed by s.52 (supervision) do not apply to the sale or offer for sale of a medicinal product:

(a) by a doctor or dentist to a patient of his . . .

The companies contended that that the words meant that the exemption for a doctor required the doctor to sell or supply the medicinal product personally and did not authorise him to delegate the sale or supply to another person. The state maintained that applying the general principles of agency and the normal principles of construction there was no requirement for the doctor to hand over medicines to his patients personally.

At the earlier hearing for judicial review, the companies failed to convince the judges of their argument and Mr Justice Owen said:

I have no hesitation in finding that if Parliament had intended doctors to be guilty of an offence in the factual situation described by the pharmacists it would have said so.

(*Pharm J* 18 October 1997 p. 634).

In dismissing the appeal, Mr Justice Stuart-Smith said:

Whatever the reason I can see no basis for imposing a far stricter regime on doctors who ex hypothesi have prescribed or ordered medicine for their patients, by requiring them not merely to supervise the supply, as in the case of pharmacists, but actually to perform the mechanical act of delivery in person.

The judge agreed with counsel for the respondents that the solution to the problem was to be found in the general principles of agency and the ordinary principles of statutory construction, i.e. '...*prima facie what a person can do himself he can do by an agent*'.

Pharm J 1 August 1998 p. 146; *The Times* 16 September 1998.

Comment: The judge said that if he had ruled in favour of the pharmacy companies he would have been making doctors criminals. It would have been criminalising something that has been widely adopted, particularly in rural areas, for many years.

Use of titles and descriptions

Norris v. Weeks (1970)

The Pharmacy Act 1954 (s.19) reads: 'it shall not be lawful for any person, unless he is a registered pharmaceutical chemist ...(b) to take or use, in connection with the sale of goods by retail, the title of chemist'.

A notice, about 1 ft high by 2.5 ft wide was displayed at Mr Weeks' drug store over goods intended for retail sale. It bore the wording on three lines, *Wyn's/Chemist/Sundries*. The word 'chemist' was in larger script than the other words and in a different colour. The magistrate dismissed a summons under section 19(1) (b) on the ground that, having regard to the articles displayed, the word *chemist* was merely descriptive of the type of goods sold.

The High Court dismissed an appeal against this decision. It was held that an offence is committed only if a person asserts that they are a chemist or takes to themselves the title 'chemist'. It could not be said that an offence is committed whenever the word 'chemist' appears.

Pharm J 14 March 1970 p. 268; *The Times* 6 March 1970.

Definitions of `a sample'

Mistry v. Norris (1985)

This case concerned the sale of a bottle of medicine containing phenobarbitone (phenobarbital) without the authority of a prescription issued by a medical practitioner, as required by the Medicines Act 1968 (s.58). The appellant argued that, as the sale had been made to an enforcement officer under the Act, it was a sample subject to section 112. Therefore, the evidence of analysis of the contents of the medicine was not admissible as the mixture had not been divided, and a portion left with the appellant, in accordance with the sampling requirements under the Act.

The Times 16 October 1985 p. 27.

Comment The appeal was dismissed by the High Court. It was held that the inspector was not acting as a sampling officer but making an ordinary purchase as any member of the public has the right to do.

Sale of Prescription Only Medicines: offence of strict liability

Pharmaceutical Society of Great Britain v. Storkwain Ltd (1986)

Section 58 of the Medicines Act 1968 provides for orders to be made specifying those medicinal products which may only be sold by retail in accordance with the prescription of an appropriate practitioner. Storkwain Ltd supplied quantities of Physeptone ampoules, Ritalin tablets and Valium tablets, all of which are Prescription Only Medicines, on the authority of two 'prescriptions' which were, in fact, forgeries. In 1984, the Society prosecuted the company for unlawfully selling those medicines contrary to section 58(2)(a) of the Act. It was submitted for Storkwain Ltd that they were unaware that the 'prescriptions' were not genuine. In the absence of any guilty knowledge (*mens rea*) of the forgeries on the part of the company, the magistrates dismissed the charges. The Society successfully appealed to the Court of Appeal, who held that an offence under section 58(2)(a) was one of strict liability and directed the magistrates to convict.

On further appeal by Storkwain Ltd, the House of Lords confirmed the decision of the Court of Appeal. It was held that guilty knowledge (*mens rea*) was a required ingredient of offences under certain sections of the Act, but section 58 was not one of those sections. That view was supported by the construction of section 58(4) and (5) and by section 121. The wording of the Prescriptions Only Order also conformed with that construction of the statute. An offence under section 58(2)(a) is, therefore, one of strict liability.

[1986] 2 All ER 635; *Pharm J* 28 June 1986 p. 829.

Is dispensing a medicine on a National Health Service prescription a `sale'?

Appleby v. Sleep (1968)

A woman obtained an NHS prescription for Penidural syrup and took it to the pharmacy for dispensing. A few days later she found a sliver of glass in the medicine. The pharmacy was charged with selling a medicine not of the quality demanded under the Food and Drugs Act 1955. The magistrates dismissed the case and ruled there was no *sale*. The Executive Council appealed to the High Court.

In dismissing the appeal Lord Parker CJ said that:

> In Pfizer Corporation v. Ministry of Health [1965] AC 512 it was held that there was no sale of a medicine to a person presenting a National Health Service prescription and that was clearly the case because, even if there was a prescription charge, the patient was not paying for the medicine itself. The sole question was whether the contract between the pharmacy and the Executive Council was a contract of sale. A chemist ...undertook to perform services ...for those services he was remunerated by the Executive Council ...not only a sum to cover the basic price of the medicine but for his general services ...the property did not pass to the Executive Council and it was not a contract of sale ...

[1968] 2 All ER 265.

Comment: The provisions of the Food and Drugs Act 1955 as they applied to medicines have since been replaced by similar provisions in the Medicines Act 1968 (s.64) (see p. 21).

Importation of medicinal products from the European Community

R v. Royal Pharmaceutical Society of Great Britain, ex parte Association of Pharmaceutical Importers and Others (1989)

The Society had adopted a provision in its Code of Ethics which, amongst other things, prohibited a pharmacist from substituting, except in an emergency, any other medicine for the medicine specifically ordered on a prescription, even if s/he believed that the quality and therapeutic effect were identical. In 1986, the Society had published a statement to the effect that this rule applied to imported medicines as well as to UK-licensed medicines. The Association, who represented companies who were involved in importing medicines from the European Community, maintained that the Society's rule infringed the provisions of the Treaty of Rome on the basis that its effect was to impose a quantitative restriction on their importing medicines – *parallel imports* – from the Community.

The European Court of Justice held that in the absence of any Community legislation regulating the doctor–pharmacist relationship, and in particular the doctor's freedom to prescribe any medicine he chose, it was for each member state to decide, within the limits of the Treaty, the degree to which they wish to protect the health of their people and how that was to be achieved. It was said that there was no evidence that the Society's rule went beyond what was necessary to achieve the objective, which was to leave the entire responsibility for the treatment of the patient in the hands of the doctor treating him/her. It followed therefore that the rule could also be justified under the Treaty on the grounds of the protection of public health.

[1989] 2 All ER 758; *Pharm J* 27 May 1989 p. 613.

Sale of prescription data: breach of confidentiality?

R v. Department of Health, ex parte Source Informatics Ltd (2000)

Source Informatics Ltd proposed a scheme whereby after they, Source Informatics, had obtained the prescribers' consent, pharmacists, for a fee, would supply anonymised information contained on NHS prescriptions for the purposes of market research. The Department of Health in a policy document entitled *The Protection and Use of Patient Information* had made clear that under common law and the Data Protection Act principles the general rule was that information given in confidence may not be disclosed without the consent of the provider of the information, i.e. doctor or pharmacist. It also stated that anonymisation, with or without aggregation, did not remove the duty of confidence towards patients who are the subject of the data, namely details on their prescriptions written by the doctor and dispensed by the pharmacist. The High Court ([1999] 4 All ER 185) agreed with the Department of Health. The Court of Appeal on judicial review reversed the decision and Mr Justice Simon Brown said:

> the patient has no proprietorial claim to the prescription form or to the information it contains...[he has] no right to control its use provided only and always that his privacy is not put at risk ...

He concluded by saying:

> Participation in Source's scheme by doctors and the pharmacists would not in my judgment expose them to any serious risk of successful breach of confidence proceedings by a patient.

The Times 18 January 2000.

Comment: This case was not appealed and it would seem that the Data Protection Act does not normally cover data which have been anonymised, i.e. detached from any details which could identify a living individual.

Meaning of professional assessment

Cathy Bosworth Horton v. Timothy Evans and Lloyds Pharmacy Ltd (2006)

Cathy Horton, an American attorney and reverend lady, had been on regular treatment with dexamethasone tablets 0.5 mg one daily since 1982. In 2001, she was returning to the USA and requested a prescription from her doctor in London, Dr Evans, for dexamethasone tablets. He supplied a prescription that called for dexamethasone tablets 4 mg for 28 days but gave no indication of dose. Mrs Horton had received seven earlier supplies of these tablets from the same pharmacy over the previous 15 months and all the supplies on the patient medication records had been recorded as 'dexamethasone 0.5 mgs-60 one to be taken daily'.

The prescription was received in Lloyds pharmacy where the pharmacist admitted that he had noticed the strength prescribed was eight times that prescribed in the past. He had checked the dosage in the *British National Formulary* (BNF) and saw no reason to question the accuracy of the prescription. With that knowledge, he had dispensed it strictly within its terms. However as 4 mg tablet were unavailable in UK he dispensed double the quantity of the 2 mg strength. The label was automatically produced by the computer system and recorded the name, quantity and strength of tablet (2 mg) supplied together with the date and name of patient.

Later Mrs Horton visited the USA and consulted a doctor in order to obtain a further prescription. This doctor was shown the bottle labelled by the Lloyd's pharmacy and, as a result, prescribed a further 90 tablets of 4 mg. Later the US doctor received a further request for a prescription and on this occasion she informed him that the normal strength of the tablets was 0.5 mg. It was at this point, that the error was discovered. Mrs Horton's health had rapidly deteriorated, she had panic attacks, loss of weight, hair loss, tried to commit suicide and developed Cushing syndrome.

Mrs Horton brought a claim before the High Court in London against the doctor, who had written the original prescription in 2001, and Lloyds Pharmacy Ltd, who had dispensed the medicine, seeking damages of £5 m based on the deterioration in her health and loss of her business and earnings. A settlement was earlier agreed with Dr Evans and the trial continued against Lloyd's.

In giving judgment, Mr Justice Keith said, 'Mrs Horton has succeeded on all the issues which this judgment has addressed and leaves the issues which arise on quantum'. Failing agreement by the parties, the matter would be referred back to the judge for his decision on the award of damages. The judge continued:

The accepted wisdom is that whenever pharmacists dispense a prescription they should consider whether the medication prescribed is suitable for the patient. That is what the Royal Pharmaceutical Society of Great Britain's Code of Medicines, Ethics and Practice requires pharmacists to do – namely 'Every prescription must be professionally assessed by a pharmacist to determine the suitability for the patient'. That is recognised by Lloyds because its branch procedures manual is to the same effect. These requirements mirror pharmacists' obligations under common law. As Stuart-Smith J said in Dwyer v Rodrick (10 February 1982) 'pharmacists...have to exercise an independent judgement to ensure that the drug is apt for the patient as well as that it conforms to the physicians requirements'.

The defence raised the issue that the pharmacist had noted the strength on the prescription was large, had checked in the BNF, found that a 4 mg dosage was within the usual therapeutic range and had, therefore, dispensed the prescription without referring to the doctor. The judge dealt with this defence thus:

> It was true that the prescription was for a strength of dexamethasone which could be properly prescribed, but the dramatic increase in strength should have alerted the pharmacist to the need to go behind the guidance in the BNF and to question the correctness of the prescription with Dr Evans or Mrs Horton ... It was no longer whether the strength came within its usual therapeutic range and could for that reason be said to be suitable for Mrs Horton.

He repeated his concern that the pharmacist had relied falsely on the BNF guidance in view of Mrs Horton's medication history as shown on the Patient Medication Records (PMR) in the pharmacy and drew attention to the Lloyds manual which read:

> If the patient already has a patient medication record on the computer, previous prescription medication details on the PMR should be studied in order to check that there has been no change to the strength or dose of the patient's medication. Any changes should be queried with the patient or the prescriber.

The judge went on to say:

> In these circumstances I have no doubt that what the pharmacist should have done was to follow the instruction in the branch procedure manual and question the correctness of the prescription with Dr Evans or Mrs Horton. Had he done that, Dr Evans' mistake would have been discovered. In failing to do that the pharmacist fell below the standards which could reasonably have been expected of a reasonably careful and competent.

Judge Keith awarded damages at £1.4 m.

N.B The earlier major case to be heard by the High Court (*Dwyer* v. *Rodrick and Others* (1982); the Migril case unreported) was similar to the current case. In the Migril case, where the doctor made a dosage mistake on the prescription, the potential mistake was not queried by the pharmacist. In that case Mr Justice Stuart-Smith in making the award said:

> pharmacists. . .have to exercise an independent judgment to ensure that the drug is apt for the patient as well as that it conforms to the physicians requirements, the pharmacist should have spotted the doctor's error, and queried the prescription with the prescriber.

The legal and professional responsibility was highlighted and established by that case and the precedent was confirmed in the current one.

[2006] EWHC 2808 (QB)

Further reading

Dale and Appelbe's Pharmacy Law and Ethics. London: Pharmaceutical Press. (Other pharmaceutical cases of historical interest are outlined in earlier editions.)

Appendix 1

Medicines Act 1968
Medicinal products

Various articles and substances are treated as medicinal products (see Chapter 1) by virtue of orders made under the Act, as follows:

Section 104(1) Orders

Orders made under section 104(1) of the Act can extend the application of specified provisions of the Act to articles and substances which are not medicinal products as defined in section 130 of the Act but which are manufactured, sold, supplied, imported or exported for use wholly or partly for a medical purpose. Two orders under this section are still extant.

1   *The Medicines (Radioactive Substances) Order 1978* (SI 1978 No. 1004) extends the application of the provisions relating to the holding of licences to the following articles and substances:

    a   Interstitial and intracavity appliances (other than nuclear powered cardiac pacemakers) which contain or are to contain a radioactive substance sealed in a container (otherwise than solely for the purpose of storage, transport or disposal) or bonded solely within material and including the immediate container or bonding that are designed to be inserted into the human body or body cavities.

    b   Surface applicators, that is to say plates, plaques and ophthalmic applicators which contain or are to contain a radioactive substance sealed in a container (otherwise than solely for the purpose of storage, transport or disposal) or bonded solely within material and including the immediate container or bonding that is designed to be brought into contact with the human body.

    c   Any apparatus capable of administering neutrons to human beings when the neutrons are administered in order to generate a radioactive substance in the person to whom they are administered for the purpose of diagnosis or research.

d   Other substances or articles (not being an instrument, apparatus or appliance) which consist of or contain or generate a radioactive substance and which:

    i   consist of or contain or generate that substance in order, when administered, to utilise the radiation emitted therefrom; and

    ii   are manufactured, sold or supplied for use wholly or mainly by being administered to one or more human beings solely by way of a test for ascertaining what effects it has when so administered.

The meaning of *administer* in relation to any apparatus in paragraph c above is modified to include the exposure of the body or any part of the body to the neutrons issued by the apparatus. The order also enables regulations to be made under section 60 prohibiting sale, supply and administration except by certain practitioners (see p. 96).

1   *The Medicines (Cyanogenetic Substances) Order 1984* (SI 1984 No. 187) extends to *cyanogenetic substances* the application of those provisions of the Act relating to dealings with products (including sale, supply or importation), the packaging and promotion of products and miscellaneous and supplementary provisions. Licensing requirements are not applied. *Cyanogenetic substances* means preparations which:

a   are presented for sale or supply under the name of, or as containing, amygdalin, laetrile or vitamin B_{17}; or

b   contain more than 0.1 per cent by weight of any substance having the formula either α-cyanobenzyl-6-Oβ-D-glucopyrosol-D-glucopyranoside or α-cyanobenzyl-Oβ-D-glucopyranosiduronic acid.

Section 105(1)(a) Orders

Orders made under section 105(1)(a) of the Act extend the application of specified provisions of the Act to certain substances which are not medicinal products but which are used in the manufacture of medicinal products. Two orders under this section have been made.

1   *The Medicines (Control of Substances for Manufacture) Order 1971* (SI 1971 No. 1200) controls the substances set out below. The terms used are defined in detail in Schedule 2 (not here reproduced). The order makes those substances subject to certain provisions of the Act concerning the holding of licences and certificates; the regulation of dealings; offences and penalties; labelling, leaflets and containers; and certain miscellaneous matters. The substances affected, and the circumstances in which they are affected, are as follows.

a   When manufactured, assembled, sold, supplied, imported or
     exported for use as an ingredient in a medicinal product *for
     parenteral injection* into human beings or animals, the following:
        amphotericin B, bacitracin, capreomycin, colistin, erythromycin,
        gentamicin, heparin, hyaluronidase, kanamycin, neomycin,
        nystatin (added by SI 1985 No. 1403), penicillin, polymyxin B,
        preparations of the pituitary (posterior lobe), streptomycin, the
        lincomycins, the rifamycins, the tetracyclines, vancomycin,
        viomycin.

b   When manufactured, assembled, sold, supplied, imported or
     exported for use as an ingredient in a medicinal product which is to
     be administered to human beings or animals by means *other than
     parenteral injection*, the following:
        gentamicin*, neomycin*, nystatin*, oxytetracycline,
        tetracycline. (*Added by SI 1985 No. 1403.)

c   When manufactured, assembled, sold, supplied, imported or
     exported for use as ingredients of *dextran injection* for human or
     animal use, the following:
        dextrans.

d   When manufactured, assembled, sold, supplied, imported or
     exported for use as an ingredient in a *medicinal product for human or
     animal use,* the following:
        antigens, antisera, antitoxins, chorionic gonadotrophin,
        corticotrophin, follicle-stimulating hormone, insulin, sera,
        streptodornase, streptokinase, toxins, vaccines.

e   When manufactured, assembled, sold, supplied, imported or
     exported for use as an ingredient in a medicinal product *for human
     use,* the following:
        preparations of blood.

f   When manufactured, assembled, sold, supplied, imported or
     exported for use as an ingredient in a medicinal product *for
     administration to animals,* the following:
        plasma; any substances wholly or partly derived from animals not
        being substances specifically mentioned in any of the above
        paragraphs.

Section 105(1)(b) and (2) Orders

Orders made under section 105(1)(b) and (2) of the Act extend the application
of specified provisions of the Act to substances which, if used without proper
safeguards, are capable of causing damage to the health of the community, or
of causing danger to the health of animals generally or of one or more species
of animals. One order has been made under this section.

The Medicines (Extension To Antimicrobial Substances) Order 1973 (SI 1973 No. 367) extends certain specified provisions of the Act concerning such matters as the holding of licences; the provision of information; the commission of offences; the prohibition of sale, supply or importation; and the promotion of sales to the following classes of substance: substances which are not medicinal products, which are or contain:

1   any of the substances commonly known as *antibiotics* being:
    a   substances synthesised by bacteria, fungi or protozoa which have antimicrobial properties, and derivatives of such substances possessing such properties;
    b   substances which are synthesised in any other way and are identical with any substances described in sub-paragraph a, of this paragraph;
    c   any salt of any of the substances described in sub-paragraphs a and b, of this paragraph;

2   any other substances *which possess antigenic properties* similar to the antigenic properties of any of the substances described in paragraph 1 above;

3   sulphanilamide (being *p*-aminobenzene sulphonamide) or any derivative of sulphanilamide which possesses antimicrobial properties, and any salt of any such substance; or

4   any derivative of the *nitrofurans* which possesses antimicrobial properties, and any salt of any such derivative.

Appendix 2

Medicines Act 1968
Prohibition of non-medicinal antimicrobial substances

Antimicrobial substances were brought within the control of the Act by an order under section 105 (see Appendix 1).

The Medicines (Prohibition of Non-Medicinal Antimicrobial Substances) Order 1977 (SI 1977 No. 2131) prohibits, subject to certain exceptions, the sale or supply of the antimicrobial substances set out in Box A2.1. The prohibition applies whether or not the substance is contained in any other substance or article, unless it is a medicinal product or an animal feeding stuff.

Box A2.1 *Prohibited substances, Part I*

Amphomycina	Nalidixic acid
Bacitracin	Nitrofurantoin
	Nitrofurazone
Candicidin	Novobiocin
Capreomycin	Nystatin
Chloramphenicol	
Cycloserine	Oleandomycin
Erythromycin	
	Paromomycin
Framycetin	
Furaltadone	Spectinomycin
Furazolidone	Spiramycin
Fusidic acid	
	Tylosin
Griseofulvin	
	Vancomycin
Hachimycin	Viomycin
	Virginiamycin

N.B. In this Part (Table A2.1):

a   a reference to any substance, other than furaltadone, shall be construed as a reference to the substance for which such name is shown in the current edition of the list of names prepared and published under section 100 of the Act; and

b   *furaltadone* means (6)-5-morpholino-methyl-3-(5-nitrofurylideneamino)-2-oxazolidine.

Table A2.1 Part II prohibited substances

Class of substance	Meaning
Amphotericins	Antimicrobial substances or mixtures of such substances produced by *Streptomyces nodosus*
Cephalosporins	Antimicrobial substances containing in their chemical structure a fused dihydrothiazine β-lactam nucleus
Gentamicins	Any antimicrobial basic substance or mixture of such substances produced by the strain *Micromonospora purpurea*, which on 1 September 1967 was numbered NRRL 2953 in the culture collection of the Northern Utilisation Research and Development Branch of the United States Department of Agriculture
Kanamycins	Any antimicrobial substance or mixture of such substances produced by *Streptomyces kanamyceticus*
Lincomycins	Antimicrobial substances produced by *Streptomyces lincolnensis* (var. *lincolnensis*). These substances are the basic amides of hygric acid or of a substituted hygric acid with 6-amino-6,8-dideoxy-1-thiogalacto-octopyranose or with substituted 6-amino-6,8-dideoxy-1-thiogalacto-octopyranose
Neomycins	Antimicrobial substances or mixtures of such substances produced by *Streptomyces fradiae* which are complex organic bases and which yield on hydrolysis with mineral acids the base neamine
Penicillins	Any antimicrobial acid which contains in its structure a fused thiazolidine β-lactam nucleus
Polymixins	Any antimicrobial substance produced by any strain of *Bacillus polymyxa*
Rifamycins	A group of related antimicrobial macrolactams produced by the growth of *Streptomyces mediterranei* and containing the chemical structure of 11-acetoxy-7,9,15-trihydroxy-13-methoxy-2,6,8,10,12-penta-methyl-pentadeca-2,4,14-trienoic acid amide attached by the nitrogen atom and by the oxygen atom in the 15-position, respectively, to the 7- and 2-positions of a 5,6,9-trioxygenated 2,4-dimethyl-1-oxonaphtho-(2,1β)-furan
Ristocetins	Antimicrobial substances produced by a strain of a *Nocardia* species referred to as *Nocardia lurida*

Table A2.1 *(continued)*	
Streptomycins	Any antimicrobial complex organic base or mixture of such bases produced by *Streptomyces griseus* which: (a) yields on hydrolysis with mineral acids the base streptidine (meso-1-3-diguanidocyclohexane-2,4,5,6-tetraol); and (b) yields on hydrolysis by a 4% solution of sodium hydroxide the substance maltol (3-hydroxy-2-methyl-8-pyrone)
Sulphanilamide	Sulphanilamide being *p*-aminobenzenesulphonamide, having any of the hydrogen atoms of either or both nitrogen atoms substituted by an equal number of univalent atoms or radicals
Tetracyclines	Antimicrobial bases which contain the chemical structure naphthacene-2-carboxamide, hydrogenated to any extent and having each of the positions 1, 3, 10, 11, 12 and 12α substituted by a hydroxyl or an oxo group

Permitted sales or supplies

Sale or supply of prohibited substances is permitted in the circumstances described below.

a   Where a sale by way of wholesale dealing is made to:
   i   a veterinary surgeon or veterinary practitioner;
   ii a person lawfully conducting a retail pharmacy business;
   iii a holder of a manufacturer's licence granted under Part II of the Act; or
   iv a person carrying on the business of selling by way of wholesale dealing.
b   Where the sale or supply is to any of the following:
   i   a public analyst appointed under section 89 of the Food and Drugs Act 1955, section 27 of the Food and Drugs (Scotland) Act 1956 or section 31 of the Food and Drugs Act (Northern Ireland) 1958;
   ii an agricultural analyst appointed under section 67 of the Agriculture Act 1970;
   iii a person duly authorised by an enforcement authority under sections 111 and 112 of the Act;
   iv a sampling officer within the meaning of Schedule 3 to the Act;
   v   universities, other institutions concerned with higher education or institutions concerned with research.
c   Griseofulvin. When sold or supplied in a fungicide for horticultural purposes and containing other ingredients in such a quantity as to render the product unfit for any medicinal purpose and unpalatable to such a degree as to prevent consumption by human beings.
d   Streptomycins as for griseofulvin plus when used, sold or supplied for use as a preservative in a product used in the artificial breeding of animals.

e   Sulphanilamide. When, as the derivative sulphaquinoxaline (not exceeding 0.5 per cent), it is sold or supplied in a product for the destruction of rats or mice, or for the manufacture of such a product. The product must also contain warfarin, or its sodium or triethanolamine derivative.

f   Sulphonamide. When, as the derivative methyl-4-aminobenzenesulphonyl carbamate, it is sold or supplied for use in the manufacture of herbicides, or contained in a product used as a herbicide for agricultural, horticultural or forestry purposes or for use in or near water or on uncultivated land.

g   Amphotericins, gentamicins, kanamycins, lincomycins, nystatin, tylosin, penicillins, and spectinomycin when used, sold or supplied for use as a preservative in a product used in the artificial breeding of animals.

Appendix 3

The Medicines (Pharmacies) (Responsible Pharmacist) Regulations SI 2008 No. 2789

These regulations come into force on 1st October 2009.
These regulations apply to all responsible pharmacists and pharmacy staff involved in a pharmacy business.

1 Absence of the responsible pharmacist

a   The maximum period for which the responsible pharmacist may be absent from the premises is two hours during the pharmacy business hours. If there is more than one responsible pharmacist during the pharmacy hours the maximum period applies to the total period of absence for all of them.

b   The responsible pharmacist must not be absent unless the arrangements set out in paragraphs 2 and 3 below are in place. Where it is not possible to put these arrangements into place arrangements must be made to ensure another pharmacist is both available and contactable to advise other pharmacy staff.

c   Where it is reasonably practical for the responsible pharmacist to be contactable during the period of absence arrangements must ensure that he can be contactable by other pharmacy staff and return with reasonable promptness if in his opinion it is necessary to secure the safe and effective running of the business.

d   The sale of General Sale Medicines may continue from the premises in the absence of the responsible pharmacist.

2 Pharmacy procedures

i   *The matters which must be covered by pharmacy procedures are:*

   a   The arrangements to secure the that medicinal products are ordered, stored, prepared, sold or supplied by retail, and disposed in a safe and effective manner b   The circumstances in which a pharmacy member of staff who is not a pharmacist may give advice on medicinal products

c   The identification of members of staff who are in the view of the responsible pharmacist competent to perform such tasks relating to the business

d   The keeping of records about the arrangements mentioned in 2a above

e   The arrangements which are to apply during the absence of the responsible pharmacist

f   The steps to be taken when there is a change of responsible pharmacist

g   The procedures to be taken when there is a complaint made against the pharmacy business

h   The procedures which should apply when a incident occurs which may indicate that the pharmacy business is not running in a safe and effective manner

i   The manner in which changes to the pharmacy procedures are notified to the pharmacy staff.

ii   *Pharmacy procedures*:

a   in writing, in electronic form, or both

b   must be available for inspection by the person carrying out the business, the superintendent (if any), the responsible pharmacist, and pharmacy staff

c   the procedures must be reviewed regularly

d   in this regulation 'pharmacy procedures' means those procedures referred to in section 71A(3) of the Medicines Act.

3 Pharmacy records

The particulars to be kept are:

a   the name of the responsible pharmacist

b   the Registration number of the responsible pharmacist in the Register of Pharmacists

c   the date and time at which the responsible pharmacist became the responsible pharmacist

d   the date and time at which the responsible pharmacist ceased to be the responsible pharmacist

e   in relation to any absence of the responsible pharmacist from the premises on a day on which they were a responsible pharmacist:

  i   the date of the absence

  ii   the time at which the absence commenced

  iii   the time at which he returned to the premises.

The Pharmacy Record

a   in writing, in electronic form, or both

b   must be available for inspection by the person carrying out the business, the superintendent (if any), the responsible pharmacist, and pharmacy staff

c   in the case of record in electronic the date on which it was created

d   in the case of written record the last day to which the record relates

e   in this regulation 'pharmacy procedures' means record referred to in section 71A(4) of the Medicines Act.

Appendix 4

Medicines Act 1968
Veterinary drugs: Pharmacy and Merchants List

The Medicines (Exemptions for Merchants in Veterinary Drugs) Order 1998 (SI 1998 No. 1044, as amended) permits the retail sale of certain categories of veterinary drugs which are listed by the Minister. This list is open to inspection at the office of the Veterinary Medicines Directorate and copies will be publicly available and published regularly (see Chapter 12). The Minister's list includes such products specified only by their product licence number and name.

The vast majority of pharmacies do not regularly handle these listed medicines, which are used in the commercial husbandry of livestock. For the convenience of pharmacists, the details of the listed cat, dog and horse wormers are set out below. They are all Pharmacy and Merchants List (PML).

Veterinary drugs saleable by pharmacists, merchants and saddlers

Tables A4.1 and A4.2 list these products

Table A4.1 Cat and dog wormers	
Marketing Authorisation No.	*Name of product*
Vm 00010/4113	Bayer Dog Wormer Tablets
Vm 00010/4115	Bayer Multi-Worm for Dogs
Vm 00715/4071	Bob Martins Easy to use Wormer Granules
Vm 00010/4102	Drontal Puppy Suspension
Vm 11188/4003	Granofen Wormer for Cats and Dogs
Vm 15476/4059	Panacur Pet Paste
Vm 11990/4014	Zerofen 22 per cent Granules for Cats and Dogs

Table A4.2 Horse wormers

Marketing Authorisation No.	Name of product
Vm 00057/4131	Equitac
Vm 0025/4069	Eqvalan Paste for Horses and Donkeys
Vm 00242/4038	Furexel
Vm 0844/4207	Multiwurma
Vm 0286/4039	Oxfendazole Horse Paste
Vm 15476/4060	Panacur Equine Guard
Vm 15476/4053	Panacur Paste
Vm 00086/4158	Panacur 22 per cent Granules Horse Wormer
Vm 15476/4009	Panacur 10 per cent Suspension
Vm 12597/4013	Pyratape-P Horse Wormer
Vm 00057/4060	Strongid-P Granules
Vm 00057/4062	Strongid-P Paste
Vm 05869/4151	Systamex Horse Paste Wormer
Vm 00242/4013	Telmin
Vm 00242/4026	Telmin B
Vm 00242/4014	Telmin Paste
Vm 00015/4052	Verdisol
Vm 11990/4017	Zerofen 22 per cent Equine Granules

Appendix 5

Misuse of Drugs Act 1971
Controlled Drugs classified for level of penalties

Schedule 2 to the Act classifies Controlled Drugs into three lists (Class A, Class B and Class C) for the purpose of the level of penalties for offences under the Act. The penalties are given in Schedule 3 (not reproduced here).

Since the Act came into force, numerous additions have been made, by Orders, to the original list of drugs in Schedule 2. In this appendix, a date shown against any drug indicates the year it was added to the list.

For the Schedules to the Misuse of Drugs Regulations, which classify Controlled Drugs according to the relevant regimes of control, see Appendix 6.

Part I: Class A drugs

1   a   The following substances and products, namely:
>Acetorphine
>Alfentanil (1984)
>Allylprodine
>Alphacetylmethadol
>Alphameprodine
>Alphamethadol
>Alphaprodine
>Anileridine
>Benzethidine
>Benzylmorphine (3-benzylmorphine)
>Betacetylmethadol
>Betameprodine
>Betamethadol
>Betaprodine
>Bezitramide
>4-Bromo-2,5-dimethoxy-α-methylphenethylamine (1975)

Bufotenine
Carfentanil (1986)
Clonitazene
Coca leaf
Cocaine
4-Cyano-2-dimethylamino-4,4-diphenylbutane
4-Cyano-1-methyl-4-phenylpiperidine
Desomorphine
Dextromoramide
Diamorphine
Diampromide
Diethylthiambutene
N,N-Diethyltryptamine
Difenoxin (1-(3-cyano-3,3-diphenylpropyl)-4-phenylpiperidine-
    4-carboxylic acid) (1975)
Dihydrocodeinone-O-carboxymethyloxime
Dihydroetorphine
Dihydromorphine
Dimenoxadole
Dimepheptanol
Dimethylthiambutene
2,5-Dimethoxy-α,4-dimethylphenethylamine
N,N-Dimethyltryptamine
Dioxaphetyl butyrate
Diphenoxylate
Dipipanone
Drotebanol (3,4-dimethoxy-17-methylmorphinan-6β,14-diol)
    (1973)
Ecgonine, and any derivative of ecgonine which is convertible to
    ecgonine or to cocaine
Ethylmethylthiambutene
Eticyclidine (1984)
Etonitazene
Etorphine
Etoxeridine
Etryptamine (1998)
Fentanyl
Furethidine
Hydromorphinol
Hydromorphone
Hydroxypethidine
N-Hydroxytenamphetamine (1990)
Isomethadone

Ketobemidone
Levomethorphan
Levomoramide
Levophenacylmorphan
Levorphanol
Lofentanil (1986)
Lysergamide
Lysergide and other *N*-alkyl derivatives of lysergamide
Mescaline
Metazocine
Methadone
Methadyl acetate
Methylamphetamine (2006)
Methyldesorphine
Methyldihydromorphine (6-methyldihydromorphine)
4-Methylaminorex (1990)
2-Methyl-3-morpholino-1,1-diphenylpropanecarboxylic acid
1-Methyl-4-phenylpiperidine-4-carboxylic acid
Metopon
Morpheridine
Morphine
Morphine methobromide, morphine *N*-oxide and other
    pentavalent nitrogen morphine derivatives
Myrophine
Nicomorphine (3,6-dinicotinoylmorphine)
Noracymethadol
Norlevorphanol
Normethadone
Normorphine
Norpipanone
Opium, whether raw, prepared or medicinal
Oxycodone
Oxymorphone
Pethidine
Phenadoxone
Phenampromide
Phenazocine
Phencyclidine (1979)
Phenomorphan
Phenoperidine
4-Phenylpiperidine-4-carboxylic acid ethyl ester
Piminodine
Piritramide

> Poppy-straw and concentrate of poppy-straw
> Proheptazine
> Properidine (1-methyl-4-phenylpiperidine-4-carboxylic acid isopropyl ester)
> Psilocin
> Racemethorphan
> Racemoramide
> Racemorphan
> Remifentanil
> Rolicyclidine (1984)
> Sufentanil (1983)
> Tenocyclidine (1984)
> Thebacon
> Thebaine
> Tilidate (1983)
> Trimeperidine

b   + any compound (not being a compound for the time being specified in sub-paragraph a above) structurally derived from tryptamine or from a ring-hydroxytryptamine by substitution at the nitrogen atom of the sidechain with one or more alkyl substituents but no other substituent

c   addition of thirty-six phenethylamine derivatives

d   + any compound (not being methoxyphenamine or a compound for the time being specified in sub-paragraph a above) structurally derived from phenethylamine, an N-alkylphenethylamine, α-methylphenethylamine, an N-alkyl-α-methylphenethylamine, α-ethylphenethylamine, or an N-alkyl-α-ethylphenethylamine by substitution in the ring to any extent with alkyl, alkoxy, alkylenedioxy or halide substituents, whether or not further substituted in the ring by one or more other univalent substituents.

[Note + sub-paragraphs b and d added by SI 1977 No. 1243.]

e   any compound (not being a compound for the time being specified in sub-paragraph a above) structurally derived from fentanyl by modification in any of the following ways, that is to say:

   i   by replacement of the phenyl portion of the phenethyl group by any heteromonocycle whether or not further substituted in the heterocycle;

   ii   by substitution in the phenethyl group with alkyl, alkenyl, alkoxy, hydroxy, halogeno, haloalkyl, amino or nitro groups;

   iii by substitution in the piperidine ring with alkyl or alkenyl groups;

      iv   by substitution in the aniline ring with alkyl, alkoxy, alkylenedioxy, halogeno or haloalkyl groups;

      v   by substitution at the 4-position of the piperidine ring with any alkoxycarbonyl or alkoxyalkyl or acyloxy group (SI 1986 No. 2230);

      vi   by replacement of the N-propionyl group by another acyl group;

   f   any compound (not being a compound for the time being specified in sub-paragraph a above) structurally derived from pethidine by modification in any of the following ways, that is to say:

      i   by replacement of the 1-methyl group by an acyl, alkyl whether or not unsaturated, benzyl or phenethyl group, whether or not further substituted;

      ii   by substitution in the piperidine ring with alkyl or alkenyl groups or with a propano bridge, whether or not further substituted;

      iii by substitution in the 4-phenyl ring with alkyl, alkoxy, aryloxy, halogeno or haloalkyl groups;

      iv   by replacement of the 4-ethoxycarbonyl by any other alkoxycarbonyl or any alkoxyalkyl or acyloxy group;

      v   by formation of an N-oxide or of a quaternary base.

2   Any stereoisomeric form of a substance for the time being specified in paragraph 1 above not being dextromethorphan or dextrorphan.

3   Any ester or ether of a substance for the time being specified in paragraph 1 or 2 above, not being a substance for the time being specified in Part II of this Schedule.

4   Any salt of a substance for the time being specified in any of paragraphs 1 to 3 above.

5   Any preparation or other product containing a substance or product for the time being specified in any of paragraphs 1 to 4 above.

Part II: Class B drugs

1   **a**   The following substances and products, namely:
       Acetyldihydrocodeine
       Amphetamine
       Codeine
       Dihydrocodeine
       Ethylmorphine (3-ethylmorphine)
       Glutethimide (1985)
       Lefetamine (1986)

Mecloqualone (1984)
Methaqualone (1984)
Methcathinone (1998)
Methylphenidate
Methylphenobarbitone [methylphenobarbital] (1984)
Nicocodine
Nicodicodine (6-nicotinoyldihydrocodeine) (1973)
Norcodeine
Pentazocine (1985)
Phenmetrazine
Pholcodine
Propiram
Zipeprol (1998)

b   any 5,5-disubstituted barbituric acid.

2   Any stereoisomeric form of a substance for the time being specified in paragraph 1 of this Part of this Schedule.

3   Any salt of a substance for the time being specified in paragraph 1 or 2 of this Part of this Schedule.

4   Any preparation or other product containing a substance or product for the time being specified in any of paragraphs 1 to 3 of this Part of this Schedule, not being a preparation falling within paragraph 6 of Part I of this Schedule.

Part III: Class C drugs

1   a   The following substances, namely:
Alprazolam
Aminorex (1998)
Benzphetamine
Bromazepam (1985)
Brotizolam (1998)
Camazepam (1985)
Cannabinol (2003)
Cannabinol derivatives(2003)
Cannabis and cannabis resin(2003)
Cathine (1986)
Cathinone (1986)
Chlordiazepoxide (1985)
Clorphentermine
Clobazam (1985)
Clonazepam (1985)
Clorazepic acid (1985)

Clotiazepam (1985)
Cloxazolam (1985)
Delorazepam (1985)
Dextropropoxyphene (1983)
Diazepam (1985)
Diethylpropion (1984)
Estazolam (1985)
Ethchlorvynol
Ethinamate (1985)
Ethyl loflazepate (1985)
N-Ethylamphetamine
Fencamfamin (1986)
Fenethylline (1986)
Fenproporex (1986)
Fludiazepam (1985)
Flunitrazepam (1985)
Flurazepam (1985)
Halazepam (1985)
Haloxazolam (1985)
4-Hydroxyl-*n*-butyril acid (2003)
Ketamine (2005)
Ketazolam
Loprazolam (1985)
Lorazepam (1985)
Lormetazepam (1985)
Mazindol (1985)
Medazepam (1985)
Mefenorex (1985)
Mephentermine
Meprobamate (1985)
Mesocarb (1998)
Methyprylone (1985)
Midazolam (1990)
Nimetazepam (1985)
Nitrazepam (1985)
Nordazepam (1985)
Oxazepam (1985)
Oxazolam (1985)
Pemoline (1989)
Phendimetrazine
Phentermine (1985)
Pinazepam (1985)
Pipradol

Prazepam (1985)
Pyrovalerone (1986)
Temazepam (1985)
Tetrazepam (1985)
Triazolam (1985)
N-Ethylamphetamine
Zolpidem.

2 Any stereoisomeric form of a substance for the time being specified in paragraph 1 of this Part of this Schedule, not being phenylpropanolamine.

3 Any salt of a substance for the time being specified in paragraph 1 or 2 of this Part of this Schedule.

4 Any preparation or other product containing a substance for the time being specified in any of paragraphs 1 to 3 of this Part of this Schedule, Part IV.

5 The following substances:
Atamestane
4-Androstene-3,17-dione
5-Androstene-3,17-diol
Bolandiol
Bolazine
Boldenone
Bolenol
Calusterone
4-Chloromethandienone
Clostebol
Drostanolone
Enestebol
Epitiostanol
Ethylestrenol
Fluoxymesterone
Formebolone
Furazabol
Mesbolone
Mestanolone
Mesterolone
Methandienone
Methandriol
Methenolone
Methyltestosterone
Metribolone
Mibolerone

Nandrolone
19-Nor-4-androstene-3,17-dione
19-Nor-4-androstene-3,17-diol
Norboletone
Norclostebol
Norethandrolone
Ovandrotone
Oxabolone
Oxandrolone
Oxymesterone
Oxymetholone
Prasterone
Propetandrol
Quinbolone
Roxibolone
Silandrone
Stanozolol
Stenbolone
Testosterone
Thiomesterone
Trenbolone

6   Any compound (not being trilostane or a compound for the time being specified in paragraph 5 above) structurally derived from 17-hydroxyandrostan-3-one or from 17-hydroxy-estran-3-one by modification in any of the following ways:

a   by further substitution at position 17 by a methyl or ethyl group;

b   by substitution to any extent at one or more positions 1, 2, 4, 6, 7, 9, 11 or 16, but at no other position;

c   by unsaturation in the carbocyclic ring system to any extent, provided that there are no more than two ethylenic bonds in any one carbocyclic ring;

d   by fusion of ring A with a heterocyclic system.

7   Any substance which is an ester or ether (or, where more than one hydroxyl function is available, both an ester and an ether) of a substance specified in paragraph 5 above or described in paragraph 6 above.

8   Chorionic gonadotrophin (HCG)
Somatotrophin
Clenbuterol
Somatrem
Non-human chorionic gonadotrophin
Somatrophin.

Meaning of certain expressions used in this schedule

For the purposes of this Schedule, the following expressions (which are not among those defined in section 37(1) of this Act) have the meanings hereby assigned to them, respectively, that is to say:

cannabinol derivatives means the following substances, except where contained in cannabis or cannabis resin, namely tetrahydro derivatives of cannabinol and 3-alkyl homologues of cannabinol or of its tetrahydro derivatives;

coca leaf means the leaf of any plant of the genus *Erythroxylon* from whose leaves cocaine can be extracted either directly or by chemical transformation;

concentrate of poppy-straw means the material produced when poppy-straw has entered into a process for the concentration of its alkaloids;

medicinal opium means raw opium which has undergone the process necessary to adapt it for medicinal use in accordance with the requirements of the *British Pharmacopoeia*, whether it is in the form of powder or is granulated or is in any other form, and whether it is or is not mixed with neutral substances;

poppy-straw means all parts, except the seeds, of the opium poppy, after mowing;

raw opium includes powdered or granulated opium but does not include medicinal opium.

Appendix 6

Misuse of Drugs Regulations 2001 (as amended)

Classification of Controlled Drugs for regimes of control

The five Schedules of Controlled Drugs appended to the Misuse of Drugs Regulations 2001 (SI 1985 No. 3998, as amended) are reproduced in this appendix. It should be used in conjunction with Chapter 17 and the tabulated summary on pp. 221–226 at the end of that chapter. They provide a full explanation of the regulations, and how they affect the drugs in the various Schedules.

Schedule 1

Controlled Drugs subject to the requirements of Regulations 14, 15, 16, 18, 19, 20, 23, 26 and 27.

1   The following substances and products, namely:
   a   4-Bromo-2,5-dimethoxy-α-methylphenethylamine
   Bufotenine
   Cannabinol: not being dronebenol or its stereoisomers
   Cannabinol derivatives
   Cannabis and cannabis resin
   Cathinone
   Coca leaf
   Concentrate of poppy-straw
   N,N-Diethyltryptamine
   2,5-Dimethoxy-4α-dimethylphenethylamine
   N,N-Dimethyltryptamine
   Eticyclidine
   Etryptamine (1998)

Fungus of any kind which contains psilocin or an ester of psilocin (2005) except when growing uncultivated or picked in order to deliver to a person authorised to possess or picked for the purpose to destroy it (2005)

N-Hydroxytenamphetamine

Lysergamide

Lysergide and other N-alkyl derivatives of lysergamide

Mescaline

Methcathinone (1998)

4-Methylaminorex

Psilocin

Raw opium

Rolicyclidine

Tenocyclidine

b   any compound (not being a compound for the time being specified in sub-paragraph a above) structurally derived from tryptamine or from a ring-hydroxy tryptamine by substitution at the nitrogen atom of the sidechain with one or more alkyl substituents but no other substituents;

c   there is a list of 36 phenethylamine derivatives;

d   any compound (not being methoxyphenamine or a compound for the time being specified in sub-paragraph a above) structurally derived from phenethylamine, an N-alkylphenethylamine, α-methylphenethylamine, an N-alkyl-α-methylphenethylamine, α-ethylphenethylamine or an N-alkyl-α-ethylphenethylamine by substitution in the ring to any extent with alkyl, alkoxy, alkylenedioxy or halide substituents, whether or not further substituted in the ring by one or more other univalent substituents;

e   any compound (not being a compound for the time being specified in Schedule 2) structurally derived from fentanyl by modification in any of the following ways, that is to say:

   i   by replacement of the phenyl portion of the phenethyl group by any heteromonocycle whether or not further substituted in the heterocycle;

   ii   by substitution in the phenethyl group with alkyl, alkenyl, alkoxy, hydroxy, halogeno, haloalkyl, amino or nitro groups;

   iii   by substitution in the piperidine ring with alkyl or alkenyl groups;

   iv   by substitution in the aniline ring with alkyl, alkoxy, alkylenedioxy, halogeno or haloalkyl groups;

   v   by substitution at the 4-position of the piperidine ring with any alkoxycarbonyl or alkoxyalkyl or acyloxy group;

      vi   by replacement of the N-propionyl group by another acyl group;

  f   any compound (not being a compound for the time being specified in Schedule 2) structurally derived from pethidine by modification in any of the following ways, that is to say:

     i   by replacement of the 1-methyl group by an acyl, alkyl whether or not unsaturated, benzyl or phenethyl group, whether or not further substituted;

    ii   by substitution in the piperidine ring with alkyl or alkenyl groups or with a propano bridge, whether or not further substituted;

   iii   by substitution in the 4-phenyl ring with alkyl, alkoxy, aryloxy, halogeno or haloalkyl groups;

    iv   by replacement of the 4-ethoxycarbonyl by any other alkoxycarbonyl or any alkoxyalkyl or acyloxy group;

    v   by formation of an N-oxide or of a quaternary base.

2   Any stereoisomeric form of a substance specified in paragraph 1.

3   Any ester or ether of a substance specified in paragraph 1 or 2.

4   Any salt of a substance specified in any of paragraphs 1 to 3.

5   Any preparation or other product containing a substance or product specified in any of paragraphs 1 to 4, not being a preparation specified in Schedule 5.

Schedule 2

Controlled Drugs subject to the requirements of Regulations 14, 15, 16, 18, 19, 20, 21, 23, 26 and 27.

1   The following substances and products, namely:

    Acetorphine
    Alfentanil
    Allylprodine
    Alphacetylmethadol
    Alphameprodine
    Alphamethadol
    Alphaprodine
    Anileridine
    Benzethidine
    Benzylmorphine (3-benzylmorphine)
    Betacetylmethadol
    Betameprodine
    Betamethadol
    Betaprodine

Bezitramide

Carfentanil

Clonitazene

Cocaine

4-Cyano-2-dimethylamino-4,4-diphenylbutane

4-Cyano-1-methyl-4-phenylpiperidine

Desomorphine

Dextromoramide

Diamorphine

Diampromide

Diethylthiambutene

Difenoxin

Dihydrocodeinone-O-carboxymethyloxine

Dihydroetorpine

Dihydromorphine

Dimenoxadole

Dimepheptanol

Dimethylthiambutene

Dioxaphetyl butyrate

Diphenoxylate

Dipipanone

Dronabinol

Drotebanol

Ecgonine, and any derivative of ecgonine which is convertible to
ecgonine or to cocaine

Ethylmethylthiambutene

Etonitazene

Etorphine

Etoxeridine

Fentanyl

Furethidine

Hydrocodone

Hydromorphinol

Hydromorphone

Hydroxypethidine

Isomethadone

Ketobemidone

Levomethorphan

Levomoramide

Levophenacylmorphan

Levorphanol

Lofentanil

Medicinal opium
Metazocine
Methadone
Methadyl acetate
Methyldesorphine
Methyldihydromorphine (6-methyldihydromorphine)
2-Methyl-3-morpholino-1,1-diphenylpropanecarboxylic acid
1-Methyl-4-phenylpiperidine-4-carboxylic acid
Metopon
Morpheridine
Morphine
Morphine methobromide, morphine N-oxide and other pentavalent
    nitrogen morphine derivatives
Myrophine
Nicomorphine
Noracymethadol
Norlevorphanol
Normethadone
Normorphine
Norpipanone
Oxycodone
Oxymorphone
Pethidine
Phenadoxone
Phenampromide
Phenazocine
Phencyclidine
Phenomorphan
Phenoperidine
4-Phenylpiperidine-4-carboxylic acid ethyl ester
Piminodine
Piritramide
Proheptazine
Properidine
Quinalbarbitone [secobarbital]
Racemethorphan
Racemoramide
Racemorphan
Remifentanil
Sufentanil
Thebacon
Thebaine

Tilidate

Trimeperidine

Zipeprol.

2   Any stereoisomeric form of a substance specified in paragraph 1 not being dextromethorphan or dextrorphan.

3   Any ester or ether of a substance specified in paragraph 1 or 2, not being a substance specified in paragraph 6.

4   Any salt of a substance specified in any of paragraphs 1 to 3.

5   Any preparation or other product containing a substance or product specified in any of paragraphs 1 to 4, not being a preparation specified in Schedule 5.

6   The following substances and products, namely:

Acetyldihydrocodeine

Amphetamine

Codeine

Dextropropoxyphene

Dihydrocodeine

Ethylmorphine (3-ethylmorphine)

Fenethylline

Glutethamide

Lefetamine

Mecloqualone

Methaqualone

Methylamphetamine

Methylphenidate

Nicocodine

Nicodicodine (6-nicotinoyldihydrocodeine)

Norcodeine

Phenmetrazine

Pholcodine

Propiram

Quinalbarbitone [secobarbital].

7   Any stereoisomeric form of a substance specified in paragraph 6.

8   Any salt of a substance specified in paragraph 6 or 7.

9   Any preparation or other product containing a substance or product specified in any of paragraphs 6 to 8, not being a preparation specified in Schedule 5.

Schedule 3

Controlled Drugs subject to the requirements of Regulations 14, 15, 16, 18, 22, 23, 24, 26 and 27.

1 The following substances, namely:
   a Benzphetamine
      Buprenorphine
      Cathine
      Chlorphentermine
      Diethylpropion
      Ethchlorvynol
      Ethinamate
      Flunitrazepam (1998)
      Mazindol
      Mephentermine
      Meprobamate
      Methylphenobarbitone [methylphenobarbital]
      Methyprylone
      Pentazocine
      Midazolam (2007)
      Phendimetrazine
      Phentermine
      Pipradrol
      Temazepam
   b any 5,5-disubstituted barbituric acid, not being quinalbarbitone
      [secobarbital].
2 Any stereoisomeric form of a substance specified in paragraph 1, not
   being phenylpropanolamine.
3 Any salt of a substance specified in paragraph 1 or 2.
4 Any preparation or other product containing a substance specified
   in any of paragraphs 1 to 3, not being a preparation specified in
   Schedule 5.

Schedule 4: Part I

Controlled Drugs excepted from the prohibition on importation, exportation
and, when in the form of a medicinal product, possession and subject to the
requirements of Regulations 22, 23, 25, 26 and 27.

1 The following substances and products, namely:
      Alprazolam
      Aminorex
      Bromazepam
      Brotizolam
      Camazepam
      Chlordiazepoxide
      Clobazam

Clonazepam
Clorazepic acid
Clotiazepam
Cloxazolam
Delorazepam
Diazepam
Estazolam
N-Ethylamphetamine
Ethyl loflazepate
Fencamfamin
Fenproporex
Fludiazepam
Flurazepam
Halazepam
Haloxazolam
4-Hydroxy-*n*-butyric acid
Ketamine (2005)
Ketazolam
Loprazolam
Lorazepam
Lormetazepam
Medazepam
Mefenorex
Mesabolene (2003)
Mesocarb
Nimetazepam
Nitrazepam
Nordazepam
Oxabolene (2003)
Oxazepam
Oxazolam
Pemoline
Pinazepam
Prazepam
Pyrovalerone
Tetrazepam
Triazolam
Zolpidem.

2 Any stereoisomeric form of a substance specified in paragraph 1.
3 Any salt of a substance specified in paragraph 1 or 2.
4 Any preparation or other product containing a substance or product specified in any of paragraphs 1 to 3, not being a preparation specified in Schedule 5.

Schedule 4: Part II

Controlled Drugs excepted from the prohibition on possession when in the form of a medicinal product; excluded from the application of offences arising from the prohibition on importation and exportation when imported or exported in the form of a medicinal product by any person for administration to himself; and subject to the requirements of Regulations 22, 23, 26 and 27.

1   The following substances and products, namely:
4-Androstene-3,17-dione
5-Androstene-3,17-diol
Atamestane
Bolandiol
Bolasterone
Bolazine
Boldenone
Bolenol
Bolmantalate
Calusterone
4-Choromethandienone
Clostebol
Drostanolone
Enestebol
Epitiostanol
Ethyloestrenol
Fluoxymesterone
Formebolone
Furazabol
Mebolazine
Mepitiostane
Mestanolone
Mesterolone
Methandienone
Methandriol
Methenolone
Methyltestosterone
Metribolone
Mibolerone
Nandrolone
19-Nor-androstene-3,17-dione
Norboletone
Norclostebol
Norethandrolone
Ovandrotone

Oxandrolone
Oxymesterone
Oxymetholone
Prasterone
Propetandrol
Quinbolone
Roxibolone
Silandrone
Stanolone
Stanozolol
Stenbolone
Testosterone
Thiomesterone
Trenbolone.

2   Any compound (not being trilostane or a compound for the time being specified in paragraph 1 of this part of this Schedule) structurally derived from 17-hydroxyandrostan-3-one or from 17-hydroxyestran-3-one by modification in any of the following ways:
   a   by further substitution at position 17 by a methyl or ethyl group;
   b   by substitution to any extent at one or more positions 1, 2, 4, 6, 7, 9, 11 or 16, but at no other position;
   c   by unsaturation in the carbocyclic ring system to any extent, provided that there are no more than two ethylenic bonds in any one carbocyclic ring;
   d   by fusion of ring A with a heterocyclic system.

3   Any substance which is an ester or ether (or, where more than one hydroxyl function is available, both an ester and an ether) of a substance specified in paragraph 1 or described in paragraph 2 of this Part of the Schedule.

4   The following substances:
   Chorionic gonadotrophin (HCG)
   Somatotrophin
   Clenbuterol
   Non-human chorionic gonadotrophin (HCG)
   Somatrem.

5   Any stereoisomeric form of a substance specified or described in any of paragraphs 1 to 4 of this Part of this Schedule.

6   Any salt of a substance specified or described in any of paragraphs 1 to 5 of this Part of this Schedule.

7   Any preparation of other product containing a substance or product specified or described in any of paragraphs 1 to 6 of this Part of the Schedule, not being a preparation specified in Schedule 5.

Schedule 5

Controlled Drugs excepted from the prohibition on importation, exportation and possession and subject to the requirements of Regulations 24 and 25.

1   (1) Any preparation of one or more of the substances to which this paragraph applies, not being a preparation designed for administration by injection, when compounded with one or more other active or inert ingredients and containing a total of not more than 100 milligrams of the substance or substances (calculated as base) per dosage unit or with a total concentration of not more than 2.5 per cent (calculated as base) in undivided preparations.
(2) The substances to which this paragraph applies are acetyldihydrocodeine, codeine, dihydrocodeine, ethylmorphine, nicocodine, nicodicodine (6-nicotinoyldihydrocodeine), norcodeine, pholcodine and their respective salts.

2   Any preparation of cocaine containing not more than 0.1 per cent of cocaine calculated as cocaine base, being a preparation compounded with one or more other active or inert ingredients in such a way that the cocaine cannot be recovered by readily applicable means or in a yield which would constitute a risk to health.

3   Any preparation of medicinal opium or of morphine containing (in either case) not more than 0.2 per cent of morphine calculated as anhydrous morphine base, being a preparation compounded with one or more other active or inert ingredients in such a way that the opium or, as the case may be, the morphine cannot be recovered by readily applicable means or in a yield which would constitute a risk to health.

4   Any preparation of dextropropoxyphene, being a preparation designed for oral administration, containing not more than 135 milligrams of dextropropoxyphene (calculated as base) per dosage unit or with a total concentration of not more than 2.5 per cent (calculated as base) in undivided preparations.

5   Any preparation of difenoxin containing, per dosage unit, not more than 0.5 milligrams of difenoxin and a quantity of atropine sulphate equivalent to at least 5 per cent of the dose of difenoxin.

6   Any preparation of diphenoxylate containing, per dosage unit, not more than 2.5 milligrams of diphenoxylate calculated as base, and a quantity of atropine sulphate equivalent to at least 1 per cent of the dose of diphenoxylate.

7   Any preparation of propiram containing, per dosage unit, not more than 100 milligrams of propiram calculated as base and compounded with at least the same amount (by weight) of methylcellulose.

8   Any powder of ipecacuanha and opium comprising:

10 per cent opium, in powder;
10 per cent ipecacuanha root, in powder; well mixed with
80 per cent of any other powdered ingredient containing no
Controlled Drug.

9   Any mixture containing one or more of the preparations specified in
    paragraphs 1 to 8, being a mixture of which none of the other ingredients
    is a Controlled Drug.

The Poisons List Order 1982

Non-medicinal poisons are listed in the Schedule to this order (SI 1982 No. 217, as amended) made under the Poisons Act 1972. Those substances in Part I of the list may not be sold by retail except by a person lawfully conducting a retail pharmacy business. Those in Part II of the list may only be sold by a person lawfully conducting a retail pharmacy business or by a person whose name is entered in a local authority's list.

The Poisons List: Part I

Aluminium phosphide

Arsenic; its compounds, other than those specified in Part II of this list

Barium, salts of, other than barium sulphate and the salts of barium specified in Part II of this list

Bromomethane

Chloropicrin

Fluoroacetic acid; its salts, fluorocetamide

Hydrogen cyanide; metal cyanides, other than ferrocyanides and ferricyanides

Lead acetates; compounds of lead with acids from fixed oils

Magnesium phosphide

Mercury, compounds of, the following:

nitrates of mercury; oxides of mercury; mercuric cyanide oxides; mercuric thiocyanate; ammonium mercuric chlorides; potassium mercuric iodides; organic compounds of mercury which contain a methyl group directly linked to the mercury atom

Oxalic acid

Phenols:

(phenol; phenolic isomers of the following: cresols, xylenols, monoethylphenols) except in substances containing less than 60 per cent, weight in weight, of phenols; compounds of phenol with a metal, except in substances containing less than the equivalent of 60 per cent, weight in weight, of phenols

Phosphorus, yellow
Strychnine; its salts, its quaternary compounds
Thallium, salts of.

The Poisons List: Part II

Aldicarb
Alpha-chloralose
Ammonia
Arsenic, compounds, of; the following:
    Calcium arsenites
    Copper acetoarsenite
    Copper arsenates
    Copper arsenites
    Lead arsenates
Barium, salts of; the following:
    Barium carbonate
    Barium silicofluoride
Carbofuran
Cycloheximide
Dinitrocresols (DNOC); their compounds with a metal or a base
Dinoseb; its compounds with a metal or a base
Dinoterb
Drazoxolon; its salts
Endosulfan
Endothal; its salts
Endrin
Fentin, compounds of
Formaldehyde
Formic acid
Hydrochloric acid
Hydrofluoric acid, alkali metal bifluorides, ammonium bifluoride, alkali
    metal fluorides, ammonium fluoride, sodium silicofluoride
Mercuric chloride, mercuric iodide, organic compounds of mercury except
    compounds of mercury which contain a methyl (CH_3) group directly linked
    to the mercury atom
Metallic oxalates
Methomyl
Nicotine; its salts; its quaternary compounds
Nitric acid
Nitrobenzene
Oxamyl
Paraquat, salts of

Phenols (as defined in Part I of this List) in substances containing less than 60 per cent, weight in weight, of phenols; compounds of phenols with a metal in substances containing less than the equivalent of 60 per cent, weight in weight, of phenols

Phosphoric acid

Phosphorus compounds, the following:

Azinphos-methyl, chlorfenvinphos, demephion, demeton-S-methyl, demeton-S-methyl sulphone, dialifos, dichlorvos, dioxathion, disulfoton, fonofus, mecarbam, mephosfolan, methidathion, mevinphos, omethoate, oxydemeton-methyl, parathion, phenkapton, phorate, phosphamidon, pirimiphos-ethyl, quinalphos, schradan, sulfotep, thiometon, thionazin, triazophos, vamidothion

Potassium hydroxide

Sodium hydroxide

Sodium nitrate

Sulphuric acid

Thiofanox

Zinc phosphide.

Appendix 8

The Poisons Rules 1982

The Poison Rules 1982 (SI 1982 No. 218, as amended), made under the Poisons Act 1972, are described in Chapter 17. In this appendix are set out eight of the Schedules to the rules. N.B. Schedules 2, 3, 6 and 7 were deleted by the Poisons Rules (Amendment) Order 1985 (SI 1985 No. 1077).

Schedule 1: Rules 5, 6, 7, 9, 10(1), 17(2) and 21(2)

Poisons included in the Poisons List to which special restrictions apply unless exempted by Rule 7 (see pp. 249 and 255–257).

Aldicarb
Alpha-chloralose
Aluminium phosphide
Arsenic; its compounds, except substances containing less than the equivalent of 0.0075 per cent of arsenic (As)
Barium, salts of (other than barium sulphate)
Bromomethane
Carbofuran
Chloropicrin
Cycloheximide
Dinitrocresols (DNOC); their compounds with a metal or a base; except winter washes containing not more than the equivalent of 5 per cent of dinitrocresols
Dinoseb; its compounds with a metal or a base
Dinoterb
Drazoxolon; its salts
Endosulfan
Endothal: its salts
Endrin
Fentin, compounds of
Fluoroacetic acid; its salts, fluoroacetamide
Hydrogen cyanide except substances containing less than 0.15 per cent, weight in weight, of hydrogen cyanide (HCN); metal cyanides, other

than ferrocyanides and ferricyanides, except substances containing less
than the equivalent of 0.1 per cent, weight in weight, of hydrogen
cyanide (HCN)

Lead, compounds of, with acids from fixed oils

Magnesium phosphide

Mercuric chloride; except substances containing less than 1 per cent of
mercuric chloride; mercuric iodide except substances containing less
than 2 per cent of mercuric iodide: nitrates of mercury except substances
containing less than the equivalent of 3 per cent, weight in weight, of
mercury (Hg); potassio-mercuric iodides except substances containing
less than the equivalent of 1 per cent of mercuric iodide; organic
compounds of mercury except substances, not being aerosols, containing
less than the equivalent of 0.2 per cent, weight in weight, of mercury (Hg)

Methomyl

Nicotine; its salts; its quaternary compounds

Oxamyl

Paraquat, salts of

Phosphorus compounds, the following:

Azinphos-methyl
Chlorfenvinphos
Demephion
Demeton-S-methyl
Demeton-S-methyl sulphone
Dichlorvos
Dioxathion
Disulfoton
Fonofos
Mecarbam
Mephosfolan
Methidathion
Mevinphos
Omethoate
Oxydemeton-methyl
Parathion
Phenkapton
Phorate
Phosphamidon
Pirimiphos-ethyl
Quinalphos
Thiometon
Thionazin
Triazophos
Vamidothion

Strychnine; its salts; its quaternary compounds; except substances
    containing less than 0.2 per cent of strychnine
Thallium, salts of
Thiofanox
Zinc phosphide.

Schedule 4: Rule 8

Articles exempted from the provisions of the Act and Rules (see p. 245)

Group I: general exemptions

Adhesives; anti-fouling compositions; builders' materials; ceramics; cosmetic products; distempers; electrical valves; enamels; explosives; fillers; fireworks; fluorescent lamps; flux in any form for use in soldering; glazes; glue; inks; lacquer solvents; loading materials; matches; medicated animal feeding stuffs; motor fuels and lubricants; paints other than pharmaceutical paints; photographic paper; pigments; plastics; propellants; rubber; varnishes; vascular plants and their seeds.

Group II: special exemptions

Table A8.1	
Poison	*Substance or article in which exempted*
Ammonia	Substances not being solutions of ammonia or preparations containing solutions of ammonia; substances containing less than 5 per cent, weight in weight, of ammonia (NH3); refrigerators
Arsenic; its compounds	Pyrites ores or sulphuric acid containing arsenic or compounds of arsenic as natural impurities; in reagent kits or reagent devices supplied for medical or veterinary purposes, substances containing less than 0.1 per cent, weight in weight, of arsanilic acid
Barium, salts of	Witherite other than finely ground witherite; barium carbonate bonded to charcoal for case hardening; fire extinguishers containing barium chloride; sealed smoke generators containing not more than 25 per cent, weight in weight, of barium carbonate
Bromomethane	Fire extinguishers
Carbofuran	Granular preparations
Drazoxolon; its salts	Treatments on seeds
Fenaminosulf	Granular preparations

(continued overleaf)

Table A8.1 *(continued)*

Formaldehyde	Substances containing less than 5 per cent, weight in weight, of formaldehyde (HCHO); photographic glazing or hardening solutions
Formic acid	Substances containing less than 25 per cent, weight in weight, of formic acid (HCOOH)
Hydrochloric acid	Substances containing less than 10 per cent, weight in weight, of hydrochloric acid
Hydrogen cyanide	Preparations of wild cherry; in reagent kits supplied for medical or veterinary purposes, substances containing less than the equivalent of 0.1 per cent, weight in weight, of hydrogen cyanide
Lead acetate	Substances containing less than the equivalent of 2.5 per cent, weight in weight, of elemental lead
Mercuric chloride	Batteries
Mercuric chloride	Treatments on seeds or bulbs
Mercuric iodide	Treatments on seeds or bulbs
Mercury organic, compounds of	Treatments on seeds or bulbs
Mercury, oxides of	Canker and wound paints (for trees) containing not more than 3 per cent, weight in weight, of yellow mercuric oxide
Methomyl	Solid substances containing not more than 1 per cent, weight in weight, of methomyl
Nicotine; its salts; its quaternary compounds	Tobacco; in cigarettes, the paper of a cigarette (any part of that paper forming part of or surrounding a filter), where that paper in each cigarette does not have more than the equivalent of 10 milligrams of nicotine; preparations in aerosol dispensers containing not more than 0.2 per cent, weight in weight, of nicotine; other liquid preparations, and solid preparations with a soap base containing not more than 7.5 per cent, weight in weight, of nicotine
Nitric acid	Substances containing less than 9 per cent, weight in weight, of nitric acid (HNO_3)
Nitrobenzene	Substances containing less than 0.1 per cent of nitrobenzene
Oxalic acid; metallic	Laundry blue; polishes; cleaning powders or scouring oxalates products containing the equivalent of not more than 10 per cent of oxalic acid dihydrate
Oxamyl	Granular preparations
Paraquat, salts of	Preparations in pellet form containing not more than 5 per cent of salts of paraquat calculated as paraquat ion (see p. 250)

Table A8.1 *(continued)*

Phenols	Creosote obtained from coal tar; liquid disinfectants or antiseptics containing phenol less than 0.5 per cent phenol and containing less than 5 per cent of other phenols (as defined in the Poisons List); motor fuel treatments not containing phenol and containing less than 2.5 per cent of other phenols; in reagent kits supplied for medical or veterinary purposes; solid substances containing less than 60 per cent of phenols; tar (coal or wood), crude or refined; in tar oil distillation fractions containing not more than 5 per cent of phenols
Phenylmercuric salts	Antiseptic dressings on toothbrushes; in textiles containing not more than 0. 01 per cent of phenylmercuric salts as bacteriostat and fungicide
Phosphoric acid	Substances containing phosphoric acid, not being descaling preparations, containing more than 50 per cent, weight in weight, of ortho-phosphoric acid
Phosphorus compounds, the following:	
Chlorfenvinphos	Treatments on seeds; granular preparations
Dichlorvos	Preparations in aerosol dispensers containing not more than 1 per cent, weight in weight, of dichlorvos; materials impregnated with dichlorvos for slow release; granular preparations; ready for use liquid preparations containing not more than 1 per cent, weight in volume, of dichlorvos
Disulfoton	Granular preparations
Fonofos	Granular preparations
Oxydemeton-methyl	Aerosol dispensers containing not more than 0.25 per cent, weight in weight, of oxydemeton-methyl
Parathion	Granular preparations
Phorate	Granular preparations
Pirimiphos-ethyl	Treatments on seeds
Thiazophos	Granular preparations
Thionazin	Granular preparations
Potassium hydroxide	Substances containing the equivalent of less than 17 per cent of total caustic alkalinity expressed as potassium hydroxide; accumulators; batteries
Sodium fluoride	Substances containing less than 3 per cent of sodium fluoride as a preservative
Sodium hydroxide	Substances containing the equivalent of less than 12 per cent of total caustic alkalinity expressed as sodium hydroxide

(continued overleaf)

Table A8.1 *(continued)*	
Sodium nitrite	Substances other than preparations containing more than 0.1 per cent of sodium nitrite for the destruction of rats or mice
Sodium silicofluoride	Substances containing less than 3 per cent of sodium silicofluoride as a preservative
Sulphuric acid	Substances containing less than 15 per cent, weight in weight, of sulphuric acid (H_2SO_4); accumulators; batteries and sealed containers in which sulphuric acid is packed together with car batteries for use in those batteries; fire extinguishers
Thiofanox	Granular preparations

In Group II in this Schedule, the expression *granular preparation* in relation to a poison means a preparation:

a   which consists of absorbent mineral or synthetic solid particles impregnated with the poison, the size of the particles being such that not more than 4 per cent, weight in weight, of the preparation is capable of passing a sieve with a mesh of 250 micrometres, and not more than 1 per cent, weight in weight, a sieve with a mesh of 150 micrometres;

b   which has an apparent density of not less than 0.4 grams per millilitre if compacted without pressure; and

c   not more than 12 per cent, weight in weight, consists of one or more poisons in respect of which an exemption is conferred by this Schedule in relation to granular preparations.

Schedule 5: Rule 10(2)

Part A

Form to which the poisons specified are restricted when sold by listed sellers of Part II poisons (see p. 256).

Table A8.2	
Poison	*Form to which sale is restricted*
Aldicarb	Preparations for use in agriculture, horticulture or forestry
Alpha-chloralose	Preparations intended for indoor use in the destruction of rats or mice and containing not more than 4 per cent, weight in weight, of alpha-

Table A8.2 *(continued)*

	chloralose, preparations intended for indoor use in the destruction of rats or mice and containing not more than 8.5 per cent, weight in weight, of alpha-chloralose, where the preparation is contained in a bag or sachet which is itself attached to the inside of a device in which the preparation is intended to be so used and the device contains not more than 3 grams of the preparation
Arsenic compounds, the following:	
Calcium arsenites	Agricultural, horticultural and forestal insecticides or fungicides
Copper acetoarsenite	Agricultural, horticultural and forestal insecticides or fungicides
Copper arsenates	Agricultural, horticultural and forestal insecticides or fungicides
Copper arsenites	Agricultural, horticultural and forestal insecticides or fungicides
Lead arsenates	Agricultural, horticultural and forestal insecticides or fungicides
Barium carbonate	Preparations for the destruction of rats or mice
Carbofuran	Preparations for use in agriculture, horticulture or forestry
Cycloheximide	Preparations for use in forestry
Dinitrocresols (DNOC); their compounds with a metal or a base	Preparations for use in agriculture, horticulture or forestry
Dinosam; its compounds with a metal or a base	Preparations for use in agriculture, horticulture or forestry
Dinoseb; its compounds with a metal or a base	Preparations for use in agriculture, horticulture or forestry
Drazoxolon; its salts	Preparations for use in agriculture, horticulture or forestry
Endosulfan	Preparations for use in agriculture, horticulture or forestry
Endothal; its salts	Preparations for use in agriculture, horticulture or forestry
Endrin	Preparations for use in agriculture, horticulture or forestry
Fentin, compounds of	Preparations for use in agriculture, horticulture or forestry

(continued overleaf)

Table A8.2 (continued)

Mercuric chloride	Agricultural, horticultural and forestal fungicides; seed and bulb dressings; insecticides
Mercuric iodide	Agricultural, horticultural and forestal fungicides; seed and bulb dressings
Mercury, organic compounds of	Agricultural, horticultural and forestal fungicides; seed and bulb dressings; solutions containing not more than 5 per cent, weight in volume, of phenylmercuric acetate for use in swimming baths
Metallic oxalates other than potassium quadroxalate	Photographic solutions or materials
Methomyl	Preparations for use in agriculture, horticulture or forestry
Nitrobenzene	Agricultural, horticultural and forestal insecticides
Oxamyl	Preparations for use in agriculture, horticulture or forestry
Paraquat, salts of	Preparations for use in agriculture, horticulture or forestry
Phosphorus compounds, the following:	Preparations for use in agriculture, horticulture or forestry
Azinphos-methyl	
Chlorfenvinphos	
Demephion	
Demeton-S-methyl	
Demeton-S-methylsulphone	
Dialifos	
Dichlorvos	
Dioxathion	
Disulfoton	
Fonofos	
Mecarbam	
Mephosfolan	
Methidathion	
Mevinphos	

Table A8.2 *(continued)*	
Omethoate	
Oxydemeton-methyl	
Parathion	
Phenkapton	
Phorate	
Phosphamidon	
Pirimiphos-ethyl	
Quinalphos	
Thiometon	
Thionazin	
Triazophos	
Vamidothion	
Thiofanox	Preparations for use in agriculture, horticulture or forestry
Zinc phosphide	Preparations for the destruction of rats or mice

Part B

Poisons which may be sold by listed sellers of Part II poisons only to persons engaged in the trade or business of agriculture, horticulture or forestry and for the purpose of that trade or business.

Aldicarb
Arsenic, compounds of
    Calcium arsenites
    Copper acetoarsenite
    Copper arsenates
    Copper arsenites
    Lead arsenates
Carbofuran
Cyclohexamide
Dinitrocresols (DNOC); their compounds with a metal or a base; except winter washes containing not more than the equivalent of 5 per cent of dinitrocresols
Dinosam; its compounds with a metal or a base

Dinoseb; its compounds with a metal or a base

Dinoterb

Drazoxolon; its salts

Endosulfan

Endothal; its salts

Endrin

Fentin; compounds of

Mercuric chloride; mercuric iodide; organic compounds of mercury, except solutions containing not more than 5 per cent, weight in volume, of phenylmercuric acetate for use in swimming baths

Methomyl

Oxamyl

Paraquat, salts of

Phosphorus compounds, the following:

  Azinphos-methyl

  Chlorfenvinphos

  Demephion

  Demeton-S-methyl

  Demeton-S-methyl sulphone

  Dialifos

  Dichlorvos

  Dioxathion

  Disulfoton

  Fonofos

  Mazidox

  Mecarbam

  Mephosfolan

  Methidathion

  Mevinphos

  Mipafox, except in the form of a cap on a stick or wire

  Omethoate

  Oxydemeton-methyl

  Parathion

  Phenkapton

  Phorate

  Phosphamidon

  Pirimiphos-ethyl

  Quinalphos

  Thiometon

  Thionazin

  Triazophos

  Vamidothion

 Thiofanox.

Schedule 8: Rule 24(1)

Form of application for entry in the list kept by a local authority under section 5 of the Act (see p. 249).

POISONS ACT 1972
(1972 c.66)

Form of application by a person to have his name entered in a local authority's list of persons entitled to sell non-medicinal poisons included in Part II of the Poisons List.

To the Chief Executive of...

I,...

being engaged in the business of...

hereby apply to have my name entered in the list kept in pursuance of section 5 of the above Act in respect of the following premises, namely,...

....

....

as a person entitled to sell from those premises non-medicinal poisons included in Part II of the Poisons List.

I hereby nominate..

....

to act as my deputy (deputies) for the sale of non-medicinal poisons in accordance with Rule 10(1) of the Poisons Rules 1982

Signature of applicant..

Date...

Schedule 9: Rule 24(2)

Format of the list to be kept by a local authority in pursuance of section 5(1) of the Act (see p. 250).

POISONS ACT 1972
(1972 c. 66)
List of persons entitled to sell non-medicinal poisons in Part II of the Poisons List

Full name	Address of premises	Description of business carried on at the premises	Name of deputy (or deputies) permitted to sell

Schedule 10: Rule 25

Certificate for the purchase of non-medicinal poison (see p. 251 and 255–257).

For the purposes of section 3(2)(a)(i) of the Poisons Act 1972 I, the undersigned, a householder
occupying (a)...
hereby certify from my knowledge of (b) ....of
(a)..
that he is a person to whom (c) .... may properly be supplied.
I further certify that (d) .... is the signature of the said
(b) ....

....
Signature of the householder giving certificate

Date

(a) Insert full postal address

(b) Insert full name of intending purchaser.

(c) Insert name of poison.

(d) Intending purchaser to sign his name here.

*Endorsement required by Rule 25 of the Poisons Rules1982 to be made by a police officer in charge of
a police station when, but only when, the householder giving the certificate is not known to the seller of
the poison to be a responsible person of good character.*

I hereby certify that in so far as is known to the police of the district in which * resides he is a
responsible person of good character.

..............................Signature of Police Officer

....Rank

..........................In charge of Police Station at

Date

*Insert full name of householder

Office Stamp of

giving the certificate.

Police Station

Schedule 11: Rule 26

Form of entry to be made in a book to be kept by sellers of poisons in accordance with section 3(2)(b) of the Act (see p. 251).

Date of Sale	Name and quantity of poisons supplied	Purchaser's			Purpose for which the poison stated to be required	Date of certificate (if any)	Name and address of person giving certificate (if any)	Signature of purchaser or, where a signed order is permitted by the Poisons Rules 1982 the date of the signed order
		Name	Address	Business, trade or occupation				

Schedule 12: Rule 12

Restriction of sale and supply of strychnine and certain other poisons (see pp. 255 and 259–261).

Part I

Cases of sale or supply to which provisions of Rule 12 do not apply.

1 The provisions of Rule 12 shall not apply in the case of the sale of substance to be exported to purchasers outside the United Kingdom.

2 The provisions of Rule 12 shall not apply in the case of the sale of a substance to a person or institution concerned with scientific education or research or chemical analysis, for the purposes of that education or research or analysis.

3 The provisions of Rule 12 shall not apply in the case of the sale of a substance by way of wholesale dealing.

4 Since September 2006, the sale or supply of strychnine is no longer approved for the control of moles (see p. 255; the following provisions of Rule 12, namely, paragraph (1) (strychnine, etc.), shall not apply in the case of the sale of a substance to:

   a an officer of DEFRA who produces a written authority in the form set out in Part III of this Schedule issued by a person duly authorised by the Minister of Agriculture, Fisheries and Food; or

   b an officer of the Department of Agriculture and Fisheries for Scotland or the Welsh Office who produces a written authority in the form set out in Part III of this Schedule issued by a person duly authorised by the Secretary of State, authorising the purchase by that officer of the substance for the purpose of killing foxes (other than foxes held in captivity) in an infected area within the meaning of the Rabies (Control) Order 1974 (SI 1974 No. 2212); so, however, that the authority in question has been issued within the preceding four weeks and the quantity sold does not exceed specified therein.

5 (1) The following provision of Rule 12, namely, paragraph (2) (fluoroacetic acid etc.), shall not apply in the case of the sale of a substance:

   a to a person producing a certificate in form 'A' of the forms set out in Part IV of this Schedule issued by the proper officer of a local authority or port health authority certifying that the substance is required for use as a rodenticide by employees of that local authority or port health authority being such use:

      i in ships or sewers in such places as are identified in the certificate; or

    ii   in such drains as are identified in the certificate, being drains which are situated in restricted areas and wholly enclosed and to which all means of access are, when not in actual use, kept closed; or

    iii in such warehouses as are identified in the certificate, being warehouses which are situated in restricted dock areas and to which all means of access are, when not in actual use, kept securely locked or barred; or

b   to a person producing a certificate in form 'B' of the said forms issued by the proper officer of a local authority or port health authority certifying that the substance is required for use as a rodenticide by such person or by the employees of such body of persons, carrying on a business of pest control, as is named in the certificate, being such use as is mentioned in sub-paragraph (1)a i or ii of this paragraph; or

c   to a person producing a certificate in form 'B' of the said forms issued, in England by a person duly authorised by DEFRA or, in Scotland or Wales, by a person duly authorised by the Secretary of State certifying that the substance is required for use as a rodenticide by officers of the Ministry of Agriculture, Fisheries and Food or of the Department of Agriculture and Fisheries for Scotland, or the Welsh Office being such use as is mentioned in sub-paragraph (1)a i or ii of this paragraph; so, however, that the certificate in question has been issued within the preceding three months and the quantity sold does not exceed the quantity specified therein.

(2) In this paragraph, the following expressions have the meanings hereby respectively assigned to them, that is to say:

dock area means an area in the vicinity of a dock as defined in section 57(1) of the Harbours Act 1964;

drain and *sewer* have the meanings respectively assigned to them by section 343(1) of the Public Health Act 1936;

local authority in Greater London means the Common Council of the City of London or the council of a London borough, elsewhere in England or Wales means the council of a county or a district and, in Scotland, means an islands or district council;

port health authority means, in England or Wales, the port health authority of the Port of London or a port health authority for the purposes of the Public Health Act 1936 and, in Scotland, a port health authority as constituted in terms of section 172 of the Public Health (Scotland) Act 1897;

restricted in relation to any area, means controlled in such manner that access to the area by unauthorised persons is in normal circumstances prevented.

6 Salts of thallium) are no longer approved for sale (see p. 257).
7 Zinc phosphide) is no longer approved for sale (see p. 257).

Part II

Strychnine is no longer approved for sale or supply for controlling moles (see p. 255).

Part III

Form of authority for the purchase of strychnine or a salt or quaternary compound thereof for killing foxes.

For the purposes of Rule 12(1) of the Poisons Rules 1982 and of paragraph 5 of Part I of Schedule 12 thereto I hereby authorise...
(an officer of [the Ministry of Agriculture, Fisheries and Food] [the Department of Agriculture and Fisheries for Scotland] [the Welsh Office]) to purchase within four weeks of the date hereof
.... of .... for the purpose of killing foxes (other than foxes held in captivity) in the following infected area (within the meaning of the Rabies (Control) Order 1974), namely the infected area in .... (locality).

....
A person authorised by [DEFRA]
[the Secretary of State for Scotland]
[the Secretary of State for Wales]

Date ....

Part IV

Forms of certificate authorising the purchase of fluoroacetic acid, a salt thereof or fluoroacetamide as a rodenticide.

Form A

Certificate authorising the purchase of fluoroacetic acid, a salt thereof or fluoroacetamide as a rodenticide for use by employees of a local authority or a port health authority (in Scotland, a port local authority or joint port authority)

For the purposes of Rule 12(2) of the Poisons Rules 1982 and of paragraph 6 of Part I of Schedule 12 thereto, I hereby certify that...
of ....is required for use by employees of.....................................
as a rodenticide in [ships] [sewers]situated at...
[the following warehouses] viz...
situated in the restricted dock area at...
being warehouses to which all means of access are, when not in actual use, kept securely locked or barred.
[the following drains] viz..
situated in the restricted area at..
being drains which are wholly enclosed and to which all means of access are, when not in actual use, kept closed.

....
The officer appointed for this purpose by
....

Date....................................

Form B

Certificate authorising the purchase of fluoroacetic acid, a salt thereof or fluoroacetamide as a rodenticide for use by a person, or the employees of a body of persons, carrying on a business of pest control or for use by officers of the Ministry of Agriculture, Fisheries and Food or of the Department of Agriculture and Fisheries for Scotland or of the Welsh Office

For the purposes of Rule 12(2) of the Poisons Rules 1982 and of paragraph 6 of Part I of Schedule 12 thereto, I hereby certify that ....
of.. is required for use by [...
......................................] [employees of] ....
[officers of the Ministry of Agriculture, Fisheries and Food/Department of Agriculture and Fisheries for Scotland/Welsh Office] as a rodenticide in:
[ships] [sewers] situated at...
[the following drains] viz..
situated in the restricted areas at...
being drains which are wholly enclosed and to which all means of access are, when not in actual, use, kept closed.

....
[The officer appointed for this purpose by]

....
[A person authorised by DEFRA]
[A person authorised by the Secretary of State for Scotland]
Date...............................   [A person authorised by the Secretary of State for Wales]

Part V

The sale or supply of salts of thallium for killing rats, mice or moles is no longer approved (see p. 261).

Appendix 9

Substances and preparations dangerous to supply

The Chemicals (Hazard Information and Packaging for Supply) Regulations 1994 (SI 1994 No. 3247, as amended) made under the Health and Safety at Work etc. Act 1974 are described in Chapter 18. An Authorised and Approved List of Dangerous Substances is set out in *Information Approved for the Classification and Labelling of Substances Dangerous for Supply* (3rd edn, January 1996, HMSO). There are five parts to the list:

Part I: List of Dangerous Substances and Articles
Part II: List of Substances Dangerous for Supply (Solvents)
Part III: List of Substances Dangerous for Supply (paints, varnishes, printing inks, adhesives and similar products)
Part IV: List of Risk Phrases
Part V: List of Safety Phrases.

The classification of and symbols for substances dangerous for supply are set out in Schedule 1 to the Regulations.

Part I

Table A9.1 lists the of 'Dangerous Substances'. N.B. The table is a selection only (see above).

Table A9.1 Some of the 'Dangerous Substances' listed in Part I			
Name of substance	**Indication of general nature of risk (references are to the relevant entry in Schedule 1)**	**Indication of particular risks (references are to the relevant entry in Part IV)**	**Indications of precautions required (references are to the relevant entry in Part V)**
	1	2	3
Acetic acid more than 90%	Corrosive	10, 35	2, 23, 36

(continued overleaf)

Table A9.1 *(continued)*

Acetone	Highly flammable	11	2, 9, 16, 23, 33
Ammonia more than 10%	Corrosive	34, 37	1/2, 7, 26, 45
Ammonia 5–10%	Irritant	36/37/38	1/2, 7, 26, 45
Amyl acetate	Flammable	10	23
Carbon tetrachloride more than 1%	Carcinogenic, toxic, dangerous for the environment	23/24/25, 40, 48/23, 59	1/2, 23, 36/37, 45, 59, 61
Chlorfenvinphos	Toxic	26/27/28	26/27/28
Chloroform	Carcinogenic, harmful	22, 38, 40, 48/20/22	2, 36/37
Copper sulphate	Harmful	22, 36/38	22
Denatured spirits			
More than 20%	Highly flammable	11, 23/25	1/2, 7, 16, 24, 45
3–20%	Harmful	20/22	1/2, 7, 16, 24, 45
Dichlorvos	Toxic	23/24/25	2, 13, 44
Ephedrine, salts of	Harmful	22	22, 25
Ethanol (ethyl alcohol)	Highly flammable	11	7, 16
Ethylene glycol	Harmful	22	2
Fluoroacetates, soluble salts	Toxic	28	1/2, 20, 22, 26, 45
Formaldehyde solution			
More than 25%	Carcinogenic, toxic	23/24/25, 34, 40, 43	1/2, 26, 36/37, 45
5–25%	Harmful	20/21/22, 36/37/38, 40, 43	51 (all)
1–5%	Harmful	40, 43	
Hydrochloric acid			
More than 25%	Corrosive	34, 37	1/2, 26, 45
10–25%	Irritant	36/37/38	1/2, 26, 45
Hydrogen peroxide			
More than 60%	Oxidising	8	1/2, 3, 28, 36/39

20–60%	Corrosive	34	45 (all)
5–20%	Irritant	36/38	
Mercurous chloride	Harmful	22	2
Mevinphos	Toxic	26/27/28	1, 13, 28, 45
Oxalic acid	Harmful	21/22	2, 24/25
Paraquat, and salts of	Toxic	26/27/28	1, 13, 45
Potassium chlorate	Oxidising, harmful	9, 20/22	2, 13, 16, 27
Potassium permanganate	Oxidising, harmful	8, 22	2
Sodium chlorate	Oxidising, harmful	9, 20/22	2, 13, 16, 27
Sodium hydroxide			
More than 5%	Corrosive	35	1/2, 26, 37/39, 45
2–5%	Corrosive	34	1/2, 26, 37/39, 45
0.5–2%	Irritant	36/38	1/2, 26, 37/39, 45
Strychnine, salts of	Toxic	26/28	1, 13, 28, 45
Sulphuric acid	Irritant	36/38	2, 26

Part IV

Indication of particular risks.

1 Explosive when dry
2 Risk of explosion by shock, friction, fire or other sources of ignition
3 Extreme risk of explosion by shock, friction, fire or other sources of ignition
4 Forms very sensitive explosive metallic compounds
5 Heating may cause an explosion
6 Explosive with or without contact with air
7 May cause fire
8 Contact with combustible material may cause fire
9 Explosive when mixed with combustible material
10 Flammable
11 Highly flammable
12 Extremely flammable
13 Extremely flammable liquefied gas
14 Reacts violently with water

15 Contact with water liberates highly flammable gases
16 Explosive when mixed with oxidising substances
17 Spontaneously flammable in air
18 In use, may form flammable/explosive vapour–air mixture
19 May form explosive peroxides
20 Harmful by inhalation
21 Harmful in contact with skin
22 Harmful if swallowed
23 Toxic by inhalation
24 Toxic in contact with skin
25 Toxic if swallowed
26 Very toxic by inhalation
27 Very toxic in contact with skin
28 Very toxic if swallowed
29 Contact with water liberates toxic gas
30 Can become highly flammable in use
31 Contact with acids liberates toxic gas
32 Contact with acids liberates very toxic gas
33 Danger of cumulative effects
34 Causes burns
35 Causes severe burns
36 Irritating to eyes
37 Irritating to respiratory system
38 Irritating to skin
39 Danger of very serious irreversible effects
40 Possible risk of irreversible effects
41 Risk of serious damage to eyes
42 May cause sensitisation by inhalation
43 May cause sensitisation by skin contact
44 Risk of explosion if heated under confinement
45 May cause cancer
46 May cause heritable genetic damage
47 May cause birth defects
48 Danger of serious damage to health by prolonged exposure

Combination of particular risks

14/15   Reacts violently with water, liberating highly flammable gases
15/29   Contact with water liberates toxic, highly flammable gas
20/21   Harmful by inhalation and in contact with skin
20/21/22   Harmful by inhalation, in contact with skin and if swallowed
20/22   Harmful by inhalation and if swallowed
21/22   Harmful in contact with skin and if swallowed

23/24	Toxic by inhalation and in contact with skin
23/24/25	Toxic by inhalation, in contact with skin and if swallowed
23/25	Toxic by inhalation and if swallowed
24/25	Toxic in contact with skin and if swallowed
26/27	Very toxic by inhalation and in contact with skin
26/27/28	Very toxic by inhalation, in contact with skin and if swallowed
26/28	Very toxic by inhalation and if swallowed
27/28	Very toxic in contact with skin and if swallowed
36/37	Irritating to eyes and respiratory system
36/37/38	Irritating to eyes, respiratory system and skin
36/38	Irritating to eyes and skin
37/38	Irritating to respiratory system and skin
42/43	May cause sensitisation by inhalation and skin contact

Part V

Indication of safety precautions required

1 Keep locked up
2 Keep out of reach of children
3 Keep in a cool place
4 Keep away from living quarters
5 Keep contents under… (appropriate liquid to be specified by the manufacturer)
6 Keep under… (inert gas to be specified by the manufacturer)
7 Keep container tightly closed
8 Keep container dry
9 Keep container in a well ventilated place
12 Do not keep the container sealed
13 Keep away from food, drink and animal feeding stuffs
14 Keep away from… (incompatible materials to be indicated by the manufacturer)
15 Keep away from heat
16 Keep away from sources of ignition – No Smoking
17 Keep away from combustible material
18 Handle and open container with care
20 When using do not eat or drink
21 When using do not smoke
22 Do not breathe dust
23 Do not breathe gas/fumes/vapour/spray (appropriate wording to be specified by manufacturer)
24 Avoid contact with skin
25 Avoid contact with eyes

26   In case of contact with eyes, rinse immediately with plenty of water and seek medical advice
27   Take off immediately all contaminated clothing
28   After contact with skin, wash immediately with plenty of... (to be specified by the manufacturer)
29   Do not empty into drains
30   Never add water to this product
33   Take precautionary measures against static discharges
34   Avoid shock and friction
35   This material and its container must be disposed of in a safe way
36   Wear suitable protective clothing
37   Wear suitable gloves
38   In case of insufficient ventilation, wear suitable respiratory equipment
39   Wear eye/face protection
40   To clean the floor and all objects contaminated by this material use... (to be specified by the manufacturer)
41   In case of fire and/or explosion do not breathe fumes
42   During fumigation/spraying wear suitable respiratory equipment (appropriate wording to be specified)
43   In case of fire, use... (indicate in the space the precise type of fire-fighting equipment; if water increases the risk, add – Never use water)
44   If you feel unwell, seek medical advice – show the label where possible
45   In case of accident or if you feel unwell, seek medical advice immediately – show the label where possible
46   If swallowed seek medical advice immediately and show this container or label
47   Keep at temperature not exceeding... degrees C (to be specified by the manufacturer)
48   Keep wetted with... (appropriate material to be specified by the manufacturer)
49   Keep only in the original container
50   Do not mix with... (to be specified by the manufacturer)
51   Use only in well ventilated areas
52   Not recommended for interior use on large surface areas

Combination of safety precautions required

1/2   Keep locked up and out of reach of children
3/7/9   Keep container tightly closed, in a cool well ventilated place
3/9   Keep in a cool, well ventilated place

3/19/14	Keep in a cool, well ventilated place away from. . . (incompatible materials to be indicated by the manufacturer)
3/9/14/49	Keep only in the original container in a cool, well ventilated place away from. . . (incompatible materials to be indicated by the manufacturer)
3/9/49	Keep only in the original container in a cool, well ventilated place
3/14	Keep in a cool place away from. . . (incompatible materials to be indicated by the manufacturer)
7/8	Keep container tightly closed and dry
7/9	Keep container tightly closed and in a well ventilated place
20/21	When using do not eat, drink or smoke
24/25	Avoid contact with skin and eyes
36/37	Wear suitable protective clothing and gloves
36/37/39	Wear suitable protective clothing, gloves and eye/face protection
36/39	Wear suitable protective clothing and eye/face protection
37/39	Wear suitable gloves and eye/face protection
47/49	Keep only in the original container at temperature not exceeding. . . degrees C (to be specified by the manufacturer).

Schedule 1 to the Regulations

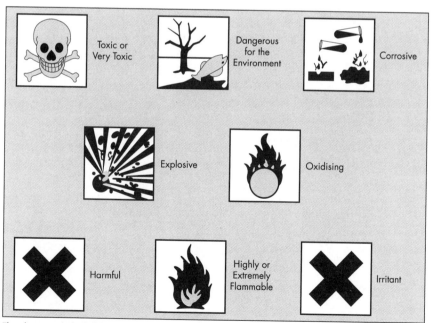

The above symbols shall be in black on an orange–yellow background.

Figure A9.1   Indication of danger.

Appendix 10

Medicines Act 1968
Patient Group Directions (PGD)
Schedule 7 to the Regulations
(SI 2000 No.1917 as amended)

Classes of individual by whom Prescription Only Medicines may be supplied or administered

Pharmacists
Registered nurses
Registered midwives
Registered health visitors
Registered ophthalmic opticians
Registered chiropodists
Registered orthoptists
Registered physiotherapists
Registered radiographers
Registered paramedics or individuals who hold a certificate of proficiency in ambulance paramedic skills issued by or with the approval of, the Secretary of State or state registered paramedics
Registered dieticians (SI 2004 No. 1189)
Registered occupational therapists (SI 2004 No. 1189)
Registered orthotists and prosthetists (SI 2004 No. 1189)
Registered speech and language therapists (SI 2004 No. 1189).

Particulars to be included in a Patient Group Direction

a   the period during which the Direction shall have effect;
b   the description or class of Prescription Only Medicine to which the Direction applies;
c   whether there are any restrictions on the quantity of medicine which may be supplied on any one occasion, and, if so, what restrictions;

d   the clinical situations which Prescription Only Medicines of that description or class may be used to treat;

e   the clinical criteria under which the person shall be eligible for treatment;

f   whether any class is excluded from treatment under the Direction and, if so what class of person;

g   whether there are any circumstances in which further advice should be sought from a doctor or dentist and if so what circumstances;

h   the pharmaceutical form or forms in which Prescription Only Medicines of that class or description are to be administered;

i   the strength, or maximum strength, at which Prescription Only Medicines of that description or class are to be administered;

j   the applicable dosage or maximum dosage;

k   the route of administration;

l   the frequency of administration;

m   any minimum or maximum period of administration applicable to Prescription Only Medicines of that description or class;

n   whether there are any relevant warnings to note and, if so, what warnings;

o   whether there is any follow up action to be taken in any circumstances and, if so, what action and in what circumstances;

p   arrangements for referral for medical advice;

q   details of the records to be kept of the supply, or the administration, of medicines under the Direction.

Index